# Transforming Corporate Social Responsibility and Business Ethics With AI

Martin Sposato
*Zayed University, UAE*

Eduardo Carlos Dittmar
*Universidad Rey Juan Carlos, Spain*

IGI Global
Scientific Publishing
Publishing Tomorrow's Research Today

Published in the United States of America by
IGI Global Scientific Publishing
701 East Chocolate Avenue
Hershey, PA, 17033, USA
Tel: 717-533-8845
Fax: 717-533-8661
Website: https://www.igi-global.com E-mail: cust@igi-global.com



Library of Congress Cataloging-in-Publication Data

Names: Sposato, Martin, 1982- editor. | Dittmar, Eduardo Carlos, editor.
Title: Transforming corporate social responsibility and business ethics with AI / edited by Martin Sposato, Eduardo Carlos Dittmar.
Description: Hershey, PA : IGI Global Scientific Publishing, [2025] | Includes bibliographical references and index. | Summary: "This book explores the intricate interplay between AI technologies and the evolving landscape of corporate ethics and social responsibility"-- Provided by publisher.
Identifiers: LCCN 2024054390 (print) | LCCN 2024054391 (ebook) | ISBN 9798369398944 (hardcover) | ISBN 9798369398951 (paperback) | ISBN 9798369398968 (ebook)
Subjects: LCSH: Social responsibility of business. | Ethics. | Artificial intelligence.
Classification: LCC HD60 .T727 2025 (print) | LCC HD60 (ebook) | DDC 658.4/080285--dc23/eng/20250409
LC record available at https://lccn.loc.gov/2024054390
LC ebook record available at https://lccn.loc.gov/2024054391

British Cataloguing in Publication Data
A Cataloguing in Publication record for this book is available from the British Library.

# Table of Contents

# Detailed Table of Contents

intelligence has to go much beyond just the parameters of credibility and benevolence, which is comparable to human relationships, and include ethical, social, and technical components that are interlinked in the collaboration between humans and machines.



Artificial Intelligence (AI) has experienced rapid penetration in our society, playing a crucial role in everyday analysis and decision making. AI integration in the financial field stands out as one of the most advanced, especially in terms of financial fraud detection and prevention. Yet, this rapid evolution of the sector brings with it several ethical and corporate social responsibility (CRS) challenges that have not yet been properly explored. This analysis provides the essential principles for understanding the use of AI in the detection of financial fraud, assessing its effectiveness, and examining the tools used to understand the conceptual framework within which ethics and CRS are defined in the application of AI. A comprehensive review of the ethical and CRS challenges inherent in the use of AI in the detection and prevention of financial fraud is conducted, along with an analysis of the different perspectives. present in the academic literature on the subject. In addition, future research directions are proposed to address these issues more comprehensively and effectively.



This study examined the top five reference companies for Generation Z, in relation to bias and responsible Artificial Intelligence (AI). Through a literature analysis on bias and the study of Law 15/2022, of July 12 (15917/2022), comprehensive for equal treatment and non-discrimination, the key factors of the study are detected to determine whether or not companies comply from an ethical point of view. The findings confirmed that all the items analyzed are complied with except for the seals on the algorithms officially. These results are essential to guide the market towards more transparent business models, which helps companies increase the trust they transmit to society. The study offers implications, limitations and future lines of research, which focus on algorithmic literacy.

This chapter examines the legal and ethical challenges of integrating artificial intelligence (AI) and automated decision-making in commercial transactions. It explores how smart contracts, algorithmic liability, and personalized consumer services are transforming traditional concepts in civil and commercial law. Through a comparative law approach, the chapter analyzes the responses of different jurisdictions, including the European Union, the United States, and Asia, to these advancements. Key topics include redefining contractual obligations, introducing "algorithmic fault" in commercial liability, and advocating for dynamic consumer protections against discriminatory pricing. The chapter also proposes innovative mechanisms for dispute resolution, such as AI-assisted mediation and electronic courts, and introduces the concept of adaptive regulation to address rapid technological changes. By doing so, it seeks to promote a fair, transparent, and ethically aligned digital marketplace.



Artificial intelligence (AI) is revolutionizing the advertising industry, offering unprecedented personalization, automation, and optimization capabilities. However, this transformation also raises critical ethical and operational concerns. This chapter examines the multifaceted influence of AI on advertising, exploring its potential benefits and inherent risks. While AI enhances efficiency and effectiveness, it also introduces challenges related to transparency, accountability, and the potential for bias and discrimination. The text similarly examines the impact of AI on creativity, highlighting the tension between automation and the preservation of the human element in compelling storytelling. Additionally, it discusses the evolving regulatory landscape, emphasizing the need for continuous adaptation to address the rapid pace of AI development. By examining these issues, this chapter aims to promote a responsible and strategic approach to AI adoption in advertising, ensuring this transformative technology's ethical and practical integration.

This chapter examines the impact of artificial intelligence (AI) on unfair competition and commercial law, emphasizing ethical implications and corporate social responsibility (CSR). AI has revolutionized market competition and intellectual property protection, providing tools for detecting infringements and optimizing strategies. However, it raises ethical challenges, including privacy concerns, market manipulation, and anticompetitive behavior. The chapter discusses how businesses can ethically use AI while upholding fair competition. It includes case studies and proposes a framework for integrating CSR into AI-driven competition, advocating for legal regulations to define ethical AI boundaries. By exploring the relationship between AI, ethics, and commercial law, the chapter aims to guide companies and policymakers in promoting responsible AI practices in the marketplace.



This chapter examines AI implementation in CSR initiatives within East Asian organizations, focusing on challenges and opportunities from traditional paternalistic leadership styles. It analyzes recent theoretical developments and empirical studies to explore how these organizations balance technological innovation and cultural preservation. The research reveals how traditional business values influence AI adoption, especially in hierarchical contexts. It highlights the importance of cultural alignment in successful AI implementation, emphasizing frameworks that accommodate both technical capabilities and cultural sensitivities. The chapter provides insights on integrating AI technologies while maintaining cultural integrity, suggesting that successful AI implementation in CSR depends on culturally sensitive approaches. It also identifies key areas for future research, including the long-term impacts of AI on organizational culture and stakeholder relationships.

# Foreword

The convergence of artificial intelligence and corporate social responsibility represents one of the most consequential developments in modern business history. As organizations worldwide grapple with the ethical implications of AI deployment while striving to meet their social responsibilities, this volume arrives at a crucial moment.

The integration of AI into business operations has moved far beyond mere efficiency gains to fundamentally reshape how organizations interact with stakeholders, make decisions, and fulfill their societal obligations. Yet this transformation brings unprecedented challenges. How do we ensure AI systems remain accountable while preserving human agency? How can organizations balance innovation with ethical considerations? How do cultural contexts influence the implementation of AI-driven CSR initiatives? These questions demand thoughtful exploration and practical frameworks for action.

What makes this volume particularly valuable is its comprehensive approach to these challenges. By combining theoretical foundations with practical applications and regional perspectives, it offers insights relevant to both scholars and practitioners. The examination of AI ethics and CSR through East Asian and Latin American lenses is especially noteworthy, as it moves beyond Western-centric approaches to consider how cultural values and local contexts shape the implementation of ethical AI practices.

The book's structure thoughtfully guides readers through this complex landscape. Beginning with foundational concepts of ethical AI culture and trust dynamics, it progresses through specific applications in areas like financial fraud detection and digital advertising, before exploring regional perspectives and emerging applications. This organization allows readers to build a robust understanding of both theoretical frameworks and practical implications.

I find the volume's treatment of trust particularly innovative. The chapter on "The Trust Paradox" challenges conventional binary views of trust and distrust in AI systems, offering a more nuanced understanding that better reflects the complexity of human-AI relationships. Similarly, the examination of how traditional East Asian business values influence AI adoption provides crucial insights for organizations operating in global contexts.

The practical value of this work cannot be overstated. For organizations developing AI governance frameworks, the book offers concrete guidance on embedding ethical considerations into AI development and deployment. The detailed case studies and regional analyses provide valuable lessons in navigating cultural nuances and operational challenges. The examination of SME experiences is particularly welcome, as smaller organizations often face unique challenges in balancing technological innovation with ethical requirements.

Looking toward the future, this volume's insights on integrating AI ethics into educational frameworks and urban development initiatives are timely and essential. As we prepare the next generation of business leaders and shape our cities' development, the frameworks and principles outlined here will be crucial in ensuring that technological advancement serves societal well-being.

Perhaps most importantly, this book demonstrates that ethical AI implementation and corporate social responsibility are not opposing forces to business success, but rather essential elements of sustainable organizational development in the digital age. The frameworks and insights presented here show how organizations can harness AI's potential while upholding their social responsibilities and ethical obligations.

As our society continues to navigate the challenges and opportunities of AI integration, this volume will serve as an essential resource for academics, business leaders, policymakers, and students. Its comprehensive treatment of both theoretical foundations and practical applications, combined with its global perspective, makes it an invaluable contribution to our understanding of how organizations can responsibly harness AI's transformative potential.

The editors and contributors have produced a work that not only advances our theoretical understanding of AI ethics and CSR but also provides practical guidance for implementing these principles in diverse organizational contexts. As we move forward in an increasingly AI-driven world, the insights and frameworks presented in this volume will be essential for anyone working at the intersection of technology, business ethics, and social responsibility.

**Angelo M. Solarino**
*University of Durham, UK*

# Preface

## CONTEMPORARY CONTEXT AND SIGNIFICANCE

The intersection of artificial intelligence (AI), corporate social responsibility (CSR), and business ethics represents one of the most critical areas of study in contemporary organizational management and technology governance. As we witness the unprecedented acceleration of AI adoption across industries, organizations face complex challenges in balancing technological innovation with ethical considerations and social responsibility. This volume emerges at a crucial juncture when the business world grapples with fundamental questions about the responsible development and deployment of AI systems while maintaining their commitment to societal welfare and sustainable development.

### Contemporary Challenges in AI Ethics and CSR

In today's rapidly evolving technological landscape, the integration of AI into business operations has transcended mere efficiency improvements to become a transformative force that reshapes organizational structures, decision-making processes, and stakeholder relationships. Organizations face unprecedented challenges in managing algorithmic bias, ensuring data privacy, maintaining transparency in AI decision-making, and addressing the societal impacts of automation. The increasing sophistication of AI systems raises complex questions about accountability, fairness, and the preservation of human agency in organizational decision-making.

Furthermore, the global nature of AI deployment introduces challenges related to cross-cultural ethical considerations, regulatory compliance across jurisdictions, and the equitable distribution of both benefits and risks. The COVID-19 pandemic has accelerated digital transformation, bringing these challenges into sharper focus while highlighting the urgent need for responsible AI governance frameworks that can adapt to rapidly changing circumstances.

The convergence of these factors necessitates a comprehensive examination of how organizations can harness AI's potential while upholding their social responsibilities and ethical obligations. The increasing public scrutiny of corporate behavior, heightened awareness of environmental sustainability, and growing demands for ethical technology governance create an imperative for organizations to develop robust frameworks for responsible AI implementation.

## Audience and Scope

This edited volume is designed to serve a diverse audience of academics, business practitioners, policy makers, and graduate students in the fields of business administration, information systems, ethics, and corporate governance. The interdisciplinary nature of the content makes it particularly valuable for professionals seeking to understand the complex interplay between technological advancement and corporate responsibility. Additionally, the book provides essential insights for organizations developing AI governance frameworks and CSR strategies in an increasingly digitalized business environment.

## Structure and Chapter Overview

The book is strategically organized into four parts, each addressing crucial aspects of the AI-CSR-ethics nexus. Part I establishes the foundational concepts and theoretical frameworks necessary for understanding the integration of AI ethics within organizational contexts. The opening chapter, "Building an Ethical AI Culture within Organizations," provides a comprehensive framework for embedding ethical considerations into organizational AI practices. It explores the critical role of leadership in fostering ethical AI development and deployment while addressing key challenges in creating cross-functional ethics teams and ensuring transparency in AI systems.

The second chapter, "The Trust Paradox: A Study on the Overlapping of Trust and Distrust Constructs," offers a novel perspective on the complex relationship between trust and distrust in AI systems. Through innovative probabilistic modeling, it challenges traditional binary views of trust and presents a more nuanced understanding of human-AI relationships.

Part II delves into specific applications and implications of AI in corporate responsibility and ethics. The third chapter, "Ethical and Corporate Social Responsibility Implications of Artificial Intelligence Application for the Detection and Prevention of Financial Fraud," presents a comprehensive analysis of AI's role in financial fraud detection while examining associated ethical challenges. This is followed by "Addressing Rights on Responsible AI in Digital Companies: The Impact of Biases and Stereotypes," which provides crucial insights into algorithmic bias and discrimination prevention in leading technology companies.

The fifth chapter, "Commercial Transactions in the Digital Era: Navigating the Legal Complexities of Algorithmic Decision-Making," offers a comparative analysis of legal frameworks governing AI-driven commercial transactions across different jurisdictions. The sixth chapter, "Navigating the AI Revolution in Advertising: Opportunities and Ethical Challenges," examines the transformation of advertising through AI while addressing critical ethical considerations in personalization and automation.

Part III provides valuable regional perspectives, focusing on East Asia and Latin America. The East Asian section begins with "AI-Driven CSR in East Asia: Navigating Leadership and Ethical Challenges," which explores the unique challenges of implementing AI-driven CSR initiatives within traditional organizational cultures. This is complemented by "Managerial Skills and Culture in East Asia: The Ethical Integration of Artificial Intelligence in Corporate Social Responsibility," which examines how cultural values influence AI ethics and CSR strategies in prominent East Asian companies.

The Latin American section offers critical insights through chapters including "Keys in the Adoption of New Technologies in Latin American SMEs: Challenges for a Sustained Growth in the AI Age" and "Barriers and Opportunities in CSR Adoption Among Latin American SMEs in the AI Age." These chapters provide comprehensive analyses of technological adoption and CSR implementation challenges specific to the region. The section also includes focused studies on Argentina's tourism industry and Costa Rica's educational reforms, demonstrating practical applications of AI and CSR in specific sectors.

Part IV concludes the volume by examining emerging applications and future directions. "Corporate Social Responsibility and AI and Their Impact on Smart Cities" explores the intersection of corporate responsibility and urban development in the context of increasing digitalization. The final chapter, "Fostering Sustainable Development in Undergraduate Students' Entrepreneurial Mindsets: Integrating Digital and AI Ethics in General Education," addresses the crucial role of education in preparing future business leaders for ethical AI implementation.

## Contemporary Relevance and Global Impact

The volume addresses pressing contemporary issues including the role of AI in pandemic response, climate change mitigation, and social equity promotion. It examines how organizations can leverage AI to enhance their CSR initiatives while navigating emerging ethical challenges. The global perspective, incorporating insights from diverse cultural contexts, provides a comprehensive understanding of how AI ethics and CSR manifest across different business environments.

## Theoretical Contributions and Academic Advancement

This volume advances theoretical understanding in several key areas. First, it develops a comprehensive framework for integrating AI ethics into existing CSR theories, proposing new constructs for understanding the relationship between technological innovation and corporate responsibility. Second, it introduces novel theoretical approaches to understanding stakeholder engagement in the context of AI deployment, extending traditional stakeholder theory to encompass artificial agents and automated decision-making systems.

The book also contributes to organizational learning theory by examining how organizations develop ethical AI capabilities and integrate them into their existing CSR frameworks. Furthermore, it advances our understanding of cross-cultural technology adoption by proposing new theoretical models for analyzing how cultural factors influence AI ethics and CSR implementation.

## Implications for Practitioners

The insights presented in this volume offer substantial practical value for business leaders, managers, and professionals involved in AI implementation and CSR initiatives. For organizational leaders, the book provides comprehensive frameworks for developing and implementing ethical AI governance structures that align with existing CSR strategies. The detailed case studies from various regional contexts offer valuable lessons in navigating cultural nuances and operational challenges in AI adoption.

Corporate executives will find particular value in the book's examination of trust-building mechanisms in AI implementation. The novel approach to understanding trust and distrust dynamics provides practical guidance for managing stakeholder relationships in the context of AI deployment. Furthermore, the chapters focusing on specific sectors such as financial services, advertising, and urban development offer industry-specific insights that can inform strategic decision-making.

For CSR professionals, the volume presents innovative approaches to integrating AI capabilities within existing sustainability frameworks. The examination of AI's role in fraud detection, bias prevention, and sustainable urban development provides practical templates for expanding CSR initiatives to encompass technological innovation. Additionally, the book's analysis of SME experiences offers valuable insights for professionals working in smaller organizations or consulting with SME clients.

HR and training professionals will benefit from the book's discussion of cultural transformation and skill development requirements for ethical AI implementation. The chapters addressing educational reform and entrepreneurial mindset development provide practical guidance for developing training programs and fostering an ethical AI culture within organizations.

## Research Implications and Academic Value

This volume makes several significant contributions to the academic discourse on AI ethics and CSR, opening new avenues for research and theoretical development. The integration of traditional CSR frameworks with emerging AI ethical considerations provides a foundation for developing new theoretical models of corporate responsibility in the digital age.

The book's examination of trust dynamics in AI systems challenges existing theoretical constructs and suggests new approaches to understanding human-AI interactions in organizational contexts. This theoretical innovation invites further research into the psychological and social dimensions of AI adoption in business settings.

For scholars in the field of comparative management, the regional perspectives offered in this volume provide rich ground for cross-cultural analysis of AI ethics and CSR implementation. The detailed examination of East Asian and Latin American contexts contributes to our understanding of how cultural factors influence technological adoption and ethical frameworks.

The volume's interdisciplinary approach, combining insights from business ethics, information systems, organizational behavior, and sustainability studies, demonstrates the value of cross-disciplinary research in understanding complex technological and social phenomena. This approach opens new possibilities for collaborative research across traditional academic boundaries.

## Methodological Contributions and Research Design

The volume makes significant contributions to research methodology in the field of AI ethics and CSR. It introduces novel approaches to studying AI implementation in organizational contexts, including innovative mixed-method designs that combine technical analysis with stakeholder perspectives. The methodological frameworks presented provide valuable tools for future researchers examining the intersection of technology and corporate responsibility.

## Future Research Directions and Emerging Trends

The rapidly evolving nature of AI technology and its increasing integration into business operations suggests several promising directions for future research. First, longitudinal studies examining the long-term impacts of AI implementation on organizational culture and stakeholder relationships are needed to understand the temporal dynamics of ethical AI adoption.

Second, the relationship between AI governance structures and traditional CSR frameworks requires further investigation. Research questions might include how organizations can effectively integrate AI ethical considerations into existing CSR reporting and monitoring systems, and how these integrated systems affect organizational performance and stakeholder trust.

Third, the role of cultural factors in shaping AI ethics and CSR practices demands more detailed examination. While this volume provides valuable insights from East Asia and Latin America, future research could explore other regional contexts and develop more comprehensive cross-cultural frameworks for ethical AI implementation.

Fourth, the specific challenges faced by SMEs in AI adoption and CSR implementation represent an important area for future research. Studies examining how smaller organizations can effectively balance resource constraints with ethical requirements in AI implementation would provide valuable insights for both theory and practice.

Fifth, the intersection of AI ethics, CSR, and sustainable development goals offers rich opportunities for future research. Studies examining how AI can contribute to achieving sustainability objectives while maintaining ethical standards could help organizations align their technological innovation with broader societal goals.

The rapid evolution of AI capabilities, particularly in areas such as natural language processing and autonomous decision-making, suggests additional research directions. Studies examining the ethical implications of increasingly sophisticated AI systems, particularly in contexts where they interface directly with stakeholders, will become increasingly important. Additionally, research investigating the role of AI in promoting and monitoring corporate sustainability initiatives promises to yield valuable insights for both theory and practice.

## Policy Implications and Regulatory Considerations

The insights presented in this volume have significant implications for policy development and regulatory frameworks. The analysis of AI implementation challenges across different jurisdictions provides valuable guidance for policymakers seeking to develop effective governance frameworks. The book's examination of successful regulatory approaches in different regional contexts offers important lessons for developing balanced and effective AI governance structures.

### Integration with Sustainable Development Goals

A unique contribution of this volume is its examination of how AI ethics and CSR initiatives align with global sustainable development objectives. The analysis provides frameworks for organizations to evaluate and enhance their AI initiatives' contribution to sustainability goals, while maintaining ethical standards and social responsibility commitments.

## CONCLUSION AND FUTURE OUTLOOK

As we move forward in an increasingly AI-driven business environment, the principles and frameworks outlined in this book will become increasingly valuable for organizations striving to balance innovation with ethical responsibility and social impact. The continuing evolution of AI technology and its applications in business contexts ensures that the themes explored in this volume will remain relevant for years to come, providing a foundation for both practical implementation and future research in this dynamic field.

The comprehensive nature of this volume, combining theoretical innovations with practical applications and regional perspectives, positions it as an essential resource for understanding and addressing the challenges of ethical AI implementation within corporate contexts. As organizations continue to navigate the complex landscape of technological advancement and social responsibility, the insights and frameworks presented here will serve as vital guides for developing sustainable and ethical approaches to AI integration in business practices.

**Martin Sposato**
*Zayed University, UAE*

**Eduardo Carlos Dittmar**
*Universidad Rey Juan Carlos, Spain*

# Section 1
# Foundations and Core Concepts

# Chapter 1
# Building an Ethical AI Culture Within Organizations

**Rohit Yadav**
https://orcid.org/0000-0002-7573-8005
*IILM University, Greater Noida, India*

## ABSTRACT

*As artificial intelligence (AI) becomes increasingly integrated into organizational practices, ensuring ethical development and deployment is critical. This chapter explores the importance of building an ethical AI culture within organizations by addressing core ethical principles, the role of leadership, and strategies for embedding ethics throughout AI development. Key areas discussed include creating cross-functional ethics teams, ensuring transparency, and fostering training and awareness of AI ethics among employees. The chapter emphasizes the significance of embedding ethical practices within AI systems to avoid biases, enhance fairness, and comply with legal and regulatory frameworks. Additionally, the societal impacts of AI, including privacy concerns, job displacement, and social equity, are explored in depth. By focusing on continuous feedback loops and stakeholder engagement, organizations can create sustainable, ethical AI systems that promote transparency, fairness, and accountability.*

## INTRODUCTION: WHY ORGANIZATIONS NEED ETHICAL AI

Organizations are the very backbone of technological innovation today, and Artificial Intelligence has become the crux for driving innovation, making processes more efficient, and fostering data-driven decision-making. While AI is slowly

DOI: 10.4018/979-8-3693-9894-4.ch001

becoming the hub of many organizational strategies, attention to the ethics of these AI systems is beginning to take its toll. Ethical AI is the practice of developing and deploying AI technologies that adhere to principles of fairness, transparency, accountability, and respect for human rights (Jobin, Ienca, & Vayena, 2019). Given the profound impact AI has on individuals, communities, and industries, organizations must recognize the critical importance of embedding ethical considerations into AI development and implementation.

Left unregulated, AI systems will feed on bias, increasing inequality and even enabling decisions that compromise privacy or undermine users' autonomy (O'Neil, 2016). It is in these risks that organizations must adopt proactive ethical frameworks that ensure that these technologies are used for the greater good and limit the potential harmful consequences. Ethical AI not only prevents the actual harm but also builds trust with the organization's stakeholders: its employees, customers, regulators, and the public at large (Dastin, 2018). At a time when data breaches, algorithmic biases, and violations of privacy have become the order of the day, ethical AI becomes the difference maker between organizations in the marketplace, helping them establish long-term reputational value (Floridi, Cowls, Beltrametti, Chatila, & Chazerand, 2018).

Additionally, responsible AI development has also become a legal imperative through governments and regulatory bodies across the world implementing legislation and standards (European Commission, 2021). Organizations failing to align their AI practices with ethical standards expose them to legal consequences, tattering down their reputation and eroding consumer confidence. Creating an ethical AI culture thus is not just corporate responsibility but a strategic issue that will definitely shape the future success of businesses in an AI-driven world.

Integrating ethical AI principles into organizational practices can allow companies to realize the full potential of AI technologies while protecting their stakeholders and society. This chapter will explore how organizations can build and sustain an ethical AI culture, with a focus on leadership, transparency, and accountability in AI systems. It will also discuss best practices, challenges, and real-world examples that can guide organizations toward a future where AI serves humanity ethically and responsibly.

## UNDERSTANDING AI ETHICS: CORE PRINCIPLES AND FRAMEWORKS

Understanding and laying down AI ethics is a set of principles and frameworks that guide the design, development, deployment, and governance of AI systems so that they align with societal values and human rights. Increased technological evolution of AI technologies raises the need to spell out the ethical challenges they pose and strategies for addressing them. Main principles of AI ethics include transparency, fairness, accountability, privacy, and inclusivity. Such principles work as groundwork to ensure that AI systems are efficient and equitable as well as trustworthy.

Transparency is the ability of AI systems to explain decisions and processes clearly and understandably. Transparency is a critical element for establishing trust with users and stakeholders, as it gives people insight into how decisions are made and whether they are fair and justified (Diakopoulos, 2016). In AI, transparency also includes openness about algorithms and data sources so that biases or manipulations in the system can be identified and corrected (Burrell, 2016).

Fairness refers to the problem of bias in AI models, such that algorithms are not discriminatory and cause disadvantage to particular groups on grounds of race, gender, or socio-economic status. Bias in AI may stem from biased data, faulty algorithms, or unequal access to technology (Barocas, Hardt, & Narayanan, 2019). To address these biases, organizations need to embrace practices such as inclusive data collection, rigorous testing for fairness, and interventions to correct biased outcomes. Fairness is often achieved by balancing competing interests and ensuring equitable treatment for all stakeholders (Eubanks, 2018).

Accountability refers to the clear responsibility for the actions and outcomes of AI systems. This is meant to ensure that, in the event of harm or unintended consequences brought about by AI systems, mechanisms are in place to hold those responsible accountable (Calo, 2015). Organizations need to establish robust governance structures, including AI ethics boards or oversight committees, to oversee the ethical deployment of AI technologies and make decisions regarding their use. Accountability is equally important in answering stakeholder concerns and dealing with breaches promptly.

Another basic ethical principle is privacy, especially in the case of AI systems that heavily rely on personal data. The implementation of strong data protection measures such as anonymization, encryption, and user consent protocols ensures respect for user privacy in AI systems (Tufekci, 2018). Organizations must also adhere to data privacy laws such as the General Data Protection Regulation (GDPR) to protect the rights of individuals and prevent legal consequences (European Commission, 2016).

Finally, the idea of inclusivity calls for the fact that AI systems are accessible and benefit all segments of society, including those who may be marginalized or underserved. Inclusivity entails designing AI systems that account for diverse needs and do not reproduce existing inequalities (West et al., 2019). This also implies making sure the AI development team is diverse, reflecting different views that can serve to minimize the potential of building technologies that help one group and hurt another.

Different ethical frameworks have been proposed to operationalize these principles. For example, the Asilomar AI Principles outline guidelines on AI safety, transparency, and ethics and advocate for research that is aligned with the public good (Stix, 2017). The OECD Principles on AI focus on responsible stewardship of AI and urge governments and organizations to ensure that AI technologies are developed in a manner that respects human rights and democratic values (OECD, 2019). In addition, organizations can use frameworks like the Fairness, Accountability, and Transparency (FAccT) Principles, which are guidelines for the assessment of the fairness and transparency of machine learning models and other AI applications (Diakopoulos et al., 2020).

In summary, for an organization interested in developing and deploying AI responsibly, it must first understand the principles of AI ethics. Transitions to the organization's approach, which should encompass transparency, fairness, accountability, privacy, and inclusivity. It is thus able to provide AI technologies that are of benefit to all stakeholders but do not do any harm. Ethical frameworks, therefore, will help guide this very complex area, providing the solid ethical underpinning that is necessary for the development of AI.

## Leadership Commitment: Tone Setting for Ethical AI

Effective leadership goes a long way in building and sustaining an ethical AI culture within the organization. Through values, accountability, and focusing on AI ethics in all matters of business activities, leaders establish the tone. In an age of skyrocketing transformation in industries due to AI technologies, organizational leaders, including executives and board members, must take a proactive approach toward making certain that AI systems are developed and deployed in an ethical manner and one aligned with ethical considerations and social values.

The commitments of leaders would have at their foundation that AI ethics is not technical, but a strategic and organizational issue. Ethical decision-making needs to be an integral part of the company's core values and should be practiced by leaders in their day-to-day life. This begins at the top, where executives lead by example, prioritize ethical considerations in AI strategy, and allocate resources for ethical governance structures (Wirtz et al., 2019). When leaders state explicitly that ethical AI is crucial, they have an environment where ethics are not treated as an add-on but as an underlying principle directing the activities of the organization.

The most prominent role of a leader in AI ethics is cultivating accountability. This calls for leaders to establish clear mechanisms on how the implications of AI systems will be overseen, especially through the development of ethics committees or oversight boards to track AI projects from development to deployment. These bodies can therefore assure constant assessment and ensure that the AI systems are used in accord with the ethical guidelines and organizational values. Leadership must also step forward and assume accountability for AI-related successes as well as failures. Transparency and accountability are warranted by their handling of ethical issues (Calo, 2015).

Organizational leaders should promote cross-functional collaboration to tackle the multidisciplinary approaches of AI ethics. AI ethics covers many domains such as technology, law, human rights, and business strategy. With that in mind, leaders must draw together diverse teams including data scientists, engineers, and legal experts down to social scientists to ensure a holistic understanding in the development of AI systems to consider ethical implications. By establishing collaboration across different departments and including ethical considerations into every stage of the AI cycle, leaders build innovative yet responsible systems (Jobin, Ienca, & Vayena, 2019).

The other critical area of commitment under leadership to AI ethics is open communication with its stakeholders outside the organization. In an environment where public trust in AI can be very fragile, open communication would then be very fundamental in enhancing credibility. The leaders must proactively communicate its AI ethics policies, efforts in overcoming potential bias, and measures used to ensure fair and transparent AI systems (Mittelstadt et al., 2016). It builds organizational trust with the consumers, regulators, and other publics who might be concerned with AI ethics; it also receives some useful feedback, which may assist in guiding ethical development of AI technologies.

However, leadership has to be more proactive in taking care that this ethical AI harmonizes with overall corporate social responsibility (CSR). AI systems not only improve the performance of a business but also enhance society. By incorporating AI ethics into CSR strategies, an organization can showcase that their ethical AI commitment goes beyond mere compliance or risk avoidance and is based on a sincere intent to create a positive social impact (Vinuesa et al., 2020). This will increase the reputation of the organization, attract top talent, and establish long-term consumer loyalty.

Finally, leaders need to make a commitment to continuous learning and adaptation in this fast-evolving area of AI ethics. The technology behind AI is rapidly changing, and so are the ethical challenges it poses. Leadership must, therefore, ensure that their understanding of AI ethics evolves with new developments, regulatory changes, and societal concerns. This commitment to ongoing learning ensures that organizations remain agile and responsive to new ethical dilemmas and opportunities as they arise (Wright, 2019).

Leadership commitment is the cornerstone of building an ethical AI culture within an organization. Executives and board members must lead by example, establish clear governance structures, foster cross-functional collaboration, engage with external stakeholders, align AI ethics with corporate social responsibility, and commit to continuous learning. By setting the tone for ethical AI, leaders create a foundation for AI systems that are not only innovative but also responsible, equitable, and aligned with societal values.

## Cross-Functional Ethics Team

The best way an organization can respond to the multi-faceted ethical challenges that AI poses is by establishing a cross-functional ethics team. AI technologies are complex and touch a wide array of domains, including technology, law, business, human rights, and societal welfare. As such, no single department or role can adequately manage the ethical considerations surrounding AI. A cross-functional team combines experts from various disciplines to ensure that AI systems are developed and implemented with a holistic understanding of their potential impacts. This team is pivotal in establishing a culture of ethical awareness and accountability, collaboration across the organization, and integrating ethical considerations into the AI development lifecycle.

The foundation of a cross-functional ethics team lies in its diversity of expertise. AI ethics is intrinsically interdisciplinary and requires the engagement of not only engineers and data scientists but also legal professionals, human rights experts, sociologists, ethicists, and business strategists. For instance, while engineers may be able to identify technical limitations and risks of AI algorithms, legal professionals will be crucial for navigating privacy laws, data protection regulations, and the changing landscape of AI-related legislation (Jobin, Ienca, & Vayena, 2019). Human rights experts can ensure that the AI systems do not violate fundamental freedoms, while sociologists can provide insights into the social implications of AI, such as its impact on marginalized groups. Business strategists can align AI ethics with organizational goals, ensuring that ethical considerations are not only respected but also integrated into the business model.

An effective cross-functional ethics team should have clearly defined roles and responsibilities. While team members will hail from diverse backgrounds, their collective objective will be to ensure that AI systems adhere to principles of ethics such as fairness, transparency, accountability, and inclusivity (Diakopoulos, 2016). A team leader or coordinator, often Chief AI Ethics Officer (CAEO) or an equivalent leadership position, should facilitate collaboration among the team members and maintain focus on ethical objectives. This leader should be equipped with powerful leadership skills as well as be well conversant in AI technology and ethics, where the team operates towards the vision of ethical AI for the long-term benefit of the organization. The team needs to continuously review AI systems along their lifecycle. This involves ascertaining ethical risks early at the stage of design, checking the system for biases in the data as well as algorithms, and ensuring mechanisms of transparency and accountability. Post-deployment, the team should remain involved, monitoring AI systems to assess impact in real-world terms, to determine unintended consequences, and make necessary adjustments. A proactive approach is the way to go: the cross-functional ethics team should not just react to issues as they arise but rather anticipate potential ethical challenges and intervene before they become critical problems (Wright, 2019).

The technical teams need to collaborate with the ethics team to ensure that ethical guidelines are operationalized into development processes. For instance, data scientists and engineers should collaborate with ethicists to perform bias audits and ensure that AI models are not perpetuating or amplifying societal inequalities inadvertently (Barocas, Hardt, & Narayanan, 2019). Similarly, legal experts should work with AI developers to ensure that data collection and usage comply with data protection laws such as the GDPR. Sociologists and human rights experts can comment on how the AI systems affect different communities, and solutions such as making systems more inclusive and accessible to different populations can be supported.

Another significant aspect of an effective cross-functional ethics team is an open and transparent communication culture. Ethical issues in AI can sometimes be complex and controversial. Therefore, team members should feel comfortable voicing concerns, proposing solutions, and challenging assumptions. Thus, it is so important that an ethical AI framework will be considered a living document—flexible and adaptable to new challenges and emerging risks. Regular deliberations, think tank meetings, and seminars ensure that all voices are heard to encourage innovation while not losing sight of ethics (Mittelstadt et al., 2016). The team also needs to be regularly trained and developed to get the latest updates on research, trends, and legal requirements in AI ethics.

Engagement with stakeholders is another essential duty for the ethics team. While the internal cross-functional team is essential, organizations must also engage with external stakeholders such as regulators, advocacy groups, and the public. The ethics team can play an important role in ensuring that AI systems are aligned with societal values and that any concerns raised by external parties are addressed (Diakopoulos et al., 2020). Engagement with external stakeholders is especially necessary given the increasing clamor for accountability in AI, from regulation and standards of ethics. The cross-functional team, therefore, collaborates with the outside parties to ensure that its organization's practices are in tandem with the wider social goals of responsibility and that they help define the industry's benchmarks for AI usage.

Finally, there is a need to empower the cross-functional ethics team with appropriate resources and authority to bring effective change within the organization. Ethical concerns should never be put to the backseat or treated as secondary issues. For the team to have meaningful impact, there is a necessity for leaders to provide them with the necessary tools, time, and autonomy to determine and modify the AI systems at will. The team must have the capability of influencing decisions and actions at different levels within an organization, be it the developmental stages of AI or deployment and then monitoring postlaunch. This must ensure that consideration of ethics within key performance indicators and business policies is maintained along with metrics meant to evaluate AI technologies on ethics (Vinuesa et al., 2020).

In conclusion, creation of a cross-functional ethics team is a good step toward an accountable AI culture. Drawing on the diversity of expertise, this team can better handle the complex and broad ethical issues that are typically found in an AI system. Through continuous assessment, collaboration, and stakeholder engagement, a cross-functional ethics team helps organizations navigate the ethical challenges of AI development and deployment, ensuring that technologies are aligned with both organizational goals and societal values. The success of such a team requires clear roles, resources, and authority, as well as a commitment to ongoing learning and adaptation in a rapidly evolving field.

## Embedding Ethical AI Practices in AI Development

Inculcating ethical AI practices in the development process is an essential step to ensure that AI systems are not only effective but also align with societal values and ethical principles. The more AI technology is integrated into various sectors such as healthcare and finance, law enforcement, and education, the greater the need for ethical considerations of its design, development, and deployment from the start. This proactive approach to AI ethics ensures that ethical considerations are not an afterthought but an integral part of the development lifecycle. By embedding these practices, organizations can build AI systems that are not only innovative and efficient but also fair, transparent, accountable, and inclusive.

The first step in embedding ethical AI practices is to establish ethical guidelines that govern AI development. These guidelines need to be founded on core ethical principles such as fairness, transparency, accountability, privacy, and inclusivity. These principles have to be turned into actionable guidelines that developers follow throughout the AI lifecycle (Diakopoulos, 2016). For example, fairness guidelines would require audits, which should review the data in training and the algorithms used periodically for biases. While transparency guidelines can require that such AI systems offer clear explanations regarding how decisions were made. Integrating these ethics into the developmental process ensures constant consideration of the ethical concerns by the design, testing, and deployment phases, as proposed by Calo in 2015.

Besides ethical guidelines, bias detection and mitigation are essential in AI development. Bias can occur at various stages: from biased data collection to biased algorithmic models. Many AI systems that are trained on biased data can unwittingly promote inequality, thus resulting in discriminatory outcomes. Hence, critical AI development practice inclusion must take into account diversified data collection with fair representation and regular algorithmic auditing and mitigative measures in preventing bias at different stages of development (Barocas, Hardt, & Narayanan, 2019). An example is how to train a developed AI model first with the diversity data of its respective population groups with the assurance of minimum or almost zero risks on algorithmic biases. In developing the model, fairness metrics and testing protocols should be instituted to check if the model outcomes disproportionately affect any group. Techniques to mitigate bias, such as re-weighting data or adjustment of model parameters, can correct these imbalances when biases are identified (Eubanks, 2018).

The embedding of ethical AI practices also emphasizes the need for transparency and explainability. With increasing complexity, it is increasingly difficult to understand how AI systems make decisions. However, if AI is to be trusted and ethically deployed, it is essential that these systems are transparent in their operations, allowing stakeholders to understand and assess the rationale behind AI-driven decisions. Transparency in AI can be gained through the development of explainable AI, where models can be designed to offer clear and understandable explanations of how they made the decisions. Those explanations are also important for user trust but also critical for the accountability and fairness with which AI systems can be scrutinized. Explainability should be one of the most prominent features of AI models that developers focus on while designing and testing them. In this regard, both technical teams and non-technical stakeholders must be able to understand why the AI outcomes are what they are (Lipton, 2018).

Accountability is another essential principle that must be inculcated into AI development practices. Ethical AI development cannot happen without well-defined lines of responsibility and accountability for the AI system's outcomes. Therefore, the organizations must be able to institute processes to track AI behavior in its lifecycle; this way, any unintended or harmful consequences that may arise due to AI actions are detected in time and can be addressed before they cause major damage. In high-stakes environments, like healthcare or criminal justice, AI systems must be regularly audited regarding their impact on users and society. Another expectation about the developers includes responsibility for meeting ethical standards about AI systems in developing those systems; in turn, the organizations shall assume responsibility about harms caused to society by AI. Responsibility should involve, first and foremost, the individual team of developing that AI as a whole including embedding ethical practice within the various strata involving decision-making mechanisms among the executive echelons, according to Calo in 2015.

Moreover, ethical AI practices involve commitment to privacy and data protection. Most AI systems work off of very large datasets, which contain a wide range of personal information. Thus, guaranteeing that these systems respect privacy is also an ethical responsibility. Organizations should, therefore, impose anonymization, encryption, and safe data storage techniques to protect users' private data. In addition, there is a need for transparency about the data collection practices and getting informed consent from users so that people are in control of how their data is being used by AI systems. Organizations must be updated on the evolving data protection laws, such as the GDPR, and ensure that their AI development practices are in compliance (Tufekci, 2018).

Organizations should embrace ethical AI frameworks and methodologies that guide the development process to further embed ethical AI practices. Frameworks such as the OECD Principles on Artificial Intelligence or the Asilomar AI Principles provide structured guidelines that organizations can integrate into their AI development practices. These frameworks advocate for AI systems that are safe, transparent, and aligned with human rights and democratic values. By embracing these frameworks, organizations ensure that their AI systems not only meet legal standards but also align with broader ethical objectives and societal good (OECD, 2019; Stix, 2017).

Finally, stakeholder engagement is critical when embedding ethical AI practices. AI systems should be developed with input from a wide range of stakeholders, including users, advocacy groups, policymakers, and external auditors. The engagement of such stakeholders helps ensure that the AI systems meet societal needs and address concerns from various groups, especially those who might be most affected by the system's deployment. Feedback from stakeholders can help in the design and testing phases of AI development, giving insights that might not be apparent to the development team alone. Regular consultations with stakeholders, including marginalized communities, help ensure that AI systems are inclusive and do not exacerbate existing inequalities (West, Whittaker, & Crawford, 2019).

In conclusion, embedding ethical AI practices into the development process is essential for ensuring that AI systems are aligned with societal values and ethical principles. By incorporating ethical guidelines, detecting and mitigating bias, ensuring transparency and explainability, establishing accountability mechanisms, safeguarding privacy, and engaging stakeholders, organizations can create AI systems that are effective, ethical, and responsible. The development of ethical AI should be regarded as an ongoing process in which all organizational levels should demonstrate commitment, and therefore should be integrated into every stage of the AI lifecycle, from conception to deployment and even beyond.

## TRAINING AND AWARENESS: BUILDING ETHICAL AI COMPETENCIES

With organizations more and more embracing AI technologies, it is critical to invest in training and awareness programs that build the ethical competencies required of all stakeholders in the development, deployment, and governance of AI. Ethical AI competencies encompass more than just technical know-how on machine learning and artificial intelligence; they imply a profound awareness of the societal, individual-level, and organizational operational impacts that AI technologies can have. The objective is to make sure that engineers and developers, business leaders, and regulators within an organization all have the knowledge and skills required to design, develop, deploy, and govern AI systems in ways that are aligned with ethical principles and societal values.

Effective training begins with a solid foundation of understanding AI ethics. The training process for AI developers and engineers involves the identification of biases in AI models, addressing privacy concerns, and understanding societal implications. That is to say, there has to be fairness, transparency, accountability, and inclusivity when these concepts translate into practical strategies throughout the development lifecycle of the AI. For instance, engineers should be trained on detecting biases in data and algorithms, applying fairness testing, and ensuring that the data applied in AI models is representative of diverse populations (Barocas, Hardt, & Narayanan, 2019). Developers must also be educated on the principles of explainable AI (XAI), which aims to make AI decisions more interpretable and transparent to both technical and non-technical stakeholders (Lipton, 2018). Understanding how and why an AI system makes a particular decision will be important in building trust while also ensuring that accountability is being addressed and whatever ethical issues occur. Cross-function training is an essential aspect of achieving a culture of responsible AI. Whereas the technical teams would most likely know how to design the AI models, other stakeholders such as business executives, legal teams, and people at the face-to-face interaction should also understand what these technologies bring to the organization. The lawyers have to understand some AI regulations; the General Data Protection Regulation, for example. This means they would need to be conversant on issues about AI-related laws with regard to the rights and regulations over personal privacy and protection. Business leaders must know the risks and ethical issues about AI so they can make well-informed decisions about adopting AI, investing in it, and governing it. Customer-facing employees should be enlightened on how AI is being used to interact with customers so that customers are transparently assured and addressed whenever there is a problem. It would be well in the businesses' interest if, through this integrated training course involving stakeholders across the organization's board, it becomes clear how and why ethics is important and relevant at each level (Jobin, Ienca, & Vayena, 2019).

Organisational culture goes along with building AI ethical competencies, starting with training of both technical as well as the ethical aspects involved with AI. Organizations need to encourage continuous learning and open discussion of the ethical implications of AI technologies. That means creating space where employees would feel free to voice concern, question assumptions, and discuss potential hazards from AI systems. Ethical considerations should be part of routine team meetings, workshops, and brainstorming to ensure that ethics is integrated at every phase of AI development from design to deployment. Organizations can foster a learning culture that values ethical awareness by integrating AI ethics into onboarding processes, offering ongoing educational resources, and access to external training programs and certifications related to AI ethics (Wright, 2019).

The most effective way of developing AI competencies is through real-world case studies and practical exercises. It is indeed challenging to learn about AI ethics in abstract terms, so giving practical examples of AI deployments in various industries can help employees understand the ethical challenges and best practices in a tangible way. These would include both successful AI implementations that followed the ethical rules and failure stories associated with the improper use of AI, including biased hiring algorithms and facial recognition systems for surveillance purposes (Eubanks, 2018). Such case studies can illustrate the consequences associated with the lack of careful consideration of ethics or the significance of responsible AI practices. Hands-on exercises and simulations can be used to help employees practice ethical decision-making by putting them in situations where they have to navigate complex ethical dilemmas related to AI technologies. These activities raise awareness and build critical thinking and problem-solving skills in the context of AI ethics (Wirtz, Göttel, & Daiser, 2019).

In addition, ethical decision-making frameworks should be included in AI training programs. These frameworks help individuals identify, analyze, and address ethical challenges in AI development. For example, frameworks like the Ethical AI Framework developed by the European Commission or the IEEE Global Initiative on Ethics of Autonomous and Intelligent Systems provide guidance on how to navigate ethical issues in AI. These frameworks provide a structured way to identify risks, weigh the potential harms and benefits of AI systems, and develop strategies for mitigating the negative impacts of AI (Diakopoulos et al., 2020). Through such integration of these frameworks in training programs, organizations can provide their employees with the tools needed to make ethical decisions throughout the development process of AI.

In addition, training and awareness initiatives must be extended to cover the concepts of inclusive design and the social impact of AI. AI systems can have profound effects on individuals and communities, especially marginalized or vulnerable populations. It is therefore critical to train teams on how to design AI systems that promote inclusivity, avoid perpetuating existing inequalities, and align with principles of justice and equity (Vinuesa et al., 2020). This would mean understanding the social implications of AI, such as how it could perpetuate bias and inequality, and developing strategies to ensure that AI systems are fair for everyone. A focus on inclusive design is not only a technical concern but also understanding the context in which the AI system will be deployed and ensuring that it does positive good in society.

Finally, external partnerships can significantly enhance training and awareness programs. Organizations can collaborate with academic institutions, professional associations, and AI ethics organizations to provide employees with access to cutting-edge research and the latest developments in AI ethics. Collaboration with external experts in AI ethics will enable organizations to keep abreast of emerging ethical challenges and best practices, ensuring that their internal training programs are relevant and comprehensive. External partnerships can also provide opportunities for employees to engage in industry-wide discussions and contribute to the development of ethical standards for AI (West, Whittaker, & Crawford, 2019).

In conclusion, it is only possible to develop AI competencies ethically within an organization by incorporating training on the technical, legal, and social aspects of AI, a culture of ethical awareness, real case studies, and frameworks for decision making in the process of development. By investing in these training and awareness initiatives, organizations can ensure that their workforce is equipped to address the ethical challenges of AI and develop technologies that are transparent, accountable, and beneficial to society. Ethical AI development is not about doing no harm but about developing AI systems with values of fairness, equity, and social responsibility. This ensures that AI technology is used to advance the best interest of human society.

Most importantly, the development of transparent and fair AI systems is one of the most important areas that can ensure artificial intelligence technologies are ethically deployed in organizations. It's essential that, in situations where AI is increasingly used for making decisions affecting individual lives—be it hiring and lending, healthcare, law enforcement, or others such decisions—the operations of such AI systems be made transparent and fair to create a sense of trust, accountability, and social responsibility. Transparent and fair AI systems help organizations avoid unintended consequences like bias, discrimination, and inequity, and they also serve to mitigate potential legal and reputational risks associated with AI deployment. This section goes into the significance of transparency and fairness in AI and discusses practical approaches for building AI systems that are both transparent and fair.

## Transparency in AI

It has to do with the capability to understand and explain how AI systems make decisions. A transparent AI system offers good insight to stakeholders about how decisions are made, which they need to trust in the outcomes produced by the AI model. Without transparency, AI systems can be seen as black boxes, where decisions are made without any understanding of how or why they were reached. This lack of understanding can erode trust in AI systems and result in a failure to hold organizations accountable for their actions.

Building transparent AI systems starts with ensuring that the algorithms and models used are interpretable and explainable. Explainable AI, also abbreviated as XAI, involves a growing research field of developing AI models that not only can perform well but also have clear explanations behind their decision-making processes. Techniques used in order to achieve explainability include model-agnostic approaches which can explain complex models such as deep neural networks and intrinsic interpretability when the models are simpler, like decision trees or linear regression models. Researchers and practitioners emphasize that systems must not only give the right output but also make it possible for end-users and developers to understand the reasoning behind such outputs (Ribeiro et al., 2016).

Auditable systems must also be prioritized, allowing independent verification of AI decision-making. This includes recording and monitoring data flows, model training processes, and system updates to leave a clear trail that can be reviewed for compliance with ethical and legal standards. Transparency is also important in the context of data usage, where organizations must disclose how they collect, store, and use data to train AI systems. This helps to mitigate concerns about data privacy and security, which are critical when dealing with sensitive personal information (Dastin, 2018).

## Fairness in AI

AI fairness refers to the concept of designing and deploying AI systems that make decisions free from bias and do not disproportionately harm certain groups based on characteristics such as race, gender, age, or socio-economic status. AI systems are most often trained from historical data; if the data, therefore, with which these models are trained are biased, so are the results learned by those AI systems-thus leading to unfair outcomes. For example, AI tools used to make hiring processes may inadvertently favour male candidates as opposed to females if the data used to train them reflects on historical patterns that were biased towards genders in recruitment.

Organizations need to identify and mitigate biases in the training data proactively to build fair AI systems. It involves conducting bias audits to see whether the data used is representative of all demographic groups and does not reinforce existing stereotypes. Fairness can also be ensured by designing AI systems that test and evaluate for discriminatory outcomes and use metrics to assess equity across different groups. The fairness metrics can involve demographic parity; the outcomes across different groups have to be comparable. Equalized odds is ensuring error rates for a given error class are identical for different groups. Hardt et al., 2016, proposed methods.

Data preprocessing can be seen as one strategy that involves cleaning and adjusting data prior to applying it to training to ensure balanced representations without any bias. Techniques of re-weighting the data or generating synthetic data of underrepresented groups can be helpful in reducing the bias from the model. Then there is algorithmic fairness where the algorithm is specifically designed not to exhibit biased decision-making, such as adding fairness constraints into the optimization process during model training. Researchers have also developed methods like adversarial debiasing, where a model is trained to produce fair outcomes while minimizing the bias introduced by the underlying data (Zhang et al., 2018).

Another way that organizations can develop fair AI systems is by integrating human oversight into automated decision-making processes. Human oversight would check AI-driven decisions to catch any inadvertent biases that the algorithm may introduce. This hybrid approach, combining machine learning with human judgment, reduces the risk of automated discrimination and can be particularly useful in high-stakes areas like criminal justice or hiring, where unfair decisions can have profound consequences on people's lives.

## Ethical Frameworks and Best Practices for Fairness and Transparency

For the development of transparent and fair AI systems, organizations can develop ethical AI frameworks that provide guidance on how transparency and fairness could be integrated in AI development processes. For example, the Fairness, Accountability, and Transparency (FAT) framework emphasizes the importance of creating AI systems that are both fair and transparent by focusing on accountability for decisions and providing mechanisms for stakeholder engagement and recourse (Dastin, 2018). This framework encourages organizations to engage with external stakeholders, including affected communities and advocacy groups, to understand the real-world impacts of AI systems and address concerns about fairness and transparency.

Another prominent framework is the IEEE Global Initiative on Ethics of Autonomous and Intelligent Systems, which outlines standards for AI development that prioritize ethical principles such as fairness, transparency, accountability, and privacy (IEEE, 2019). These guidelines offer concrete steps organizations can take to ensure that their AI systems align with societal values and ethical norms, providing a roadmap for companies striving to create systems that uphold human dignity and respect fundamental rights.

## ONGOING EVALUATION AND IMPROVEMENT

Building transparent and fair AI systems is not a one-time effort but requires continuous evaluation and improvement. As AI technologies evolve and new challenges emerge, organizations must set up monitoring systems to track the performance and fairness of deployed models. This includes periodically updating models to address data drift and ensuring that new data does not introduce unintended bias. Additionally, organizations should be prepared to retrain models if evidence emerges that they are producing biased or unfair outcomes.

Independent third-party audits can also increase transparency and accountancy of the AI system. The audits assess whether the system operates according to ethical standards and also according to the general requirements of law in that specific jurisdiction. Independent third-party audits safeguard against unethical practices and, unintentionally, causing damage. Finally, regular feedback loop between the affected stakeholders and companies, including the users, customers, and regulatory bodies, will ensure that fairness and transparency concerns can be addressed and that AI systems continue to evolve in responsible ways.

In conclusion, building transparent and fair AI systems is a process that demands proactive and multi-faceted approaches. Organizations can develop AI systems that create trust, adhere to ethical standards, and further a just and equitable society by focusing on interpretability, data fairness, human oversight, and ongoing evaluation. Ethical AI development is not about compliance with legal or regulatory requirements but creating AI systems that benefit all stakeholders and avoid harm.

## Ethics in AI Deployment and Operations

The ethical issues of AI go beyond the development phase into deployment and operations stages, where the AI systems are put into practice and interact with real-world users and environments. AI systems must therefore be deployed and operated ethically to maintain public trust, achieve fairness, and avoid harm. Proper management of ethical considerations by AI systems deployed in critical sectors is very important. Critical sectors include healthcare, criminal justice, finance, and education, among others. Ethical management of AI systems during deployment calls for constant oversight, transparency, accountability, and responsiveness to emerging issues in real-world data and use.

The first consideration for ethical deployment involves achieving alignment with desired outcomes. Organizations need to take a very keen interest in reviewing whether the system operates in compliance with its ethics guidelines and the purposes it was made to achieve, which includes finding out whether it behaves as one would expect or delivers results compatible with organizational values and social good. Regular pre-deployment audits would be necessary in order to appraise the risk, bias, and ethical concerns of an AI system. Such audits may detect hidden issues about data privacy, algorithmic fairness, and unforeseen consequences that could have gone undetected at the design phase. For instance, if an AI system intended to assist in hiring processes has inadvertently been found to favor specific demographic groups due to biased training data, such concerns must be rectified before widespread deployment (Dastin, 2018).

Once an AI system is in place, mechanisms for monitoring and evaluation need to be in place to ensure that it remains ethical. An AI system is dynamic, and its behavior changes over time because of the interactions with new data and environments. Continuous monitoring helps identify any shifts in the outcomes of the AI system that could result in ethical violations, such as discriminatory patterns or biased predictions. These monitoring systems should track the accuracy and performance of AI but also its impact on fairness, transparency, privacy, and accountability. For instance, in sectors such as health care, high-stakes AI systems should be regularly evaluated so that they are not inadvertently contributing to exacerbating health disparities or inequitable treatment outcomes (Obermeyer et al., 2019). Regular ethics audits and impact assessments should be incorporated into the operational workflow to address these concerns and make adjustments as necessary.

Another critical component of ethical AI deployment is ensuring transparency in AI operations. As AI systems make decisions that directly impact individuals, users have the right to understand how those decisions are made. Transparency is crucial for both user trust and accountability. Organizations should ensure that AI systems are designed to provide explanations for their decisions in a manner that is understandable to the end-users. This is aligned with the principles of explainable AI (XAI), which focuses on making complex models more interpretable (Lipton, 2018). For example, in financial services, an AI system that determines creditworthiness must be able to explain the factors influencing its decision to both the applicant and the regulatory bodies, especially when adverse decisions are made. This transparency not only helps users understand the reasoning behind AI-generated decisions but also ensures that organizations are accountable for the systems they deploy.

Further, the respect for user consent and autonomy is necessary when AI is deployed, particularly where personal or sensitive data is concerned. There should be greater transparency about how that data is used and whether decisions will be based on human judgment or automatically by the AI. This has far-reaching applications in industries such as health, where AI may decide upon treatment plans or predict outcomes for patients. Organizations would need to get consent from the users, clarifying their rights regarding the data that is being used through AI systems, how this data is going to be processed, and how the decisions made may affect them. For instance, the doctors using AI for diagnosis must inform their patients on how the AI tools will be used in their treatment and to what extent human intervention will still prevail in decision-making. The users should also be allowed to opt out of specific AI systems if they feel uneasy about the usage or risks involved.

The issue of accountability is central during the operational phase of deployment because people's choices are made by AI systems, so accountability structures that determine who is responsible in the event of failures must be well spelled out. Mechanisms for tracing decision pathways in AI must also be included during design for tracing accountability in case of harmful or biased outcomes. This may include the following: logging of decisions made by the system, creation of audit trails, or escalation procedures if there is a problem in terms of ethics. If an AI system deployed in the context of law enforcement bases arrest recommendations on biased data that resulted in an unjust arrest, there must be a ready mechanism to investigate and bring relevant accountability measures on people who deployed the system. Besides that, accountability should not lie on the developers alone, but be put within the organization and institutional governance framework (Calo, 2015).

In addition to that, response to ethical concerns during the operation stage is a necessity. This is because in deploying and utilizing the AI system in real-world scenarios, some new ethical concerns may be observed or other undesirable effects may manifest. There should be feedback loops within the organization where users, stakeholders, and affected communities can raise ethical concerns about AI operations. The feedback received should be responded to in a timely manner, and there should be a procedure in place to modify or halt the use of the system if there are identified ethical issues. These feedback loops should be designed to engage diverse stakeholders, especially those who may be disproportionately affected by AI systems, such as marginalized groups or vulnerable populations (O'Neil, 2016). For example, AI systems used in hiring or criminal justice can have a disproportionate impact on underrepresented groups, and it is important for organizations to have mechanisms to gather and respond to their concerns.

One of the key ethical considerations with the deployment of AI systems is that they tend to amplify already existing social inequalities. AI systems are trained on historical data, and if the data reflects biased or unequal treatment, these biases are likely to be perpetuated in AI outcomes. Thus, there is a strong need for organizations to implement strategies for mitigating bias in AI operations. This could include periodically checking the fairness of AI decisions, applying bias correction algorithms, or engaging external experts to review the fairness of AI systems. Sometimes, this might mean that adjustments are continually made to the AI models based on real-world performance data and user feedback to ensure that they do not harm underrepresented or vulnerable groups.

Lastly, ethical AI deployment requires a continued commitment to data protection and privacy. The ethical use of data is essential in preventing harm, especially when AI systems are based on sensitive information. Organizations need to ensure that they are not violating privacy regulations such as the GDPR or the California Consumer Privacy Act (CCPA), ensuring personal information is safe, and implementing strong security measures to protect against data breaches. It therefore goes beyond AI model development but includes the secure handling of data throughout the life cycle of operating an AI system, as suggested by Tufekci (2018).

Overall, ethics for AI deployment and operations requires adequate planning, real-time oversight, and commitment to fairness, accountability, and transparency. By ensuring AI systems align with intended ethical outcomes, regularly monitoring their performance, providing transparency in decision-making, respecting user consent, and maintaining responsiveness to emerging concerns, organizations can deploy AI in ways that benefit society and minimize harm. Ethical deployment practices not only build trust with users but also ensure that AI technologies contribute positively to individuals and communities without exacerbating inequality or causing unintended negative consequences.

## Creating an Ethical AI Feedback Loop

The ethical AI feedback loop is an important aspect for ensuring accountability, transparency, and conformity of AI systems to ethical principles in the course of their lifecycle. In the course of deployment and operation in real-world environments, new ethical challenges and risks can emerge. A well-designed feedback loop will enable organizations to continuously assess the performance of AI systems, address emerging ethical concerns, and make the necessary adjustments to prevent harm. The feedback loop ensures that AI technologies align with an organization's ethical standards while building trust among users, stakeholders, and the public. It is a dynamic process that encourages continuous improvement and responsiveness to ethical issues, ensuring that AI systems remain safe, equitable, and transparent over time.

The first step in creating an effective ethical feedback loop is to establish clear ethical guidelines and objectives at the outset. Organizations must define what ethical principles will guide the development, deployment, and operations of AI systems. Some of these could include fairness, transparency, accountability, privacy, and inclusiveness. When implemented into the AI design and development phase, this allows organizations to establish a fundamental ethical AI feedback loop that will be measurable throughout the life cycle of the system. Ethical standards must be revisited regularly in the feedback process to enable organizations to adapt their strategies with new insights and challenges arising (Jobin, Ienca, & Vayena, 2019).

The most important part of the ethical feedback loop is the real-time monitoring of AI systems after deployment. Even though AI systems can be rigorously tested during development, real-world use often poses unforeseen challenges, such as shifts in data distributions or changes in user behavior. Continuous monitoring allows organizations to track AI system performance in real time, ensuring that it operates according to ethical standards. For instance, if an AI system used in hiring processes begins to exhibit biased behavior toward certain demographic groups, continuous monitoring can identify these disparities early on, enabling corrective action to be taken. Regular audits and checks on algorithmic decisions are critical to detect biases, inaccuracies, or harmful outcomes that may not have been evident in the testing process (Binns, 2018). The monitoring must cover technical performance as well as ethical impact with defined metrics to measure fairness, transparency, and other ethical benchmarks.

The feedback loop must also include mechanisms for stakeholder engagement. Ethical concerns are not limited to internal assessments; they should also involve feedback from external stakeholders, including users, customers, regulatory bodies, advocacy groups, and affected communities. For example, in high-stakes AI applications like healthcare or criminal justice, it is important to solicit feedback from vulnerable populations who may be disproportionately affected by biased or unfair decisions. The organization should provide channels that are accessible and clear to the stakeholders on reporting concerns, sharing experiences, and giving their opinions about the AI system's ethical performance. This may include conducting surveys, having user forums, using social media platforms, or organizing community outreach programs. Through these channels, the organizations will hear the voice of those who have been affected by the AI system, providing the organizations with information on real-world implications that could help improve the system (O'Neil, 2016).

Human oversight is another very important component of an ethical AI feedback loop. AI systems are powerful tools, but they may sometimes make mistakes or produce results that are difficult to interpret. Human oversight ensures that decisions made by AI systems are subject to review and intervention when necessary. Human oversight is in many critical applications not only an ethical requirement but also a legal one. For instance, in healthcare, AI can aid in decision-making regarding diagnosis, but an expert health care provider has to evaluate and validate the conclusions by AI before applying them. In an autonomous vehicle, even though the system is enabled to make driving decisions, human drivers should always be alert and on standby in case of a human takeover. Mechanisms for human-in-the-loop guarantee that AI decisions are inspected for fairness, safety, and suitableness to ethics (Levesque, 2017).

Therefore, in an ethical AI feedback loop, there should also be iterative improvement of the system based on its feedback and performance data. When ethics or technical failures are identified in the system, organizations must provide procedures for correcting and updating their AI system. For instance, if a hiring process AI system is determined to be biased against certain demographic groups, the organization can adjust the model, retrain it with more representative data, or implement additional fairness algorithms. Iterative improvement requires commitment to continuous learning and adaptation to ensure that the AI system evolves in response to changing ethical standards, societal expectations, and technological advancements. This implies that there should be post-deployment investments for maintaining and upgrading the AI system as challenges and risks arise over a much longer time horizon after the deployment phase has begun (Rahwan et al., 2019).

A third and crucial feature of an ethical feedback loop is to provide transparency and explainability over how the received feedback will help to enhance AI systems. With the aid of transparency, the system assures internal and external stakeholders about what happens to the feedback provided for incorporating into its operations and decision-making. Suppose a user finds an AI-driven loan approval system prone to bias and reports this; in that case, transparency will mean providing a clear explanation of how the system will be reviewed and adjusted for their feedback. Explainability also extends to how changes to the system are communicated. When an AI model is modified to address bias, there should be some form of explanation of what was changed, why that was necessary, and how it is expected to improve the ethical performance of the system (Lipton, 2018). Transparency in the feedback loop increases trust, ensuring that stakeholders feel their concerns are taken seriously and that corrective actions are being taken in good faith.

Data privacy and security are crucial in the context of AI feedback loops. During the feedback process, organizations may collect user data, feedback, and operational data from AI systems. The handling of such data must be responsible, according to privacy regulations like the General Data Protection Regulation (GDPR) or the California Consumer Privacy Act (CCPA). Organizations must be transparent about what data is being collected, how it will be used, and who will have access to it. This builds trust and protects user rights and privacy during the feedback process. In addition, feedback mechanisms must include security protocols to protect the sensitive data that is gathered within the loop against breaches or misuse (Tufekci, 2018).

Lastly, accountability is at the heart of an ethical AI feedback loop. Organizations must be able to delineate clear lines of responsibility for action on feedback and ethical improvements in AI systems. This includes responsibility to both the individual and teams involved in review and action taken on feedback. For instance, an ethics committee or a specific AI ethics officer could be given the responsibility of reviewing reports, monitoring systems, and ensuring that the ethical concerns are addressed in an effective and timely manner. Accountability structures allow feedback to never go without answer and allow organizations to assume full responsibility over an ethically well-functioning AI system.

Therefore, developing the ethical AI feedback loop is an adaptive and evolving practice that must follow careful planning with transparency and effective engagement of stakeholder inputs accompanied by human overviews with steady improvements. Feedback from internal and external sources should be incorporated to monitor AI systems in real-time and make iterative adjustments to keep AI technologies aligned with ethical principles and societal values. This feedback loop helps build trust, prevents harm, and fosters the responsible use of AI systems that benefit individuals, organizations, and society at large.

## LEGAL, REGULATORY, AND SOCIETAL IMPACTS OF ETHICAL AI

Artificial Intelligence (AI), recently, has brought out deep ethical, legal, and societal concerns with its increasing integration into the face of various industries and everyday life. The autonomy and pervasiveness of AI systems raise critical questions affecting existing legal frameworks; it calls for new approaches towards regulation; it has drastic implications on society. Ensuring the ethical use of AI involves not only adherence to ethical principles within organizations but also compliance with evolving legal standards and recognition of broader societal impacts. Understanding the legal, regulatory, and societal impacts of AI is essential for organizations striving to develop and deploy AI responsibly, while also managing risks and fostering trust among stakeholders.

## Legal Effects of Ethical AI

Legal impacts of ethical AI relate more or less to how AI-related laws and regulations have changed. As far as technological change is concerned, the process has always been a bit slow, at least regarding traditional lawmaking. Yet today, AI-based systems are taking their places everywhere from healthcare and criminal justice systems to finance and self-driving cars; this forces the governments to bring legal frameworks for unique AI-specific issues. The legal implications of AI are wide-ranging, involving liability, intellectual property, data privacy, and discrimination.

A particularly sensitive issue regarding the law involves liability. Whose fault would it be when an AI causes damage? How does one sue for damages or take responsibility if a self-driving car crashes, or if an AI-powered diagnostic system renders a wrong diagnosis? Accordingly, liability laws would need to be drafted appropriately so that current liability laws could not handle these questions effectively (Gunning et al., 2019). In some situations, AI acts in ways that cannot be completely predictable, which hinders legal responsibility assignment. The developer, user, or manufacturer of the AI system should be held liable for harm; otherwise a new category of liability - AI-specific liability - is introduced (Calo, 2015).

This raises a critical area of legal concern: data privacy. An AI system often relies upon vast amounts of data to make decisions as well as train models on such data, much of which may be sensitive personal information. With the spotlight now on the collection, storage, and use of personal data, laws like the European Union's General Data Protection Regulation (GDPR) and the California Consumer Privacy Act (CCPA) have raised the bar for organizations collecting data from individuals. The ethical AI system needs to be designed to comply with these regulations, thereby protecting individual privacy and costly legal ramifications. For example, the right to access data, rectify data, or delete data is given to the individual under the GDPR, which affects the way data collection and storage are designed in the AI system (Voigt & Von dem Bussche, 2017).

Legal question regarding discrimination- Ethical AI is contingent upon considerations toward discrimination. AI systems fed with biased data create the problem of aggravating and even perpetuating what exists, which could violate anti-discrimination laws. For instance, if an AI hiring algorithm somehow favors one group of people against another, that may violate, for example, the Civil Rights Act or equal employment opportunity laws in the U.S. or anti-discrimination laws in any other jurisdiction. According to O'Neil (2016), legal scholars would argue that these regulations must make provisions for how algorithmic discrimination might occur and ensure that an AI system must be designed and tested to eliminate biased outcomes.

## Regulatory Impact of Ethical AI

Regulatory frameworks for AI are being developed to meet the ethical challenges that these technologies present. In response to the rapid growth of AI, governments and international organizations are proposing various regulations and guidelines to ensure that AI development and deployment align with ethical standards, mitigate harm, and protect public safety.

At the national level, countries are introducing or contemplating AI-specific regulations to address concerns about ethics, accountability, and safety. For instance, the European Commission proposed the Artificial Intelligence Act in 2021, which aims to regulate high-risk AI applications such as biometric identification, critical infrastructure, and law enforcement (European Commission, 2021). This regulation is aimed at ensuring that AI systems are developed and deployed in a manner that respects fundamental rights, including privacy, non-discrimination, and transparency. Similarly, in the U.S., there is no federal AI law, but various states and regulatory bodies are making rules to ensure that the applications of AI are transparent and that the risks are managed (Calo, 2015). The regulatory framework in the U.S. has been evolving as a response to growing concerns over the misuse of AI in surveillance and criminal justice.

Apart from national regulatory measures, an international cooperation framework would be necessary because of the global nature of AI technologies. Ethical issues related to AI are cross-border issues since AI systems usually cross borders with data flows. International organizations such as the Organisation for Economic Co-operation and Development (OECD) and the United Nations are responding to this need by working on putting together general standards and frameworks that should guide the development and application of ethical AI (OECD, 2021). These guidelines focus on the transparency, accountability, and non-discrimination in AI systems and push for the responsible use of AI in healthcare, security, and finance.

One of the main aspects of regulation is that the ethical AI frameworks have to be enforceable. This involves mechanisms for auditing AI systems and ensuring accountability of organizations for any violations of ethical or legal standards. Governments may need to develop new regulatory bodies or empower existing ones to monitor and enforce AI compliance, as AI technologies continue to evolve faster than traditional regulatory bodies can adapt (Rahwan et al., 2019).

## Societal Impacts of Ethical AI

The impact of AI on society is broad, ranging from employment and privacy to access to justice and social equity. In fact, ethical AI has to consider broader implications of the deployment of the AI to ensure it brings benefit to the entire society without adding to the list of harmful practices or contributing to inequality.

Among the primary concerns related to the adoption of AI, job displacement ranks first. Automation and AI-based systems are a potential disruptor in labor markets. The industries affected most would include manufacturing, transportation, and customer service. AI could create new opportunities and enhance productivity but may lead to job loss and income inequality. Societies must find a way to cope with these changes through education, reskilling, and social safety nets. Ethical AI deployment should consider social impacts of automation and AI, taking care not to disadvantage workers with technological advancements more than others do (Brynjolfsson & McAfee, 2014).

Bias and discrimination are also central societal issues related to AI. If not carefully designed and monitored, AI systems can perpetuate existing biases in data, which lead to discriminatory outcomes that disadvantage marginalized groups. This can cause much harm in the sectors like criminal justice, where AI gadgets are used to make predictive policies or risk assessment that may target certain racial or ethnic groups more than others. The AI must work to ensure that it is fair, non-discriminatory, and transparent to prevent societal harm. Societies must ensure that ethical AI systems will not exacerbate societal divisions but contribute to social equity and justice (Eubanks, 2018).

The other critical issue for society is privacy. As AI systems often require access to vast amounts of personal data, the privacy of individuals is at risk of being compromised. In ethical AI, therefore, privacy must be protected, and individuals should have control over their personal data. Rules such as the GDPR and CCPA are crucial for protecting the privacy of individuals, but AI systems also need to be designed with the principles of privacy by design that protect data from the beginning (Tufekci, 2018).

Trust is a broader societal issue that relates to the use of deployed AI systems. For AI to be widespread and accepted and integrated into the society, one needs to assure that these systems are working with ethics and transparently. Therefore, trust develops through transparency, accountability, and fairness, and if these values are the priorities of any organization, their AI systems contribute positively to the society. Absence of such trust can have public resistance for AI systems; otherwise, there is a fear that AI would not benefit humanity.

In conclusion, the impact of ethical AI is legal, regulatory, and societal. Legal frameworks must be aligned to address liabilities, data privacy, and discrimination. Regulatory bodies must ensure the development and deployment of AI in ethically sound processes with proper safeguards to protect the individual and the community. AI, on the societal level, must be applied in ways that promote social equity, transparency, and accountability. By dealing with these legal, regulatory, and societal challenges, organizations can ensure that AI benefits society and causes the least harm and meets the highest ethical standards.

## CONCLUSION: BUILDING A SUSTAINABLE ETHICAL AI CULTURE

Never before has ethical AI been more needed. As AI technologies become increasingly sophisticated and pervasive, organizations face the challenge of ensuring that these systems are developed and deployed in a manner that is aligned with ethical principles, legal standards, and societal expectations. Throughout this chapter, we have considered the different aspects of building an ethical AI culture in organizations, from understanding core AI ethics principles, leadership commitment, cross-functional teams, and embedding ethics into AI development processes. These are the efforts that would help to minimize the risks related to AI, such as algorithmic bias, discrimination, data privacy concerns, and job displacement.

Leadership commitment forms one of the foundational elements for a sustainable ethical AI culture. Leadership will have set the tone for how matters of ethics will be considered in an organization. Executives and decision-makers must lead on ethical AI, ensuring these values cascade from strategy and development to deployment and long-term operation. By infusing ethics into the organizational DNA, leaders not only cultivate an atmosphere of trust and accountability but also navigate their organizations through the daunting complexity of implementing ethical AI.

Secondly, establish a cross-functional team with diverse input, as many functions of the organization are being affected by AI, and, hence, multiple disciplines will have to be accounted for in such ethics. These teams by experts in technology, law, ethics, human resources and other competent areas can work together to identify risks, formulate guidelines, and assess the ethical implications of AI systems at every stage of development and deployment.

No less important is the continuous employee education and training in ethical AI practices. The ethical AI competencies are developed in the workforce, which implies that developers as well as decision-makers in an organization can identify and respond to any ethical issues arising in their processes. Through the encouragement of awareness and responsibility, it will ensure the designing of AI systems that are based on fairness, transparency, and accountability. Such training programs can include not just the technical application of AI, but also broader impacts on the society and their ethics, for which employees working on such assignments would be exposed.

Transparency and fairness are critical principles in the development of ethical AI systems. The ability to explain AI decision-making processes and ensure that systems operate without bias is paramount. Transparency fosters trust among users, stakeholders, and the public, while fairness ensures that AI systems do not perpetuate or amplify societal inequalities. Organizations must develop mechanisms to regularly evaluate AI systems, monitor their outputs, and make adjustments when necessary to avoid harm and ensure ethical compliance.

The feedback mechanism in AI systems is a critical element of an organization's long-term commitment to ethical AI. With the establishment of a feedback mechanism that involves the participation of internal and external stakeholders, organizations can monitor the real-world performance of AI systems and respond to emerging issues in a timely manner. This iterative process of evaluation and adjustment enables organizations continuously to improve ethical standards for their AI technologies and maintain accountability throughout the lifecycle.

Moreover, organizations should be aware of the significant legal, regulatory, and societal implications of AI systems. Organizations need to address the challenging legal and ethical dilemmas presented by AI technologies in order to maintain compliance with new regulations and standards, both nationally and internationally. The failure to achieve this can lead to legal liability, reputational damage, and a loss of public trust. The deployment of AI systems also needs to consider societal issues, such as the potential for AI to contribute to inequality or job displacement. Ethical AI should contribute to the common good, promote social equity, and ensure that vulnerable populations are not disproportionately harmed.

Ultimately, building an ethical AI culture within organizations is a continuous journey that requires commitment, collaboration, and ongoing efforts from all levels of the organization. In fact, although the last few years have seen important steps forward, there is still a lot of work to be done in ensuring that AI is developed and deployed in ways that reflect the values of fairness, transparency, and accountability. It is in such an arena where ethics must take the forefront, beginning with the design phase through deployment, ensuring that the created AI technology serves a better tomorrow with responsibility and safety and serves society at large.

As AI continues to evolve, so must our approach to its ethical implications. Organizations can not only avoid risks but also seize opportunities to innovate in ways that are aligned with the public good by fostering a culture of ethical AI. Ethical AI is not just a compliance issue—it is a critical component of sustainable, responsible innovation that can shape a better future for all.

## REFERENCES


Barocas, S., Hardt, M., & Narayanan, A. (2019). *Fairness and machine learning: Limitations and opportunities*. https://fairmlbook.org

Binns, R. (2018). Fairness in machine learning: Lessons from political philosophy. *Proceedings of the 2018 CHI Conference on Human Factors in Computing Systems*, 1-14. DOI: 10.1145/3173574.3173982

Brynjolfsson, E., & McAfee, A. (2014). *The second machine age: Work, progress, and prosperity in a time of brilliant technologies*. W.W. Norton & Company.

Burrell, J. (2016). How the machine 'thinks': Understanding opacity in machine learning algorithms. *Big Data & Society*, 3(1), 1–12. DOI: 10.1177/2053951715622512

Calo, R. (2015). Robots in American law. *U.C. Davis Law Review*, 49(1), 65–124. DOI: 10.2139/ssrn.2584400

Dastin, J. (2018). Amazon scraps secret AI recruiting tool that showed bias against women. *Reuters*. https://www.reuters.com/article/us-amazon-com-jobs-automation-insight-idUSKCN1MK08G

Diakopoulos, N. (2016). *Automating the news: How algorithms are reshaping journalism*. Columbia University Press.

Diakopoulos, N., Friedler, S. A., Pesta, B., & Wallach, H. (2020). *Fairness, accountability, and transparency in machine learning: A survey*. Springer., DOI: 10.1007/s11023-019-09506-3

Eubanks, V. (2018). *Automating inequality: How high-tech tools profile, police, and punish the poor*. St. Martin's Press.

European Commission. (2016). *General Data Protection Regulation (GDPR)*. https://gdpr-info.eu

European Commission. (2021). *Proposal for a regulation laying down harmonized rules on artificial intelligence (Artificial Intelligence Act)*. https://ec.europa.eu/info/business-economy-euro/banking-and-finance/financial-markets/securities-markets/financial-regulation/ai-acts_en

Floridi, L., Cowls, J., Beltrametti, M., Chatila, R., Chazerand, P., Dignum, V., Luetge, C., Madelin, R., Pagallo, U., Rossi, F., Schafer, B., Valcke, P., & Vayena, E. (2018). AI4People—An ethical framework for a good AI society: Opportunities, risks, principles, and recommendations. *Minds and Machines*, 28(4), 689–707. DOI: 10.1007/s11023-018-9482-5 PMID: 30930541

Gunning, D., Aha, D., & McGovern, A. (2019). *Explainable artificial intelligence (XAI)*. DARPA. https://www.darpa.mil/program/explainable-artificial-intelligence

Hardt, M., Price, E., & Srebro, N. (2016). Equality of opportunity in supervised learning. *Proceedings of the 30th International Conference on Neural Information Processing Systems*, 3315-3323.

IEEE. (2019). *IEEE 7000-2021: Standard for ethics in autonomous and intelligent systems*. IEEE. https://standards.ieee.org/standards/7000

Jobin, A., Ienca, M., & Vayena, E. (2019). The global landscape of AI ethics guidelines. *Nature Machine Intelligence*, 1(9), 389–399. DOI: 10.1038/s42256-019-0088-2

Levesque, H. (2017). *Artificial intelligence: A guide for thinking humans*. Penguin Press.

Lipton, Z. C. (2018). The mythos of model interpretability. *Communications of the ACM*, 61(12), 36–43. DOI: 10.1145/3233231

Mittelstadt, B. D., Allo, P., Taddeo, M., Wachter, S., & Floridi, L. (2016). The ethics of algorithms: Mapping the debate. *Big Data & Society*, 3(2), 1–21. DOI: 10.1177/2053951716679679

O'Neil, C. (2016). *Weapons of math destruction: How big data increases inequality and threatens democracy*. Crown Publishing Group.

Obermeyer, Z., Powers, B. W., Vogeli, C., & Mullainathan, S. (2019). Dissecting racial bias in an algorithm used to manage the health of populations. *Science*, 366(6464), 447–453. DOI: 10.1126/science.aax2342 PMID: 31649194

OECD. (2019). *OECD Principles on Artificial Intelligence*. https://www.oecd.org/going-digital/ai/principles/

OECD. (2021). *Recommendation of the Council on Artificial Intelligence*. OECD. https://www.oecd.org/digital/ai/

Rahwan, I., Cebrian, M., & Robles, D.. (2019). Machine behaviour. *Nature*, 568(7753), 477–486. DOI: 10.1038/s41586-019-1138-y PMID: 31019318

Ribeiro, M. T., Singh, S., & Guestrin, C. (2016). "Why should I trust you?": Explaining the predictions of any classifier. *Proceedings of the 22nd ACM SIGKDD International Conference on Knowledge Discovery and Data Mining*, 1135-1144.

Stix, C. (2017). *Asilomar AI Principles*. Future of Life Institute. https://futureoflife.org/ai-principles/

Tufekci, Z. (2018). *Twitter and tear gas: The power and fragility of networked protest*. Yale University Press.

Vinuesa, R., Azizpour, H., Leite, I., Aken, M. V., & Schiebinger, L. (2020). The role of artificial intelligence in achieving the Sustainable Development Goals. *Nature Communications*, 11(1), 233. DOI: 10.1038/s41467-019-14108-y PMID: 31932590

Voigt, P., & Von dem Bussche, A. (2017). *The EU General Data Protection Regulation (GDPR): A practical guide*. Springer. DOI: 10.1007/978-3-319-57959-7

West, S. M., Whittaker, M., & Crawford, K. (2019). Discriminating systems: Gender, race, and power in AI. *AI Now Institute Report 2019*. https://ainowinstitute.org/aienow19.pdf

Wirtz, B. W., Göttel, V., & Daiser, P. (2019). Artificial intelligence and the digital transformation of business models. *Electronic Markets*, 29, 535–551. DOI: 10.1007/s12525-019-00354-3

Wright, S. (2019). Artificial intelligence ethics and governance: Challenges and opportunities. *AI & Society*, 34(3), 553–561. DOI: 10.1007/s00146-019-00879-6

Zhang, B. H., Lemoine, B., & Dastin, J. (2018). Mitigating bias in algorithmic decision-making systems: A survey of fairness techniques. *Proceedings of the 2018 IEEE International Conference on Data Science and Advanced Analytics (DSAA)*, 279-288.

# Chapter 2
# The Trust Paradox:
## A Study on the Overlapping of Trust and Distrust Constructs

**Pedro Brazo**
https://orcid.org/0000-0002-8858-6813
*University of Seville, Spain*

**Felix Velicia-Martin**
https://orcid.org/0000-0003-2300-6256
*University of Seville, Spain*

**Pedro R. Palos-Sanchez**
https://orcid.org/0000-0001-9966-0698
*University of Seville, Spain*

## ABSTRACT

*This chapter discusses the complicated interplay between trust and distrust in artificial intelligence. It argues against the prevalent view of trust and distrust as two contrary states, providing theoretical foundations for the existence of overlapping states in decision-making processes. This revolutionary view is corroborated with both theoretical analysis and methodological novelties by applying a probabilistic model based on the Beta distribution. Thus, it becomes clear that trust in artificial intelligence has to go much beyond just the parameters of credibility and benevolence, which is comparable to human relationships, and include ethical, social, and technical components that are interlinked in the collaboration between humans and machines.*

DOI: 10.4018/979-8-3693-9894-4.ch002

## INTRODUCTION

The rapid advancement of artificial intelligence (AI) has brought about a new era in technology and decision-making, unparalleled in opportunities and complex ethical and moral issues. AI presents several major ethical concerns for society: bias and discrimination, privacy and surveillance, and the risk of system malfunctions and misuse. These issues raise difficult questions about the role of AI in decision-making. While AI offers significant potential for economic and social development, its implementation also exposes users to risks, from reinforcing social prejudices (Köbis et al., 2021) to the dangers of mass surveillance (Hu et al., 2024; Mobilio, 2023; Sedky et al., 2005), and privacy violations in areas like healthcare (Borda et al., 2022). These challenges highlight the need for careful ethical consideration of AI's impact, as it becomes a powerful tool full of both commitment and jeopardy, much like the duality of Dr. Jekyll and Mr. Hyde.

Given AI's worldwide reach and impact, evaluating the concepts of trust and distrust in these technologies is critical for its ethical development and implementation (Bécue et al., 2021; Gasser, 2023). Indeed, despite the widespread acceptance of trust in all types of relationships, the potential for trust betrayal has received little attention. While trust often denotes a collaborative engagement between agents in a relationship that is featured by shared expectations of ethical behavior, however, distrust denotes a break from such collaborative standards, often appearing as opportunistic behavior (Arrow, 1974). Inside the trust construct appear credibility and benevolence, two foundational sources of trust, stressing this contrast. According to the literature, credibility refers to a seller's attributes, especially in the areas of expertise, honesty, and reliability. On the other hand, benevolence points to the vendor having a personal stake in the customer's satisfaction (Garbarino & Lee, 2003; Sirdeshmukh et al., 2002). Under these precedents, distrust might be seen as the exact opposite of trust, as the absence of trust (Cho, 2006).

As AI increases in importance, expanding to encompass increasingly diverse partnerships, buyers' and suppliers' views become obsolete and limited, due to the entrance into the scene of other agents. The use of artificial intelligence has led to the existence of new relations and types of trust. Traditionally, the literature identifies four groups of trust-based relationships: (1) between individuals or between groups, (2) between individuals and organizations, (3) between organizations, and (4) between individuals and technology (Söllner et al., 2016). However, with the advent of artificial intelligence, a new model has evolved, creating a new type of agent that interacts transversally with all the previous agents: the machine learning agent. This new agent interacts autonomously, transforming the previous four groups of trust-based relationships into (1) individuals-individuals-AI, (2) individuals-organizations-AI, (3) organizations-organizations-AI, and (4) technology-AI. This means that there is no remuneration for the transaction anymore (buyers' and suppliers' views), and trust cannot be evaluated only based on personal credibility and benevolence because this machine code, invented by a human being, has learned also from the human credibility and benevolence default.

In light of the antecedents mentioned above the following research questions serve as a framework for this investigation. What separates distrust from trust? Are they separate structures, or do they reflect the two extremes of a single continuum? Should trust and mistrust also be assessed using different measures?

This study takes a two-part approach. First, it explores the concept of trust, how it's currently measured, and emerging theories on the growing importance of distrust. Second, it offers a new perspective on trust and distrust, suggesting they should be seen as a probabilistic function rather than a simple dichotomy.

## THEORETICAL BACKGROUND

The constructs of trust and distrust have undergone extensive scholarly investigation across a multitude of disciplines, including psychology (Rempel et al., 1985; Rotter, 1967), sociology (Coleman, 1990; Luhmann, 2018), organizational behavior (Dirks & Ferrin, 2001; Mayer et al., 1995), and more recently, computer science and artificial intelligence (Graziani et al., 2023; Lewis & Marsh, 2022).

Following Rousseau et al. (1998) and Mayer et al. (1995), trust is often described as a psychological state that involves the willingness to be vulnerable and is based on favorable expectations about another party's intentions or actions. Mistrust involves aspects of wariness, suspicion, and a lack of confidence in the other party and should not simply be seen as the absence of trust (Hardin, 2004; Lewicki et al., 1998). In light of the given circumstances, trust can perhaps be defined not simply as the absence of doubt, but as a synthesis of judgment, acceptance of risk, and uncertainty management.

Trust is a high-order construct (see Figure 1) that integrates multiple dimensions to represent its theoretical complexity. Trust is conceptualized as a higher-order latent variable through second-order components comprising credibility and benevolence, each further defined by subdimensions such as credibility (competence, reliability, and trustworthiness) and benevolence (altruism, and goodwill). This hierarchical approach allows researchers to model trust as a multidimensional construct, capturing its holistic nature while retaining the specialties required for the assessment of separate dimensions.

## Trust and Credibility

Credibility is a multidimensional artifact, operationalized through a range of indicators, such as competence, trustworthiness, and reliability (see Figure 1). Following McKnight et al. (1998), in the context of organizations, credibility is frequently operationalized through measurements of competence, which may include technical ability and prior performance achievements. Competence refers to reputation, credibility, and transparency; however, this feature could be much more as a perceived quality, human quality, rather than of a computer product (Tseng & Fogg, 1999). Credibility also has to do with the user's expertise. People are more likely to perceive an AI technology as credible when they lack expertise, so they tend to be less skeptical about a technology that has been developed to help them.

*Figure 1. TRUST High-Order Construct (HOC) model*

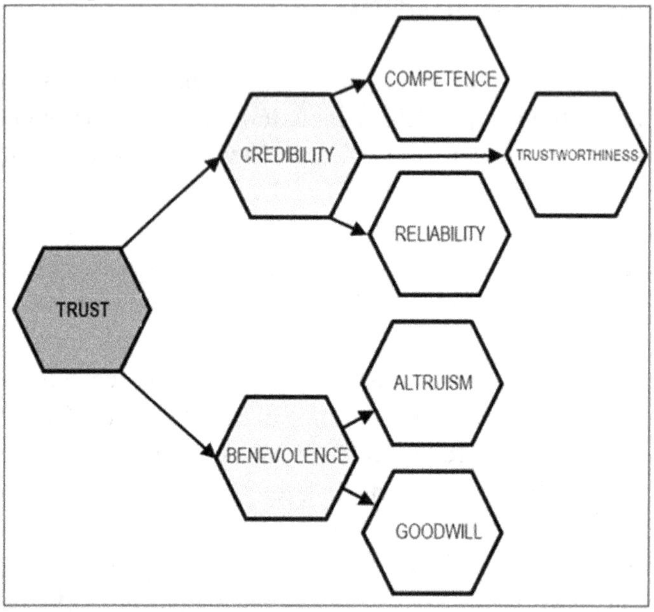


*Source: Own Elaboration*

Credibility assessment (see Table 1) can be particularly useful when integrating AI-based recommendations into a decision-making process. It emphasizes that trust is not binary: It depends on both the technical integrity of the AI and the credibility of those guiding or overseeing it. By applying this framework, organizations can determine the appropriate level of scrutiny, verification, or trust to assign to any AI-supported action or decision. (1) In the upper left quadrant, both parties are credible: AI is credible because it produces reliable results and the user/organization is confident in AI products (although perhaps not very qualified). At this stage, the organization can have confidence in the results of AI. Good faith is ensured by the user's credibility and the lack of technical expertise by the user is mitigated by the demonstrated credibility of the AI. (2) In the upper right quadrant, the AI is credible and reliable, but the user's credibility in the proposed solution is questionable. While AI suggests that the result is probably good, user involvement calls for caution. The result may still be usable, but it is prudent to review, add supervision, or seek a second opinion before fully acting on the information. (3) The bottom-left quadrant: the user can trust the AI, yet they are less knowledgeable. The tool may not be fully reliable in its domain. The output cannot be relied on directly, even if the credibility of the user is certain. More verification, such as by an outside expert or performing additional testing, would be required before making decisions based on AI tools. Fourth, (4) the lower right quadrant when neither the AI technology nor the user can be trusted. It is safest to reject the result from the AI tools in this case. Having no reliable basis on both sides—user and AI Tech—the risk of acting on misinformation is too high. It would force the organization to look for alternative tools, additional data, or more credible human input to guide decision-making.

*Table 1. Decision matrix for AI credibility assessment*

| **Decision matrix** | | **USER** | |
|---|---|---|---|
| | | **Credible / Lack of expertise** | **No Credible/Own Expertise** |
| AI Tech | Credible | (1) Full Acceptance | (2) Cautious Acceptance |
| | Not Credible | (3) Further Verification | (4) Full Rejection |

Source: Own Elaboration

When determining credibility, we also must pay special attention to truthfulness and reliability (see Figure 1). Butler (1991) and Lewicki et al. (1998), define truthworthiness as the belief that the trustee is acting in good faith and is unlikely to mislead, defraud, or manipulate the trustor. Trustworthiness in the field of artificial intelligence can be operationalized through a system's commitment to ethical standards, the absence of dishonest behavior, and the general recognition of its capabilities and limitations (Floridi & Taddeo, 2016).

The reliability of the trustee's behavior over some time creates a sense of predictability and trustworthiness (McKnight et al., 1998; Zand, 1972). Reliability in the domain of artificial intelligence can be operationalized by system efficiency, output consistency, and resistance to faults or failures (Soni et al., 2019).

These attributes are also of key relevance to the sense of system trustworthiness in organizational contexts, as well as in the artificial intelligence context.

## Trust and Benevolence

Benevolence is typically operationalized in organizational settings with measures of goodwill and altruism (see Figure 1). Altruism represents acts that are intended to benefit the trustor for which there is no expectation of reward, while goodwill represents the trustee's wish to do more than their duty to help the trustor (Blau, 1964; Gefen, 2000).

Benevolence goes beyond merely transactional agreements and entails things like after-sales assistance, individual support, and a readiness to resolve conflicts in the buyer's favor (Palmatier et al., 2006; Pavlou & Gefen, 2005). The seller's concern for the buyer's well-being acts as a sign of benevolence, which in turn instigates trust in the relationship that exists between the two individuals. Benevolence represents a human capacity that is not usually associated with machines. Consequently, it can be anticipated that the absence of empathy in AI will extend to and adversely influence views on its benevolence when compared to a human manager, which may be regarded as a critical determinant in individuals' decisions to place trust in AI management (Li & Bitterly, 2024).

Benevolence, in this context of systems and especially artificial intelligence, can be operationalized through design elements of the system that put the user's well-being first. These may include features that improve the quality of life or ability to do a job, transparent data usage regulations, and user-friendly interfaces (Lee & See, 2004; Vance et al., 2008).

# METHODOLOGY

This research comprises a Scoping Review (ScR) to investigate distrust in artificial intelligence. Although systematic literature reviews have traditionally been the most recognized and extensive methodology, scoping literature reviews have emerged as an alternative to traditional literature review methodologies in several medical and social science domains (Anderson et al., 2008).

A ScR is a broad form of literature review that aims to provide an overview or map of existing data relevant to a large research subject (Miake-Lye et al., 2016; Tricco et al., 2015). Unlike systematic reviews, which are intended to deal with specific, typically observation-oriented issues through a rigorous examination of the quality and conclusions of the included research, scoping reviews are more exploratory in nature (Rumrill et al., 2010). They are particularly effective in identifying key ideas, hypotheses, sources, and evidence gaps in the existing literature. Scoping reviews, in general, do not contain an in-depth evaluation of the data or an assessment of the risk of bias in the studies included, except for the particular importance required by the review objectives.

The primary reason we used a scoping review in our study was to clarify key concepts and definitions in the literature. Scoping reviews are ideal for this since they enable the identification and mapping of many characteristics or concepts present in academic papers or studies (Cacchione, 2016). The scoping review approach is suitable in our scenario since we have no intention to answer a pragmatic question or provide evidence to inform practice. Rather, our objective is to provide an overview of how certain significant concepts or definitions have been addressed in the literature, and therefore a more nuanced knowledge of these terms (Anderson et al., 2008; Arksey & O'Malley, 2005).

## RESULTS AND DISCUSSIONS

### General Approximation

The general purpose of this review of the literature is to use a kind of dialectical reasoning to examine and resolve the research questions proposed in our investigation. We made use of the DIMENSIONS database for this commitment. This relatively new database, which is used for academic research, has completely changed the way metadata is analyzed outside of bibliometrics (Hook et al., 2018). According to Ordua-Malea and Delgado-López-Cózar (2018) and Thelwall (2018), it is seen as a democratization of scholarly data and a substitute for WoS and Scopus. The term distrust was combined into a single Boolean search expression. A Boolean search string was used for the terms 'distrust' and 'artificial intelligence'. We restricted our search to 'journal articles' in English that were published between 2015 and 2023. The results were then grouped according to activities or industry sectors to create a hierarchy (Butler, 2010; Rousseau & Leuven, 2018). The Dimensions database categorizes and gives the research topics a code, enabling a more accurate analysis and filtering of the results. In this instance, we highlight the codes '46 Information and Computing Sciences', '35 Commerce, Management, Tourism and Services', and '42 Health Sciences' as the most notable areas of study. 174 matches were discovered in all.

*Table 2. Fields of research by publication, citations, and citation means*

| Field of Research | Publications | Citations | Citation Mean |
|---|---|---|---|
| 46 Information and Computing Sciences | 54 | 767 | 14,2 |
| 35 Commerce, Management, Tourism, and Services | 23 | 247 | 10,74 |
| 42 Health Sciences | 18 | 394 | 21,89 |
| 44 Human Society | 18 | 358 | 19,89 |
| 32 Biomedical and Clinical Sciences | 15 | 344 | 22,93 |
| 47 Language, Communication, and Culture | 11 | 106 | 9,64 |
| 48 Law and Legal Studies | 10 | 15 | 1,5 |
| 50 Philosophy and Religious Studies | 10 | 97 | 9,7 |
| 36 Creative Arts and Writing | 8 | 84 | 10,5 |
| 52 Psychology | 7 | 173 | 24,71 |

Source: Own Elaboration. Data Extracted from Dimension Database

Figure 2, which records the number of publications on distrust from 2015 to 2023, shows a clear growing trend, which is particularly evident from 2019 on. The lack of academic output over the first years (2014–2018) implies that the subject was still developing and receiving little academic attention. In the years immediately afterward-2019-2023-there is a striking increase, culminating in 23 publications in 2022 and 26 in 2023. The increase in publications could be an indication that distrust has moved from the margin to the center of academic discussion, perhaps as a result of recent developments in society, politics, or techniques that call for urgent scholarly investigation.

*Figure 2. Publications on 'distrust' and AI between 2015 and 2023*

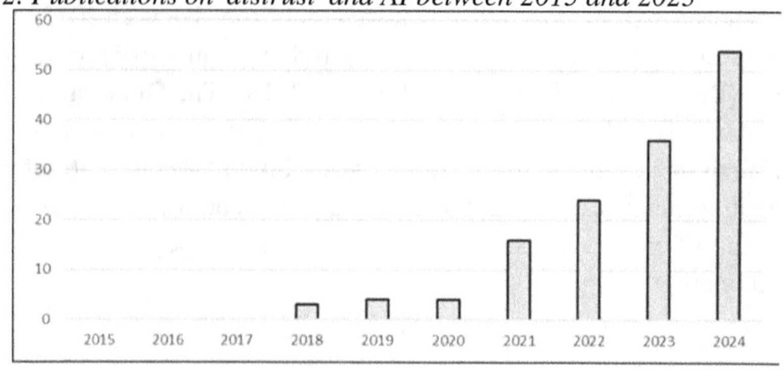


*Source: Own Elaboration. Data extracted from Dimensions database*

We divide economic activities according to the Australian and New Zealand Standard Research Classification (ANZSRC) 2020 code (Bode et al., 2018; Herzog & Lunn, 2018). Figure 3 and Figure 4 provide a view of the academic landscape in various research fields. It shows differences in the total number of publications and the average number of citations per economic field.

*Figure 3. Number of publications in each research category*

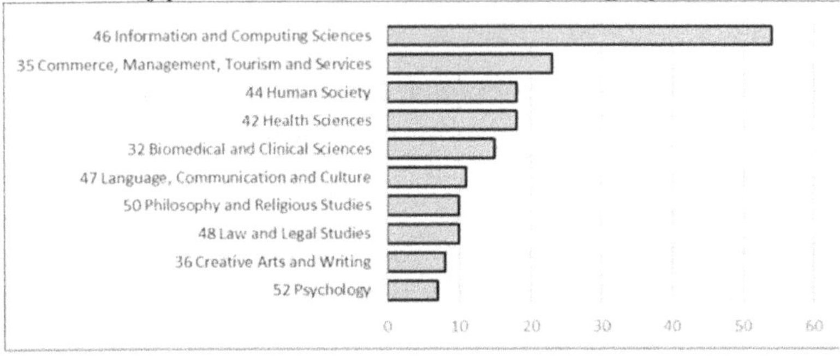


*Source: Own Elaboration. Data extracted from Dimensions database*

*Figure 4. Citation mean in each research category*

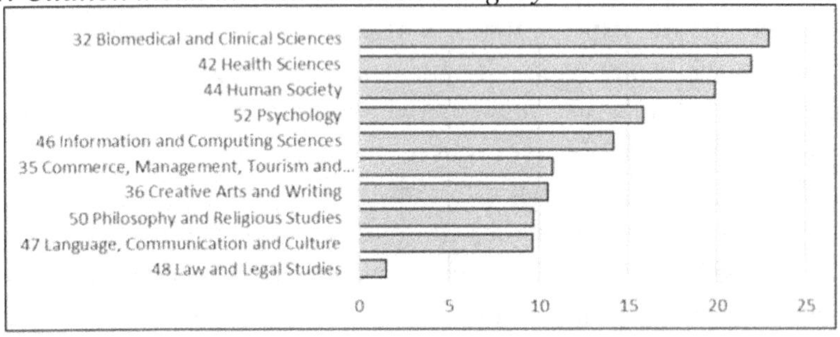


*Source: Own elaboration. Data extracted from Dimensions database*

Table 2 lists the number of publications, total citations, and mean citation rate, while Figures 2, 3, and 4 show the academic production by discipline. A first glance at this table reveals its asymmetry, which underlines the differences in research volume and academic influence. Thus, "Information and Computing Sciences" is the category coming out as most prolific concerning the volume of publication; however, it only moderates in its citation mean to indicate that high productivity does not always mean high research impact. 'Biomedical and Clinical Sciences' has fewer publications, though it does come with the highest citation mean to show exceptional influence and quality per publication. The 'Health Sciences' field shows a strong output and citation impact. However, 'Creative Arts and Writing' and 'Law and Legal Studies' present low results in both categories, thus showing minimal research activity and influence. 'Psychology' has a middle-level citation impact but a lower numbers of publications, which could be indicative of focused and significant research—it is a call for analysis of variance in academic indicators.

## Origins of Distrust

The concept of distrust has been examined in various disciplines and has evolved over time (see Table 3). The term's genesis can be dated to at least the first decade of the 1970s, when significant contributions offered various viewpoints on the nature of distrust (sometimes so-called mistrust).

According to Deutsch's theory (1973), distrust follows from selecting a known course of action over another course of action that might have more harmful than beneficial consequences. By this definition, distrust is fundamentally risk-averse behavior. To minimize the possibility of adverse consequences, individuals or organizations can opt for a safer versus a riskier course of action. So, according to Deutsch, distrust is also a strategic response to insecurity, in addition to being an emotional or psychological state.

In 1979, Austin & Worchel defined distrust as a feeling of the possibility of threat and, therefore, an expectation of harm. This definition marks the affective nature of distrust while putting much emphasis on its predictive aspect. According to Austin & Worchel, mistrust puts a person on alert for eventual harm, and this alertness may influence subsequent actions and decisions.

Dunn (1988) gave a somewhat different view in describing distrust as a hesitation that leads a person to try other alternatives. Rather than passively avoiding danger, the trustee is searching for alternatives; thus, mistrust has an active aspect. In the context of interpersonal relations, where distrust might lead people to seek other social connections or resources, Dunn's concept may be especially applicable.

In conclusion, the concept of distrust has complex historical roots that include strategic, proactive, and emotional aspects. A logical perspective on risk aversion underlies Deutsch's definition. Although Austin & Worchel's concept emphasizes emotional and psychological preparation for possible injury, Dunn's definition places more emphasis on the proactive search for alternatives. Since each of these definitions adds to a sophisticated understanding of distrust, it becomes a multidimensional and complex artifact that applies to many different academic fields, each of them related to different constructs (see Table 3 and Table 4).

*Table 3. The origins of distrust*

| Authors | Year | Definition | Construct |
|---|---|---|---|
| Deutsch | 1973 | Avoiding an ambiguous path has more possible negative consequences than positive consequences. | Suspicion |
| Austin & Worchel | 1979 | A sense of readiness for danger and anticipation of discomfort | Discomfort |
| Dunn | 1988 | Diffidence or doubt that makes one try to find other means | Doubt |

Source: Own elaboration

## Distrust in Artificial Intelligence

The concept of AI can be so wide-ranging that it includes whatever a machine can do that replicates human behavior (Lee et al., 2023; Minsky M, 1968). The general notion of AI links a task typically performed by humans to machine code. This broad definition of AI not only does not assist us in defining what comprises AI in general and what does not, but it also leads to doubt, misinformation, and misuse (De Bruyn et al., 2020). Taking into account the previous considerations, given that AI is based on mimicking human behavior, distrust is more plausible than trust in artificial intelligence (Savage, 2019; Woolgar, 1985).

The idea of distrusting artificial intelligence (AI) has evolved differently if compared to the traditional distrust concept (Hardin, 2004; Lewicki et al., 1998). Distrust linked to AI has changed dramatically in the last few years and has taken various forms in different spheres of society. This period that we analyze, from 2015 to 2024, shows us the extraordinary importance of trust-distrust duality, and the idea of distrust has gone through many stages down the ages, unfolding in different fields.

## Health Science

In the medical area, the concept of distrust has evolved in a complex way. Today, the doctor-patient contact takes place face-to-face. With the development of AI systems, two further forms of interaction are possible: either the doctor's diagnosis and/or treatment decisions are supported by the AI system while having contact with the patient, or the doctor could be substituted by the AI system, in which case the patient has contact with a chatbot - that is, a machine-only (Riedl et al., 2024). Recent scholarship has turned its focus to the complex relationship between technology and health care, more precisely to the distrust of artificial intelligence and mandatory vaccination (Cobianchi et al., 2023; Sallam et al., 2023). With an increasing number of citations for publications issued after 2020, including Gao et al. (2020) and Ongena et al. (2020), one notices the rising trend in concern about the role of technology in nourishing distrust of AI in health care.

## Information Technology and Computer Science

In the area of information technology, the emphasis has been on the social and business dimensions of distrust. Gremillion et al. (2016) investigated the impact of distrust in the context of military technology, while Dwork et al. (2022) and Schepman et al. (2023) investigated the social and business dimensions of skepticism and distrust in AI.

## Components of Social and Cultural Interest

Other studies on social concerns, such as social and media issues, like those by Molina et al. (2023) and Karpus et al. (2021), have looked at how social and moral values and beliefs foster distrust. Moral values and traditional customs are the stumbling blocks to the development of AI. These findings show that distrust is not only a state of mind but also culturally and socially constructed.

## Other Businesses

It would seem that structural and institutional problems weigh organizations down and contribute to the development of distrust. In the smart city context, Leung et al. et al.(2023) examine distrust between residents and the government whereas Prasad et al. (2017) examine it between the supply chain channel partners. These disparate studies demonstrate the complexity with which distrust emerges to be founded on a multitude of factors that include governance and institutional design.

*Table 4. Chronological framework of scholarly contributions to the concept of distrust/mistrust across various sectors, annotated with citation metrics*

| Framework | Year | Authors | Definition of trust / mistrust | Cites |
|---|---|---|---|---|
| Human-Computer Interaction | (2023) | Schepman, Astrid et al. | Corporate distrust leads to negative attitudes toward AI | 11 |
| Medical Science | (2023) | Sallam, Malik et al. | Mistrust and resistance mentioned in the context of compulsory vaccination | 8 |
| Medical Science | (2023) | Cobianchi, Lorenzo et al. | Mistrust associated with lack of knowledge about AI-related aspects | 5 |
| Medical Science | (2023) | Kim, Michelle B. et al. | Medical mistrust contributed to the hesitancy of the HPV vaccine. | 2 |
| Urban Planning | (2023) | Leung, Kevin Y. K. et al. | Mistrust between people and the government in the context of smart cities | 7 |

continued on following page

*Table 4. Continued*

| Framework | Year | Authors | Definition of trust / mistrust | Cites |
|---|---|---|---|---|
| Computer Scie & Law | (2022) | Dwork, Cynthia et al. | Social distrust of AI comes from various sources. | 2 |
| Media & Society | (2022) | Molina, Maria D. et al. | Distrust in humans predicts greater trust in AI. | 5 |
| Medical Science | (2022) | Starke, Georg et al. | Misplaced trust and distrust in medical AI | 1 |
| Statistics & Society | (2022) | Hand, David J. | Mistrust could be aggravated by misuse and misunderstanding of statistical methods. | 6 |
| Ethics & Philosophy | (2021) | Braun, Matthias et al. | Significance of distrust in societal deliberation about trustworthy AI | 14 |
| Medical Science | (2021) | Saunkeah, Bobby et al. | Mistrust and reluctance to participate in research among American Indian/Alaska Native communities | 15 |
| Medical Science | (2021) | Martinho, Andreia et al. | Distrust in private tech companies and the need for regulatory oversight in health AI | 13 |
| Social Dilemmas | (2021) | Karpus, Jurgis et al. | Humans exploit benevolent AI, indicating weaker cooperative dispositions toward AI. | 7 |
| Commun. Studies | (2020) | Lobera, Josep et al. | Opposition to AI is more likely among those with egalitarian values and privacy concerns. | 19 |
| Medical Science | (2020) | Ongena, Yfke P. et al. | Distrust and accountability among patients regarding AI in radiology | 53 |
| Medical Science | (2020) | Gao, Shuqing et al. | Distrust of related companies and lack of trust in AI are reasons for negative attitudes towards medical AI | 43 |
| Medical Science | (2020) | Skewes, Monica C. et al. | Unethical and stigmatizing research has engendered distrust in many Native communities. | 20 |
| Medical Science | (2020) | Mazurowski, Maciej A. | A potential misalignment of interests could create distrust toward the field of AI in radiology. | 15 |
| Medical Science | (2018) | James, Rosalina D. et al. | Mistrust in research among urban American Indian and Alaskan communities | 18 |
| Medical Science | (2022) | McClelland, Shearwood et al. | Mistrust and barriers to cancer screening among American Indian populations | 18 |
| Medical Science | (2018) | Isaacson, Mary J. et al. | Trust/Respect and Mistrust in Culturally Acceptable Palliative / EOL Care for Indigenous People | 16 |
| Medical Science | (2018) | Houghtaling, Bailey et al. | Stressors, including mistrust and substance abuse, impact breastfeeding knowledge and practice in an American Indian community. | 12 |
| Medical Science | (2017) | Guadagnolo, B. Ashleigh et al. | Disparities in cancer care access and outcomes for American Indian populations | 38 |
| Medical Science | (2017) | Enoch, Mary-Anne et al. | Mistrust and unique hurdles in getting consent from tribes for research on alcohol use disorders | 28 |

continued on following page

*Table 4. Continued*

| Framework | Year | Authors | Definition of trust / mistrust | Cites |
|---|---|---|---|---|
| Medical Science | (2017) | Goodwin, Elizabeth A. et al. | Treatment barriers influence social quality of life and indicate mistrust in American Indian/Alaska Native breast cancer survivors. | 15 |
| Medical Science | (2017) | Wille, Stephanie M. et al. | Barriers to healthcare include discrimination and mistrust for American Indians experiencing homelessness. | 15 |
| Medical Science | (2017) | Nesoff, Elizabeth D. et al. | Distrust in the health care system among rural American Indian populations in the context of myocardial infarction | 5 |
| Supply Chain Management | (2017) | Prasad, T. V. S. R. K. et al. | Distrust among channel partners in decentralized supply chains | 1 |
| Medical Science | (2016) | Hernández-Mulero, N. et al. | Interpersonal distrust in the context of athletic identity and eating disorders | 5 |
| Military Technology | (2016) | Gremillion, Gregory M. et al. | Analysis of trust in autonomy for convoy operations, including distrust and disuse of autonomy | 3 |
| Medical Science | (2015) | Tiwari, Tamanna et al. | Distrust related to racial differences and physical and environmental barriers in an American Indian community | 4 |

Source: Own Elaboration from WOS

## The Future of the Mistrust Concept

Rapid technological advancements, particularly in AI and data analytics, are predicted to have an impact on the future of distrust/mistrust. As AI is integrated into more businesses, it is projected that the dimensions of distrust will expand to include ethical, social, and even philosophical concerns (Aljabri et al., 2023). The increasing number of citations for contemporary publications implies that scientific and social interest is growing (see Table 5).

*Table 5. A frequency-based analysis of the attributes of the construct of mistrust across disciplines*

| Cluster | Attributes of Mistrust | Frequency of Citation |
|---|---|---|
| Medical Science | Lack of Knowledge | 5 |
| | Cultural Sensitivity | 4 |
| | Barriers to Access | 4 |
| | Distrust of System | 3 |

continued on following page

*Table 5. Continued*

| Cluster | Attributes of Mistrust | Frequency of Citation |
|---|---|---|
| Technology & Computer Science | Privacy Concerns | 3 |
| | Corporate Distrust | 2 |
| | Misuse and Misunderstanding | 2 |
| Social & Cultural Factors | Racial and Ethnic Factors | 5 |
| | Community Perceptions | 3 |
| | Egalitarian Values | 1 |
| Systemic and Institutional Factors | Lack of Transparency | 2 |
| | Quality of Local Systems | 2 |
| | Regulatory Oversight | 2 |
| Psychological Factors | Low Priority | 1 |
| | Perfectionism | 1 |

Source: Own Elaboration

## Ethical Implications of Bot Abuse in Political and Economics Contexts

Table 6 highlights bot abuse in political and economic contexts, emphasizing disinformation's ethical challenges and the pressing need for frameworks to combat manipulation and restore trust in AI systems.

In 2023, Diaz Ruiz noted how the misinformation process is seeded under the aspect of truthiness, like the case of the 'flat earth movement.'

*Table 6. Ethical implications of bot abuse in political and economic contexts*

| Year | Authors | Bot Use | Context | Misuse |
|---|---|---|---|---|
| (2022) | Wu, Liang et al. | Definition, Manipulation, and Detection | Social Media | Misinformation |
| (2022) | Herasimenka, Aliaksandr et al. | Communication Resource Mobilization | Anti-Vaccination Campaigns | Disinformation, Monetization |
| (2023) | Diaz Ruiz, Carlos A. | Seeding Misinformation: Flat Earth. | Society | Disinformation, Fake News |
| (2024) | Nilsson, Thomas Royal; Spezzano, Francesca | Algorithmic Contribution to Misinformation | Social Networks | Misinformation Dissemination |
| (2024) | Mulcahy, Rory; Barnes, Renee | Sharing of Misinformation by Influencers | Social Media | Misinformation, Consumer Deception |

Source: Own Elaboration

Apparent state-sponsored campaigns by Russia and China have grown increasingly aggressive by 2024. Pathak and Spezzano discuss how bots manipulate the narratives on geopolitical conflicts to create erosions of unity among international allies. Concretely, Chinese networks disseminate misinformation with efforts to discredit human rights abuses and advance state propaganda.

In 2024, Mulcahy and Barnes revealed another dimension in which bots exploited social media influencers to perpetuate fake stories. This has further nurtured public distrust in digital ecosystems. It is not that easy to rebuild confidence in AI technologies either.

Bot abuses are becoming increasingly sophisticated; this demands an immediate need for reforms in ethics as well as detection technologies. Without these reforms, the benefits from AI will perpetually be undermined through disinformation-fueled ongoing suspicion of technology.

## A Change in the Trust-Distrust Paradigm Measurement

In the field of artificial intelligence, the conceptual division between trust and distrust is explored in this study, delving into the approach that advocates that both variables cannot be measured identically because they are constructs that can occur at the same time in an overlapping manner in the same decision-making process, breaking the axiom of orthogonality that has been in force in the related literature.

Traditionally, trust has been measured as a dummy variable, say *T*, where it can only take values *T*=0 (denoting distrust) or *T*=1 (denoting trust). When analyzing such a variable, the theoretical stream of research assumes that both magnitudes are mutually exclusive, which implies the absence of overlap: a system is either trustworthy or, on the contrary, untrustworthy. However, we never fully trust or distrust, so neither full trust nor distrust is possible (Marsh & Dibben, 2005). However, let us assume the orthogonality assumption and examine whether it would be possible to model T in such a way that the overlap of trust and distrust, which we define as a superposition state by similarity to quantum superposition states in computer systems, would be possible.

If we introduce the concept of orthogonality in the variable, transforming it into orthogonal vectors in a two-dimensional vector space, we have the following:

$$v_0 = \binom{1}{0} \; y \; v_1 = \binom{1}{0}$$

We define a superposition state (ψ) for T, which combines trust and distrust, represented as a linear combination of the trust and distrust states:

$$\psi = \alpha v_0 + \beta v_1$$

where $|\alpha^2|+|\beta^2|=1$
In probabilistic terms, this implies:

$$P(T = 0) = |\alpha^2| \; y \; P(T = 1) = |\beta^2|$$

The variable T in this superposition state can therefore probabilistically represent both trust and distrust simultaneously. The orthogonality condition ensures that the states of trust and distrust are independent and mutually exclusive when observed individually; however, in an overlapping state, the dummy variable T would not exclusively reflect trust or distrust, but a combination of both, and an overlapping state can be assumed in probabilistic terms as can be seen in Figure 5.

*Figure 5. Orthogonality configuration and linear combination of trust and distrust*

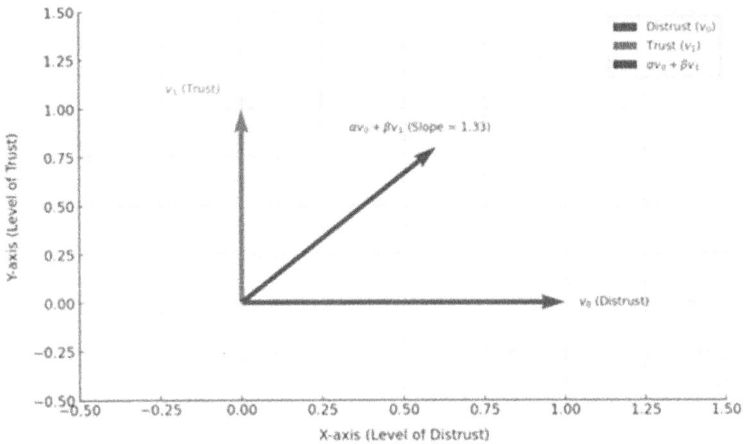


In recent years, the idea of the superposition of binary states has risen in hand with the field of quantum decision-making and Grover´s quantum search algorithm (Ashtiani & Abdollahi Azgomi, 2019). A suitable alternative under the superposition model could be a beta-probabilistic distribution.

The Beta distribution is chosen appropriately as:

1. It allows modeling a variable that can take continuous values between 0 and 1, that is, a continuous mixture from distrust to trust.
2. The beta distribution has shape parameters (α and β) that can regulate the 'intensity' or measure of trust and distrust and can therefore provide a way of modeling the two states within a certain probabilistic proportion. The Beta distribution has a probability density function given by:

$$f(x;\alpha,\beta) = B(\alpha,\beta)^* x^{\alpha-1} * (1-x)^{\beta-1}$$

Where:

- $x$ is the random variable in the range [0, 1],
- α and β are parameters that control the shape of the distribution,
- B(α,β) is the Beta function, which normalizes the distribution.

The Beta distribution is defined as:

$$f(x;\alpha,\beta) = \frac{x^{\alpha-1}(1-x)^{\beta-1}}{B(\alpha,\beta)}, 0 \leq x \leq 1$$

where $B(\alpha,\beta)$ is the Beta function, which normalizes the distribution and is given by:

$$B(\alpha,\beta) = \int_0^1 x^{\alpha-1}(1-x)^{\beta-1}dx$$

To ensure $f(x;\alpha,\beta)$ integrates to 1, we use the normalization of beta distribution:

$$\int_0^1 x^{\alpha-1}(1-x)^{\beta-1}dx = 1$$

Substituting $f(x;\alpha,\beta)$ into the integral:

$$\int_0^1 \frac{x^{\alpha-1}(1-x)^{\beta-1}dx}{B(\alpha,\beta)} = 1$$

Since $B(\alpha,\beta)$ is defined as

$$B(\alpha,\beta) = \int_0^1 x^{\alpha-1}(1-x)^{\beta-1}dx$$

The normalization condition holds because dividing by $B(\alpha,\beta)$ ensures the integral evaluates to 1.

According to the previous demonstration, assuming $\alpha$=3 and $\beta$=2, the beta distribution is:

$$B(3,2) = \int_0^1 x^{3-1}(1-x)^{2-1}dx = \int_0^1 x^2(1-x)^2 dx = \int_0^1 x^2 dx - \int_0^1 x^3 dx = \frac{x^3}{3}\Big|_0^1 - \frac{x^4}{4}\Big|_0^1$$

Then the probability density function becomes

Where
Which could be plotted as follows in Figure 6:

*Figure 6. State of trust according to beta distribution probability density function*

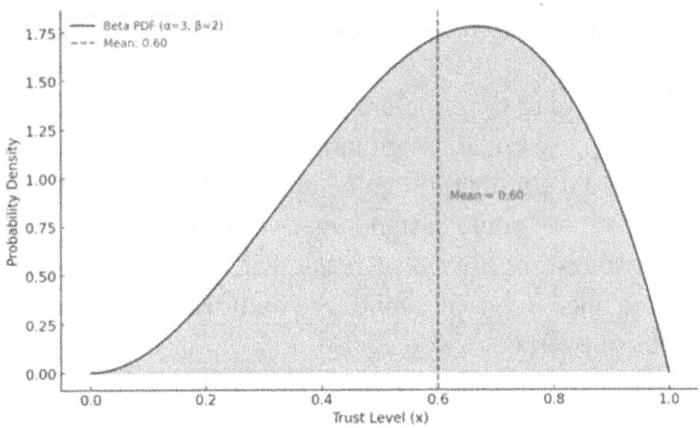


If we invert the coefficients and plot again, we would obtain beta distribution for trust, distrust, and the superposition state.

*Figure 7. State of superposition according to beta distribution probability density function*

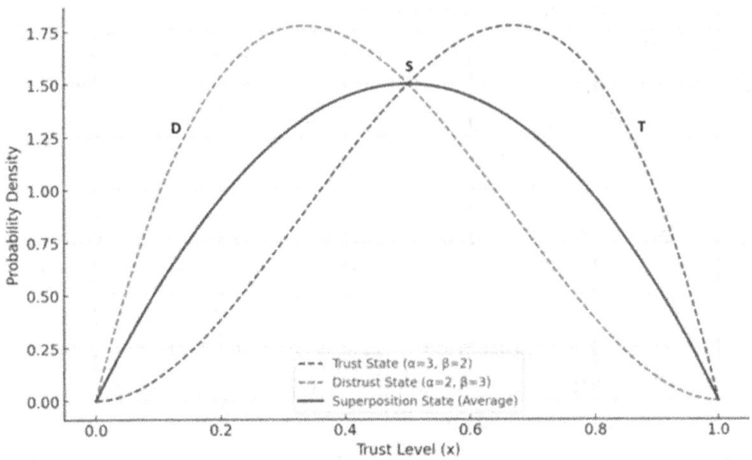

## Interpretation of the Model

By adjusting the parameters α and β, we can make the distribution skew towards 0 (distrust), see red dotted line D, or towards 1 (trust), see blue dotted line T, or maintain an equilibrium between the two (S), reflecting the probabilistic nature and the possibility of 'overlap' between the trust and distrust states.

- If we would require to have the probability to be more inclined toward trust (value close to 1), we could assign larger values to α.
- If we would need the probability to be more inclined towards distrust, that is, a value close to 0, we could assign larger values to β.
- Where both values are alike, the result will stay in an intermediate state, reflecting a balance between confidence and distrust, as would be expected from the idea of overlap.

This distribution allows us to capture the uncertainty and variability in the state of trust in a system under superposition, when users may have a combination of trust and distrust with probabilities rather than a unique deterministic state. In such a context, so long as we can use this distribution in an aprioristic way, we could use it to extract both parameters from a specific situation within a decision-making process. So, in this latter decision-making process:

- If $\alpha>\beta$ (T), the distribution will be skewed towards 1 (see Figures 6 and 7), hence a greater tendency towards trustiness.
- If $\beta>\alpha$ (D), the distribution will be skewed toward 0, reflecting a greater tendency toward distrust.
- If $\alpha\approx\beta$ (S), the distribution will be centered around 0.5, reflecting the balance between trust and distrust (see Figure 7).

This statistical model with the Beta distribution enables us to capture the representation of the overlapping states of confidence and distrust in an AI system.

- Expectation provides an average measure of trust in the system, while variance reflects the uncertainty or dispersion of that confidence.
- By tuning the parameters α and β, we can represent different degrees of inclination toward trust or distrust, thus modeling those situations where users may feel both trust and distrust in variable proportions.

In a nutshell, the Beta distribution is a flexible modeling tool in systems where the notion of trust is not binary, but a probabilistic integration of trust and distrust that befits the notion of overlap.

## CONCLUSIONS, IMPLICATIONS, AND FUTURE LINES OF INVESTIGATION

This study does indeed give a very critical view of the many complexities of distrust in an increasingly misinformation-influenced socio-economic environment, along with rapidly declining social trust. This investigation insists on the need for understanding the role of AI and bots as agents of misinformation in shaping decision-making processes and changing public opinion.

As a concept insinuated as separate from trust, this is a domain that has traditionally been scarcely academically observed. Whereas trust and distrust have conventionally been viewed as opposite sides of the one continuum, this paper develops a rationale for operationalizing distrust as a separate construct. It fits well into the recent calls for research in that respect, such as Six and Latusek (2023), claiming that specific frameworks should be developed since the dynamics of distrust-embedded relationships, especially in contexts involving AI technologies and their misuse, cannot be caught well by the existing ones.

This study gives a comparison of how the bots grew from the simple tasks of data harvesting to identity fraud and complex operations. These have now been expanded to include the spread of fake news, political propaganda, and even financial fraud. This sophistication is not an issue of technology but rather one that cuts across many dimensions: psychological, ethical, and governance-related aspects. The findings underlined one uncomfortable fact: the growing capability of bots to spread misinformation on digital platforms is increasingly difficult to counter, compounding their impact on public trust and individual decision-making.

The development of a new approach to the concept of the trust-distrust paradigm, therefore, carries immense implications for society: the more the public relies on these platforms for information, the more difficult it will be to find ways to distinguish credible sources from manipulated content. In this situation, the vicious circle is that the more advanced and global the bots, the more they will undermine trust in AI technologies. This, in turn, inhibits the more general spread of AI into our lives in areas such as health, education, and governance. The arguments presented here are effective in demonstrating that the developing complexity cycle of bots, together with the reduction in trust, must be slowed if misinformation's societal cost is to be reduced.

Another important contribution of this investigation is its call for combined and rapid efforts toward creating tools for understanding and measuring distrust. It points out the need for scale and framework validation that can quantify distrust as a distinct phenomenon, different from trust. Such a scale is necessary not just to advance academic research but also to inform practical strategies regarding neutralizing misinformation. Offering a better insight into what constitutes distrust, these frames could support initiatives to restore public confidence both in digital platforms and the technology dependence on which they rely.

It also brings into light some ethical and policy dimensions regarding the misuse of the bots. It encourages an interdisciplinary approach; it brings experts from computer science, psychology, ethics, and public policy together. Collaboration is required to develop solutions that not only detect and eliminate dangerous bots but also rebuild trust in AI systems. The operationalization of distrust in the paper is very timely since this shows the need for a proactive response to a growing societal crisis.

From this, the study frames a very powerful picture of how AI and bots challenge established truths in an era of misinformation. It does so with a critical argument that these technologies are powerful tools in advancing human potential on one hand, while they tend to undermine decision-making processes and shape public opinion in the most troubling ways. Operating these challenges calls for effort in operationalizing and validating distrust as the cardinal point of scholarly inquiry and practical intervention. In that way, society will be able to somewhat neutralize the negative effects of misinformation so that AI technologies serve responsible and socially useful goals. The article presents an engaging summary of the complications surrounding the concept of untrust, particularly in the current socio-political environment marked by misinformation and falling social trust. It advocates for more integrated research into the role of AI and bots as misinformation agents in decision-making, laying the groundwork for future academic research aimed at increasing our understanding of this crucial topic.

Based on the thorough research and analysis offered, an obvious conclusion arises regarding the role of bots in altering decision-making processes and influencing public opinion through the propagation of misinformation. The research shows a significant growth in the sophistication of AI-powered bots, notably their capacity to propagate misinformation across several platforms (Hajli et al., 2022; Shao et al., 2018). This trend is an urgent societal issue that directly addresses the study question of the impact of AI technologies, notably bots, on public trust and decision-making.

This study introduces the Beta model, a significant methodological innovation, as a method for modeling overlapping states of trust and distrust. In contrast to conventional binary models, which assume trust and distrust are 'either-or' notions, the Beta distribution offers a probabilistic way of treating trust and distrust simultaneously, both in coexistence and in variability. This work formalizes a 'superposition state,' in which both trust and distrust contribute to influencing decision processes. The model parameters of the Beta distribution enable more fine-grained representations of trust dynamics from strong trust through intermediate uncertainty to strong distrust. In its most poignant usage, this probabilistic perspective is especially useful, as it relates to AI and bots where users tend to be mixed on trust and skepticism in roughly equal parts. The Beta distribution framework not only provides a richer theoretical framework for the dynamics of trust-distrust but also provides for the design of artificial intelligence systems and interventions that must recognize the fluid and complex nature of user trust.

This chapter concludes with the thesis that artificial intelligence and bots are becoming increasingly powerful instruments to take advantage of decision-making and misinformation to construct public opinion. Understanding, measuring, and mitigating skepticism on this trend calls for a multidiscipline approach. This perspective views operationalizing and validating distrust as not just scholarly endeavors but as core activities in responding to the growing societal crisis.

Based on these wide-ranging findings, several important recommendations arise for academic research, policymakers, entrepreneurs, and practitioners. First, there is a clear need to develop and test frameworks and tools that are squarely aimed at measuring distrust as a distinct construct, moving beyond traditional trust-distrust continua. This would foster a much better understanding of the relationship between trust and distrust with particular reference to de context of artificial intelligence and automation. Second, there must be interdisciplinary cooperation: computer scientists, psychologists, ethicists, and experts on public policy are needed to develop technologies for the effective detection of harmful bots and to work out ethical criteria for the implementation of AI; likewise, policymakers and organizations in this regard need to concentrate on public awareness about digital literacy that would help people—especially young persons—to distinguish fake news from reality and evaluate sources more aptly. Lastly, the use of models like the Beta distribution opens up possibilities for incorporating the dynamics of trust-distrust in the architecture of artificial intelligence systems—ensuring, therefore, that the technologies will be deployed in ways that support societal objectives instead of eroding them. These approaches respond to the overriding need to reduce the societal consequences of misinformation and build a more resilient socio-digital environment.

## REFERENCES


Aljabri, M., Zagrouba, R., Shaahid, A., Alnasser, F., Saleh, A., & Alomari, D. M. (2023). Machine learning-based social media bot detection: A comprehensive literature review. *Social Network Analysis and Mining*, 13(1), 20. Advance online publication. DOI: 10.1007/s13278-022-01020-5

Anderson, S., Allen, P., Peckham, S., & Goodwin, N. (2008). Asking the right questions: Scoping studies in the commissioning of research on the organisation and delivery of health services. *Health Research Policy and Systems*, 6(1), 7. Advance online publication. DOI: 10.1186/1478-4505-6-7 PMID: 18613961

Arksey, H., & O'Malley, L. (2005). Scoping studies: Towards a methodological framework. *International Journal of Social Research Methodology*, 8(1), 19–32. DOI: 10.1080/1364557032000119616

Arrow, K. J. (1974). Limited Knowledge and Economic Analysis. *The American Economic Review*, 64(February), 1–10. https://papers.ssrn.com/sol3/papers.cfm?abstract_id=1506319

Ashtiani, M., & Abdollahi Azgomi, M. (2019). A novel trust evolution algorithm based on a quantum-like model of computational trust. *Cognition Technology and Work*, 21(2), 201–224. DOI: 10.1007/s10111-018-0496-9

Austin, W. G., & Worchel, S. (1979). *The social psychology of intergroup relations*. Brooks Cole Publishing.

Bécue, A., Praça, I., & Gama, J. (2021). Artificial intelligence, cyber-threats and Industry 4.0: Challenges and opportunities. *Artificial Intelligence Review*, 54(5), 3849–3886. DOI: 10.1007/s10462-020-09942-2

Blau, P. (1964). *Power and exchange in social life*. J Wiley & Sons.

Bode, C., Herzog, C., Hook, D., & McGrath, R. (2018). *A guide to the Dimensions data approach. Dimensions Report*. Digital Science.

Borda, A., Molnar, A., Neesham, C., & Kostkova, P. (2022). Ethical Issues in AI-Enabled Disease Surveillance: Perspectives from Global Health. *Applied Sciences (Basel, Switzerland)*, 12(8), 3890. Advance online publication. DOI: 10.3390/app12083890

Braun, M., Bleher, H., & Hummel, P. (2021). A Leap of Faith: Is There a Formula for "Trustworthy" AI? *The Hastings Center Report*, 51(3), 17–22. DOI: 10.1002/hast.1207 PMID: 33606288

Butler, J.Jr. (1991). Toward Understanding and Measuring Conditions of Trust: Evolution of a Conditions of Trust Inventory. *Journal of Management*, 17(3), 643–663. DOI: 10.1177/014920639101700307

Butler, L. (2010). An alternative to WoS subject categories: redefining journal sets for closer alignment to a national classification scheme. *Eleventh International Conference on Science and Technology Indicators*, 62.

Cacchione, P. Z. (2016). The Evolving Methodology of Scoping Reviews. *Clinical Nursing Research*, 25(2), 115–119. DOI: 10.1177/1054773816637493 PMID: 26976609

Cho, J. (2006). The mechanism of trust and distrust formation and their relational outcomes. *Journal of Retailing*, 82(1), 25–35. DOI: 10.1016/j.jretai.2005.11.002

Cobianchi, L., Piccolo, D., Dal Mas, F., Agnoletti, V., Ansaloni, L., Balch, J., Biffl, W., Butturini, G., Catena, F., Coccolini, F., Denicolai, S., De Simone, B., Frigerio, I., Fugazzola, P., Marseglia, G., Marseglia, G. R., Martellucci, J., Modenese, M., Previtali, P., & Zese, M. (2023). Surgeons' perspectives on artificial intelligence to support clinical decision-making in trauma and emergency contexts: Results from an international survey. *World Journal of Emergency Surgery; WJES*, 18(1). Advance online publication. DOI: 10.1186/s13017-022-00467-3 PMID: 36597105

Coleman, J. S. (1990). Foundations of Social Theory. In *Foundations of Social Theory* (Vol. 69, Issue 2, p. 993). DOI: 10.2307/2579680

De Bruyn, A., Viswanathan, V., Beh, Y. S., Brock, J. K. U., & von Wangenheim, F. (2020). Artificial Intelligence and Marketing: Pitfalls and Opportunities. *Journal of Interactive Marketing*, 51(1), 91–105. DOI: 10.1016/j.intmar.2020.04.007

Deutsch, M. (1973). The Resolution of Conflict. *The American Behavioral Scientist*, 17(2), 248–248. DOI: 10.1177/000276427301700206

Diaz Ruiz, C., & Nilsson, T. (2023). Disinformation and Echo Chambers: How Disinformation Circulates on Social Media Through Identity-Driven Controversies. *Journal of Public Policy & Marketing*, 42(1), 18–35. DOI: 10.1177/07439156221103852

Dirks, K. T., & Ferrin, D. L. (2001). The Role of Trust in Organizational Settings. *Organization Science*, 12(4), 450–467. DOI: 10.1287/orsc.12.4.450.10640

Dunn, J. (1988). Ch. 5: Trust and Political Agency. In *Trust: Making and Breaking Cooperative Relations* (pp. 73–93). Basil Blackwell. DOI: 10.2307/591021

Dwork, C., & Minow, M. (2022). Distrust of Artificial Intelligence: Sources & Responses from Computer Science & Law. *Daedalus*, 151(2), 309–321. DOI: 10.1162/daed_a_01918

Enoch, M. A., & Albaugh, B. J. (2017). Review: Genetic and environmental risk factors for alcohol use disorders in American Indians and Alaskan Natives. *The American Journal on Addictions*, 26(5), 461–468. DOI: 10.1111/ajad.12420 PMID: 27599369

Floridi, L., & Taddeo, M. (2016). What is data ethics? *Philosophical Transactions. Series A, Mathematical, Physical, and Engineering Sciences*, 374(2083), 20160360. Advance online publication. DOI: 10.1098/rsta.2016.0360 PMID: 28336805

Gao, S., He, L., Chen, Y., Li, D., & Lai, K. (2020). Public Perception of Artificial Intelligence in Medical Care: Content Analysis of Social Media. *J Med Internet Res 2020;22(7):E16649*Https://Www.Jmir.Org/2020/7/E16649*, 22*(7), e16649. DOI: 10.2196/16649

Garbarino, E., & Lee, O. F. (2003). Dynamic Pricing in Internet Retail: Effects on Consumer Trust. *Psychology and Marketing*, 20(6), 495–513. DOI: 10.1002/mar.10084

Gasser, U. (2023). An EU landmark for AI governance. *Science*, 380(6651), 1203. DOI: 10.1126/science.adj1627 PMID: 37319234

Gefen, D. (2000). E-commerce: The role of familiarity and trust. *Omega*, 28(6), 725–737. DOI: 10.1016/S0305-0483(00)00021-9

Goodwin, E. A., Burhansstipanov, L., Dignan, M., Jones, K. L., & Kaur, J. S. (2017). The Experience of Treatment Barriers and Their Influence on Quality of Life in American Indian/Alaska Native Breast Cancer Survivors. *Cancer*, 123(5), 861–868. DOI: 10.1002/cncr.30406 PMID: 27763688

Graziani, M., Dutkiewicz, L., Calvaresi, D., Amorim, J. P., Yordanova, K., Vered, M., Nair, R., Abreu, P. H., Blanke, T., Pulignano, V., Prior, J. O., Lauwaert, L., Reijers, W., Depeursinge, A., Andrearczyk, V., & Müller, H. (2023). A global taxonomy of interpretable AI: Unifying the terminology for the technical and social sciences. *Artificial Intelligence Review*, 56(4), 3473–3504. DOI: 10.1007/s10462-022-10256-8 PMID: 36092822

Gremillion, G. M., Metcalfe, J. S., Marathe, A. R., Paul, V. J., Christensen, J., Drnec, K., Haynes, B., & Atwater, C. (2016). Analysis of trust in autonomy for convoy operations. In T. George, A. K. Dutta, & M. S. Islam (Eds.), *Micro- and Nanotechnology Sensors, Systems, and Applications VIII* (Vol. 9836, Issue Conference on Micro-and Nanotechnology Sensors, Systems, and Applications VIII. DOI: 10.1117/12.2224009

Guadagnolo, B. A., Petereit, D. G., & Coleman, C. N. (2017). Cancer Care Access and Outcomes for American Indian Populations in the United States: Challenges and Models for Progress. *Seminars in Radiation Oncology*, 27(2), 143–149. DOI: 10.1016/j.semradonc.2016.11.006 PMID: 28325240

Hajli, N., Saeed, U., Tajvidi, M., & Shirazi, F. (2022). Social Bots and the Spread of Disinformation in Social Media: The Challenges of Artificial Intelligence. *British Journal of Management*, 33(3), 1238–1253. DOI: 10.1111/1467-8551.12554

Hand, D. J. (2022). Trustworthiness of statistical inference. *Journal of the Royal Statistical Society. Series A, (Statistics in Society)*, 185(1), 329–347. DOI: 10.1111/rssa.12752

Hardin, R. (2004). Distrust. In Hardin, R. (Ed.), *Distrust* (pp. 3–33). Russell Sage Foundation.

Herasimenka, A. (2022). Communication resource mobilization. *Journal of Communication*. Advance online publication. DOI: 10.1093/joc/jqac043 PMID: 37016634

Hernández-Mulero, N., & Berengüí, R. (2016). No Title. *Cuadernos de Psicología del Deporte*, 16(2), 37–44.

Herzog, C., & Lunn, B. K. (2018). *Issue 1* (Vol. 117). Response to the letter 'Field classification of publications in Dimensions: a first case study testing its reliability and validity.' In *Scientometrics*. Springer Netherlands., DOI: 10.1007/s11192-018-2854-z

Hook, D. W., Porter, S. J., & Herzog, C. (2018). Dimensions: Building Context for Search and Evaluation. *Frontiers in Research Metrics and Analytics*, 3, 23. Advance online publication. DOI: 10.3389/frma.2018.00023

Houghtaling, B., Byker Shanks, C., Ahmed, S., & Rink, E. (2018). Grandmother and health care professional breastfeeding perspectives provide opportunities for health promotion in an American Indian community. *Social Science & Medicine*, 208, 80–88. DOI: 10.1016/j.socscimed.2018.05.017 PMID: 29772397

Hu, X., Li, S., Huang, T., Tang, B., Huai, R., & Chen, L. (2024). How Simulation Helps Autonomous Driving: A Survey of Sim2real, Digital Twins, and Parallel Intelligence. *IEEE Transactions on Intelligent Vehicles*, 9(1), 593–612. DOI: 10.1109/TIV.2023.3312777

Isaacson, M. J., & Lynch, A. R. (2018). Culturally Relevant Palliative and End-of-Life Care for U.S. Indigenous Populations: An Integrative Review. *Journal of Transcultural Nursing*, 29(2), 180–191. DOI: 10.1177/1043659617720980 PMID: 28826379

James, R. D., West, K. M., Claw, K. G., EchoHawk, A., Dodge, L., Dominguez, A., Taualii, M., Forquera, R., Thummel, K., & Burke, W. (1613–1616). EchoHawk, A., Dodge, L., Dominguez, A., Taualii, M., Forquera, R., Thummel, K., & Burke, W. (2018). Responsible research with urban American Indians and Alaska natives. *American Journal of Public Health*, 108(12), 1613–1616. Advance online publication. DOI: 10.2105/AJPH.2018.304708 PMID: 30359103

Karpus, J., Krueger, A., Verba, J. T., Bahrami, B., & Deroy, O. (2021). Algorithm exploitation: Humans are keen to exploit benevolent AI. *iScience*, 24(6), 102679. Advance online publication. DOI: 10.1016/j.isci.2021.102679 PMID: 34189440

Kim, E., Shin, J., Kwon, Y., & Park, B. (2023). EMG-Based Dynamic Hand Gesture Recognition Using Edge AI for Human-Robot Interaction. *Electronics (Basel)*, 12(7), 1541. Advance online publication. DOI: 10.3390/electronics12071541

Köbis, N., Bonnefon, J. F., & Rahwan, I. (2021). Bad machines corrupt good morals. *Nature Human Behaviour*, 5(6), 679–685. DOI: 10.1038/s41562-021-01128-2 PMID: 34083752

Lee, J. D., & See, K. A. (2004). Trust in automation: Designing for appropriate reliance. *Human Factors*, 46(1), 50–80. DOI: 10.1518/hfes.46.1.50.30392 PMID: 15151155

Lee, M., Scheepers, H., Lui, A. K. H., & Ngai, E. W. T. (2023). The implementation of artificial intelligence in organizations: A systematic literature review. *Information & Management*, 60(5), 103816. DOI: 10.1016/j.im.2023.103816

Leung, K. Y. K., & Lee, H. Y. (2023). Implementing the smart city: Who has a say? Some insights from Hong Kong. *International Journal of Urban Sciences*, 27(sup1, S1), 124–148. DOI: 10.1080/12265934.2021.1997634

Lewicki, R. J., McAllister, D. J., & Bies, R. J. (1998). Trust and Distrust: New Relationships and Realities. *Academy of Management Review*, 23(3), 438. DOI: 10.2307/259288

Lewis, P. R., & Marsh, S. (2022). What is it like to trust a rock? A functionalist perspective on trust and trustworthiness in artificial intelligence. *Cognitive Systems Research*, 72, 33–49. DOI: 10.1016/j.cogsys.2021.11.001

Li, M., & Bitterly, T. B. (2024). How Perceived Lack of Benevolence Harms Trust of Artificial Intelligence Management. *The Journal of Applied Psychology*, 109(11), 1794–1816. Advance online publication. DOI: 10.1037/apl0001200 PMID: 38815093

Lobera, J., Fernández Rodríguez, C. J., & Torres-Albero, C. (2020). Privacy, Values and Machines: Predicting Opposition to Artificial Intelligence. *Communication Studies*, 71(3), 448–465. DOI: 10.1080/10510974.2020.1736114

Luhmann, N. (2018). *Trust and power*. John Wiley & Sons.

Marsh, S., & Dibben, M. R. (2005). Trust, untrust, distrust and mistrust - An exploration of the dark(er) side. *Lecture Notes in Computer Science*, 3477, 17–33. DOI: 10.1007/11429760_2

Martinho, A., Kroesen, M., & Chorus, C. (2021). A healthy debate: Exploring the views of medical doctors on the ethics of artificial intelligence. *Artificial Intelligence in Medicine*, 121, 102190. Advance online publication. DOI: 10.1016/j.artmed.2021.102190 PMID: 34763805

Mayer, R. C., Davis, J. H., & Schoorman, F. D. (1995). An Integrative Model Of Organizational Trust. *Academy of Management Review*, 20(3), 709–734. DOI: 10.2307/258792

Mazurowski, M. A. (2020). Artificial Intelligence in Radiology: Some Ethical Considerations for Radiologists and Algorithm Developers. *Academic Radiology*, 27(1), 127–129. DOI: 10.1016/j.acra.2019.04.024 PMID: 31818378

McClelland, R. S. (2022). Generative design and digital manufacturing: using AI and robots to build lightweight instrument structures. In R. B. Johnson, V. N. Mahajan, S. Thibault, & A. Padilla-Vivanco (Eds.), *CURRENT DEVELOPMENTS IN LENS DESIGN AND OPTICAL ENGINEERING XXIII* (Vol. 12217, Issue Conference on Current Developments in Lens Design and Optical Engineering XXIII Part of SPIE Optics and Photonics Conference CL-San Diego, CA, p. 37). DOI: 10.1117/12.2646476

McKnight, D. H., Cummings, L. L., & Chervany, N. L. (1998). Initial trust formation in new organizational relationships. *Academy of Management Review*, 23(3), 473–490. DOI: 10.2307/259290

Miake-Lye, I. M., Hempel, S., Shanman, R., & Shekelle, P. G. (2016). What is an evidence map? A systematic review of published evidence maps and their definitions, methods, and products. *Systematic Reviews*, 5(1), 28. Advance online publication. DOI: 10.1186/s13643-016-0204-x PMID: 26864942

Minsky M. (1968). *Semantic Information Processing*.

Mobilio, G. (2023). Your face is not new to me – Regulating the surveillance power of facial recognition technologies. *Internet Policy Review*, 12(1). Advance online publication. DOI: 10.14763/2023.1.1699

Molina, M. D., & Sundar, S. S. (2022). Does distrust in humans predict greater trust in AI? Role of individual differences in user responses to content moderation. *New Media & Society*. Advance online publication. DOI: 10.1177/14614448221103534

Molina, M. D., Wang, J., Sundar, S. S., Le, T., & DiRusso, C. (2023). Reading, Commenting and Sharing of Fake News: How Online Bandwagons and Bots Dictate User Engagement. *Communication Research*, 50(6), 667–694. DOI: 10.1177/00936502211073398

Mulcahy, R., & Barnes, R. (2024). Sharing of misinformation by influencers. *Australasian Marketing Journal*. Advance online publication. DOI: 10.1177/14413582241273987

Nesoff, E. D., Brownstein, J. N., Veazie, M., O'Leary, M., & Brody, E. A. (2017). Time-to-Treatment for Myocardial Infarction: Barriers and Facilitators Perceived by American Indians in Three Regions. *Journal of Community Health*, 42(1), 129–138. DOI: 10.1007/s10900-016-0239-x PMID: 27613739

Ongena, Y. P., Haan, M., Yakar, D., & Kwee, T. C. (2020). Patients' views on the implementation of artificial intelligence in radiology: Development and validation of a standardized questionnaire. *European Radiology*, 30(2), 1033–1040. DOI: 10.1007/s00330-019-06486-0 PMID: 31705254

Orduña-Malea, E., & Delgado-López-Cózar, E. (2018). Dimensions: Redescubriendo el ecosistema de la información científica. *El Profesional de la Información*, 27(2), 420–431. DOI: 10.3145/epi.2018.mar.21

Palmatier, R. W., Dant, R. P., Grewal, D., & Evans, K. R. (2006). Factors influencing the effectiveness of relationship marketing: A meta-analysis. *Journal of Marketing*, 70(4), 136–153. DOI: 10.1509/jmkg.70.4.136

Pathak, R., & Spezzano, F. (2024). Algorithmic contribution to misinformation. *ACM Transactions on the Web*. Advance online publication. DOI: 10.1145/3616088

Pavlou, P. A., & Gefen, D. (2005). Psychological contract violation in online marketplaces: Antecedents, consequences, and moderating role. *Information Systems Research*, 16(4), 372–399. DOI: 10.1287/isre.1050.0065

Prasad, T. V. S. R. K., Srinivas, K., & Srinivas, C. (2017). Decentralized production-distribution planning in multi-echelon supply chain network using intelligent agents. *OPSEARCH*, 54(2), 217–232. DOI: 10.1007/s12597-016-0277-2

Rempel, J. K., Holmes, J. G., & Zanna, M. P. (1985). Trust in Close Relationships. *Journal of Personality and Social Psychology*, 49(1), 95–112. DOI: 10.1037/0022-3514.49.1.95 PMID: 11474726

Riedl, R., Hogeterp, S. A., & Reuter, M. (2024). Do patients prefer a human doctor, artificial intelligence, or a blend, and is this preference dependent on medical discipline? Empirical evidence and implications for medical practice. *Frontiers in Psychology*, 15, 1422177. Advance online publication. DOI: 10.3389/fpsyg.2024.1422177 PMID: 39188871

Rotter, J. B. (1967). A new scale for the measurement of interpersonal trust. *Journal of Personality*, 35(4), 651–665. DOI: 10.1111/j.1467-6494.1967.tb01454.x PMID: 4865583

Rousseau, D. M., Sitkin, S. B., Burt, R. S., & Camerer, C. (1998). Not so different after all: A cross-discipline view of trust. *Academy of Management Review*, 23(3), 393–404. DOI: 10.5465/amr.1998.926617

Rousseau, R., & Leuven, K. U. (2018). The Australian and New Zealand Fields of Research (FoR) Codes. *ISSI Newsletter*, 14(3), 59–61.

Rumrill, P. D., Fitzgerald, S. M., & Merchant, W. R. (2010). Using scoping literature reviews as a means of understanding and interpreting existing literature. *Work (Reading, Mass.)*, 35(3), 399–404. DOI: 10.3233/WOR-2010-0998 PMID: 20364059

Sallam, M., Salim, N. A., Al-Tammemi, A. B., Barakat, M., Fayyad, D., Hallit, S., Harapan, H., Hallit, R., & Mahafzah, A. (2023). ChatGPT Output Regarding Compulsory Vaccination and COVID-19 Vaccine Conspiracy: A Descriptive Study at the Outset of a Paradigm Shift in Online Search for Information. *Cureus*, 15(2). Advance online publication. DOI: 10.7759/cureus.35029 PMID: 36819954

Saunkeah, B., Beans, J. A., Peercy, M. T., Hiratsuka, V. Y., & Spicer, P. (2021). Extending Research Protections to Tribal Communities. *The American Journal of Bioethics*, 21(10), 5–12. DOI: 10.1080/15265161.2020.1865477 PMID: 33449863

Savage, N. (2019). How AI and neuroscience drive each other forwards. *Nature*, 571(7766), S15–S17. DOI: 10.1038/d41586-019-02212-4 PMID: 31341311

Schepman, A., & Rodway, P. (2023). The General Attitudes towards Artificial Intelligence Scale (GAAIS): Confirmatory Validation and Associations with Personality, Corporate Distrust, and General Trust. *International Journal of Human-Computer Interaction*, 39(13), 2724–2741. DOI: 10.1080/10447318.2022.2085400

Sedky, M. H., Moniri, M., & Chibelushi, C. C. (2005). Smart video surveillance for workplace applications: Implications, technologies and requirements. In J. J. Villanueva (Ed.), *Proceedings of the 5th IASTED International Conference on Visualization, Imaging, and Image Processing, VIIP 2005* (Issues 5th IASTED International Conference on Visualization, Imaging, and Image Processing, pp. 737–742).

Shao, C., Hui, P. M., Cui, P., Jiang, X., & Peng, Y. (2018). Tracking and Characterizing the Competition of Fact Checking and Misinformation: Case Studies. *IEEE Access : Practical Innovations, Open Solutions*, 6, 75327–75341. DOI: 10.1109/ACCESS.2018.2881037

Sirdeshmukh, D., Singh, J., & Sabol, B. (2002). Consumer trust, value, and loyalty in relational exchanges. *Journal of Marketing*, 66(1), 15–37. DOI: 10.1509/jmkg.66.1.15.18449

Six, F. E., & Latusek, D. (2023). Distrust: A critical review exploring a universal distrust sequence. *Journal of Trust Research*, 13(1), 1–23. DOI: 10.1080/21515581.2023.2184376

Skewes, M. C., Gonzalez, V. M., Gameon, J. A., FireMoon, P., Salois, E., Rasmus, S. M., Lewis, J. P., Gardner, S. A., Ricker, A., & Reum, M. (2020). Health Disparities Research with American Indian Communities: The Importance of Trust and Transparency. *American Journal of Community Psychology*, 66(3–4), 302–313. DOI: 10.1002/ajcp.12445 PMID: 32652706

Söllner, M., Benbasat, I., Gefen, D., Leimeister, J. M., & Pavlou, P. A. (2016). *Trust*. MIS Quarterly Research Curations., DOI: 10.25300/MISQ/2019/curations/10312016

Soni, N., Sharma, E. K., Singh, N., & Kapoor, A. (2019). *Impact of Artificial Intelligence on Businesses: from Research, Innovation, Market Deployment to Future Shifts in Business Models*. http://arxiv.org/abs/1905.02092

Starke, G., & Ienca, M. (2022). Misplaced Trust and Distrust: How Not to Engage with Medical Artificial Intelligence. *Cambridge Quarterly of Healthcare Ethics*, •••, 1–10. DOI: 10.1017/S0963180122000445 PMID: 36263755

Thelwall, M. (2018). Dimensions: A competitor to Scopus and the Web of Science? *Journal of Informetrics*, 12(2), 430–435. DOI: 10.1016/j.joi.2018.03.006

Tiwari, T., Albino, J., & Batliner, T. S. (2015). Challenges faced in engaging American Indian mothers in an early childhood caries preventive trial. *International Journal of Dentistry*, 2015, 1–5. Advance online publication. DOI: 10.1155/2015/179189 PMID: 26089905

Tricco, A. C., Antony, J., Zarin, W., Strifler, L., Ghassemi, M., Ivory, J., Perrier, L., Hutton, B., Moher, D., & Straus, S. E. (2015). A scoping review of rapid review methods. *BMC Medicine*, 13(1), 224. Advance online publication. DOI: 10.1186/s12916-015-0465-6 PMID: 26377409

Tseng, S., & Fogg, B. J. (1999). Credibility and computing technology. *Communications of the ACM*, 42(5), 39–44. DOI: 10.1145/301353.301402

Vance, A., Elie-dit-cosaque, C., & Straub, D. W. (2008). Examining trust in information technology artifacts: The effects of system quality and culture. *Journal of Management Information Systems*, 24(4), 73–100. DOI: 10.2753/MIS0742-1222240403

Wille, S. M., Kemp, K. A., Greenfield, B. L., & Walls, M. L. (2017). Barriers to healthcare for American indians experiencing homelessness. *Journal of Social Distress and the Homeless*, 26(1), 1–8. DOI: 10.1080/10530789.2016.1265211 PMID: 29375241

Woolgar, S. (1985). Why not a sociology of machines? the case of sociology and artificial intelligence. *Sociology*, 19(4), 557–572. DOI: 10.1177/0038038585019004005

Wu, L. (2022). Definition, manipulation, and detection. *SIGKDD Explorations*. Advance online publication. DOI: 10.1145/3373464.3373475

Zand, D. (1972). Trust and managerial problem solving. *Administrative Science Quarterly*, 17(2), 229–239. DOI: 10.2307/2393957

## KEY TERMS AND DEFINITIONS

**Artificial Intelligence:** The capability of machines that emulate the behavior or decision-making aptitude of man. AI technologies within this context include bots and machine learning systems used in several applications.

**Benevolence:** That aspect of trust that shows the goodwill and non-exploitative intentions of a trustee, often operationalized through user-friendly designs and systems that put the user first.

**Beta Distribution:** A statistical model of the probabilistic combination of trust and distrust. It allows for a continuous spectrum of states between complete trust (1) and complete distrust (0).

**Bots:** These are automated programs designed to do specific tasks, ranging from benign data gathering to malicious ones, like dispersing misinformation or conducting identity fraud.

**Credibility:** The degree of perceived competence, honesty, and reliability in a trustee, especially in the domains of AI or organizational relations.

**Distrust:** A particular disposition of wariness regarding other parties' intentions and/or actions.

**Ethical AI:** The design and deployment of AI applications in ethical standards for trustworthy, transparent, and reliable outputs that aim at the center of user needs.

**Misinformation:** Information that is incorrect or misleading, which is circulated intentionally or unintentionally and influences the processes of decision-making in public opinion. In a perspective related to AI, this kind of information is usually propagated through bots.

**Public Trust:** Collective confidence that society places in institutions, technologies, or systems; this is crucial for acceptance and success regarding such innovations as AI.

**State of Superposition Trust-Distrust:** It consists of a probabilistic framework in which, instead of trust and distrust being complementary states, they coexist for specific portions; hence, the dynamics of decision-making can be nuanced in situations involving artificial intelligence.

**Superposition State:** Adopted from quantum mechanics and applied here to explain that there exists a state of mutual exclusiveness where trust and distrust will be possible, each with some probability.

**Trust:** A psychological condition, the willingness to be vulnerable, based on favorable expectations about the intentions or actions of others, often including elements involving perceptions of credibility, benevolence, and reliability.

**Vicious Loop of Distrust:** A situation in which the growing sophistication of bots in spreading misinformation feeds public mistrust in AI, which delays the adoption and potential benefits of AI technologies.

# Chapter 3
# Ethical and Corporate Social Responsibility:
## Implications of Artificial Intelligence Application for the Detection and Prevention of Financial Fraud

**María-Elena Lindez-Macarro**
*Universidad Rey Juan Carlos, Spain*

**Felix Villalba-Romero**
https://orcid.org/0000-0002-0608-6365
*Universidad de Málaga, Spain*

## ABSTRACT

*Artificial Intelligence (AI) has experienced rapid penetration in our society, playing a crucial role in everyday analysis and decision making. AI integration in the financial field stands out as one of the most advanced, especially in terms of financial fraud detection and prevention. Yet, this rapid evolution of the sector brings with it several ethical and corporate social responsibility (CRS) challenges that have not yet been properly explored. This analysis provides the essential principles for understanding the use of AI in the detection of financial fraud, assessing its effectiveness, and examining the tools used to understand the conceptual framework within which ethics and CRS are defined in the application of AI. A comprehensive review of the ethical and CRS challenges inherent in the use of AI in the detection and prevention of financial fraud is conducted, along with an analysis of the different perspectives. present in the academic literature on the subject. In addition, future research directions are proposed to address these issues more comprehensively and effectively.*

DOI: 10.4018/979-8-3693-9894-4.ch003

## 1. INTRODUCTION

As the implementation of artificial intelligence (AI) systems steadily progresses in the financial sphere, academics and researchers have turned their focus towards analysing the socio-economic and political implications of this emerging phenomenon (Gomes et al., 2020; Kamruzzaman, 2022; Kumar et al., 2023). Academic interest continues to grow given the potential of AI and the wide range of benefits AI provides such as automation and efficiency of processes (Iadanza et al., 2022), analysis of large datasets (Dutta et al., 2020), innovation and development (Mannuru et al., 2023) and process optimization (Igwegbe et al., 2023); as well as diverse application like medicine, marketing, finance or agriculture (Yang et al., 2021; Lorkowski et al., 2021; Hasan et al., 2023; Majeed et al., 2024).

However, the greater complexity of this technology has certain negative aspects. For the incorporation of AI, companies face challenges such as changing infrastructures, development and maintenance costs, and lack of specialised professionals. Nevertheless, the most important challenge lies in the ethical and corporate social responsibility (CSR), which pose unprecedented problems for society. The pervasiveness of AI raises several questions about equity, transparency, and automated decision-making, demanding rigorous scrutiny to mitigate potential negative implications for various strata of the population (Elliott et al., 2021). According to Zhao & Fariñas (2022), companies and governments must make collective efforts to achieve responsible and sustainable AI through a proactive regulatory framework backed by rigorous corporate policies and reporting (Vinuesa et. Al, 2020).

Other important issue lies on the way to integrate technological progress, such as AI implementation and cope with issues, considering the diverse business practices and cultural values of societies (Hofstede, 2001); and future AI impacts in internet business, perception and autonomy, as well as in Internet of Thing (IoT) and technologies such as blockchain (Lee et al., 2018). While in Western countries any AI implementation effort need to integrate individual rights and freedom to maximize profit, Asian countries place stronger emphasis on collective well-being and societal harmony. For example, AI implementation should emphasize on collective-welfare and institutional respect in China (Ding, 2018), respect hierarchical structures and employee welfare in Japan, or show technological prowess and social equity (Kim & Chung, 2019; Zhang et al., 2022). In this regard, a global approach needs to consider the diversity of culturally aligned CSR to be worldwide accepted (Wilson & van der Velden, 2022) or even include enough flexibility to adapt their AI strategies to different ethic and value priority, balancing innovation with ethical responsibilities (Minkkinen et al., 2022).

The integration of AI in the financial sector has focused on its application for the detection and prevention of financial fraud, leading to multiple lines of research and innovation (Ryman-Tubb et al., 2018; Li, 2022; Mill et al., 2023). The implementation of AI to combat financial fraud has led to quicker and more efficient identification of fraudulent actions, minimizing financial losses when fraud occurs (Bansal et al., 2024), as well as achieving better financial security, while providing a quick response to consumers affected by fraudulent activities and giving them more transparency and explainability in these situations (Zhou et al., 2023). Investment in security must be paramount as generative AI is also a tool used by fraudsters to their advantage, which explain the main part of the increase in fraudulent activity. As a results, main concerns stem from AI processes and how its mechanisms confront with ethics and social responsibility issues at the same time as fighting financial fraud, which have not fully been addressed by current research in financial fraud, which is the main contribution of this research.

The incorporation of AI in finance highlights its potential to transform fraud detection, enhance security, and improve transparency, but also underscores unresolved ethical challenges. This chapter explores how AI mechanisms intersect with ethics, social responsibility, and culturally diverse business practices, emphasizing the need for globally adaptable, responsible frameworks. By addressing these gaps, this research aims to contribute to a deeper understanding of AI's societal implications and its role in fostering innovation while safeguarding ethical principles.

The structure of this research consists of the following Section 2 which briefly present the methodology. Section 3 includes the theoretical framework and Section 4 the applications methodological development. Section 5 analyses the ethical and CSR challenges while section 6 presents the discussion and research agenda. Finally, section 7 contains the conclusions of the study.

## 2. METHODOLOGY

This research aims to set a theoretical framework that may be used as a base to apply AI to fraud detection and prevention, considering ethical and social responsibility implications. This framework offers basic definitions and requires conceptualisation, and responds to the main challenges derived from the use of AI in financial fraud detection from an ethical and social responsibility views.

Therefore, this research formulates the following research questions (RQs):

RQ1: Definition of AI, AI ethics and CSR in AI.

RQ2: How is AI applied to the detection and prevention of financial fraud?

RQ3: Is there published evidence that AI acts as an effective tool for the prevention and detection of financial fraud?
RQ4: What are the ethical and CSR challenges facing the use of AI as a tool for the detection and prevention of financial fraud?

The research questions posed align with the objectives of this research: (1) to understand what AI and how ethics and CSR are defined in this context, (2) to understand how AI is applied for fraud detection and prevention, (3) to check whether it is effective according to the existing literature, and (4) the ethical and CSR challenges that exist in the area.

To achieve the main objective of this work and answer the research questions, an extensive literature review has been conducted as well as the expert's reviews in the field.

Literature reviews play a crucial role in establishing a solid foundation for scientific research. Various methodologies have been developed to conduct effective literature reviews in different fields. Ramdhani and Ramdhani (2014) propose a verification methodology for research frameworks based on literature reviews, emphasizing analytical, conceptual, logical, and operational approaches. Chukwuere (2023) compares eleven different literature review methodologies in information systems research, highlighting their strengths and weaknesses to guide researchers in selecting appropriate methods. To enhance quantitative literature reviews, Laghrabli et al. (2015) introduce a novel framework using association rules analysis, which helps identify relationships between variables and explore new research directions. These studies collectively demonstrate the importance of selecting suitable literature review methodologies and offer innovative approaches to improve the quality and precision of research across various disciplines. A tool for semantic indexing and similarity queries can enhance literature review methods by improving efficiency, quality, and comprehensiveness (Koukal et al., 2014). As Cowell (2012), points out, literature reviews can be a rigorous research strategy if the scientific method is applied to ensure a standardized approach.

As a result, the review of the literature has been integrated in a framework which outlines the main challenges in financial fraud detection and prevention.

## 3. THEORETICAL FRAMEWORK

In this section, we dive into a comprehensive analysis of AI concept and ethics and CRS from an AI perspective. Thus, research question 1 is answered in this section.

## 3.1. Artificial Intelligence (AI) Concept

As one of the fields of research and innovation that has evolved the most in recent years, AI is defined as the science that allows computers to execute tasks that require human intelligence (Finocchiaro, 2023). The European Commission, in its proposal for a European Regulation on artificial intelligence, establishes AI as: "a computer program developed with one or more of the techniques and approaches listed in Annex I and which, for a given set of defined objectives by the human being, generates results such as content, predictions, recommendations or decisions that influence the environments with which they interact" (European Parliament & Council, 2024).

AI has become an efficient and practical tool that is already part of a vast majority of activity sectors such as telecommunications, finance, and the automotive industry (Choi, 2021; Tan et al., 2022). The significant advance of AI is due to the expansion of applications and accessibility of tools, methods, and theories, facilitating their use (Cantrell & Zhang, 2018). Institutions as relevant in the field of robotics as the Stanford Robotics Center (SRC) work together with other institutions on AI projects. For example, in one of these projects, the SRC is trying to define the responsible use of AI technology together with the Human-Centered Artificial Intelligence Institute (HAI), with the aim of addressing the technical, social and economic challenges of robotics in areas such as health, education, sustainability and work (Stanford University, 2024). Computer scientists have identified three levels of AI based on the expected growth of its ability to analyse data and make predictions: narrow AI, general AI and superintelligence AI (Mersha et al., 2024). This classification is based on the level of capability and understanding that AI systems possess. AI systems designed to perform specific tasks without general awareness and understanding of the world are called weak AI and operate within a limited range of functions, while general AI systems could understand, learn and apply knowledge in a human-like manner. This includes the ability to reason, solve problems and understand complex concepts (Arrieta et al., 2019; Russell & Norvig, 1995; Searle, 1980). Nowadays, there is currently narrow AI and general AI. Most companies use narrow AI.

The evolution of AI can be traced through the advances driven by Google. At the beginning of the 21st century, machine learning was used for spell checkers, followed by Google Translate five years later. In 2012, deep learning began to be applied to speech recognition and large-scale training. In 2013, Word2Vec revolutionised natural language processing, while AtariDQN did the same with deep learning. Subsequently, neural networks and methodologies such as distillation were introduced, making it easier to work with complex models and facial recognition. Since 2016, investment in AI for security, preventive medicine, genomics and ethical principles has intensified. In recent years, advances have been almost monthly, achieving consistent milestones in natural language processing, image generation, conversational modelling, music, video and medical diagnostics (Google, 2025).

AI researcher Nick Bostrom defines the superintelligence as "an intellect far smarter than the best human brains in virtually every field, including scientific creativity, general wisdom, and social skills." (Bostrom, 2014). We are likely to see general AI appear in our lifetime, endowing machines with the ability to interact in human-like ways when working alongside humans (Baum, 2018; Brundage, 2015).

## 3.2. AI Ethics

Ethics is the set of moral principles that guide human interaction and decision-making, with the objective of improving the general well-being of society, protecting personal integrity, human dignity, and the rights of the most vulnerable individuals (Wirtz et al., 2018). From the AI approach, ethics refers to morality and the preference for a certain line of action in the development, implementation, and use of AI (Jobin & Ienca, 2019; Kaplan & Haenlein, 2020; Lin, 2016), as well as the protection against the inaccurate or unfair bias that algorithms may apply and the threat to privacy (Davenport et al., 2019).

Traditional ethics have been affected in business processes from automated decision-making and the comprehensibility of business models to labour relations by AI systems (Sison et al., 2023). Therefore, the ethical responsibility of public and private companies developing AI technology becomes crucially important. (Martin, 2018).

## 3.3. Corporate Social Responsibility in AI

Corporate Social responsibility (CSR) is a form of anticipatory reflection on the possible impacts of research on society, which involves aligning scientific research with the needs of society, the environment and democratically held values (Kumar et al., 2022; Politi, 2024). In the context of AI, CSR involves considering how AI can contribute to social good and align with shared values in society (Cath et al., 2017), as well as mitigate potential negative consequences and maximize benefits such as equity and transparency (Helfat et al., 2023).

AI forces companies to re-evaluate their performance in terms of transparency and accountability, organisational culture, responsibility in the use of technologies and collaboration between public and private interests (Fioravante, 2024). Hence, it is necessary to align the adoption of AI with the company's overall CSR strategy, using AI to improve the company's sustainability as well as to address social and environmental issues (Ahdadou et al., 2024; Pai & Chandra, 2022).

The fast progress of artificial intelligence in recent years has developed new concepts and generated new challenges, which require a consensus identification and regulatory effort for appropriate management. A conceptual framework, developed in this section, is needed to capture the new concepts and ethical and CRS implications, in the implementation of diverse AI applications.

## 4. AI APPLICATION TO THE DETECTION AND PREVENTION OF FINANCIAL FRAUD

Throughout this section, the main AI trends and technologies in the field of financial fraud and their effectiveness will be developed according to existing literature. Thus, research questions 2 and 3 are answered in this section.

### 4.1. Transaction Pattern Analysis

Monitoring financial transactions may be crucial to detect and prevent financial crime, such as fraud, money laundering and terrorist financing. Fraudsters use AI for the creation of fake content, more persuasive phishing that is personalised to the target audience, or attacks against biometric systems such as facial, voice or fingerprint recognition systems in banking access or security systems, which can lead to huge financial damage and loss of consumer trust. Pattern analysis involves identifying and analysing modes of behaviours which may suggest illegal activity. Using the pattern analysis technique, AI can analyse large volumes of financial data, identifying patterns in transactions and anomalies that may indicate fraudulent activities (Zheng et al., 2024). When AI algorithms identify anomalous patterns, they proceed to segment financial data into different categories, facilitating the identification of atypical behaviours within each segment (Dasari & Kaluri, 2024). Additionally, this tool can include the identification of correlations between different financial variables and the prediction of possible fraud scenarios based on the available data (Innan et al., 2023), as well as data visualization tools that simplify the detection of trends, patterns, and anomalies in financial data (Qiu & Luo, 2024).

Finally, pattern analysis-based systems offer the ability to detect fraud in real time by continuously monitoring financial transactions and triggering alerts when suspicious patterns are identified, while adapting and learning from new data to improve their accuracy in fraud detection (Maashi et al., 2023; Yang et al., 2023).

## 4.2. Machine Learning (ML)

Machine Learning (ML) is often defined as the capability of a machine to imitate intelligent human behaviour and thus, computer systems are able to learn and adapt by using algorithms and statistical models. This is a fundamental tool in data science that allows systems to learn and improve their performance with the experience gained from data (Ghoddusi et al., 2019). In the detection and prevention of financial fraud, ML extracts key information from data to predict and generate new insights (Zhou et al., 2023). The ML life cycle begins with Feature Engineering, which involves the selection and manipulation of data to transform it into useful features. Once the data is collected, automatic algorithms are generated capable of learning and acting autonomously in various situations, making it crucial to feed them with large volumes of data for their effectiveness (Martínez, 2016). The main strength of ML lies in its ability to continuously adapt and detect fraudulent activity in real time, marking a significant advance in cybersecurity. However, fraudsters also use it to carry out massive attacks and circumvent antivirus and protection systems.

Within ML, Supervised Learning and Unsupervised Learning are prominent approaches. The first uses annotated training data to guide the system in associating labels to training examples, making it valuable in problem classification (Sood et al., 2023). In contrast, Unsupervised Learning identifies patterns without specifying labels, and its models include Principal Component Analysis (PCA), which reduces the dimensionality of the data for better visualization and analysis (Beattie & Esmonde-White, 2021).

## 4.3. Natural Language Processing (NLP)

A machine learning technology that gives computers the ability to interpret, manipulate and comprehend human language is Natural Language Processing (NPL). Unlike structured information, which can be organized in tables or matrices with neatly labelled rows and columns, unstructured information as the human language is confusing and difficult to understand.

To deal with unstructured information, computers start with segmentation, meaning take one sentence at a time. Then they divide the information into small pieces of information, called tokens, and once they have been sorted into a structure according to their meaning, NLP algorithms can work with them (Belz, 2022; Feder et al., 2022; Hamilton et al., 2024; Martinez, 2010).

The use of natural language processing (NLP) focuses on improving customer support and trend analysis, analysing fraud attempts by examining language and sentiment patterns (Faccia, 2023). Specifically, NPL detects inconsistencies or subtle clues in language that indicate whether an attempt is being made to hide information in a document (Chang et al., 2022; Faccia et al., 2023).

Cheng and Cai (2023) state that the use of NLP has led to a significant improvement in fraud detection capabilities. Along the same lines, Ebner et al. (2023) consider it a crucial technique to understand the content of messages and proactively alert people at risk, significantly contributing to the protection of consumers against financial fraud.

### 4.4. Neural Networks

A neural network is an AI method that teaches computers to process data and mimics the communication of neurons in the human brain using electronic circuits. Neurons receive signals, modify them, and transmit them to other neurons via axons. In this system, the perceptron acts as an individual neuron, with an input layer, hidden layers and an output layer. The signal enters the input layer, is processed by algorithms in the hidden layers, and the result is transmitted to the output layer (Guresen & Kayakutlu, 2011; Mangrulkar, 1990; Medhat, 2012; Xie et al., 2022).

The popularity of neural networks as a Deep Learning (DL) technique is due to their ability to identify and combine crucial features from unstructured data, achieving high performance without any domain knowledge (Zhu et al., 2021). In their study, Krambia-Kapardis et al. (2010) obtained an average of 90% accuracy in the fraud detection prediction model using artificial neural networks, thus demonstrating that they can be used to identify companies prone to fraud.

Likewise, Cherif et al. (2023) highlights that the use of AI such as neural networks is becoming essential for the detection of credit card fraud, while Almazroi and Ayub (2023) underlines its importance for detecting fraud in online payments. Projects such as those by Adler and Shavit (2024), aimed at understanding neural networks, focus on superposition computation, which brings significant advances in improving the applicability and efficiency of these networks in various disciplines.

### 4.5. Adversary Generative Networks (GANs)

Generative Adversarial Networks (GANs) are a system of two neural networks, the generator and the discriminator, which compete during training. The generator creates synthetic data similar to real data, while the discriminator attempts to distinguish between generated and real data (Cheah et al., 2023; Zhang et al., 2023).

In financial fraud detection, GANs generate synthetic samples of fraud data to address class imbalance. This interaction improves the generation of minority fraud samples, balancing the proportion between fraud and non-fraud in the data sets, which strengthens the detection of financial frauds (Chen et al., 2018; Jin et al., 2020). GANs have experienced significant development due to their versatility and usefulness, with multiple variants being proposed to improve their applicability (Strelcenia & Prakoonwit, 2023).

### 4.6. Social Media and Online Behaviour

Social media are online platforms that allow users to connect, interact, and share information with other people over the Internet (Lai et al., 2017). These platforms facilitate communication and interaction between individuals, groups, and organizations, thus creating virtual communities where relationships can be established, collaborate, share ideas and stay informed on various topics (Guo et al., 2021).

Social media can be used to detect financial fraud in various ways, such as through data exploration, analysis of relationships and connections, extraction of relevant data, implementation of algorithms and automated processes or the use of metadata and provenance that facilitate the organization of the information collected (Jamshidi & Hashemi, 2012; Diaz-Granados et al., 2015). Analysing behaviour patterns which derivates from the engagement with the online environment is used in fraud detection.

In this section main AI applications, namely Transaction Pattern Analysis, Machine Learning (ML), Natural Language Processing (NLP), Neural Network, Generative Adversarial Networks (GANs), the use of social media and online behaviour, have been identified and briefly introduced, as the most relevant applications for the financial fraud detection and prevention.

Nevertheless, an effective use of these applications raises ethical concerns and issues which means corporate social responsibility challenges and ethical dilemmas. Moreover, corporations and organisations need to address and manage these challenges and involve key stakeholders to face them.

## 5. ETHICAL AND CORPORATE SOCIAL RESPONSIBILITY CHALLENGES IN AI APPLICATIONS FOR FINANCIAL FRAUD DETECTION AND PREVENTION

AI is part of our lives, and its influence is growing, so it is crucial that people who design, develop, deploy, acquire, and use AI understand how to use AI ethics and CRS to minimize harm and optimize benefits. This section exhaustively analyses the main ethical and social responsibility challenges that AI applications generate for companies and consumers. Accordingly, this section addresses the answer to research question 4.

## 5.1. Privacy

Aiming to train AI models to deal with financial fraud, massive amounts of data need to be incorporated into them (Cui et al., 2022). Banking entities and digital financial corporations (Fintechs) store in their systems enormous amounts of personal data of their clients, as well as their daily financial transactions (Gai et al., 2017). This data can be classified as personal information (PI), relating to an identified or identifiable person, such as a name or postcode, and as sensitive personal information (SPI) which, if compromised, could be misused to harm or cause problems for an individual (Carmody et al., 2021; Fayoumi et al., 2022).

If a model is trained with personal or sensitive information without applying any privacy controls, there is a risk that this data may be used improperly, compromising the privacy and security of customers, and losing control over the possession of their data (Albayati et al., 2020; Cam & Kiet, 2023; Khan et al., 2023). However, another issue arises. The definition of privacy differs according to the country we are in, as well as the types of data to which this term applies (Walters et al., 2019).

As stated by Firdaus et al. (2018), it is crucial to find ways to ensure data confidentiality while using AI to effectively detect and prevent fraud. Privacy controls that can be applied during model training as model anonymisation and differential privacy or after model training, data minimisation. In the process of anonymisation, identifiable information is removed or modified from individuals' data to protect their privacy (Galbusera & Cina, 2024; Weber et al., 2024), while differential privacy ensures that the probability of any outcome of a learning algorithm does not change when modifying a single record in the training data, so that an adversary cannot infer information about a specific record (Zhu & Yu, 2019; Zhu et al., 2021). Finally, data minimisation reduces the amount of data that is collected and processed by limiting the SPI that is held and shared, helping to protect users' privacy (Razaque et al., 2022; Yaraziz et al., 2022).

## 5.2. Explainability

The importance of explainability lies in its epistemic and ethical benefits, as it provides insight into the extent to which the use of AI models meets the standards set by the other principles (Adams, 2023). AI tools must be able to provide clear and understandable explanations of how they reached certain conclusions or decisions (Nayak & Chandiramani, 2022; Harbinja et al., 2023), which helps to reduce errors and anticipate the strengths and weaknesses of the model, as well as to avoid unexpected behaviour in production (López-Úbeda et al., 2023).

In the pursuit of model explainability, it is important not to confuse with interpretability, as these are different ways of understanding how the model works. Interpretability is the degree to which an observer can understand the cause of a decision. It is the success rate with which humans can predict the outcome of an AI output, while explainability goes a step further and examines how the AI system arrived at an outcome (Aslam et al., 2022; Nicodeme, 2020; Tiwary et al., 2024). Improving explainability and interpretability of AI models allows companies to remain competitive in the marketplace, gain customer confidence and build trust in reliable AI (Adadi & Berrada, 2018; Firdaus et al., 2022; Pagliari et al., 2022).

## 5.3. Transparency

Transparency has become an essential pillar of the implementation of AI for the detection and prevention of financial fraud. Financial institutions are responsible for facilitating customers' understanding of how automated fraud detection systems work, thus avoiding undermining trust in the system and raising concerns about privacy protection (Van Bekkum & Borgesius, 2021).

Ensuring the collection of personal and financial data through appropriate customer consent is a key challenge that financial institutions must address (Yerima & Bashar, 2022). The absence of transparency can lead to social and psychological consequences such as distrust of technology and a strong sense of powerlessness, which can have a profound impact on mental health (Nannini et al., 2024).

Transparency is about revealing information related to the data used to build AI systems, making design decisions along the way, creating models, evaluating the models and implementing the models (Johnson et al., 2022). Governance ensures that the process followed during creation and implementation follows internal policies to create reliable AI, increase public confidence and legitimise the decisions taken (De Fine Licht & De Fine Licht, 2020; Win & Beydoun, 2020).

By increasing transparency, we can improve governance. Therefore, it is important that the roles of the participants in the AI systems process and the responsibilities that each of them takes are well defined, harmonising the processes carried out (Francisco & Linnér, 2023; Sakyoud et al., 2023; Shneiderman, 2020).

## 5.4. Impartiality

Training plays a critical role in the development of machine learning and AI systems for financial fraud detection. This process involves the use of models and historical data sets, which can introduce inherent biases if not managed properly

(Dong et al., 2022). In general, bias is a systematic error, but in the context of fairness, the problem revolves around unintended bias. Unintended bias gives some groups or individuals a systematic advantage and other groups or individuals a systematic disadvantage, perpetuating social inequalities (Chu et al., 2021; Ranard et al., 2024). In the judicial context, for example, the influence of implicit biases in judges' decisions can compromise the perception of justice and fairness in the legal system. This can lead to widespread distrust of judicial institutions, affecting the legitimacy of the system and people's willingness to participate in it (Schneider & Weber, 2024).

These biases, which may be related to demographic variables such as gender, race, or age, have the potential to bias associations between certain fraudulent behaviours and specific population characteristics (Cruz et al., 2021). Consequently, AI models can inadvertently replicate existing social biases and generate discriminatory decisions (Fiore et al., 2019; Zheng et al., 2023).

This phenomenon highlights the critical importance of addressing algorithmic bias during the training of AI models to ensure fairness and objectivity in their application and the need for human oversight and continuous evaluation in the development of rules for algorithmic software (Simos et al., 2022).

## 5.5. Solidity

AI provides multiple and sophisticated tools to combat financial fraud, but each of them has weaknesses that make them vulnerable to criminal attacks (Hu et al., 2021). Analyzing the vulnerabilities and robustness of the models applied in fraud detection is imperative for companies that use them, especially financial and insurance companies due to the characteristics of the information they possess (Amerirad et al., 2023). Different techniques can be used in this process, such as the DeepFense online defence framework proposed by Rouhani et al. (2018) or the automated verification framework based on Satisfiability Modulo Theory (SMT) by Huang et al. (2017). However, the goal of different methodologies should be the same: to develop robust and resilient countermeasures for different types of likely adversary scenarios to provide reliable infrastructure in AI environments (Sengupta et al., 2020). Interacting with AI systems that fail or are perceived as unreliable can generate stress, anxiety and frustration for users. This is especially relevant in contexts where AI is used for critical tasks or where it is expected to improve quality of life. It is therefore imperative to ensure the robustness of these technologies (Hamon et al., 2024).

## 5.6. Responsibility and Accountability

Accountability focuses on the responsibility that people, organizations, or institutions have to inform and justify their actions before interested parties, assuming the consequences of the decisions made, being a fundamental principle in governance, management, and decision-making process (Kieslich et al., 2022; Taher et al., 2024). The complexity of AI models has made it difficult to determine the responsible authority, hindering accountability and the protection of basic rights of citizens (Horneber & Laumer, 2023; Zajko, 2023).

According to London (2019), it is essential to promote accountability and ensure that machine learning systems do not become covert tools to arbitrarily interfere with the autonomy of stakeholders. The importance of accountability has led the European Commission to incorporate it as one of the seven requirements of trustworthy AI, while highlighting auditability and the guarantee of adequate and accessible remediation as key factors to consider in the implementation of AI (European Commission, 2019).

## 5.7. Impact on Decision Making

The impact of using AI on decision making in financial organizations is significant (Sabharwal et al., 2024). According to Pinheiro et al. (2023), the development of intelligent routines to support complex decision making is not always simple, presenting difficulties related to the abundance of available data sources, the number of legal regulations that must be met, and the need to incorporate transparency, auditability, standardization, and desirable reuse in information technology systems. In compliance with Giest & Klievink (2022), the integration of AI in decision-making should be encourage, as it promotes innovation in areas such as the public sector.

However, the automation generated by AI tools does not exempt the need for human supervision or the importance of a correct interpretation of the results obtained to make informed decisions, especially in critical situations where decisions based solely on algorithms could have significant consequences (De Barros et al., 2017; Jesus et al., 2021). Likewise, companies must ensure effective appeal mechanisms in case of errors made in decision-making, both because of humans and AI (Kanika et al., 2022).

## 5.8. Legislation and Regulatory Framework

The Council and the European Parliament have reached a provisional agreement on what is the first Artificial Intelligence (AI) Regulation, based on the European Commission's 2021 proposal to create the EU's first regulatory framework for AI

(European Commission, 2019; European Commission, 2023). The key objectives of this law are to ensure that Artificial Intelligence systems introduced on the European market are safe and respect citizens' rights while stimulating investment and innovation in the field of AI in Europe (European Commission, 2023).

At a global level, politicians and competent authorities are working to review their country's financial, data protection and administrative legislation (Huh, 2022; Ridzuan et al., 2024), promoting the importance of complying with constitutional principles and human rights to ensure transparency and explainability of AI systems, which may require a strong legal framework (Kuzniacki et al., 2022; Lee et al., 2018). In 2023, AI became a key US policy issue, driven by Biden's executive order, which established risk-based industry standards and promoted transparency. In 2024, these policies are expected to be implemented through the new Artificial Intelligence Safety Institute, while Congress evaluates proposals on transparency, deepfakes and platform accountability, however, the new US president has repealed the law against AI risks (Jiménez, 2025; MIT Technology Review, 2024).

Meanwhile, regulation of AI in China has been fragmented, with specific rules for areas such as algorithms and deepfakes. In 2023, a possible comprehensive law was announced, although implementation could take years. In the meantime, companies must register their models with the government, which limits foreign competition and reinforces state control, favouring Chinese companies but restricting competition and online expression.

A global increase in AI regulation is expected in the coming years, with Africa highlighted by the African Union's potential strategy to boost competitiveness and protect consumers. Countries such as Rwanda, Nigeria and South Africa are already moving forward with national policies. Bodies such as the UN and OECD are working on standards that could facilitate regulatory harmonisation at a global level. At the geopolitical level, differences between democratic and authoritarian approaches to AI development will become more pronounced, forcing companies to decide whether to prioritise global expansion or focus on local markets.

Assuring security from the development phase of AI technology and continuously monitoring and updating to prevent problems is essential to steer the development of AI in a positive direction (Jang, 2024). Legislative authorities face new challenges such as the legal personification of AI, responsibility for the consequences of the implementation of these tools and the continuous evolution and transformation of AI technology that makes legislation obsolete and inadequate in noticeably short periods of time (King et al., 2019; Azzutti, 2022; Novelli, 2022).

## 5.9. Fraudulent Misinformation

Recent advancements in AI technologies have exacerbated the challenges of misinformation and financial fraud.

Generative AI models can produce compelling but fabricated content, complicating detection efforts (Xu et al., 2023; Shoaib et al., 2023). Manipulating narrative frames into precise information can generate misinformation, requiring innovative detection approaches using large language models and deep neural networks (Wang et al., 2024).

To combat AI-generated misinformation, researchers propose examining manipulation traces at signal, perceptual, semantic, and human levels (Xu et al., 2023) and multifaceted strategies including advanced detection algorithms, cross-platform collaboration, and policy initiatives (Shoaib et al., 2023).

In the financial sector, artificial intelligence and machine learning techniques offer promising solutions for fraud prevention by identifying legitimate and fraudulent behaviors (Agarwal, 2021). However, challenges remain, such as evolving fraud patterns and the need for model interpretability.

While data science in finance offers opportunities for improved customer experiences and cutting-edge solutions, it also raises ethical concerns, potential biases, and data security issues (Zheng et al., 2023). Fraudsters are increasingly using AI-based tools such as WormGPT and FraudGPT to create misleading information and scam unsuspecting victims, requiring the evolution of fraud detection techniques (Sina, 2023). The proliferation of Artificial Intelligence Generated Content (AIGC), which uses AI to assist or replace manual content generation by generating content based on user-inputted keywords, further complicates the detection of misinformation, making traditional approaches inadequate (Xu et al., 2023).

As financial institutions adopt advanced technologies such as OpenAI to protect customers from fraud, they must also address the ethical challenges posed by generative AI in algorithmic trading and fraud detection (Zheng et al., 2023; Sina, 2023).

This section has presented most relevant challenges found in the literature derived from AI Implementation for the financial fraud detection and prevention, as well as important considerations on some of the most AI-based tools and techniques, explaining some of the difficulties to cope with the presented challenges.

The result of this research is a holistic theoretical framework for financial fraud detection and prevention, which gather a conceptualisation process including concepts, ethical and social responsibility concerns for the framing of AI applications, that eventually contribute to copying the identified challenges, as is represented in figure 1.

*Figure 1. Financial fraud detection and prevention theoretical framework*

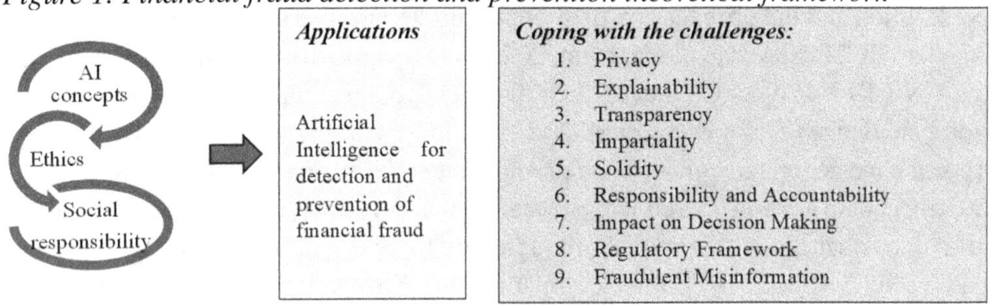


## 6. DISCUSSION AND RESEARCH AGENDA

In recent years, the exponential penetration of AI has been pivotal, triggering a profound transformation across a wide range of economic sectors and catalysing the transition to the fourth industrial revolution (Mannuru et al., 2023). AI impact is particularly relevant in the financial sector and cybersecurity, becoming a protection mechanism for consumers (Kim, 2019). Companies such as and Paypal and Capital One, reports significant progress using data science techniques and machine learning models to detect and prevent financial fraud and surveys show great customers satisfaction. Similarly, credit cards companies, such as Visa and MasterCard, have used AI applications. This shows a trend to use technology-based detection services for many companies in the financial sector. Nonetheless, the rapid development of AI and the increasing reliance on AI tools bring the emergence of ethical threats and dilemmas, as well as concerns related to social responsibility (Borenstein et al., 2021; Biondi et al., 2023; Van Den Berg et al., 2024). Moraes (2024) highlights the relevance of integrating experts from multiple disciplines and sectors in the creation of regulatory frameworks for artificial intelligence (AI). This encompasses the collaboration of regulators, private sector representatives, academics and members of civil society, promoting a broader and more diverse view on the challenges and possibilities posed by AI.

Some notable episodes have highlighted the ethical challenges inherent in the implementation of AI in business (see Table1), such as evidence of gender bias in Amazon's AI-based recruitment tool, the manifestation of racist and sexist comments by Microsoft's chatbot, which culminated in its retirement, as well as the deadly incidents associated with Tesla's autonomous systems (Sison et al., 2023). Other case includes discriminatory behaviour in ranking algorithm affecting the decision-making process. In fraud detection, there have also been cases where AI presents ethical challenges, such as the SyRI case in the Netherlands, where cases of unfair persecution and the propagation of xenophobic stereotypes were reported (Züger & Asghari, 2022; Newman & Mintrom, 2023). On the positive side, it is also reported the UNICEF's Project Connect which may be a good example to overcome the solidity challenge (Züger & Asghari, 2022). Chinese companies such as Alibaba and Tecent have generated concerns on privacy data (Verma et al., 2021; Nishant et al., 2020) but also are considered like a role model in privacy policy within the country after deep changes in their policy, though they force consumers to accept it private data policies (Fu, 2019). Other companies, i.e. Softbank poses human oversight concerns in AI development and governance (Sigfrids et al., 2023).

These incidents are a tangible demonstration of the imperative to continue researching and improving AI tools, ensuring their alignment with ethical guidelines and the fundamental values of society.

*Table 1. Examples of ethical concerns in case studies*

| Case study | Ethical concern | Challenge | Reference |
|---|---|---|---|
| Amazon | Evidence of gender bias | Impartiality | Sison et al., 2023<br>Claudy et al, 2022 |
| Microsoft's chatbot | Racist and sexist comments | Transparency | Sison et al., 2023<br>Daza & Ilozumba, 2022 |
| Deliveroo, food delivery platform | Discriminatory behaviour in reputational-ranking algorithm | Impact on Decision Making | Piccininni, 2022 |
| Tesla's autonomous systems | Deadly incidents associated | Responsibility and accountability | Sison et al., 2023<br>Leben, 2023 |
| SyRI (Dutch welfare fraud detection project) | Unfair persecution and the propagation of xenophobic stereotypes.<br>No public interest AI approach, nor deliberative and participatory design | Misinformation<br>Regulatory Framework | Züger Asghari, 2022<br><br>Newman & Mintrom, 2023 |
| UNICEF's Project Connect | Public interest AI, open for validation to others, use an open-source tool | Solidity | Züger & Asghari, 2022 |
| Alibaba (e-commerce platform) | data privacy and consumer autonomy | Privacy | Fu, 2019<br>Verma et al., 2021 |
| Softbank | human oversight to ensure fairness and transparency | Fairness and transparency | Sigfrids et al., 2023 |
| Tecent (Tech conglomerate) | data privacy, potential misuse of technology, surveillance, | Privacy<br>Fraudulent misinformation | Fu, 2019<br>Nishant et al., 2020 |

In their work to detect financial fraud, the various AI models require high-quality financial transaction data, machine learning algorithms, the construction of predictive models based on historical data, the ability to adapt to new fraudulent techniques, and the ability to interpret results to assist analysts, requiring high investments by companies to adapt their infrastructures, train staff in new processes and recruit specialised personnel (Kapadiya et al., 2022; Mishra, 2023; Souza et al., 2024). In addition to these barriers to incorporating AI, companies may face difficulties in finding huge amounts of reliable data to feed into these systems, adaptation to legacy systems from other companies, legal restrictions that restrict the proper training of algorithms, or employee resistance to incorporating AI into operational processes.

The massive collection of personal data for the training of AI algorithms poses significant challenges in terms of privacy and protection of sensitive consumer data (Awosika et al., 2024; Baabdullah et al., 2024; Deng et al., 2023; Zaimi et al., 2023). This carries the inherent risk of potential misuse or compromise of personal information during fraud detection operations, which can lead to a profound negative impact on consumer trust (Mhlanga, 2020; Xiong et al., 2021). Furthermore, if training data contains biases, such as racial or gender discrimination, algorithms can perpetuate and amplify these biases (Lokanan, 2022; Truby, 2020), leading to unfair prosecution, inequity, and errors in decision-making. The complex nature of the Artificial Intelligence algorithms used in financial fraud detection can complicate the understanding of the decisions made, which impacts on the identification of possible errors in the process (Mytnyk et al., 2023). This complexity can result in a lack of transparency and explainability in the procedure (Boustani, 2021; Fukas et al., 2022; Kesa & Kerikmäe, 2020). Due to the ethical dilemmas present, it is imperative to institute mechanisms that clarify decision-making responsibility and ensure accountability within a sound legal framework when AI is used for the detection and prevention of financial fraud (Yang et al., 2021; Kong et al., 2024). This framework should include an appropriate compensation system for clients and consumers in case of harm (Ali et al., 2022).

To address these challenges, global governmental entities, international organisations, and technology giants have implemented concerted actions and reached consensus to build trust in AI (Zhang et al., 2021). These actions focus on data protection or the auditing of algorithms. However, the scale of AI's negative influence requires going further by regulating clear legal frameworks at the international level, encouraging ethical oversight and combating misinformation. Additionally, considerable international research and public-private collaboration is required to promote the benefits of AI, while managing and reducing the associated risks to consumers and society at large.

## 7. CONCLUSIONS

This study sheds light on an area that is continually evolving, the ethics and social responsibility in using AI to prevent and detect financial fraud. Throughout this research, both theoretical and empirical knowledge have been detailed to provide a global vision of the line of research. The analysis of the literature makes clear the importance of AI to detect financial fraud and how integrated this technology is in the financial sector and the detection of financial fraud. Continuing to research AI and its ethical and social implications can foster innovation and the advancement of numerous areas of knowledge. This research leads to the following conclusions:

1. The application of AI systems for the detection of financial fraud raises a significant number of ethical issues faced by financial institutions and governmental organisations.
2. The incorporation of customers' personal and financial information by banks and FinTechs raises ethical dilemmas related to privacy and data control by consumers, eroding their privacy and exposing them to the public and to fraudsters. This scenario exposes them to anxiety and fear of vulnerability, post-violation of privacy stress, distrust and feelings of powerlessness and lack of control.
3. At the same time, the various AI models aimed at detecting financial fraud exhibit deficiencies and vulnerabilities that make them susceptible to exploitation by criminals, leading to a direct threat to the security of customers' personal data, increasing feelings of helplessness and insecurity.
4. Datasets used in training algorithms can also lead to biased decisions if they contain inherent biases related to gender, ethnicity, or age, which could result in the erroneous association of certain demographic groups with fraudulent behaviour and the perpetuation of social inequalities, negatively impacting vulnerable groups.
5. Achieving transparency in the fraud detection procedure using AI is still a work in progress, which results in a lack of clarity as to the explainability of errors and creates mistrust among consumers.
6. The use of Artificial Intelligence has catalysed a significant change in the decision-making process, supported by the capabilities provided by this technology.
7. It is essential to thoroughly understand and analyse the results derived from the application of AI, while maintaining rigorous oversight of the entire process. The question of accountability for the actions undertaken by the various entities making use of AI emerges as a fundamental ethical dilemma that still requires further academic development, given its complexity and its compelling relevance in safeguarding citizens' rights.

8. In order to secure individuals and entities against the potential threats inherent in the use of Artificial Intelligence, it is essential to establish an international legal framework that is both robust and adaptable to the constant evolution of technological innovation.
9. While AI offers considerable potential to improve the detection and prevention of financial fraud, its implementation requires a cautious and multidisciplinary approach. Collaboration between public and private sectors, investment in research to mitigate bias and improve transparency, as well as the promotion of digital literacy among consumers, are essential aspects of addressing the ethical and social challenges intrinsic in this technology.
10. The path towards an ethical and corporate socially responsible use of AI in the detection and prevention of financial fraud involves a continuous commitment to critical reflection by institutions and academics, responsible innovation and the search for a balance between effectiveness in the fight against fraud and respect for individual and collective rights.

Research on the ethical and social responsibility implications of AI in financial fraud detection and prevention is a line of research with enormous potential that has not yet been sufficiently explored. Future lines of research could analyse the impact on fairness and accuracy of fraud detection as a function of algorithmic biases, as well as examine the impact of the use of AI in fraud detection on digital financial inclusion and consumer digital financial literacy and education. The establishment of a clear legal and ethical framework for the use of AI in financial fraud is essential to protect society from the risks associated with AI as well as encouraging ethical oversight and combating misinformation. Thus, the academic community needs to focus on these topics to provide policymakers and authorities with deeper specific recommendations according to the discipline of implementation of the technologies and to the evolution of AI.

## REFERENCES


Adadi, A., & Berrada, M. (2018). Peeking Inside the Black-Box: A Survey on Explainable Artificial Intelligence (XAI). *IEEE Access : Practical Innovations, Open Solutions*, 6, 52138–52160. DOI: 10.1109/ACCESS.2018.2870052

Adams, J. (2023). Defending explicability as a principle for the ethics of artificial intelligence in medicine. *Medicine, Health Care, and Philosophy*, 26(4), 615–623. DOI: 10.1007/s11019-023-10175-7 PMID: 37642834

Adler, M., & Shavit, N. (2024). On the Complexity of Neural Computation in Superposition. CSAIL Technical Reports (July 1, 2003 - present). https://hdl.handle.net/1721.1/157073

Agarwal, S. (2021). Artificial Intelligence Techniques of Fraud Prevention. In Applications of Artificial Intelligence in Business and Finance (pp. 113-132). Apple Academic Press. DOI: 10.1201/9781003129639-6

Ahdadou, M., Aajly, A., & Tahrouch, M. (2024). Enhancing corporate governance through AI: A systematic literature review. *Technology Analysis and Strategic Management*, •••, 1–14. DOI: 10.1080/09537325.2024.2326120

Albayati, H., Kim, S. K., & Rho, J. J. (2020). Accepting financial transactions using blockchain technology and cryptocurrency: A customer perspective approach. *Technology in Society*, 62, 101320. DOI: 10.1016/j.techsoc.2020.101320

Ali, A., Razak, S. A., Othman, S. H., Eisa, T. A. E., Al-Dhaqm, A., Nasser, M., Elhassan, T., Elshafie, H., & Saif, A. (2022). Financial Fraud Detection Based on Machine Learning: A Systematic Literature Review. *Applied Sciences (Basel, Switzerland)*, 12(19), 9637. DOI: 10.3390/app12199637

Almazroi, A. A., & Ayub, N. (2023). Online Payment fraud detection model using machine learning techniques. *IEEE Access : Practical Innovations, Open Solutions*, 11, 137188–137203. DOI: 10.1109/ACCESS.2023.3339226

Amerirad, B., Cattaneo, M., Kenett, R. S., & Luciano, E. (2023). Adversarial Artificial Intelligence in Insurance: From an Example to Some Potential Remedies. *Risks*, 11(1), 20. DOI: 10.3390/risks11010020

Arrieta, A. B., Díaz-Rodríguez, N., Del Ser, J., Bennetot, A., Tabik, S., Barbado, A., Garcia, S., Gil-Lopez, S., Molina, D., Benjamins, R., Chatila, R., & Herrera, F. (2019). Explainable Artificial Intelligence (XAI): Concepts, taxonomies, opportunities and challenges toward responsible AI. *Information Fusion*, 58, 82–115. DOI: 10.1016/j.inffus.2019.12.012

Aslam, N., Khan, I. U., Mirza, S., AlOwayed, A., Anis, F. M., Aljuaid, R. M., & Baageel, R. (2022). Interpretable Machine Learning Models for Malicious Domains Detection Using Explainable Artificial Intelligence (XAI). *Sustainability (Basel)*, 14(12), 7375. DOI: 10.3390/su14127375

Awosika, T., Shukla, R. M., & Pranggono, B. (2024). Transparency and Privacy: The Role of Explainable AI and Federated Learning in Financial Fraud Detection. *IEEE Access : Practical Innovations, Open Solutions*, 1, 64551–64560. Advance online publication. DOI: 10.1109/ACCESS.2024.3394528

Azzutti, A. (2022). AI trading and the limits of EU law enforcement in deterring market manipulation. Computer Law And Security Report. *Computer Law & Security Report*, 45, 105690. DOI: 10.1016/j.clsr.2022.105690

Baabdullah, T., Alzahrani, A., Rawat, D. B., & Liu, C. (2024). Efficiency of Federated Learning and Blockchain in Preserving Privacy and Enhancing the Performance of Credit Card Fraud Detection (CCFD) Systems. *Future Internet*, 16(6), 196. DOI: 10.3390/fi16060196

Bansal, K., Paliwal, A. C., & Singh, A. K. (2024). *Analysis of the benefits of artificial intelligence and human personality study on online fraud detection*. International Journal Of Law And Management./International Journal Of Law And Management., DOI: 10.1108/IJLMA-08-2023-0198

Baum, S. (2018). Countering superintelligence misinformation. *Information (Basel)*, 9(10), 244. DOI: 10.3390/info9100244

Beattie, J. R., & Esmonde-White, F. W. L. (2021). Exploration of Principal Component Analysis: Deriving Principal Component Analysis Visually Using Spectra. *Applied Spectroscopy*, 75(4), 361–375. DOI: 10.1177/0003702820987847 PMID: 33393349

Belz, A. (2022). A Metrological Perspective on Reproducibility in NLP*. *Computational Linguistics*, 48(4), 1125–1135. DOI: 10.1162/coli_a_00448

Biondi, G., Cagnoni, S., Capobianco, R., Franzoni, V., Lisi, F. A., Milani, A., & Vallverdú, J. (2023). Editorial: Ethical design of artificial intelligence-based systems for decision making. *Frontiers in Artificial Intelligence*, 6, 1250209. Advance online publication. DOI: 10.3389/frai.2023.1250209 PMID: 37554695

Borenstein, J., Grodzinsky, F. S., Howard, A., Miller, K. W., & Wolf, M. J. (2021). AI Ethics: A Long History and a Recent Burst of Attention. *Computer*, 54(1), 96–102. DOI: 10.1109/MC.2020.3034950

Bostrom, N. (2014). *Superintelligence: Paths, dangers, strategies*. Oxford University Press.

Boustani, N. M. (2021). Artificial intelligence impact on banks clients and employees in an Asian developing country. *Journal of Asia Business Studies*, 16(2), 267–278. DOI: 10.1108/JABS-09-2020-0376

Brundage, M. (2015). Taking superintelligence seriously. *Futures*, 72, 32–35. DOI: 10.1016/j.futures.2015.07.009

Cam, N. T., & Kiet, V. T. (2023). FlwrBC: Incentive Mechanism Design for Federated Learning by Using Blockchain. *IEEE Access : Practical Innovations, Open Solutions*, 11, 107855–107866. DOI: 10.1109/ACCESS.2023.3320045

Cantrell, B., & Zhang, Z. (2018). A third intelligence. *Landscape Architecture Frontiers*, 6(2), 42. DOI: 10.15302/J-LAF-20180205

Carmody, J., Shringarpure, S., & Van de Venter, G. (2021). AI and privacy concerns: A smart meter case study. *Journal Of Information Communication And Ethics In Society*, 19(4), 492–505. DOI: 10.1108/JICES-04-2021-0042

Cath, C., Wachter, S., Mittelstadt, B., Taddeo, M., & Floridi, L. (2017). Artificial Intelligence and the 'Good Society': The US, EU, and UK approach. *Science and Engineering Ethics*. Advance online publication. DOI: 10.1007/s11948-017-9901-7 PMID: 28353045

Chang, J., Yen, N. Y., & Hung, J. C. (2022). Design of a NLP-empowered finance fraud awareness model: The anti-fraud chatbot for fraud detection and fraud classification as an instance. Journal Of Ambient Intelligence & Humanized Computing. *Journal of Ambient Intelligence and Humanized Computing*, 13(10), 4663–4679. DOI: 10.1007/s12652-021-03512-2

Cheah, P. C. Y., Yang, Y., & Lee, B. G. (2023). Enhancing Financial Fraud Detection through Addressing Class Imbalance Using Hybrid SMOTE-GAN Techniques. *International Journal Of Financial Studies*, 11(3), 110. DOI: 10.3390/ijfs11030110

Chen, J., Shen, Y., & Ali, R. (2018). Credit Card Fraud Detection Using Sparse Autoencoder and Generative Adversarial Network. 2018 IEEE 9th Annual Information Technology, *Electronics and Mobile Communication Conference (IEMCON)*. https://doi.org/DOI: 10.1109/IEMCON.2018.8614815

Cheng, C., & Cai, W. (2023). Double-weight LDA extracting keywords for financial fraud detection system. *Multimedia Tools and Applications*, 83(17), 50757–50781. Advance online publication. DOI: 10.1007/s11042-023-17334-1

Cherif, A., Badhib, A., Ammar, H., Alshehri, S., Kalkatawi, M., & Imine, A. (2023). Credit card fraud detection in the era of disruptive technologies: A systematic review. Journal Of King Saud University. Computer And Information Sciences/Ma ala am'a Al-malīk Saud : Ùlm Al- asib Wa Al-ma'lumat, 35(1), 145-174. https://doi.org/DOI: 10.1016/j.jksuci.2022.11.008

Choi, Á. (2021). España ante la Revolución Industrial 4.0: Mercado laboral y formación. *Araucaria*, 47(47), 479–505. DOI: 10.12795/araucaria.2021.i47.21

Chukwuere, J. E. (2023). Exploring Literature Review Methodologies in Information Systems Research: A Comparative Study. [ELDN]. *Education & Learning in Developing Nations*, 1(2), 38–46. DOI: 10.26480/eldn.02.2023.74.82

Claudy, M. C., Aquino, K., & Graso, M. (2022). Artificial intelligence can't be charmed: The effects of impartiality on laypeople's algorithmic preferences. *Frontiers in Psychology*, 13, 898027. DOI: 10.3389/fpsyg.2022.898027 PMID: 35846643

Comisión Europea (CE). (2021). Proposal for a Regulation of the European Parliament and of the Council on Harmonised Rules in the field of Artificial Intelligence (Artificial Intelligence Act) and amending certain legislative acts of the Union. Brussels, 21.04.2021. https://eur-lex.europa.eu/legal-content/ES/TXT/?uri=CELEX:52021PC0206

Cowell, J. M. (2012). Literature reviews as a research strategy. *The Journal of School Nursing: the Official Publication of the National Association of School Nurses*, 28(5), 326–327. DOI: 10.1177/1059840512458666 PMID: 23012244

Cruz, A. F., Saleiro, P., Belem, C., Soares, C., & Bizarro, P. (2021). Promoting Fairness through Hyperparameter Optimization. *2021 IEEE International Conference On Data Mining (ICDM)*. https://doi.org/DOI: 10.1109/ICDM51629.2021.00119

Cui, X., Chang, Y., Yang, C., Cong, Z., Wang, B., & Leng, Y. (2022). Development and Trends in Artificial Intelligence in Critical Care Medicine: A Bibliometric Analysis of Related Research over the Period of 2010–2021. *Journal of Personalized Medicine*, 13(1), 50. DOI: 10.3390/jpm13010050 PMID: 36675711

Dasari, S., & Kaluri, R. (2024). An Effective Classification of DDoS Attacks in a Distributed Network by Adopting Hierarchical Machine Learning and Hyperparameters Optimization Techniques. *IEEE Access : Practical Innovations, Open Solutions*, 12, 10834–10845. DOI: 10.1109/ACCESS.2024.3352281

Davenport, T. H., Guha, A., Grewal, D., & Breßgott, T. (2019). How artificial intelligence will change the future of marketing. *Journal of the Academy of Marketing Science*, 48(1), 24–42. DOI: 10.1007/s11747-019-00696-0

Daza, M. T., & Ilozumba, U. J. (2022). A survey of AI ethics in business literature: Maps and trends between 2000 and 2021. *Frontiers in Psychology*, 13, 1042661. DOI: 10.3389/fpsyg.2022.1042661 PMID: 36600712

De Barros, R. S. M., De Lima Cabral, D. R., Gonçalves, P. M., & De Carvalho Santos, S. G. T. (2017). RDDM: Reactive drift detection method. *Expert Systems with Applications*, 90, 344–355. DOI: 10.1016/j.eswa.2017.08.023

De Fine Licht, K., & De Fine Licht, J. (2020). Artificial intelligence, transparency, and public decision-making. *AI & Society*, 35(4), 917–926. DOI: 10.1007/s00146-020-00960-w

Deng, W., Liang, G., Yu, C., Yao, K., Wang, C., & Zhang, X. (2023). An Early Warning Model of Telecommunication Network Fraud Based on User Portrait. Computers, Materials & Continua/Computers. *Computers, Materials & Continua*, 75(1), 1561–1576. DOI: 10.32604/cmc.2023.035016

Diaz-Granados, M., Diaz-Montes, J., & Parashar, M. (2015). Investigating insurance fraud using social media. *Proceedings 2015 IEEE International Conference on Big Data*, pp.1344-1349. https://doi.org/DOI: 10.1109/BigData.2015.7363893

Ding, J. (2018). Deciphering China's AI Dream: The Context, Components, Capabilities, and Consequences of China's Strategy to Lead the World in AI. Future of Humanity Institute, University of Oxford. https://www.fhi.ox.ac.uk/wp-content/uploads/Deciphering_Chinas_AI-Dream.pdf

Dong, Y., Liu, N., Jalaian, B., & Li, J. (2022). EDITS: Modeling and Mitigating Data Bias for Graph Neural Networks. *Proceedings Of The ACM Web Conference 2022*. https://doi.org/DOI: 10.1145/3485447.3512173

Dutta, A., Deb, T., & Pathak, S. (2020). Automated Data Harmonization (ADH) using Artificial Intelligence (AI). OPSEARCH/Opsearch, 58(2), 257-275. https://doi.org/DOI: 10.1007/s12597-020-00467-4

Ebner, N., Pehlivanoglu, D., & Shoenfelt, A. (2023). *Financial Fraud and Deception in Aging*. Advances In Geriatric Medicine And Research., DOI: 10.31219/osf.io/ay4jw

Elliott, K., Price, R., Shaw, P., Spiliotopoulos, T., Ng, M., Coopamootoo, K., & Van Moorsel, A. (2021). Towards an Equitable Digital Society: Artificial Intelligence (AI) and Corporate Digital Responsibility (CDR). *Society*, 58(3), 179–188. DOI: 10.1007/s12115-021-00594-8 PMID: 34149122

European Commission. (2019) Ethics guidelines for trustworthy AI. https://digital-strategy.ec.europa.eu/en/library/ethics-guidelines-trustworthy-ai

European Commission. (2023). The Commission welcomes the political agreement on the Artificial Intelligence Act [Press release] https://ec.europa.eu/commission/presscorner/api/files/document/print/es/ip_23_6473/IP_23_6473_ES.pdf

European Parliament & Council. (2024). *Regulation laying down harmonised rules on artificial intelligence (PE-CONS 24/24). (EC) No 300/2008, (EU) No 167/2013, (EU) No 168/2013, (EU) 2018/858, (EU) 2018/1139 and (EU) 2019/2144 and Directives 2014/90/EU, (EU) 2016/797 and (EU) 2020/1828*. Artificial Intelligence Act.

Faccia, A. (2023). National Payment Switches and the Power of Cognitive Computing against Fintech Fraud. *Big Data and Cognitive Computing*, 7(2), 76. DOI: 10.3390/bdcc7020076

Faccia, A., McDonald, J. A. K., & George, B. (2023). NLP Sentiment Analysis and Accounting Transparency: A New Era of Financial Record Keeping. *Computers*, 13(1), 5. DOI: 10.3390/computers13010005

Fayoumi, M. A., Odeh, A., Keshta, I., Aboshgifa, A., AlHajahjeh, T., & Abdulraheem, R. (2022). Email phishing detection based on naïve Bayes, Random Forests, and SVM classifications: A comparative study. 2022 IEEE 12th Annual Computing And Communication Workshop And Conference (CCWC). https://doi.org/DOI: 10.1109/CCWC54503.2022.9720757

Feder, A., Keith, K. A., Manzoor, E., Pryzant, R., Sridhar, D., Wood-Doughty, Z., Eisenstein, J., Grimmer, J., Reichart, R., Roberts, M. E., Stewart, B. M., Veitch, V., & Yang, D. (2022). Causal Inference in Natural Language Processing: Estimation, Prediction, Interpretation and Beyond. *Transactions of the Association for Computational Linguistics*, 10, 1138–1158. DOI: 10.1162/tacl_a_00511

Finocchiaro, G. D. (2023). The regulation of artificial intelligence. *AI & Society*. Advance online publication. DOI: 10.1007/s00146-023-01650-z

Fioravante, R. (2024). Beyond the Business Case for Responsible Artificial Intelligence: Strategic CSR in Light of Digital Washing and the Moral Human Argument. *Sustainability (Basel)*, 16(3), 1232. DOI: 10.3390/su16031232

Fiore, U., De Santis, A., Perla, F., Zanetti, P., & Palmieri, F. (2019). Using generative adversarial networks for improving classification effectiveness in credit card fraud detection. *Information Sciences*, 479, 448–455. DOI: 10.1016/j.ins.2017.12.030

Firdaus, A., Anuar, N. B., Karim, A., & Razak, M. F. A. (2018). Discovering optimal features using static analysis and a genetic search based method for Android malware detection. Frontiers Of Information Technology & Electronic Engineering/Frontiers Of Informaion Technology & Electronic Engineering, 19(6), 712-736. https://doi.org/DOI: 10.1631/FITEE.1601491

Firdaus, R., Xue, Y., Gang, L., & Ali, M. S. E. (2022). Artificial Intelligence and Human Psychology in Online Transaction Fraud. *Frontiers in Psychology*, 13, 947234. Advance online publication. DOI: 10.3389/fpsyg.2022.947234 PMID: 36304851

Francisco, M., & Linnér, B. (2023). AI and the governance of sustainable development. An idea analysis of the European Union, the United Nations, and the World Economic Forum. *Environmental Science & Policy*, 150, 103590. DOI: 10.1016/j.envsci.2023.103590

Fu, T. (2019). China's personal information protection in a data-driven economy: A privacy policy study of Alibaba, Baidu and Tencent. *Global Media and Communication*, 15(2), 195–213. DOI: 10.1177/1742766519846644

Fukas, P., Rebstadt, J., Menzel, L., & Thomas, O. (2022). Towards Explainable Artificial Intelligence in Financial Fraud Detection: Using Shapley Additive Explanations to Explore Feature Importance. En Lecture notes in computer science (pp. 109-126). DOI: 10.1007/978-3-031-07472-1_7

Gai, K., Qiu, M., Sun, X., & Zhao, H. (2017). Security and Privacy Issues: A Survey on FinTech. En Lecture notes in computer science (pp. 236-247). DOI: 10.1007/978-3-319-52015-5_24

Galbusera, F., & Cina, A. (2024). Image annotation and curation in radiology: An overview for machine learning practitioners. *European Radiology Experimental*, 8(1), 11. Advance online publication. DOI: 10.1186/s41747-023-00408-y PMID: 38316659

Ghoddusi, H., Creamer, G. G., & Rafizadeh, N. (2019). Machine learning in energy economics and finance: A review. *Energy Economics*, 81, 709–727. DOI: 10.1016/j.eneco.2019.05.006

Giest, S. N., & Klievink, B. (2022). More than a digital system: How AI is changing the role of bureaucrats in different organizational contexts. *Public Management Review*, 26(2), 379–398. DOI: 10.1080/14719037.2022.2095001

Gomes, M. G., Da Silva, V. H. C., Pinto, L. F. R., Centoamore, P., Digiesi, S., Facchini, F., & De Oliveira Neto, G. C. (2020). Economic, Environmental and Social Gains of the Implementation of Artificial Intelligence at Dam Operations toward Industry 4.0 Principles. Sustainability, 12(9), 3604. https://doi.org/ (2025). Making AI helpful for everyone. Google IA. https://ai.googleDOI: 10.3390/su12093604Google

Guo, Z., Cho, J., Chen, I., Sengupta, S., Hong, M., & Mitra, T. (2021). Online Social Deception and Its Countermeasures: A Survey. *IEEE Access : Practical Innovations, Open Solutions*, 9, 1770–1806. DOI: 10.1109/ACCESS.2020.3047337

Guresen, E., & Kayakutlu, G. (2011). Definition of artificial neural networks with comparison to other networks. *Procedia Computer Science*, 3, 426–433. DOI: 10.1016/j.procs.2010.12.071

Hamilton, S. A., Ambrosy, A. P., Parikh, R. V., Tan, T. C., Fitzpatrick, J. K., Avula, H. R., Sandhu, A. T., Ku, I. A., Go, A. S., Sax, D., & Bhatt, A. S. (2024). Applying natural language processing to identify emergency department and observation encounters for worsening heart failure. *ESC Heart Failure*, 11(5), 2542–2545. Advance online publication. DOI: 10.1002/ehf2.14829 PMID: 38741373

Hamon, R., Junklewitz, H., Garrido, J. S., & Sanchez, I. (2024). Three Challenges to Secure AI Systems in the Context of AI Regulations. *IEEE Access : Practical Innovations, Open Solutions*, 12, 61022–61035. DOI: 10.1109/ACCESS.2024.3391021

Harbinja, E., Edwards, L., & McVey, M. (2023). Governing ghostbots. Computer Law And Security Report. *Computer Law & Security Report*, 48, 105791. DOI: 10.1016/j.clsr.2023.105791

Hasan, Z., Vaz, D., Athota, V. S., Désiré, S. S. M., & Pereira, V. (2023). Can artificial intelligence (AI) manage behavioural biases among financial planners? *Journal of Global Information Management*, 31(2), 1–18. DOI: 10.4018/JGIM.321728

Helfat, C. E., Kaul, A., Ketchen, D. J.Jr, Barney, J. B., Chatain, O., & Singh, H. (2023). Renewing the resource-based view: New contexts, new concepts, and new methods. *Strategic Management Journal*, 44(6), 1357–1390. DOI: 10.1002/smj.3500

Hofstede, G. (2001). *Culture's Consequences: Comparing Values, Behaviors, Institutions, and Organizations Across Nations* (2nd ed.). SAGE Publications.

Horneber, D., & Laumer, S. (2023). Algorithmic accountability. *Business & Information Systems Engineering*, 65(6), 723–730. DOI: 10.1007/s12599-023-00817-8

Hu, Y., Kuang, W., Qin, Z., Li, K., Zhang, J., Gao, Y., Li, W., & Li, K. (2021). Artificial Intelligence Security: Threats and Countermeasures. *ACM Computing Surveys*, 55(1), 1–36. DOI: 10.1145/3487890

Huang, X., Kwiatkowska, M., Wang, S., & Wu, M. (2017). Safety Verification of Deep Neural Networks. En Lecture notes in computer science (pp. 3-29). https://doi.org/DOI: 10.1007/978-3-319-63387-9_1

Huh, Y. K. (2022). Legal Implications of Financial Supervision with Artificial Intelligence. *The Korean Journal of Securities Law*, 23(1), 221–250. https://www.webofscience.com/wos/alldb/full-record/KJD:ART002839443

Iadanza, E., Benincasa, G., Ventisette, I., & Gherardelli, M. (2022). Automatic Classification of Hospital Settings through Artificial Intelligence. *Electronics (Basel)*, 11(11), 1697. DOI: 10.3390/electronics11111697

Igwegbe, C. A., Obi, C. C., Ohale, P. E., Ahmadi, S., Onukwuli, O. D., Nwabanne, J. T., & Białowiec, A. (2023). Modelling and optimisation of electrocoagulation/flocculation recovery of effluent from land-based aquaculture by artificial intelligence (AI) approaches. *Environmental Science and Pollution Research International*, 30(27), 70897–70917. DOI: 10.1007/s11356-023-27387-2 PMID: 37160520

Innan, N., Khan, M. A., & Беннаи, M. (2023). Financial fraud detection: A comparative study of quantum machine learning models. *International Journal of Quantum Information*, 22(02), 2350044. Advance online publication. DOI: 10.1142/S0219749923500442

Jamshidi, S., & Hashemi, M. R. (2012). *An efficient data enrichment scheme for fraud detection using social network analysis. 2012 SIXTH INTERNATIONAL SYMPOSIUM ON TELECOMMUNICATIONS.* IST., DOI: 10.1109/ISTEL.2012.6483147

Jang, S. (2024). Recent Trends and Implications for Artificial Intelligence Regulation. Science. *Technology and Law*, 15(1), 153–174. DOI: 10.34267/cbstl.2024.15.1.153

Jesus, S., Belém, C., Balayan, V., Bento, J., Saleiro, P., Bizarro, P., & Gama, J. (2021). How can I choose an explainer? *Proceedings of the 2021 ACM Conference on Fairness, Accountability, and Transparency*, pp.805-815. https://doi.org/DOI: 10.1145/3442188.3445941

Jiménez, M. (2025, 21 enero). Trump barre la era Biden con una avalancha de decretos contra la inmigración, la agenda verde y la diversidad. El País. https://elpais.com/internacional/2025-01-20/trump-barre-la-era-biden-con-una-avalancha-de-decretos-contra-la-inmigracion-la-agenda-verde-y-la-diversidad.html

Jin, Q., Lin, R., & Yang, F. (2020). E-WACGAN: Enhanced Generative Model of Signaling Data Based on WGAN-GP and ACGAN. *IEEE Systems Journal*, 14(3), 3289–3300. DOI: 10.1109/JSYST.2019.2935457

Jobin, A., Ienca, M., & Vayena, E. (2019). The global landscape of AI ethics guidelines. *Nature Machine Intelligence*, 1(9), 389–399. DOI: 10.1038/s42256-019-0088-2

Johnson, M., Albizri, A., Harfouche, A., & Fosso-Wamba, S. (2022). Integrating human knowledge into artificial intelligence for complex and ill-structured problems: Informed artificial intelligence. *International Journal of Information Management*, 64, 102479. DOI: 10.1016/j.ijinfomgt.2022.102479

Kamruzzaman, M. M. (2022). Impact of Social Media on Geopolitics and Economic Growth: Mitigating the Risks by Developing Artificial Intelligence and Cognitive Computing Tools. *Computational Intelligence and Neuroscience*, 2022, 1–12. DOI: 10.1155/2022/7988894 PMID: 35602647

Kanika, S., Singla, J., Kashif Bashir, A., Nam, Y., UI Hasan, N., & Tariq, U. (2022). Handling Class Imbalance in Online Transaction Fraud Detection. Computers, Materials & Continua/Computers. *Computers, Materials & Continua*, 70(2), 2861–2877. DOI: 10.32604/cmc.2022.019990

Kapadiya, K., Patel, U., Gupta, R., Alshehri, M. D., Tanwar, S., Sharma, G., & Bokoro, P. N. (2022). Blockchain and AI-Empowered Healthcare Insurance Fraud Detection: An Analysis, Architecture, and Future Prospects. *IEEE Access : Practical Innovations, Open Solutions*, 10, 79606–79627. DOI: 10.1109/ACCESS.2022.3194569

Kaplan, A., & Haenlein, M. (2020). Rulers of the world, unite! The challenges and opportunities of artificial intelligence. *Business Horizons*, 63(1), 37–50. DOI: 10.1016/j.bushor.2019.09.003

Kesa, A., & Kerikmäe, T. (2020). Artificial Intelligence and the GDPR: Inevitable Nemeses? TalTech Journal Of European Studies/TalTech. *Journal of European Studies*, 10(3), 68–90. DOI: 10.1515/bjes-2020-0022

Khan, H. U., Malik, M. Z., Nazir, S., & Khan, F. (2023). Utilizing Bio Metric System for Enhancing Cyber Security in Banking Sector: A Systematic Analysis. *IEEE Access : Practical Innovations, Open Solutions*, 11, 80181–80198. DOI: 10.1109/ACCESS.2023.3298824

Kim, D. J. (2019). Digital Economy and FinTech in the view of Consumer Protection. *The Journal of Comparative Private Law*, 26(3), 285–330. https://www.webofscience.com/wos/alldb/full-record/KJD:ART002501742

Kim, S., & Chung, S. (2019). Explaining organizational responsiveness to emerging regulatory pressure: The case of illegal overwork in South Korea. *Human Relations*, 72(9), 1436–1461.

King, T. C., Aggarwal, N., Taddeo, M., & Floridi, L. (2019). Artificial Intelligence Crime: An Interdisciplinary Analysis of Foreseeable Threats and Solutions. *Science and Engineering Ethics*, 26(1), 89–120. DOI: 10.1007/s11948-018-00081-0 PMID: 30767109

Kong, M., Li, R., Wang, J., Li, X., Jin, S., Xie, W., Hou, M., & Cao, C. (2024). CFTNet: A robust credit card fraud detection model enhanced by counterfactual data augmentation. *Neural Computing & Applications*, 36(15), 8607–8623. DOI: 10.1007/s00521-024-09546-9

Koukal, A., Gleue, C., & Breitner, M. (2014). Enhancing Literature Review Methods-Evaluation of a Literature Search Approach based on Latent Semantic Indexing.

Krambia-Kapardis, M., Christodoulou, C., & Agathocleous, M. (2010). Neural networks: The panacea in fraud detection? *Managerial Auditing Journal*, 25(7), 659–678. DOI: 10.1108/02686901011061342

Kumar, A., Bhattacharyya, S. S., & Krishnamoorthy, B. (2023). Automation-augmentation paradox in organizational artificial intelligence technology deployment capabilities; an empirical investigation for achieving simultaneous economic and social benefits. *Journal of Enterprise Information Management*, 36(6), 1556–1582. DOI: 10.1108/JEIM-09-2022-0307

Kumar, S., Sharma, D., Rao, S., Lim, W. M., & Mangla, S. K. (2022). Past, present, and future of sustainable finance: Insights from big data analytics through machine learning of scholarly research. Annals Of Operation Research. *Annals of Operations Research*. Advance online publication. DOI: 10.1007/s10479-021-04410-8 PMID: 35002001

Kuzniacki, B., Almada, M., Tyliński, K., & Górski, Ł. (2022). Requirements for Tax XAI Under Constitutional Principles and Human Rights. En Lecture notes in computer science (pp. 221-238). https://doi.org/DOI: 10.1007/978-3-031-15565-9_14

Laghrabli, S., Benabbou, L., & Berrado, A. (2015, October). A new methodology for literature review analysis using association rules mining. In 2015 10th International Conference on Intelligent Systems: Theories and Applications (SITA) (pp. 1-6). IEEE. DOI: 10.1109/SITA.2015.7358394

Lai, C. Y., Li, Y., & Lin, L. F. (2017). A social referral appraising mechanism for the e-marketplace. *Information & Management*, 54(3), 269–280. DOI: 10.1016/j.im.2016.07.001

Leben, D. (2023). Explainable AI as evidence of fair decisions. *Frontiers in Psychology*, 14, 1069426. DOI: 10.3389/fpsyg.2023.1069426 PMID: 36865358

Lee, K. F., Triolo, P., & Kania, E. (2018). AI Superpowers: China, Silicon Valley, and the New World Order. Houghton Mifflin Harcourt.

Lee, K. Y., Kwon, H. Y., & Lim, J. I. (2018). Legal Consideration on the Use of Artificial Intelligence Technology and Self-regulation in Financial Sector: Focused on Robo-Advisors. En Lecture notes in computer science (pp. 323-335). https://doi.org/DOI: 10.1007/978-3-319-93563-8_27

Li, J. (2022). E-Commerce Fraud Detection Model by Computer Artificial Intelligence Data Mining. *Computational Intelligence and Neuroscience*, 2022, 1–9. DOI: 10.1155/2022/7498025 PMID: 35586101

Lin, P. (2016). Why ethics matters for autonomous cars. In Lin, L. A. P., Abney, K., & Bekey, G. A. (Eds.), *Robot ethics: The ethical and social implications of robotics* (pp. 69–85). MIT Press.

Lokanan, M. (2022). The determinants of investment fraud: A machine learning and artificial intelligence approach. *Frontiers in Big Data*, 5, 961039. Advance online publication. DOI: 10.3389/fdata.2022.961039 PMID: 36299659

London, A. J. (2019). Artificial Intelligence and Black-Box Medical Decisions: Accuracy versus Explainability. *The Hastings Center Report*, 49(1), 15–21. DOI: 10.1002/hast.973 PMID: 30790315

López-Úbeda, P., Martín-Noguerol, T., & Luna, A. (2023). Radiology, explicability and AI: Closing the gap. *European Radiology*, 33(12), 9466–9468. DOI: 10.1007/s00330-023-09902-8 PMID: 37410108

Lorkowski, J., Kolaszyńska, O., & Pokorski, M. (2021). Artificial Intelligence and Precision Medicine: A Perspective. En Advances in experimental medicine and biology (pp. 1-11). https://doi.org/DOI: 10.1007/5584_2021_652

Maashi, M., Alabduallah, B. I., & Kouki, F. (2023b). Sustainable Financial Fraud Detection Using Garra Rufa Fish Optimization Algorithm with Ensemble Deep Learning. *Sustainability (Basel)*, 15(18), 13301. DOI: 10.3390/su151813301

Majeed, Y., Fu, L., & He, L. (2024). Editorial: Artificial intelligence-of-things (AIoT) in precision agriculture. *Frontiers in Plant Science*, 15, 1369791. Advance online publication. DOI: 10.3389/fpls.2024.1369791 PMID: 38344185

Mangrulkar, S. (1990). Artificial neural systems. *ISA Transactions*, 29(1), 5–7. DOI: 10.1016/0019-0578(90)90024-F PMID: 2307576

Mannuru, N. R., Shahriar, S., Teel, Z. A., Wang, T., Lund, B. D., Tijani, S., Pohboon, C. O., Agbaji, D., Alhassan, J., Galley, J., Kousari, R., Ogbadu-Oladapo, L., Saurav, S. K., Srivastava, A., Tummuru, S. P., Uppala, S., & Vaidya, P. (2023). Artificial intelligence in developing countries: The impact of generative artificial intelligence (AI) technologies for development. *Information Development*, 02666669231200628. Advance online publication. DOI: 10.1177/02666669231200628

Martin, K. (2018). Ethical Implications and Accountability of Algorithms. *Journal of Business Ethics*, 160(4), 835–850. DOI: 10.1007/s10551-018-3921-3

Martinez, A. R. (2010). Natural language processing. *Wiley Interdisciplinary Reviews: Computational Statistics*, 2(3), 352–357. DOI: 10.1002/wics.76

Martínez, R. (2016). Fraud Detection Using Deep Learning. https://cybercamp.es/cybercamp2016/sites/default/files/contenidos/material/cybercamp2016-fraud_detection_using_deep_learning-ruben_martinez.pdf

Medhat, M. (2012). Artificial intelligence methods applied for quantitative analysis of natural radioactive sources. *Annals of Nuclear Energy*, 45, 73–79. DOI: 10.1016/j.anucene.2012.02.013

Mersha, M., Lam, K., Wood, J., AlShami, A., & Kalita, J. (2024). Explainable artificial intelligence: A survey of needs, techniques, applications, and future direction. *Neurocomputing*, 128111, 128111. Advance online publication. DOI: 10.1016/j.neucom.2024.128111

Mhlanga, D. (2020). Industry 4.0 in Finance: The Impact of Artificial Intelligence (AI) on Digital Financial Inclusion. *International Journal Of Financial Studies*, 8(3), 45. DOI: 10.3390/ijfs8030045

Mill, E. R., Garn, W., Ryman-Tubb, N. F., & Turner, C. (2023). Opportunities in real time fraud detection: An explainable artificial intelligence (XAI) Research Agenda. *International Journal of Advanced Computer Science and Applications*, 14(5), 1172–1186. https://www.webofscience.com/wos/alldb/full-record/WOS:001015077500001. DOI: 10.14569/IJACSA.2023.01405121

Minkkinen, M., Niukkanen, A., & Mäntymäki, M. (2022). What about investors? ESG analyses as tools for ethics-based AI auditing. *AI & Society*. Advance online publication. DOI: 10.1007/s00146-022-01415-0

Mishra, S. (2023). Exploring the Impact of AI-Based Cyber Security Financial Sector Management. *Applied Sciences (Basel, Switzerland)*, 13(10), 5875. DOI: 10.3390/app13105875

MIT Technology Review (2024). Vuelta al mundo por las regulaciones de la IA en 2024. Opinno. https://www.technologyreview.es/s/16069/vuelta-al-mundo-por-las-regulaciones-de-la-ia-en-2024

Moraes, T. (2024). Ethical AI Regulatory Sandboxes: Insights from cyberspace regulation and Internet governance. *2nd International Symposium On Trustworthy Autonomous Systems*, 10, 1-10. DOI: 10.1145/3686038.3686049

Mytnyk, B., Tkachyk, O., Shakhovska, N., Fedushko, S., & Syerov, Y. (2023). Application of Artificial Intelligence for Fraudulent Banking Operations Recognition. *Big Data and Cognitive Computing*, 7(2), 93. DOI: 10.3390/bdcc7020093

Nannini, L., Alonso-Moral, J. M., Catala, A., Lama, M., & Barro, S. (2024). Operationalizing Explainable Artificial Intelligence in the European Union Regulatory Ecosystem. *IEEE Intelligent Systems*, 39(4), 37–48. DOI: 10.1109/MIS.2024.3383155

Nayak, S., & Chandiramani, J. (2022). A crisis that changed the banking scenario in India: Exploring the role of ethics in business. *Asian Journal Of Business Ethics*, 11(S1), 7–32. DOI: 10.1007/s13520-022-00151-4

Newman, J., & Mintrom, M. (2023). Mapping the discourse on evidence-based policy, artificial intelligence, and the ethical practice of policy analysis. *Journal of European Public Policy*, 30(9), 1839–1859. DOI: 10.1080/13501763.2023.2193223

Nicodeme, C. (2020). Build confidence and acceptance of AI-based decision support systems - Explainable and liable AI. 13th IEEE International Conference On Human System Interaction (IEEE HSI). DOI: 10.1109/HSI49210.2020.9142668

Nishant, R., Kennedy, M., & Corbett, J. (2020). Artificial intelligence for sustainability: Challenges, opportunities, and a research agenda. *International Journal of Information Management*, 53, 102104. DOI: 10.1016/j.ijinfomgt.2020.102104

Novelli, C. (2022). Legal personhood for the integration of AI systems in the social context: A study hypothesis. *AI & Society*, 38(4), 1347–1359. DOI: 10.1007/s00146-021-01384-w

Pagliari, M., Chambon, V., & Berberian, B. (2022). What is new with Artificial Intelligence? Human–agent interactions through the lens of social agency. *Frontiers in Psychology*, 13, 954444. Advance online publication. DOI: 10.3389/fpsyg.2022.954444 PMID: 36248519

Pai, V., & Chandra, S. (2022). Exploring Factors Influencing Organizational Adoption of Artificial Intelligence (AI) in Corporate Social Responsibility (CSR) Initiatives. *Pacific Asia Journal Of The Association For Information Systems*, 14, 82–115. DOI: 10.17705/1pais.14504

Piccininni, M. (2022). Counterfactual fairness: The case study of a food delivery platform's reputational-ranking algorithm. *Frontiers in Psychology*, 13, 1015100. DOI: 10.3389/fpsyg.2022.1015100 PMID: 36389466

Pinheiro, A. F., Santos, W. B., & De Lima Neto, F. B. (2023). Intelligent Framework to Support Technology and Business Specialists in the Public Sector. *IEEE Access : Practical Innovations, Open Solutions*, 11, 15655–15679. DOI: 10.1109/ACCESS.2023.3243195

Politi, V. (2024). Who ought to look towards the horizon? A qualitative study on the collective social responsibility of scientific research. *European Journal for Philosophy of Science*, 14(2), 19. Advance online publication. DOI: 10.1007/s13194-024-00580-x

Qiu, S., & Luo, Y. (2024). How to detect and forecast corporate fraud by media reports? An approach using machine learning and qualitative comparative analysis. *Journal of Forecasting*, 43(1), 58–80. DOI: 10.1002/for.3022

Ramdhani, M. A., & Ramdhani, A. (2014). Verification of research logical framework based on literature review. *International Journal of Basic and Applied Science*, 3(2), 1–9.

Ranard, B. L., Park, S., Jia, Y., Zhang, Y., Alwan, F., Celi, L. A., & Lusczek, E. R. (2024). Minimizing bias when using artificial intelligence in critical care medicine. *Journal of Critical Care*, 82, 154796. DOI: 10.1016/j.jcrc.2024.154796 PMID: 38552451

Razaque, A., Alotaibi, B., Alotaibi, M., Hussain, S., Alotaibi, A., & Jotsov, V. (2022). Clickbait detection using deep recurrent neural network. *Applied Sciences (Basel, Switzerland)*, 12(1), 504. DOI: 10.3390/app12010504

Ridzuan, N. N., Masri, M., Anshari, M., Fitriyani, N. L., & Syafrudin, M. (2024). AI in the Financial Sector: The Line between Innovation, Regulation and Ethical Responsibility. *Information (Basel)*, 15(8), 432. DOI: 10.3390/info15080432

Rouhani, B. D., Samragh, M., Javaheripi, M., Javidi, T., & Koushanfar, F. (2018). DeepFense. 2018 IEEE/ACM INTERNATIONAL CONFERENCE ON COMPUTER-AIDED DESIGN (ICCAD). *Digest of Technical Papers*, 1–8. Advance online publication. DOI: 10.1145/3240765.3240791

Russell, S. J., & Norvig, P. (1995). Artificial intelligence: A modern approach. *Choice (Chicago, Ill.)*, 33(03), 33–1577. DOI: 10.5860/CHOICE.33-1577

Ryman-Tubb, N. F., Krause, P., & Garn, W. (2018). How Artificial Intelligence and machine learning research impacts payment card fraud detection: A survey and industry benchmark. *Engineering Applications of Artificial Intelligence*, 76, 130–157. DOI: 10.1016/j.engappai.2018.07.008

Sabharwal, R., Miah, S. J., Wamba, S. F., & Cook, P. (2024). Extending application of explainable artificial intelligence for managers in financial organizations. Annals Of Operation Research. *Annals of Operations Research*. Advance online publication. DOI: 10.1007/s10479-024-05825-9

Sakyoud, Z., Aaroud, A., & Akodadi, K. (2023). Optimization of purchasing business process in Moroccan public universities based on COBIT and artificial intelligence techniques. *Kybernetes*, 53(5), 1607–1635. DOI: 10.1108/K-02-2022-0167

Schneider, D., & Weber, K. (2024). AI for decision support: What are possible futures, social impacts, regulatory options, ethical conundrums and agency constellations? TATuP - Zeitschrift Für Technikfolgenabschätzung In Theorie Und Praxis, 33(1), 8-54. DOI: 10.14512/tatup.33.1.08

Searle, J. (1980). Minds, brains, and programs. *Behavioral and Brain Sciences*, 3(3), 417–424. DOI: 10.1017/S0140525X00005756

Sengupta, S., Basak, S., Saikia, P., Paul, S., Tsalavoutis, V., Atiah, F., Ravi, V., & Peters, A. (2020). A review of deep learning with special emphasis on architectures, applications and recent trends. *Knowledge-Based Systems*, 194, 105596. DOI: 10.1016/j.knosys.2020.105596

Shneiderman, B. (2020). Bridging the Gap Between Ethics and Practice. *ACM Transactions on Interactive Intelligent Systems*, 10(4), 1–31. DOI: 10.1145/3419764

Shoaib, M. R., Wang, Z., Ahvanooey, M. T., & Zhao, J. (2023). Deepfakes, misinformation, and disinformation in the era of frontier AI, generative AI, and large AI models. In *2023 International Conference on Computer and Applications (ICCA)* (pp. 1-7). IEEE DOI: 10.1109/ICCA59364.2023.10401723

Sigfrids, A., Leikas, J., Salo-Pöntinen, H., & Koskimies, E. (2023). Human-centricity in AI governance: A systemic approach. *Frontiers in Artificial Intelligence*, 6, 976887. DOI: 10.3389/frai.2023.976887 PMID: 36872934

Simos, T. E., Katsikis, V. N., & Mourtas, S. D. (2022). A multi-input with multi-function activated weights and structure determination neuronet for classification problems and applications in firm fraud and loan approval. *Applied Soft Computing*, 127, 109351. DOI: 10.1016/j.asoc.2022.109351

Sina, A. (2023). Open AI and its Impact on Fraud Detection in Financial Industry. Journal of Knowledge Learning and Science Technology ISSN: 2959-6386 (online), 2(3), 263-281. DOI: 10.60087/jklst.vol2.n3.p281

Sison, A., Ferrero, I., Ruiz, P. G., & Kim, T. W. (2023). Editorial: Artificial intelligence (AI) ethics in business. *Frontiers in Psychology*, 14, 1258721. Advance online publication. DOI: 10.3389/fpsyg.2023.1258721 PMID: 37771802

Sood, P., Sharma, C., Nijjer, S., & Sakhuja, S. (2023). Review the role of artificial intelligence in detecting and preventing financial fraud using natural language processing. *International Journal of System Assurance Engineering and Management*, 14(6), 2120–2135. DOI: 10.1007/s13198-023-02043-7

Souza, M. A., Gouveia, H. T. V., Ferreira, A. A., De Lima Neta, R. M., Neto, O. N., Da Silva Lira, M. M., Torres, G. L., & De Aquino, R. R. B. (2024). Detection of Non-Technical Losses on a Smart Distribution Grid Based on Artificial Intelligence Models. *Energies*, 17(7), 1729. DOI: 10.3390/en17071729

Stanford University. (2024). Stanford HAI and Stanford Robotics Center Launch New Partnership (2024, 29 octubre). Stanford HAI. https://hai.stanford.edu/news/stanford-hai-and-stanford-robotics-center-launch-new-partnership

Strelcenia, E., & Prakoonwit, S. (2023). A Survey on GAN Techniques for Data Augmentation to Address the Imbalanced Data Issues in Credit Card Fraud Detection. *Machine Learning And Knowledge Extraction*, 5(1), 304–329. DOI: 10.3390/make5010019

Taher, S. S., Ameen, S. Y., & Ahmed, J. A. (2024). Advanced Fraud Detection in Blockchain Transactions: An Ensemble Learning and Explainable AI Approach. Engineering, Technology And Applied Science Research/Engineering, Technology And. *Applied Scientific Research*, 14(1), 12822–12830. DOI: 10.48084/etasr.6641

Talaei, J., Yang, A., Takishova, T., & Masialeti, M. (2024). How Does Cost Leadership Strategy Suppress the Performance Benefits of Explainability of AI Applications in Organizations? *Journal of Global Information Management*, 32(1), 1–23. DOI: 10.4018/JGIM.354062

Tan, Z., Liu, B., & Wu, A. (2022). Artificial Intelligence and Feature Identification Based Global Perception of Power Consumer: Definition, Structure, and Applications. *Frontiers in Energy Research*, 10, 907027. Advance online publication. DOI: 10.3389/fenrg.2022.907027

Tiwary, N., Noah, S. A. M., Fauzi, F., & Yee, T. S. (2024). Max Explainability Score–A quantitative metric for explainability evaluation in knowledge graph-based recommendations. *Computers & Electrical Engineering*, 116, 109190. DOI: 10.1016/j.compeleceng.2024.109190

Truby, J. (2020). Governing Artificial Intelligence to benefit the UN Sustainable Development Goals. *Sustainable Development (Bradford)*, 28(4), 946–959. DOI: 10.1002/sd.2048

Van Bekkum, M., & Borgesius, F. Z. (2021). Digital welfare fraud detection and the Dutch SyRI judgment. *European Journal of Social Security*, 23(4), 323–340. DOI: 10.1177/13882627211031257

Van Den Berg, M., Gerlings, J., & Kim, J. (2024). Empirical Research on Ensuring Ethical AI in Fraud Detection of Insurance Claims: A Field Study of Dutch Insurers. En Communications in computer and information science (pp. 106-114). https://doi.org/DOI: 10.1007/978-3-031-50485-3_9

Verma, S., Sharma, R., Deb, S., & Maitra, D. (2021). Artificial intelligence in marketing: Systematic review and future research direction. *International Journal of Information Management Data Insights*, 1(1), 100002. DOI: 10.1016/j.jjimei.2020.100002

Vinuesa, R., Azizpour, H., Leite, I., Balaam, M., Dignum, V., Domisch, S., Felländer, A., Langhans, S. D., Tegmark, M., & Fuso Nerini, F. (2020). The role of artificial intelligence in achieving the Sustainable Development Goals. *Nature Communications*, 11(1), 233. DOI: 10.1038/s41467-019-14108-y PMID: 31932590

Walters, R., Trakman, L., & Zeller, B. (2019). Jurisdictional [Comparative] Differences. En DATA PROTECTION LAW: A COMPARATIVE ANALYSIS OF ASIA-PACIFIC AND EUROPEAN APPROACHES (pp. 265-290). https://doi.org/DOI: 10.1007/978-981-13-8110-2_11

Wang, G., Frederick, R., Duan, J., Wong, W., Rupar, V., Li, W., & Bai, Q. (2024). Detecting misinformation through Framing Theory: the Frame Element-based Model. arXiv preprint arXiv:2402.15525.

Weber, M. T., Schaaf, J., Storf, H., Wagner, T. O., Berger, A., & Noll, R. (2024). Editing Physicians' Responses Using GPT-4 for Academic Research. *Studies in Health Technology and Informatics*. Advance online publication. DOI: 10.3233/SHTI240019 PMID: 38682512

Wilson, C., & van der Velden, M. (2022). Sustainable AI: An integrated model to guide public sector decision-making. *Technology in Society*, 68, 101926. DOI: 10.1016/j.techsoc.2022.101926

Win, K. T., & Beydoun, G. (2020). Preface: Towards the Next Generation of Information Systems: Enhancing Traceability and Transparency. AJIS. Australasian Journal Of Information Systems/AJIS. Australian Journal Of Information Systems. *AJIS. Australasian Journal of Information Systems*, 24. Advance online publication. DOI: 10.3127/ajis.v24i0.2823

Wirtz, J., Patterson, P. G., Kunz, W. H., Gruber, T., Lu, V. N., Paluch, S., & Martins, A. (2018). Brave new world: Service robots in the frontline. *Journal of Service Management*, 29(5), 907–931. DOI: 10.1108/JOSM-04-2018-0119

Xie, J., Dmour, A. A., & Lakys, Y. (2022). Application of Nonlinear Fractional Differential Equations in Computer Artificial Intelligence Algorithms. *Applied Mathematics And Nonlinear Sciences*, 8(1), 1145–1154. DOI: 10.2478/amns.2022.2.0101

Xiong, T., Ma, Z., Li, Z., & Dai, J. (2021). The analysis of influence mechanism for internet financial fraud identification and user behavior based on machine learning approaches. *International Journal of System Assurance Engineering and Management*, 13(S3), 996–1007. DOI: 10.1007/s13198-021-01181-0

Xu, D., Fan, S., & Kankanhalli, M. (2023). Combating misinformation in the era of generative AI models. In *Proceedings of the 31st ACM International Conference on Multimedia* (pp. 9291-9298) DOI: 10.1145/3581783.3612704

Yang, J., Tang, Z., Guan, Z., Hua, W., Wei, M., Wang, C., & Gu, C. (2021). Automatic Feature Engineering-Based Optimization Method for Car Loan Fraud Detection. *Discrete Dynamics in Nature and Society*, 2021, 1–10. DOI: 10.1155/2021/6077540

Yang, X., Li, H., Ni, L., & Li, T. (2021). Application of Artificial Intelligence in Precision Marketing. *Journal of Organizational and End User Computing*, 33(4), 209–219. DOI: 10.4018/JOEUC.20210701.oa10

Yang, X., Zhang, C., Sun, Y., Pang, K., Li, J., Wa, S., & Lv, C. (2023). FinChain-BERT: A High-Accuracy Automatic Fraud Detection Model Based on NLP Methods for Financial Scenarios. *Information (Basel)*, 14(9), 499. DOI: 10.3390/info14090499

Yaraziz, M. S., Jalili, A., Gheisari, M., & Liu, Y. (2022). Recent trends towards privacy-preservation in Internet of Things, its challenges and future directions. *IET Circuits, Devices & Systems*, 17(2), 53–61. DOI: 10.1049/cds2.12138

Yerima, S. Y., & Bashar, A. (2022). *Semi-supervised novelty detection with one class SVM for SMS spam detection. 2022 29TH INTERNATIONAL CONFERENCE ON SYSTEMS, SIGNALS AND IMAGE PROCESSING.* IWSSIP., DOI: 10.1109/IWSSIP55020.2022.9854496

Zaimi, R., Hafidi, M., & Lamia, M. (2023). A deep learning approach to detect phishing websites using CNN for privacy protection. *Intelligent Decision Technologies*, 17(3), 713–728. DOI: 10.3233/IDT-220307

Zajko, M. (2023). Automated government benefits and welfare surveillance. *Surveillance & Society*, 21(3), 246–258. https://www.webofscience.com/wos/alldb/full-record/WOS:001078822300002. DOI: 10.24908/ss.v21i3.16107

Zhang, D., Mishra, S., Brynjolfsson, E., Etchemendy, J., Ganguli, D., Grosz, B., Lyons, T., Manyika, J., Niebles, J. C., Sellitto, M., Shoham, Y., Clark, J., & Perrault, R. (2022). *The AI Index 2022 Annual Report. AI Index Steering Committee, Stanford Institute for Human-Centered AI.* Stanford University.

Zhang, T., Qin, Y., & Li, Q. (2021). Trusted Artificial Intelligence: Technique Requirements and Best Practices. 2021 INTERNATIONAL CONFERENCE ON CYBERWORLDS (CW 2021), pp.303-306. https://doi.org/DOI: 10.1109/CW52790.2021.00058

Zhang, W., Zhang, S., Chen, J., & Huang, H. (2023). *CCFD-GAN: Credit Card Fraud Detection Based on Generative Adversarial Networks Enhanced by Penalty Mechanism. 2023 INTERNATIONAL JOINT CONFERENCE ON NEURAL NETWORKS.* IJCNN., DOI: 10.1109/IJCNN54540.2023.10191810

Zhao, J., & Fariñas, B. G. (2022). Artificial Intelligence and Sustainable Decisions. *European Business Organization Law Review*, 24(1), 1–39. DOI: 10.1007/s40804-022-00262-2

Zheng, X., Gildea, E., Chai, S., Zhang, T., & Wang, S. (2023). Data Science in Finance: Challenges and Opportunities. *AI*, 5(1), 55–71. DOI: 10.3390/ai5010004

Zheng, X., Gildea, E., Chai, S., Zhang, T., & Wang, S. (2023). Data science in finance: Challenges and opportunities. *AI*, 5(1), 55–71. DOI: 10.3390/ai5010004

Zheng, X., Li, J., Lu, M., & Wang, F. (2024). New Paradigm for Economic and Financial Research With Generative AI: Impact and Perspective. *IEEE Transactions on Computational Social Systems*, 11(3), 1–11. DOI: 10.1109/TCSS.2023.3334306

Zhou, Y., Li, H., Xiao, Z., & Qiu, J. (2023). A user-centered explainable artificial intelligence approach for financial fraud detection. *Finance Research Letters*, 58, 104309. DOI: 10.1016/j.frl.2023.104309

Zhu, T., Ye, D., Wang, W., Zhou, W., & Yu, P. (2021). More Than Privacy: Applying Differential Privacy in Key Areas of Artificial Intelligence. *IEEE Transactions on Knowledge and Data Engineering*, 1. Advance online publication. DOI: 10.1109/TKDE.2020.3014246

Zhu, T., & Yu, P. S. (2019). Applying Differential Privacy Mechanism in Artificial Intelligence. *39th IEEE International Conference On Distributed Computing Systems (ICDCS)*. DOI: 10.1109/ICDCS.2019.00159

Zhu, X., Ao, X., Qin, Z., Chang, Y., Liu, Y., He, Q., & Li, J. (2021). Intelligent financial fraud detection practices in post-pandemic era. *Innovation (Cambridge (Mass.))*, 2(4), 100176. DOI: 10.1016/j.xinn.2021.100176 PMID: 34806059

Züger, T., & Asghari, H. (2022). AI for the public. How public interest theory shifts the discourse on AI. *AI & Society*, 38(2), 815–828. DOI: 10.1007/s00146-022-01480-5

# Section 2
# AI Ethics and Corporate Responsibility

# Chapter 4
# Addressing Rights on Responsible AI in Digital Companies: The Impact of Biases and Stereotypes

**Cristina Gallego-Gomez**
https://orcid.org/0000-0002-7477-520X
*Universidad Rey Juan Carlos, Spain*

**Carmen Llovet**
*Universidad Antonio de Nebrija, Spain*

## ABSTRACT

*This study examined the top five reference companies for Generation Z, in relation to bias and responsible Artificial Intelligence (AI). Through a literature analysis on bias and the study of Law 15/2022, of July 12 (15917/2022), comprehensive for equal treatment and non-discrimination, the key factors of the study are detected to determine whether or not companies comply from an ethical point of view. The findings confirmed that all the items analyzed are complied with except for the seals on the algorithms officially. These results are essential to guide the market towards more transparent business models, which helps companies increase the trust they transmit to society. The study offers implications, limitations and future lines of research, which focus on algorithmic literacy.*

DOI: 10.4018/979-8-3693-9894-4.ch004

## 1. INTRODUCTION

This work explores the role of artificial intelligence (AI) in major companies like YouTube, Netflix, Amazon, Google, and Instagram, which are popular among Generation Z. While AI aims to automate tasks, it also raises ethical concerns, particularly with issues like "Deepfake" content, which manipulates text, images, and audio to appear real. The research focuses on how these companies address gender bias and stereotypes in their AI applications through corporate social responsibility (CSR) actions and identifies good practices for other companies.

These companies are influential in shaping young people's digital experiences but also contribute to issues like overexposure to harmful content, especially for women and adolescents, who are more vulnerable to gender stereotypes. Despite significant technological development, there is a gap in AI literacy, with children and young people lacking education on how to use these technologies safely.

The study reveals that while these companies are making efforts to combat biases, transparency in AI practices is often lacking in their CSR reports. Additionally, legislative action is growing, with several countries proposing bills to regulate AI. The study concludes by highlighting the need for more inclusive AI practices and suggests future research to explore these issues in smaller companies and other sectors.

AI is transforming various sectors, from improving governance in smart cities (Kumi et al., 2024) and enhancing education with provocative concepts (Lundberg & Mozelius, 2024) to detecting hate speech and solving intellectual property issues in media literacy (Gongane et al., 2024; Subiela-Hernández et al., 2023). In business, AI boosts competitiveness by enhancing consumer engagement through chatbots (Pathak et al., 2025), improving supply chain management and content personalization (Hemachandran & Rodriguez, 2023), and enabling advanced media techniques like facial recognition and video processing (Bayazitov et al., 2024).

However, there are also ethical considerations regarding the risks AI introduces, such as privacy violations (Cai, 2024), gender biases in representation (Sedkaoui & Benaichouba, 2024), and social biases in AI-generated content (Taveekitworachai et al., 2023), as well as psychological and social harms from deepfakes (Lundberg & Mozelius, 2024; Sanchez-Acedo et al., 2024). These issues extend to the commercial sphere, where AI impacts various sectors like security, media, and political campaigns (Nour & Gelfand, 2022), with Generation Z's exposure to AI and the Metaverse influencing the digital entertainment landscape (Connock, 2024; Das & Gochhait, 2023).

AI's impact extends beyond the legal and financial realms to influence communication, media, and consumer behavior. Legal frameworks are emerging to address AI's role in datafication, social media, and digital journalism (Gálvez, 2024), and there is a need for interoperability in AI management (Hallur et al., 2021).

Moreover, we also find challenges in the commercial sphere. AI can provoke consumer insecurity, calling for more humanized advertisements (Alhjarah et al., 2024) and addressing issues like greenwashing and femvertising (Lima & Casais, 2021). Companies must adhere to transparency and disclose environmental, social, and governance (ESG) objectives (Grishunin et al., 2022), while AI literacy becomes essential for young people to navigate digital spaces safely (Audenhove et al., 2024). Educational efforts should focus on developing critical literacy, identifying sources, and understanding AI-generated content (Bustos Díaz & Martin-Vicario, 2024; Garriga et al., 2024).

Generation Z, the first digital-native generation, is highly engaged with AI-driven technologies, which impact education, social interaction, and consumer behavior (Gupta et al., 2024). This generation is also increasingly aware of issues related to diversity, equity, and inclusion, with an opportunity to promote positive change (Low et al., 2023). However, despite their positive attitude toward AI, concerns persist about information overload, data privacy, and mental health (IAB & Mazzin, 2024).

Some studies reveal that this generation, while aware of AI, still faces challenges with managing academic integrity, privacy, and misinformation (Acosta Enríquez et al., 2024), and experiences discomfort with algorithmic ambiguity and the lack of regulation to address AI biases (Gupta et al., 2024). These concerns lead to the suggestion of using more humanized and critically designed AI models (Rapp et al., 2025).

However, they are not the only interest group related to AI. There are different profiles involved in the development of artificial intelligence as stakeholders. AI developers face technical limitations due to the novelty of the technology and the lack of regulation. In this sense, regulatory bodies have limitations, since the creation of standards is slow compared to the advancement of technology.

For their part, researchers from academic centers lack resources and it is civil rights organizations that ensure the defense of vulnerable groups in their access to this type of tools. Together with them, as a group that raises its voice, there are users, who present an attitude in line with equity values.

## 2. THE IMPACT OF AI BIASES AND GENDER STEREOTYPES

We could point out several lines of work around biases, with detected problems and possible solutions in the following table 1:

*Table 1. Problems and solutions to gender biases generated by AI. Source. Own elaboration*

| Problems | Solutions |
|---|---|
| underrepresentation of women in images in scientific advancements and natural environments | association with technology developers |
| gender stereotypes of both men and women, aesthetic | inclusive text and image generators |
| linguistic and photographic biases | exhaustive tests |
| incomplete or poorly labeled patterns that reinforce biases | notification channels so that end users can communicate the problems experienced |
| personalized recommendation algorithms | train the models with Generation Z language |

## 2.1. Studies on Gender Bias in AI

GenAI is reshaping industries by enhancing business models and fostering innovation, yet it faces challenges in addressing ethical concerns such as biases and privacy issues (Sedkaoui & Benaichouba, 2024). Gender biases in digital spaces are evident, with male faces predominating and women being underrepresented, particularly older women in digital representations of assistive devices (Chen et al., 2024; Zorrilla-Muñoz et al., 2024).

AI-generated content often perpetuates gender stereotypes, as seen in various AI platforms and workplace images, reinforcing existing human biases (Hu & Kurylo, 2024; García-Ull & Lázaro, 2023). A feminist analysis of AI discourse highlights gender as a critical category, with AI reproducing gender stereotypes and underrepresenting women in scientific and technological narratives (Carstensen & Ganz, 2023; Gai et al., 2024).

However, efforts to combat these biases are emerging, with AI models being trained to remove gender stereotypes and promote equal representation, offering a more inclusive approach to media content (Low et al., 2023; Ortega Fernández & Rodríguez Hernández, 2024).

Additionally, partnerships between tech developers and companies like Cemex emphasize the need for objective, inclusive AI models to ensure fairer and more representative outcomes (United Nations Global Compact & Accenture, 2024).

## 2.2. Biases in Artificial Intelligence in the Regulatory Frame

The United Nations Global Compact and Accenture (2024) have created a guide to help develop sustainable development goals through AI, though they highlight biases as a significant implementation challenge. The use of AI can inadvertently perpetuate gender, racial, and other biases, as biases from model design and incomplete training data can be reflected in the digital world. AI can also be affected by automation bias, where users may overly trust model outputs without sufficient analysis.

Governance, transparency, and reproducibility are necessary to mitigate errors, bias, and toxicity (United Nations Global Compact & Accenture, 2024: 40). AI regulation addresses bias as a high-risk category due to its potential to affect people's lives and human rights. Law 15/2022 in Spain, part of EU law, mandates equal treatment and non-discrimination, reinforcing the need to protect against discrimination in AI use, particularly in judicial systems and data-driven decision-making.

This regulation is complemented by the General Data Protection Regulation (GDPR), which protects privacy, and the Artificial Intelligence Tort Liability Directive, which addresses damages caused by AI systems. Spain's National Artificial Intelligence Strategy also includes the Digital Rights Charter and initiatives for AI governance, which aim to regulate AI use in areas like social media, advertising, and automated decision-making processes, with clear criteria for non-discrimination across various personal and social characteristics.

## 3. METHODOLOGY

To carry out this study, an exhaustive documentary search has been carried out to offer an updated analysis of the literature, mainly due to two factors: 1) The volume of works related to AI, which requires adapting the descriptors to the topic of study 2) The field of study is evolving rapidly, which forces researchers to offer updated information for greater value contribution.

To carry out the analysis, the following steps have been carried out:

- Exhaustive search for relevant articles in databases
- Selection using reproducible criteria of the articles that are included in the review
- Description of the design and selection of articles
- Data synthesis and interpretation of results

Based on this, the bibliographic review consists of a search in the Scopus database, since it is the main database due to the advantages it presents according to Stahlschmidt & Stephen (2020). The descriptors used are the following: AI and youth literacy, AI and iGen, AI and Z generation, AI and social media and corporate social responsibility, AI and media entertainment, AI and media gender stereotypes, AI and stereotypes in the title and abstract fields.

Likewise, artificial intelligence has been framed within the sustainable development goals (United Nations Global Compact & Accenture, 2024) since AI technologies could help achieve them if they are used responsibly and are accessible to all people.

Therefore, the same descriptors have been used to complement the search on Scopus, using the Web of Science (WoS), with the following results shown in figure 1, 220 documents have been found, redefined by the "open access" criteria, and in the last 5 years, 216 are written in English, and the country where most literature is produced is the United States (80/220). An image of the total number of articles published with the related SDGs is offered. SDG number 3 "Good health and well-being" is the most predominant in the literature, accounting for 23.6% of total production, followed by SDG 4 "Quality education" and SDG 10 "reduction of inequalities".

*Figure 1. SDGs predominant in scientific works with the descriptors used.*

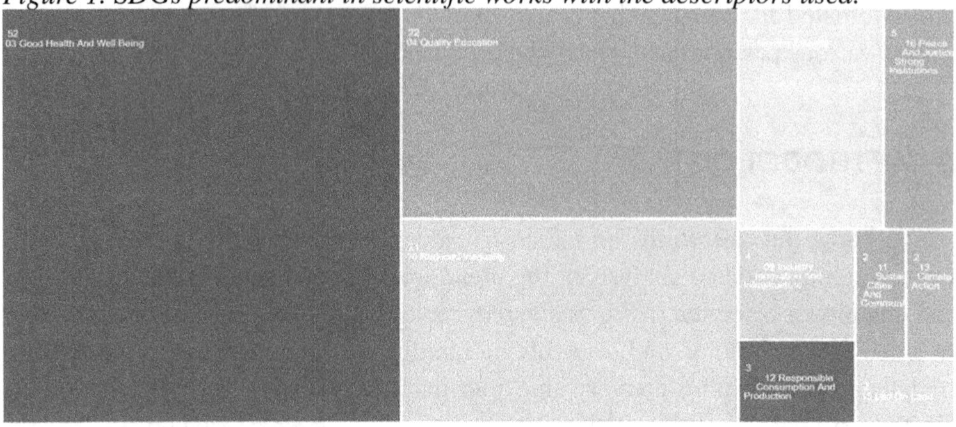


*Source: WOS (2024)*

In the same way that the study by Borden et al. (2024) analyses Facebook's public communication on the data policy provided by artificial intelligence and detects the lack of clarity in how it is stored or used, this research analyses whether the most attractive companies for young people of Generation Z, belonging to the technology sector -YouTube, Netflix, Amazon, Google and Instagram-, comply with the criteria indicated by Law 15/2022 for equal treatment and non-discrimination.

Therefore, as part of the methodology, a content analysis of the information on the corporate website of a sample of companies has been applied during the time period following the publication of Law 15/2022 in July, until July 2024.

To effectively address biases and harmful content, several practical actions can be implemented:

1. **Content moderation and removal**: It's crucial to remove synthetic or altered content, such as hate speech, harassment, explicit violence, and other harmful materials. This helps create a safer, more respectful online space. The moderation should also target biases related to political views, gender, and sexual orientation to foster a more inclusive digital environment.
2. **Promoting inclusion through representation**: Companies like Netflix are working to improve inclusion by assessing diversity metrics such as gender, ethnicity, LGBTQ+ representation, and disability in entertainment content. This not only promotes more diverse storytelling but also ensures that underrepresented groups see themselves reflected in the media they consume.
3. **Enhanced accessibility features**: Platforms like Netflix are adding accessibility features, such as assistive listening, brightness controls, screen readers, and voice commands, to improve the user experience for people with disabilities. These inclusivity efforts ensure that all users, regardless of their abilities, can enjoy the content equally.
4. **Diversity in AI:** Amazon focuses on creating fair and responsible AI by promoting team diversity and providing resources to develop inclusive AI and machine learning solutions. This is critical in ensuring that AI models are not only effective but also free from biases related to race, gender, and other factors.
5. **Responsible AI principles:** companies like Google are prioritizing responsible AI development by focusing on privacy, security, safety, accountability, and ethical use. They work on making AI systems more inclusive, like the Monk Skin Tone Scale, to ensure better representation in datasets. Project Relate, an Android app by Google, further exemplifies inclusivity by helping people with non-standard speech communicate more effectively through speech-to-text transcription and voice repetition.
6. **Comprehensive digital principles**: across all sectors, implementing principles for responsible content moderation and AI development is key to building a fair, trustworthy, and safe digital space. This includes addressing content that may cause harm or spread misinformation, and focusing on transparency, privacy, and security to ensure ethical AI deployment.

In practice, these actions translate into a comprehensive strategy to mitigate bias, ensure accessibility, and foster inclusion, all while maintaining user safety and promoting fairness across platforms and AI systems.

## 4. ANALYSIS OF THE RESULTS

**Content Moderation and Removal**

Taking as a reference the corporate pages of the five large companies analyzed, Table 2 shows which of the 10 criteria of equal treatment and non-discrimination highlighted in Law 15/2022 are followed by the companies preferred by Gen Z:

*Table 2. Equal treatment and non-discrimination criteria. Own elaboration based on Law 15/2022*

| 10 criteria for equal treatment and non-discrimination | | | You Tube | Netflix | Amazon | Google | Instagram |
|---|---|---|---|---|---|---|---|
| *In the media* | 1 | **Accessible** treatment and format of information, in its content and programming | X | X | X | X | X |
| | 2 | promotion of a **non-stereotyped image** of different people and population groups | X | X | X | X | X |
| | 3 | Promotion of **language** and messages against discrimination and intolerance | X | X | X | X | X |
| | 4 | prevention and elimination of content that violates the **right to equal treatment** | X | X | X | X | X |
| | 5 | Prohibition of communication containing elements of **discrimination** | X | X | X | X | X |
| *In AI and algorithms* | 6 | **Bias minimization** | X | X | X | X | X |
| | 7 | **transparency and accountability** | X | X | X | X | X |
| | 8 | Reliable ethics that respect **fundamental rights,** following the recommendations of the European Union in this regard | X | X | X | X | X |
| | 9 | impact assessments that determine possible **discriminatory bias** | X | X | X | X | X |
| | 10 | **quality seals of algorithms** | | | | | |

### 4.1. Accessibility

Although all platforms comply with the criteria regarding regulated biases, some stand out in the explicit information regarding them. In the media, accessibility is more important on Netflix than on other platforms where there are no such specific mentions of the topic. Netflix offers a robust audio description. Additionally, it has subtitles and captions for the deaf or hard of hearing (SDH).

Compatibility with screen readers and keyboard navigation and allows configuring accessibility settings by profile. The social networks in the study do not have it as developed despite having frequent interaction on their platform, although in the case of Instagram it allows users to add descriptions so that images are understandable by screen readers. It should be noted that the seal of global standards such as the Web Content Accessibility Guidelines (WCAG) has not been found on the websites.

*Figure 2. Communication of Netflix's accessibility systems within your help center.*

*Source: Netflix (n.d.a; n.d.b)*

## 4.2. Inclusion and Discrimination

The law prohibits all forms of discrimination based on personal characteristics, such as gender, racial or ethnic origin, religion, disability, age, sexual orientation, gender identity, among others, and a clear policy in this direction is explicitly found on all company websites, so they comply with the regulations on equal treatment and non-discrimination as part of their business commitment. All the companies analyzed have a space dedicated as part of their transparency to publicize how they fight against these biases. Despite these actions, companies must continue to follow the line of transparency in the face of the new challenges posed by artificial intelligence, such as the limitation of algorithms, which can in turn give rise to new biases.

In particular, the companies give details of how they approach the process of removing harmful messages in the case of Instagram and YouTube specify the process of reviewing these messages. YouTube has a program called "YouTube Creators for Change" that gives voice to different people and helps them create their social impact through this program made up of anonymous people, who reflect on difficult conversations.

Below are examples of the communication of equality and non-discrimination by the companies most valued by generation Z (figure 3, figure 4, figure 5).

*Figure 3. Google's commitments to equality and non-discrimination.*

## Our commitments

### Promoting sustainable equality in our workplace

Creating meaningful change starts within our own company. Strengthening our commitment to racial equity and inclusion will help Google build more useful products for our users and everyone else. To that end, we are announcing a number of commitments aimed at establishing a sustainable playing field for our Black community.

- Work to improve the representation of the African-descendant community in management positions and commit to improving the representation of minority groups at the management level by 30% by 2025
- Increase efforts to address representation issues by focusing on recruitment, retention and promotion at all levels
- Working to inspire a deeper sense of inclusion and belonging in Googlers in general and in our Black community in particular
- Establish various anti-racist educational programs with a global vision that can be extended to all Googlers
- More effectively promote the physical and mental health and well-being of our African-descendant community
- Increasing supplier diversity
- Taking responsibility

*Source: Google (n.d.a; n.d.b; n.d.c)*

*Figure 4. Instagram's (Meta) measures for equality and non-discrimination.*

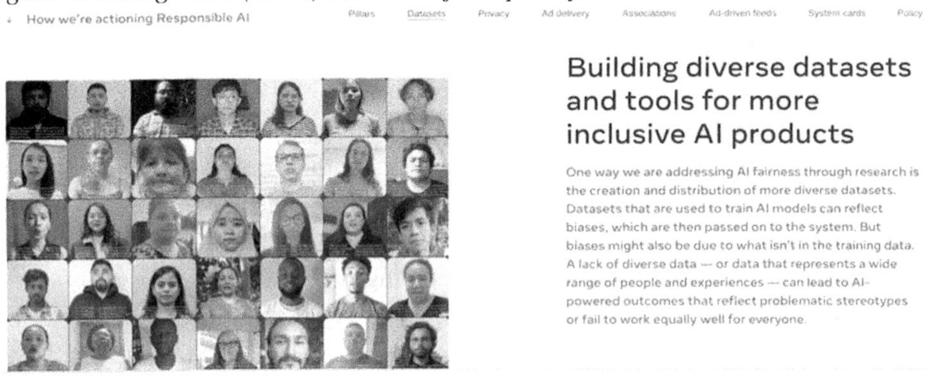


*Source: Instagram (n.d.)*

*Figure 5. Instagram's (Meta) measures for equality and non-discrimination.*

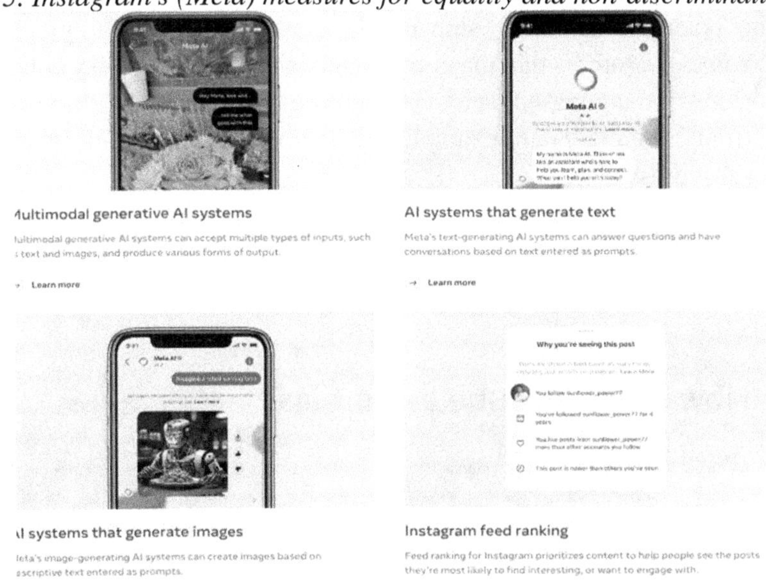


*Source: Instagram (n.d.)*

## 4.3. Bias

Regarding AI and the algorithms they use, it should be noted that none of the companies analyzed have formal quality seals for their AI algorithms.

All of them are based on the use of ethical principles, internal reviews through transparency principles and the use of audit tools by their own teams/employees to ensure their quality and responsibility. Although these mechanisms are useful, the absence of external certifications can be a limitation in terms of public trust and transparency and can sometimes lead to incurring cognitive biases.

In this sense, Amazon has been involved in incurring biases in facial recognition, especially in erroneous identifications related to gender and race (Kleinman 2019). For their part, the rest of the companies declare a scrupulous procedure in this regard, so much so that YouTube uses Google policies and in Netflix the algorithms are designed to minimize biases in content recommendation. It is precisely in these actions where content companies run the greatest risk of perpetuating biases, since confirmation biases can easily occur, showing the user only what they want to see, perpetuating polarization, or only showing the most viewed content, giving an advantage to some over others that may become invisible, or in the very construction of the algorithm, having biased data.

Below (figures 6 and 7) are examples of how the companies most valued by Generation Z address biases.

*Figure 6. YouTube's commitments.*

OUR COMMITMENTS

### How does YouTube avoid bias?

We do our best to ensure that our systems are not designed with bias against certain individuals or groups based on their political views or other attributes, such as gender or sexual orientation. The goal of our platform has always been to give a voice to a wide variety of people and to enable users from all over the world to share content.

*Source: YouTube (n.d.a)*

*Figure 7. YouTube's commitments.*

**What processes does YouTube follow to ensure that its systems do not contain unwanted harmful bias?**

The team that trains our search and discovery systems is made up of people from all over the world. The guidelines they follow are public domain . Our search and recommendation systems are not designed to filter or demote videos or channels based on particular political viewpoints.

*Source: YouTube (n.d.b)*

YouTube (n.d.) puts the spotlight on content creators to promote inclusion, diversity, and transparency, so much so that on its website, it states the following:

Transparency tools for altered or synthetic content: will be available in Creator Studio to help creators report when they upload significantly altered or synthetic content that appears real (including the use of generative AI). Creators will be required to disclose this information when the content is realistic and therefore may give users the impression that real people, places or events appear. Depending on the information disclosed, certain tags will appear in the description of the videos. In addition, if the content is related to sensitive topics (such as health, news, elections or finance), a tag will also be displayed in the video itself or in the player window.

Amazon, Google and Instagram have specific pages where they address the use of responsible AI (Table 2). All of the companies analyzed have the challenge of developing and using algorithms in an ethical, equitable and transparent manner, ensuring that technologies are inclusive and respect human rights. All of them fight through their algorithms to mitigate biases, although in different ways. It has already been mentioned that YouTube has education in AI through specific programs, Google for its part has ethical research centers, and Amazon has improved its transparency as can be seen in Image 6, and strives to make a fairer company in all its facets, including the products it sells, and fighting with Alexa, its virtual assistant, to be inclusive in terms of accent, language and accessibility needs.

## 4.4. Transparency

In terms of transparency, Instagram has greatly improved its policy due to its growing impact on society, and being a network with a high impact on young people. That is why, as shown in figures 8 and 9, the recommendation systems that Instagram makes to its users are detailed, all of which have AI. Through messages such as "Why are you seeing this post", Instagram offers explanations about how its algorithms prioritize content in the feed, Stories, Reels and the Explore section.

*Figure 8. Amazon Inclusion, diversity and equity.*

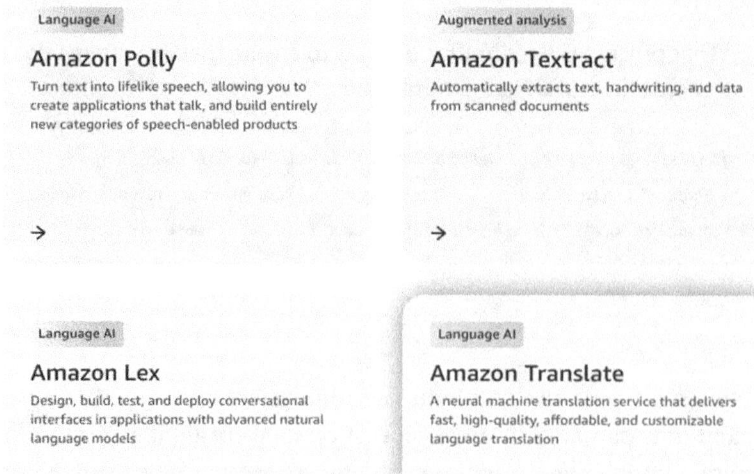


*Source: Amazon Web Services (n.d.)*

*Figure 9. Amazon commitment with responsible AI.*

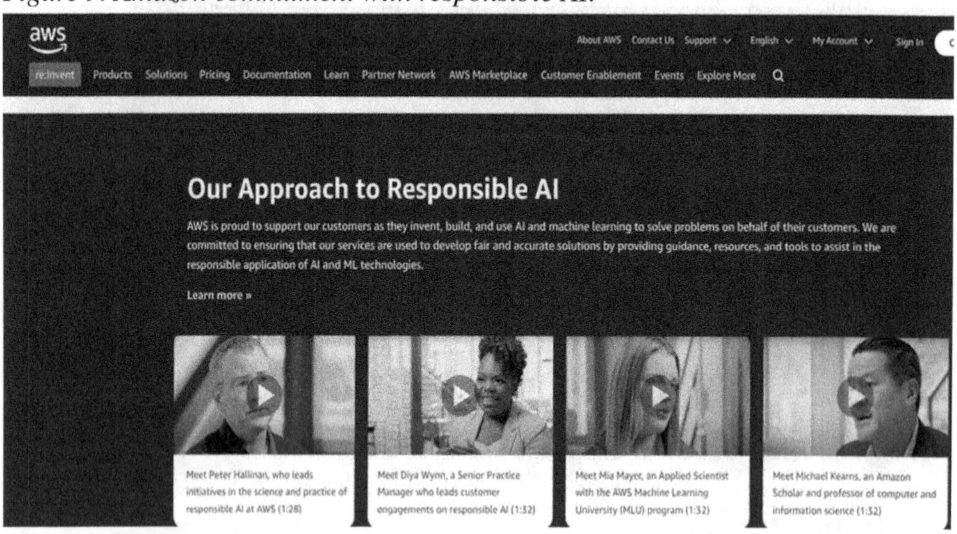


*Source: Amazon Web Services (n.d.)*

*Figure 10. Amazon's approach to responsible AI and inclusion policies.*

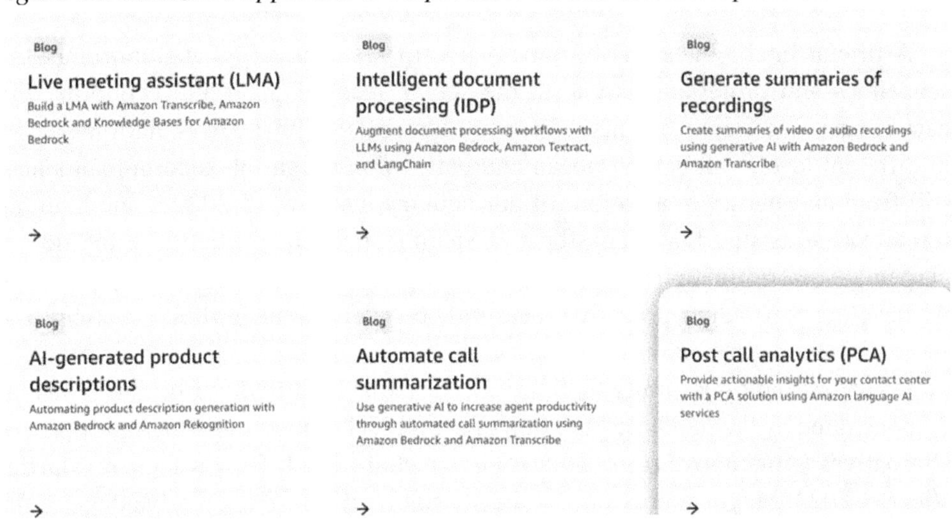


*Source: Amazon (n.d.)*

*Figure 11. Transparency center and recommended systems of Instagram.*

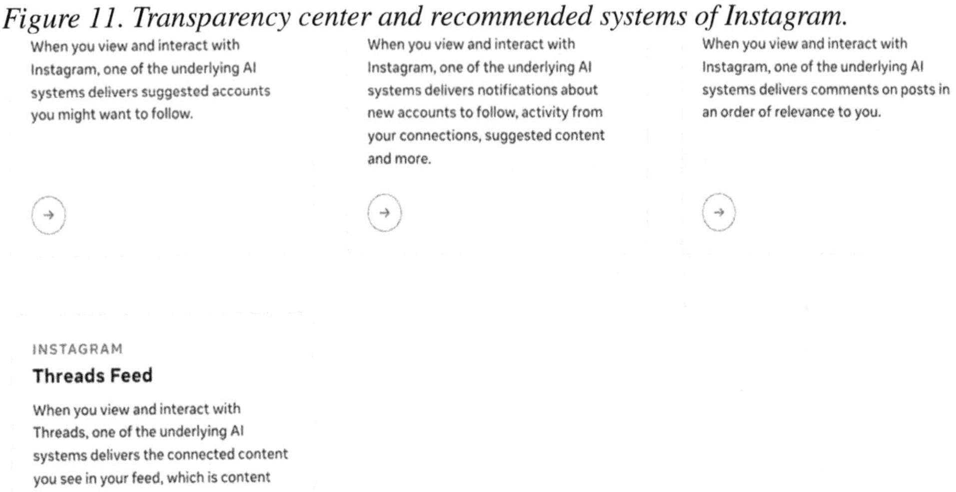


*Source: Meta (n.d.)*

## 5. CONCLUSION

Artificial intelligence has become a line of research of great importance for academics and professionals due to the social, technological and economic impact it has on different agents. There are already established regulations on AI in different levels -global, european and national– though the accomplishment is still from an internal motivation. In our country the Law 15/2022 is an essential framework to ensure that AI systems in Spain respect equal treatment and do not perpetuate discrimination. It imposes clear responsibilities on both companies and AI developers to adopt proactive measures, be transparent in their practices and avoid discriminatory biases.

GenZ has the opportunity to claim the sustainable attitude of digital firms, as demonstrated by the purchase intention of ecological products and their proposal of alternatives (Audenhove et al., 2024; Garriga et al., 2024; Bustos Díaz & Martín-Vicario, 2024; Mayiwar et al., 2024). Furthermore, if Gen Z takes advantage of the numerous resources supplied by digital enterprises and learns to claim the practices that are required to be followed, the humanization of AI that Gen Z seeks may be expanded beyond design to other vital domains (Rapp et al, 2025).

The analysis of the companies show that all of them comply with the specific criteria of non-discrimination, enacting practices that help users understand how they carry out processes and specific actions of equality. In particular, Google is the company that provides the most information in this regard through a specific microsite dedicated to the social impact of its products and its policies. These results confirm the trend that companies meet corporate social responsibility guidelines in the use of AI (Hua et al, 2024). However, these companies, which have had to improve their ethical behavior, have also engaged in stereotypes. This is the case of Google Translate, which had to adjust its algorithms to reduce gender bias in translations that favored stereotypes. (Google AI Blog, 2019)

Google and Netflix are also the ones that offer the most transparency regarding accessibility, which provides inclusion, despite not having seals from official organizations such as the Web Content Accessibility Guidelines (WCAG). Previous studies (Hemachandran & Rodŕguez, 2023; Pathak et al., 2025) revealed that AI can boost competitiveness by connecting with customers in a more personal way. On the other hand, gaps in consciousness regarding access to the researched digital corporations are definitely larger in more vulnerable audiences, such as GenZ, who are unfamiliar with the ambiguity of algorithms (Gupta et al., 2024).

It should be noted that in the aspects analyzed regarding the content of the websites, there is a commitment to eliminating biases in a corporate manner in all companies as a demonstrating the global effort (United Nations Global Compact & Accenture, 2024; Ortega Fernández & Rodríguez Hernández, 2024) to introduce solutions to avoid perpetuating real stereotypes -gender, race, aesthetics, etc- in the virtual world (García-Ull & Lázaro, 2023; Gai et al, 2024; Carstensen & Ganz, 2023). And it's encouraging that some of the solutions come from the same Generation Z (Low et al, 2024).

The conclusion is that the companies show their commitments in different ways. Not all companies declare principles of responsible AI as such, of the five analyzed, three of them do: Amazon, Google and Meta (instagram). However, Amazon and Meta direct this service to their clients and users while Google explains how they manage it in their company. Youtube and Meta (Instagram), as part of their transparency, focus on being very strict in complying with their internal policies, which in the case of Youtube, specifically warn of equality policies, and have specific programs that give voice to different people to include ethical principles in their developments, and Google has specific ethics departments in this line.

In the case of Meta, they are transparent with users so that in the case of content considered harmful, they can detect it and warn their users. They explain to the user why they see the content that appears to them on Instagram. What is more significant from the information presented on the websites is to verify the efficiency of those transparency rules, which might be applied to these digital enterprises in the same way that Radwan and Russo did in 2024.

In addition to having the characteristics of being a social network that follows guidelines for action regarding AI, Instagram announces in detail how they use AI to make the platform smarter and to the user's liking through the recommendations of various intelligences used at the same time. These measures are in line with the studies that remark the benefits of the AI in media literacy (Gongane et al., 2024; Subiela-Hernández et al., 2023) and specially among Gen Z to develop skills on AI (Acosta-Enríquez et al., 2024; Kinnula et al, 2024).

In relation with gender stereotypes found in previous studies (Chen et al, 2024; Zorrilla-Muñoz et al, 2024, Hu & Kurylo, 2024), our study finds that while in countries such as Norway, a law has been announced that will prohibit influencers and brands from publishing images on social networks that have been retouched using filters (or other editing tools) without notice (Navarro, 2021), Tik Tok, although not among the companies analyzed, has been the first social network that will put an end to beauty filters in an effort to protect minors. The measure that will be implemented in Spain is intended to ensure that the platform is a safe place and does not encourage behaviors that may cause some type of body dysmorphia (Cherre, 2024).

A significant finding is that none of the companies analyzed has quality seals for the algorithms. On their pages they detail how they carry out the evaluations and try to offer all the transparency parameters, but without a doubt, quality seals would be an effective tool to increase their efficiency and fight against biases. Especially in companies like Amazon (due to history) and social networks, they are prone by their nature to fall into biases for actions such as recommendations. In this regard the risks mentioned by several studies -privacy, mental health- (IAB & Mazzin, 2024) emphasize the need of media literacy to vulnerable audiences.

The major technology companies discussed make available to users in their policies the monitoring they carry out to avoid sessions in their algorithms. All the analyzed examples have internal audits on a regular basis. In addition, the training and awareness of developers allows them to detect more inclusive practices.

## 5.1. Limitations

The limitations found are theoretical and practical. Regarding the theoretical limitations, when searching for specialized literature it is difficult to discern the articles that apply to the study in a specific way. In the last five years, the increase in research related to artificial intelligence has grown significantly, which makes the review difficult. A search on the Web of Science returns 220 Open Access documents on the subject of this research in the last five years.

Regarding the practical limitations, the companies analyzed are presented with web pages that in turn host other websites with different services and external links, such as the Amazon policy that redirects to YouTube, which has nothing to do with their companies. Meta redirects to Instagram, although in this case it belongs to the same group. Therefore, the information is not always accessible and is located on internal pages, which can mean a loss of information, both for this analysis and for the user. Furthermore, all information on corporate policies is mostly presented in web format. There is no space with all corporate social responsibility reports, which makes searching difficult, since the site map does not return results on corporate websites such as YouTube.

## 5.2. Practical and Theoretical Implications of the Study

Theoretical studies on artificial intelligence (AI) systems have important implications in various areas due to the multidisciplinary nature of their development, where the technical, communication and regulatory parts are fundamental parameters in the construction. Ethics committees in companies have a primary role in identifying and preventing social problems.

This study provides a framework for Generation Z in their perception of the companies they prefer. Additionally, it shows how the use of algorithms can lead to bias, although there is a desire to mitigate it, so the community in general is recommended to be critical of the content found through these systems and not to trust recommendation systems to avoid losing the perspective of opinion, since the recommendations are based solely on tastes and interests, discarding those different opinions.

## 5.3. Future Lines

As future lines, specific studies of AI biases are established, in the fields detected as sensitive in the regulation such as health, justice, security or employment. Additionally, it would be possible to study how the companies subject to this study act in the fields where biases are classified as dangerous. In this regard, emerging trends in AI bias mitigation, such as emerging technologies, new regulatory frameworks, changing social expectations, industry initiatives, and the economic impact or financial implications, would necessitate further investigation.

A possible future line of research is to complement this study with the participation of GenZ users to detect whether the main areas of social responsibility that have been detected on the company's websites are reflected in the perceptions of consumers as social commitment, thus detecting which values are most attractive to young people and whether this is the reason for their success/attractiveness among young people. As a second line of research, it would be interesting to know how different countries address biased policies that have a recognized impact on vulnerable audiences. A third line of research related to literacy is identified. Detecting the behavior of users and how they detect (or not) the biases of the platforms they use daily, such as social networks. In this sense, it would be necessary to analyze how companies educate users about IA bias by analyzing training programs, user awareness, and educational resources.

A third line of research focuses on the practical ramifications of a systematic evaluation of policy effectiveness will contribute to a more comparative analysis between companies. There are several questions on practical aspects to inquiry such as:

- identifying technical challenges and solutions (resource constraints, organizational resistance, regulatory compliance difficulties),
- analyzing how bias is measured and tracked (via specific KPIs, benchmarking approaches),
- asking for communication strategies to validate their bias mitigation efforts (third party audits, user feedback mechanisms, internal review processes, continuous monitoring approaches, industry collaboration),
- providing examples of bias incidents (how companies responded, lessons learned, changes implemented) and potential solutions to identify biases or difficulties in implementing anti-bias measures and what solutions were practiced by the companies.

This line will necessitate the use of qualitative research approaches such as interviews or focus groups with the major corporations. A data-driven case study methodology, including strengths and weaknesses, best practices, and divergences, would also enable a systematic comparison of firms and the determination of the real-world impact of their actions.

Finally, it would be interesting to examine cross-industry initiatives (via industry standards, shared sources, and collaborative research) as well as international comparisons of approaches.

This research did not receive any specific grant from any funding agency in the public, commercial or not-for-profit sectors. Funding for this research was provided by the author(s) of the article.

## REFERENCES


Acosta-Enriquez, B. G., Arbulú Ballesteros, M. A., Arbulu Perez Vargas, C. G., Orellana Ulloa, M. N., Gutiérrez Ulloa, C. R., Pizarro Romero, J. M., Gutiérrez Jaramillo, N. D., Cuenca Orellana, H. U., Ayala Anzoátegui, D. X., & López Roca, C. (2024). Knowledge, attitudes, and perceived Ethics regarding the use of ChatGPT among generation Z university students. *International Journal for Educational Integrity*, 20(1), 10. DOI: 10.1007/s40979-024-00157-4

Aldaihani, F. M. F., & Asadul Islam, S. G. (2024). Harnessing Green Purchase Intention of Generation Z Consumers through Green Marketing Strategies. *Business Strategy & Development*, 7(3), e419. Advance online publication. DOI: 10.1002/bsd2.419

Aleman, E., & Martínez, R. (2024). 'It's Like They Are Using Our Data Against Us.' Counter-Cartographies of AI Literacy. *Reading Research Quarterly*, 59(4), 665–677. DOI: 10.1002/rrq.574

Aljarah, A., Ibrahim, B., & López, M. (2024). *AI, we do not trust! The nexus between awareness of falsity in AI-generated CSR ads and online brand engagement, Internet Research, Vol. ahead-of-print No. ahead-of-print.* DOI: 10.1108/INTR-12-2023-1156

Amazon (17 de diciembre de 2021). *Amazon refuerza su compromiso con la igualdad de género.*https://www.aboutamazon.es/noticias/trabajar-en-amazon/amazon-refuerza-su-compromiso-con-la-igualdad-de-genero

Amazon Web Services. (n.d). *Inclusión, diversidad y equidad en AWS.*https://aws.amazon.com/es/diversity-inclusion/?nc1=f_cc

Amazon Web Services. (n.d.). *Inteligencia artificial› Servicios de IA.*https://aws.amazon.com/ai/services/?nc1=h_ls

Van Audenhove, L., Vermeire, L., Van den Broeck, W., & Demeulenaere, A. (2024). Data literacy in the new EU DigComp 2.2 framework how DigComp defines competences on artificial intelligence, internet of things and data. Information and Learning Sciences, 125(5/6), 406-436.

Bayazitov, D., Kozhakhmet, K., Omirali, A., & Zhumaliyeva, R. (2024). Leveraging Amazon Web Services for Cloud Storage and AI Algo*rithm Integration: A Comprehensive Analysis.Applied Mathematics & Information Sciences*, 18(6), 1235–1246. DOI: 10.18576/amis/180606

Boatwright, B. C., & White, C. (2020). Is Privacy Dead? Does It Matter? How Facebook Frames Its Data Policy Through Public Communication. *Journal of Public Interest Communications*, 4(1), 78–101. DOI: 10.32473/jpic.v4.i1.p78

Borden, S.L., Codina, L. & Ufarte-Ruiz, M.-J. (2024). Introduction. Our Relationships with GenAI and the Media: Testing the Limits of Transparency, Trust and Moral Agency. *Communication and Society* 37 (4 Special), 217–21. .DOI: 10.15581/003.37.4.217-221

Bustos Díaz, J., & Martin-Vicario, L. (2024). Media Literacy in a Hyperconnected World: From Social Networks to Artificial Intelligencel Alfabetización Mediática En Un Mundo Hiperconectado: De Las Redes Sociales a La Inteligencia Artificial. *European Public and Social Innovation Review*, 9, 1–17. DOI: 10.31637/epsir-2024-1241

Cai, L. (2024). Realities vs Expectations: Children's Perception and Imagination of AI. *International Journal of Technology and Design Education*, 34(5), 1687–1704. DOI: 10.1007/s10798-024-09879-5

Carstensen, T., & Ganz, K. (2023). Gendered AI: German News Media Discourse on the Future of Work. *AI & Society*. Advance online publication. DOI: 10.1007/s00146-023-01747-5

Chen, Y., Zhai, Y., & Sun, S. (2024). The Gendered Lens of AI: Examining News Imagery across Digital Spaces. *Journal of Computer-Mediated Communication*, 29(1), zmad047. Advance online publication. DOI: 10.1093/jcmc/zmad047

Cheng, Y., & Jiang, H. (2020). How Do AI-Driven Chatbots Impact User Experience? Examining Gratifications, Perceived Privacy Risk, Satisfaction, Loyalty, and Continued Use. *Journal of Broadcasting & Electronic Media*, 64(4), 592–614. DOI: 10.1080/08838151.2020.1834296

Cherre, I. (november 28, 2024). TikTok prohibirá los filtros de belleza para proteger a los menores. *La Vanguardia*.https://www.lavanguardia.com/andro4all/tiktok/tiktok-prohibira-los-filtros-de-belleza-para-proteger-a-los-menores

Connock, A. (2024). *Media Management and Live Experience: Sports, Culture, Entertainment and Events*. Routledge., DOI: 10.4324/9781003435167

Das, S., & Gochhait, S. (2023). *Digital Entertainment as Next Evolution in Service Sector: Emerging Digital Solutions in Reshaping Different Industries*. Palgrave McMillan., DOI: 10.1007/978-981-19-8121-0

De Freitas, L. C., & Neves de Moura Filho, R. (2022). Aesthetic Normalization of Gender in the Instagram Application: A Portrait of the Brazilian Woman. *Computer Law & Security Report*, 47, 105753. Advance online publication. DOI: 10.1016/j.clsr.2022.105753

Doshi, T. (May 11, 2022). Improving skin tone representation across Google. *Blog Google*. https://blog.google/products/search/monk-skin-tone-scale

Gai, X., Sainz de Baranda Andújar, C., & Franco, Y. G. (2024). Las Fotografías Que Ilustran Las Informaciones Sobre Inteligencia Artificial En Los Medios Españoles (2017-2021). Un Análisis Desde La Perspectiva de Género[1]. *Historia y Comunicacion Social*, 29(1), 201–218. DOI: 10.5209/hics.95830

Gálvez, C. (2024). Scientific Map of Artificial Intelligence in Communication (2004-2024) | Mapa Científico de La Inteligencia Artificial En Comunicación (2004-2024). *European Public and Social Innovation Review*, 9, 1–17. Advance online publication. DOI: 10.31637/epsir-2024-947

García-Ull, F. J., & Lázaro, M. M. (2023). Gender Stereotypes in AI-Generated Images | Estereotipos de Género En Imágenes Generadas Mediante Inteligencia Artificial. *El Profesional de la Información*, 32(5), e320505. Advance online publication. DOI: 10.3145/epi.2023.sep.05

Garriga, M., Ruiz-Incertis, R., & Magallón-Rosa, R. (2024). Artificial Intelligence, Disinformation and Media Literacy Proposals around Deepfakes | Inteligencia Artificial, Desinformación y Propuestas de Alfabetización En Torno a Los Deepfakes. *Observatorio (OBS*)*, •••, 175–194. DOI: 10.15847/obsOBS18520242445

Gautam, A., Joshi, R. K., Narula, A., & Sharma, N. (2024). Mitigating Human Rights Violations Caused by Deepfake Technology. *Library Progress International 44*(3), 4628–4737. https://bpasjournals.com/library-science/index.php/journal/article/view/1283/800

Geca (2024). Informe 'Generación Z'. *Spain Audiovisual Hub*.https://spainaudiovisualhub.mineco.gob.es/content/dam/seteleco-hub-audiovisual/resources/pdf/GECA_Informe_generacion_Z.pdf

Gongane, V. U., Munot, M. V., & Anuse, A. D. (2024). A Survey of Explainable AI Techniques for Detection of Fake News and Hate Speech on Social Media Platforms. *Journal of Computational Social Science*, 7(1), 587–623. DOI: 10.1007/s42001-024-00248-9

Google. (n.d.a). *Applying AI to help solve society's biggest challenges and improve lives*.https://ai.google/advancing-ai/social-impact

Google. (n.d.b). *Our principles*https://ai.google/responsibility/principles/#our-ai-principles-in-action

Google. (n.d.c). *Communication made easier*https://sites.research.google/relate

Google, A. I. Blog (2019). *Reducing gender bias in Google Translate.* Retrieved from https://ai.googleblog.com/2019/12/reducing-gender-bias-in-google.html

Grishunin, S., Naumova, E., Burova, E., Suloeva, S., & Nekrasova, T. (2022). The Impact of Sustainability Disclosures on Value of Companies Following Digital Transformation Strategies. *International Journal of Technology*, 13(7), 1432–1441. DOI: 10.14716/ijtech.v13i7.6194

Gupta, A., Pranathy, R. S., Binny, M., Chellasamy, A., Nagarathinam, A., Pachiyappan, S., & Bhagat, S. (2024). Voices of the Future: Generation Z's Views on AI's Ethical and Social Impact. *Studies in Systems. Decision and Control.*, 223, 367–386. Advance online publication. DOI: 10.1007/978-3-031-51997-0_31

Hallur, G. G., Prabhu, S., & Aslekar, A. (2021). Entertainment in Era of AI, Big Data & IoT. In S. Das & S. Gochhait (eds) *Digital Entertainment* (pp.87-109). Palgrave Macmillan. https://doi.org/DOI: 10.1007/978-981-15-9724-4_5

Hemachandran, K. & Rodriguez, R.V. (2023). *Artificial Intelligence for Business: An Implementation Guide Containing Practical and Industry-Specific Case Studies.* https://doi.org/.DOI: 10.4324/9781003358411

Hu, Y. & Kurylo, A.D. (2024). *Screaming out Loud in the Communication Classroom: Asian Stereotypes and the Fallibility of Image Generating Artificial Intelligence (AI). The Role of Generative AI in the Communication Classroom.* DOI: 10.4018/979-8-3693-0831-8.ch012

Hua, X., Hasan, N. A. M., De Costa, F., & Qiao, W. (2024). Opportunities or Challenges? The Interplay between Artificial Intelligence and Corporate Social Responsibility Communication. *Business Systems Research*, 15(1), 131–157. DOI: 10.2478/bsrj-2024-0007

IAB & Mazzin. (2024). *Guía para conectar con la Generación Z.*https://iabspain.es/iab-spain-y-mazinn-presentan-la-2a-edicion-de-la-guia-para-conectar-con-la-generacion-z/

Instagram (n.d.). *PROGRAMS. Instagram fosters communities of support*https://about.instagram.com/community/programs

Kinnula, M., Durall Gazulla, E., Hirvonen, N., Malmberg, J., & Haukipuro, L. (2024). Nurturing Systems Thinking among Young People by Developing Business Ideas on Sustainable AI. *International Journal of Child-Computer Interaction*, 40, 100656. Advance online publication. DOI: 10.1016/j.ijcci.2024.100656

Kleinman, Z. (February 4, 2019). Amazon: Facial recognition bias claims are 'misleading. *BBC News.*https://www.bbc.com/news/technology-47117299

Kotilainen, S., Okkonen, J., Vuorio, J., & Leisti, K. (2020). *Youth Media Education in the Age of Algorithm-Driven Social Media. The Handbook of Media Education Research.* DOI: 10.1002/9781119166900.ch10

Kumar, P. C., Cotter, K., & Cabrera, L. Y. (2024). Taking Responsibility for Meaning and Mattering: An Agential Realist Approach to Generative AI and Literacy. *Reading Research Quarterly*, 59(4), 570–578. DOI: 10.1002/rrq.570

Kumi, S., Snow, C., Lomotey, R. K., & Deters, R. (2024). Uncovering Concerns of Citizens Through Machine Learning and Social Network Sentiment Analysis. *IEEE Access : Practical Innovations, Open Solutions*, 12, 94885–94913. DOI: 10.1109/ACCESS.2024.3426329

Law 15/2022, of July 12 (15917/2022), for equal treatment and non-discrimination *BOE*https://www.boe.es/buscar/pdf/2022/BOE-A-2022-11589-consolidado.pdf

Lima, A. M., & Casais, B. (2021). Consumer Reactions towards Femvertising: A Netnographic Study. *Corporate Communications*, 26(3), 605–621. DOI: 10.1108/CCIJ-02-2021-0018

Lin, Y.-P. (2021). Media Literacy in an Age of Artificial Intelligence: An Exploratory Research from Hmc. *Taiwan Journal of East Asian Studies*, 18(1), 1–42. DOI: 10.6163/TJEAS.202106_18(1).0001

Low, B., Lavin, D., Du, C. R., & Fang, C. (2023). Risk-Informed and AI-Based Bias Detection on Gender, Race, and Income Using Gen-Z Survey Data. *IEEE Access : Practical Innovations, Open Solutions*, 11, 88317–88328. DOI: 10.1109/ACCESS.2023.3305636

Lundberg, E., & Mozelius, P. (2024). The Potential Effects of Deepfakes on News Media and Entertainment. *AI & Society*. Advance online publication. DOI: 10.1007/s00146-024-02072-1

Marimekala, D., & Lamb, J. (2024). Impact of Generative AI Adoption in Academia and How It Influences Ethics, Cognitive Thinking and AI Singularity. *IEEE Integrated STEM Education Conference, ISEC 2024*. DOI: 10.1109/ISEC61299.2024.10664756

Mayiwar, L., Asutay, E., Tinghög, G., Västfjäll, D., & Barrafrem, K. (2024). Determinants of Digital Well-Being. *AI & Society*. Advance online publication. DOI: 10.1007/s00146-024-02071-2

Meta (n.d.b). *El compromiso de Meta es proteger a las personas y darles la posibilidad de expresarse.*https://transparency.meta.com/es-es/

Meta (n.d.c). Nuestro método para explicar el sistema de clasificación. https://transparency.meta.com/features/explaining-ranking/#facebook_ai_systems

Meta (n.d.a). *Responsible AI. Driven by our belief that AI should benefit everyone.* https://ai.meta.com/responsible-ai/

Montero Carretero, L. (May, 28, 2023). El fin de la era del 'todo vale' para la inteligencia artificial. *ABC*https://www.abc.es/economia/fin-era-vale-inteligencia-artificial-20230528014912-nt.html

Nader, K., Toprac, P., Scott, S., & Baker, S. (2024). Public Understanding of Artificial Intelligence through Entertainment Media. *AI & Society*, 39(2), 713–726. DOI: 10.1007/s00146-022-01427-w PMID: 35400854

Navarro, T. (August 24, 2021). Los filtros de Instagram que ayudan a escapar de los límites del mundo físico. *El País*. https://elpais.com/ideas/2021-08-29/los-filtros-de-instagram-que-ayudan-a-escapar-de-los-limites-del-mundo-fisico.html

Netflix (n.d.). *Accesibilidad en Netflix*. https://help.netflix.com/es-es/node/116022

Netflix (n.d.). *Inclusión y diversidad.*https://about.netflix.com/es_es/inclusion

Nour, N., & Gelfand, J. (2022). Deepfakes: A Digital Transformation Leads to Misinformation. *Grey Journal 18* (2), 85–94. https://doi.org/DOI: 10.26069/greynet-2022-000.471-gg

Ortega Fernández, E. A., & Rodríguez Hernández, J. (2024). Sesgo en la inteligencia artificial y su impacto en el aprendizaje de estudiantes que utilizan ChatGPT. In Almazán-López, O. (Ed.), *IA, educación y medios de comunicación: modelo TRIC* (pp. 59–78). Dykinson.

Pathak, K., Prakash, G., Samadhiya, A., Kumar, A., & Luthra, S. (2025). Impact of Gen-AI Chatbots on Consumer Services Experiences and Behaviors: Focusing on the Sensation of Awe and Usage Intentions through a Cybernetic Lens. *Journal of Retailing and Consumer Services*, 82, 104120. Advance online publication. DOI: 10.1016/j.jretconser.2024.104120

Prates, M. O. R., Avelar, P. H., & Lamb, L. C. (2020). Assessing Gender Bias in Machine Translation: A Case Study with Google Translate. *Neural Computing & Applications*, 32(10), 6363–6381. DOI: 10.1007/s00521-019-04144-6

Radwan, E. K. A., & Russo, A. (2024). Web-Based Corporate Social Responsibility Disclosure Practices: A Systematic Literature Review and Research Directions. *Corporate Social Responsibility and Environmental Management*, 31(5), 5049–5106. DOI: 10.1002/csr.2841

Rapp, A., Di Lodovico, C., Torrielli, F., & Di Caro, L. (2025). How Do People Experience the Images Created by Generative Artificial Intelligence? An Exploration of People's Perceptions, Appraisals, and Emotions Related to a Gen-AI Text-to-Image Model and Its Creations. *International Journal of Human-Computer Studies*, 193, 103375. Advance online publication. DOI: 10.1016/j.ijhcs.2024.103375

European Parliament (2016). Reglamento (UE) 2016/679 del Parlamento Europeo y del Consejo.https://www.boe.es/doue/2016/119/L00001-00088.pdf

European Parliament (2024). Reglamento (UE) 2024/1689 del Parlamento Europeo y del Consejo. https://www.boe.es/buscar/doc.php?id=DOUE-L-2024-81079

Rival Technologies. (May 11, 2023). *YouTube, Netflix and Amazon are Gen Z's Top Brands in 2023, New Research From Rival Group Finds.*https://www.rivaltech.com/gen-z-brand-power-index

Sanchez-Acedo, A., Carbonell-Alcocer, A., Gertrudix, M. & Rubio-Tamayo, J.L. (2024). The Challenges of Media and Information Literacy in the Artificial Intelligence Ecology: Deepfakes and Misinformation. *Communication and Society 37* (4 Special), 223–39. .DOI: 10.15581/003.37.4.223-239

Sedkaoui, S., & Benaichoub, R. (2024). Generative AI as a Transformative Force for Innovation: A Review of Opportunities, Applications and Challenges. *European Journal of Innovation Management*. Advance online publication. DOI: 10.1108/EJIM-02-2024-0129

Stahlschmidt, S., & Stephen, D. (2020). Comparison of web of science, scopus and dimensions databases. KB forschungspoolprojekt, 1-37. https://www.bibliometrie.info/downloads/DZHW-Comparison-DIM-SCP-WOS.PDF

Sterbenk, Y., Champlin, S., Windels, K., & Shelton, S. (2022). Is Femvertising the New Greenwashing? Examining Corporate Commitment to Gender Equality. *Journal of Business Ethics*, 177(3), 491–505. DOI: 10.1007/s10551-021-04755-x

Subiela-Hernández, B. H., Gómez-Company, A., & Vizcaíno-Laorga, R. (2023). Retos y oportunidades en la lucha contra la desinformación y los derechos de autor en Periodismo: MediaVerse (IA, blockchain y smart contracts). *Estudios sobre el Mensaje Periodístico*, 29(4), 869–880. DOI: 10.5209/esmp.88081

Taveekitworachai, P., Gursesli, M. C., Abdullah, F., Chen, S., Cala, F., Guazzini, A., Lanata, A., & Thawonmas, R. (2023). Journey of ChatGPT from Prompts to Stories in Games: The Positive, the Negative, and the Neutral. *IEEE International Conference on Consumer Electronics* - Berlin, ICCE-Berlin, 202–3. https://doi.org/ DOI: 10.1109/ICCE-Berlin58801.2023.10375663

United Nations Global Compact & Accenture. (2024). *Inteligencia artificial generativa para los objetivos mundiales. Guía del sector privado para acelerar el desarrollo sostenible con la tecnología.*https://www.pactomundial.org/biblioteca/inteligencia-artificial-generativa-para-los-objetivos-mundiales/

YouTube. (n.d.). *Nuestro enfoque sobre la IA.*https://www.youtube.com/intl/ALL_es/howyoutubeworks/our-commitments/responsible-ai/

YouTube. (n.d.). *¿Cómo evita YouTube los sesgos?*https://www.youtube.com/intl/ALL_es/howyoutubeworks/our-commitments/preventing-bias/

Zorrilla-Muñoz, V., Moyano, D. L., Marcos Carvajal, C., & Agulló-Tomás, M. S. (2024). Towards Equitable Representations of Ageing: Evaluation of Gender, Territories, Aids and Artificial Intelligence. *Land (Basel)*, 13(8), 1304. Advance online publication. DOI: 10.3390/land13081304

## KEY TERMS AND DEFINITIONS

**Algorithmic Literacy:** Formation regarding the usage of technology that includes artificial intelligence.

**Artificial Intelligence:** Generating text and graphics from data

**Biases in Artificial Intelligence:** Techniques to provide information that are not objective, complete, or true because algorithms emphasize some items over others. As a result, the people involved in the story had their rights violated.

**Generation Z:** The young people born in the final decade of the twentieth century.

**Gender Stereotypes:** A method of producing bias that involves lowering the perception of one gender, typically the feminine.

**iGen:** The younger generation has been influenced by the Internet since birth.

**Responsible AI:** The commitment of individuals or organizations to operate in ways that protect the rights of all participating in the AI process, such as openness and privacy.

# APPENDIX

## Regulatory Framework of AI in Spain

The first AI guideline, determined by the Global Compact, focuses on transparency and regular testing of AI systems to avoid bias and ensure proper functioning. It also stresses the importance of managing automation bias, engaging staff, and providing reporting channels for end users to address issues (United Nations Global Compact & Accenture, 2024: 55). Additionally, Law 15/2022 (15917/2022) complements the Artificial Intelligence Regulation, aiming to protect fundamental rights, security, and trust through a risk-based approach. AI systems are classified by risk level: unacceptable risk systems are prohibited due to their threat to rights; high risk systems are strictly regulated due to their significant impact; limited risk systems require additional transparency; and minimal or zero risk systems have few restrictions.

*Figure 12. Risk levels in the use of AI Regulation of AI.*

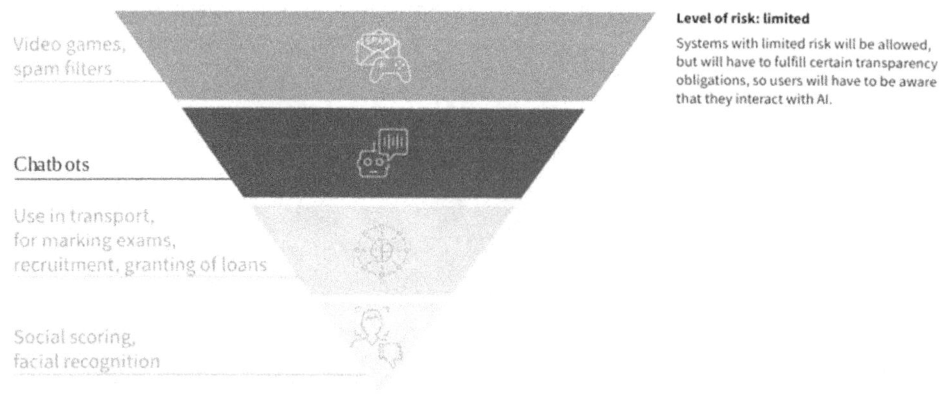


*Law 15/2022 of July 12*

Law 15/2022, of July 12, applies to the rights and obligations of individuals or entities in Spain, regardless of nationality or residence. It aims to prevent, eliminate, and correct all forms of discrimination in both public and private sectors. The regulation highlights that biases in AI can have serious consequences, particularly in areas like security (e.g., facial recognition), healthcare (e.g., diagnostic and treatment applications), justice (e.g., legal decision-making), and employment selection, where they could violate fundamental rights.

# Chapter 5
# Commercial Transactions in the Digital Era:
## Navigating the Legal Complexities of Algorithmic Decision-Making

**David López Jiménez**
https://orcid.org/0000-0002-7013-9556
*EAE Business School, Spain & UNIE Universidad, Spain*

## ABSTRACT

*This chapter examines the legal and ethical challenges of integrating artificial intelligence (AI) and automated decision-making in commercial transactions. It explores how smart contracts, algorithmic liability, and personalized consumer services are transforming traditional concepts in civil and commercial law. Through a comparative law approach, the chapter analyzes the responses of different jurisdictions, including the European Union, the United States, and Asia, to these advancements. Key topics include redefining contractual obligations, introducing "algorithmic fault" in commercial liability, and advocating for dynamic consumer protections against discriminatory pricing. The chapter also proposes innovative mechanisms for dispute resolution, such as AI-assisted mediation and electronic courts, and introduces the concept of adaptive regulation to address rapid technological changes. By doing so, it seeks to promote a fair, transparent, and ethically aligned digital marketplace.*

## INTRODUCTION

In recent years, Artificial Intelligence (AI) has transformed the commercial landscape, introducing profound changes in how businesses operate, engage with customers, and manage contractual obligations. The deployment of AI-driven

DOI: 10.4018/979-8-3693-9894-4.ch005

automated decision-making systems has accelerated business processes, enabled innovative services, and created new opportunities for growth. At the same time, these technologies have raised significant ethical and legal challenges that disrupt traditional notions of commerce and contract law (Ajunwa, 2020; Leal, 2022). Civil and commercial law, which has historically governed business relationships and obligations, now confronts the complex task of adapting to these rapid technological advances.

AI's impact on commerce is particularly evident in the growing use of automated processes for contract execution, market analysis, and consumer engagement. The advent of smart contracts—self-executing contracts with the terms of the agreement directly written into code—has revolutionized traditional contracting models, raising questions about how consent is formed, how contractual obligations are enforced, and what legal remedies are available when these automated systems fail or cause harm (Anderson, 2022; Miller, 2018). Automated decision-making systems also present novel scenarios of liability, as decisions are increasingly made without direct human intervention, challenging established legal principles such as fault, negligence, and diligence. Furthermore, the use of algorithms in personalizing prices and services introduces new forms of discrimination and consumer vulnerability, necessitating a reevaluation of consumer protection laws (Barocas & Barocas, 2016; Narayanan, 2023).

These technological shifts call for an updated legal framework that can address the complexities of algorithmic decision-making in commercial activities while promoting ethical practices and fair competition. This chapter aims to explore the legal frontiers of algorithmic decision-making in commerce, focusing on the intersection of smart contracts, algorithmic liability, consumer protection, and the evolution of civil and commercial law. By adopting a comparative law approach, the chapter will analyze how various jurisdictions, including the European Union, the United States, and Asian countries, are addressing the regulation of automated commercial transactions. It will also propose innovative legal mechanisms and adaptive regulatory frameworks designed to protect consumer rights, ensure fair competition, and foster technological progress responsibly (Ajunwa, 2020; Leal, 2022).

The incorporation of automated decision-making systems into commerce has raised a host of new legal challenges that cannot be adequately addressed by existing legal norms alone. Traditionally, commercial law has relied on well-defined concepts of consent, liability, and contractual obligations to regulate business transactions. However, the rise of AI has blurred these concepts, creating situations where contractual obligations are executed autonomously, often without explicit human oversight, and where liability becomes difficult to assign.

For instance, when a smart contract autonomously executes a transaction based on pre-programmed conditions, questions arise about how informed consent is ensured, who bears responsibility for potential errors in the contract's execution, and how disputes should be resolved when the contract operates outside human control. Similarly, the use of AI in market surveillance, pricing, and consumer profiling raises concerns about discrimination, privacy violations, and the potential for algorithmic abuse in commercial practices. Without adequate legal adaptation, these issues can undermine the integrity of commerce, erode consumer trust, and lead to unfair competitive environments.

Different jurisdictions have begun to recognize the need for legal frameworks that specifically address the challenges posed by algorithmic decision-making. The European Union, for example, has introduced regulatory proposals, such as the Artificial Intelligence Act (AI Act), aimed at creating legal standards for AI's use in various domains, including commerce. Similarly, the United States has seen a growing body of case law addressing issues related to smart contracts, algorithmic liability, and digital consumer protection. In Asia, countries like China and Japan are developing guidelines for automated decision-making that emphasize the importance of transparency, accountability, and consumer rights. This comparative analysis will highlight the strengths and limitations of existing regulatory approaches, laying the groundwork for proposing a dynamic regulatory framework capable of responding to technological advancements.

The examination of legal frameworks governing automated decision-making in commerce is of paramount importance for several reasons. First, the integrity of commercial transactions relies on a legal system that can effectively manage the complexities introduced by AI. By providing clear rules on consent formation, liability, and dispute resolution in automated environments, the law can ensure that commercial activities remain fair, transparent, and predictable. This is particularly vital as businesses increasingly rely on automated systems to handle a range of transactions, from supply chain management to online consumer sales.

Second, addressing the legal implications of algorithmic decision-making is crucial for protecting consumer rights. In highly automated digital environments, consumers are often subject to personalized pricing, targeted advertising, and automated contractual clauses that may be difficult to understand or challenge. Without robust legal protections, consumers risk being exploited by practices such as discriminatory pricing, algorithmic bias, and abusive contract terms generated through automated processes. Therefore, the law must evolve to empower consumers to exercise their rights effectively in this new commercial landscape.

Third, establishing an adaptive regulatory framework for AI in commerce is essential for fostering innovation while safeguarding ethical standards. While overregulation can stifle technological progress, a lack of clear legal guidelines can lead to the misuse of AI, resulting in market distortions, anticompetitive behaviors, and erosion of consumer trust (Miller, 2018). By proposing legal mechanisms that promote responsible AI use, this chapter seeks to strike a balance between encouraging innovation and ensuring that commercial practices align with societal values of fairness, transparency, and accountability.

The ongoing digital transformation of commerce, driven by AI and automated decision-making systems, necessitates a reevaluation of traditional legal concepts and regulatory frameworks. This chapter will contribute to the discourse by offering an in-depth analysis of the legal challenges and opportunities associated with AI in commercial transactions. By exploring comparative legal approaches and proposing adaptive regulatory mechanisms, the chapter seeks to foster a commercial landscape where innovation, ethical responsibility, and consumer rights coexist harmoniously. As the digital era continues to reshape commerce, it is imperative that civil and commercial law evolve to address the ethical implications and legal complexities of algorithmic decision-making.

## AUTOMATED DECISION-MAKING AND ITS IMPACT ON COMMERCIAL TRANSACTIONS

The advent of AI and automated decision-making systems has fundamentally transformed the landscape of commercial transactions. Traditional models of commerce, which rely on human negotiation, consent, and the establishment of contractual obligations, are being replaced or supplemented by smart contracts and algorithm-driven processes. These changes have introduced new legal complexities, necessitating a reevaluation of core concepts in civil and commercial law. This section delves into the theoretical implications of automated decision-making in commerce, addressing issues such as contractual obligations, algorithmic liability, consumer protection, and adaptive regulation.

### Smart Contracts and Automated Processes: Rethinking Traditional Contracts

A major advancement in the field of automated decision-making is the emergence of smart contracts. These are contracts that automatically execute themselves, with the terms and conditions of the agreement encoded directly into computer programs. When predefined conditions are met, the contract automatically executes its terms without requiring human intervention. For example, in a supply chain transaction, a smart contract could automatically release payment to a supplier upon confirmation of product delivery, thereby streamlining the transaction process (Anderson, 2022).

Smart contracts challenge traditional legal notions of contract formation, performance, and enforcement. Traditional contracts require a clear expression of intent, negotiation, and mutual consent. With smart contracts, these elements become embedded in coded instructions, raising questions about the validity of consent and the ability of parties to understand the contract's implications. In legal theory, consent must be informed and freely given. However, the complexity of smart contract code may obscure its terms from the average participant, potentially leading to disputes over the validity of consent (Bowling et al., 2017).

Moreover, smart contracts introduce questions about contractual autonomy and the possibility of error. In conventional contracts, parties have the autonomy to renegotiate terms or address unforeseen circumstances. Smart contracts, in contrast, operate on rigid pre-coded conditions, leaving little room for flexibility once the contract is executed (Leal, 2022). Errors in the code, unforeseen events, or changes in circumstances can result in outcomes that may not reflect the parties' original intentions, leading to legal disputes over the fulfillment of contractual obligations.

The theoretical debate extends to the legal capacity of automated systems to execute contracts. Since smart contracts function autonomously, some legal scholars argue that they lack the capacity to enter into contracts in the traditional sense (Scholz, 2021). Civil and commercial law traditionally requires a party to have legal capacity and intention to create legal relations. With smart contracts, these concepts become blurred, as the execution of contractual terms is delegated to algorithms. This raises the question: can an automated system legally "consent" to contractual obligations, or should the law recognize new forms of contractual capacity specific to automated processes?

## Algorithmic Liability in Commercial Transactions

The increasing use of automated decision-making in commerce brings to the forefront the issue of liability. In traditional commercial law, liability is typically grounded in principles of fault, negligence, and diligence. When human actors make decisions that lead to harm or contractual breaches, they can be held liable based on their actions, intentions, or lack of care. However, in an environment where algorithms and AI systems make autonomous decisions, assigning liability becomes more complex (Berman, 2018; Crootof et al., 2023).

The concept of "algorithmic fault" emerges as a critical aspect of this discussion. Algorithmic fault refers to errors or biases in an automated system that result in harm or unfair commercial practices. For example, an AI pricing algorithm that discriminates against certain consumer groups based on their data profiles may engage in unethical behavior that could lead to legal claims (Citron & Pasquale, 2014). The challenge lies in determining who bears responsibility for such algorithmic faults. Is it the developer who designed the algorithm, the business that deploys it, or the AI system itself?

In response to these questions, legal theorists propose the notion of "technological diligence" as a standard for evaluating liability in automated environments. Technological diligence involves the careful design, testing, and monitoring of AI systems to ensure that they operate fairly and accurately (Peterson, 2017). Businesses deploying automated decision-making tools would be required to demonstrate that they have exercised technological diligence in developing and implementing their algorithms, thereby reducing the risk of harm or unfair practices. This approach aligns with traditional civil law concepts of duty of care but adapts them to the context of autonomous systems.

Another dimension of algorithmic liability concerns extracontractual scenarios, where automated processes cause harm to third parties outside the scope of a contractual relationship. For instance, if an automated advertising algorithm disseminates false information about a competitor's product, this could result in reputational damage and potential financial loss. In such cases, existing civil law principles on torts, defamation, and unfair competition must be adapted to address the automated nature of the harm. Theoretical discussions in this area explore whether AI systems should be treated as autonomous agents with distinct liability or whether liability should be attributed solely to their human operators (Buchanan & O'Connell, 2006).

## Consumer Protection in the Era of Algorithmic Personalization

Automated decision-making significantly influences consumer transactions, particularly through personalized services and dynamic pricing models. AI algorithms analyze vast amounts of consumer data to tailor offerings, adjust prices, and recommend products based on individual profiles. While these practices enhance consumer experiences and market efficiency, they also raise critical legal concerns regarding discrimination, transparency, and the potential for exploitative commercial practices (Hurley, 2003; Jeffers, 2020).

One of the primary concerns in this context is algorithmic discrimination. Personalization algorithms often rely on data patterns that can inadvertently reinforce biases, leading to differential treatment of consumers based on characteristics such as age, gender, location, or socioeconomic status. For example, an AI system might offer higher prices to consumers in wealthier neighborhoods, resulting in price discrimination that may be ethically and legally problematic. In commercial law, the principle of equal treatment is fundamental to ensuring fairness in market transactions. The challenge is to develop legal standards that can detect, assess, and address algorithmic discrimination in a manner that protects consumers while allowing for legitimate personalization practices (Barocas & Selbst, 2016).

Automated processes also give rise to concerns about the use of "abusive algorithmic clauses" in consumer contracts. These are contract terms generated or applied automatically by algorithms, often without clear disclosure or the consumer's informed consent. For instance, an e-commerce platform's terms of service might include clauses that limit consumer rights or impose unfair penalties, implemented automatically through the platform's algorithms. The opacity of these automated processes makes it difficult for consumers to understand the contract terms they are bound to, raising questions about how the law should regulate the formation and enforcement of such clauses (Citron & Pasquale, 2014). Theoretical approaches to this issue advocate for enhanced transparency requirements and mechanisms that empower consumers to challenge unfair automated clauses in court or through arbitration.

## The Need for Adaptive Regulation in an Automated Environment

Given the rapid evolution of automated decision-making technologies, traditional commercial law faces the challenge of keeping pace with technological changes. Static legal frameworks may become outdated or ineffective in addressing the nuances of AI-driven commerce. Therefore, the concept of adaptive regulation has emerged as a theoretical solution to this problem.

Adaptive regulation refers to the creation of dynamic legal frameworks that can automatically adjust to technological advancements and emerging commercial practices. This approach involves the use of regulatory mechanisms, such as "sandbox" environments for testing new technologies, periodic reviews of regulatory standards, and the incorporation of technological tools (e.g., AI algorithms) in regulatory processes. The goal is to develop laws that are flexible enough to respond to the complexities of automated commerce while maintaining legal certainty and protecting consumer rights.

The theoretical debate around adaptive regulation also explores the role of international cooperation in developing harmonized legal standards for algorithmic decision-making. As commerce becomes increasingly global, differing regulatory approaches across jurisdictions create challenges for businesses and consumers alike. Comparative law analysis can provide valuable insights into best practices and guide the development of cohesive regulatory frameworks that address both local and global dimensions of algorithmic commerce.

Automated decision-making in commercial transactions presents multifaceted challenges that extend beyond traditional legal doctrines. From redefining contractual obligations in smart contracts to addressing algorithmic liability and protecting consumers from discrimination, the impact of AI on commerce necessitates a reimagining of civil and commercial law. The theoretical discussions outlined in this section lay the foundation for examining how legal frameworks can evolve to meet these challenges, promoting a marketplace that balances technological innovation with ethical responsibility and fairness.

## TRANSFORMATION OF COMMERCE: AUTOMATED DECISION-MAKING AND NEW CONTRACTUAL MODELS

Today, traditional contracting models, which relied on manual negotiation, mutual consent, and human judgment, are increasingly being replaced or supplemented by automated processes and smart contracts. This shift changes how transactions are executed and raises new legal and ethical questions about consent, autonomy, liability, and the potential for errors in these automated systems. In this section, we explore how AI and automated processes are redefining contractual relationships, highlighting the complexities and opportunities these technologies introduce to commercial law (Canale, 2021; Ruster, 2020; Scholz, 2021).

### Automated Contracts: Beyond Traditional Models

The conventional model of contract formation involves negotiation, mutual consent, and the expression of a clear intention to create legally binding obligations. This process is typically characterized by a sequence of offer, acceptance, and consideration. However, with the introduction of smart contracts—self-executing contracts with terms directly embedded into code—this traditional model has been disrupted.

A smart contract is a set of programmed instructions that automatically execute specified actions when predefined conditions are met. For example, in an insurance transaction, a smart contract could be programmed to automatically process and release payments when data from a weather monitoring system confirms a natural disaster, such as a hurricane. This automation enhances efficiency, reduces the need for intermediaries, and minimizes the potential for human error.

However, this paradigm shift raises important legal questions. Can a contract truly be considered a "contract" if it is executed by an algorithm rather than human intention? Traditional contract law requires a "meeting of the minds" or mutual assent between parties. In the context of smart contracts, this mutual assent is expressed through code, which may not be easily comprehensible to all parties involved, particularly those who lack technical expertise. This opacity poses challenges to the concept of informed consent, as parties may not fully understand the conditions and implications embedded in the contract's code (Leal, 2019).

Moreover, smart contracts operate within a rigid framework. Unlike traditional contracts, which can be amended through mutual agreement in response to changing circumstances, smart contracts automatically enforce their terms without room for negotiation or flexibility. This rigidity introduces potential risks: if a flaw exists in the code or if unforeseen events occur, the automated execution could result in unintended outcomes. For example, a glitch in a smart contract might release payments prematurely or fail to account for exceptional situations, such as a force majeure evento (Scholz, 2021). These scenarios highlight the need for legal mechanisms to address errors and adapt to the dynamic nature of commercial relationships.

Another critical issue is the degree of autonomy granted to automated systems in executing contracts. In traditional contracts, parties have control over their obligations and can exercise judgment in fulfilling them. In contrast, smart contracts delegate decision-making to algorithms, which operate independently once programmed. This autonomy raises questions about the legal capacity of automated systems. For instance, can an AI-driven agent be considered a legal entity capable of entering into contracts, or should its actions always be attributed to the human or corporate entity that deploys it?

Legal scholars debate the concept of "digital personhood," which suggests that autonomous systems could be granted a form of legal recognition to operate within specified parameters (Canale, 2021). However, this idea is controversial, as it challenges existing legal frameworks that define contractual capacity based on human characteristics such as intention, understanding, and the ability to assume liability. To address these challenges, some jurisdictions are considering the creation of legal statuses for AI systems, potentially treating them as "agents" of the deploying party rather than independent actors. This approach would allow for contractual obligations to be enforced while maintaining the human element of legal responsibility.

## Algorithmic Consent and Errors in Automated Processes

Automated contracting processes also introduce complexities related to consent and the possibility of errors. In traditional contracts, consent is typically expressed through written or verbal agreement, ensuring that both parties clearly understand their obligations. In automated environments, consent is embedded in code, executed through algorithms that may not be easily interpreted by the average participant. This raises significant questions about whether consent is truly informed and voluntary.

In the context of smart contracts, consent is expressed through the acceptance of the contract's programmed terms. However, understanding these terms requires a certain level of technical knowledge, as the contract's provisions are often coded in complex algorithms. For example, a smart contract used in a decentralized finance (DeFi) application may include provisions that dynamically adjust interest rates based on market conditions. While this may provide financial advantages, participants may not fully comprehend the algorithm's decision-making processes, potentially resulting in outcomes that differ from their expectations.

The opacity of these algorithms challenges the principle of informed consent, which is a cornerstone of contract law. In response, some legal scholars advocate for the implementation of "algorithmic transparency" in automated contracts. This concept involves providing clear explanations of how an algorithm operates, including its decision-making logic, risk factors, and potential outcomes. By enhancing transparency, parties can make more informed decisions about their participation in automated contracts, thereby aligning algorithmic processes with the legal standard of informed consent.

The self-executing nature of smart contracts introduces the risk of errors that can have significant legal implications. These errors may arise from flaws in the code, incorrect input data, or unforeseen events that the algorithm fails to account for. For instance, a smart contract designed to facilitate the automated transfer of goods could malfunction if the data source it relies on becomes unavailable or provides inaccurate information, resulting in the delivery of incorrect goods or quantities.

Addressing these errors poses a challenge within the traditional legal framework. In human-driven contracts, errors can be corrected through negotiation, legal intervention, or the application of doctrines such as mistake or misrepresentation. However, smart contracts lack this flexibility, as they are programmed to execute their terms automatically. One potential solution is to incorporate "escape clauses" or "kill switches" within the code, allowing parties to pause or terminate the contract in the event of an error or unexpected situation. These clauses would provide a mechanism for human intervention, enabling parties to renegotiate or seek legal remedies as necessary.

## The Need for Legal Reforms to Address New Contractual Models

The emergence of smart contracts and automated decision-making necessitates a reexamination of legal doctrines and the development of new regulatory frameworks. Some scholars argue for the establishment of an "automated commercial code" that specifically addresses the unique characteristics of AI-driven transactions. Such a code could include provisions on algorithmic consent, error correction mechanisms, and the delineation of liability in automated environments (Anderson et al., 2005; Scholz, 2021).

Furthermore, there is a need for adaptive regulation that can evolve alongside technological advancements. Legal reforms could introduce requirements for algorithmic transparency, mandating that businesses disclose the operation of their automated processes in a clear and accessible manner. Additionally, the law could establish standards for technological diligence, holding companies accountable for the design, testing, and monitoring of their smart contracts and automated systems (Peterson, 2017).

Automated decision-making and smart contracts are reshaping commercial transactions, challenging traditional legal concepts such as consent, flexibility, and liability. While these technologies offer significant benefits in terms of efficiency and accuracy, they also introduce complexities that necessitate careful legal scrutiny. By exploring these theoretical issues, this section underscores the importance of developing legal frameworks that address the unique characteristics of automated transactions, ensuring that commerce in the digital era remains fair, transparent, and aligned with the principles of civil and commercial law.

## CIVIL AND COMMERCIAL LIABILITY: REDEFINING ALGORITHMIC LIABILITY

The integration of automated decision-making and AI into commercial activities has brought forth new forms of risk and liability. Traditional concepts of civil and commercial liability—based on fault, negligence, and intent—must now be reconsidered in light of the unique characteristics of AI systems that operate autonomously. This section examines the complexities of "algorithmic liability," exploring how civil law can adapt to address issues of fault and diligence in an environment where algorithms make decisions that can directly impact consumers, businesses, and third parties. We will discuss new theoretical concepts, such as "algorithmic fault" and "technological diligence," as well as mechanisms for regulating liability in cases of harm caused by automated commercial practices.

### Understanding Algorithmic Liability in Commercial Activities

In conventional commercial transactions, liability is often based on a party's actions or omissions. For example, if a business fails to meet the terms of a contract due to negligence, it can be held liable for any resulting damages. However, in scenarios where AI systems autonomously make decisions, determining liability becomes more complex. Who is responsible when an algorithm's decision leads to a harmful outcome? Is it the developer, the business deploying the system, or the algorithm itself?

Algorithmic fault is a concept that attempts to address this complexity. It refers to situations where an AI system's decision-making process contains flaws, such as bias, errors in data processing, or unintended consequences, leading to damages or losses. For example, an AI-driven loan approval system that exhibits bias against certain demographic groups might unjustly deny credit to individuals, resulting in financial harm and potential legal disputes. Establishing fault in such cases requires examining the AI system's design, the data it uses, and the decision-making criteria embedded in its algorithms.

To manage these situations, the concept of technological diligence has been introduced. This refers to the obligation of businesses and developers to design, implement, and monitor AI systems in a manner that minimizes the risk of harm. Technological diligence may include regular audits of AI algorithms, updating systems to correct known biases, and ensuring that the data used in decision-making processes is accurate and representative. The failure to exercise technological diligence can be construed as a form of negligence, leading to liability for damages caused by the AI system.

## Distinguishing Between Contractual and Extracontractual Liability in Automated Environments

In automated commerce, liability issues can arise both within the scope of contractual relationships and in extracontractual (tort) contexts. Distinguishing between these two areas is essential for determining the applicable legal principles and remedies.

Contractual liability occurs when one party fails to fulfill its obligations as outlined in a contract. In the context of automated decision-making, this might involve an AI system executing a transaction in a manner that breaches the contractual terms, such as delivering goods of substandard quality or failing to meet delivery deadlines. The rigid nature of smart contracts can exacerbate these issues, as the automated system may not allow for renegotiation or rectification in response to unexpected circumstances. In such cases, establishing liability may hinge on whether the business exercised technological diligence in programming and monitoring the AI system.

Extracontractual liability (or tort liability) arises when an AI system causes harm to third parties outside of any contractual relationship. For example, an AI-powered advertising algorithm that spreads false or misleading information about a competitor's product could result in reputational damage and financial losses. Addressing extracontractual liability in automated environments involves applying traditional civil law principles, such as fault, causation, and harm, to the actions of AI systems. Legal scholars debate whether AI systems should be treated as autonomous agents capable of committing torts or whether liability should be attributed to the humans or companies behind these systems.

## Regulatory Mechanisms for Addressing Algorithmic Liability

To address the complexities of algorithmic liability, regulatory frameworks must evolve to encompass new forms of risk associated with AI-driven commerce. Several mechanisms have been proposed to establish clear standards for liability and to guide businesses in the responsible deployment of AI systems (Langenbucher, 2021; Packin & Lev-Aretz, 2016).

One approach to regulating algorithmic liability is to require businesses to conduct regular audits of their AI systems. These audits would involve examining the algorithms' decision-making processes, data inputs, and outcomes to identify potential biases, errors, and risks of harm. By implementing mandatory audits, regulators can encourage businesses to exercise technological diligence and proactively address issues that may lead to liability. Moreover, audits can serve as evidence in legal disputes, demonstrating that a business took reasonable steps to ensure its AI systems operated fairly and accurately.

In some contexts, such as financial services, healthcare, and autonomous vehicles, the deployment of AI systems presents significant risks to public welfare. For these high-risk applications, legal scholars have suggested adopting a strict liability regime, where businesses deploying the AI system are automatically held liable for any harm caused, regardless of fault or negligence. This approach provides a strong incentive for businesses to implement rigorous safety measures and oversight. However, it also raises concerns about stifling innovation, as strict liability may deter companies from investing in AI technologies due to the potential for costly liability (Langenbucher, 2021).

Given the unpredictability of AI outcomes, businesses could be required to obtain insurance coverage for potential damages caused by their automated systems. AI insurance policies would provide a financial safety net, enabling companies to compensate victims while distributing the risk across multiple stakeholders. Additionally, the establishment of risk-sharing mechanisms, such as industry-wide compensation funds, could help manage liability in cases where AI systems cause widespread or systemic harm (Packin & Lev-Aretz, 2016).

## Algorithmic Defamation and Misleading Advertising: Navigating Liability in Commercial Practices

Automated decision-making is increasingly used in marketing and advertising, where algorithms tailor content and promotional messages based on data analytics and consumer profiling. However, these practices introduce new risks of liability, particularly in the areas of defamation and misleading advertising.

Defamation occurs when false or misleading statements harm an individual's or company's reputation. In the context of automated commerce, AI-powered systems may inadvertently generate defamatory content. For instance, an algorithm designed to compare products might incorrectly present a competitor's product in a negative light, causing reputational damage. Determining liability in such cases is complex, as the defamatory statement is produced by an autonomous system rather than a human actor. Current legal frameworks are beginning to adapt by attributing responsibility to the business deploying the AI system, especially if it failed to exercise technological diligence in monitoring and controlling the algorithm's outputs.

Automated advertising algorithms can also lead to misleading or deceptive practices, such as exaggerating the benefits of a product or concealing its limitations. The dynamic nature of these algorithms, which adjust content based on consumer data in real time, makes it difficult to identify and regulate potentially misleading messages. Legal solutions to this problem include imposing strict guidelines for transparency in algorithmic advertising, requiring businesses to clearly disclose how AI-driven promotions are generated and what data sources they rely on.

## The Need for Adaptive Liability Frameworks

Given the rapid evolution of AI technologies, a static approach to algorithmic liability may prove insufficient. Instead, there is a growing consensus on the need for adaptive liability frameworks that can respond to emerging risks and technological advancements. Such frameworks could involve periodic reviews of liability standards, the establishment of AI ethics committees within companies to oversee the deployment of automated systems, and the creation of regulatory sandboxes that allow businesses to test new AI applications under controlled conditions. These adaptive measures would enable the legal system to address new forms of algorithmic harm while providing businesses with guidance on responsible practices.

Algorithmic liability in commercial transactions presents complex legal challenges that require a rethinking of traditional concepts of fault, negligence, and contract breach. By introducing new standards such as technological diligence and exploring mechanisms like algorithmic audits, strict liability, and risk-sharing, the legal system can begin to address the unique risks posed by automated decision-making. As AI continues to reshape commerce, adaptive regulatory frameworks will be essential for ensuring that businesses deploy AI responsibly, safeguard consumer rights, and maintain the integrity of the marketplace.

## COMPARATIVE LAW: REGULATORY TRENDS AND ADAPTIVE REGULATION

The widespread use of AI and automated decision-making systems in commerce has presented new challenges to civil and commercial law, necessitating a reevaluation of legal frameworks across different jurisdictions. Various regions, including the European Union (EU), the United States, and Asia, have approached the regulation of AI with different strategies, reflecting their unique legal traditions, market structures, and ethical priorities. This section provides a comparative analysis of these regulatory trends, highlighting key legal initiatives and exploring the concept of adaptive regulation—legal frameworks designed to evolve in response to rapid technological changes. By examining international regulatory efforts, this section aims to identify best practices and propose a dynamic regulatory model that balances innovation with ethical standards in AI-driven commerce (Edwards & Veale, 2017; Hildebrandt, 2015; Zarsky, 2016).

### European Union: The AI Act and Digital Market Regulation

The European Union (EU) has been at the forefront of AI regulation, adopting a comprehensive approach that emphasizes human rights, data protection, and market fairness. The AI Act, proposed in 2021, represents one of the most ambitious attempts to establish a regulatory framework for AI systems, including those used in commercial transactions. The AI Act classifies AI systems into different risk categories—unacceptable, high-risk, limited risk, and minimal risk—each subject to varying levels of regulation. Commercial applications, such as AI-driven credit scoring, automated hiring processes, and personalized pricing algorithms, are typically categorized as high-risk and are therefore subject to strict compliance requirements.

The AI Act imposes several obligations on businesses deploying high-risk AI systems, including requirements for transparency, risk assessment, human oversight, and compliance with data governance standards. For instance, companies must ensure that their AI systems are transparent and explainable, allowing affected individuals to understand how decisions are made. Additionally, businesses must conduct regular audits to identify and mitigate risks associated with their AI applications.

One of the most groundbreaking aspects of the AI Act is its emphasis on algorithmic transparency. The Act requires businesses to disclose when consumers are interacting with AI systems, providing information on the system's operation and its potential impacts on decision-making. This transparency is particularly relevant in commercial transactions, where consumers may be subject to automated decisions that affect their access to services, pricing, and contractual terms. By mandating transparency, the EU aims to protect consumer rights and prevent discriminatory practices in AI-driven commerce (Hildebrandt, 2015).

Furthermore, the EU's Digital Markets Act (DMA) complements the AI Act by targeting the market power of large digital platforms. The DMA imposes obligations on "gatekeepers"—dominant platforms that control access to digital markets—requiring them to ensure fair competition, data portability, and the interoperability of services. By regulating these gatekeepers, the DMA seeks to prevent the misuse of algorithmic decision-making to manipulate markets, stifle competition, or engage in unfair practices.

## United States: Sector-Specific Regulation and Liability Considerations

In contrast to the EU's comprehensive approach, the United States has adopted a more sector-specific regulatory strategy. Rather than establishing overarching AI legislation, the U.S. focuses on regulating AI within specific industries, such as finance, healthcare, and consumer protection. This fragmented approach reflects the U.S. legal tradition, which often relies on a combination of federal, state, and industry-specific regulations to address emerging challenges.

The U.S. regulatory framework for financial services is an example of sector-specific regulation. The Equal Credit Opportunity Act (ECOA) and the Fair Credit Reporting Act (FCRA), enforced by agencies such as the Consumer Financial Protection Bureau (CFPB), provide safeguards against discriminatory practices in lending and credit scoring. As financial institutions increasingly use AI algorithms to make lending decisions, these regulations have been adapted to address algorithmic bias and ensure fairness in automated credit assessments.

The U.S. approach to data privacy is governed by laws such as the California Consumer Privacy Act (CCPA) and the Federal Trade Commission Act (FTC Act), which grant consumers rights over their personal data and prohibit unfair or deceptive business practices. While not specifically designed for AI, these laws have been used to address concerns related to data-driven decision-making in commerce. For example, the FTC has issued guidance on AI and data analytics, emphasizing the need for transparency, accuracy, and fairness in AI-driven marketing and consumer profiling.

The U.S. legal system has also begun to address the issue of liability in AI-driven commerce. Courts are grappling with questions of fault and negligence in cases where automated systems cause harm. While there is no uniform standard for algorithmic liability, several court decisions suggest that businesses deploying AI systems may be held liable if they fail to exercise reasonable care in designing, testing, and monitoring these systems. This evolving case law underscores the importance of technological diligence as a legal standard for managing the risks associated with AI in commercial transactions.

## Asia: Regulatory Developments and Ethical Guidelines

In Asia, the regulation of AI in commerce is characterized by a combination of government-led initiatives, industry self-regulation, and ethical guidelines. Countries like China, Japan, and Singapore have taken proactive steps to establish regulatory frameworks that balance technological innovation with ethical considerations.

China's approach to AI regulation is driven by its ambition to become a global leader in AI while maintaining control over its digital economy. The Personal Information Protection Law (PIPL), enacted in 2021, sets strict requirements for data collection, processing, and sharing, emphasizing individual consent and the protection of personal information. Additionally, the Cybersecurity Law and sector-specific guidelines, such as the Guidelines on Automated Decision-Making in Financial Services, provide regulatory oversight of AI applications in areas such as credit scoring, insurance, and e-commerce.

China also highlights ethical AI through its Ethical Standards for AI framework, which encourages transparency, fairness, and non-discrimination in AI systems. Businesses are encouraged to incorporate ethical principles into their AI development and deployment, particularly in commercial activities that impact consumer welfare. While these guidelines are not legally binding, they reflect China's efforts to integrate ethical considerations into its regulatory landscape.

On the other side, Japan's regulatory approach focuses on balancing innovation with human-centric values. The Artificial Intelligence Technology Strategy, developed by Japan's Cabinet Office, outlines a vision for responsible AI development that respects human rights, privacy, and social norms. Japan's Act on the Protection of Personal Information (APPI) provides a legal framework for data privacy, regulating the collection and use of personal data in AI-driven commerce. The APPI's recent amendments strengthen individuals' rights over their data and impose obligations on businesses to ensure data accuracy and security.

In the case of Singapore it has positioned itself as a hub for AI governance, promoting ethical AI use through initiatives such as the Model AI Governance Framework. This framework provides guidelines for businesses on implementing

AI in a transparent, explainable, and accountable manner. While voluntary, the framework serves as a reference for companies seeking to align their AI practices with ethical standards, particularly in commercial applications such as financial services and retail.

## The Concept of Adaptive Regulation

Given the rapid pace of AI development, static regulatory frameworks risk becoming obsolete or ineffective. To address this challenge, the concept of adaptive regulation has gained prominence in legal theory and policy discussions. Adaptive regulation refers to legal frameworks designed to evolve in response to technological advancements and changes in commercial practices. This approach combines flexibility with legal certainty, allowing regulations to adapt to new risks while providing businesses with clear compliance guidelines. In this sense, several mechanisms can facilitate adaptive regulation in the context of AI-driven commerce.

For instance, regulatory sandboxes allow businesses to test new AI applications in a controlled environment under the supervision of regulators. This approach enables companies to experiment with innovative technologies while adhering to ethical standards and safety requirements. The data and insights generated from sandbox trials inform the development of adaptive regulations that address potential risks without stifling innovation. The United Kingdom's Financial Conduct Authority (FCA) pioneered the use of sandboxes in the financial sector, and this model has been adopted in various jurisdictions, including Singapore.

Adaptive regulation involves the use of another type of instruments, the dynamic rule-making processes, where regulatory standards are periodically reviewed and updated to reflect technological changes. For example, regulators could establish AI audit requirements that evolve over time, incorporating new evaluation metrics for algorithmic transparency, bias detection, and data protection. By implementing dynamic rules, legal frameworks can remain relevant and responsive to emerging risks in AI-driven commerce.

To facilitate adaptive regulation, authorities may develop algorithmic tools that monitor AI systems in real time, assessing their compliance with legal standards. These tools could automatically flag potential violations, such as discriminatory pricing or misleading advertising, allowing regulators to intervene promptly. By integrating technology into regulatory processes, adaptive frameworks can enhance oversight and ensure that AI-driven commerce aligns with ethical and legal norms.

## Proposal for a Global Adaptive Regulatory Framework

Given the cross-border nature of digital commerce, a coordinated international approach is necessary to address the challenges of AI in commercial transactions. In this sense, it is proposed the development of a global adaptive regulatory framework that harmonizes key legal standards while allowing for jurisdictional flexibility.

This framework could include core principles that establish universal guidelines, such as transparency, fairness, and accountability, to govern the use of AI in commerce. It would also incorporate dynamic compliance mechanisms, like regular audits and regulatory sandboxes, to ensure regulations can adapt to technological advancements. Additionally, the framework would promote international cooperation by fostering dialogue and collaboration among regulators, businesses, and policymakers, facilitating the sharing of best practices and the development of coherent policies.

The comparative analysis of regulatory trends in the EU, the U.S., and Asia reveals a diversity of approaches to managing the complexities of AI-driven commerce. While the EU leads with a comprehensive regulatory framework focused on human rights and market fairness, the U.S. adopts a sector-specific strategy that emphasizes technological diligence. Meanwhile, Asian countries are integrating ethical guidelines into their regulatory models. The concept of adaptive regulation emerges as a promising solution, offering a dynamic and flexible approach to address the evolving risks of AI in commercial activities. By learning from these varied approaches, it is possible to design a global regulatory framework that balances innovation with the ethical use of AI, fostering a competitive and fair digital marketplace.

# THE ROLE OF DISPUTE RESOLUTION MECHANISMS IN AI-DRIVEN COMMERCE

The integration of AI and automated decision-making systems into commercial transactions has transformed how businesses operate, and it has also introduced novel legal complexities that challenge traditional dispute resolution mechanisms. Given the autonomous nature of algorithmic processes and the often opaque manner in which AI systems make decisions, traditional court-based dispute resolution may prove inadequate for addressing the multifaceted conflicts that arise in this context. This section examines the challenges of resolving disputes in AI-driven commerce and proposes innovative mechanisms, including AI-assisted mediation, electronic courts, and alternative dispute resolution (ADR) methods. By analyzing these mechanisms, this section aims to delineate how they can be adapted to meet the unique needs of digital marketplaces, ensuring both fairness and legal certainty.

## Traditional Dispute Resolution and its Limitations in AI-Driven Commerce

Traditional dispute resolution mechanisms, primarily litigation in courts, have long served as the cornerstone for addressing conflicts in commercial transactions. These mechanisms are founded on principles such as due process, the right to a fair trial, and the adversarial system, which involves the presentation of evidence and arguments before an impartial judge or jury. However, AI-driven commerce poses unique challenges to these traditional forms of dispute resolution (Kaufmann-Kohler & Schultz, 2004; Reed, 2020).

First, the technical complexity of AI and automated decision-making systems often requires specialized knowledge that exceeds the expertise of generalist courts. For example, disputes involving smart contracts or algorithmic pricing may necessitate an in-depth understanding of blockchain technology, machine learning algorithms, or data analytics. Traditional courts may lack the resources or expertise to adequately evaluate such technical evidence, potentially leading to inconsistent or uninformed judgments (Reed, 2020).

Second, the speed at which AI systems operate in commercial transactions contrasts sharply with the often slow and procedural nature of court-based dispute resolution. AI-driven commerce involves real-time decision-making, dynamic pricing, and instantaneous contract execution, leaving little room for the protracted timelines typical of traditional litigation. This mismatch can result in delayed justice and ongoing harm to the parties involved, undermining the very objectives of civil and commercial law: fairness, efficiency, and the protection of legitimate interests.

Third, the cross-border nature of AI-driven commerce introduces jurisdictional challenges. Transactions facilitated by AI often transcend national boundaries, involving parties from different legal systems with varying regulations and standards. Resolving disputes through traditional courts becomes complicated when determining which jurisdiction's laws apply and how to enforce judgments across borders. This legal fragmentation increases the cost and uncertainty of litigation and may result in inconsistent outcomes that weaken the integrity of global digital markets.

## AI-Assisted Mediation and Arbitration: A New Frontier in Dispute Resolution

To address the limitations of traditional dispute resolution, legal scholars and practitioners are exploring AI-assisted mediation and arbitration as innovative alternatives tailored to the digital economy. These methods leverage AI technology to facilitate efficient, fair, and cost-effective resolutions, aligning with the dynamic and cross-border nature of modern commerce (Katsh & Rabinovich-Einy, 2017; De Girolamo, 2019).

Mediation is a voluntary process in which a neutral third party (the mediator) assists disputing parties in reaching a mutually acceptable agreement. AI-assisted mediation introduces algorithmic tools to enhance the process by analyzing data, identifying potential areas of compromise, and providing real-time feedback to the parties. For instance, an AI system could analyze patterns in past disputes, assess the strengths and weaknesses of each party's position, and suggest potential settlement terms based on comparable cases.

The use of AI in mediation offers several advantages. It can reduce the time and costs associated with traditional mediation, streamline the negotiation process, and provide objective, data-driven insights that help parties make informed decisions. However, AI-assisted mediation also raises ethical and legal concerns. For example, the neutrality and fairness of the AI mediator must be ensured, particularly regarding data bias and transparency in the algorithmic decision-making process. To address these concerns, legal frameworks governing AI-assisted mediation should incorporate standards for algorithmic transparency, impartiality, and the right to human oversight, ensuring that AI tools support rather than undermine the principles of fairness and autonomy in dispute resolution.

Arbitration is a binding dispute resolution process in which an arbitrator (or panel of arbitrators) renders a decision based on the evidence and arguments presented by the parties. AI-assisted arbitration involves the use of algorithms to manage case files, evaluate evidence, and even provide recommendations to the arbitrators. For example, AI systems can automate the review of contracts, identify relevant clauses, and detect potential breaches, thereby expediting the resolution process.

The potential for AI to facilitate arbitration is particularly relevant in the context of smart contracts. Given their self-executing nature, smart contracts operate on predefined conditions that, when met, automatically trigger specific outcomes. When disputes arise—such as errors in code execution or unforeseen external factors—the rigid structure of smart contracts may leave little room for manual intervention. AI-assisted arbitration can address these issues by quickly analyzing the smart contract's code, verifying its execution, and recommending tailored solutions based on the contract's original intent. This approach enhances the flexibility of automated transactions and provides a means to resolve disputes without undermining the integrity of the self-executing model.

Nonetheless, AI-assisted arbitration also requires careful legal scrutiny. Questions about the enforceability of AI-generated decisions, the safeguarding of procedural fairness, and the protection of parties' rights to appeal must be addressed. Furthermore, the confidentiality and security of data processed by AI systems during arbitration are paramount, especially given the sensitivity of commercial information.

Therefore, the integration of AI into arbitration must be accompanied by regulatory safeguards that uphold the principles of due process, confidentiality, and the right to challenge arbitral decisions.

## Electronic Courts and Online Dispute Resolution (ODR) in the Digital Marketplace

In response to the jurisdictional and logistical challenges posed by AI-driven commerce, several jurisdictions have developed electronic courts and online dispute resolution (ODR) platforms as mechanisms for resolving disputes in the digital era. These platforms offer a virtual forum where parties can submit evidence, make arguments, and receive legally binding decisions without the need for physical courtrooms. By embracing digital technology, electronic courts and ODR platforms aim to make justice more accessible, efficient, and adaptable to the needs of cross-border transactions (Rule, 2017; Cortés, 2018).

Electronic courts represent an extension of traditional courts into the digital realm, utilizing online portals for case management, electronic filing of documents, and virtual hearings. Some electronic courts, particularly in jurisdictions like Singapore and the Netherlands, have begun to incorporate AI tools to assist judges in managing caseloads, analyzing evidence, and identifying relevant legal precedents. In AI-driven commerce disputes, electronic courts offer the advantage of specialized knowledge and streamlined procedures, allowing for expedited resolutions that align with the pace of digital transactions.

However, the use of AI in electronic courts raises important questions regarding judicial discretion and the integrity of the legal process. While AI can assist in case management and legal analysis, it is essential that human judges retain ultimate decision-making authority to ensure that each case is evaluated on its individual merits. To balance the benefits of AI assistance with the preservation of judicial integrity, legal systems must establish clear guidelines for the use of AI in electronic courts, including standards for algorithmic accuracy, bias mitigation, and human oversight (Cortés, 2018).

ODR platforms offer a fully digital alternative to traditional litigation and arbitration, enabling parties to resolve disputes through automated negotiation, mediation, or arbitration processes. In AI-driven commerce, ODR platforms are particularly suited to handling high-volume, low-value disputes, such as those arising from online sales, dynamic pricing, or automated contractual clauses. For example, an ODR system could use AI algorithms to automatically evaluate claims, match them with relevant legal standards, and propose settlement options, reducing the time and costs involved in manual dispute resolution.

The effectiveness of ODR in AI-driven commerce depends on several factors, including the platform's ability to handle complex algorithmic disputes, the protection of consumer rights, and the enforcement of ODR decisions across jurisdictions. To enhance the credibility and fairness of ODR, regulatory frameworks should establish minimum standards for transparency, data protection, and the right to human intervention when disputes involve sensitive or high-stakes issues. Additionally, international cooperation is needed to ensure the mutual recognition and enforcement of ODR outcomes, providing a cohesive legal environment for global digital markets.

## Harmonizing Dispute Resolution Mechanisms With Algorithmic Commerce

The evolution of AI-driven commerce calls for the development of dispute resolution mechanisms that are efficient, accessible, and tailored to the unique characteristics of algorithmic transactions. This section proposes a multi-layered approach to harmonize dispute resolution in the digital marketplace.

First, traditional courts and arbitration institutions should integrate AI tools to improve case management, expedite legal analysis, and assist judges and arbitrators in navigating the technical complexities of algorithmic disputes. To ensure fairness, this integration must include safeguards that preserve judicial discretion, prevent algorithmic bias, and protect the rights of all parties involved.

Second, jurisdictions should consider establishing dedicated forums for AI-related disputes, such as specialized AI courts or arbitration panels. These forums, staffed with experts in AI technology and commercial law, would provide tailored procedures for resolving issues involving smart contracts, algorithmic liability, and digital consumer rights. This approach ensures decisions are informed by both legal principles and technological realities.

Third, the use of AI-assisted mediation and arbitration should be encouraged to provide flexible and cost-effective alternatives to traditional litigation. Regulatory frameworks must establish clear standards for AI-assisted ADR, including requirements for algorithmic transparency, neutrality, and human oversight. These measures ensure that such mechanisms promote fairness while upholding legal standards in digital transactions.

Finally, international cooperation is essential to address the jurisdictional challenges of AI-driven commerce. Agreements should be developed to enable the mutual recognition and enforcement of electronic court and ODR decisions. By harmonizing cross-border legal standards, this approach can create a reliable legal environment for businesses and consumers to resolve disputes in the global digital marketplace.

The rise of AI and automated decision-making in commerce demands a reimagining of dispute resolution mechanisms. By embracing AI-assisted mediation, electronic courts, and ODR platforms, the legal system can adapt to the complexities of digital transactions while safeguarding the principles of fairness, transparency, and accountability. Moving forward, the development of harmonized dispute resolution frameworks—supported by international cooperation and adaptive regulation—will be essential for promoting trust and stability in the rapidly evolving landscape of algorithmic commerce.

## PROPOSING ADAPTIVE REGULATORY FRAMEWORKS FOR ALGORITHMIC COMMERCE

The rapid evolution of AI and automated decision-making in commercial transactions necessitates the development of regulatory frameworks that are responsive to technological innovations and grounded in the principles of fairness, transparency, and accountability. The existing legal paradigms, designed primarily for human-mediated commerce, face significant limitations when applied to algorithmic processes that operate autonomously, often across multiple jurisdictions. This section proposes an adaptive regulatory framework that can address the complexities of AI-driven commerce, balancing the need for innovation with the imperative to protect consumer rights, ensure market integrity, and maintain ethical standards.

### The Principles of an Adaptive Regulatory Framework

An adaptive regulatory framework for algorithmic commerce must be built on core principles that guide the design, implementation, and enforcement of regulations. These principles act as benchmarks for evaluating AI system behavior while providing regulators with the flexibility to respond to technological advancements (Kaal & Vermeulen, 2017; Veale & Edwards, 2018; Zuboff, 2019).

The principle of transparency addresses the complexity of AI-driven commercial transactions, where algorithms often operate in ways that are not easily understandable to the average consumer or business. Businesses deploying AI systems must provide clear and accessible information about how decisions are made, including the data used, the logic behind decision-making processes, and potential implications for consumers. By counteracting the "black box" nature of AI systems, this principle enables stakeholders to evaluate operations, detect biases, and challenge unfair practices.

To clarify responsibility in AI-driven decision-making, the framework must establish accountability mechanisms. As algorithms increasingly take on decision-making roles, traditional lines of responsibility in commerce become blurred. Businesses must remain accountable for the outcomes of their AI systems, which requires defining obligations for developers, deployers, and operators. These obligations should include ensuring data quality, maintaining algorithmic integrity, and mitigating harm caused by automated processes.

The principle of fairness is vital to addressing risks of discrimination and inequality introduced by AI systems, particularly in areas like personalized pricing, marketing, and consumer profiling. AI systems must be designed and implemented to prevent unjustified discrimination or exploitation of vulnerable groups. Regulatory frameworks should incorporate standards that prohibit algorithmic bias, promote equitable treatment, and provide avenues for consumers to seek redress when outcomes are unfair.

Given the dynamic nature of AI technologies, regulations must be adaptable to technological advancements. This adaptability can be achieved through mechanisms like periodic reviews of regulatory standards, the use of regulatory sandboxes to test new AI applications, and the incorporation of technological tools—such as AI algorithms—in regulatory oversight. By embedding flexibility into the framework, regulators can address emerging risks while supporting innovation. The global nature of digital commerce necessitates international cooperation and the harmonization of standards. Cross-border mechanisms are crucial to ensure the consistent application of regulations, mutual recognition of decisions, and effective enforcement across jurisdictions.

## Designing Dynamic Compliance Mechanisms

To operationalize the principles outlined above, an adaptive regulatory framework should incorporate dynamic compliance mechanisms that allow businesses and regulators to respond effectively to the evolving landscape of algorithmic commerce.

On the one hand, businesses deploying AI systems in commerce should be required to conduct algorithmic impact assessments (AIAs) before and after implementation. These assessments would evaluate the potential risks associated with AI applications, including biases, privacy concerns, and the potential for discriminatory outcomes. AIAs should also involve a thorough review of the data inputs, algorithmic logic, and decision-making criteria used by the AI system. By requiring regular AIAs, the regulatory framework ensures that businesses proactively address risks, maintain compliance with ethical standards, and adapt to changing technological and market conditions (Wachter et al., 2017).

On the other hand, mandatory algorithmic audits should serve as a core component of adaptive regulation, like financial audits. Businesses would be required to submit their AI systems to regular, independent audits that examine their design, data sources, and decision-making processes. These audits would identify potential biases, errors, and unfair practices, providing an evidence-based foundation for regulatory action if necessary. Additionally, businesses should publish transparency reports detailing the operation of their AI systems, including metrics on their impact on consumers and market competition. This level of transparency enhances accountability and allows regulators, consumers, and stakeholders to monitor the fairness and integrity of algorithmic commerce (Pasquale, 2015).

Besides, the regulatory framework should define clear standards for algorithmic compliance, outlining the technical and procedural requirements that AI systems must meet. These standards could include requirements for algorithmic explainability, data accuracy, non-discrimination, and safeguards against malicious or unintended outcomes. Compliance with these standards would be mandatory for businesses deploying AI in commerce, with non-compliance subject to penalties, fines, or restrictions on the use of certain algorithms. To keep pace with technological advancements, these standards should be subject to periodic review and updates, incorporating new insights and best practices from the field of AI ethics and governance.

## Regulatory Sandboxes and Experimental Legal Regimes

Given the nascent and rapidly evolving nature of AI technologies, it is essential to provide businesses with a controlled environment in which they can experiment with innovative AI applications while ensuring consumer protection and legal compliance. Regulatory sandboxes offer a solution by allowing businesses to test new AI-driven products, services, and business models under the supervision of regulatory authorities (Arner et al., 2017).

In the sandbox model, regulators set up a framework where businesses can trial their AI applications on a limited scale and within predefined boundaries. During this testing phase, companies can identify and address potential legal and ethical issues, such as biases in decision-making, data privacy concerns, and the implications of automated contract execution. The insights gained from sandbox testing can then inform the development of permanent regulatory standards and compliance requirements, providing a pathway for innovative technologies to enter the market responsibly.

Sandboxes facilitate a feedback loop between regulators and businesses, allowing for continuous dialogue and knowledge sharing. This iterative process enables regulators to develop a nuanced understanding of emerging technologies and adjust regulatory standards accordingly. For example, if sandbox trials reveal that certain AI applications pose a high risk of algorithmic discrimination, regulators can refine compliance requirements, such as mandating more robust bias detection and mitigation measures. By adopting this adaptive approach, the regulatory framework remains flexible, responsive, and informed by real-world developments in AI.

Regulatory sandboxes can also serve as a platform for international cooperation, where cross-border pilot programs enable regulators from different jurisdictions to collaborate on developing harmonized standards for algorithmic commerce. By aligning their sandbox frameworks, countries can facilitate the mutual recognition of AI compliance, reduce regulatory fragmentation, and promote a cohesive global environment for digital markets.

## Enforcing Adaptive Regulation and Consumer Protections

Enforcement is a critical component of any regulatory framework, and adaptive regulation for algorithmic commerce must include mechanisms that both deter non-compliance and empower consumers to protect their rights.

An adaptive regulatory framework should involve the creation of dedicated AI oversight authorities with the expertise to monitor, investigate, and enforce compliance in algorithmic commerce. These authorities would be responsible for reviewing algorithmic audits, conducting investigations into reported incidents of algorithmic bias or misconduct, and imposing penalties for violations. To ensure transparency and public trust, these authorities should operate independently and be granted the power to compel businesses to disclose relevant information about their AI systems.

Consumers must have access to clear rights and mechanisms for redress in cases where algorithmic decisions result in unfair treatment, discrimination, or harm. The regulatory framework should establish a comprehensive set of consumer rights, including the right to know when an algorithm is used in a decision-making process, the right to explanation and contestation, and the right to access remedies in the event of harm. Additionally, regulators should develop streamlined procedures for consumer complaints, including the use of ODR platforms to handle algorithmic commerce disputes efficiently and fairly.

Given the cross-border nature of digital commerce, adaptive regulation must include mechanisms for international enforcement cooperation. Regulatory authorities should collaborate on establishing reciprocal agreements for the recognition and enforcement of compliance standards, investigations, and sanctions. This cooperation is vital for addressing challenges such as data transfer, jurisdictional conflicts, and the enforcement of consumer protections across national boundaries.

## The Road Ahead: Implementing an Adaptive Regulatory Framework for a Fair Digital Marketplace

The proposed adaptive regulatory framework represents a forward-looking approach to managing the complexities of AI-driven commerce. By integrating principles of transparency, accountability, fairness, adaptability, and cross-border cooperation, the framework aims to create a legal environment that supports innovation while safeguarding the interests of consumers and market participants. Implementing this framework will require coordinated efforts among governments, businesses, legal practitioners, and technologists, as well as a commitment to continuous evaluation and refinement.

In the rapidly evolving digital marketplace, where AI and automated decision-making reshape the nature of commercial transactions, an adaptive regulatory framework is not merely a legal necessity but an ethical imperative. By embracing dynamic compliance mechanisms, fostering regulatory experimentation through sandboxes, and promoting robust consumer protections, the legal system can navigate the challenges of algorithmic commerce and ensure that technological progress aligns with the values of justice, equity, and accountability.

As the digital era advances, the adaptive regulation of algorithmic commerce will be central to building a marketplace that is technologically innovative, fair, transparent, and human-centered. The development and implementation of such a framework will define the trajectory of digital markets, ensuring that they remain competitive, inclusive, and aligned with societal values in the age of AI.

## CONCLUSION

The digital age has brought forth a significant transformation in commerce, driven by AI and automated decision-making systems. These advancements have redefined traditional business models, introduced efficiencies, and expanded market reach in unprecedented ways. However, they have simultaneously exposed the limitations of current civil and commercial laws, revealing the necessity for adaptive legal frameworks capable of addressing the challenges of algorithmic commerce. This chapter has delved into the intricate legal, ethical, and regulatory complexities associated with AI-driven transactions and proposed an adaptive, multi-layered approach for regulating this dynamic marketplace. This conclusion summarizes key insights, emphasizes the necessity of a balanced regulatory framework, and outlines a path forward for fostering a responsible and equitable digital marketplace.

AI and automated decision-making have fundamentally changed commercial transactions. From smart contracts and personalized pricing to consumer profiling, these technologies offer numerous benefits, including cost reductions, increased efficiency, and enhanced market insights. Nevertheless, they introduce complexities that disrupt established legal concepts such as consent, liability, and consumer protection. The rise of algorithmic commerce has blurred traditional legal boundaries, necessitating a reevaluation of core concepts within civil and commercial law.

This chapter has highlighted the need to rethink legal concepts considering automated decision-making. Smart contracts challenge traditional ideas about contract formation, especially in terms of consent and the ability to modify terms in automated environments. Algorithmic liability creates scenarios where fault, negligence, and responsibility are difficult to assign. Additionally, algorithms used in personalizing consumer experiences introduce risks of discrimination, unfair practices, and potential consumer exploitation. Jurisdictions worldwide are beginning to address these challenges. The European Union (EU) has developed comprehensive legislation like the AI Act and Digital Markets Act, emphasizing transparency and consumer protection. In contrast, the United States has taken a sector-specific approach, focusing on finance, data privacy, and consumer rights. Asian countries have adopted a combination of regulatory measures and ethical guidelines, balancing innovation with oversight. This diversity of approaches underscores the complexity of harmonizing global standards for algorithmic commerce.

A central theme of this chapter is the call for an adaptive regulatory framework tailored to the evolving nature of AI-driven commerce. Static legal structures are inadequate given the rapid pace of technological advancements, leading to gaps in protections and inconsistencies in law application. In contrast, an adaptive framework can respond dynamically to the shifting landscape of algorithmic commerce, promoting an environment where innovation coexists with ethical and legal safeguards.

Such a framework would incorporate principles of transparency, accountability, fairness, adaptability, and cross-border cooperation. By adopting these principles, regulators can ensure that businesses deploying AI respect consumer rights, uphold market integrity, and mitigate the risks of algorithmic abuse. Mechanisms like algorithmic impact assessments (AIAs), mandatory audits, regulatory sandboxes, and robust consumer protections form the foundation of this approach, providing the flexibility needed to accommodate technological changes while ensuring legal certainty.

The need for adaptability is particularly critical in cross-border commerce. Given the global nature of digital markets, regulatory fragmentation can result in legal ambiguities, higher compliance costs, and difficulties in enforcing consumer protections. International cooperation and harmonization of standards are therefore essential for building a coherent regulatory environment for algorithmic commerce. Aligning legal standards, promoting mutual recognition of compliance mechanisms, and facilitating data exchange between jurisdictions can help create a unified approach to managing the complexities of AI in commerce.

Another vital aspect explored is the development of dispute resolution mechanisms suitable for algorithmic commerce. Traditional litigation processes—often slow, jurisdictionally limited, and lacking technological expertise—are increasingly inadequate for resolving disputes stemming from AI-driven transactions. The chapter advocates for AI-assisted mediation, electronic courts, and ODR platforms as viable alternatives that offer efficiency, accessibility, and cross-border applicability.

The future of dispute resolution in algorithmic commerce hinges on these mechanisms' ability to adapt to technological advances while maintaining principles of fairness, transparency, and due process. AI-assisted mediation and arbitration can offer flexible, cost-effective alternatives to traditional litigation, particularly for high-volume, low-value disputes typical of digital markets. Electronic courts and ODR platforms further extend access to justice, allowing parties to resolve conflicts in virtual environments that transcend national boundaries.

However, these dispute resolution forms must be supported by regulatory safeguards. Integrating AI tools in legal processes should include standards for algorithmic neutrality, accuracy, and human oversight to ensure that outcomes are just and legally sound. Establishing AI-specific forums, staffed with experts in AI technology and commercial law, could provide tailored procedures for resolving disputes involving smart contracts, algorithmic liability, and digital consumer rights.

The ongoing digital transformation of commerce presents both immense opportunities and significant challenges. While AI and automated decision-making can drive economic growth and market efficiency, they also raise ethical concerns. Algorithmic bias, discriminatory pricing, opaque decision-making processes, and data privacy violations threaten consumer trust and market fairness. The role of regulation is not just to restrict harmful practices but to foster a digital marketplace where technological progress aligns with societal values.

Achieving this balance requires a nuanced approach. Overregulation risks stifling innovation and limiting the benefits AI can bring to commerce, while underregulation leaves consumers vulnerable to exploitation and market distortions. The adaptive regulatory framework proposed in this chapter seeks to strike a balance by establishing clear standards for ethical AI use while allowing for technological experimentation and growth. By mandating transparency, enforcing algorithmic accountability, and protecting consumer rights, the framework creates an environment where responsible innovation can thrive.

Regulating AI in commercial transactions is a dynamic and evolving challenge. The legal system must continuously adapt to the complexities of algorithmic commerce to ensure that technological advancements do not undermine consumer rights, market integrity, or ethical standards. The proposed adaptive regulatory framework offers a comprehensive path forward, combining compliance mechanisms, flexible legal standards, and cross-border cooperation to create a balanced and equitable digital marketplace.

Implementing this framework will require coordinated efforts from governments, businesses, legal professionals, technologists, and consumers. Governments must lead by establishing strong regulatory authorities, promoting international cooperation, and embedding principles of transparency, accountability, and fairness in digital markets. Businesses, in turn, must act as stewards of responsible AI use, committing to ethical practices, algorithmic integrity, and proactive risk management. Consumers should be empowered with the rights, tools, and knowledge necessary to navigate and challenge algorithmic commerce effectively.

As AI continues to reshape commerce, evolving civil and commercial law will play a crucial role in guiding this transformation toward a future that is technologically advanced, just, inclusive, and aligned with human values. Building a regulatory framework that is adaptive, ethical, and globally cohesive will lay the foundation for a digital marketplace where innovation, consumer protection, and fair competition can harmoniously coexist. This is the promise and the responsibility of algorithmic commerce in the digital era.

## FUTURE LINES OF RESEARCH

The evolving landscape of algorithmic commerce continues to present numerous questions and challenges that demand further academic exploration. This chapter has laid the groundwork for understanding the legal and ethical implications of AI-driven transactions, yet there remain critical aspects that require deeper investigation. Future research must focus on adaptive regulation, the complexities of algorithmic decision-making, and how emerging technologies intersect with existing legal frameworks. This discussion will identify key future research areas, emphasizing the need for a multidisciplinary approach to ensure a fair, transparent, and accountable digital marketplace.

One major area requiring exploration is algorithmic liability, particularly the question of responsibility when autonomous systems cause harm. Traditional legal concepts like fault, negligence, and vicarious liability need to be reconsidered in the context of AI. Future research should examine how liability is allocated among AI developers, operators, and users, especially when these entities span multiple jurisdictions. Establishing standards of "technological diligence" for risk mitigation efforts in AI deployment is another crucial topic. There is also a debate on whether AI systems should be recognized as autonomous legal entities capable of bearing responsibility, or if liability should always revert to the human or corporate actors involved. Interdisciplinary research, integrating law, computer science, ethics, and economics, is essential here, and empirical studies could offer real-world insights into practical liability frameworks.

Implementing adaptive regulation on a global scale presents a complex set of questions. Future research must investigate how regulatory harmonization can be achieved across jurisdictions with differing legal traditions and market structures. Key questions include how international legal standards for AI in commerce could be developed and enforced, especially in the face of different national regulations, such as the European Union's AI Act and the United States' sector-specific approaches. The role of international organizations, such as the United Nations and the World Trade Organization, in facilitating global consensus on AI regulation is another important aspect to explore. Additionally, research on regulatory sandboxes and experimental legal regimes can provide insights into the best practices for adaptive regulation, helping to ensure consumer protections keep pace with the rapid development of AI.

As AI systems increasingly shape consumer experiences through personalized pricing, targeted advertising, and automated contracts, it is crucial to study how these technologies can be designed to respect consumer rights and promote fairness. Future research must focus on developing algorithmic fairness criteria and methods for detecting and mitigating biases in AI-driven commercial practices, especially in critical sectors such as finance, insurance, and e-commerce. The role of transparency in fostering consumer trust, including tools like explainable AI and algorithmic impact assessments, needs to be further examined. Mechanisms to enhance consumer autonomy and control over their data, such as consumer-driven data governance models, are also worthy of in-depth investigation. Effective strategies for consumer protection in an increasingly automated marketplace require a multidisciplinary approach, combining law, ethics, data science, and consumer behavior studies.

The rise of AI-assisted mediation, electronic courts, and ODR platforms has opened new avenues for resolving commercial disputes. However, further research is needed to refine these mechanisms and assess their long-term viability. Key research directions include studying the legal and ethical implications of AI-generated decisions in mediation and arbitration, particularly regarding procedural fairness, neutrality, and enforceability. Investigating how AI can be integrated into electronic courts and its impact on judicial discretion and human oversight is another important research avenue. Evaluating the effectiveness of ODR platforms in handling cross-border disputes, including challenges related to jurisdiction, data protection, and decision enforcement, can provide valuable insights into best practices for these emerging systems. Empirical research, such as case studies of existing AI-assisted dispute resolution platforms, will inform the development of standards for these mechanisms.

The extensive use of consumer data in AI-driven commerce raises significant privacy concerns. Future research must explore the intersection of AI, data privacy laws, and commercial law to create a cohesive regulatory framework that balances personal information protection with business innovation. Areas for exploration include the adequacy of current data privacy regulations, such as the GDPR and CCPA, in addressing AI-driven commerce, particularly in terms of data collection, consent, and data subject rights. Additionally, the potential of privacy-preserving AI techniques like differential privacy and federated learning to comply with privacy laws should be investigated. Research into operationalizing data portability and enhancing consumer control over personal information in AI-driven markets can also contribute to more transparent and consumer-empowered commerce practices.

Smart contracts and automated decision-making are disrupting traditional contractual frameworks, necessitating a reevaluation of how commercial relationships are negotiated, executed, and enforced in the digital era. Future research should examine the development of legal standards for smart contracts, including the validity of algorithmic consent and the resolution of unforeseen events. The potential for new commercial models, such as decentralized autonomous organizations (DAOs), to operate within existing legal frameworks, and their impact on corporate liability, governance, and contract law, must also be analyzed. Additionally, exploring the concept of digital personhood for AI systems and the implications of granting limited legal recognition to autonomous agents in commercial transactions could offer a basis for developing adaptive commercial codes tailored to algorithmic transactions.

The complexities of AI-driven markets call for a multidisciplinary approach, involving legal scholars, technologists, ethicists, economists, and policymakers. Collaborative efforts such as interdisciplinary conferences, joint policy initiatives, and cross-sector working groups will be essential for developing solutions that are technically viable, legally sound, and ethically aligned. Ongoing research is crucial for shaping adaptive regulations that safeguard consumer interests, ensure fairness, and foster a responsible digital marketplace. Engaging in this inquiry will help build a future where algorithmic commerce aligns with the principles of justice, equity, and human dignity, while driving economic growth.

Future research must tackle the legal, ethical, and technical aspects of algorithmic commerce. This includes addressing liability, regulation, consumer protection, dispute resolution, privacy, and new commercial models. By focusing on these areas through a collaborative, interdisciplinary lens, scholars and policymakers can help ensure that AI-driven commerce evolves in a way that is equitable, transparent, and socially responsible.

## REFERENCES


Ajunwa, I. (2020). The paradox of automation as anti-bias intervention. *Cardozo Law Review*, 41, 1671–1742. DOI: 10.2139/ssrn.2746078

Anderson, R. (2022). The dawn of credit scoring. In *Credit intelligence and modelling: many paths through the forest of credit rating and scoring* (pp. 281–314). Oxford University Press., DOI: 10.1093/oso/9780192844194.003.0008

Anderson, T., Schum, D., & Twining, W. (2005). *Analysis of Evidence* (2nd ed.). Cambridge University Press., DOI: 10.1017/CBO9780511610585

Arner, D. W., Barberis, J., & Buckley, R. P. (2017). FinTech, RegTech and the Reconceptualization of Financial Regulation. *Northwestern Journal of International Law & Business*, 37(3), 371–413.

Barocas, S., & Barocas, A. D. (2016). Big data's disparate impact. *California Law Review*, 104, 671–732. . doi: DOI: 10.2139/ssrn.2477899

Berman, E. (2018). A government of laws and not of machines. *SSRN*, 98, 1277–1355. DOI: 10.2139/ssrn.3098995

Bowling, B., Marks, A., & Keenan, C. (2017). Automated justice? Technology, crime, and social control. In *The Oxford Handbook of Law, Regulation, and Technology* (pp. 705–730). Oxford University Press., DOI: 10.1093/oxfordhb/9780199680832.013.32

Buchanan, L., & O'Connell, A. (2006). A brief history of decision making. *Harvard Business Review*, 84(1), 32–41. https://hbr.org/2006/01/a-brief-history-of-decision-making PMID: 16447367

Canale, D. (2021). The opacity of law: On the hidden impact of experts' opinion on legal decision-making. *Law and Philosophy*, 40(5), 509–543. DOI: 10.1007/s10982-021-09408-8

Citron, D. K., & Pasquale, F. (2014). The scored society: Due process for automated predictions. *Washington Law Review (Seattle, Wash.)*, 89(1), 1–33.

Cortés, P. (2018). *Online Dispute Resolution for Consumers in the European Union*. Routledge., DOI: 10.4324/9780203847756

Crootof, R., Kaminski, M. E., & Price, W. N.II. (2023). Humans in the loop. *SSRN*, 76(2), 429–510. DOI: 10.2139/ssrn.4066781

De Girolamo, D. (2019). Rethinking the role of the mediator: Promoting party autonomy through informed decision-making. *Journal of Law and Society*, 46(1), 64–91. DOI: 10.1111/jols.12160

Edwards, L., & Veale, M. (2017). Slave to the algorithm? Why a "right to an explanation" is probably not the remedy you are looking for. *Duke Law and Technology Review*, 16(1), 18–84. DOI: 10.31228/osf.io/97upg

Hildebrandt, M. (2015). *Smart technologies and the end(s) of law: Novel entanglements of law and technology*. Edward Elgar Publishing. DOI: 10.4337/9781849808774

Huq, A. Z. (2020). A right to a human decision. *Virginia Law Review*, 106(3), 611–688.

Hurley, S. L. (2003). *Justice, Luck, and Knowledge*. Harvard University Press.

Jeffers, M. T. (2020). Luck and the limits of equality. *Philosophical Papers*, 49(3), 397–429. DOI: 10.1080/05568641.2020.1762114

Kaal, W. A., & Vermeulen, E. P. M. (2017). How to regulate disruptive innovation – From facts to data. *SSRN*, 57(2), 169–190. DOI: 10.2139/ssrn.2808044

Katsh, E., & Rabinovich-Einy, O. (2017). *Digital Justice: Technology and the Internet of Disputes*. Oxford University Press. DOI: 10.1093/acprof:oso/9780190464585.001.0001

Kaufmann-Kohler, G., & Schultz, T. (2004). *Online Dispute Resolution: Challenges for Contemporary Justice*. Kluwer Law International.

Langenbucher, K. (2021). Zur Regulierung des Kreditscoring. *Europäische Zeitschrift Für Wirtschaftsrecht*, 22, 961–963.

Leal, A. A. (2019). Aspetos jurídicos da análise de dados na Internet (big data analytics) nos setores bancário e financeiro: proteção de dados pessoais e deveres de informação. In *FinTech—Desafios da Tecnologia Financeira* (2nd ed.). Almedina.

Leal, A. A. (2022). Decisões, algoritmos e interpretabilidade em ambiente negocial. Sobre o dever de explicação das decisões algorítmicas. *Lisbon Law Review*, 63(1–2), 65–148.

Miller, A. P. (2018). Want less-biased decisions? use algorithms. *Harvard Business Review*. Retrieved from: https://hbr.org/2018/07/want-less-biased-decisions-use-algorithms

Narayanan, A. (2023). Understanding social media recommendation algorithms. *Knight First Amendment Institute at Columbia University*. Retrieved from: https://knightcolumbia.org/content/understanding-social-media-recommendation-algorithms

Packin, N. G., & Lev-Aretz, Y. (2016). On social credit and the right to be unnetworked. *Columbia Business Law Review*, 2, 339–425. DOI: 10.7916/cblr.v2016i2.1739

Pasquale, F. (2015). *The Black Box Society: The Secret Algorithms That Control Money and Information*. Harvard University Press. DOI: 10.4159/harvard.9780674736061

Peterson, M. (2017). *An introduction to decision theory* (2nd ed.). Cambridge University Press., DOI: 10.1017/9781316585061

Reed, C. (2020). *Law, Technology and the Internet*. Cambridge University Press., DOI: 10.1017/CBO9780511808791

Rule, C. (2017). *The New Handshake: Online Dispute Resolution and the Future of Consumer Protection*. American Bar Association.

Ruster, A. (2020). Willenserklärungen Mittels Autonomer Systeme? Zum Vertragsschluss bei Einsatz künstlicher Intelligenz (Teil 2). *Juristische Rundschau*, 12(12), 639–649. DOI: 10.1515/juru-2020-0059

Scholz, L. H. (2021). Algorithms and contract law. In *The Cambridge Handbook of the Law of Algorithms* (pp. 141–152). Cambridge University Press.

Veale, M., & Edwards, L. (2018). Clarity, surprises, and further questions in the GDPR's provisions on automated decision-making and profiling. *Computer Law & Security Review*, 34(2), 398–404. DOI: 10.1016/j.clsr.2017.12.002

Wachter, S., Mittelstadt, B., & Floridi, L. (2017). Why a right to explanation of automated decision-making does not exist in the General Data Protection Regulation. *International Data Privacy Law*, 7(2), 76–99. DOI: 10.1093/idpl/ipx005

Zarsky, T. Z. (2016). The trouble with algorithmic decisions: An analytic road map to examine efficiency and fairness in automated and opaque decision-making. *Science, Technology & Human Values*, 41(1), 118–132. DOI: 10.1177/0162243915605575

Zuboff, S. (2019). *The Age of Surveillance Capitalism: The Fight for a Human Future at the New Frontier of Power*. PublicAffairs.

# Chapter 6
# Navigating the AI Revolution in Advertising:
## Opportunities and Ethical Challenges

**Park Beede**
https://orcid.org/0000-0001-7923-4245
*Zayed University, UAE*

## ABSTRACT

*Artificial intelligence (AI) is revolutionizing the advertising industry, offering unprecedented personalization, automation, and optimization capabilities. However, this transformation also raises critical ethical and operational concerns. This chapter examines the multifaceted influence of AI on advertising, exploring its potential benefits and inherent risks. While AI enhances efficiency and effectiveness, it also introduces challenges related to transparency, accountability, and the potential for bias and discrimination. The text similarly examines the impact of AI on creativity, highlighting the tension between automation and the preservation of the human element in compelling storytelling. Additionally, it discusses the evolving regulatory landscape, emphasizing the need for continuous adaptation to address the rapid pace of AI development. By examining these issues, this chapter aims to promote a responsible and strategic approach to AI adoption in advertising, ensuring this transformative technology's ethical and practical integration.*

DOI: 10.4018/979-8-3693-9894-4.ch006

## INTRODUCTION

The rapid development of artificial intelligence (AI) technologies and tools is radically reshaping various traditional business sectors, including the advertising industry. Recently, AI tools have revolutionized advertising campaigns and corporate communications, making them more streamlined, personalized, and optimized. AI has fundamentally altered how brands interact with their target audiences, from hyper-personalized content creation to automated ad placements.

While AI's impact on advertising is often focused on benefits associated with efficiencies and effectiveness, it also introduces new ethical and operational concerns. Several issues arise from the adoption of AI in advertising, which calls for the attention of advertisers and regulators alike. First, the reliance on AI-driven automation raises questions about transparency and accountability. As decision-making processes become more complex and less human-driven, overseeing the welfare of individuals targeted with content becomes more challenging, leading to potential biases and unintended discrimination (Pasquale, 2015). Furthermore, the rapid pace of AI development has outpaced regulatory frameworks, with concerns about data privacy and surveillance marketing practices arising. The misuse of consumer data and its potential to infringe on privacy rights has sparked debates about the ethical implications of AI (Zuboff, 2019). The comprehensive AI Act in the EU is an example of how legal frameworks are trying to catch up. However, these regulations often need frequent revision to address the rapidly evolving AI landscape.

One of the most pressing concerns in the advertising industry is the potential negative impact and the looming threat of AI on creativity. Whereas AI tools like natural language generation and image synthesis can create content at scale, there is a real risk that this could lead to a commoditization of creativity, resulting in advertisements that lack emotional resonance. This is not just a risk but a challenge that advertisers must face. The tension between automation and creativity is not just a key consideration but a battleground for the future of advertising. Advertisers must balance and actively apply the efficiencies offered by AI with the need to preserve a human touch essential for compelling storytelling and brand connection.

Given the numerous emerging issues, advertisers must approach AI adoption with a strategic perspective and responsible mindset. This approach ensures that AI tools safeguard user welfare, promote ethical implementation, and balance technological advances with human creativity. Ignoring these concerns may lead to consumer distrust, regulatory pushback, and a decline in the overall effectiveness of AI-enhanced advertising strategies. This chapter explores critical, creative context issues arising from AI technologies in advertising and their ethical implications, plotting a course for further inquiry.

## THE RISE OF AUTOMATION: A HISTORICAL PERSPECTIVE ON AI IN ADVERTISING AND MARKETING

The advertising and marketing landscape constantly evolves, adapting to technological advancements and shifting consumer behaviors. One of the most transformative forces in recent decades has been the rise of artificial intelligence (AI). While intelligent machines crafting persuasive messages and optimizing campaigns may seem futuristic, the origins of AI in marketing appeared long ago.

### Early Days (1950s-1980s): Laying the Foundation

The adoption of AI in marketing began in the mid-20th century, coinciding with the birth of AI itself. Pioneers in computer science laid the groundwork for concepts like machine learning, but the practical applications in advertising were limited due to constraints in computing power and data availability. Early forays into AI-powered marketing primarily involved rule-based systems for targeting consumers. These systems, though simple, could automate basic tasks like direct mail targeting (Govender, 2023). For instance, a company could program a system to send specific catalogs to customers based on their past purchase history, such as a rudimentary personalization form.

### Rise of Data and Machine Learning (1990s-2000s): The Internet Revolution

The advent of the internet in the 1990s ushered in a new era for advertising and marketing. The explosion of online data created unprecedented opportunities for targeted advertising and personalized messaging. Basic algorithms began to be employed for tasks like ad placement and keyword targeting. As computing power grew and machine learning algorithms matured, marketers harnessed these technologies for more sophisticated applications. Predictive modeling allows marketers to anticipate customer behavior and assess campaign effectiveness, while personalization algorithms customize advertisements and offers based on user's online activities and preferences (Kotras, 2020). This era also saw the rise of search engine optimization (SEO), where algorithms played a critical role in determining the visibility of websites in search results.

## AI-Powered Marketing (2010s-Present): The Age of Hyper-Personalization

The convergence of big data and deep learning algorithms in the 2010s propelled AI in marketing to new heights. Programmatic advertising emerged, automating ad buying and placement in real-time. Natural Language Processing (NLP) enabled the development of chatbots, sentiment analysis tools, and AI-powered content generation. Computer vision algorithms began analyzing images and videos to develop insights into consumer behavior and preferences (Nanne et al., 2020). AI is now employed to create hyper-personalized customer experiences across various touchpoints, such as email marketing and social media interactions. Nevertheless, this rapid evolution has raised ethical issues, particularly around data privacy, algorithmic bias, and transparency.

The evolution of artificial intelligence in advertising and marketing has shown impressive progress, moving from basic rule-driven systems to sophisticated algorithms that shape today's marketing landscape. As AI advances, it will significantly change how brands connect with consumers, enabling unprecedented personalization and engagement. Nevertheless, managing this evolution with care is essential, prioritizing ethical considerations in developing and using AI in the marketing industry.

# AI-POWERED PERSONALIZATION

The digital age has ushered in an era of unparalleled data collection, providing businesses with a wealth of information about consumer behavior. AI has emerged as a powerful tool to leverage this data, enabling highly personalized advertising and marketing experiences. By analyzing extensive consumer data, AI algorithms can forecast personal preferences, interests, and needs, enabling marketers to provide customized content with exceptional accuracy.

One of the essential ways AI enables personalized advertising is through predictive analytics. AI algorithms can analyze past consumer behavior, such as purchase history, website browsing activity, and social media interactions, to predict future actions and preferences (Jannach et al., 2018). This allows marketers to anticipate what products or services a consumer might be interested in and deliver targeted advertisements accordingly. For example, suppose a consumer frequently purchases running shoes online and follows fitness influencers on social media. In that case, AI algorithms can infer an interest in fitness and display ads for related products, such as sportswear, fitness trackers, or gym memberships.

Additionally, AI enables the development of dynamic content that adjusts in real time according to user interactions. This means that the content a consumer sees can change based on their current behavior and engagement (Hollebeek and Macky, 2019). For instance, if a consumer lingers on a particular product page, AI algorithms can trigger a pop-up ad offering a discount or free shipping to incentivize a purchase. This dynamic adaptation of content ensures that consumers are consistently exposed to the most relevant and engaging information, increasing the likelihood of conversion.

AI also plays a crucial role in customer segmentation, dividing consumers into distinct groups based on shared characteristics and behaviors (Wedel and Kamakura, 2000). This allows marketers to tailor their messaging and offers to specific audience segments, increasing the effectiveness of their campaigns. For example, a clothing retailer might use AI to segment customers based on their preferred styles, sizes, and price points, enabling them to deliver personalized recommendations and promotions.

The benefits of AI-powered personalization extend beyond targeted advertising. It also enhances the overall customer experience by providing relevant product recommendations, personalized search results, and customized website experiences (Tam and Ho, 2005). By anticipating customer needs and preferences, AI helps businesses create a seamless and satisfying shopping journey.

However, the rise of AI in targeted advertising also raises ethical concerns. Issues such as algorithmic bias, data privacy, and the potential for manipulation require careful consideration (Zuiderveen Borgesius, 2018). Businesses must use AI responsibly and transparently, ensuring that consumer data is handled ethically, privacy is paramount, and personalization efforts do not infringe on individual autonomy.

## The Double-Edged Sword of Personalization: Navigating Data Privacy and Ethical Considerations in the Age of AI

One of the principal concerns pertains to the potential for infringements on privacy. AI-driven personalization relies on collecting and analyzing vast quantities of personal data, including browsing history, purchase records, social media activity, and even location data. If mishandled or misused, this data can expose individuals to privacy risks such as identity theft, discrimination, and manipulation. Zuboff (2019) argues that the pervasive surveillance enabled by data-driven technologies creates a "surveillance capitalism" in which individuals are reduced to mere data points, their privacy eroded for tech companies' profit.

Furthermore, the lack of transparency and control over how personal data is used in AI systems exacerbates privacy concerns. Consumers are often unaware of the extent of data collection and the intricate workings of AI algorithms. This opacity can lead to powerlessness and distrust, as individuals feel they have little control over their data. Solove (2006) highlights the importance of "digital personhood" and the need for individuals to have agency over their personal information in the digital realm.

Another challenge is the potential for bias and discrimination. AI algorithms are trained on historical data, often reflecting societal biases. If not carefully addressed, AI systems can amplify and perpetuate these biases, leading to discriminatory outcomes in advertising and marketing campaigns. For instance, an algorithm trained on data that reflects gender stereotypes in certain professions may inadvertently target job advertisements for those professions based on gender, perpetuating existing inequalities. O'Neil (2017) warns of the dangers of "Weapons of Math Destruction," algorithms that embed and amplify human biases, leading to unfair and discriminatory outcomes.

To navigate these challenges, a multifaceted approach is required. Firstly, robust data privacy regulations are essential. Frameworks such as Europe's General Data Protection Regulation (GDPR) provide a foundation for protecting individual privacy rights. These regulations should be strengthened and adapted to the evolving AI landscape, ensuring transparency, accountability, and user control over personal data.

Secondly, ethical considerations must be embedded in the design and development of AI systems. This includes promoting fairness, transparency, and accountability in algorithmic decision-making. Techniques like differential privacy and federated learning can help mitigate privacy risks while enabling personalized experiences.

Finally, consumer education and awareness are crucial. Individuals must be informed about how their data is used and empowered to make informed choices about their privacy. This includes promoting digital literacy and encouraging critical thinking about the ethical implications of AI-driven personalization. By implementing robust regulations, promoting ethical AI development, and empowering consumers, we can harness the benefits of AI while mitigating the risks.

## PREDICTIVE ANALYTICS AND CUSTOMER INSIGHTS

Predicting consumer behavior has historically been a critical goal for marketers. Traditional methods of uncovering insights, such as surveys and focus groups, offer glimpses into consumer preferences, but they are often reactive and limited in scope. However, the advent of AI has revolutionized this landscape, offering powerful tools to predict future actions with increasing accuracy.

At the heart of this revolution lies AI's capacity to analyze vast quantities of data with unprecedented speed and precision. Machine learning algorithms, a subset of AI, excel at identifying patterns and trends within these datasets that would be impossible for humans to detect. To create comprehensive consumer profiles, these algorithms can sift through diverse data sources, including purchase history, online browsing activity, social media interactions, and demographic data.

One of AI's critical strengths in predictive analytics is its ability to uncover non-linear relationships and complex interactions within data. Traditional statistical methods often assume linear relationships, which may not accurately reflect the nuances of consumer behavior. Machine learning algorithms, in contrast, can identify subtle patterns and correlations, leading to more precise predictions. For instance, a study by Liu et al. (2020) demonstrated that a deep learning model outperformed traditional regression models in predicting customer churn by considering complex interactions between customer attributes and behaviors.

Furthermore, AI algorithms can adapt and learn over time. The algorithms refine their models as new data becomes available, leading to increasingly accurate predictions. This dynamic learning capability is crucial in the ever-evolving landscape of consumer behavior, where trends and preferences shift rapidly. A study by Kumar et al. (2019) showed that AI-powered recommendation systems that continuously learn from user interactions can significantly improve their accuracy in predicting future product preferences.

Predictive analytics, a vital area of advanced analytics, utilizes historical data, statistical methods, and machine learning to forecast future results. This proactive strategy has taken root in marketing and advertising, transforming how companies comprehend, target, and connect with their customers. By employing the power of prediction, marketers can optimize campaigns, personalize customer experiences, and drive revenue growth.

However, implementing predictive analytics in marketing is not without its challenges. Ethical considerations, data privacy, and the potential for algorithmic bias must be carefully addressed to ensure this technology's responsible and equitable use. Marketers must prioritize transparency and accountability in their data collection and analysis practices, ensuring that predictive models enhance customer experiences, not exploit them.

By harnessing the power of prediction, marketers can gain a deeper understanding of customer behavior, optimize campaign performance, and deliver personalized experiences that drive business growth. At the same time, it is crucial to approach this technology with a responsible and ethical mindset, ensuring that data privacy and algorithmic equality are prioritized. As predictive analytics continues to evolve, it promises to revolutionize the marketing landscape further, enabling businesses to connect with their customers in more meaningful, impactful, and hopefully equitable ways.

## The Imperative of Data Accuracy and Continuous Refinement in AI Models

The growth of AI models, particularly machine learning algorithms, is increasingly employed to personalize customer experiences, optimize campaigns, and automate tasks. The effectiveness of these models hinges critically on the accuracy of the data they are trained on and the ongoing refinement of their algorithms. This section explores the challenges associated with data accuracy in AI and emphasizes the necessity of continuous model refinement for optimal performance.

Data accuracy poses a significant challenge in AI applications. Inaccurate, incomplete, or biased data can lead to flawed models that produce unreliable or discriminatory results. This is particularly concerning in advertising and marketing, where AI targets specific demographics and personalizes content (Akter et al., 2022).

Several factors contribute to data inaccuracy:

- The process of data collection itself can introduce errors. This can be due to faulty instruments, human error in data entry, or incomplete data capture.
- Data preprocessing involves cleaning, transforming, and preparing raw data for model training. Errors in this stage, such as incorrect data normalization or feature scaling, can propagate through the model and affect its accuracy.
- Data bias occurs when the data used to train an AI model reflects existing societal biases. This can lead to models perpetuating and amplifying these biases, resulting in unfair or discriminatory outcomes. For instance, a model trained on historical data that reflects gender bias in hiring may inadvertently discriminate against female candidates.

Even with accurate and unbiased data, AI models require continuous refinement to maintain optimal performance. This is because the real-world environment is dynamic and constantly evolving. Concept drift reflects the relationship between input data and output variables, which changes over time. This can be due to shifts in consumer behavior, market trends, or the emergence of new technologies. For example, a model developed to predict customer preferences based on pre-pandemic data may become less accurate as consumer behavior evolves in the post-pandemic world.

Model degradation is when a machine learning model's performance worsens over time. This happens because the real-world data the model encounters after deployment can differ significantly from the data it was trained on. Over time, AI models' performance can degrade due to data drift, model complexity, and the accumulation of minor errors. Regular monitoring and retraining are essential to prevent performance degradation and maintain model accuracy and relevance.

Addressing data accuracy challenges and ensuring continuous model refinement requires a multi-faceted approach. Implementing robust data quality assurance processes is crucial for ensuring the accuracy and completeness of data. This includes data validation, data cleansing, and data auditing. Identifying and mitigating bias in data is essential for building fair and equitable AI models. This can involve data augmentation, re-sampling, and algorithmic fairness constraints. Monitoring model performance is necessary to detect and address issues such as concept drift and model degradation. Regular retraining of models with updated data is crucial for maintaining accuracy and relevance. Lastly, incorporating human oversight in the AI lifecycle can help ensure data accuracy, identify potential biases, and validate model outputs.

Data accuracy and continuous model refinement are critical for the successful implementation of AI in advertising and marketing. Model degradation is often an inevitable part of the AI lifecycle. By understanding its causes and applying appropriate mitigation strategies, organizations can ensure that their AI systems remain accurate, reliable, and trustworthy.

## AI-ENHANCED CONTENT CREATION

Artificial intelligence is rapidly transforming the marketing content landscape, automating tasks previously thought to be the exclusive domain of human creativity. This section provides an overview of AI's role in generating and optimizing marketing content, focusing on its applications in copywriting, image generation, and video editing.

AI-powered copywriting tools leverage natural language processing (NLP) and machine learning (ML) algorithms to generate various forms of marketing copy, including website content, social media posts, email newsletters, and product descriptions. These tools can analyze vast amounts of data to identify patterns and trends in language use, enabling them to produce human-quality copy tailored to specific target audiences and optimized for search engines.

For instance, Jasper.ai and Copy.ai are popular platforms that offer AI-powered copywriting tools. These platforms can generate different creative text formats, translate languages, and answer questions in a relevant manner, even if they are open-ended, challenging, or strange (Jasper.ai, 2024). A study by Huang and Rust (2018) found that AI-generated content can be as effective as human-generated content in driving customer engagement, particularly in tasks such as writing product descriptions and social media posts.

AI is also used to generate visually compelling marketing images. Generative adversarial networks (GANs) and diffusion models can create realistic pictures from textual descriptions, enabling marketers to quickly and easily generate campaign visuals. This technology is beneficial for creating product mockups, social media graphics, and website banners.

DALL-E 2, developed by OpenAI, is a prominent example of an AI image generator. It can create realistic and creative images from a user-provided text description, offering a powerful tool for marketers to visualize their ideas (OpenAI, 2024). Furthermore, platforms like Midjourney allow users to generate images based on specific artistic styles or desired moods, further expanding the creative possibilities.

AI streamlines video editing by automating time-consuming tasks such as video transcription, scene detection, and object tracking. AI-powered video editing tools can also analyze video content to identify critical moments and suggest optimal cuts, transitions, and music. This technology enables marketers to create engaging video content for platforms like YouTube, Instagram, and TikTok.

Runway ML is an example of an AI-powered video editing platform that offers tools for style transfer, image synthesis, and motion tracking (Runway ML, 2024). These tools significantly reduce the time and effort required to produce high-quality video content. Research by Anantrasirichai and Bull (2022) indicates that AI can substantially improve the efficiency and effectiveness of video editing, allowing marketers to produce more engaging content with fewer resources.

AI is revolutionizing the way marketers create and optimize content. By automating tedious tasks and providing contextual suggestions, AI tools enable marketers to focus on strategic planning and creative ideation. As AI technology evolves, we can expect even more innovative applications to emerge, further blurring the lines between human and machine creativity in marketing and advertising.

## AI's Impact on Creativity in Advertising

AI's influence on advertising creativity has sparked both excitement and concern. AI technologies, particularly in content generation, data analysis, and personalization, are increasingly integrated into creative processes that once relied solely on human intuition and imagination. By automating repetitive and data-driven tasks, AI has freed up time for creative professionals to focus on higher-order thinking, such as developing novel concepts and storytelling. However, the integration of AI also raises critical questions about the future of creativity, originality, and the human role in advertising.

## Automation of Creative Tasks

AI-powered tools have revolutionized the way advertisements are created and distributed. Algorithms can now generate personalized content for different audience segments, offering tailored messaging that resonates with individual consumers based on their preferences, browsing behavior, and demographics. For instance, AI-driven platforms like Persado and Phrasee use natural language processing (NLP) to optimize ad copy, testing thousands of variations to determine which phrases will yield the highest engagement (Khurana et al., 2023). These tools provide valuable insights into consumer psychology and preferences, enabling advertisers to craft more compelling and relevant content.

Moreover, AI can automatically generate visual content, such as banners, images, and videos. Tools like Adobe Sensei leverage machine learning to assist with design tasks, from color adjustments to layout suggestions. Such platforms analyze previous successful designs and consumer interactions, recommending design elements that are statistically more likely to succeed. This level of automation, while efficient, raises questions about the uniqueness of AI-generated content. There is a growing concern that over-reliance on AI could lead to a homogenization of ads, where content, although optimized for performance, becomes formulaic and devoid of creative innovation.

## AI-Driven Personalization vs. Creativity

One of AI's most significant contributions to advertising is its ability to hyper-personalize content. AI analyzes vast amounts of consumer data to craft advertisements that appeal to specific individuals down to their most nuanced preferences. This ability to tailor messages to an audience at scale has increased brand engagement and return on investment (ROI). For example, Netflix and Amazon employ AI algorithms to recommend shows or products based on user data, effectively acting as personalized advertisements (Rafieian and Yoganarasimhan, 2023).

However, this level of personalization also poses challenges to creativity. The creative process, traditionally, has involved a degree of risk-taking and pushing the boundaries of conventional norms. AI, conversely, bases its decisions on patterns and historical data, which could lead to "safe" choices that are less likely to push creative boundaries. In other words, while AI may help refine and optimize content for specific audiences, it may also stifle the kind of imaginative leaps that drive truly innovative advertising.

## The Role of AI in Creative Collaboration

Rather than replacing human creativity, AI is increasingly seen as a collaborator in the creative process. AI tools can assist human creatives by generating initial ideas or suggesting alternatives based on data analysis. This allows creative professionals to focus on higher-level tasks, such as storytelling and emotional resonance. This "human-AI collaboration" is already evident in campaigns like Coca-Cola's "Taste the Feeling," where AI analyzed data to suggest which emotions and images most likely engage consumers. Still, human designers and copywriters shaped the final creative direction (Springer, 2024).

This collaborative approach highlights AI's potential to act as a creative assistant rather than a replacement. AI can quickly generate and test multiple creative iterations, allowing humans to experiment with a broader range of concepts than would be possible without technological assistance. In this sense, AI enhances creativity by providing more data-driven insights and alternatives, expanding the toolkit available to human advertisers.

## Risks of Commoditizing Creativity

Despite AI's potential to enhance creative processes, there is a risk that it could commoditize creativity. When AI tools are used to generate large volumes of content quickly and efficiently, the uniqueness and originality of creative work may be diluted. This commoditization could lead to a proliferation of generic ads that rely heavily on past performance data, resulting in advertising that feels formulaic and lacks emotional depth.

The tension between AI's efficiency and the need for emotionally resonant, original content is a significant issue for advertisers. While AI-generated content may improve metrics such as click-through rates (CTRs) or conversions, it may not evoke the same emotional engagement or brand loyalty as ads deeply rooted in human experiences and emotions. As such, advertisers must balance leveraging AI for optimization and ensuring creativity remains at the heart of their campaigns.

# FUTURE DIRECTIONS FOR AI AND CREATIVITY

As AI continues to evolve, its role in advertising creativity will likely become even more sophisticated. Emerging technologies, such as generative adversarial networks (GANs), have the potential to create highly original and realistic content, from hyper-realistic visuals to emotionally nuanced text (Goodfellow et al., 2014). These advancements could further blur the line between human and machine-generated creativity, raising questions about authorship, intellectual property, and the future of creative work in advertising.

Ultimately, the critical challenge for advertisers will be using AI to enhance — not replace — human creativity. Advertisers should focus on how AI can be harnessed to generate new ideas, refine creative concepts, and deliver personalized experiences while ensuring that the emotional and narrative aspects of advertising remain driven by human insight. This approach will allow advertisers to stay competitive in an AI-driven world without losing the core elements of creativity that make their brands unique.

## Case Studies of AI in Creative Campaigns

The application of AI in advertising campaigns has yielded both highly successful results and notable challenges. Analyzing real-world case studies, we can better understand how AI has effectively enhanced creativity and where it has fallen short. Four case studies highlight AI's potential and limitations in advertising, shedding light on the complexities of blending technology with creative processes.

1. Nike's AI-Powered "Nike By You" Campaign

   Overview:

Nike's "Nike By You" campaign is a prime example of AI being used to elevate personalization in advertising. Launched in 2020, the campaign allowed consumers to design their sneakers through an AI-powered interface (Lindecrantz et al., 2020). The system utilized machine learning algorithms to recommend design choices based on users' past interactions, preferences, and trending styles.

AI Integration:

The AI behind the campaign analyzed user data to suggest color combinations, styles, and other design elements likely to resonate with individual customers. It also monitored global fashion trends in real time, ensuring user suggestions were personalized and aligned with the latest design aesthetics. Moreover, the system allowed users to explore limitless combinations while maintaining brand cohesion by subtly guiding the design process.

Success Factors:

- Personalization: The campaign successfully tapped the demand for personalized products, enhancing customer engagement and brand loyalty.

AI's ability to offer tailored recommendations resulted in increased customer satisfaction.

- Creativity enhancement: Instead of stifling creativity, AI empowered users to express their creativity by offering suggestions and ideas they might not have considered. This blend of user input and AI support resulted in unique designs for each customer.
- Sales impact: The "Nike By You" campaign generated significant consumer interest, boosting sales and positive brand engagement. Nike reported a noticeable increase in conversions as customers responded well to the individualized product offerings.

Observations:

The effectiveness of this campaign highlights how AI can enhance creativity by serving as a tool for user empowerment. AI can drive customer satisfaction and business success when designed to augment rather than dictate creative choices.

2. Lexus' AI-Written Commercial

Overview:

Lexus collaborated with IBM Watson in 2018 to create the first AI-generated advertisement for its ES model. The ad was designed to highlight the car's advanced safety features and was written entirely by AI, using a dataset of award-winning commercials to inform its creative decisions (Snee and Smulowitz, 2021).

AI Integration:

IBM Watson's AI analyzed 15 years of automotive and luxury brand advertisements, focusing on those that had won prestigious creative awards. The system identified common patterns, themes, and emotional triggers in successful ads. It then synthesized these insights into a script, which human directors brought to life.

Success Factors:

- Data-driven creativity: The AI-generated script captured key emotional elements that resonated with viewers, such as safety, family, and the importance of human connection, aligning with the core values of the Lexus brand.
- Publicity: The novelty of an AI-written ad generated significant media attention and public interest, further amplifying the campaign's reach. The campaign was lauded for showcasing the potential of AI in

the creative process, even in the highly subjective realm of emotional storytelling.

Observations:

This case demonstrated that AI can successfully contribute to creative content combined with human oversight. The AI-generated script provided a foundation, but the final product benefited from human execution in directing, acting, and emotional nuance.

3. Burger King's AI-Generated Slogans

Overview:

In 2018, Burger King experimented with AI-generated slogans in a humorous campaign, allowing AI to "write" marketing slogans for their products (Sherman, 2018). The experiment was intended to be comedic, but it resulted in widespread confusion.

AI Integration:

The AI system was trained on existing fast-food slogans, brand messages, and product descriptions. However, instead of producing applicable advertising copy, the AI-generated a series of nonsensical and bizarre slogans, such as "The Whopper lives in a bun mansion" and "It is like a sandwich, but in no way."

Challenges:

- Lack of coherence: The slogans generated by the AI were nonsensical and did not communicate the intended brand message. While the campaign was meant to be humorous, many viewers were confused and did not understand the point of the experiment.
- Missed connection: The campaign did not resonate with consumers, as the AI-generated content lacked clarity and failed to communicate any meaningful or persuasive message about the products.
- Marketing misstep: Although Burger King framed the campaign as a humorous exploration of AI's creative potential, it ultimately failed to contribute positively to brand perception. The campaign was seen as a gimmick rather than an effective use of AI in marketing.

Observations:

This case underscores AI's limitations in generating creative content that resonates with audiences. While AI is influential in data-driven optimization, it still struggles with tasks that require originality, coherence, and a deep understanding of human humor or emotion. Creative campaigns that rely too heavily on AI without sufficient human oversight may backfire.

4. Apple iPad AI-Themed Crush Campaign

Overview:

While visually striking, Apple's recent iPad advertisement has been met with widespread criticism and can be considered a misstep in effectively communicating the product's value proposition. The ad depicts a hydraulic press crushing various objects representing traditional creative tools, such as musical instruments and art supplies, culminating in the reveal of the new iPad Pro. This imagery, set against the ironically nostalgic soundtrack of Sonny and Cher's "All I Ever Need Is You," has sparked outrage among artists and creatives who interpret the ad as a symbolic annihilation of human artistry by technology (Smith, 2024; di Placido, 2024).

AI Integration:

While the "iPad Crush" advertisement does not employ AI in its visual execution, it plays a pivotal role in the broader campaign strategy. The primary reason for the ad's failure lies in its misinterpretation. While Apple likely intended to showcase the iPad's versatility and power as a comprehensive creative tool, the execution inadvertently conveyed a message of technological dominance over human expression.

Challenges:

- Ambiguous symbolism: The act of crushing creative tools can be seen as dismissive of the effort and skill involved in traditional art forms rather than celebrating the iPad's potential to augment them.
- Lack of context: The ad fails to demonstrate how the iPad empowers creativity. It focuses on destroying traditional tools without effectively showcasing the iPad's creative capabilities.
- Tone-deafness to current anxieties: The ad comes at a time when concerns about the impact of AI on creative fields are heightened, with ongoing strikes by Hollywood writers and actors partly motivated by the perceived threat of AI-generated content.

Observations:

In essence, while aiming to highlight the iPad's creative potential, Apple's ad instead triggered anxieties about the role of technology in art and inadvertently alienated a key segment of its target audience. This is a cautionary tale for brands seeking to leverage AI in their advertising, emphasizing the importance of nuanced messaging, clear communication, and sensitivity to broader cultural conversations.

## CONCLUSION

The use of AI in advertising campaigns has produced remarkable successes and high-profile failures. Successful applications, such as Nike's 'Nike By You' campaign and Lexus's AI-written commercial, demonstrate how AI can enhance creativity, personalization, and audience engagement when used strategically. These cases show that AI can be a powerful tool to augment human creativity, offering data-driven insights and supporting the creative process. The potential benefits of AI in advertising, such as increased efficiency and personalized experiences, should not be overlooked.

However, campaigns like Burger King's AI-powered slogan experiment reveal AI's limitations in handling tasks that require emotional intelligence, nuance, and authenticity. These cases emphasize the importance of balancing automation and human oversight in creative processes. Moreover, they raise ethical concerns about using AI in advertising, particularly regarding transparency and consumer trust.

Ultimately, AI has the potential to revolutionize advertising creativity, but it must be deployed with care, ensuring that human judgment and creativity remain at the forefront of campaign development. This reassures the audience about the irreplaceable role of human creativity in the industry.

## The Rise of Synthetic Media in Advertising

The advent of synthetic media encompasses a spectrum of media formats, including AI-generated images, videos, voices, and even virtual avatars. The growing adoption of synthetic media in advertising presents a compelling paradox, offering unprecedented creative opportunities and raising significant ethical concerns. This section will delve into the development and growing use of synthetic media in advertising, examining its impact, benefits, and potential drawbacks.

The roots of synthetic media can be traced back to the early development of computer graphics and AI research. However, recent breakthroughs in deep learning, particularly in generative adversarial networks (GANs) and natural language processing (NLP), have propelled the capabilities of synthetic media generation to new heights. GANs, for instance, enable the creation of highly realistic images, videos, and voices by having two neural networks compete in the learning process (Goodfellow et al., 2014).

The advertising industry has been quick to recognize synthetic media's potential. Its applications range from creating virtual influencers and generating personalized advertising content to producing cost-effective and time-efficient marketing campaigns. For example, brands like KFC and Lil Miquela have leveraged AI-generated virtual avatars to engage with audiences in novel ways (Sorosrungruang et al., 2024). Synthetic media also allows for the creation of hyper-realistic product demonstrations and interactive experiences, blurring the lines between the physical and digital worlds.

Synthetic content and deepfakes allow brands to create dynamic, engaging, personalized content. For instance, Kietzmann et al. (2021) highlight how deepfakes can reshape the way ads are made but also note potential risks related to consumer trust and deception. In this direction, there is growing concern about the impact of deepfakes on consumer trust. Sivathanu et al. (2023) demonstrate how AI-based deepfake ads can influence online shopping intentions and warn of potential damage to brand credibility if consumers feel misled.

The impact of synthetic media on advertising is multifaceted. On the one hand, it offers numerous benefits. It can substantially reduce the cost and time associated with traditional media production, allowing advertisers to create more content with fewer resources. Moreover, synthetic media enables personalized advertising experiences tailored to individual consumer preferences, potentially leading to higher engagement and conversion rates. The ability to create virtual influencers and brand ambassadors who are perpetually youthful and controversy-free also presents an alluring prospect for marketers, exciting the audience about the possibilities of synthetic media.

However, the rise of synthetic media also raises significant concerns. The potential for misuse, particularly in creating deepfakes and spreading misinformation, poses a severe threat (Chesney and Citron, 2019). The ethical implications of using AI-generated virtual beings to influence consumer behavior are also a subject of ongoing debate. Additionally, there are concerns about job displacement within the creative industry as AI-powered tools become more sophisticated.

Synthetic media rapidly reshapes the advertising landscape, offering unprecedented opportunities and challenges. While its potential benefits are undeniable, proactively addressing the ethical and societal implications is crucial. Achieving a balance between innovation and responsible use will be essential to harnessing synthetic media's full potential in advertising while mitigating its risks.

## Development of Deepfakes

The term "deepfake" originated in 2017 and is derived from the underlying technology, deep learning. A subset of machine learning, deep learning algorithms enable the creation of highly realistic and convincing fake videos, images, and audio recordings. These algorithms learn patterns and features from vast datasets of natural media, allowing them to generate synthetic content virtually indistinguishable from authentic material.

Deepfakes can create highly realistic but insincere representations, potentially deceiving consumers. The hyper-realism of deepfakes can blur the line between reality and fiction in ads, leading to ethical concerns about manipulation (Kietzmann et al., 2021). A primary concern for advertisers is the subsequent erosion of trust between brands and consumers. Campbell et al. (2022) explore how brands may lose credibility if the public sees deepfake technology as deceptive or unethical. For content creators, deepfake technology often involves manipulating personal likenesses without consent. Kalpokas and Kalpokiene (2022) note that deepfakes can easily enable unauthorized use of celebrity identities in marketing without their approval, which infringes on privacy rights.

Early deepfake techniques relied on methods like autoencoders and generative adversarial networks (GANs). Autoencoders are neural networks trained to reconstruct input data, while GANs consist of two networks, a generator and a discriminator, that compete against each other to create realistic synthetic content. Recent advancements have introduced more sophisticated techniques, such as StyleGAN2 and DeepFaceLab, which further enhance the quality and realism of deepfakes.

The advertising industry has quickly recognized the potential of deepfakes to create innovative and engaging campaigns. Deepfakes offer several advantages over traditional advertising methods, including:

- Cost-effectiveness: Deepfakes can reduce the need for expensive photoshoots, celebrity endorsements, and location shoots.
- Personalization: Deepfakes enable personalized advertising experiences, tailoring content to individual viewers' preferences and demographics.
- Creativity: Deepfakes unlock new creative possibilities, allowing advertisers to resurrect historical figures, de-age actors, and create fantastical scenarios.

With rapid developments in synthetic content creation, ethical advertising practices require transparency about deepfakes. Studies identify the importance of disclosing deepfakes in ads to maintain ethical integrity and avoid manipulation (Karpinska-Krakowiak and Eisend, 2024). The legal implications of synthetic content and deepfakes are a significant concern. Van der Sloot and Wagensveld

(2022) discuss the challenges of regulating deepfakes, especially in advertising, where the line between entertainment and deception can be blurry. The absence of clear regulations surrounding deepfake use in advertising creates a gray area in accountability, emphasizing the need for policies that address deepfake misuse in media and advertising (Van der Sloot and Wagensveld, 2022).

The rise of deepfakes in advertising has sparked considerable debate, citing both benefits and concerns. On the one hand, deepfakes can capture viewers' attention and create memorable experiences, increasing engagement with advertising content. Advertisers can use deepfakes to tell more compelling and immersive stories, forging deeper connections with audiences. Deepfakes can also make advertising more accessible to diverse audiences, efficiently transcending language and cultural barriers.

However, a variety of concerns also arise. Deepfakes that spread false information and manipulate public opinion can result in misinformation and manipulation, threatening trust and credibility. Using deepfakes raises ethical concerns regarding consent, privacy, and potential harm. Lastly, the automation potential of deepfakes may lead to job displacement in the advertising industry, particularly for actors and voiceover artists.

Deepfakes have emerged as a transformative force in the advertising industry, offering exciting possibilities for creativity and innovation. However, their use also raises significant ethical and societal concerns. As deepfake technology evolves, advertisers, policymakers, and the public must engage in thoughtful dialogue and establish guidelines to ensure the responsible and ethical use of deepfakes in advertising.

## Ethical and Societal Implications

AI systems, particularly those used in advertising, learn from vast datasets of existing information. If these datasets reflect societal biases, the AI models can inadvertently perpetuate and even amplify these biases in their output. This can lead to discriminatory advertising practices, such as targeting certain products or services to specific demographic groups based on stereotypes or excluding certain groups altogether (Gao et al., 2023).

For instance, a study by Lambrecht and Tucker (2019) found that online advertising algorithms were more likely to display ads for high-paying jobs to men than women, perpetuating gender bias in the workplace. This bias can be subtle and difficult to detect, yet it can have significant consequences for individuals and society.

Synthetic media, including deepfakes, pose a significant ethical challenge in advertising. Deepfakes are incredibly realistic AI-generated videos or audio recordings that can make people appear to say or do things they never did. While they have the potential for creative applications, they can also be used to deceive and manipulate audiences. Imagine a deepfake of a celebrity endorsing a product they never actually used or a political candidate making false statements in a doctored video. This can erode trust in advertising and media, making it difficult for consumers to distinguish between real and fabricated.

Advertisements that rely on deepfake technology should ensure transparency about using synthetic voices or images. Without clear disclosure, consumers are left unaware that their content is artificially generated, leading to ethical concerns about dishonesty and the erosion of authenticity in media. In this context, companies and advertisers have an ethical responsibility to prevent the misuse of AI technologies that could perpetuate false narratives or harm individuals. Organizations must create robust guidelines and policies for the ethical deployment of deepfake technology (Floridi et al., 2018). Proactively adopting ethical standards can harness deepfake technology responsibly, avoiding potential social backlash or regulatory challenges while enhancing consumer engagement.

Beyond bias and deepfakes, the increasing use of AI in advertising raises broader societal concerns. As AI algorithms become more sophisticated, they can personalize ads to an unprecedented degree, potentially leading to filter bubbles and echo chambers where individuals are exposed only to information that confirms their existing beliefs. This can further polarize society and hinder informed decision-making.

Moreover, the pervasive use of AI in advertising can contribute to a culture of materialistic consumerism. By constantly bombarding individuals with targeted ads, AI algorithms can manipulate their desires and create artificial needs, leading to overconsumption and environmental damage.

Overall, the use of AI in advertising presents a complex ethical landscape. While AI offers exciting possibilities for creativity and efficiency, it also carries the potential for bias, manipulation, and societal harm. Advertisers, policymakers, and consumers must be aware of these ethical considerations and work together to ensure that AI is used responsibly and ethically in the advertising industry. The rapid integration of AI into advertising practices necessitates critically examining the ethical implications and a robust framework for responsible development and deployment. Transparency, accountability, and ethical considerations must be paramount to diminish potential risks and ensure AI serves the best interests of consumers and society.

Transparency in AI advertising mandates that consumers be fully informed when interacting with AI-driven systems and understand how these systems influence their choices. This includes disclosing the use of AI in generating content, targeting advertisements, and personalizing user experiences (Kumar and Suthar, 2024). As Selbst and Powles (2018) state, “meaningful transparency” requires not only disclosing the presence of AI but also providing understandable explanations of how AI systems function and impact consumers. This enables individuals to make informed decisions and fosters trust between consumers and advertisers.

Accountability is essential in ensuring that AI systems are used responsibly and ethically. This requires establishing clear lines of responsibility for the outcomes of AI-driven advertising. When AI systems produce harmful or discriminatory outcomes, mechanisms must be established to identify the responsible parties and hold them accountable. This can involve developing robust auditing and monitoring systems and establishing clear ethical guidelines for AI development and deployment in advertising.

Responsible AI development in advertising entails a commitment to ethical considerations throughout the entire lifecycle of AI systems. This includes ensuring that AI models are trained on diverse and unbiased datasets to prevent perpetuating stereotypes and discriminatory practices. It also involves designing AI systems that respect user privacy and autonomy, avoiding manipulative techniques that exploit cognitive biases or vulnerabilities.

Furthermore, responsible AI development requires ongoing monitoring and evaluation to mitigate unintended consequences. This includes engaging in open dialogue with key stakeholders, including consumers, researchers, and policymakers, to ensure that AI in advertising aligns with societal values and expectations.

Thus, the ethical challenges posed by AI in advertising demand a comprehensive approach that prioritizes transparency, accountability, and responsible development. By embracing these principles, we can harness AI's potential to enhance the advertising landscape while safeguarding consumers' interests and promoting a more equitable and trustworthy digital environment.

## The Societal Implications of AI in Advertising

While the AI transformation promises increased efficiency and personalization, it also carries significant societal implications that warrant careful consideration. The industry should focus on three critical areas of concern: job displacement, perceived credibility, and the exacerbation of the digital divide.

AI's ability to automate tasks previously performed by humans raises concerns about job displacement within the advertising sector. Algorithms can generate creative content, target specific demographics, and optimize ad spending with minimal human intervention. This automation threatens roles traditionally held by copywriters, media buyers, and even creative directors. A 2020 report by McKinsey Global Institute estimated that AI could automate up to 45% of tasks currently performed by marketing and sales professionals (Chui et al., 2020). While some argue that AI will create new jobs requiring different skill sets, the transition may be challenging for those displaced, leading to potential unemployment and economic disruption.

The rise of AI-generated content and personalized advertising can blur the lines between authentic communication and manipulation, impacting the perceived credibility of advertising messages. Consumers may find it difficult to distinguish between genuine recommendations and AI-powered nudges, eroding trust in brands and the advertising ecosystem. Furthermore, the use of deepfakes and synthetic media raises ethical concerns about deception and the potential for misuse. A study by Newman and Schwarz (2023) found that deepfakes can significantly influence people's perceptions and attitudes, highlighting the potential for AI to be used for malicious purposes in advertising.

AI-powered advertising relies heavily on data and digital infrastructure. This dependence can exacerbate the digital divide, further marginalizing communities with limited access to technology or digital literacy skills. While beneficial for those with consistent internet access, personalized advertising can exclude individuals from receiving relevant information or opportunities, reinforcing existing inequalities. This disparity can have far-reaching consequences, impacting access to education, employment, and essential services. Van Laar et al. (2019) argue that digital skills are increasingly crucial for social and economic participation, emphasizing the need to address the digital divide and ensure equitable access to the benefits of AI in advertising.

Given these issues, integrating AI in advertising presents a complex interplay of opportunities and challenges. While it offers the potential for increased efficiency and personalization, it also raises critical concerns. Addressing these societal implications will require proactive measures from policymakers, industry leaders, and educators to ensure a responsible and equitable transition into the age of AI-powered advertising.

## Implications for Future Research

The rapid evolution of AI is poised to revolutionize marketing communications, presenting both exciting opportunities and complex challenges. As AI-powered tools become increasingly sophisticated, they develop the potential to reshape how brands interact with consumers and how consumers make purchasing decisions. To fully understand this transformative technology, it is essential to identify critical areas for future research and explore the long-term impact of AI on consumer behavior and brand relationships.

Overall, the ethical implications of AI in marketing communications should be charted. As AI algorithms become increasingly adept at personalization and targeting, questions arise about the potential for manipulation, bias, and invasion of privacy. The hyper-personalization of tailored marketing messages can lead to more relevant and engaging experiences while raising concerns about filter bubbles and echo chambers. Future research should investigate the ethical boundaries of AI in marketing, examining how to ensure fairness, transparency, and accountability in its application.

AI's impact on consumer trust and brand loyalty is significant, given the rapid growth in technology tools. For example, AI-powered chatbots and virtual assistants are increasingly used to interact with customers. These tools can provide instant and personalized customer support, improving satisfaction and loyalty. Research is needed to understand how these interactions influence consumer trust and brand loyalty. Marketers must ensure these AI-driven interactions are not impersonal or frustrating. Do consumers perceive AI-driven interactions as authentic and valuable, or do they erode trust in the brand?

As an emerging technology, the role of AI in shaping consumer preferences and decision-making should be explored. AI algorithms can analyze vast amounts of data to predict consumer preferences and personalize marketing messages. This anticipatory marketing can create seamless and personalized experiences but raises ethical concerns about manipulation and privacy. Future research should explore how this personalization influences consumer decision-making processes and potentially shapes their preferences over time.

Lastly, the impact of AI on the marketing profession is already evident. As AI automates routine tasks and takes on more complex responsibilities, how will the role of marketing professionals evolve? Research is needed to understand the skills and knowledge required for marketers to thrive in an AI-driven landscape.

AI is poised to revolutionize marketing communications, offering unprecedented personalization, efficiency, and engagement opportunities. However, further research is essential to understanding the ethical implications, long-term impact on consumer behavior, and evolving role of marketing professionals in this AI-driven landscape. By addressing these challenges and harnessing the power of AI responsibly, brands can build stronger relationships with consumers and create a more engaging and personalized customer experience.

## Navigating the Complexities of AI in Advertising

The advent of AI in advertising presents a dynamic landscape fraught with intricate challenges and promising opportunities. Addressing these complexities necessitates a concerted effort from various disciplines, fostering an integrated understanding of this transformative technology's ethical, societal, and technological implications. Tackling these multifaceted challenges requires a collaborative approach that transcends disciplinary boundaries. Computer scientists can contribute their technical expertise to develop AI systems that are transparent, fair, and accountable. Social scientists can provide insights into AI's psychological and sociological impacts on consumer behavior and societal values. Legal scholars can offer guidance on regulatory frameworks to mitigate risks associated with AI in advertising. This interdisciplinary synergy can foster a comprehensive understanding of the complex connections among technology, society, and ethics.

While the AI revolution offers significant potential benefits, adopting AI in advertising and marketing is equally challenging. To minimize risks and ensure the ethical use of AI, businesses must prioritize responsible AI development. This includes robust data privacy procedures and security measures to protect consumer data. It also means ensuring AI algorithms are trained on diverse, unbiased data to avoid discriminatory outcomes. Developing transparent and explainable AI systems is imperative, allowing humans to understand how decisions are made. Maintaining human oversight of AI systems is essential to ensure they are used ethically and responsibly.

The rapid advancements in AI are undeniably transforming the marketing landscape. Businesses that embrace these technologies can gain a significant competitive advantage. This includes improving customer engagement and loyalty, optimizing marketing campaigns and budgets, gaining a deeper understanding of consumer behavior, and developing innovative products and services. AI is a technological advance and a strategic imperative for businesses to embrace in this evolving landscape. By adopting AI responsibly and ethically, businesses can exploit its power to enhance customer experiences, drive growth, and shape the future of marketing.

## REFERENCES


Akter, S., Dwivedi, Y. K., Sajib, S., Biswas, K., Bandara, R. J., & Michael, K. (2022). Algorithmic bias in machine learning-based marketing models. *Journal of Business Research*, 144, 201–216. DOI: 10.1016/j.jbusres.2022.01.083

Anantrasirichai, N., & Bull, D. (2022). Artificial intelligence in the creative industries: A review. *Artificial Intelligence Review*, 55(1), 589–656. DOI: 10.1007/s10462-021-10039-7

Campbell, C., Plangger, K., Sands, S., Kietzmann, J., & Bates, K. (2022). How deepfakes and artificial intelligence could reshape the advertising industry: The coming reality of AI fakes and their potential impact on consumer behavior. *Journal of Advertising Research*, 62(3), 241–251. DOI: 10.2501/JAR-2022-017

Chesney, B., & Citron, D. (2019). Deep fakes: A looming challenge for privacy, democracy, and national security. *California Law Review*, 107, 1753. DOI: 10.15779/Z38RV0D15J

Chui, M., Evers, M., & Zheng, A. (2020). How the bio revolution could transform the competitive landscape. *The McKinsey Quarterly*, 7, •••. https://www.mckinsey.com/~/media/McKinsey/Business%20Functions/McKinsey%20Digital/Our%20Insights/How%20the%20Bio%20Revolution%20could%20transform%20the%20competitive%20landscape/How-the-Bio-Revolution-could-transform-the-competitive-landscape.pdf

di Placido, D. (2024, May 10). Apple's iPad Pro 'crush' controversy. *Forbes*. Retrieved from https://www.forbes.com/sites/danidiplacido/2024/05/09/the-backlash-against-apples-new-ipad-pro-ad-explained/

Floridi, L., Cowls, J., Beltrametti, M., Chatila, R., Chazerand, P., Dignum, V., Luetge, C., Madelin, R., Pagallo, U., Rossi, F., Schafer, B., Valcke, P., & Vayena, E. (2018). AI4People—an ethical framework for a good AI society: Opportunities, risks, principles, and recommendations. *Minds and Machines*, 28(4), 689–707. DOI: 10.1007/s11023-018-9482-5 PMID: 30930541

Gao, B., Wang, Y., Xie, H., Hu, Y., & Hu, Y. (2023). Artificial intelligence in advertising: Advancements, challenges, and ethical considerations in targeting, personalization, content creation, and ad optimization. *SAGE Open*, 13(4), 21582440231210759. Advance online publication. DOI: 10.1177/21582440231210759

Goodfellow, I., Pouget-Abadie, J., Mirza, M., Xu, B., Warde-Farley, D., Ozair, S., Courville, A., & Bengio, Y. (2014). Generative adversarial nets. *Advances in Neural Information Processing Systems, 27.* https://proceedings.neurips.cc/paper_files/paper/2014/file/5ca3e9b122f61f8f06494c97b1afccf3-Paper.pdf

Govender, K. (2023). *Age of Agency: Rise with AI.* CRC Press. DOI: 10.4324/9781032684895

Hollebeek, L. D., & Macky, K. (2019). Digital content marketing's role in fostering consumer engagement, trust, and value: Framework, fundamental propositions, and implications. *Journal of Interactive Marketing*, 45(1), 27–41. DOI: 10.1016/j.intmar.2018.07.003

Huang, M. H., & Rust, R. T. (2018). Artificial intelligence in service. *Journal of Service Research*, 21(2), 155–172. DOI: 10.1177/1094670517752459

Jannach, D., Zanker, M., Felfernig, A., & Friedrich, G. (2018). *Recommender Systems: An Introduction.* Cambridge University Press.

Jasper, A. I. (2024, November 2). *AI content generation for marketing and sales.* Jasper. Retrieved from https://www.jasper.ai/

Kalpokas, I., & Kalpokiene, J. (2022). *Deepfakes: A realistic assessment of potentials, risks, and policy regulation.* Springer Nature. DOI: 10.1007/978-3-030-93802-4

Karpinska-Krakowiak, M., & Eisend, M. (2024). Realistic Portrayals of Untrue Information: The Effects of Deepfaked Ads and Different Types of Disclosures. *Journal of Advertising*, •••, 1–11. DOI: 10.1080/00913367.2024.2306415

Khurana, D., Koli, A., Khatter, K., & Singh, S. (2023). Natural language processing: State of the art, current trends and challenges. *Multimedia Tools and Applications*, 82(3), 3713–3744. DOI: 10.1007/s11042-022-13428-4 PMID: 35855771

Kietzmann, J., Mills, A. J., & Plangger, K. (2020). Deepfakes: Perspectives on the future "reality" of advertising and branding. *International Journal of Advertising*, 40(3), 473–485. DOI: 10.1080/02650487.2020.1834211

Kotras, B. (2020). Mass personalization: Predictive marketing algorithms and the reshaping of consumer knowledge. *Big Data & Society*, 7(2), 2053951720951581. Advance online publication. DOI: 10.1177/2053951720951581

Kumar, D., & Suthar, N. (2024). Ethical and legal challenges of AI in marketing: an exploration of solutions. *Journal of Information, Communication and Ethics in Society*, 22(1), 124-144. https://doi-org.zulib.idm.oclc.org/10.1108/JICES-05-2023-0068

Kumar, V., Rajan, B., Venkatesan, R., & Lecinski, J. (2019). Understanding the role of artificial intelligence in personalized engagement marketing. *California Management Review*, 61(4), 135–155. DOI: 10.1177/0008125619859317

Lambrecht, A., & Tucker, C. (2019). Algorithmic bias? An empirical study of apparent gender-based discrimination in the display of STEM career ads. *Management Science*, 65(7), 2966–2981. DOI: 10.1287/mnsc.2018.3093

Lindecrantz, E., Tjon Pian Gi, M., & Zerbi, S. (2020, April 28). Personalizing the customer experience: Driving differentiation in retail. *McKinsey and Company*. https://www.mckinsey.com/industries/retail/our-insights/personalizing-the-customer-experience-driving-differentiation-in-retail

Liu, X., Xie, M., Wen, X., Chen, R., Ge, Y., Duffield, N., & Wang, N. (2020). Micro-and macro-level churn analysis of large-scale mobile games. *Knowledge and Information Systems*, 62(4), 1465–1496. DOI: 10.1007/s10115-019-01394-7

Nanne, A. J., Antheunis, M. L., Van Der Lee, C. G., Postma, E. O., Wubben, S., & Van Noort, G. (2020). The use of computer vision to analyze brand-related user generated image content. *Journal of Interactive Marketing*, 50(1), 156–167. https://doi-org.zulib.idm.oclc.org/10.1016/j.intmar.2019.09.003. DOI: 10.1016/j.intmar.2019.09.003

Newman, E. J., & Schwarz, N. (2023). Misinformed by images: How images influence perceptions of truth and what can be done about it. *Current Opinion in Psychology*, 101778. Advance online publication. DOI: 10.1016/j.copsyc.2023.101778 PMID: 38134526

O'Neil, C. (2017). *Weapons of math destruction: How big data increases inequality and threatens democracy*. Crown.

Open, A. I. (2024, November 2). DALL·E 2 is an AI system that can create realistic images and art from a description in natural language. OpenAI. Retrieved from https://openai.com/index/dall-e-2/

Pasquale, F. (2015). *The black box society: The secret algorithms that control money and information*. Harvard University Press. DOI: 10.4159/harvard.9780674736061

Rafieian, O. and Yoganarasimhan, H. (2023). AI and personalization. *Artificial Intelligence in Marketing*, 77-102. DOI: 10.1108/S1548-643520230000020004

Runway, M. L. (2024, November 2). Introducing Act-One – Generate expressive character performances inside [Alpha. Retrieved from https://app.runwayml.com/video-tools/teams/]. *GEN*, 3, •••.

Selbst, A., & Powles, J. (2018, January). "Meaningful information" and the right to explanation. In *conference on fairness, accountability and transparency* (pp. 48-48). PMLR. https://proceedings.mlr.press/v81/selbst18a.html

Sherman, E. (2018, September 27). Burger King skewers AI mania in hilarious ad, but hits one tone-deaf note. *Inc.* Retrieved from https://adage.com/article/digital-marketing-ad-tech-news/burger-king-generative-ai-contest-builds-fans-weird-whoppers/2540371

Sivathanu, B., Pillai, R., & Metri, B. (2023). Customers' online shopping intention by watching AI-based deepfake advertisements. *International Journal of Retail & Distribution Management*, 51(1), 124–145. DOI: 10.1108/IJRDM-12-2021-0583

Smith, P. (2024, May 10). Apple ad fail shows why we fear AI. *Financial Review*. https://www.afr.com/technology/apple-ad-fail-shows-why-we-fear-ai-20240510-p5jcgo

Snee, B. J., & Smulowitz, S. M. (2021). It's Alive!: Reanimating the Author in the Age of Artificially Intelligent Advertising. *Popular Culture Studies Journal, 9*(1), 249-264. https://www.mpcaaca.org/_files/ugd/5a6d69_8e82e21052d34aa8b5b744fc56f30913.pdf

Solove, D. J. (2006). *The Digital Person: Technology and Privacy in the Information Age*. NYU Press.

Sorosrungruang, T., Ameen, N., & Hackley, C. (2024). How real is real enough? Unveiling the diverse power of generative AI-enabled virtual influencers and the dynamics of human responses. *Psychology and Marketing*, 41(12), 3124–3143. Advance online publication. DOI: 10.1002/mar.22105

Springer, J. (2024, June 5). 5 ways Coke is using AI to enhance its marketing. *Ad-Age*.https://adage.com/article/digital-marketing-ad-tech-news/how-coke-using-ai-enhance-marketing/2563521

Tam, K. Y., & Ho, S. Y. (2005). Web personalization as a persuasion strategy: An elaboration likelihood model perspective. *Information Systems Research*, 16(3), 271–291. DOI: 10.1287/isre.1050.0058

Van der Sloot, B., & Wagensveld, Y. (2022). Deepfakes: Regulatory challenges for the synthetic society. *Computer Law & Security Report*, 46, 105716. DOI: 10.1016/j.clsr.2022.105716

Van Laar, E., van Deursen, A. J., van Dijk, J. A., & De Haan, J. (2019). Determinants of 21st-century digital skills: A large-scale survey among working professionals. *Computers in Human Behavior*, 100, 93–104. DOI: 10.1016/j.chb.2019.06.017

Wedel, M., & Kamakura, W. A. (2000). *Market segmentation: Conceptual and methodological foundations*. Springer Science and Business Media. DOI: 10.1007/978-1-4615-4651-1

Zuboff, S. (2019). *The Age of Surveillance Capitalism: The Fight for a Human Future at the New Frontier of Power* (1st ed.). PublicAffairs.

Zuiderveen Borgesius, F. (2018). Discrimination, artificial intelligence, and algorithmic decision-making. *Council of Europe, Directorate General of Democracy*, 42. https://hdl.handle.net/11245.1/7bdabff5-c1d9-484f-81f2-e469e03e2360

## ADDITIONAL READING

De Bruyn, A., Viswanathan, V., Beh, Y. S., Brock, J. K. U., & Von Wangenheim, F. (2020). Artificial intelligence and marketing: Pitfalls and opportunities. *Journal of Interactive Marketing*, 51(1), 91–105. DOI: 10.1016/j.intmar.2020.04.007

Gao, B., Wang, Y., Xie, H., Hu, Y., & Hu, Y. (2023). Artificial intelligence in advertising: Advancements, challenges, and ethical considerations in targeting, personalization, content creation, and ad optimization. *SAGE Open*, 13(4), 21582440231210759. Advance online publication. DOI: 10.1177/21582440231210759

Li, H. (2019). Special section introduction: Artificial intelligence and advertising. *Journal of Advertising*, 48(4), 333–337. DOI: 10.1080/00913367.2019.1654947

Rodgers, S. (2021). Themed issue introduction: Promises and perils of artificial intelligence and advertising. *Journal of Advertising*, 50(1), 1–10. DOI: 10.1080/00913367.2020.1868233

Sterne, J. (2017). *Artificial intelligence for marketing: practical applications*. John Wiley and Sons. DOI: 10.1002/9781119406341

Verma, S., Sharma, R., Deb, S., & Maitra, D. (2021). Artificial intelligence in marketing: Systematic review and future research direction. *International Journal of Information Management Data Insights*, 1(1), 100002. DOI: 10.1016/j.jjimei.2020.100002

Vlačić, B., Corbo, L., Silva, S. C., & Dabić, M. (2021). The evolving role of artificial intelligence in marketing: A review and research agenda. *Journal of Business Research*, 128, 187–203. DOI: 10.1016/j.jbusres.2021.01.055

## KEY TERMS AND DEFINITIONS

**Advertising:** Advertising, in its broadest sense, transcends the mere promotion of products or services. It encompasses a complex interplay of communication effects that shape perceptions, attitudes, and behaviors across individuals and society. This definition underscores the need to understand advertising's diverse roles and potential impacts critically. It encourages a holistic perspective that considers this powerful communication tool's ethical, social, and cultural dimensions.

**Artificial Intelligence:** Artificial intelligence (AI) can be defined as the ability of a computer to perform tasks that humans usually do. At its core, AI aims to replicate or simulate human cognitive functions, such as learning, problem-solving, and decision-making. The fundamental goal is to create machines that can exhibit intelligent behavior and augment human capabilities.

**Automation:** In the context of advertising, automation refers to the utilization of technology to streamline and expedite tasks that were previously performed manually. This encompasses various processes, including ad creation, campaign management, data analysis, and customer targeting.

**Deepfake:** The term "deepfake" in advertising refers to synthetic media, primarily generated through artificial intelligence (AI) techniques like deep learning, to fabricate or manipulate visual or auditory content. This technology allows for creating highly realistic and convincing depictions of individuals.

**Optimization:** Optimization refers to the strategic process of continuously refining various aspects of an advertising campaign to maximize its effectiveness and achieve desired outcomes. This involves systematically analyzing data, identifying areas for improvement, and implementing adjustments to enhance performance.

**Personalization:** Personalization in advertising refers to tailoring advertisements to individual consumers based on their unique characteristics, preferences, and behaviors. This approach aims to deliver more relevant and engaging content to each consumer, increasing the likelihood of conversion.

**Synthetic Media:** Synthetic media, in the context of advertising, refers to the artificial production, manipulation, or modification of media content using artificial intelligence (AI) technologies. A key characteristic of synthetic media is its ability to blur the lines between reality and artificiality.

# Chapter 7
# Artificial Intelligence and Unfair Competition: Legal Strategies for Ethical and Responsible Business Practices

**David López Jiménez**
https://orcid.org/0000-0002-7013-9556
*EAE Business School, Spain & UNIE Universidad, Spain*

## ABSTRACT

*This chapter examines the impact of artificial intelligence (AI) on unfair competition and commercial law, emphasizing ethical implications and corporate social responsibility (CSR). AI has revolutionized market competition and intellectual property protection, providing tools for detecting infringements and optimizing strategies. However, it raises ethical challenges, including privacy concerns, market manipulation, and anticompetitive behavior. The chapter discusses how businesses can ethically use AI while upholding fair competition. It includes case studies and proposes a framework for integrating CSR into AI-driven competition, advocating for legal regulations to define ethical AI boundaries. By exploring the relationship between AI, ethics, and commercial law, the chapter aims to guide companies and policymakers in promoting responsible AI practices in the marketplace.*

## INTRODUCTION

In today's rapidly evolving global commercial landscape, artificial intelligence (AI) has emerged as a transformative force, redefining how companies compete, innovate, and protect their intellectual property assets. AI's ability to process vast amounts of data, identify patterns, and automate decision-making processes has

DOI: 10.4018/979-8-3693-9894-4.ch007

enabled businesses to gain a competitive edge and optimize various aspects of their operations, from market surveillance to customer engagement ((Kaplan & Haenlein, 2020)). However, the growing reliance on AI has also introduced new challenges and ethical dilemmas, particularly in the realm of unfair competition and commercial law. This chapter explores these complex issues, focusing on how AI can both serve as a tool for safeguarding against unfair competition and simultaneously introduce significant ethical concerns in business practices.

AI technologies have given rise to novel forms of commercial strategies, allowing companies to monitor market trends, identify potential intellectual property infringements, and adjust their competitive tactics with unprecedented precision. For instance, AI-driven algorithms can scan online marketplaces to detect counterfeit goods, identify unauthorized use of trademarks, and monitor competitors' activities. This enhanced surveillance capacity provides businesses with the tools necessary to protect their assets effectively and respond quickly to infringements, promoting a more transparent and fair competitive environment (Sharma et al., 2021).

However, the same AI technologies that offer these protective capabilities also present ethical challenges. Automated systems used for market monitoring may cross the line into intrusive data collection, potentially infringing on the privacy rights of consumers and competitors. Similarly, AI algorithms employed for dynamic pricing and market analysis can lead to practices that may be viewed as anticompetitive, such as price-fixing or the exploitation of market dominance. These practices raise important questions about the ethical boundaries of AI use in commerce, as well as the need for legal frameworks that address the implications of AI on fair competition (Calo, 2017).

Moreover, AI's impact on business ethics extends to corporate social responsibility (CSR). In an era where consumers and stakeholders increasingly demand ethical conduct from companies, CSR has become a critical component of business strategy. Companies are not only expected to protect their commercial interests but also to operate in a manner that respects the rights of competitors, consumers, and society at large. The integration of CSR principles into AI-driven business practices is essential to ensure that technological advancements do not compromise fairness, transparency, and respect for the broader market ecosystem (Floridi et al., 2018). Therefore, this chapter seeks to address the pressing need for legal and ethical guidelines that guide companies in using AI responsibly within the competitive landscape.

AI's role in commercial competition is multifaceted, offering both defensive mechanisms against unfair competition and tools for strategic market positioning. On the defensive side, AI technologies empower companies to safeguard their intellectual property (IP) assets. Automated systems can continuously scan the internet for unauthorized use of trademarks, patents, and copyrighted material, providing early detection and facilitating swift enforcement actions. For example, AI-powered image recognition software can identify counterfeit products bearing a company's logo or design, alerting businesses to potential infringements in real-time. These capabilities enhance the protection of IP rights and contribute to a more equitable market where businesses can compete on the merits of their innovations and brand value.

In addition to protecting IP, AI serves as a strategic tool that enables companies to gather competitive intelligence, optimize pricing strategies, and improve customer targeting. Machine learning algorithms analyze vast datasets, including market trends, consumer behaviors, and competitors' activities, allowing companies to make data-driven decisions that enhance their market positioning. However, these practices introduce ethical concerns, particularly when the use of AI encroaches on the boundaries of fair competition. For instance, dynamic pricing algorithms, while beneficial for optimizing profit margins, can inadvertently lead to price discrimination or collusion-like outcomes when multiple companies employ similar algorithms that interact with each other in the marketplace.

The ethical challenges posed by AI are further complicated by its potential to disrupt market dynamics. AI can enable large corporations to consolidate their market dominance by leveraging advanced technologies that smaller competitors may lack access to. This raises questions about the fairness of AI-driven competition, as it may exacerbate existing market inequalities and limit opportunities for smaller firms to participate in the market on an equal footing. Thus, while AI offers significant advantages in terms of operational efficiency and market protection, it also poses critical ethical and legal dilemmas that need to be addressed within the framework of commercial law.

Unfair competition refers to business practices that deceive consumers, infringe upon the rights of competitors, or distort market conditions in ways that undermine fair trade. With the rise of AI, new forms of unfair competition have emerged, necessitating a re-examination of existing ethical standards and legal regulations. One prominent example is the use of AI for automated market surveillance. While monitoring competitors' activities is a legitimate business practice, the use of AI-driven data scraping and analysis tools can border on invasive behavior, raising concerns about the ethics of collecting and utilizing competitors' data without consent.

Another concern relates to AI-enabled price optimization algorithms. These systems can dynamically adjust prices based on market demand, competitor pricing, and consumer behavior data. While this may lead to efficient market outcomes, it also carries the risk of facilitating implicit collusion, where algorithms learn to avoid price competition without direct coordination between firms. Such behavior can harm consumers by keeping prices artificially high and limiting the benefits of market competition. This scenario underscores the need for clear ethical guidelines that define the acceptable use of AI in pricing strategies, as well as legal frameworks that prevent anticompetitive practices in the digital economy.

Additionally, AI's capacity for large-scale data processing presents ethical issues related to privacy and the potential misuse of personal information. Companies using AI for targeted advertising or customer segmentation must navigate the delicate balance between leveraging consumer data for competitive advantage and respecting individuals' privacy rights. The use of AI to monitor consumer behavior, predict purchasing preferences, and tailor marketing strategies raises concerns about consent, data security, and the potential for discriminatory practices. These issues highlight the importance of embedding CSR principles into AI-driven business operations, ensuring that the pursuit of market success does not come at the expense of ethical conduct and consumer trust.

In light of these challenges, corporate social responsibility (CSR) emerges as a vital framework for guiding the ethical use of AI in commercial competition. CSR emphasizes the idea that businesses have a responsibility not just to their shareholders, but to a broader set of stakeholders, including employees, consumers, competitors, and society as a whole. Integrating CSR principles into AI practices means that companies must go beyond legal compliance and proactively address the ethical implications of their use of AI technologies.

One way companies can incorporate CSR into their AI strategies is by implementing transparency and accountability measures. For instance, firms can disclose their use of AI algorithms for market surveillance, pricing, and customer engagement, providing stakeholders with insights into how data is collected, processed, and used. Furthermore, companies can establish internal ethics committees to oversee AI practices, ensuring that they align with both legal requirements and ethical standards. By taking these steps, businesses can demonstrate their commitment to fair competition, consumer protection, and the responsible use of technology.

Another aspect of CSR in the context of AI involves fostering a culture of ethical awareness within the organization. This includes providing training for employees and management on the ethical challenges associated with AI, promoting a corporate mindset that prioritizes ethical decision-making, and encouraging open dialogue about the potential risks and benefits of AI implementation. In doing so, companies can create an environment where ethical considerations are integrated into strategic business decisions, particularly those involving AI and competitive practices.

The ethical complexities introduced by AI in commercial competition highlight the need for adaptive legal frameworks that can address the unique challenges posed by these technologies. Current competition laws and regulations, while providing a foundation for fair business practices, may not fully encompass the nuances of AI-driven market behaviors. For instance, traditional antitrust laws designed to prevent collusion and monopolistic practices may struggle to address the subtleties of algorithmic pricing and automated market monitoring.

In this context, commercial regulations must evolve to set clear boundaries for AI use in competition. This includes defining what constitutes ethical AI practices, setting standards for data collection and usage, and establishing mechanisms for algorithmic accountability. Moreover, regulatory authorities should consider implementing guidelines that require companies to conduct AI audits, ensuring that their algorithms do not engage in unfair or anticompetitive behavior. These regulatory measures, when combined with a corporate commitment to CSR, can help foster an environment where AI is used to enhance, rather than undermine, the integrity of the marketplace.

AI's transformative impact on commercial competition presents both opportunities and challenges for businesses and regulators alike. While AI provides companies with powerful tools to protect their intellectual property, optimize market strategies, and compete more effectively, it also introduces significant ethical and legal concerns that must be addressed. As companies navigate the complexities of AI-driven competition, the integration of corporate social responsibility principles and the development of adaptive legal frameworks will be crucial in promoting fair and ethical business practices.

This chapter will explore these issues in greater depth, examining the ways in which AI can be harnessed responsibly within the competitive landscape. Through case studies, legal analysis, and a proposed framework for ethical AI integration, the discussion aims to contribute to the global discourse on AI, commercial law, and business ethics. By doing so, it seeks to guide companies, policymakers, and legal professionals in understanding and addressing the ethical challenges of AI in commercial competition, fostering a marketplace that upholds fairness, transparency, and social responsibility.

## AI AND THE TRANSFORMATION OF BUSINESS PRACTICES IN COMMERCIAL LAW

Artificial intelligence (AI) has significantly transformed business practices in recent years, introducing new methods for managing operations, enhancing customer experiences, and protecting intellectual property. In the context of commercial law, AI's capabilities for data analysis, market surveillance, and decision-making have created both opportunities and challenges for businesses. This transformation not only changes the competitive landscape but also raises important questions about how AI aligns with ethical principles and the standards of fair competition.

## AI as a Transformative Force in Market Dynamics

The integration of AI into business practices has fundamentally altered how companies engage with the market and each other. AI technologies enable businesses to analyze vast amounts of data, identify market trends, and implement strategies with an unprecedented level of precision. In particular, AI-driven analytics tools allow companies to monitor competitor activities, assess consumer behaviors, and adjust their market positioning in real-time. This increased responsiveness can enhance competitive strategies, enabling companies to optimize pricing, tailor marketing efforts, and respond to market demands more effectively than ever before (Jarrahi, 2018).

One key area where AI has significantly impacted business practices is in the detection of intellectual property (IP) infringements. Traditionally, companies relied on manual methods and legal teams to monitor for trademark and patent violations. However, AI technologies have introduced automated systems capable of scanning websites, marketplaces, and social media platforms for unauthorized use of copyrighted content, trademarks, and patented designs. For example, image recognition algorithms can identify counterfeit products by comparing online listings against a company's catalog of proprietary images. This real-time surveillance allows companies to address IP violations swiftly, enhancing their ability to protect their assets and maintain a competitive Edge (Vinuesa et al., 2020).

Furthermore, AI is employed to conduct comprehensive market surveillance, gathering data on competitors' product launches, pricing strategies, and promotional activities. Advanced natural language processing (NLP) algorithms can analyze textual data from news articles, press releases, and social media posts to provide businesses with actionable insights about their market environment. However, the use of AI for such purposes raises ethical questions regarding the boundaries of acceptable market monitoring. While gathering market intelligence is a legitimate business practice, AI's capacity for extensive data collection and analysis can blur the lines between competitive strategy and invasive surveillance.

## The Dual Nature of AI in Commercial Law: Protection and Ethical Concerns

AI's role in commercial law is inherently dualistic. On the one hand, it serves as a powerful tool for companies to protect their assets and enforce intellectual property rights, thereby promoting a fair and transparent market. On the other hand, its use introduces ethical concerns, especially when AI-driven practices challenge the boundaries of fair competition and privacy.

AI as a protective mechanism: From a legal perspective, AI strengthens the enforcement of intellectual property laws. AI systems can detect unauthorized use of trademarks, copyrighted material, and patented technologies across digital platforms, providing companies with concrete evidence for legal actions. This level of automated vigilance not only acts as a deterrent to potential infringers but also ensures a more equitable market by upholding intellectual property rights. For example, AI-based monitoring tools can detect trademark violations in real-time, allowing companies to issue cease-and-desist letters promptly, thereby protecting their brand integrity.

In addition, AI facilitates trademark and patent registration processes. AI algorithms can analyze existing patent databases to identify potential overlaps, helping companies avoid infringing on pre-existing patents during product development. This use of AI streamlines legal compliance, reducing the likelihood of costly litigation and fostering a market environment where innovation and creativity are respected and protected.

AI as an ethical concern: Despite these protective benefits, the use of AI in market surveillance and IP enforcement raises significant ethical issues. One major concern is the potential for AI-driven practices to infringe on privacy and intellectual autonomy. For instance, AI algorithms that scan online content for trademark violations may inadvertently collect personal data, leading to potential privacy violations. Moreover, AI's capacity to monitor competitors' activities extensively can raise questions about the ethics of market intelligence gathering. Where does the line between legitimate market analysis and unethical surveillance lie?

Another ethical concern relates to the potential misuse of AI in anticompetitive practices. Advanced AI algorithms can be employed for dynamic pricing, adjusting product prices in response to market fluctuations and competitor pricing strategies. While dynamic pricing can be a legitimate business strategy, it can also lead to unintended collusion or price-fixing behaviors, particularly when multiple companies use similar AI algorithms that interact in predictable ways. This scenario poses a legal and ethical challenge, as it may distort market dynamics and harm consumer interests. Thus, while AI offers powerful tools for competition and market protection, its application must be carefully managed to avoid undermining the principles of fair competition.

## AI, Data Collection, and the Ethical Limits of Market Surveillance

AI-driven market surveillance relies heavily on data collection and analysis. Companies use AI to monitor digital marketplaces, websites, and even competitors' customer interactions to gather insights that inform their competitive strategies. However, this practice raises critical questions about data ethics, particularly in terms of privacy, consent, and the ethical limits of competitive intelligence (Martin & Murphy, 2017).

AI technologies can mine vast amounts of data from various sources, including public databases, social media platforms, and e-commerce sites. For instance, machine learning algorithms can analyze consumer reviews and purchasing patterns to identify emerging market trends, helping businesses tailor their products and marketing strategies accordingly. While this use of AI can provide valuable business intelligence, it also poses ethical challenges. The indiscriminate collection of data, even if publicly available, can infringe on individual privacy rights and lead to the misuse of personal information (Zeng et al., 2021).

In the context of commercial law, the ethical use of AI for market surveillance must be considered within the framework of data protection regulations, such as the General Data Protection Regulation (GDPR) in the European Union and other emerging data privacy laws in jurisdictions like China and Japan. These regulations establish legal standards for data collection, processing, and use, requiring companies to obtain consent for the collection of personal data and to ensure transparency in their data practices. However, the rapid advancement of AI technologies often outpaces the development of legal norms, leaving a gray area in terms of how AI-based market surveillance should be conducted ethically (Kaminski, 2019).

To address these ethical concerns, companies must adopt a corporate social responsibility (CSR) approach that emphasizes transparency, accountability, and respect for individual rights. For example, businesses should be transparent about their use of AI in market surveillance, clearly communicating their data collection practices and the purposes for which the data will be used. Moreover, companies can implement internal policies and oversight mechanisms to ensure that AI-driven surveillance does not violate privacy rights or engage in unethical monitoring of competitors. By incorporating ethical considerations into their use of AI, companies can leverage the technology's benefits while upholding their social responsibilities and fostering a competitive environment grounded in fairness and respect for legal and ethical standards.

## The Need for Legal Frameworks to Guide AI-Driven Business Practices

Given the transformative impact of AI on commercial practices, there is a growing need for legal frameworks that define the boundaries of acceptable AI use in competition. Current commercial laws, particularly those related to intellectual property, privacy, and competition, provide a foundation for regulating business conduct. However, the unique capabilities of AI—such as its ability to process vast amounts of data, make autonomous decisions, and adapt to changing market conditions—require a reevaluation of existing legal norms (Wachter et al., 2017).

Legal frameworks must address several key aspects of AI-driven business practices. First, they should establish clear guidelines on the ethical collection and use of data, ensuring that AI technologies are employed in ways that respect privacy and individual rights. Second, regulations should define the limits of market surveillance, delineating what constitutes fair market analysis versus intrusive or anticompetitive behavior. Third, legal standards must govern the use of AI in pricing strategies, preventing algorithmic collusion and other forms of market manipulation that could harm consumers and distort competition (Calvano et al., 2020).

In addition to regulatory measures, the development of industry standards and best practices for ethical AI use can help guide companies in aligning their competitive strategies with CSR principles. These standards might include requirements for algorithmic audits, transparency in AI usage, and mechanisms for ensuring human oversight in AI-driven decision-making processes. By fostering a culture of ethical AI use within the commercial sector, legal frameworks and industry guidelines can promote a marketplace where innovation thrives, competition remains fair, and business practices align with societal values and legal norms.

# UNFAIR COMPETITION IN THE AGE OF AI: ETHICAL AND LEGAL DILEMMAS

Artificial intelligence (AI) has transformed how companies engage in competition, enabling them to develop more sophisticated strategies for market positioning, customer targeting, and operational efficiency. However, the capabilities of AI also introduce ethical and legal dilemmas, particularly when its application encroaches upon the principles of fair competition. AI can be harnessed in ways that distort markets, infringe upon consumer rights, and create barriers for competitors, thereby raising critical questions about the ethical use of AI in business. This section delves into the complexities of unfair competition in the AI era, exploring practices that push the boundaries of legality and ethical standards and highlighting the urgent need for updated regulations and responsible corporate strategies.

## AI-Powered Pricing: Between Efficiency and Collusion

One of the most notable applications of AI in competitive strategies is dynamic pricing, where algorithms automatically adjust product prices in real-time based on market conditions, demand fluctuations, and competitor pricing. While this practice can optimize sales and improve market responsiveness, it presents a gray area in terms of fair competition. AI-powered pricing systems have the potential to unintentionally lead to anticompetitive behaviors, such as algorithmic collusion, where independent companies' pricing algorithms engage in parallel behavior that resembles price-fixing.

Unlike traditional price-fixing, which requires explicit agreement between competitors, algorithmic collusion occurs when AI systems learn from market data and adjust prices in a way that avoids direct competition. For example, multiple companies using similar AI-driven pricing algorithms might learn to maintain stable prices that maximize profits without explicitly communicating with one another. This phenomenon is particularly problematic because it can result in artificially inflated prices, harming consumer welfare and distorting the competitive market dynamics. Legal frameworks, such as antitrust laws, traditionally focus on preventing explicit collusion, leaving a regulatory gap when it comes to the implicit, algorithm-driven pricing behaviors of AI.

The ethical implications of AI-driven pricing go beyond market manipulation. Dynamic pricing algorithms can lead to price discrimination, where different consumers are charged varying prices for the same product or service based on factors like location, purchasing history, or even the type of device they use to make the purchase. While personalized pricing can be seen as a way to cater to specific consumer segments, it raises concerns about fairness and transparency. For instance, charging higher prices to customers based on their perceived ability to pay can create an inequitable marketplace, undermining trust and potentially violating principles of corporate social responsibility (CSR).

Addressing these dilemmas requires a nuanced approach. On one hand, companies must leverage AI to remain competitive and meet market demands. On the other hand, they need to ensure that their pricing strategies align with ethical standards, promoting fairness and avoiding practices that can be construed as collusion or discrimination. This challenge underscores the importance of corporate oversight and algorithmic audits to monitor AI systems for behaviors that could lead to unintended anticompetitive outcomes.

## AI and Data Exploitation: Surveillance, Privacy, and Competitive Intelligence

AI's capacity to process vast amounts of data has revolutionized market research, enabling companies to gain deep insights into consumer behaviors, preferences, and trends. However, this data-driven advantage often leads to ethical and legal concerns, particularly when it involves the exploitation of data in ways that intrude on privacy, manipulate consumer behavior, or unfairly target competitors (Wachter et al., 2017).

Modern AI systems, such as those utilizing machine learning and natural language processing (NLP), can mine data from an extensive array of sources, including social media, online shopping behaviors, and even competitors' websites. These tools provide companies with a wealth of information that can be used to refine marketing strategies, improve customer segmentation, and outmaneuver rivals (Tene & Polonetsky, 2013). While collecting publicly available information is generally considered legitimate, the use of AI to aggregate and analyze this data at scale can create privacy risks and raise ethical questions.

For example, AI systems that monitor online interactions may inadvertently collect personal data, leading to potential violations of data privacy laws, such as the European Union's General Data Protection Regulation (GDPR). This legal risk is exacerbated by AI's ability to combine disparate pieces of data to create detailed consumer profiles, often without the individuals' explicit consent (Kaminski, 2019). Such practices not only risk breaching privacy regulations but also threaten the ethical standards of consumer rights and autonomy. From a CSR perspective, companies must carefully navigate the use of AI for data collection, ensuring that their competitive intelligence efforts do not infringe on privacy or misuse personal information.

In addition to privacy concerns, AI-driven market surveillance can cross into the realm of unethical competitive practices. For instance, companies can use AI to scrape competitors' websites, analyzing product offerings, pricing models, and customer feedback (Zarsky, 2016). While gathering competitive intelligence is a standard business practice, the use of automated AI tools for surveillance can become ethically questionable, especially if it involves accessing proprietary or restricted information. In some cases, these actions may even violate laws governing unfair competition and trade secrets, depending on how the data is obtained and used.

Therefore, companies must adopt clear ethical guidelines for AI-driven market research and data analysis. Transparency in data practices, informed consent, and respect for privacy rights are fundamental principles that should guide AI's application in competitive intelligence. Furthermore, implementing internal policies and oversight mechanisms to ensure compliance with data protection laws and ethical standards is crucial for maintaining the integrity of competitive practices in the age of AI.

## AI in Advertising and Consumer Manipulation: Ethical Considerations

AI's growing role in advertising and customer engagement introduces another layer of ethical complexity. AI-driven algorithms enable companies to target consumers with personalized advertisements, recommendations, and promotions based on their browsing history, purchasing habits, and even emotional responses. While personalized advertising can enhance customer experiences and drive sales, it also poses ethical risks related to manipulation and the exploitation of consumer vulnerabilities.

One area of concern is the use of AI to create highly targeted advertising campaigns that leverage psychological profiling. By analyzing consumer data, AI can identify individual preferences, fears, and desires, tailoring marketing messages to evoke specific emotional responses. This level of personalization, while effective, raises questions about the ethical limits of influencing consumer behavior. When does tailored advertising cross the line into manipulation? For example, using AI to target consumers with ads for products they are likely to buy impulsively based on psychological triggers can be seen as exploiting their vulnerabilities rather than serving their genuine needs.

Moreover, AI's role in filtering information for consumers, such as recommending news articles or products, can create echo chambers that reinforce existing biases and limit exposure to diverse perspectives. This practice can distort consumer decision-making, as individuals are presented with a curated reality that aligns with their previous behaviors. Such algorithmic filtering not only affects consumer autonomy but also raises broader concerns about the social impact of AI on public discourse and market dynamics.

From a commercial law perspective, these practices intersect with issues of consumer protection and unfair competition. Regulatory frameworks in many jurisdictions are beginning to address the ethical use of AI in advertising, mandating transparency and consumer rights to opt-out of targeted marketing. Companies must navigate these legal requirements while adhering to ethical principles that prioritize consumer welfare. Incorporating CSR principles into advertising strategies involves adopting practices that are not only legally compliant but also respectful of consumer autonomy and well-being.

## Barriers to Entry and Market Power: AI's Impact on Competition

AI's advanced capabilities and the substantial investment required to develop and implement sophisticated AI systems can create significant barriers to entry for smaller companies and new market entrants. Larger corporations that can afford to deploy state-of-the-art AI technologies gain a competitive advantage, consolidating their market power and potentially creating oligopolistic market structures. This dynamic raises ethical concerns about the fairness of AI-driven competition and the risk of market dominance.

AI-enabled companies can leverage their technological edge to outpace competitors in areas such as product development, market surveillance, and customer engagement. For instance, large online platforms use AI to analyze consumer behavior patterns and optimize their offerings, creating ecosystems that are difficult for smaller competitors to penetrate. Additionally, these platforms can use AI to set prices that deter new entrants or to acquire emerging competitors before they can grow into legitimate market threats. This concentration of market power can stifle innovation and limit consumer choices, challenging the ideals of a competitive and diverse marketplace.

The ethical dilemma here lies in balancing the legitimate business use of AI to achieve competitive advantage with the need to preserve a market environment that fosters innovation and fair competition. This challenge requires not only self-regulation by companies, guided by CSR principles, but also the establishment of regulatory frameworks that promote market accessibility and prevent the abuse of AI-driven market power. Legal measures, such as antitrust laws, must adapt to address the ways in which AI can alter competitive dynamics and create new forms of market concentration.

# AI AS A TOOL FOR PROTECTING INTELLECTUAL PROPERTY AND PROMOTING FAIR COMPETITION

While artificial intelligence (AI) has sparked ethical and legal concerns regarding unfair competition, it also presents significant opportunities for promoting fair competition and protecting intellectual property (IP). As businesses navigate an increasingly complex market landscape, the implementation of AI technologies for safeguarding trademarks, copyrights, and patents has become an essential aspect of commercial strategy. By leveraging AI's capabilities, companies can monitor market activities, identify IP infringements, and address unfair practices with a level of efficiency previously unattainable. However, these protective mechanisms must be balanced with ethical considerations to ensure that AI not only defends a company's commercial interests but also fosters a competitive marketplace that respects both the spirit and letter of the law.

## AI in Trademark and Copyright Protection

In the digital age, the unauthorized use of trademarks and copyrighted material poses a significant threat to businesses. Counterfeit products, unauthorized reproductions, and intellectual property theft undermine brand integrity, consumer trust, and market competition. AI offers advanced tools for identifying such violations, allowing companies to protect their brand assets and enforce their IP rights more effectively.

**Trademark monitoring and enforcement:** One of AI's most impactful applications in intellectual property management is automated trademark surveillance. Companies can use AI-powered image recognition and natural language processing (NLP) technologies to monitor the digital landscape for potential trademark infringements. For example, AI systems can scan websites, e-commerce platforms, and social media for logos, product names, and slogans that resemble a company's registered trademarks. By comparing these findings against a database of registered marks, AI can quickly detect potential violations, enabling companies to take swift action.

This automation significantly reduces the time and cost traditionally associated with trademark monitoring, making it more feasible for companies to protect their IP assets on a global scale. In addition, AI can prioritize potential threats based on factors like the similarity of the infringement, market reach, and impact on brand value, helping legal teams to focus their efforts on the most critical cases. For instance, when a major sportswear brand detects counterfeit products bearing its logo on an online marketplace, AI systems can automatically generate detailed reports, including evidence of infringement, to support legal claims.

**Copyright protection in the digital domain:** Similarly, AI is transforming how companies protect their copyrighted content. Digital watermarking and content recognition technologies allow AI systems to scan the internet for unauthorized reproductions of copyrighted material, such as images, music, videos, and written content. When instances of infringement are detected, AI can alert the copyright holder, providing detailed information about the location and nature of the violation. This process not only strengthens copyright enforcement but also acts as a deterrent against unauthorized use, as potential infringers become aware of the heightened likelihood of detection.

The use of AI in this context supports fair competition by ensuring that original creators retain control over their intellectual property, preventing others from unfairly profiting from their creative work. For example, a company that has invested heavily in creating high-quality digital content can use AI to protect its assets, ensuring that competitors do not replicate or distribute the content without authorization. This protection promotes a competitive environment where innovation and creativity are rewarded, rather than undermined by illicit copying.

## Patent Analysis and Protection Through AI

AI's capacity for processing vast quantities of data and identifying patterns has also revolutionized patent analysis. Patent infringement and unauthorized use of patented technology present significant challenges in many industries, particularly in high-tech fields such as pharmaceuticals, electronics, and software. AI offers companies powerful tools for patent protection, enabling them to monitor technological developments, identify potential infringements, and ensure compliance with existing patents (Trappey et al., 2017).

**Patent searches and due diligence:** Before a company seeks to file a new patent, it must conduct a comprehensive search to ensure that its invention does not infringe on existing patents. AI-based tools have significantly enhanced this process by rapidly scanning patent databases and identifying relevant documents that may contain similar or overlapping technologies. These AI systems use natural language processing and machine learning algorithms to analyze patent literature, technical specifications, and scientific publications, providing legal teams with insights that inform their patent strategy (Chien, 2019).

AI's ability to conduct exhaustive searches and assess the novelty of an invention helps companies navigate the complexities of the patent landscape, reducing the risk of unintentional infringement. This proactive approach not only protects a company's intellectual property but also upholds the integrity of the competitive market by ensuring that new products and technologies do not violate existing IP rights.

**Monitoring for patent infringement:** Once a patent is granted, AI can assist in monitoring for potential infringements in the market. AI-driven systems can track industry developments, analyze competitors' patent filings, and examine new products for similarities to a company's patented technology. When an infringement is detected, AI can generate detailed reports that include evidence of violation, technical comparisons, and legal analyses to support enforcement actions (Zhang et al., 2021). This level of surveillance is particularly valuable in industries where technological advancements occur rapidly, and the risk of IP infringement is high.

The use of AI in patent protection not only benefits individual companies but also promotes fair competition by creating a marketplace where innovative products and technologies are safeguarded against exploitation. When businesses know that their patents are actively monitored and protected, they are more likely to invest in research and development, fostering an environment that rewards innovation and drives technological progress.

## Balancing AI's Protective Functions With Ethical Considerations

While AI offers robust mechanisms for protecting intellectual property and promoting fair competition, its use must be carefully balanced with ethical considerations. Automated surveillance and enforcement activities, if left unchecked, can potentially lead to overreach, privacy violations, and aggressive legal strategies that may stifle competition. Therefore, companies must adopt an ethical framework when employing AI for IP protection, ensuring that their actions align with both legal standards and corporate social responsibility (CSR) principles.

**Transparency and due process:** One of the key ethical concerns in using AI for IP protection is the risk of false positives—instances where AI systems mistakenly identify legitimate uses as infringements. Given the high stakes of IP enforcement, it is crucial for companies to incorporate human oversight into their AI processes. Before taking legal action, companies should conduct a thorough review of AI-generated findings to verify their accuracy and ensure that enforcement efforts are justified. This practice not only minimizes the risk of wrongful claims but also upholds principles of fairness and due process, preventing the misuse of IP rights as a tool for bullying smaller competitors or limiting market access.

**Data privacy in IP surveillance:** AI's effectiveness in market surveillance often hinges on its ability to collect and analyze large amounts of data. However, this data-driven approach raises privacy concerns, particularly when monitoring online activities, consumer behaviors, or competitor websites. Companies must establish clear policies regarding the types of data they collect and the methods used to obtain it, ensuring compliance with privacy regulations and ethical standards. For example, when using AI to detect copyright violations on social media platforms, businesses should avoid collecting unnecessary personal data and implement safeguards to protect user privacy. By adopting a privacy-conscious approach, companies can respect individual rights while pursuing legitimate IP protection activities.

**Collaboration and standards for ethical IP enforcement:** To foster a marketplace that values both IP protection and fair competition, industry stakeholders should collaborate to develop standards and best practices for the ethical use of AI in IP enforcement. This collaboration can involve establishing industry-wide guidelines on AI surveillance, promoting transparency in IP protection activities, and creating mechanisms for resolving disputes amicably before resorting to litigation. For instance, companies could participate in industry consortia that facilitate information sharing about potential IP infringements, allowing for collective monitoring and the development of a unified response to counterfeiting and piracy.

### AI-Driven IP Protection as a Foundation for a Fair Competitive Environment

The use of AI in IP protection contributes to a marketplace where innovation and creativity are safeguarded, creating a more equitable competitive environment. By enforcing intellectual property rights effectively, AI helps ensure that businesses are rewarded for their investments in research, development, and branding, deterring counterfeiters and free-riders from exploiting the market unfairly. However, this protective function must be exercised responsibly, guided by an ethical framework that promotes transparency, fairness, and respect for privacy.

Moreover, AI-driven IP protection can foster a level playing field, particularly for smaller companies and startups that may lack the resources to engage in extensive market surveillance manually. By automating IP enforcement, AI provides these firms with access to tools that allow them to protect their assets and compete more effectively in the market. This democratization of IP protection helps maintain a diverse and dynamic marketplace where innovation is not solely the domain of large corporations.

AI serves as a powerful tool for promoting fair competition through the protection of intellectual property. When used ethically and within the boundaries of legal frameworks, AI can reinforce market integrity, support innovation, and enhance consumer trust. However, businesses must remain vigilant in balancing their protective strategies with ethical considerations, ensuring that AI's application in IP enforcement aligns with broader social responsibilities and the principles of a just marketplace. By doing so, companies can harness AI's potential to foster a competitive environment that is not only technologically advanced but also equitable and respectful of the rights of all market participants.

## COMMERCIAL REGULATION AND LEGAL STRATEGIES FOR ETHICAL AI PRACTICES

As artificial intelligence (AI) becomes increasingly integrated into commercial operations, the need for robust and adaptive legal frameworks to regulate AI practices has become more urgent. While AI offers vast opportunities for efficiency and market optimization, its potential for misuse raises concerns about anticompetitive behaviors, privacy violations, and the erosion of fair competition principles. Traditional commercial law, designed primarily for a pre-digital marketplace, must evolve to address the unique challenges posed by AI. This section explores the current gaps in commercial regulation concerning AI and proposes strategic legal measures to promote ethical AI practices. By fostering transparency, accountability, and fairness, these legal strategies aim to guide businesses toward a responsible use of AI that aligns with both corporate social responsibility (CSR) and competitive integrity.

## The Limitations of Existing Commercial Regulations

Existing commercial regulations, including competition laws, intellectual property protections, and consumer rights, were established in an era that did not anticipate the rapid development of AI. As a result, these laws often fall short in addressing the nuances of AI-driven business practices. For example, antitrust laws are primarily designed to prevent explicit collusion between firms, yet they struggle to address scenarios where AI algorithms, operating independently, lead to market behaviors resembling price-fixing or exclusionary practices. Similarly, intellectual property laws provide mechanisms for enforcing trademarks and patents but do not fully account for the automated nature of AI surveillance and enforcement activities.

**Antitrust and competition law challenges:** One of the most significant regulatory challenges is how to adapt antitrust laws to the realities of AI-enabled competition. AI algorithms can make autonomous decisions about pricing, inventory management, and market entry, potentially leading to behaviors that reduce competition. For instance, when multiple companies employ AI-driven dynamic pricing algorithms, these systems can learn to avoid direct competition, resulting in parallel pricing strategies that effectively stabilize prices without explicit collusion. This phenomenon, often referred to as "algorithmic collusion," falls into a legal gray area, as traditional antitrust laws focus on human agreements and communications rather than the autonomous actions of algorithms.

Additionally, large companies that deploy sophisticated AI technologies may gain a disproportionate advantage in the marketplace, creating barriers to entry for smaller competitors. AI's capacity to analyze market data, predict trends, and optimize operations can reinforce the dominance of established players, leading to market concentration and the potential abuse of market power. Existing competition laws may not adequately address these dynamics, as they often focus on overtly monopolistic practices rather than the subtler effects of AI-driven competitive strategies.

**Intellectual property law and AI enforcement:** While intellectual property laws play a crucial role in protecting trademarks, copyrights, and patents, they face new challenges in the age of AI. The automated nature of AI surveillance for IP enforcement raises questions about the legality and ethicality of collecting data across digital platforms. Current IP laws do not clearly define the boundaries of AI's role in monitoring potential violations, leading to concerns about overreach and the potential misuse of surveillance technologies. Moreover, the international nature of digital commerce complicates the enforcement of IP rights, as companies must navigate varying legal standards across jurisdictions.

**Privacy regulations and consumer rights:** Privacy laws, such as the General Data Protection Regulation (GDPR) in the European Union, address some aspects of AI-driven data collection, emphasizing consent, transparency, and data protection. However, many jurisdictions still lack comprehensive privacy regulations that address AI's capacity to process personal data for commercial purposes. As companies increasingly use AI to collect and analyze consumer information, there is a growing need for regulations that set clear standards for ethical data use, ensure consumer rights, and establish accountability mechanisms for potential violations.

## Defining Boundaries for AI Use in Competition: Regulatory Proposals

To address the regulatory gaps surrounding AI in commerce, it is essential to define clear boundaries for AI use in competitive practices. Regulatory bodies must develop frameworks that guide businesses in employing AI ethically, preventing the technology from being used to distort market dynamics or infringe upon consumer rights (Pasquale, 2015). The following proposals offer strategic directions for establishing such boundaries within commercial regulation.

**Algorithmic transparency and audits:** One of the key measures for ensuring ethical AI use is to mandate algorithmic transparency. Companies that employ AI for competitive practices, such as pricing, market analysis, or customer segmentation, should be required to disclose their use of AI and provide information about how these systems operate. This transparency enables regulatory authorities to monitor AI behaviors for potential anticompetitive effects and holds companies accountable for their algorithms' actions (Diakopoulos, 2016).

In addition to transparency, regular algorithmic audits should be required to assess whether AI systems adhere to ethical standards and comply with competition laws. These audits can evaluate how algorithms make decisions, identify potential biases, and detect behaviors that may lead to market manipulation or consumer discrimination (Brundage et al., 2020). By implementing a structured audit process, regulators can ensure that companies' AI practices align with legal requirements and corporate social responsibility principles.

**Prohibiting algorithmic collusion:** Given the risks associated with algorithmic collusion, commercial regulations should explicitly prohibit AI systems from engaging in practices that resemble price-fixing or coordinated market behaviors. This prohibition could involve setting legal guidelines that define what constitutes unacceptable algorithmic interaction, such as price signaling or market partitioning.

To enforce these guidelines, regulatory bodies could implement monitoring mechanisms that detect patterns of parallel pricing among companies using AI-driven dynamic pricing strategies (Ezrachi & Stucke, 2016). If evidence of algorithmic collusion is found, companies should be held accountable, facing penalties similar to those for traditional antitrust violations.

**Data protection and ethical AI surveillance:** Regulations must also address the ethical implications of AI-driven market surveillance, particularly concerning data privacy. Commercial laws should establish clear standards for the collection, processing, and use of data by AI systems, emphasizing the principles of consent, transparency, and data minimization (Zarsky, 2016). For instance, companies should be required to obtain explicit consent from consumers before collecting personal data for AI analysis. Additionally, data minimization practices should be enforced to ensure that only necessary information is collected and used for legitimate business purposes.

To prevent the misuse of AI for intrusive market surveillance, regulations should define the limits of data collection regarding competitors' activities. While gathering publicly available information may be permissible, using AI to access proprietary or confidential data should be prohibited. By setting these boundaries, regulators can protect the competitive integrity of the marketplace while allowing businesses to leverage AI ethically.

**Establishing an international framework for IP enforcement:** Given the global nature of digital commerce, there is a pressing need for an international framework that standardizes the use of AI in intellectual property (IP) enforcement. This framework could involve collaborative efforts between countries to harmonize IP laws, facilitate cross-border enforcement, and create mechanisms for resolving disputes arising from AI-driven IP monitoring (Hughes, 2019). For example, international guidelines could define the acceptable scope of AI surveillance for copyright infringement, ensuring that such practices do not infringe on privacy rights or violate the laws of different jurisdictions.

## Legal Strategies for Corporate Compliance With Ethical AI Use

In addition to regulatory measures, companies themselves must adopt legal strategies to ensure compliance with ethical AI use in commercial practices. These strategies include developing internal policies, implementing oversight mechanisms, and fostering a corporate culture that prioritizes ethical decision-making.

**Developing AI ethics policies:** Companies should establish comprehensive AI ethics policies that outline the ethical principles and legal standards governing the use of AI within their operations. These policies should cover aspects such as data privacy, algorithmic transparency, and the fair use of AI in competition. For example, a company's AI ethics policy might include guidelines on conducting regular algorithmic audits, respecting consumer privacy rights, and avoiding practices that could lead to implicit collusion. By codifying these principles into formal policies, businesses can create a clear framework for ethical AI use that aligns with both commercial regulations and CSR objectives.

**Creating AI ethics committees:** To oversee the implementation of ethical AI practices, companies can form internal AI ethics committees comprising legal experts, data scientists, and business leaders. These committees would be responsible for reviewing AI-driven strategies, monitoring compliance with ethical guidelines, and addressing any ethical concerns that arise in the course of business operations. By involving diverse perspectives, AI ethics committees can help ensure that AI practices reflect a balance between competitive goals and ethical considerations, fostering responsible innovation.

**Training and awareness programs:** Legal compliance with ethical AI practices also requires fostering a culture of awareness and responsibility among employees. Companies should implement training programs that educate employees about the legal and ethical implications of AI, including the risks of anticompetitive behavior, privacy violations, and algorithmic biases. By raising awareness, businesses can empower their workforce to make informed decisions that support ethical AI use and align with regulatory standards.

### Collaborative Regulation and Industry Standards

In addition to formal regulations, collaborative efforts between regulatory bodies, industry stakeholders, and academia are essential for developing best practices and standards for ethical AI use in commerce. Industry associations, for example, can play a pivotal role in creating voluntary guidelines that set benchmarks for ethical AI practices, promoting transparency, accountability, and fair competition. By fostering dialogue and cooperation, these collaborative initiatives can bridge the gap between regulation and practice, ensuring that AI technologies contribute positively to market dynamics and societal well-being.

## PROPOSING A FRAMEWORK FOR SOCIAL RESPONSIBILITY IN AI-DRIVEN COMPETITION

In an era where artificial intelligence (AI) is transforming business strategies, competitive dynamics, and market behaviors, companies face the growing imperative to align their AI-driven practices with principles of corporate social responsibility (CSR). A framework for responsible AI use in competition is not only crucial for maintaining ethical standards but also for fostering trust, promoting fairness, and ensuring long-term sustainability in the marketplace. This section proposes a strategic framework for companies to adopt ethical AI practices that balance competitive advantages with societal welfare. By emphasizing transparency, fairness, and accountability, the proposed framework seeks to integrate CSR into AI-driven competition, ensuring that technological innovation contributes positively to both businesses and society.

## Guiding Principles for an Ethical AI-CSR Framework

The foundation of any responsible AI-CSR framework lies in establishing core principles that guide the ethical use of AI in competitive environments. These principles must align with both legal standards and CSR values, serving as a compass for companies to navigate the complexities of AI-driven competition. The following principles form the bedrock of this proposed framework:

**Transparency:** Transparency is a critical component of ethical AI use. Companies should be open about how they employ AI in their operations, including pricing algorithms, market surveillance, and customer engagement. This transparency extends to disclosing the data sources used for AI analysis, the methodologies behind algorithmic decisions, and the potential impacts on consumers and competitors. By fostering transparency, companies can build trust with stakeholders and create an environment where AI practices are subject to scrutiny and informed debate.

**Fairness:** AI-driven competition must be grounded in fairness, ensuring that practices do not exploit consumers, exclude competitors, or create unjust market advantages. This principle involves actively avoiding discriminatory pricing, predatory strategies, and data misuse. It also means implementing measures to mitigate biases in AI algorithms that may lead to unfair outcomes. Fairness in AI use reinforces the integrity of the marketplace and supports the creation of an equitable competitive landscape.

**Accountability:** Companies must be accountable for the outcomes of their AI systems. This includes taking responsibility for unintended consequences, such as algorithmic biases, privacy infringements, and anticompetitive behaviors. Establishing accountability mechanisms, such as internal review processes, ethics committees, and external audits, ensures that AI practices align with both ethical standards and legal requirements.

**Respect for privacy:** In the context of AI, respecting privacy is paramount. Companies should implement data protection policies that prioritize consent, data minimization, and secure handling of personal information. The ethical use of AI requires that businesses not only comply with existing privacy regulations but also proactively adopt practices that protect individuals' rights in the digital environment.

**Inclusivity and stakeholder engagement:** Ethical AI use should involve the perspectives of diverse stakeholders, including employees, customers, regulators, and industry partners. Engaging with these groups fosters a more comprehensive understanding of AI's societal impact and helps companies design AI practices that consider the interests of all parties involved. Inclusivity in AI decision-making is vital for ensuring that AI-driven strategies reflect broader societal values, not just corporate interests.

## Implementation Strategies for Ethical AI in Competition

While guiding principles establish the moral and ethical direction of AI use, companies must adopt concrete implementation strategies to operationalize these principles effectively. These strategies involve creating policies, systems, and practices that embed ethical considerations into AI-driven competitive activities.

**Adopting AI codes of conduct:** A formal code of conduct for AI use provides companies with a structured set of guidelines that articulate how AI should be applied ethically in business operations. This code should encompass the company's commitments to transparency, fairness, data privacy, and accountability. For example, a code of conduct might include provisions requiring regular audits of pricing algorithms to prevent discrimination, setting standards for data collection that protect consumer privacy, and mandating the disclosure of AI's role in customer interactions.

By adopting an AI code of conduct, companies signal their dedication to ethical practices and set clear expectations for employees and stakeholders. Furthermore, such a code provides a reference point for evaluating AI practices, guiding decision-making, and resolving ethical dilemmas that arise in the course of competition.

**Establishing internal AI ethics committees:** To ensure that AI practices align with CSR values, companies should form internal AI ethics committees comprising representatives from legal, technical, and business departments. These committees play a critical role in overseeing AI deployment, conducting risk assessments, and evaluating the ethical implications of AI-driven strategies. For instance, an AI ethics committee might review the introduction of a new pricing algorithm, assessing its potential impact on different consumer groups and identifying any risks of implicit collusion or unfair discrimination.

By facilitating cross-functional collaboration, AI ethics committees help companies navigate the complex interplay between business objectives, legal compliance, and ethical standards. Their work is essential for creating a culture of accountability and ethical vigilance, where AI practices are subject to regular scrutiny and improvement.

**Implementing algorithmic audits:** Regular audits of AI systems are a cornerstone of responsible AI use. These audits involve evaluating algorithms for biases, fairness, and compliance with both internal policies and external regulations. For example, an audit might examine whether a company's customer segmentation algorithm disproportionately disadvantages certain demographic groups, leading to unequal pricing or access to services.

Algorithmic audits also provide a mechanism for identifying unintended consequences of AI use, such as discriminatory outcomes or market behaviors that verge on anticompetitive practices. By continuously monitoring AI systems, companies can make informed adjustments to algorithms, ensuring that their AI practices remain ethical and aligned with CSR principles.

**Transparency initiatives and stakeholder communication:** Companies should adopt transparency initiatives that facilitate open communication with stakeholders about their AI use. This could involve publishing reports detailing how AI is employed in key business areas, the data sources used, and the measures taken to ensure ethical practices. Additionally, companies can establish channels for feedback and dialogue with customers, competitors, and regulatory bodies, fostering an environment of mutual trust and accountability.

For example, a company might create a public "AI ethics report" that outlines its approach to ethical AI, provides insights into its algorithmic decision-making processes, and describes its efforts to protect consumer privacy. Such transparency not only builds trust but also allows stakeholders to hold companies accountable for their AI practices, promoting a competitive environment that is both fair and responsible.

## Legal and Regulatory Engagement

The responsible use of AI in competition requires companies to actively engage with the evolving legal landscape. By collaborating with regulators and participating in policy discussions, businesses can help shape regulations that foster ethical AI use while supporting innovation and market competitiveness (Floridi et al., 2018).

**Collaborating with regulatory bodies:** Companies should work with regulatory authorities to develop industry standards and guidelines for ethical AI use. By participating in public consultations, industry roundtables, and policy development processes, businesses can contribute their expertise and insights to the creation of balanced regulations that address the complexities of AI-driven competition (Wachter, Mittelstadt, & Floridi, 2017).

Such collaboration also allows companies to stay informed about regulatory developments, ensuring that their AI practices remain compliant with legal standards. For instance, companies can engage with antitrust regulators to explore how their dynamic pricing algorithms interact with market dynamics, identifying potential risks of algorithmic collusion and implementing safeguards accordingly (Ezrachi & Stucke, 2016).

**Promoting industry self-regulation:** In addition to formal regulations, industry self-regulation plays a critical role in promoting ethical AI practices. Companies can participate in industry associations and consortia that establish voluntary codes of conduct, best practices, and certification programs for AI use. By adhering to these standards, companies demonstrate their commitment to responsible AI use and help set a benchmark for ethical behavior across the industry.

For example, a consortium of e-commerce companies might develop a voluntary code of conduct for dynamic pricing, outlining principles for transparency, fairness, and consumer protection. Companies that adopt this code can undergo periodic reviews and receive certifications that attest to their compliance with ethical standards, enhancing their reputation and credibility in the market.

## The Benefits of a Socially Responsible AI Framework

Implementing a framework for socially responsible AI use in competition offers several benefits for both companies and the broader market. By prioritizing transparency, fairness, and accountability, businesses can build trust with consumers, strengthen their brand reputation, and mitigate legal and ethical risks associated with AI practices (Wilson et al., 2017). Moreover, ethical AI use fosters a competitive environment where innovation thrives, market opportunities are accessible, and consumer welfare is protected (Schwartz, 2019).

From a CSR perspective, adopting an ethical AI framework enables companies to align their business strategies with societal values, contributing to the public good while achieving commercial success (Jobin et al., 2019). By demonstrating a commitment to responsible AI use, businesses can differentiate themselves in the marketplace, attracting customers, investors, and partners who prioritize ethical considerations (Cath et al., 2018).

## Toward a Holistic Approach to AI-Driven Competition

The integration of AI into competitive practices presents both challenges and opportunities for companies seeking to navigate the complex interplay between technological innovation and ethical standards. The framework proposed in this section offers a roadmap for companies to employ AI in ways that enhance competitiveness while upholding principles of corporate social responsibility. By adopting guiding principles, implementing strategic practices, and engaging with legal and regulatory developments, businesses can leverage AI ethically, fostering a marketplace that is fair, transparent, and inclusive (Floridi, 2018).

Ultimately, the adoption of a socially responsible AI framework is not just a matter of compliance or risk management—it is a strategic imperative for building sustainable business models that contribute positively to society. As AI continues to shape the future of competition, companies that embrace ethical practices will be well-positioned to lead the market, earning the trust and loyalty of consumers and stakeholders in an increasingly digital economy.

## CONCLUSION

The integration of artificial intelligence (AI) into business operations and competitive strategies has fundamentally transformed the commercial landscape, introducing unprecedented efficiencies, market insights, and opportunities for intellectual property protection. However, these advancements come with complex ethical, legal, and societal challenges that require careful navigation. As AI-driven practices become increasingly prevalent, companies face a dual imperative: to harness AI for competitive advantage while ensuring that its use aligns with the principles of corporate social responsibility (CSR) and fosters a fair and transparent marketplace. This chapter has explored the intricate interplay between AI, unfair competition, intellectual property protection, and commercial regulation, culminating in the proposal of a framework for ethical AI use in competition.

One of the central themes of this chapter has been the need to balance the potential of AI as an innovative tool for market competition with the ethical imperative to maintain fairness and transparency. AI technologies have reshaped the competitive environment by enabling companies to automate pricing, monitor markets, protect intellectual property, and tailor their strategies based on vast amounts of data. Yet, these capabilities also introduce risks of market manipulation, data exploitation, privacy violations, and unfair competitive practices, which threaten the integrity of the marketplace.

The framework proposed in this chapter advocates for a balanced approach that emphasizes transparency, fairness, accountability, respect for privacy, and stakeholder engagement. By embedding these principles into AI practices, companies can navigate the complexities of AI-driven competition responsibly. This balance is not only crucial for upholding ethical standards but also for fostering consumer trust, ensuring regulatory compliance, and promoting a marketplace where innovation thrives alongside equity and inclusion.

The chapter has highlighted several ethical dilemmas associated with AI in competition, including algorithmic collusion, dynamic pricing, market surveillance, and data exploitation. These dilemmas underscore the need for companies to carefully assess the potential consequences of their AI strategies. For example, while dynamic pricing algorithms can optimize revenues and respond to market demands, they can also lead to price discrimination or implicit collusion that undermines market fairness. Similarly, AI-driven market surveillance enhances the ability to protect intellectual property but can encroach on privacy rights and involve questionable data collection practices.

Addressing these dilemmas requires a nuanced approach that integrates CSR principles into AI-driven practices. Companies must prioritize ethical considerations such as consumer welfare, privacy protection, and non-discrimination in their AI use. This involves not only adhering to legal standards but also going beyond compliance to adopt ethical guidelines and self-regulatory practices that reflect a genuine commitment to responsible competition. By doing so, businesses can mitigate the ethical risks of AI while leveraging its capabilities to enhance market efficiency and innovation.

The chapter has emphasized the critical role of commercial regulation in shaping the ethical use of AI in competition. Existing laws, particularly those related to antitrust, intellectual property, and data privacy, provide a foundational framework for regulating business practices. However, the rapid advancement of AI has exposed gaps in these regulations, highlighting the need for more adaptive legal strategies that address the unique challenges posed by AI technologies.

Regulatory proposals discussed in the chapter include mandating algorithmic transparency, implementing regular audits, prohibiting algorithmic collusion, and establishing clear standards for data collection and use. These measures aim to ensure that AI practices do not infringe upon the principles of fair competition, consumer rights, or market accessibility. By setting boundaries for AI use, commercial regulations can provide companies with a clearer understanding of their legal and ethical obligations, promoting a level playing field where businesses can compete on the merits of their innovation and integrity.

However, regulation alone is not sufficient to address the ethical complexities of AI. The chapter also advocates for industry self-regulation and collaboration with regulatory bodies to develop best practices and standards for ethical AI use. This dual approach—combining formal regulations with voluntary codes of conduct and industry guidelines—offers a comprehensive strategy for fostering a responsible AI-driven marketplace.

In addition to regulatory engagement, the chapter has outlined practical strategies for companies to implement ethical AI practices within their competitive activities. The proposed framework includes adopting AI codes of conduct, establishing internal

AI ethics committees, conducting regular algorithmic audits, and promoting transparency through stakeholder communication. These strategies serve as mechanisms for operationalizing ethical principles, ensuring that AI-driven competition aligns with both legal standards and CSR values.

By adopting an AI code of conduct, companies can define their commitments to ethical AI use, setting clear guidelines for transparency, fairness, and privacy protection. AI ethics committees provide oversight and accountability, offering a platform for evaluating the ethical implications of AI strategies and making informed decisions that prioritize societal welfare alongside business objectives. Regular audits are essential for monitoring algorithms for biases, discriminatory outcomes, and potential anticompetitive behaviors, enabling companies to take corrective action when necessary.

Transparency initiatives, such as publishing AI ethics reports and engaging in dialogue with stakeholders, further reinforce the company's commitment to ethical practices. By openly communicating how AI is used, companies can build trust with consumers, regulators, and partners, fostering a culture of accountability and inclusivity in the marketplace.

The adoption of a socially responsible AI framework offers numerous benefits for companies and society at large. From a business perspective, integrating ethical principles into AI practices enhances the company's reputation, builds consumer trust, and reduces the risk of legal challenges. Ethical AI use also supports long-term market sustainability by promoting competition based on innovation and value creation rather than exploitative practices.

For society, a responsible AI framework contributes to a marketplace where consumers are protected, privacy rights are respected, and diverse competitors have a fair opportunity to succeed. By addressing the ethical challenges of AI, companies can help shape a market environment that reflects societal values, supports economic inclusion, and encourages technological progress that benefits all stakeholders.

The ethical integration of AI in business competition is not merely a matter of compliance with legal requirements—it is a strategic choice that reflects a company's commitment to societal welfare and sustainable market practices. As companies continue to adopt AI technologies, they must do so with a sense of responsibility, recognizing the broader impact of their competitive strategies on consumers, competitors, and society. By adopting the framework proposed in this chapter, businesses can lead the way in setting a new standard for ethical AI use, one that balances innovation with fairness, transparency, and respect for human rights.

AI's role in competition is a powerful force that can drive market efficiency, innovation, and growth. However, its potential for misuse underscores the importance of establishing robust ethical guidelines and regulatory measures. The future of AI in commerce depends on our ability to shape its use in ways that promote not just competitive success but also the common good. By embracing ethical AI practices, companies can contribute to a marketplace that is not only technologically advanced but also just, equitable, and sustainable.

## FUTURE DIRECTIONS AND ONGOING CHALLENGES

Despite the advances in developing a framework for ethical AI use, the field continues to evolve, presenting new challenges and questions. The rapid pace of AI development necessitates ongoing research and dialogue to address emerging ethical issues and refine legal frameworks. For example, as AI systems become more autonomous and capable of making complex decisions, questions arise about the extent of human oversight required and how accountability should be assigned for AI-driven actions.

Moreover, the global nature of AI-driven commerce calls for international cooperation in establishing standards and regulations that harmonize practices across jurisdictions. Cross-border collaboration is essential to address issues such as intellectual property enforcement, data privacy, and algorithmic accountability in the international marketplace.

## REFERENCES


Brundage, M., Avin, S., Clark, J., . . .. (2020). Toward Trustworthy AI Development: Mechanisms for Supporting Verifiable Claims. *arXiv preprint arXiv:2004.07213.*

Calo, R. (2017). Artificial Intelligence Policy: A Primer and Roadmap. *University of California, Davis Law Review*, 51(2), 399–435.

Calvano, E., Calzolari, G., Denicolò, V., & Pastorello, S. (2020). Artificial Intelligence, Algorithmic Pricing, and Collusion. *The American Economic Review*, 110(10), 3267–3297. DOI: 10.1257/aer.20190623

Cath, C., Wachter, S., Mittelstadt, B., Taddeo, M., & Floridi, L. (2018). Artificial Intelligence and the 'Good Society': The US, EU, and UK Approach. *Science and Engineering Ethics*, 24(2), 505–528. PMID: 28353045

Chien, C. V. (2019). Predicting Patent Litigation. *Texas Law Review*, 97(2), 383–452.

Diakopoulos, N. (2016). Accountability in Algorithmic Decision Making. *Communications of the ACM*, 59(2), 56–62. DOI: 10.1145/2844110

Ezrachi, A., & Stucke, M. E. (2016). *Virtual Competition: The Promise and Perils of the Algorithm-Driven Economy*. Harvard University Press. DOI: 10.4159/9780674973336

Floridi, L. (2018). Soft Ethics and the Governance of the Digital. *Philosophy & Technology*, 31(1), 1–8. DOI: 10.1007/s13347-018-0303-9 PMID: 30322997

Floridi, L., Cowls, J., Beltrametti, M., Chatila, R., Chazerand, P., Dignum, V., Luetge, C., Madelin, R., Pagallo, U., Rossi, F., Schafer, B., Valcke, P., & Vayena, E. (2018). AI4People—An Ethical Framework for a Good AI Society: Opportunities, Risks, Principles, and Recommendations. *Minds and Machines*, 28(4), 689–707. DOI: 10.1007/s11023-018-9482-5 PMID: 30930541

Floridi, L., Cowls, J., & King, T. C.. (2018). AI4People—An Ethical Framework for a Good AI Society: Opportunities, Risks, Principles, and Recommendations. *Minds and Machines*, 28(4), 689–707. DOI: 10.1007/s11023-018-9482-5 PMID: 30930541

Hughes, J. (2019). The Law of Intellectual Property: The Need for a Global Framework. *Intellectual Property Quarterly*, 3, 214–232.

Jarrahi, M. H. (2018). Artificial Intelligence and the Future of Work: Human-AI Symbiosis in Organizational Decision Making. *Business Horizons*, 61(4), 577–586. DOI: 10.1016/j.bushor.2018.03.007

Jobin, A., Ienca, M., & Vayena, E. (2019). The Global Landscape of AI Ethics Guidelines. *Nature Machine Intelligence*, 1(9), 389–399. DOI: 10.1038/s42256-019-0088-2

Kaminski, M. E. (2019). The Right to Explanation, Explained. *Berkeley Technology Law Journal*, 34(1), 189–218.

Kaplan, A., & Haenlein, M. (2020). Rulers of the World, Unite! The Challenges and Opportunities of Artificial Intelligence. *Business Horizons*, 63(1), 37–50. DOI: 10.1016/j.bushor.2019.09.003

Martin, K., & Murphy, P. (2017). The Ethics of Big Data: Current and Future Challenges. *Business Horizons*, 60(2), 211–220.

Pasquale, F. (2015). *The Black Box Society: The Secret Algorithms That Control Money and Information*. Harvard University Press. DOI: 10.4159/harvard.9780674736061

Schwartz, P. M. (2019). Data Protection Law and the Ethical Use of Analytics. *Berkeley Technology Law Journal*, 34(2), 1121–1178.

Sharma, A., Garg, A., & Sujeet, K. (2021). Artificial Intelligence and Intellectual Property: Evolving Strategies for IP Management. *Journal of Intellectual Property Rights*, 26(1), 22–31.

Tene, O., & Polonetsky, J. (2013). Big data for all: Privacy and user control in the age of analytics. *Northwestern Journal of Technology and Intellectual Property*, 11(5), 239–273.

Trappey, A. J., Wu, C. Y., Taghaboni-Dutta, F., & Trappey, C. V. (2017). Using patent data for technology forecasting: China RFID patent analysis. *Advanced Engineering Informatics*, 31, 105–120.

Vinuesa, R., Azizpour, H., Leite, I., Balaam, M., Dignum, V., Domisch, S., & Nerini, F. F. (2020). The Role of Artificial Intelligence in Achieving the Sustainable Development Goals. *Nature Communications*, 11(1), 233. DOI: 10.1038/s41467-019-14108-y PMID: 31932590

Wachter, S., Mittelstadt, B., & Floridi, L. (2017). Why a Right to Explanation of Automated Decision-Making Does Not Exist in the General Data Protection Regulation. *International Data Privacy Law*, 7(2), 76–99. DOI: 10.1093/idpl/ipx005

Wilson, H. J., Daugherty, P. R., & Bianzino, N. (2017). The Jobs That Artificial Intelligence Will Create. *MIT Sloan Management Review*, 58(4), 14–16.

Yeung, K. (2018). Algorithmic Regulation: A Critical Interrogation. *Regulation & Governance*, 12(4), 505–523. DOI: 10.1111/rego.12158

Zarsky, T. Z. (2016). Incompatible: The GDPR in the Age of Big Data. *Seton Hall Law Review*, 47(4), 995–1020.

Zeng, Y., Chen, P., & Luo, W. (2021). The Role of Data Ethics in AI Development. *International Journal of Information Management*, 56, 102208.

Zhang, L., Chen, Y., & Yin, Y. (2021). AI-enabled patent intelligence for competitive technical analysis. *Technological Forecasting and Social Change*, 163, 120442.

# Section 3
# Regional Perspectives and Applications

# Chapter 8
# AI-Driven CSR in East Asia:
## Navigating Leadership and Ethical Challenges

**Jenny Patricia Vargas Portillo**
https://orcid.org/0000-0002-0226-3053
*Universidad de Sevilla, Spain*

## ABSTRACT

*This chapter examines AI implementation in CSR initiatives within East Asian organizations, focusing on challenges and opportunities from traditional paternalistic leadership styles. It analyzes recent theoretical developments and empirical studies to explore how these organizations balance technological innovation and cultural preservation. The research reveals how traditional business values influence AI adoption, especially in hierarchical contexts. It highlights the importance of cultural alignment in successful AI implementation, emphasizing frameworks that accommodate both technical capabilities and cultural sensitivities. The chapter provides insights on integrating AI technologies while maintaining cultural integrity, suggesting that successful AI implementation in CSR depends on culturally sensitive approaches. It also identifies key areas for future research, including the long-term impacts of AI on organizational culture and stakeholder relationships.*

## INTRODUCTION

The integration of Artificial Intelligence (AI) into Corporate Social Responsibility (CSR) initiatives has emerged as a transformative force in global business practices, particularly within the context of East Asian business cultures. The rapid

DOI: 10.4018/979-8-3693-9894-4.ch008

advancement of AI technologies, as noted by Wang (2021), has fundamentally altered the landscape of organizational decision-making and leadership approaches. This transformation has been especially pronounced in East Asian contexts, where traditional paternalistic leadership styles intersect with technological innovation. The relationship between AI implementation and organizational leadership has been extensively examined in recent literature, with particular attention paid to the unique challenges and opportunities presented by this technological revolution (Kaur et al., 2022).

The significance of this chapter lies in its comprehensive examination of how AI-driven CSR initiatives are being shaped by and are reshaping traditional East Asian business practices. Through careful analysis of both theoretical frameworks and practical implementations, this work contributes to the growing body of knowledge regarding the intersection of technological innovation and cultural preservation in organizational contexts. As emphasized by Jiménez et al. (2021), the successful integration of AI technologies depends heavily on the strength of cooperative relationships and cultural alignment within organizational structures. This chapter addresses this crucial intersection by providing a detailed examination of how East Asian organizations navigate the complex dynamics between technological advancement and traditional business values.

The contemporary business landscape in East Asia has been characterized by rapid technological advancement coupled with strong cultural traditions, creating unique challenges for organizations implementing AI-driven initiatives. As explored by Meng (2024), the integration of AI technologies in organizational contexts presents both opportunities and challenges, particularly in environments where traditional structures remain strong. This dynamic has created a pressing need for frameworks that can guide organizations through the complex process of technological adoption while preserving cultural values and maintaining organizational harmony. The examination of these frameworks represents a significant contribution to both theoretical understanding and practical implementation strategies.

The scope of this investigation encompasses several key areas that have been identified as critical to understanding AI implementation in East Asian organizational contexts. These areas include the evolution of leadership practices in response to AI integration, as explored by Sposato (2024), the development of ethical frameworks that accommodate both technological capabilities and cultural values, as examined by Zhang et al. (2022), and the transformation of stakeholder engagement processes in AI-enhanced environments, as analyzed by Seo et al. (2021). Through examination of these interconnected dimensions, this chapter provides valuable insights into how organizations can effectively balance innovation with tradition while maintaining cultural integrity.

Recent developments in AI technology and its applications in CSR have further complicated the implementation landscape for East Asian organizations. The work of Fullan et al. (2024) has highlighted the increasing importance of developing comprehensive approaches to leadership development that address both technical and cultural considerations. These developments have created new challenges for organizations seeking to maintain traditional values while leveraging advanced technological capabilities. The exploration of these challenges and potential solutions represents another significant contribution of this chapter to the existing literature.

This work makes several significant contributions to the field. First, it provides a comprehensive framework for understanding how AI implementation affects and is affected by traditional East Asian leadership approaches. Second, it offers practical insights into the development of culturally sensitive implementation strategies that can help organizations navigate the complex landscape of technological innovation. Third, it presents a detailed analysis of how ethical considerations in AI implementation must be adapted to accommodate East Asian cultural values and business practices. As noted by Wang et al. (2021), these insights are particularly crucial as organizations seek to create symbiotic relationships between human judgment and artificial intelligence capabilities.

The structure of this chapter has been carefully designed to progress from theoretical foundations through practical implications to future considerations. Initially, the theoretical framework underlying AI integration in East Asian contexts is examined, followed by an analysis of how leadership practices are evolving in response to technological innovation. Subsequent sections explore ethical considerations, methodological approaches, cultural dimensions, and organizational learning processes. The chapter concludes with an examination of practical implications, future directions, and strategic considerations for organizations seeking to implement AI-driven CSR initiatives while maintaining cultural sensitivity.

Furthermore, this chapter addresses the growing need for empirical evidence regarding the effectiveness of different implementation approaches in East Asian contexts. As highlighted by Ouyang et al. (2022), successful AI implementation depends heavily on systematic approaches that account for both technical and cultural considerations. The analysis presented here contributes to this understanding by examining various implementation strategies and their outcomes across different organizational contexts. This examination provides valuable insights for both researchers and practitioners seeking to understand and improve AI implementation processes in East Asian organizations.

## THEORETICAL FRAMEWORK AND CONTEXT

The theoretical underpinning of AI integration in East Asian business contexts has been shaped by several key frameworks and cultural considerations that warrant deeper examination. The concept of trustworthy artificial intelligence, as elaborated by Kaur et al. (2022), provides a foundation for understanding how AI systems can be effectively implemented within organizational structures while maintaining ethical standards. This framework becomes particularly relevant when considered alongside the traditional paternalistic leadership styles prevalent in East Asian business cultures. The symbiotic relationship between human decision-making and artificial intelligence, as described by Wang (2021), suggests that successful integration requires a careful balance between technological capabilities and human oversight.

The integration of AI technologies within East Asian organizational contexts has been influenced by multiple theoretical perspectives on organizational learning and innovation adoption. According to Jiménez et al. (2021), the triple helix model of innovation provides valuable insights into how organizations can effectively coordinate technological advancement with existing cultural practices. This model emphasizes the importance of cooperation and relationship-building in successful innovation implementation, aspects that align closely with traditional East Asian business values.

The theoretical framework must also account for the unique characteristics of East Asian leadership approaches. Wang et al. (2021) have identified significant relationships between organizational support systems and the successful implementation of AI initiatives, particularly in contexts where traditional hierarchical structures remain strong. The integration of AI technologies has been found to both challenge and reinforce existing power structures within organizations, creating complex dynamics that must be carefully managed. As noted by Kuleto et al. (2021), the opportunities and challenges presented by AI implementation often intersect with established organizational hierarchies and decision-making processes.

Furthermore, the theoretical framework must consider the role of cultural values in shaping technology adoption patterns. Ouyang et al. (2022) have demonstrated through systematic review that successful AI implementation in organizational contexts depends heavily on cultural alignment and stakeholder acceptance. This finding is particularly relevant in East Asian contexts, where collective decision-making and consensus-building often play crucial roles in organizational change processes. The theoretical understanding of AI integration must therefore account for both technical capabilities and cultural considerations.

The framework also encompasses considerations of ethical implementation and governance structures. Zhang et al. (2022) have emphasized the importance of establishing clear ethical guidelines and regulatory frameworks for AI implementation in organizational contexts. These considerations become particularly significant in East Asian business environments, where traditional values regarding authority, responsibility, and social harmony must be reconciled with the demands of technological innovation. The theoretical framework must therefore address both the technical and ethical dimensions of AI implementation, while remaining sensitive to cultural contexts and organizational traditions.

Additionally, the theoretical understanding of AI integration must account for the evolving nature of leadership development in technological contexts. Recent work by Sposato (2024) has highlighted the importance of adapting leadership training and development approaches to accommodate AI implementation, particularly in traditional business environments. This adaptation process must be understood within the broader context of organizational change and cultural preservation, as organizations seek to maintain their cultural identity while pursuing technological innovation.

The transformation of leadership practices in response to AI integration has been documented across various sectors. Sposato (2024) has observed that leadership training and development have undergone significant changes in response to AI implementation, particularly in traditional business environments. The integration of AI technologies has necessitated a reconceptualization of leadership roles, with traditional paternalistic approaches being adapted to accommodate technological innovation. This evolution has been particularly noticeable in East Asian contexts, where cultural values and technological advancement must be carefully balanced.

## ETHICAL CONSIDERATIONS AND IMPLEMENTATION CHALLENGES

The ethical implications of AI implementation in CSR initiatives within East Asian organizational contexts have been revealed to be multifaceted and deeply intertwined with cultural values. The traditional Confucian principles that underpin many East Asian business practices have been observed to significantly influence how ethical considerations are conceptualized and addressed. As noted by Zhang et al. (2022), the establishment of ethical guidelines and regulatory frameworks for AI implementation must be approached through a culturally sensitive lens that acknowledges the distinct characteristics of East Asian organizational structures.

The ethical decision-making framework in East Asian contexts has been found to be particularly influenced by collective responsibility and harmonious relationships. According to Nguyen et al. (2022), the implementation of AI technologies must be guided by ethical principles that extend beyond individual rights to encompass collective wellbeing and social harmony. This consideration has been demonstrated to be especially pertinent in contexts where organizational decisions are traditionally made through consensus-building processes and where the impact on collective welfare is prioritized over individual outcomes.

Data privacy and security considerations in East Asian organizations have been observed to reflect a unique balance between technological advancement and cultural values. The protection of sensitive information has been approached through what Wang et al. (2021) describe as a "symbiotic relationship" between traditional trust-based systems and modern technological safeguards. This relationship has been found to require careful attention to both technical security measures and cultural expectations regarding information sharing and protection. The implementation of data protection frameworks has been noted to necessitate consideration of local cultural norms regarding privacy and the collective ownership of information.

The social impact assessment of AI implementation in East Asian contexts has been revealed to require particular attention to relationship networks and social hierarchies. As emphasized by Kaur et al. (2022), the development of trustworthy AI systems must account for the complex web of social relationships that characterize East Asian business environments. The impact assessment process has been found to necessitate consideration of both direct effects on organizational stakeholders and broader implications for social harmony and collective wellbeing.

The ethical framework for AI implementation has been observed to require specific attention to power dynamics within East Asian organizational structures. According to Kuleto et al. (2021), the opportunities and challenges presented by AI implementation often intersect with established hierarchical relationships and decision-making processes. The ethical considerations must therefore address not only technical capabilities but also the preservation of important cultural values regarding authority and responsibility.

Knowledge protection and intellectual property considerations have been found to present unique challenges in East Asian contexts. The traditional emphasis on knowledge sharing and collective learning has been noted to require careful balance with modern requirements for data protection and intellectual property rights. As observed by Ouyang et al. (2022), successful AI implementation depends heavily on establishing frameworks that protect sensitive information while maintaining cultural values regarding knowledge transfer and collective benefit.

The ethical implications of AI-driven decision-making processes have been demonstrated to require particular attention in East Asian organizational contexts. The traditional emphasis on human judgment and relationship-based decision-making has been found to necessitate careful consideration of how AI systems can support rather than replace human wisdom. As noted by Wang (2021), the creation of symbiotic relationships between human judgment and artificial intelligence capabilities requires careful attention to ethical principles that preserve cultural values while leveraging technological advantages.

The development of ethical frameworks for AI implementation has been observed to require specific attention to stakeholder engagement processes. According to Seo et al. (2021), the impact of AI on stakeholder relationships must be carefully managed to maintain meaningful connections while leveraging technological capabilities. The ethical framework must therefore address both the technical aspects of AI implementation and the preservation of important relationship networks that characterize East Asian business environments.

The future development of ethical guidelines for AI implementation has been noted to require ongoing attention to evolving cultural dynamics. As emphasized by ElSayary (2024), the integration of AI technologies can enhance organizational capabilities while requiring careful attention to cultural preservation and ethical considerations. The ethical framework must therefore remain adaptable while maintaining core cultural values and principles that guide organizational behavior in East Asian contexts.

This comprehensive approach to ethical considerations has been demonstrated to be essential for successful AI implementation in East Asian organizational contexts. The framework must continue to evolve while maintaining sensitivity to cultural values and traditions that have historically guided business practices in these environments.

## METHODOLOGICAL APPROACHES TO AI INTEGRATION

The implementation of AI in organizational contexts has been approached through multiple methodological frameworks, each offering distinct insights into the integration process. The importance of rigorous research methods in understanding organizational transformations has been emphasized by Bell et al. (2022), particularly when examining the intersection of technology and traditional business practices. A comprehensive understanding of these methodological approaches has been deemed essential for successful AI integration, especially within the unique cultural and organizational contexts of East Asian institutions.

The foundational methodological framework has been constructed through both empirical and non-empirical approaches, as outlined by Dan (2017). Empirical methodologies have been employed to gather quantitative data on implementation outcomes, while non-empirical approaches have provided valuable insights into the theoretical underpinnings of AI integration. This dual approach has been particularly valuable in East Asian contexts, where traditional business practices must be carefully considered alongside technological innovation.

Systematic review methodologies have emerged as a crucial tool in understanding AI implementation patterns. As demonstrated by Ouyang et al. (2022), comprehensive reviews of empirical research have revealed significant patterns in AI adoption within organizational contexts. These systematic approaches have been particularly valuable in identifying key success factors and potential barriers to implementation, especially in traditional business environments where cultural considerations play a crucial role.

The assessment of AI integration has been further enhanced through mixed-methods approaches, as evidenced in recent studies. According to Pucchio et al. (2022), cross-sectional mixed-methods studies have provided valuable insights into organizational readiness and implementation challenges. This methodological approach has been particularly effective in capturing both quantitative metrics of implementation success and qualitative insights into cultural adaptation processes.

Longitudinal research methodologies have been employed to track the evolution of AI integration over time. Wang et al. (2021) have identified significant relationships between organizational support systems and implementation success through extended observation periods. These longitudinal approaches have been essential in understanding how organizations adapt to technological change while maintaining cultural integrity.

Action research methodologies have been increasingly utilized to study AI implementation in real-world contexts. Bell et al. (2018) have proposed comprehensive approaches for conducting actionable research within organizational settings, particularly noting the importance of stakeholder engagement in the research process. This methodological framework has been especially valuable in East Asian contexts, where collective decision-making processes often play crucial roles in technological adoption.

The evaluation of AI integration has also been approached through case study methodologies. As demonstrated by Kuleto et al. (2021), detailed case studies have revealed various opportunities and challenges in the implementation of AI and machine learning in organizational contexts. These case studies have provided valuable insights into the specific challenges faced by organizations attempting to balance technological innovation with cultural preservation.

Quantitative methodologies have been employed to measure the impact of AI implementation on organizational performance. According to Deo et al. (2020), modern AI model development has required sophisticated quantitative approaches to evaluate implementation success. These methodological frameworks have been particularly valuable in assessing the technical aspects of AI integration while maintaining sensitivity to organizational contexts.

Qualitative research approaches have been utilized to understand the human dimensions of AI integration. As noted by Thomas (2006), general inductive approaches have been valuable in analyzing qualitative evaluation data related to technological implementation. These methodological frameworks have been especially important in understanding how organizational stakeholders adapt to and interact with AI systems.

The development of implementation frameworks has been informed by comparative methodologies. Research by Xia et al. (2022) has employed comparative approaches to identify common patterns and unique challenges across different organizational contexts. These comparative frameworks have been particularly valuable in understanding how cultural factors influence AI integration processes.

Throughout these various methodological approaches, the importance of cultural sensitivity has been consistently emphasized. The successful integration of AI technologies has been found to require careful consideration of both technical capabilities and cultural contexts, as highlighted by Wang (2021) in studies of symbiotic relationships between human judgment and artificial intelligence capabilities. This cultural awareness has been integrated into methodological frameworks through careful attention to stakeholder engagement and organizational values.

The methodological approaches to AI integration continue to evolve as new technologies emerge and organizational needs change. Future research directions may include the development of more sophisticated mixed-methods approaches that can better capture the complex interplay between technological innovation and cultural preservation in East Asian organizational contexts (Sposato, 2015).

## Cultural Dimensions and Organizational Learning

The relationship between cultural values and technological innovation has been examined through the lens of organizational learning theory. Wang et al. (2021) have identified significant correlations between organizational support systems and the successful implementation of AI initiatives. In East Asian contexts, the traditional emphasis on collective learning and hierarchical knowledge transfer has influenced how organizations approach AI integration. The integration process has been found to be most effective when it aligns with existing cultural values while promoting innovation and adaptation. According to Jiménez et al. (2021), the success of innovation initiatives often depends on the strength of cooperative relationships within organizational structures.

## Leadership Development and AI Competencies

The development of leadership capabilities in AI-enhanced environments has been identified as a critical consideration for East Asian organizations. Through recent empirical studies, several key challenges and opportunities in the development of AI-aware leadership practices have been identified by Fullan et al. (2024), with particular attention being paid to the complex intersection between traditional leadership approaches and technological innovation. The traditional paternalistic leadership model has necessitated significant adaptation to accommodate the technical and ethical demands of AI implementation, while the cultural values that have historically defined East Asian business practices have been carefully preserved.

The integration of AI competencies into leadership development programs has demanded a fundamental reconsideration of traditional training approaches. According to Meng (2024), the convergence of big data and AI in leadership practices has presented both opportunities and challenges, particularly in contexts where traditional hierarchical structures remain prevalent. The development of AI competencies among leaders has been found to require not only technical understanding but also a sophisticated appreciation of the cultural implications of technological change. This dual requirement has led to the emergence of new approaches to leadership development that emphasize both technical literacy and cultural sensitivity.

The transformation of leadership practices in response to AI integration has been particularly pronounced in organizational contexts where traditional values regarding authority and decision-making must be reconciled with the capabilities and limitations of AI systems. Wang (2021) has emphasized the importance of developing symbiotic relationships between human judgment and artificial intelligence capabilities, noting that effective leadership in AI-enhanced environments requires a careful balance between technological reliance and human oversight. This balance has been found to be especially critical in East Asian contexts, where cultural values regarding collective decision-making and hierarchical authority structures must be carefully maintained.

The evolution of leadership competencies has been significantly influenced by changing patterns of stakeholder engagement in AI-enhanced environments. As noted by Seo et al. (2021), substantial shifts in interaction patterns between leaders and organizational stakeholders have been observed, necessitating the development of new competencies related to stakeholder communication and technological mediation. These changes have been particularly pronounced in East Asian contexts, where traditional relationship-building approaches have required careful adaptation to accommodate technological innovation while preserving cultural values.

The ethical dimensions of AI leadership development have received increased attention in contemporary organizational contexts. Through comprehensive research, Nguyen et al. (2022) have identified the critical importance of incorporating ethical principles into AI-related leadership development programs. The integration of ethical considerations has been found to be particularly crucial in East Asian environments, where traditional values regarding social responsibility and collective welfare play significant roles in organizational decision-making. Leaders have been required to develop competencies not only in the technical aspects of AI implementation but also in managing the ethical implications of technological innovation within culturally sensitive environments.

Recent developments in leadership training methodologies have been shaped by the need for comprehensive approaches that address both technological and cultural considerations. As demonstrated by Sposato (2024), the importance of developing integrated approaches to leadership training has been emphasized, with particular attention being paid to the balance between innovation and tradition. These approaches have been designed to address not only the technical aspects of AI implementation but also the cultural and organizational implications of technological change. The success of such programs has been found to depend heavily on their ability to maintain cultural sensitivity while promoting technological innovation and adaptation.

The role of organizational support systems in leadership development has been identified as a critical success factor in AI implementation initiatives. According to Kuleto et al. (2021), various opportunities and challenges in the implementation of AI and machine learning in organizational contexts have been observed, with particular emphasis being placed on the importance of sustained leadership development initiatives. These initiatives have been required to balance the need for technical competency development with the preservation of traditional leadership values and approaches.

The impact of AI integration on leadership communication patterns has been extensively studied in recent research. Wang et al. (2021) have identified significant correlations between organizational support systems and successful AI implementation, particularly noting the importance of leadership engagement in technology adoption processes. The development of communication competencies has been found to be most effective when integrated into existing organizational frameworks while acknowledging the unique characteristics of East Asian business cultures.

The future trajectory of leadership development in AI-enhanced environments has been shaped by emerging technological capabilities and evolving organizational needs. As emphasized by ElSayary (2024), the integration of AI technologies can enhance organizational capabilities while requiring careful attention to cultural preservation and ethical considerations. Leadership development programs have been required to evolve continuously to address these changing needs while maintaining alignment with traditional values and cultural practices.

Through this comprehensive approach to leadership development, the integration of AI competencies has been achieved while preserving important cultural values and organizational traditions. The success of these initiatives has been found to depend heavily on organizations' ability to maintain balance between technological innovation and cultural preservation, particularly in East Asian contexts where traditional leadership approaches continue to play significant roles in organizational success.

## PRACTICAL IMPLICATIONS FOR CSR IMPLEMENTATION

The practical implications of AI integration in CSR initiatives have been observed to extend across multiple organizational dimensions in East Asian contexts. In recent empirical studies, it has been demonstrated that the integration of AI technologies can significantly enhance organizational learning and metacognitive capabilities (ElSayary, 2024). The implementation process in East Asian contexts must be carefully balanced against traditional approaches to corporate responsibility and stakeholder engagement, with particular attention paid to cultural sensitivities and established business practices.

The effectiveness of AI-driven CSR initiatives has been found to be significantly influenced by organizational readiness and support systems. According to Wang et al. (2021), the successful implementation of AI technologies depends heavily on the establishment of comprehensive support structures that align with existing organizational processes. These support systems must be designed to accommodate both technical requirements and cultural considerations, particularly in contexts where traditional decision-making approaches remain prevalent.

The integration of AI technologies in CSR practices has been observed to require specific attention to knowledge management processes. As noted by Popenici and Kerr (2017), the successful implementation of AI initiatives depends heavily on organizations' ability to effectively manage and transfer knowledge across different organizational levels. This requirement becomes particularly significant in East Asian contexts, where traditional knowledge-sharing practices must be carefully balanced with technological innovation.

Stakeholder engagement processes have been identified as critical factors in successful AI implementation. Research by Seo et al. (2021) has revealed significant patterns in stakeholder interaction within AI-enhanced environments, particularly noting the importance of maintaining meaningful relationships while leveraging technological capabilities. The implementation process must therefore address both technical requirements and social dimensions of stakeholder engagement, with particular attention paid to preserving traditional relationship networks.

The development of implementation frameworks has been found to require careful consideration of cultural factors. According to Ouyang et al. (2022), successful implementation of AI technologies in organizational contexts depends on systematic approaches that account for both technical and cultural considerations. These frameworks must be designed to accommodate traditional decision-making processes while promoting technological innovation and adaptation.

Training and development requirements have been identified as crucial elements of successful AI implementation. Research by Kuleto et al. (2021) has revealed various opportunities and challenges in the implementation of AI and machine learning in organizational contexts, particularly noting the importance of comprehensive training programs. These programs must be designed to address both technical competencies and cultural considerations, ensuring that staff at all levels can effectively engage with AI-driven CSR initiatives.

The monitoring and evaluation of AI-driven CSR initiatives has been found to require specific attention to both technical and social metrics. As emphasized by Zhang et al. (2022), the establishment of clear evaluation frameworks must address both quantitative performance indicators and qualitative social impacts. These frameworks must be designed to capture both the technical effectiveness of AI implementations and their broader social implications.

Resource allocation considerations have been identified as critical factors in successful implementation. According to Meng (2024), the integration of AI technologies in organizational contexts presents both opportunities and challenges regarding resource distribution and utilization. Organizations must carefully balance investments in technical infrastructure with investments in human capital development and cultural preservation.

The adaptation of existing CSR practices to accommodate AI capabilities has been found to require careful attention to organizational change management. Research by Sposato (2024) has revealed the importance of developing comprehensive change management strategies that address both technical and cultural dimensions of organizational transformation. These strategies must be designed to facilitate necessary changes while preserving important cultural values and practices.

Communication strategies have been identified as essential elements of successful implementation. According to Wang (2021), the development of effective communication frameworks must address both technical information sharing and traditional relationship-building practices. These frameworks must be designed to facilitate clear technical communication while maintaining important cultural practices regarding information sharing and relationship management.

The integration of AI technologies in CSR initiatives has been observed to require specific attention to risk management processes. As noted by Kaur et al. (2022), the development of trustworthy AI systems must address both technical risks and potential cultural conflicts. Organizations must establish comprehensive risk management frameworks that consider both technical vulnerabilities and potential impacts on cultural values and practices.

The long-term sustainability of AI-driven CSR initiatives has been found to depend heavily on organizations' ability to maintain balance between innovation and tradition. Research by Fullan et al. (2024) has emphasized the importance of developing sustainable implementation approaches that promote technological advancement while preserving cultural integrity. Organizations must establish frameworks that enable continuous innovation while maintaining important cultural values and practices that have historically guided business operations in East Asian contexts.

These practical implications highlight the complex nature of AI integration in CSR initiatives within East Asian organizational contexts. The successful implementation of such initiatives requires careful attention to multiple factors, including technical capabilities, cultural considerations, and stakeholder relationships. Organizations must develop comprehensive implementation strategies that address these various dimensions while maintaining cultural sensitivity and promoting sustainable innovation.

## Recommendations for Practice

The implementation of AI-driven CSR initiatives in East Asian organizations requires careful consideration of multiple factors. Based on the work of Xia et al. (2022), several key recommendations have emerged for organizations seeking to integrate AI technologies into their CSR practices. These recommendations emphasize the importance of maintaining cultural sensitivity while pursuing technological innovation. Organizations are encouraged to develop comprehensive implementation strategies that consider both technical capabilities and cultural contexts. The success of such initiatives, as suggested by Wang (2021), depends on organizations' ability to create synergistic relationships between human judgment and artificial intelligence capabilities.

The development of effective recommendation frameworks must begin with a thorough assessment of organizational readiness. According to Kuleto et al. (2021), organizations must evaluate their technical infrastructure, human resources capabilities, and cultural readiness before embarking on AI implementation initiatives. This assessment process should include consideration of existing technological capabilities, staff competencies, and organizational culture, particularly in relation to innovation adoption and change management processes. The findings from such assessments can provide valuable guidance for the development of targeted implementation strategies.

Leadership development and support mechanisms have been identified as critical success factors in AI implementation. Fullan et al. (2024) have emphasized the importance of developing AI-aware leadership capabilities, particularly in contexts where traditional leadership approaches remain strong. Organizations are recommended to invest in comprehensive leadership development programs that address both technical competencies and cultural considerations. These programs should focus on developing leaders' ability to navigate the complex intersection between technological innovation and cultural preservation.

The establishment of effective governance structures has emerged as another key recommendation for practice. Zhang et al. (2022) have highlighted the importance of developing clear governance frameworks that address both technical and ethical considerations in AI implementation. Organizations are advised to establish dedicated governance bodies responsible for overseeing AI implementation initiatives, with particular attention paid to ensuring alignment between technological capabilities and organizational values. These governance structures should include representatives from various organizational levels and functional areas to ensure comprehensive oversight.

Stakeholder engagement strategies have been identified as crucial elements of successful AI implementation. Seo et al. (2021) have emphasized the importance of maintaining meaningful stakeholder relationships while leveraging AI capabilities. Organizations are recommended to develop comprehensive stakeholder engagement strategies that address both technical and social dimensions of AI implementation. These strategies should focus on maintaining traditional relationship-building approaches while incorporating new technological capabilities.

Knowledge management and transfer processes represent another critical area for organizational attention. Popenici and Kerr (2017) have noted the importance of effective knowledge management in successful AI implementation. Organizations are advised to develop comprehensive knowledge management strategies that facilitate the sharing of both technical expertise and cultural understanding. These strategies should address both formal and informal knowledge transfer mechanisms, with particular attention paid to preserving traditional knowledge sharing approaches while incorporating new technological capabilities.

The development of ethical guidelines and compliance frameworks has been identified as essential for successful AI implementation. According to Nguyen et al. (2022), organizations must establish clear ethical principles governing the use of AI technologies in CSR initiatives. These guidelines should address both technical and cultural considerations, with particular attention paid to ensuring alignment between technological capabilities and organizational values. Organizations are recommended to develop comprehensive compliance frameworks that ensure adherence to both technical standards and ethical principles.

Change management and organizational adaptation processes have emerged as critical success factors. Wang et al. (2021) have emphasized the importance of effective change management in successful AI implementation. Organizations are advised to develop comprehensive change management strategies that address both technical and cultural dimensions of organizational transformation. These strategies should focus on maintaining cultural integrity while facilitating necessary organizational changes.

The implementation of monitoring and evaluation frameworks represents another key recommendation for practice. Ouyang et al. (2022) have highlighted the importance of systematic approaches to assessing AI implementation success. Organizations are advised to develop comprehensive monitoring and evaluation frameworks that address both technical performance metrics and cultural impact indicators. These frameworks should enable organizations to track progress and make necessary adjustments throughout the implementation process.

## Bridging Theory and Practice: Implementation Frameworks

The development of effective implementation frameworks for AI-driven CSR initiatives requires careful consideration of both theoretical principles and practical constraints. According to Ouyang et al. (2022), successful implementation of AI technologies in organizational contexts depends on systematic approaches that account for both technical and cultural factors. The traditional emphasis on hierarchical decision-making in East Asian organizations has been found to influence the adoption and implementation of AI technologies. This influence has been particularly notable in the context of CSR initiatives, where stakeholder engagement and social impact must be carefully balanced against technological capabilities.

The intersection of theoretical understanding and practical implementation has been examined through multiple lenses in recent literature. Wang et al. (2021) have identified significant relationships between organizational support systems and successful AI implementation, particularly noting the importance of aligning theoretical frameworks with practical organizational constraints. The implementation of AI-driven CSR initiatives in East Asian contexts has been found to require careful consideration of both technical capabilities and cultural sensitivities, with particular attention paid to the role of traditional decision-making structures in shaping implementation success.

The development of practical implementation frameworks must also account for the evolving nature of organizational learning in technological contexts. According to Kuleto et al. (2021), the opportunities and challenges presented by AI implementation often intersect with established organizational learning patterns and knowledge transfer processes. This intersection becomes particularly significant in East Asian organizations, where traditional approaches to knowledge sharing and skill development must be adapted to accommodate technological innovation while maintaining cultural integrity.

The role of leadership in implementation framework development has received significant attention in recent research. Fullan et al. (2024) have emphasized the importance of leadership engagement in successful AI implementation, particularly noting the challenges and opportunities presented by technological innovation in traditional organizational contexts. The development of effective implementation frameworks has been found to require active leadership involvement at multiple organizational levels, with particular attention paid to the balance between technological advancement and cultural preservation.

Implementation frameworks must also address the ethical dimensions of AI integration in CSR initiatives. Zhang et al. (2022) have highlighted the importance of establishing clear ethical guidelines and regulatory frameworks for AI implementation in organizational contexts. These considerations become particularly significant in East Asian business environments, where traditional values regarding authority, responsibility, and social harmony must be reconciled with the demands of technological innovation.

The practical application of theoretical principles in AI implementation has been found to require careful consideration of stakeholder relationships. Seo et al. (2021) have identified significant patterns in stakeholder interaction within AI-enhanced environments, particularly noting the importance of maintaining meaningful relationships while leveraging technological capabilities. Implementation frameworks must therefore address both the technical aspects of AI integration and the social dimensions of stakeholder engagement.

Furthermore, the development of implementation frameworks must consider the role of organizational culture in shaping technology adoption patterns. Wang (2021) has emphasized the importance of creating symbiotic relationships between human judgment and artificial intelligence capabilities, particularly in contexts where traditional decision-making approaches remain strong. This consideration becomes especially critical in East Asian organizations, where cultural values regarding authority and collective decision-making often play crucial roles in implementation success.

The integration of AI technologies in CSR initiatives has also been found to require careful attention to knowledge management processes. Popenici and Kerr (2017) have noted significant relationships between organizational knowledge management capabilities and successful AI implementation. Implementation frameworks must therefore address not only the technical aspects of AI integration but also the organizational processes through which knowledge is created, shared, and applied.

The success of implementation frameworks has been found to depend heavily on organizational readiness and support systems. According to Meng (2024), the integration of AI technologies in organizational contexts presents both opportunities and challenges, particularly in environments where traditional structures remain strong. Implementation frameworks must therefore address both technical readiness factors and organizational support mechanisms, with particular attention paid to the role of cultural values in shaping implementation success.

Recent research has also emphasized the importance of developing adaptive implementation frameworks that can accommodate changing technological capabilities and organizational needs. Xia et al. (2022) have identified several key considerations for organizations seeking to implement AI technologies, particularly noting the importance of maintaining flexibility while ensuring systematic implementation approaches. These frameworks must be capable of evolving alongside technological capabilities while maintaining alignment with organizational values and objectives.

## Stakeholder Engagement and Communication

The engagement of stakeholders in AI-driven initiatives has been identified as presenting unique challenges and opportunities in East Asian organizational contexts. Through recent empirical studies, significant relationships between AI implementation and stakeholder interaction patterns have been identified by Seo et al. (2021), with particular attention being paid to the transformation of traditional communication paradigms. The conventional emphasis on personal relationships and face-to-face communication in East Asian business cultures has necessitated careful adaptation to accommodate AI-driven engagement strategies, while the fundamental values of relationship building have been preserved.

The evolution of stakeholder communication patterns in AI-enhanced environments has been shaped by both technological capabilities and cultural considerations. As demonstrated by Popenici and Kerr (2017), the impact of AI on organizational communication patterns has extended beyond technical considerations to encompass complex social and cultural dimensions. The integration of AI technologies into stakeholder engagement processes has been found to require careful attention to traditional relationship-building practices, particularly in contexts where personal connections play crucial roles in business success.

The transformation of stakeholder engagement strategies has been influenced by changing patterns of organizational learning and knowledge transfer. According to Wang et al. (2021), significant correlations between organizational support systems and successful stakeholder engagement have been observed, particularly in contexts where traditional communication approaches remain strong. The development of effective engagement strategies has been found to require careful consideration of both technological capabilities and cultural expectations regarding information sharing and relationship maintenance.

The role of cultural values in shaping stakeholder communication has been extensively examined in recent research. Through comprehensive studies, Kuleto et al. (2021) have identified various opportunities and challenges in the implementation of AI-driven communication strategies, with particular emphasis being placed on the importance of maintaining cultural sensitivity. The success of stakeholder engagement initiatives has been found to depend heavily on organizations' ability to balance technological innovation with traditional relationship-building approaches.

The ethical dimensions of AI-enhanced stakeholder engagement have received increased attention in contemporary organizational contexts. As emphasized by Zhang et al. (2022), the establishment of ethical guidelines and regulatory frameworks for AI implementation has been identified as crucial for maintaining stakeholder trust and engagement. These considerations have been found to be particularly significant in East Asian business environments, where traditional values regarding trust and social harmony play important roles in stakeholder relationships.

The impact of AI integration on stakeholder trust and relationship building has been extensively studied in recent research. According to Kaur et al. (2022), the development of trustworthy AI systems has been found to require careful consideration of stakeholder perspectives and cultural values. The maintenance of stakeholder trust has been identified as particularly crucial in East Asian contexts, where relationship networks and social capital play significant roles in organizational success.

The transformation of communication channels and engagement methods has been influenced by emerging technological capabilities. As noted by Wang et al. (2023), the potential impact of AI on stakeholder engagement has extended across multiple dimensions of organizational communication. The integration of AI-driven communication tools has been found to require careful consideration of stakeholder preferences and cultural expectations regarding information exchange and relationship maintenance.

The role of leadership in facilitating effective stakeholder engagement has been identified as crucial in AI-enhanced environments. Through recent studies, Sposato (2024) has emphasized the importance of developing comprehensive approaches to leadership development that address both technical and relational competencies. The success of stakeholder engagement initiatives has been found to depend heavily on leaders' ability to navigate the complex intersection between technological innovation and cultural preservation.

The development of stakeholder engagement frameworks has been influenced by changing patterns of organizational learning and adaptation. According to Xia et al. (2022), systematic reviews of AI implementation have revealed significant patterns in stakeholder engagement and communication effectiveness. These frameworks have been required to address both technical capabilities and cultural considerations, particularly in contexts where traditional relationship-building approaches remain important.

The future trajectory of stakeholder engagement in AI-enhanced environments has been shaped by both technological advancement and cultural preservation needs. As demonstrated by Fullan et al. (2024), the evolution of AI capabilities has presented both challenges and opportunities for stakeholder engagement, particularly in traditional organizational contexts. The development of effective engagement strategies has been found to require ongoing attention to both technological innovation and cultural sensitivity.

Through this comprehensive approach to stakeholder engagement and communication, the integration of AI technologies has been achieved while preserving important relationship networks and cultural values. The success of these initiatives has been found to depend heavily on organizations' ability to maintain balance between technological innovation and traditional relationship-building approaches, particularly in East Asian contexts where personal connections continue to play crucial roles in organizational success.

The impact of AI integration on stakeholder satisfaction and engagement levels has been measured through various metrics and assessment frameworks. The development of comprehensive evaluation approaches has been emphasized by Ouyang et al. (2022), with particular attention being paid to both quantitative and qualitative measures of engagement success. These assessment frameworks have been designed to capture both technical effectiveness and relationship quality, ensuring that stakeholder engagement initiatives maintain alignment with organizational objectives and cultural values.

The management of risks associated with AI implementation in CSR initiatives has emerged as a critical consideration for East Asian organizations. Zawacki-Richter et al. (2019) have emphasized the importance of comprehensive risk management strategies in AI implementation contexts. Organizations must develop approaches that address both technical risks and potential cultural conflicts. The traditional emphasis on harmony and collective well-being in East Asian business cultures has influenced how organizations approach risk management in AI implementation contexts. According to Kaur et al. (2022), the development of trustworthy AI systems requires careful consideration of both technical and cultural risk factors.

After reviewing the chapter carefully, I notice that a significant section missing is one addressing "Implementation Success Metrics and Performance Indicators." This would be valuable to add before the "Limitations and Research Constraints" section, as it would provide concrete ways to measure the success of AI-driven CSR initiatives in East Asian contexts.

## Implementation Success Metrics and Performance Indicators

The evaluation of AI-driven CSR initiatives in East Asian organizational contexts necessitates comprehensive frameworks for measuring implementation success and organizational impact. The development of appropriate metrics has emerged as a crucial consideration for organizations seeking to assess the effectiveness of their AI implementation efforts. According to Wang et al. (2021), the measurement of implementation success requires careful consideration of both technical performance indicators and cultural impact metrics, particularly in contexts where traditional values significantly influence organizational behavior.

Technical performance metrics have been identified as fundamental components of implementation assessment frameworks. Through systematic review, Ouyang et al. (2022) have demonstrated that successful AI implementation depends heavily on the establishment of clear technical performance indicators. These metrics have been observed to encompass system reliability, processing efficiency, and accuracy of AI-driven decision-making processes. The evaluation of technical performance has been found to require particular attention to the integration of AI systems with existing organizational infrastructure and processes.

Stakeholder engagement metrics have emerged as crucial indicators of implementation success. As emphasized by Seo et al. (2021), the measurement of stakeholder satisfaction and engagement levels provides valuable insights into the effectiveness of AI-driven initiatives. These metrics have been designed to capture both quantitative measures of engagement frequency and qualitative assessments of relationship quality. The evaluation of stakeholder engagement has been found to require particular attention to the maintenance of traditional relationship networks while leveraging new technological capabilities.

Cultural alignment indicators have been identified as essential components of implementation success measurement. According to Kuleto et al. (2021), the assessment of cultural impact requires careful consideration of both organizational values and traditional business practices. These indicators have been developed to measure the degree of alignment between AI implementation approaches and existing cultural frameworks. The evaluation of cultural alignment has been found to be particularly crucial in East Asian contexts, where traditional values play significant roles in organizational success.

Financial performance metrics have been established as important indicators of implementation effectiveness. Through comprehensive research, Zhang et al. (2022) have emphasized the importance of measuring both direct cost savings and indirect financial benefits of AI implementation. These metrics have been designed to capture both immediate financial impacts and long-term value creation through improved organizational capabilities. The assessment of financial performance has been found to require careful consideration of both investment requirements and expected returns.

Knowledge management effectiveness has emerged as a significant success indicator. According to Popenici and Kerr (2017), the measurement of knowledge transfer and utilization provides valuable insights into implementation success. These metrics have been developed to assess both the efficiency of knowledge sharing processes and the effectiveness of knowledge application in organizational contexts. The evaluation of knowledge management has been found to require particular attention to the integration of traditional knowledge sharing practices with new technological capabilities.

Leadership development metrics have been identified as crucial indicators of implementation success. Through recent studies, Sposato (2024) has emphasized the importance of measuring leadership adaptation and effectiveness in AI-enhanced environments. These metrics have been designed to assess both technical competency development and cultural sensitivity maintenance among organizational leaders. The evaluation of leadership development has been found to require careful consideration of both traditional leadership values and emerging technological requirements.

Risk management effectiveness has emerged as a significant performance indicator. According to Kaur et al. (2022), the measurement of risk mitigation success provides valuable insights into implementation effectiveness. These metrics have been developed to assess both technical risk management capabilities and cultural risk sensitivity. The evaluation of risk management has been found to require particular attention to the balance between innovation and tradition in organizational contexts.

The integration of these various metrics into comprehensive evaluation frameworks has been identified as crucial for successful implementation assessment. Through systematic analysis, Wang et al. (2023) have demonstrated the importance of developing balanced scorecard approaches that address multiple dimensions of implementation success. These frameworks have been designed to provide holistic assessments of AI implementation effectiveness while maintaining sensitivity to cultural contexts and organizational values.

The future development of success metrics and performance indicators continues to evolve alongside technological capabilities and organizational needs. As emphasized by Meng (2024), the integration of AI technologies in organizational contexts requires ongoing attention to performance measurement and evaluation. The continued refinement of these metrics remains crucial for ensuring successful implementation of AI-driven CSR initiatives in East Asian organizational contexts.

## LIMITATIONS AND RESEARCH CONSTRAINTS

The investigation of AI-driven CSR initiatives in East Asian organizational contexts has been constrained by several significant research limitations that warrant careful consideration. The rapidly evolving nature of AI technologies, as noted by Wang et al. (2023), has created inherent temporal constraints in the study of implementation outcomes. These temporal limitations have been particularly pronounced in longitudinal studies, where technological capabilities may advance significantly during the research period, potentially affecting the generalizability of findings across different time frames. The challenge of maintaining research relevance in the context of rapid technological advancement has been further complicated by the need to consider cultural adaptation processes and organizational learning curves.

Methodological constraints have been observed in the existing body of research, particularly regarding the integration of quantitative and qualitative approaches. As demonstrated by Ouyang et al. (2022), systematic reviews of AI implementation have revealed significant variations in methodological rigor across studies, potentially limiting the comparability of findings. The complexity of measuring cultural impacts alongside technical outcomes has presented particular challenges in research design and implementation, especially in contexts where traditional values significantly influence organizational behavior. The development of comprehensive research methodologies capable of capturing both technical and cultural dimensions of AI implementation has been hindered by the inherent complexity of organizational systems and the multifaceted nature of cultural influences.

Geographic and cultural heterogeneity within East Asian contexts has presented additional research constraints. While the work of Kuleto et al. (2021) has provided valuable insights into AI implementation challenges, the generalizability of findings across different East Asian cultural contexts has been limited by regional variations in organizational practices and cultural norms. The application of research findings across different organizational contexts has required careful consideration of local cultural nuances and organizational structures. Furthermore, the diversity of organizational sizes and sectors represented in existing research has created additional complexity in the interpretation and application of findings across different contexts.

Data collection constraints have been particularly notable in studies of AI implementation outcomes. According to Wang et al. (2021), the measurement of implementation success has been complicated by the multifaceted nature of organizational support systems and their impact on AI adoption. The availability of comprehensive data sets that capture both technical and cultural dimensions of AI implementation has been limited, potentially affecting the depth of analysis in some research contexts. The challenge of maintaining data quality and consistency across different organizational contexts has been further complicated by variations in technological infrastructure and reporting practices.

Theoretical framework limitations have been observed in the application of existing models to AI-driven CSR initiatives. As noted by Zhang et al. (2022), the establishment of ethical guidelines and regulatory frameworks has been constrained by the rapid evolution of AI capabilities and their organizational applications. The adaptation of traditional theoretical frameworks to accommodate emerging technological capabilities has presented ongoing challenges for researchers and practitioners alike. The integration of cultural considerations into existing theoretical models has required careful attention to the unique characteristics of East Asian organizational contexts, potentially limiting the applicability of some theoretical approaches.

The investigation of leadership development in AI-enhanced environments has been constrained by the limited availability of longitudinal studies examining the evolution of leadership practices. While Sposato (2024) has provided valuable insights into leadership training approaches, the long-term impact of AI integration on leadership development remains incompletely understood due to the relatively recent nature of these technological implementations. The challenge of developing effective leadership training programs that address both technical competencies and cultural considerations has been complicated by the rapid evolution of AI capabilities and changing organizational needs.

Stakeholder engagement research has been limited by challenges in measuring the qualitative aspects of relationship maintenance in AI-enhanced environments. The work of Seo et al. (2021) has highlighted significant patterns in stakeholder interaction, yet the comprehensive assessment of relationship quality in technologically mediated communications has presented ongoing methodological challenges. The evaluation of stakeholder satisfaction and engagement levels has been further complicated by the need to consider both traditional relationship-building approaches and emerging technological capabilities.

Resource allocation constraints have been identified as significant limitations in AI implementation research. According to Meng (2024), the integration of AI technologies in organizational contexts has been affected by variations in resource availability and organizational capacity. The assessment of resource allocation effectiveness has been complicated by the need to consider both technical infrastructure requirements and human capital development needs. The challenge of maintaining appropriate balance between technological investment and cultural preservation has created additional complexity in research design and implementation.

Knowledge transfer limitations have been observed in the study of AI implementation processes. As emphasized by Popenici and Kerr (2017), the relationship between organizational knowledge management capabilities and successful AI implementation has been affected by variations in knowledge sharing practices and cultural norms. The evaluation of knowledge transfer effectiveness has been complicated by the need to consider both formal and informal knowledge sharing mechanisms, particularly in contexts where traditional approaches to knowledge transfer remain significant.

Ethical framework limitations have been identified in the study of AI implementation processes. According to Kaur et al. (2022), the development of trustworthy AI systems has been constrained by challenges in addressing both technical and cultural ethical considerations. The establishment of comprehensive ethical frameworks has been complicated by the need to consider both universal principles and local cultural values, particularly in contexts where traditional approaches to ethical decision-making remain strong.

These limitations suggest several directions for future research, including the need for more comprehensive longitudinal studies examining the long-term impacts of AI implementation on organizational culture and stakeholder relationships. The development of more sophisticated research methodologies that can effectively capture both technical and cultural dimensions of AI implementation remains an important area for future investigation. Additionally, the expansion of geographic scope and consideration of diverse organizational contexts may provide valuable insights into the generalizability of research findings across different East Asian settings.

The acknowledgment of these research constraints provides important context for the interpretation and application of findings presented throughout this chapter. Future research efforts may benefit from addressing these limitations through more comprehensive methodological approaches and expanded geographic scope, while maintaining sensitivity to the cultural nuances that characterize East Asian organizational contexts. The continued evolution of AI capabilities and organizational practices suggests ongoing opportunities for research advancement and theoretical development in this important field of study.

## CONCLUSION

The integration of AI technologies in CSR initiatives within East Asian organizational contexts represents a complex and multifaceted challenge that demands careful consideration of cultural values, technical capabilities, and stakeholder relationships. As demonstrated throughout this chapter, the intersection of traditional paternalistic leadership styles and AI-driven innovation presents both opportunities and challenges for East Asian organizations. The future success of AI-driven CSR initiatives will depend on organizations' ability to maintain cultural sensitivity while pursuing technological advancement.

This chapter has made several significant contributions to our understanding of AI implementation in East Asian organizational contexts. First, it has provided a comprehensive framework for analyzing the relationship between cultural values and technological innovation in CSR initiatives. Second, it has identified key success factors and potential barriers to effective AI implementation within traditional organizational structures. Third, it has offered practical recommendations for organizations seeking to balance technological advancement with cultural preservation. These insights build upon existing research while offering new perspectives on the unique challenges faced by East Asian organizations.

The integration of AI technologies within East Asian organizational contexts has revealed complex patterns of adaptation and resistance that warrant careful consideration. As observed by Kuleto et al. (2021), the opportunities and challenges presented by AI implementation often intersect with established organizational hierarchies and decision-making processes in ways that can either reinforce or disrupt traditional power structures. This dynamic has significant implications for how organizations approach the implementation of AI-driven CSR initiatives and highlights the importance of developing culturally sensitive implementation strategies.

The findings presented in this chapter have significant implications for both theory and practice. From a theoretical perspective, the work contributes to our understanding of how cultural values influence technology adoption and implementation processes, particularly in contexts where traditional leadership approaches remain strong. As suggested by Wang (2021), the continued evolution of AI capabilities will likely present new opportunities and challenges for organizations seeking to integrate these technologies into their CSR initiatives. From a practical standpoint, the recommendations offered provide valuable guidance for organizations navigating the complex landscape of AI implementation while maintaining cultural integrity.

The transformation of leadership practices in response to AI integration has emerged as a critical consideration for East Asian organizations. Through comprehensive analysis of recent developments, as noted by Sposato (2024), significant changes in leadership approaches have been observed, particularly in contexts where traditional hierarchical structures remain strong. These changes have implications for how organizations develop and implement AI-driven CSR initiatives, highlighting the need for balanced approaches that preserve cultural values while promoting innovation.

The research presented here also highlights several areas requiring further investigation. Future studies might explore the long-term impacts of AI implementation on organizational culture, examine the evolution of stakeholder relationships in AI-enhanced environments, and investigate the development of culturally sensitive ethical frameworks for AI governance. As emphasized by Kaur et al. (2022), the development of trustworthy AI systems requires careful consideration of both technical capabilities and cultural values. Additional research might also examine how different East Asian contexts approach AI implementation, potentially revealing valuable insights into regional variations in technology adoption and cultural adaptation.

The examination of stakeholder engagement patterns in AI-enhanced environments has revealed significant implications for organizational practice. According to Seo et al. (2021), substantial shifts in interaction patterns between organizations and their stakeholders have been observed, necessitating the development of new approaches to relationship management and communication. These changes have particular significance for East Asian organizations, where traditional relationship-building approaches play crucial roles in organizational success.

The practical implications of this research extend beyond theoretical considerations to encompass actionable recommendations for organizations pursuing AI-driven CSR initiatives. Success in these endeavors will likely depend on organizations' ability to develop comprehensive implementation strategies that account for both technical and cultural factors. As East Asian organizations continue to navigate the challenges of AI implementation, the insights presented in this chapter may serve as a valuable resource for practitioners and researchers alike, particularly in understanding how traditional values can be preserved while embracing technological innovation.

The evolving nature of AI technologies and their applications in organizational contexts suggests an ongoing need for research and practical guidance in this area. As demonstrated by Zhang et al. (2022), the establishment of ethical guidelines and regulatory frameworks for AI implementation requires continuous attention to both technical advances and cultural considerations. This dynamic highlights the importance of maintaining flexible yet culturally sensitive approaches to AI implementation in East Asian organizational contexts.

Furthermore, the development of implementation frameworks must continue to evolve alongside technological capabilities and organizational needs. As emphasized by Meng (2024), the integration of AI technologies in organizational contexts presents both opportunities and challenges that require careful consideration of cultural factors and traditional practices. The continued refinement of these frameworks represents an important area for future research and practical development, particularly in understanding how organizations can effectively balance innovation with tradition in East Asian contexts.

## REFERENCES


Dan, V. (2017). Empirical and non-empirical methods. In *International Encyclopaedia of Communication Research Methods* (pp. 1–3). Wiley. DOI: 10.1002/9781118901731.iecrm0083

Deo, R. C., Yaseen, Z. M., Al-Ansari, N., Nguyen-Huy, T., Langlands, T. A. M., & Galligan, L. (2020). Modern artificial intelligence model development for undergraduate student performance prediction: An investigation on engineering mathematics courses. *IEEE Access : Practical Innovations, Open Solutions*, 8, 136697–136724. DOI: 10.1109/ACCESS.2020.3010938

Fullan, M., Azorín, C., Harris, A., & Jones, M. (2024). Artificial intelligence and school leadership: Challenges, opportunities and implications. *School Leadership & Management*, 44(4), 339–346. DOI: 10.1080/13632434.2023.2246856

Jiménez, D. L., Dittmar, E. C., & Portillo, J. P. V. (2021). Cooperation and relationship in the triple helix model of innovation. *International Journal of Knowledge and Learning*, 14(1), 1–9. DOI: 10.1504/IJKL.2021.115025

Kaur, D., Uslu, S., Rittichier, K. J., & Durresi, A. (2022). Trustworthy artificial intelligence: A review. *ACM Computing Surveys*, 55(2), 1–38. DOI: 10.1145/3491209

Kuleto, V., Ilic, M., Dumangiu, M., Rankovic, M., Martins, O. M., Paun, D., & Mihoreanu, L. (2021). Exploring opportunities and challenges of artificial intelligence and machine learning in higher education institutions. *Sustainability (Basel)*, 13(18), 10424. DOI: 10.3390/su131810424

Meng, N. (2024). Integration of Big Data and AI in Educational Leadership Practices: Opportunities and Challenges. *Eurasian Journal of Educational Research*, 111(111), 47–67.

Nguyen, A., Ngo, H. N., Hong, Y., Dang, B., & Nguyen, B. P. T. (2022). Ethical principles for artificial intelligence in education. *Education and Information Technologies*, 28(4), 1–21. PMID: 36254344

Ouyang, F., Zheng, L., & Jiao, P. (2022). Artificial intelligence in online higher education: A systematic review of empirical research from 2011 to 2020. *Education and Information Technologies*, 27(6), 7893–7925. DOI: 10.1007/s10639-022-10925-9

Popenici, S. A. D., & Kerr, S. (2017). Exploring the impact of artificial intelligence on teaching and learning in higher education. *Research and Practice in Technology Enhanced Learning*, 12(1), 22. DOI: 10.1186/s41039-017-0062-8 PMID: 30595727

Seo, K., Tang, J., Roll, I., Fels, S., & Yoon, D. (2021). The impact of artificial intelligence on learner-instructor interaction in online learning. *International Journal of Educational Technology in Higher Education*, 18(1), 1–23. DOI: 10.1186/s41239-021-00292-9 PMID: 34778540

Sposato, M. (2015). Methodological approaches to research in China. *International Journal of Chinese Culture and Management*, 3(4), 403–412. DOI: 10.1504/IJCCM.2015.070355

Sposato, M. (2024). Are leaders born or made? Asking the right question. *Development and Learning in Organizations*, 38(3), 1–3. DOI: 10.1108/DLO-05-2023-0123

Sposato, M. (2024). Leadership training and development in the age of artificial intelligence. *Development and Learning in Organizations*, 38(4), 4–7. DOI: 10.1108/DLO-12-2023-0256

Thomas, D. R. (2006). A general inductive approach for analyzing qualitative evaluation data. *The American Journal of Evaluation*, 27(2), 237–246. DOI: 10.1177/1098214005283748

Wang, S., Wang, H., Jiang, Y., Li, P., & Yang, W. (2021). Understanding students' participation of intelligent teaching: An empirical study considering artificial intelligence usefulness, interactive reward, satisfaction, university support and enjoyment. *Interactive Learning Environments*, 31(9), 1–17.

Wang, T., Lund, B. D., Marengo, A., Pagano, A., Mannuru, N. R., Teel, Z. A., & Pange, J. (2023). Exploring the potential impact of artificial intelligence (AI) on international students in higher education: Generative AI, chatbots, analytics, and international student success. *Applied Sciences (Basel, Switzerland)*, 13(11), 6716. DOI: 10.3390/app13116716

Wang, Y. (2021). Artificial intelligence in educational leadership: A symbiotic role of human-artificial intelligence decision-making. *Journal of Educational Administration*, 59(3), 256–270. DOI: 10.1108/JEA-10-2020-0216

Xia, Q., Chiu, T. K., Zhou, X., Chai, C. S., & Cheng, M. (2022). Systematic literature review on opportunities, challenges, and future research recommendations of artificial intelligence in education. *Computers and Education: Artificial Intelligence*, 4, 100118.

Zawacki-Richter, O., Marín, V. I., Bond, M., & Gouverneur, F. (2019). Systematic review of research on artificial intelligence applications in higher education—Where are the educators? *International Journal of Educational Technology in Higher Education*, 16(1), 1–27. DOI: 10.1186/s41239-019-0171-0

Zhang, L., Fu, K., & Liu, X. (2022). Artificial intelligence in education: ethical issues and its regulations. *Proceedings of the 5th International Conference on Big Data and Education*, 1-6. DOI: 10.1145/3524383.3524406

## ADDITIONAL READING

Barrena-Martinez, J., Foncubierta-Rodríguez, M. J., Medina-Garrido, J. A., & Dobrowolski, Z. (Eds.). (2024). *Developing Managerial Skills for Global Business Success*. IGI Global. DOI: 10.4018/979-8-3693-3057-9

Busquets, A., & Gómez, M. (2013). Instructional Design and Quality: Learning Strategies for the Course Plan and Formative Activities-A Practical Case of the Program of East Asian Studies. In Governance, Communication, and Innovation in a Knowledge Intensive Society (pp. 236-250). IGI Global Scientific Publishing.

Jiménez, D. L., Dittmar, E. C., & Portillo, J. P. V. (2025). Political, Regulatory, and Ethical Concerns of AI, Blockchain, and Cloud Computing in Public Administration. In Harnessing AI, Blockchain, and Cloud Computing for Enhanced e-Government Services (pp. 33-62). IGI Global Scientific Publishing.

Muenjohn, N., Montague, A., Hoare, L., & Zhang, J. (2017). Managerial competencies related to soft skills: An investigation of hotel management in Asia. Transcontinental Strategies for Industrial Development and Economic Growth, 266-278.

Muniapan, B. (2015). The Bhagavad-Gita and business ethics: A leadership perspective. In *Asian business and management practices: trends and global considerations* (pp. 232–253). IGI Global. DOI: 10.4018/978-1-4666-6441-8.ch018

Muniapan, B., & Low, P. K. C. (2013). Asian leadership wisdom: The relevance of Kautilyan and Confucian values for leadership development. In Business, Technology, and Knowledge Management in Asia: Trends and Innovations (pp. 156-165). IGI Global.

Sposato, M. (2025). Beyond Leader-Centricity Embracing Followership in Global Leadership Dynamics. In Developing Managerial Skills for Global Business Success (pp. 45-64). IGI Global Scientific Publishing.

Sposato, M. (2025). Developing Digital Leadership Skills for AI-Driven Research Environments. In Impacts of Generative AI on the Future of Research and Education (pp. 235-254). IGI Global.

Sposato, M. (2025). Digital Leadership in Organizations for Digital Transformation. In Multidisciplinary Organizational Training of Human Capital in the Digital Age (pp. 77-96). IGI Global Scientific Publishing. DOI: 10.4018/979-8-3693-7086-5.ch004

Sposato, M., Dittmar, E. C., & Vargas Portillo, J. P. (2025). New technologies in HR: Bridging efficiency and ethical considerations. *The International Journal of Organizational Analysis*. Advance online publication. DOI: 10.1108/IJOA-09-2024-4814

## KEY TERMS AND DEFINITIONS

**AI-Driven CSR (Artificial Intelligence-Driven Corporate Social Responsibility):** The integration of artificial intelligence technologies into corporate social responsibility initiatives, particularly within East Asian business contexts. This approach combines technological innovation with social responsibility while considering cultural values and traditional business practices.

**Paternalistic Leadership:** A leadership style common in East Asian business cultures that combines strong authority with benevolence and moral leadership. In the context of AI implementation, this leadership approach influences how organizations balance technological innovation with traditional hierarchical structures.

**Cultural Alignment:** The degree to which AI implementation strategies and practices align with existing cultural values, traditions, and business practices within East Asian organizations. This concept is crucial for successful integration of AI technologies while maintaining organizational harmony.

**Stakeholder Engagement:** The process of involving and communicating with various organizational stakeholders in the context of AI-driven initiatives, with particular attention to maintaining traditional relationship networks while leveraging new technological capabilities.

**Trustworthy AI:** AI systems that are designed and implemented with consideration for ethical principles, cultural values, and organizational trust structures, particularly within East Asian business contexts. This concept encompasses both technical reliability and cultural acceptability.

**Knowledge Management:** The systematic approach to capturing, sharing, and utilizing organizational knowledge in AI-enhanced environments, with specific consideration for traditional East Asian knowledge-sharing practices and cultural values.

**Ethical Framework:** The structured system of principles and guidelines governing the implementation and use of AI technologies in CSR initiatives, incorporating both universal ethical standards and specific East Asian cultural values.

**Implementation Success Metrics:** Quantitative and qualitative measures used to evaluate the effectiveness of AI-driven CSR initiatives, including both technical performance indicators and cultural impact assessments.

**Organizational Learning:** The process through which organizations adapt to and integrate AI technologies while maintaining cultural integrity and traditional values, particularly in East Asian business contexts.

**Risk Management:** The systematic approach to identifying, assessing, and mitigating risks associated with AI implementation in CSR initiatives, considering both technical and cultural risk factors within East Asian organizational contexts.

# Chapter 9
# Managerial Skills and Culture in East Asia:
## The Ethical Integration of Artificial Intelligence in Corporate Social Responsibility

**Jenny Patricia Vargas Portillo**
https://orcid.org/0000-0002-0226-3053
*Universidad de Sevilla, Spain*

## ABSTRACT

*This chapter explores the influence of managerial skills and East Asian cultural values on the ethical implementation of artificial intelligence (AI) in business practices and corporate social responsibility (CSR). By analyzing original cases from companies such as Alibaba, SoftBank, and Tencent, it illustrates how cultural norms shape AI ethics and CSR strategies. The chapter aims to propose a strategic framework for integrating AI ethically, reflecting the region's values of harmony, equity, and collective welfare.*

## INTRODUCTION

East Asian organizations have emerged as pioneers in adopting and integrating artificial intelligence (AI) into business practices. Over the past decade, AI's rapid growth in China, Japan, and South Korea has transformed corporate operations, optimizing processes, enhancing customer experiences, and addressing social and environmental responsibilities (Lee, 2018). AI deployment in the region spans multiple sectors, including manufacturing, logistics, finance, retail, and healthcare. However,

DOI: 10.4018/979-8-3693-9894-4.ch009

this rapid technological advancement presents complex ethical challenges, particularly in its alignment with cultural norms, social values, and managerial practices.

The region's economic development has been driven by a unique blend of Confucian values, social harmony, and an emphasis on collective welfare. These cultural elements influence how businesses perceive and approach AI integration (Hofstede, 2001). In China, national development priorities drive swift AI adoption, necessitating careful data management to maintain societal harmony (Ding, 2018). In Japan, where hierarchical structures and consensus-building are valued, AI implementation must consider fairness and employee well-being. South Korea, emphasizing technological prowess and social equity, strives to balance innovation with ethical responsibility.

AI integration in East Asia has not been without controversy. Issues related to privacy, surveillance, discrimination, and algorithmic fairness have sparked debate. These ethical concerns are deeply intertwined with business ethics and legal frameworks unique to each country. For instance, AI-driven consumer profiling in China raises questions about data privacy, while Japan grapples with fairness and transparency in AI-driven human resource management. Similarly, South Korean firms must navigate ethical boundaries in personalized marketing.

This chapter explores these ethical dilemmas through a cultural and managerial lens, examining how East Asian businesses reconcile AI implementation with corporate social responsibility (CSR) and regional cultural values. By analyzing case studies from leading companies such as Alibaba and SoftBank, we aim to highlight the interplay between cultural norms, ethical considerations, and AI's role in corporate governance.

The exploration of these issues is particularly relevant in the current global business environment, where AI technologies are reshaping industries and redefining competitive advantages. East Asian countries, with their rapid technological development and influential market presence, offer a unique perspective on how AI can be harnessed ethically and responsibly. The strategies and practices developed by companies in this region not only influence local business operations but also serve as a reference for organizations worldwide seeking to integrate AI in a manner that aligns with societal expectations and ethical norms.

The complexity of AI ethics in East Asia is compounded by the region's diverse socio-political landscapes and regulatory environments. In China, the government plays a central role in promoting AI development as part of its national strategy for technological leadership. This state-driven approach influences how companies navigate ethical issues, as they must balance corporate interests with national priorities and social harmony (Zhang et al., 2021). Chinese companies like Alibaba, known for their aggressive use of AI in e-commerce and logistics, face the challenge of optimizing operational efficiency while adhering to evolving standards of data privacy and consumer rights. The Chinese government's recent regulations on data security and consumer protection further underscore the need for businesses to integrate ethical considerations into their AI strategies.

In contrast, Japan's approach to AI ethics is shaped by its long-standing cultural values of respect, collectivism, and a deep sense of social responsibility. Japanese companies must carefully manage the integration of AI in a way that supports labor relations and fosters trust among employees and customers. The introduction of AI in the workplace, particularly in decision-making and human resource management, is approached with caution to ensure that it aligns with the cultural expectations of fairness, hierarchy, and collective welfare. For instance, companies like SoftBank navigate these challenges by implementing AI systems that complement human oversight, emphasizing transparency and inclusivity in their CSR practices.

South Korea, positioned between China's state-driven model and Japan's culturally conservative approach, adopts a balanced strategy that emphasizes technological innovation alongside social welfare. Korean businesses are at the forefront of AI research and application, particularly in sectors such as finance, healthcare, and entertainment. However, this rapid technological adoption also brings forth ethical concerns, especially in areas like customer segmentation and personalized marketing. South Korean companies must be vigilant in managing issues related to data privacy, consumer protection, and potential biases in AI algorithms, ensuring that their practices uphold social equity and align with cultural values of respect and community welfare.

This chapter also aims to propose a culturally sensitive framework for integrating AI into CSR practices in East Asian organizations. The framework advocates for transparency in the deployment of AI, human oversight in automated decision-making processes, and the incorporation of CSR strategies that reflect regional cultural values, such as equity, harmony, and community well-being (Kim & Chung, 2019). This approach not only addresses ethical concerns but also enables companies to enhance their reputational capital, foster public trust, and create long-term value for stakeholders.

## ARTIFICIAL INTELLIGENCE AND BUSINESS PRACTICES IN EAST ASIA

AI has become a transformative force in East Asian business practices, permeating various sectors and reshaping traditional corporate operations. The integration of AI technologies into business activities such as marketing, supply chain management, human resources, and customer service has allowed companies to achieve unprecedented levels of efficiency, personalization, and innovation. However, AI adoption in East Asia is uniquely influenced by regional cultural values, societal expectations, and distinctive managerial practices, which impact how companies navigate the ethical implications of these advanced technologies.

## Cultural Influence on AI Adoption in East Asian Businesses

East Asia comprises diverse cultures with rich historical and philosophical traditions that continue to influence modern business practices. Countries like China, Japan, and South Korea share certain cultural traits, such as collectivism, hierarchical social structures, and a strong emphasis on harmony and social welfare. These cultural values significantly shape how companies approach AI adoption and integrate it into their business models (Lee et al., 2018).

In China, a strong focus on efficiency, technological advancement, and economic growth drives rapid AI integration in corporate operations. The Chinese ethos, deeply rooted in Confucianism, values harmony and collective well-being, influencing how companies handle data privacy and consumer welfare in AI-driven applications. Chinese technology firms, often aligned with national goals of economic modernization and technological leadership, receive extensive government support for AI research and development. This backing encourages companies to adopt AI rapidly to maintain both domestic and global competitiveness. Additionally, the Chinese government's proactive stance on AI regulation and development creates an environment where businesses are incentivized to innovate while adhering to ethical standards. This dynamic interplay between government policies and corporate strategies ensures that AI technologies are deployed in ways that align with societal values and national priorities (Ding, 2018).

Similarly, Japan's cultural values, influenced by Confucian and Buddhist principles, emphasize hierarchy, collective responsibility, and social order. Consequently, Japanese businesses approach AI adoption with caution, ensuring that technology aligns with labor relations and workplace harmony. This cultural framework significantly impacts managerial decisions concerning AI ethics, particularly in areas such as privacy, surveillance, and employee welfare. Japanese companies often implement AI systems that complement human oversight rather than replace it, reflecting a deep-seated respect for human judgment and the importance of maintaining social harmony. For instance, in the context of human resource management, AI tools are used to support decision-making processes while preserving the hierarchical and consensual nature of Japanese corporate culture. This approach helps mitigate potential ethical concerns and fosters trust among employees and stakeholders (Hofstede, 2001).

South Korea, another major player in AI adoption, balances its emphasis on technological innovation with a strong commitment to social welfare. South Korean businesses widely implement AI to improve customer experiences and optimize operations. However, given the cultural importance of balancing innovation with social harmony, companies must carefully consider the ethical and societal implications of AI use (Zhang et al., 2022). South Korean firms are known for their proactive stance on addressing ethical challenges, such as data privacy and algorithmic fairness. This commitment to ethical AI practices is often driven by a cultural emphasis on social equity and community welfare.

## AI Integration in Operations and Marketing: Case Studies of Alibaba and Naver

### Alibaba: AI in E-Commerce and Consumer Data Management

Alibaba, one of China's largest and most influential technology conglomerates, exemplifies AI integration in business. As an e-commerce leader, Alibaba employs advanced AI-driven algorithms to analyze consumer data and deliver personalized shopping experiences. Its AI-powered recommendation systems enhance customer satisfaction by tailoring product suggestions to individual users, optimizing sales processes, and reinforcing market dominance (Bawack et al., 2022).

However, this extensive AI integration raises ethical concerns regarding data privacy and consumer autonomy. Chinese consumers are becoming increasingly aware of how their data is collected and utilized for personalized marketing. While China's regulatory landscape supports rapid technological progress, societal expectations of harmony and discretion necessitate responsible data governance. In response, Alibaba has introduced transparency-focused policies and user control mechanisms to address privacy concerns, reflecting the importance of ethical AI management in maintaining consumer trust (Verma et al., 2021).

### Naver: AI in Personalized Advertising and Ethical Boundaries

Naver, South Korea's leading online platform, presents another case of AI integration, particularly in marketing and customer engagement. Using AI-driven algorithms, Naver profiles users based on their online behaviors and preferences, delivering personalized advertisements tailored to individual needs. This approach enhances the user experience while increasing the effectiveness of targeted marketing, aligning with South Korea's strong cultural emphasis on technological advancement and consumer satisfaction (Kar et al., 2022).

However, concerns regarding privacy infringement and potential discrimination in AI-driven user segmentation have led to ethical debates. Given that South Korean culture places high value on individual rights and societal welfare, companies like Naver face pressure to balance innovation with ethical responsibility. In response, Naver has initiated internal reviews and public consultations to develop AI ethics guidelines that align with the nation's cultural expectations of fairness and consumer protection. The company's proactive approach highlights how cultural values shape responsible AI integration (Wilson & van der Velden, 2022).

## AI in Human Resources and Internal Management: The SoftBank Case

### SoftBank: AI in Employee Performance Management and Hierarchical Dynamics

In Japan, SoftBank serves as a prominent example of how AI is being integrated into human resource operations while navigating cultural values and ethical considerations. SoftBank employs AI-driven systems to assess employee performance, optimize task allocation, and streamline HR processes. The company aims to leverage AI to enhance efficiency and reduce biases in employee evaluations, aligning with Japan's cultural emphasis on fairness, labor respect, and technological innovation (Papetti et al., 2020).

Nevertheless, implementing AI in human resource management within the Japanese context presents unique challenges. Japanese society values hierarchical workplace structures, collective responsibility, and employee welfare. Consequently, SoftBank must carefully balance AI adoption with maintaining traditional labor relations and ensuring employee trust. To address these challenges, the company has implemented privacy policies and feedback mechanisms that integrate human oversight, ensuring fairness and transparency in AI-driven HR processes (Sigfrids et al., 2023).

SoftBank's approach underscores the importance of cultural sensitivity in AI adoption. By involving employees in decision-making and respecting hierarchical norms, the company has successfully aligned AI integration with Japanese cultural expectations. This case exemplifies the role of managerial skills in ethical AI implementation, highlighting the need for business leaders to navigate cultural complexities, engage stakeholders, and adapt AI strategies accordingly (Staniškienė & Stankevičiūtė, 2018).

## Ethical Implications of AI-Driven Business Practices in East Asia

The cases of Alibaba, Naver, and SoftBank highlight that AI integration in East Asian business practices is not only about technological advancement but also involves navigating ethical and cultural complexities. The region's unique cultural norms significantly influence how companies approach AI-related ethical challenges, such as data privacy, employee welfare, and consumer rights.

In China, the societal value placed on harmony and technological progress drives companies to adopt AI in ways that emphasize efficiency while attempting to address ethical concerns. Alibaba's efforts to develop data governance policies indicate a growing awareness of the need to balance technological capabilities with ethical responsibilities.

Similarly, in South Korea, the integration of AI into business practices like personalized advertising is shaped by cultural norms that prioritize both innovation and social welfare. Naver's ongoing efforts to establish ethical guidelines for AI usage demonstrate the influence of cultural values in defining the ethical boundaries of AI implementation.

In Japan, the integration of AI into internal management processes, as seen in SoftBank's case, reveals the interplay between technological innovation and traditional labor relations. Japanese companies are compelled to respect hierarchical structures and employee welfare while adopting AI to enhance productivity and fairness.

## The Role of Culture in Shaping AI Integration

The integration of AI into East Asian business practices is profoundly influenced by cultural values, societal norms, and managerial competencies. As demonstrated by the cases of Alibaba, Naver, and SoftBank, companies must navigate ethical dilemmas related to data privacy, consumer welfare, and labor relations while ensuring alignment with cultural expectations. This intricate interplay between technology, ethics, and cultural identity requires business leaders to possess not only technical expertise but also cultural awareness, ethical judgment, and stakeholder engagement capabilities (Nishant et al., 2020).

Ultimately, the ethical and effective integration of AI in East Asian businesses depends on a culturally adapted approach that balances innovation with societal values. As the region continues to lead in AI adoption, understanding the cultural underpinnings of AI implementation will be essential for companies seeking to develop strategies that align with both business goals and societal expectations. By embedding cultural sensitivity into AI governance frameworks, East Asian organizations can foster responsible AI adoption and contribute to sustainable corporate development (Vinuesa et al., 2020).

## ETHICAL AND CULTURAL DILEMMAS IN AI IMPLEMENTATION

The integration of AI into business practices in East Asia presents a set of complex ethical and cultural dilemmas. These dilemmas arise from the intersection of advanced technologies with regional cultural norms, societal expectations, and diverse regulatory landscapes. As AI-driven systems permeate areas such as customer segmentation, marketing, human resources, and decision-making processes, companies in East Asia are faced with unique challenges that require careful consideration of both ethical principles and cultural values (Lee, 2021).

### The Complexity of Ethical Dilemmas in East Asian AI Practices

East Asia, with its rapid technological advancements and strong emphasis on societal harmony, presents a dynamic environment where businesses must balance innovation with ethical responsibilities. AI implementation in this context is not just about optimizing operations; it also involves navigating sensitive issues related to privacy, fairness, discrimination, and transparency (Minkkinen et al., 2022).

One of the primary ethical concerns in AI adoption is data privacy. AI systems, particularly those used in customer segmentation and personalized marketing, rely on vast amounts of personal data to function effectively. The collection, processing, and utilization of this data raise concerns about individuals' right to privacy and the potential for misuse. In China, Japan, and South Korea, cultural values that emphasize harmony, respect, and social welfare influence how companies address these privacy issues. In contrast to Western approaches that often focus on individual rights, East Asian societies place a stronger emphasis on collective well-being and societal harmony, shaping the ethical standards that guide AI implementation.

Another key ethical dilemma relates to discrimination and fairness in AI-driven decision-making processes. AI algorithms used in areas such as customer profiling, hiring, and performance evaluation can inadvertently introduce biases that lead to unfair outcomes. In South Korea, for example, the use of AI for customer segmentation in marketing has sparked debates over whether AI-driven recommendations and advertising may unintentionally discriminate against certain consumer groups. Korean cultural norms that value social equity and community welfare compel businesses to scrutinize their AI practices and address any potential biases in their algorithms.

Transparency and accountability are additional ethical considerations in AI implementation. As AI systems become increasingly complex, the "black box" nature of certain AI models poses challenges for businesses seeking to ensure that their decisions are understandable, explainable, and justifiable to stakeholders. In Japan, the cultural emphasis on trust, respect for hierarchy, and collective responsibility drives companies to implement AI in ways that are transparent and accountable to both employees and society. However, achieving this level of transparency often requires significant managerial skill and a deep understanding of AI technology and its implications.

## Cultural Dimensions Shaping Ethical Dilemmas

Cultural values in East Asia play a crucial role in shaping how businesses perceive and address the ethical dilemmas associated with AI implementation. Concepts such as collectivism, harmony, and respect for hierarchy influence corporate decision-making processes, guiding companies to adopt AI in ways that align with societal expectations (Awan et al., 2018).

In East Asian cultures, the collective well-being often takes precedence over individual interests. This cultural orientation affects how businesses manage AI-related ethical challenges, particularly those involving data privacy and consumer rights. In China, for example, the use of AI in customer profiling and targeted marketing is generally accepted if it contributes to economic growth and social harmony. However, companies like Alibaba have been pushed to balance this drive for technological efficiency with the need to protect consumer privacy and maintain public trust. The cultural emphasis on harmony compels companies to adopt AI practices that do not disrupt societal balance, reflecting a deep-seated belief in the importance of discretion and mutual respect.

The Japanese cultural value placed on hierarchical structures and labor relations significantly shapes how companies implement AI in internal management processes. Japanese businesses, such as SoftBank, must navigate the ethical dilemmas posed by AI-driven employee performance evaluations while respecting traditional norms of workplace hierarchy and collective decision-making. This dynamic requires managers to involve employees in discussions about AI integration and develop policies that address concerns over job security, privacy, and fairness. By fostering a culture of transparency and inclusivity, Japanese companies can mitigate potential conflicts between technological innovation and cultural expectations (Lee, 2021).

The rapid adoption of AI in South Korea is often balanced against cultural norms that prioritize social welfare and equity. Korean companies like Naver face ethical dilemmas in using AI for customer segmentation and advertising, as they must consider the potential impact of these practices on social equity. Korean culture's strong focus on balancing economic progress with social harmony drives companies to adopt AI responsibly, ensuring that their strategies do not inadvertently harm certain consumer groups or violate societal norms of fairness and respect (Vinuesa et al., 2020).

## Case Studies of Ethical Dilemmas in East Asian Companies

### Naver: AI-Driven Customer Segmentation and Privacy Concerns

Naver, a South Korean internet conglomerate, provides a compelling case study of the ethical dilemmas arising from AI implementation. The company uses AI algorithms to profile users and provide personalized advertisements based on their online behavior and preferences. While this approach enhances user experience and aligns with South Korea's technological and consumer-oriented culture, it also raises significant ethical questions about privacy and discrimination (Kar et al., 2022).

South Korean society places a high value on social harmony and individual rights, and concerns have been voiced about the extent to which AI-driven customer segmentation may infringe on user privacy. Additionally, the possibility that AI algorithms could create or reinforce discriminatory patterns in advertising has led to public debate. Korean companies like Naver are thus compelled to reassess their AI practices and adopt ethical guidelines that reflect cultural expectations of social equity and privacy.

In response, Naver has taken steps to enhance transparency and user control over data. The company has introduced features that allow users to manage their data preferences and opt out of certain types of personalized advertising. This case illustrates how cultural norms and ethical considerations drive East Asian companies to adapt their AI strategies, emphasizing a need for transparency, user empowerment, and respect for societal values.

### Tencent: AI in Social Welfare and Surveillance

Tencent, a leading Chinese technology conglomerate, faces a different set of ethical dilemmas in its AI practices. Tencent has developed AI systems aimed at improving public services, such as health care and urban management, reflecting the Chinese cultural emphasis on collective welfare and technological progress. However, the use of AI in these areas also raises concerns about surveillance, data privacy, and the potential misuse of technology (Nishant et al., 2020).

In China, societal norms often prioritize social stability and economic growth, which can sometimes justify extensive data collection for public welfare purposes. Nevertheless, Chinese companies like Tencent are increasingly aware of the need to address privacy concerns and ethical issues related to AI surveillance. In response, Tencent has started to implement internal guidelines that emphasize responsible data use, transparency, and user consent. The company's engagement with civil society and regulators illustrates how ethical considerations and cultural values intersect, guiding businesses toward more responsible AI practices.

## The Role of Managerial Skills in Addressing Ethical Dilemmas

Successfully navigating the ethical and cultural dilemmas of AI implementation in East Asia requires advanced managerial skills, including ethical leadership, intercultural sensitivity, and decision-making under uncertainty. Managers must be adept at understanding and interpreting cultural norms, engaging with stakeholders, and developing strategies that align with both corporate objectives and societal expectations.

For example, in Japanese companies like SoftBank, managers play a pivotal role in facilitating discussions about AI adoption, ensuring that employee concerns are addressed, and that AI practices reflect cultural values of respect, fairness, and collective decision-making. In China and South Korea, managers must balance the drive for technological innovation with the need to protect consumer privacy and promote social harmony. This balancing act requires technical expertise and a deep understanding of the cultural and ethical implications of AI technologies.

In East Asia, the ability to navigate these ethical dilemmas is increasingly seen as a core managerial competency. Companies that successfully integrate AI into their business practices in an ethical and culturally sensitive manner are more likely to maintain public trust, enhance their corporate reputation, and achieve long-term success in the digital era.

The ethical dilemmas associated with AI implementation in East Asian businesses are deeply intertwined with regional cultural norms and values. Issues related to privacy, fairness, transparency, and social welfare present complex challenges that require companies to go beyond mere technological adoption. East Asian companies must navigate these ethical complexities in ways that align with cultural expectations, demonstrating respect for societal values while advancing their business objectives.

As illustrated by the cases of Naver and Tencent, cultural norms significantly shape how companies address AI-related ethical issues, driving them to adopt practices that reflect collective welfare, social equity, and respect for privacy. Managerial skills play a critical role in guiding organizations through these dilemmas, emphasizing the importance of ethical leadership, stakeholder engagement, and cultural sensitivity.

Understanding the cultural dimensions of AI implementation is essential for developing ethical and effective AI strategies in East Asia. As AI continues to evolve and become more integrated into business practices, companies in the region will need to adapt their approaches to navigate the dynamic interplay between technology, ethics, and cultural values.

## Cross-Cultural Awareness, Sensitivity and Strategic Adaptability

One of the foremost skills that managers in East Asia must possess is cross-cultural awareness and sensitivity. AI technologies do not operate in a vacuum; they are implemented within specific cultural contexts that shape both the perception of AI and the ethical considerations associated with its use. Therefore, managers need to have a deep understanding of the cultural values and social norms that influence stakeholders' attitudes toward AI. For example, the importance of harmony in Chinese society, respect for hierarchy in Japanese corporate culture, and the balance between technological innovation and social welfare in South Korea all impact how AI should be managed ethically.

Cross-cultural awareness involves more than simply recognizing cultural differences; it requires an active engagement with these differences to inform ethical AI strategies. For instance, when implementing AI in customer services, managers must be sensitive to cultural concerns about privacy and data usage. In China, where societal harmony and trust are crucial, managers need to be aware that consumers may view the collection of personal data as a potential threat to social stability. Thus, managers should design AI systems and policies that are transparent, prioritize user consent, and clearly communicate how data will be used to avoid public distrust.

In Japan, managers must consider the cultural emphasis on group harmony and collective decision-making when implementing AI in human resource operations. This might involve incorporating AI tools that facilitate, rather than dictate, decision-making processes, thereby preserving the sense of collective agency and respect within the organizational hierarchy. Cross-cultural sensitivity helps managers align AI implementation with these cultural values, ensuring that the technology serves to enhance, rather than disrupt, established corporate and societal norms.

AI technologies are constantly evolving, and their applications in business contexts are expanding. In East Asia, where the pace of technological adoption is particularly rapid, managers must be strategically adaptable to navigate the ethical implications of these changes effectively. Strategic adaptability refers to the ability of managers to adjust strategies, policies, and operational practices in response to new developments in AI, as well as shifts in societal attitudes and regulatory landscapes.

One aspect of strategic adaptability is the proactive identification of potential ethical issues before they escalate. For example, as facial recognition technology becomes more prevalent in China for purposes ranging from security to personalized marketing, managers must anticipate public concerns about surveillance and privacy. A strategically adaptable manager would not only ensure that the company complies with current regulations but also develop internal guidelines that go beyond legal requirements to address ethical considerations and public sentiment. This might involve limiting the use of facial recognition technology in certain contexts or implementing stricter data protection measures to alleviate privacy concerns.

In addition, strategic adaptability requires managers to remain informed about regional and global trends in AI ethics, including changes in laws, standards, and public expectations. In Japan, where the government actively promotes AI development while advocating for ethical guidelines, managers need to stay abreast of policy discussions to align their corporate practices with national objectives and ethical standards. By doing so, they can position their companies as responsible innovators, gaining public trust and competitive advantage.

## Stakeholder Engagement, Transparency and Ethical AI Frameworks

Engaging with a broad range of stakeholders is essential for ethical AI management in East Asia. Stakeholder engagement involves actively seeking input from various parties affected by AI implementation, including employees, customers, regulatory authorities, and civil society organizations. In the context of East Asia, where societal harmony and collective well-being are highly valued, engaging stakeholders ensures that AI practices align with community expectations and ethical norms (Staniškienė & Stankevičiūtė, 2018).

For instance, in South Korea, companies like Naver have started to engage with civil society organizations to address concerns related to AI-driven personalization and privacy. Managers leading such initiatives demonstrate an understanding of the importance of transparency and inclusiveness in decision-making processes. By involving stakeholders in discussions about AI's potential risks and benefits, managers can build consensus and co-develop ethical guidelines that reflect a shared commitment to societal welfare.

Transparency is a key component of stakeholder engagement. In Japan, where trust and mutual respect form the foundation of business relationships, companies need to be transparent about how AI systems are used, especially in sensitive areas such as employee performance evaluation or customer data management. Managers should provide clear information about the AI technologies in use, their purposes, and the safeguards in place to protect privacy and fairness. This approach not only addresses ethical concerns but also fosters trust among stakeholders, reinforcing the company's reputation for responsible AI practices (Sigfrids et al., 2023).

Beyond individual skills, managers in East Asia must work toward building ethical AI frameworks that are specifically tailored to the cultural and societal contexts of the region. This involves developing a comprehensive strategy that encompasses ethical guidelines, governance structures, and accountability mechanisms. Managers play a central role in shaping these frameworks, ensuring that they reflect both global best practices and local cultural values.

In China, where technological progress and economic growth are prioritized, managers should integrate ethical AI frameworks that emphasize transparency, data security, and consumer consent. They should lead the creation of internal policies that guide AI usage, focusing on aligning technological capabilities with the values of social harmony and collective welfare. By doing so, managers can foster an environment in which AI is used responsibly to benefit both the company and society at large.

In Japan, ethical AI frameworks might focus more on employee welfare, transparency in decision-making, and the preservation of workplace harmony. Managers are tasked with the responsibility of ensuring that AI systems, particularly those used in human resources, are implemented in ways that support fair treatment, respect for hierarchy, and collective involvement. This might involve establishing review boards or ethics committees that include employee representatives, providing an additional layer of oversight and ensuring that AI applications do not disrupt the cultural fabric of the workplace.

## AI for Environmental Sustainability and Resource Optimization

### Tencent's AI-Driven Energy Management

Tencent, a leading Chinese technology conglomerate, offers a prominent example of using AI for environmental CSR. Tencent has developed AI systems that monitor and optimize energy consumption within its data centers, significantly reducing the company's carbon footprint. These AI systems analyze vast amounts of operational data in real-time to identify patterns of energy use and suggest adjustments to improve efficiency. By implementing AI in this way, Tencent aligns its business practices with China's national focus on green development and sustainability.

However, the use of AI for environmental purposes also raises ethical considerations related to data privacy and the potential for AI misuse. For instance, while AI-driven monitoring can enhance energy efficiency, it may involve extensive data collection from various sources, including sensors and user interactions. Tencent's approach to addressing these ethical concerns involves developing internal guidelines that prioritize transparency, user consent, and the ethical use of AI technologies. This commitment to ethical AI use not only strengthens Tencent's CSR strategy but also reflects the Chinese cultural emphasis on social harmony and collective welfare.

### Toyota's AI in Sustainable Manufacturing

In Japan, companies like Toyota have integrated AI into their CSR efforts to support sustainable manufacturing processes. Toyota employs AI in its production lines to optimize resource use, reduce waste, and enhance energy efficiency. The company's AI-driven systems monitor every aspect of the production process, from material sourcing to assembly, to identify opportunities for reducing environmental impact. This approach reflects Japan's cultural values of harmony with nature and responsible use of resources.

Furthermore, Toyota has expanded its AI applications beyond internal operations to include environmentally friendly products, such as electric and hybrid vehicles that incorporate AI for enhanced energy management. This commitment to sustainability aligns with the Japanese cultural ideal of 'mottainai,' which emphasizes the importance of minimizing waste and respecting resources. By integrating AI into its CSR strategy, Toyota not only advances its business goals but also contributes to societal well-being and environmental stewardship.

## AI in Social Welfare and Community Engagement

### SoftBank's AI for Disaster Response and Community Support

In Japan, SoftBank has utilized AI as part of its CSR initiatives to support disaster response and community engagement. Japan, prone to natural disasters such as earthquakes and typhoons, has a strong cultural emphasis on preparedness and community solidarity. SoftBank has developed AI-driven platforms that provide real-time information and coordination support during disasters. These platforms use AI to analyze data from sensors, social media, and emergency services to offer timely insights for disaster management and resource allocation.

Through this AI application, SoftBank demonstrates its commitment to community welfare and societal resilience. The company's approach is culturally aligned with the Japanese values of social harmony and collective responsibility. By using AI to enhance its disaster response capabilities, SoftBank contributes to the well-being of communities, positioning itself as a socially responsible corporation that goes beyond mere profit-making to address critical societal challenges.

## Naver's AI in Education and Social Equity

In South Korea, Naver has integrated AI into its CSR initiatives focused on education and social equity. Naver's AI-powered educational platforms provide personalized learning experiences, helping to bridge gaps in educational access and quality. These platforms use AI algorithms to tailor learning content to the needs of individual students, offering support to those who might otherwise be left behind in traditional educational systems.

This use of AI aligns with the South Korean cultural emphasis on social equity and the importance of education in societal progress. However, Naver also faces ethical challenges related to data privacy and the potential for biased algorithmic outcomes. To address these issues, Naver has implemented robust data protection measures and ethical guidelines that promote fairness, transparency, and inclusivity in AI-driven education. By doing so, Naver not only fulfills its CSR commitments but also reinforces the cultural values of equity and social welfare.

# Addressing the Ethical Challenges of AI in CSR

While the integration of AI into CSR initiatives offers numerous benefits, it also presents ethical challenges that companies in East Asia must navigate carefully. One such challenge is the potential misuse of AI, particularly when it comes to data privacy and surveillance. For example, AI systems used for environmental monitoring or social welfare may collect large amounts of personal data, raising concerns about privacy violations and data security.

To address these ethical challenges, East Asian companies are increasingly developing AI governance frameworks that emphasize ethical use, transparency, and accountability. Tencent, for instance, has adopted internal policies that guide the ethical application of AI in its CSR activities, ensuring that user data is collected and processed in ways that respect privacy and consent. Similarly, Toyota and SoftBank have established ethical guidelines for AI that align with their respective cultural contexts, prioritizing societal welfare, transparency, and stakeholder engagement.

Another ethical consideration is ensuring that AI-driven CSR initiatives do not inadvertently reinforce social inequalities or biases. In the realm of AI in education, companies like Naver are actively working to mitigate algorithmic biases and promote inclusivity. This involves regularly auditing AI systems for fairness, involving diverse stakeholders in the design process, and promoting transparency in AI decision-making.

The integration of AI into CSR initiatives in East Asia reflects a region-specific approach that is shaped by cultural values, societal expectations, and ethical considerations. Companies like Tencent, Toyota, SoftBank, and Naver illustrate how AI can be used to advance CSR goals in areas such as environmental sustainability, social welfare, disaster response, and education. However, the successful incorporation of AI into CSR also requires careful management of ethical challenges, including data privacy, transparency, and fairness (Vinuesa et al., 2020).

By aligning their AI-driven CSR strategies with regional cultural norms and values, East Asian companies can foster trust, enhance their social impact, and demonstrate their commitment to responsible business practices. This culturally sensitive approach to AI in CSR underscores the importance of ethical leadership, strategic adaptability, and stakeholder engagement in achieving not only business success but also societal well-being.

AI serves as a powerful tool for East Asian companies to advance their CSR initiatives in ways that resonate with cultural ideals of harmony, collective welfare, and responsibility. As the region continues to lead in AI adoption, the lessons learned from these CSR practices offer valuable insights for global businesses seeking to integrate AI into their social responsibility efforts in a manner that is both ethical and culturally relevant (Wilson & van der Velden, 2022).

## DEVELOPING A CULTURALLY SENSITIVE FRAMEWORK FOR AI AND CSR

The ethical integration of AI into CSR strategies in East Asia necessitates a nuanced and culturally sensitive framework. This framework must reflect the region's unique cultural values, societal norms, and ethical standards, while simultaneously addressing the technical and operational challenges posed by AI technologies. Given the diversity within East Asia, a one-size-fits-all model would be insufficient. Instead, the framework proposed here considers specific regional attributes, emphasizing transparency, human oversight, cultural alignment, and stakeholder engagement as core pillars. This section develops a comprehensive, culturally sensitive framework for AI and CSR that East Asian companies can use to guide their strategies, ensuring that AI serves not just corporate objectives, but the broader goals of societal well-being and harmony.

A culturally sensitive AI-CSR framework for East Asia should be rooted in core principles that reflect the region's societal values and ethical considerations. These principles provide a foundation upon which businesses can build their AI and CSR strategies, guiding decision-making processes and ensuring that AI applications align with cultural expectations.

In East Asian cultures, especially in Japan and South Korea, trust is a cornerstone of business and social interactions. Therefore, transparency in how AI technologies are used within CSR initiatives is essential. Companies must openly communicate their AI practices, including how data is collected, processed, and utilized, to foster trust among stakeholders. Moreover, accountability mechanisms should be in place to address any ethical concerns or negative impacts arising from AI use. This principle aligns with the cultural values of honesty, respect, and social responsibility, which are highly regarded in the region.

The East Asian cultural focus on harmony, collective welfare, and respect for human dignity necessitates a human-centric approach to AI implementation in CSR. AI should be seen as a tool that supports human decision-making rather than replacing it entirely. Human oversight ensures that ethical considerations, cultural values, and societal welfare are prioritized in AI-driven processes. For example, in Japanese companies, AI systems used for employee performance evaluation should incorporate human review to maintain fairness and respect for traditional workplace hierarchies. Similarly, in China, AI used for social welfare initiatives should involve community consultation to align technological interventions with local needs and expectations.

The integration of AI into CSR practices must reflect the cultural values and ethical norms specific to each East Asian society. In China, where collectivism and social harmony are central, CSR initiatives should leverage AI to promote societal benefits, such as environmental sustainability and equitable access to services. In South Korea, the emphasis on social equity means that AI-CSR strategies should actively work to reduce disparities and support vulnerable populations. By incorporating cultural alignment into their AI strategies, companies can ensure that their actions resonate with societal values and reinforce their commitment to responsible and ethical business practices.

## Strategic Implementation of a Culturally Sensitive AI-CSR Framework

Establishing robust AI governance structures is critical to ensuring that AI-CSR initiatives adhere to ethical guidelines and cultural values. Companies should form interdisciplinary AI ethics committees that include members from various departments, such as technology, legal, human resources, and CSR. This diversity ensures that multiple perspectives are considered in AI decision-making processes, fostering a holistic approach to ethics and cultural sensitivity. In East Asia, where hierarchy and collective decision-making are culturally significant, these committees can also include representatives from employee groups and external stakeholders, such as community leaders and government officials. This inclusive governance model aligns with regional cultural norms and promotes transparency and accountability.

Before implementing AI technologies in CSR projects, companies should conduct comprehensive ethical impact assessments. These assessments evaluate the potential cultural, social, and ethical implications of AI use, identifying risks related to privacy, bias, and social equity. For instance, in South Korea, where social equity is a priority, companies might assess how AI-driven customer segmentation could affect different demographic groups and take steps to mitigate discriminatory outcomes. Ethical impact assessments help companies anticipate and address potential conflicts between technological capabilities and cultural values, ensuring that their AI-CSR practices are both responsible and culturally aligned.

Given the collectivist cultural context in many East Asian societies, involving stakeholders in the AI-CSR process is crucial. Companies should actively seek input from employees, customers, community members, and regulatory bodies to inform their AI strategies. This engagement can take various forms, including surveys, focus groups, public forums, and collaborative workshops. In China, for example, companies can work with local communities to design AI-driven environmental monitoring systems, ensuring that the technology is tailored to meet specific community needs and preferences. In Japan, employee involvement in discussions about AI implementation in human resource management can foster a sense of ownership and trust, aligning with the cultural value of group harmony.

Continuous monitoring and evaluation are vital to maintaining the ethical integrity of AI-CSR initiatives. Companies should conduct regular audits of their AI systems to ensure compliance with ethical standards, data protection regulations, and cultural norms. These audits should include assessments of algorithmic fairness, data privacy practices, and the social impact of AI applications. In South Korea, for instance, companies can periodically review their AI-driven marketing strategies to identify and rectify any biases that may arise in customer segmentation, reflecting a commitment to social equity and consumer welfare. Regular evaluations enable companies to adapt their strategies in response to evolving ethical challenges and cultural dynamics.

## Tailoring AI-CSR Practices to Specific East Asian Contexts

### China: Leveraging AI for Collective Welfare and Sustainability

While the core principles and strategic components of the framework provide a general guide, companies must tailor their AI-CSR practices to the specific cultural, regulatory, and business environments of each East Asian country. This tailored approach ensures that AI integration resonates with local societal values and meets the expectations of diverse stakeholders. In China, the government's emphasis on technological progress and societal welfare provides a unique context for AI-CSR integration. Companies should align their AI strategies with national priorities, such as poverty alleviation, environmental sustainability, and public health. For example, technology firms can develop AI-driven platforms for smart agriculture, optimizing resource use and improving food security, which aligns with the Chinese cultural value of social harmony and collective well-being. Additionally, companies can partner with government agencies to ensure that AI systems comply with data protection regulations and ethical guidelines, reinforcing their commitment to responsible innovation.

## Japan: Emphasizing Harmony, Inclusivity, and Ethical Stewardship

In Japan, CSR practices are closely linked to the cultural values of harmony, environmental stewardship, and respect for societal order. Companies implementing AI in their CSR strategies should prioritize inclusivity, transparency, and ethical reflection. For instance, Japanese firms can incorporate AI in waste management and recycling programs, using the technology to optimize resource use while respecting community input. Additionally, in human resource management, AI tools should be designed to facilitate fair and respectful employee evaluations, with human oversight to prevent bias and uphold traditional workplace values. By embedding cultural sensitivity into their AI-CSR practices, Japanese companies can maintain public trust and reinforce their reputation for ethical business conduct.

## South Korea: Fostering Social Equity and Technological Innovation

South Korea's CSR practices are shaped by the cultural emphasis on technological innovation and social equity. Companies in South Korea should use AI to address societal challenges, such as educational disparities and healthcare access, while ensuring that their practices do not exacerbate social inequalities. For example, technology firms can develop AI-powered educational platforms that provide personalized learning experiences, helping to bridge gaps in educational quality and access. However, companies must also implement robust data protection measures and ethical guidelines to safeguard user privacy and ensure fairness. By focusing on social equity and community welfare, South Korean companies can integrate AI into their CSR initiatives in a way that reflects the country's cultural values and societal goals.

## Toward a Holistic and Culturally Informed AI-CSR Framework

The development of a culturally sensitive AI-CSR framework for East Asia requires a holistic approach that considers regional values, ethical norms, and stakeholder expectations. By grounding their AI-CSR strategies in core principles such as transparency, human-centric oversight, cultural alignment, and stakeholder engagement, companies can navigate the complexities of AI ethics while fulfilling their social responsibilities. The strategic components of this framework, including ethical governance, impact assessments, and regular audits, provide a practical guide for companies seeking to implement AI ethically in their CSR initiatives.

Transparency is essential for building trust among stakeholders. Companies must openly communicate their AI practices, including how data is collected, processed, and utilized. This openness helps to demystify AI technologies and ensures that stakeholders are aware of the ethical considerations involved. Transparent practices also facilitate accountability, allowing companies to address any ethical concerns or negative impacts arising from AI use.

AI should be seen as a tool that supports human decision-making rather than replacing it entirely. Human oversight ensures that ethical considerations, cultural values, and societal welfare are prioritized in AI-driven processes. This principle is particularly important in East Asian cultures, where respect for human dignity and collective welfare are highly valued. Human-centric oversight helps to maintain fairness and prevent biases in AI applications.

Engaging with a broad range of stakeholders is crucial for ethical AI management. Companies should actively seek input from employees, customers, community members, and regulatory bodies to inform their AI strategies. This engagement ensures that AI practices align with community expectations and ethical norms. It also fosters a sense of ownership and trust among stakeholders, reinforcing the company's commitment to responsible AI use.

Establishing robust AI governance structures is critical to ensuring that AI-CSR initiatives adhere to ethical guidelines and cultural values. Companies should form interdisciplinary AI ethics committees that include members from various departments, such as technology, legal, human resources, and CSR. This diversity ensures that multiple perspectives are considered in AI decision-making processes, fostering a holistic approach to ethics and cultural sensitivity.

Before implementing AI technologies in CSR projects, companies should conduct comprehensive ethical impact assessments. These assessments evaluate the potential cultural, social, and ethical implications of AI use, identifying risks related to privacy, bias, and social equity. Ethical impact assessments help companies anticipate and address potential conflicts between technological capabilities and cultural values, ensuring that their AI-CSR practices are both responsible and culturally aligned.

Continuous monitoring and evaluation are vital to maintaining the ethical integrity of AI-CSR initiatives. Companies should conduct regular audits of their AI systems to ensure compliance with ethical standards, data protection regulations, and cultural norms. These audits should include assessments of algorithmic fairness, data privacy practices, and the social impact of AI applications. Regular evaluations enable companies to adapt their strategies in response to evolving ethical challenges and cultural dynamics.

Furthermore, the tailored application of the framework to specific East Asian contexts ensures that AI integration resonates with local cultural values and addresses the unique societal challenges of each country. As AI continues to evolve and shape the future of business and society, East Asian companies have the opportunity to lead by example, demonstrating how culturally sensitive and ethically grounded AI practices can contribute to sustainable development and societal well-being.

The proposed framework serves as a roadmap for East Asian companies to align their AI-driven CSR strategies with the region's cultural and ethical landscapes. By adopting this framework, businesses can foster public trust, enhance their social impact, and position themselves as responsible innovators in an increasingly digital world. This culturally informed approach not only benefits the companies themselves but also promotes a more equitable, harmonious, and sustainable future for East Asian societies.

## FUTURE LINES OF RESEARCH

Despite the comprehensive exploration of AI integration in East Asian business practices and CSR presented in this work, several areas warrant further investigation. The rapid evolution of AI technologies and the complex interplay with regional cultural norms necessitate ongoing scholarly attention to better understand the emerging ethical, societal, and managerial challenges.

While the study of comparative analysis of AI-CSR practices across East Asia has primarily focused on China, Japan, and South Korea, future research could extend to other East Asian countries, such as Taiwan, Singapore, and Vietnam. A comparative analysis of AI-CSR practices in these diverse cultural and regulatory contexts would deepen our understanding of how regional variations in societal values, legal frameworks, and business environments shape the ethical integration of AI. This approach could uncover best practices and potential pitfalls that transcend national boundaries, informing global discourse on responsible AI adoption.

As AI increasingly permeates human resource management, performance evaluation, and workforce planning, future research should investigate its implications for labor relations in East Asia. Given the region's cultural emphasis on collective welfare, job security, and respect for hierarchy, it is crucial to explore how companies can balance the efficiency gains from AI-driven decision-making with the preservation of employee welfare and workplace harmony. Studies could also examine the role of managerial skills in fostering an inclusive environment that addresses employees' concerns regarding AI, promoting transparency and fairness.

Another promising line of research lies in examining how East Asian AI-CSR practices align with or diverge from global standards and regulations. As East Asian companies expand their international operations, they face the challenge of navigating diverse ethical landscapes and legal requirements. Understanding the interaction between regional cultural norms and global AI ethics standards can provide insights into developing universal guidelines for ethical AI implementation. Such research could explore how East Asian companies adapt their culturally sensitive AI strategies to meet international expectations and the implications for cross-cultural business ethics.

This study proposes a culturally sensitive framework for AI integration into CSR in East Asia. Future research could focus on the practical development and application of AI governance models tailored to specific industries or sectors within the region. Exploring how organizations design and implement governance structures that incorporate ethical guidelines, cultural values, and stakeholder engagement mechanisms can offer actionable strategies for responsible AI use. This line of research would also benefit from investigating the role of cross-cultural training in enhancing managers' abilities to navigate the ethical complexities of AI in a diverse and dynamic regional context.

With the growing use of AI in fields like education, healthcare, and marketing, there is a critical need to examine how AI can be leveraged to address social inequities while mitigating the risks of bias and discrimination. Research should focus on identifying best practices for implementing AI-driven solutions that align with the region's cultural emphasis on social harmony and collective welfare. Studies could also explore the impact of AI on marginalized communities and the effectiveness of regulatory and ethical safeguards in protecting vulnerable groups.

Finally, future research should consider conducting longitudinal studies to assess the long-term impact of AI integration on CSR initiatives and societal well-being. By tracking the evolution of AI ethics, stakeholder perceptions, and corporate practices over time, researchers can provide valuable insights into the sustainability of AI-driven CSR strategies. This approach would help identify factors that contribute to the successful and ethical use of AI in East Asian businesses, offering lessons for other regions seeking to navigate the ethical challenges of technological advancement. The ongoing development of AI technologies and their integration into business practices present a dynamic field for future research. By exploring these lines of inquiry, scholars can contribute to a more nuanced understanding of how culturally sensitive and ethically grounded AI practices can promote not only corporate success but also societal progress in East Asia and beyond.

## CONCLUSION

The ethical integration of artificial intelligence (AI) in East Asian business practices presents a complex interplay of technological innovation, cultural values, and managerial challenges. This chapter has explored how companies in China, Japan, and South Korea navigate the implementation of AI while adhering to regional cultural norms and ethical considerations. The findings reveal several key insights that contribute to our understanding of AI integration in corporate social responsibility (CSR) initiatives within the East Asian context.

First, the successful integration of AI into business practices requires a deep understanding of and respect for regional cultural values. East Asian societies, characterized by their emphasis on collective welfare, social harmony, and hierarchical relationships, approach AI implementation differently from Western counterparts. Companies like Alibaba, SoftBank, and Naver have demonstrated that effective AI integration must align with these cultural foundations while addressing modern ethical challenges such as data privacy, algorithmic fairness, and transparency.

The research highlights the critical role of managerial skills in navigating the ethical complexities of AI implementation. Successful managers in East Asian organizations must possess technical expertise, cultural sensitivity and ethical judgment. These skills are essential for balancing the efficiency gains of AI with societal expectations and cultural values. The cases examined show that managers who effectively engage stakeholders, maintain transparency, and prioritize ethical considerations are better positioned to implement AI solutions that benefit both their organizations and society at large.

Cultural differences across East Asian countries significantly influence how organizations approach AI integration. In China, where national development priorities and social harmony are paramount, companies focus on aligning AI initiatives with collective welfare and governmental objectives. Japanese organizations emphasize consensus-building and workplace harmony, implementing AI systems that complement rather than disrupt traditional labor relations. South Korean firms balance technological innovation with social equity, demonstrating how cultural values shape the ethical boundaries of AI implementation.

The development of culturally sensitive frameworks for AI integration emerges as a crucial factor in successful implementation. These frameworks must consider transparency and accountability mechanisms that align with cultural expectations of trust and responsibility. They should incorporate stakeholder engagement processes that respect hierarchical structures while ensuring inclusive participation. Furthermore, ethical guidelines must reflect regional values while meeting global standards, and human oversight systems should balance automation with cultural preferences for human interaction.

The research also reveals the importance of industry-specific adaptations in AI integration. Different sectors face unique challenges and opportunities in implementing AI ethically. For instance, e-commerce companies must navigate consumer privacy concerns while optimizing user experience, whereas manufacturing firms focus on balancing workforce automation with employee welfare. This sectoral variation requires flexible frameworks that can accommodate different business contexts while maintaining cultural sensitivity.

The role of CSR in AI implementation has emerged as a critical consideration. East Asian companies increasingly recognize that responsible AI practices must extend beyond regulatory compliance to address broader societal concerns. This approach aligns with the regional emphasis on corporate responsibility and social harmony. Companies that successfully integrate AI into their CSR initiatives demonstrate how technology can contribute to social welfare while maintaining cultural values.

Looking forward, several challenges and opportunities warrant attention. The rapid evolution of AI technologies requires organizations to continuously adapt their ethical frameworks and management practices. This dynamic environment demands ongoing development of managerial capabilities and organizational structures that can respond to emerging ethical challenges while preserving cultural values.

Furthermore, the globalization of business operations presents East Asian companies with the challenge of maintaining cultural sensitivity while meeting international standards and expectations. This balancing act requires sophisticated management approaches that can reconcile local cultural values with global ethical principles in AI implementation.

The research also highlights the need for enhanced collaboration between industry, academia, and government bodies in developing ethical AI frameworks. Such collaboration can help establish best practices that reflect cultural values while promoting innovation and social responsibility. The experiences of East Asian companies offer valuable lessons for organizations worldwide seeking to implement AI ethically and responsibly.

Organizations should invest in developing managers' cultural competencies alongside technical skills, while ensuring ethical frameworks for AI implementation remain flexible enough to accommodate cultural nuances while maintaining core principles. Stakeholder engagement should reflect cultural preferences for consensus-building and collective decision-making, and regular assessment of AI impacts on social harmony and workplace relationships remains essential.

Areas requiring further investigation include the long-term effects of AI integration on organizational culture and social relationships, the development of culturally specific metrics for measuring ethical AI implementation, the role of cross-cultural learning in improving AI governance frameworks, and the impact of emerging technologies on traditional cultural values and business practices.

In conclusion, the ethical integration of AI in East Asian business practices requires a sophisticated understanding of cultural values, managerial capabilities, and ethical considerations. Success in this endeavor demands more than technical expertise; it requires cultural sensitivity, ethical judgment, and strategic adaptability. The experiences of East Asian companies provide valuable insights for organizations worldwide, demonstrating how cultural values can guide responsible AI implementation while promoting innovation and social welfare.

As AI continues to transform business practices, the ability to navigate cultural and ethical considerations will become increasingly important. Organizations that can successfully balance technological advancement with cultural values and ethical responsibilities will be better positioned to achieve sustainable success in the evolving digital landscape. The East Asian approach to AI integration, characterized by its emphasis on collective welfare, harmony, and ethical responsibility, offers important lessons for global business practices in the AI era.

## REFERENCES


Awan, U., Kraslawski, A., & Huiskonen, J. (2018). Governing interfirm relationships for social sustainability: The relationship between governance mechanisms, sustainable collaboration, and cultural intelligence. *Sustainability (Basel)*, 10(12), 4473. DOI: 10.3390/su10124473

Bawack, R. E., Wamba, S. F., Carillo, K. D. A., & Akter, S. (2022). Artificial intelligence in E-Commerce: A bibliometric study and literature review. *Electronic Markets*, 32(1), 297–338. DOI: 10.1007/s12525-022-00537-z PMID: 35600916

Ding, J. (2018). *Deciphering China's AI Dream: The Context, Components, Capabilities, and Consequences of China's Strategy to Lead the World in AI*. Future of Humanity Institute, University of Oxford. https://www.fhi.ox.ac.uk/wp-content/uploads/Deciphering_Chinas_AI-Dream.pdf

Hofstede, G. (2001). *Culture's Consequences: Comparing Values, Behaviors, Institutions, and Organizations Across Nations* (2nd ed.). SAGE Publications.

Kar, A. K., Choudhary, S. K., & Singh, V. K. (2022). How can artificial intelligence impact sustainability: A systematic literature review. *Journal of Cleaner Production*, 376, 134120. DOI: 10.1016/j.jclepro.2022.134120

Kim, S., & Chung, S. (2019). Explaining organizational responsiveness to emerging regulatory pressure: The case of illegal overwork in South Korea. *Human Relations*, 72(9), 1436–1461.

Lee, K. (2021). A Systematic Review on Social Sustainability of Artificial Intelligence in Product Design. *Sustainability (Basel)*, 13(5), 2668. Advance online publication. DOI: 10.3390/su13052668

Lee, K. F., Triolo, P., & Kania, E. (2018). *AI Superpowers: China, Silicon Valley, and the New World Order*. Houghton Mifflin Harcourt.

Minkkinen, M., Niukkanen, A., & Mäntymäki, M. (2022). What about investors? ESG analyses as tools for ethics-based AI auditing. *AI & Society*. Advance online publication. DOI: 10.1007/s00146-022-01415-0

Nishant, R., Kennedy, M., & Corbett, J. (2020). Artificial intelligence for sustainability: Challenges, opportunities, and a research agenda. *International Journal of Information Management*, 53, 102104. DOI: 10.1016/j.ijinfomgt.2020.102104

Papetti, A., Gregori, F., Pandolfi, M., Peruzzini, M., & Germani, M. (2020). A method to improve workers' well-being toward human-centered connected factories. *Journal of Computational Design and Engineering*, 7(5), 630–643. DOI: 10.1093/jcde/qwaa047

Sigfrids, A., Leikas, J., Salo-Pöntinen, H., & Koskimies, E. (2023). Human-centricity in AI governance: A systemic approach. *Frontiers in Artificial Intelligence*, 6, 976887. DOI: 10.3389/frai.2023.976887 PMID: 36872934

Staniškienė, E., & Stankevičiūtė, Ž. (2018). Social sustainability measurement framework: The case of employee perspective in a CSR-committed organisation. *Journal of Cleaner Production*, 188, 708–719. DOI: 10.1016/j.jclepro.2018.03.269

Verma, S., Sharma, R., Deb, S., & Maitra, D. (2021). Artificial intelligence in marketing: Systematic review and future research direction. *International Journal of Information Management Data Insights*, 1(1), 100002. DOI: 10.1016/j.jjimei.2020.100002

Vinuesa, R., Azizpour, H., Leite, I., Balaam, M., Dignum, V., Domisch, S., Felländer, A., Langhans, S. D., Tegmark, M., & Fuso Nerini, F. (2020). The role of artificial intelligence in achieving the Sustainable Development Goals. *Nature Communications*, 11(1), 233. DOI: 10.1038/s41467-019-14108-y PMID: 31932590

Wilson, C., & van der Velden, M. (2022). Sustainable AI: An integrated model to guide public sector decision-making. *Technology in Society*, 68, 101926. DOI: 10.1016/j.techsoc.2022.101926

Zhang, D., Mishra, S., Brynjolfsson, E., Etchemendy, J., Ganguli, D., Grosz, B., Lyons, T., Manyika, J., Niebles, J. C., Sellitto, M., Shoham, Y., Clark, J., & Perrault, R. (2021). *The AI Index 2021 Annual Report*. AI Index Steering Committee, Human-Centered AI Institute, Stanford University.

Zhang, D., Mishra, S., Brynjolfsson, E., Etchemendy, J., Ganguli, D., Grosz, B., Lyons, T., Manyika, J., Niebles, J. C., Sellitto, M., Shoham, Y., Clark, J., & Perrault, R. (2022). *The AI Index 2022 Annual Report*. AI Index Steering Committee, Stanford Institute for Human-Centered AI, Stanford University.

# Chapter 10
# Keys in the Adoption of New Technologies in Latin American SMEs:
## Challenges for a Sustained Growth in the AI Age

**Eduardo Carlos Dittmar**
https://orcid.org/0000-0002-8087-2444
*Universidad Rey Juan Carlos, Spain*

**Víctor Manuel Castillo Girón**
https://orcid.org/0000-0002-8307-2952
*Universidad de Guadalajara, Mexico*

## ABSTRACT

*This research examines the integration of advanced technologies, particularly Artificial Intelligence (AI), in Small and Medium-sized Enterprises (SMEs) across Latin America. It addresses a gap in scholarship regarding technological advancement in regional SMEs. Our study, based on data from 306 SME executives in six countries, reveals a growing trend towards technology adoption, especially in customer-oriented sectors, driven by desires for improved operational efficiency and productivity. Major barriers include high initial costs and lack of skilled personnel. The findings highlight the need for tailored digital advancement strategies in Latin America, considering the unique motivations, challenges, and operational contexts of SMEs. This study offers insights for policymakers, tech industry leaders, and SME decision-makers navigating technological transformation in the AI era, emphasizing the importance of strategic alignment, comprehensive implementation across business areas, and addressing workforce skill gaps for successful digital evolution.*

DOI: 10.4018/979-8-3693-9894-4.ch010

## INTRODUCTION

The digital transformation sweeping across the global business landscape has emerged as a defining challenge for enterprises of all sizes, with particularly profound implications for Small and Medium-sized Enterprises (SMEs) in Latin America. As we navigate the complexities of an increasingly interconnected and technologically driven world, the ability of these businesses to adapt and innovate has become a critical determinant of their success and longevity. This phenomenon is especially significant in Latin America, a region characterized by its vibrant economic potential and growing integration into the global market.

In the rapidly evolving landscape of global business, the adoption of new technologies has become a critical factor in determining the success and longevity of enterprises. This phenomenon is particularly significant for SMEs in Latin America, a region characterized by its dynamic economic growth and increasing integration into the global market (Liñán et al., 2020). As we stand on the beginning of a new era dominated by artificial intelligence (AI) and other advanced technologies, the challenges and opportunities facing Latin American SMEs are more pronounced than ever.

The technological revolution, often referred to as the Fourth Industrial Revolution or Industry 4.0, has started a new paradigm of business operations. This paradigm shift is marked by the convergence of digital, physical, and biological technologies, fundamentally altering the way companies operate, compete, and deliver value to their customers. For Latin American SMEs, which form the backbone of the region's economy, embracing these technological advancements is not just an option but a necessity for sustained growth and competitiveness in the global marketplace (Ferraro & Rojo, 2018).

However, the path to technological adoption has challenges for these businesses. Limited resources, both financial and human, often constrain the ability of SMEs to invest in and implement new technologies (Molina-Ycaza & Sánchez-Riofrío, 2016). Moreover, the rapid pace of technological change can be overwhelming, making it difficult for smaller enterprises to keep up with the latest innovations and integrate them effectively into their operations. The skills gap in the workforce, coupled with resistance to change among employees and management, further complicates the adoption process (Akpan et al., 2022).

Despite these challenges, the potential benefits of technological adoption for Latin American SMEs are immense. Enhanced productivity, improved operational efficiency, and increased competitiveness are just a few of the advantages that come with successful implementation of new technologies (Ramírez-Solis et al., 2022). In an age where data is often referred to as the new oil, the ability to collect, analyze, and leverage information can provide SMEs with unprecedented insights into their business operations, customer behavior, and market trends. This, in turn, can lead to more informed decision-making and strategic planning (Hansen & Bøgh, 2021).

The rise of AI and machine learning technologies presents both opportunities and challenges for SMEs in the region. On one hand, these technologies offer the potential for automation of routine tasks, freeing up human resources for more value-added activities. They can also provide sophisticated analytics capabilities that were previously available only to large corporations with significant IT budgets. On the other hand, the implementation of AI systems requires specialized skills and knowledge that may be in short supply in many Latin American countries (Mishrif & Khan, 2023).

Customer expectations are also evolving rapidly in the digital age. With the proliferation of smartphones and high-speed internet access, consumers in Latin America are increasingly demanding seamless, personalized experiences across all touchpoints. For SMEs, this means that adopting customer-facing technologies such as e-commerce platforms, mobile apps, and chatbots is becoming essential for customer retention and growth (Schnarch, 2013).

Security and privacy concerns add another layer of complexity to the technological adoption process. As SMEs increasingly rely on digital systems and collect more customer data, they become potential targets for cyberattacks. Ensuring robust cybersecurity measures and compliance with data protection regulations is very important, yet it can be a significant challenge for smaller businesses with limited IT resources (López Jiménez et al., 2021).

In this context, identifying the key factors that enable successful adoption of new technologies becomes paramount for Latin American SMEs. This involves understanding the types of technologies available and their potential applications and developing strategies to overcome the barriers to adoption. It requires a holistic approach that addresses issues of organizational culture, skills development, financial planning, and risk management.

This article aims to explore these key factors, examining the challenges faced by Latin American SMEs in adopting new technologies and proposing strategies for overcoming them. By analyzing the interplay between innovation, productivity, internal processes, customer relationships, and human capital, we seek to provide a comprehensive framework for understanding and navigating the complexities of technological adoption in the AI age.

## CONCEPTUAL FRAMEWORK

The adoption of new technologies by SMEs in Latin America represents a multifaceted process influenced by internal and external factors. This conceptual framework serves as a foundation for comprehending the key elements shaping technology adoption in this context, with the transformative potential of AI. As SMEs navigate the complexities of an increasingly digital marketplace, their ability to integrate cutting-edge technologies, including AI-driven solutions, into their operations becomes crucial for maintaining competitiveness and driving growth.

At its core, technology adoption in SMEs is propelled by the imperative to remain competitive in a rapidly evolving digital landscape. This process extends beyond the mere acquisition of new tools and systems; it encompasses the holistic integration of these technologies into existing business processes and the cultivation of novel capabilities within the organization. AI, in particular, stands out as a transformative force, offering SMEs unprecedented opportunities to enhance decision-making, automate routine tasks, and unlock new avenues for innovation across various business functions (Arranz et al., 2023).

The framework for technology adoption in Latin American SMEs comprises several interconnected components, each playing a relevant role in the overall digital transformation journey. It begins by examining the diverse array of technologies available and their potential applications across different business contexts. This includes emerging technologies such as AI, IoT, cloud computing, and blockchain, as well as more established digital tools like CRM systems and ERP software.

Innovation capacity emerges as an axis in this study, referring to an SME's ability to adopt new technologies and to adapt and innovate based on these adoptions. This capacity is inextricably linked to the concepts of flexibility and adaptability, which are essential for SMEs operating in the dynamic Latin American market. AI plays a significant role in enhancing innovation capacity by enabling SMEs to analyze vast amounts of data, identify patterns, and generate insights that can drive product development, process improvements, and business model innovations (Schwaeke et al., 2024).

The dimensions of productivity, costs, competitiveness, and efficiency form other important factors. The adoption of new technologies, especially AI-powered solutions, is often motivated by the potential for improved operational efficiency and reduced costs, which in turn can strengthen an SME's competitiveness in both local and global markets. AI technologies, such as machine learning algorithms and robotic process automation, offer SMEs the opportunity to streamline operations, optimize resource allocation, and enhance overall productivity. Research has shown that the adoption of AI can have a significant positive impact on labor productivity, offering substantial benefits for SMEs (Damioli et al., 2021).

Internal information management and decision-making processes constitute a key consideration. New technologies, particularly AI-driven analytics tools, can significantly augment an SME's ability to collect, analyze, and utilize data for strategic decision-making. This aspect deepens into how technology adoption, especially the integration of AI systems, can lead to more informed, timely, and data-driven business decisions, enabling SMEs to respond more effectively to market changes and customer needs (Karuppiah et al., 2023).

Another important factor is the human element, which encompasses aspects such as collaboration between employees. This can be facilitated and enhanced through the adoption of new communication and project management technologies. It also considers the challenges of resistance to change and the skills gap that often accompanies the introduction of new technologies. Customer retention is another important component, reflecting the potential of new technologies to enhance customer experiences, personalize services, and build stronger, long-term relationships with clients (Van & Gómez, 2015).

Besides, the considerations of security and privacy, which have become increasingly important in the digital age, are very relevant to be mentioned. As SMEs adopt new technologies, they must also implement robust measures to protect sensitive data and comply with evolving regulatory requirements (López Jiménez et al., 2022).

## Types of New Technologies

The technological landscape for SMEs in Latin America is evolving, offering a diverse array of tools and systems that can significantly enhance business operations and competitiveness. The Internet of Things (IoT) applications, spanning from research and innovation to market deployment, offer a wide range of opportunities for SMEs to enhance their operations and create new value propositions (Vermesan & Friess, 2014). At the forefront of this technological revolution is AI, which serves as a cornerstone for many emerging technologies and applications. AI's ability to process vast amounts of data, recognize patterns, and make predictions is revolutionizing how SMEs approach various aspects of their business, from customer service to supply chain management (Pigola et al., 2021).

Cloud computing stands out as a fundamental technology enabling digital transformation for Latin American SMEs. By providing scalable and flexible IT infrastructure without the need for significant upfront investments, cloud services allow SMEs to access advanced computing resources, including AI-powered analytics and machine learning platforms. This democratization of technology levels the playing field, enabling smaller businesses to leverage capabilities previously available only to large corporations. Cloud-based solutions also facilitate remote work and collaboration, which have become increasingly important in the post-pandemic business environment (CEPAL, 2021).

The IoT represents another transformative technology for SMEs in the region. By connecting physical devices to the internet, IoT enables real-time data collection and monitoring across various business processes. In manufacturing and logistics, IoT sensors can track inventory levels, monitor equipment performance, and optimize supply chain operations. The Industrial Internet of Things (IIoT) presents both opportunities and challenges for manufacturing businesses in emerging economies, offering potential for significant improvements in operational efficiency (Peter et al., 2023). When combined with AI algorithms, IoT data can provide predictive insights, allowing SMEs to anticipate maintenance needs, prevent downtime, and improve overall operational efficiency (Hansen & Bøgh, 2021). Furthermore, the integration of IoT with AI and vehicle telematics offers new opportunities for sustainable growth in SMEs (Agbonyin et al., 2024).

Blockchain technology, while still in its early stages of adoption among Latin American SMEs, offers promising applications in areas such as supply chain transparency, secure transactions, and digital identity verification. For SMEs involved in international trade, blockchain can streamline cross-border transactions, reduce fraud, and enhance traceability of goods. As the technology matures and becomes more accessible, it has the potential to address longstanding challenges related to trust and transparency in business relationships (Bican & Brem, 2020).

Mobile technologies continue to play a relevant role in the digital transformation of Latin American SMEs. With high smartphone penetration rates across the region, mobile apps and responsive web platforms enable SMEs to reach customers, manage operations, and facilitate transactions on-the-go. AI-powered chatbots and virtual assistants, integrated into mobile platforms, allow SMEs to provide 24/7 customer support and personalized services at scale, enhancing customer engagement and satisfaction (Schnarch, 2013).

Data analytics and business intelligence tools, often powered by AI algorithms, are becoming increasingly important for SMEs seeking to make data-driven decisions. These technologies enable businesses to gain insights from their operational data, customer interactions, and market trends. Advanced analytics can help SMEs optimize pricing strategies, identify new market opportunities, and personalize marketing efforts. As these tools become more user-friendly and accessible through cloud-based platforms, even SMEs with limited technical expertise can harness the power of data analytics to drive growth and innovation (Ramírez-Solis et al., 2022).

Robotic Process Automation (RPA) is emerging as a valuable technology for SMEs looking to streamline repetitive tasks and improve operational efficiency. By automating routine processes in areas such as accounting, human resources, and customer service, RPA frees up employees to focus on higher-value activities. When combined with AI capabilities, such as Natural Language Processing (NLP) and machine learning, RPA can handle increasingly complex tasks, adapting to changing business rules and improving its performance over time (Atieh et al., 2023).

Augmented Reality (AR) and Virtual Reality (VR) technologies are opening new possibilities for SMEs in sectors such as retail, education, and tourism. These immersive technologies can enhance customer experiences, facilitate remote training and collaboration, and create innovative marketing opportunities. For example, AR apps can allow customers to visualize products in their own space before making a purchase, while VR can offer virtual tours or interactive learning experiences (Bhuiyan et al., 2024).

Cybersecurity technologies, while not always considered "new," are continuously evolving to address the growing threats in the digital landscape. For Latin American SMEs embarking on digital transformation journeys, robust cybersecurity solutions are essential to protect sensitive data, maintain customer trust, and ensure business continuity. AI-powered security tools can provide real-time threat detection and automated responses to cyber attacks, offering SMEs a level of protection previously available only to larger enterprises with dedicated IT security teams.

As these technologies continue to evolve and converge, they create new opportunities for innovation and growth among Latin American SMEs. The key challenge for these businesses lies in identifying the most relevant technologies for their specific needs and effectively integrating them into their operations. By leveraging these new technologies, particularly AI-driven solutions, SMEs can enhance their competitiveness, improve operational efficiency, and drive sustainable growth in the digital age.

## Innovation, Flexibility and Adaptability

Today, innovation, flexibility, and adaptability have become critical success factors for SMEs in Latin America. These interconnected attributes enable businesses to leverage new technologies effectively, respond to market changes swiftly, and maintain competitiveness in an increasingly digital economy. The integration of AI into business processes has further amplified the importance of these qualities, as it offers unprecedented opportunities for innovation while demanding greater flexibility and adaptability from organizations.

Innovation in the context of Latin American SMEs extends beyond the mere adoption of new technologies. It encompasses the ability to creatively apply these technologies to solve existing problems, improve processes, and create new value propositions. AI serves as a powerful catalyst for innovation, enabling SMEs to develop novel products, services, and business models. Moreover, AI acts as an enabler for other technologies, amplifying their potential and creating synergies that can drive innovation in SMEs (Kulkov et al., 2024). For instance, AI-powered predictive analytics can help SMEs anticipate market trends and customer needs, facilitating proactive innovation rather than reactive adaptation.

Flexibility in the digital age refers to an SME's capacity to quickly adjust its operations, strategies, and resource allocation in response to technological advancements and market shifts. This attribute is particularly important when implementing AI solutions, as they often require businesses to reimagine their processes and organizational structures. Flexible SMEs can more easily experiment with different AI applications, pivot their strategies based on data-driven insights, and scale their technological investments as needed (Arranz et al., 2023).

Adaptability, closely linked to flexibility, involves the broader organizational capability to embrace change and thrive in uncertain environments. For Latin American SMEs, adaptability is essential in navigating the challenges and opportunities presented by rapid technological progress, especially in AI. Adaptable organizations foster a culture of continuous learning, encouraging employees to acquire new skills and embrace AI-augmented work processes. This cultural shift is vital for successful digital transformation and long-term sustainability in an AI-driven economy (Akpan et al., 2022).

The synergy between innovation, flexibility, and adaptability creates a powerful framework for SMEs to harness the potential of new technologies. Innovative SMEs that remain flexible in their approach and adaptable to change are better positioned to exploit the benefits of AI and other emerging technologies. For example, an adaptable SME might more readily adopt AI-powered chatbots for customer service, flexibly integrating this technology into their existing systems while innovatively using the gathered data to improve product offerings (Karuppiah et al., 2023).

However, cultivating these attributes presents significant challenges for many Latin American SMEs. Resource constraints, risk aversion, and deeply ingrained traditional business practices can hinder innovation efforts and resist change. Overcoming these barriers requires a strategic approach that balances short-term stability with long-term vision. SMEs can start by fostering a culture of experimentation and learning, where failures are viewed as opportunities for growth rather than setbacks.

To enhance flexibility and adaptability, SMEs can adopt agile methodologies and lean startup principles, which emphasize iterative development, rapid prototyping, and customer feedback. These approaches are particularly well-suited to AI projects, which often require continuous refinement and adaptation. By breaking down large initiatives into smaller, manageable tasks, SMEs can reduce the risk associated with innovation while maintaining the flexibility to adjust course as needed (Mancini & González, 2021).

Collaboration and partnerships play a relevant role in fostering innovation, flexibility, and adaptability among Latin American SMEs. By forming alliances with technology providers, academic institutions, and other businesses, SMEs can access expertise, share risks, and accelerate their innovation processes. Collaborative ecosystems, such as innovation hubs and incubators, provide valuable platforms for SMEs to experiment with AI and other emerging technologies in a supportive environment.

Government policies and support programs can significantly impact the innovation capacity and adaptability of SMEs in the region. Initiatives that promote digital literacy, provide access to AI tools and training, and offer financial incentives for technology adoption can help create an enabling environment for SMEs to innovate and adapt. Policymakers should also consider regulatory frameworks that encourage responsible AI adoption while protecting SMEs from potential risks associated with rapid technological change (Heredia Zurita & Dini, 2021).

As AI and other emerging technologies continue to reshape the business landscape, the ability of Latin American SMEs to innovate, remain flexible, and adapt will be important determinants of their success. By embracing these qualities and leveraging the transformative power of AI, SMEs can not only survive but thrive in the digital age, contributing to economic growth and technological advancement across the region.

## Productivity, Costs, Competitiveness and Efficiency

The adoption of new technologies, particularly AI-driven solutions, offers Latin American SMEs unprecedented opportunities to enhance their productivity, optimize costs, boost competitiveness, and improve overall efficiency. These interconnected factors form the backbone of sustainable growth and success in an increasingly digital marketplace (Ramírez-Solis et al., 2022).

Productivity gains through technology adoption can be substantial for SMEs in the region. AI-powered automation tools can streamline repetitive tasks, freeing up human resources for more strategic, value-adding activities. For instance, machine learning algorithms can analyze production data to identify bottlenecks and suggest process improvements, leading to increased output with the same or fewer inputs. NLP technologies can automate customer service inquiries, allowing staff to focus on complex issues that require human judgment and empathy (Hansen & Bøgh, 2021).

Cost optimization is another significant benefit of implementing new technologies. While initial investments in AI and other advanced systems may seem daunting for SMEs with limited resources, the long-term cost savings can be substantial. Cloud-based AI services, for example, allow businesses to access sophisticated analytics capabilities without the need for expensive in-house infrastructure. Predictive maintenance systems can reduce downtime and extend the lifespan of equipment, cutting repair and replacement costs. Moreover, AI-driven energy management systems can significantly lower utility expenses by optimizing resource usage (Atieh et al., 2023).

Competitiveness in the global market is increasingly tied to an SME's ability to leverage technology effectively. AI-enabled data analytics can provide Latin American SMEs with valuable insights into market trends, customer preferences, and competitor strategies. This information allows businesses to make data-driven decisions, tailor their offerings to specific market needs, and identify new growth opportunities. Additionally, AI-powered personalization tools can enhance customer experiences, fostering loyalty and differentiating SMEs from their competitors (Bianchi et al., 2017).

Efficiency improvements are often the most immediate and tangible benefits of technology adoption for SMEs. AI algorithms can optimize supply chain management, reducing inventory costs and improving delivery times. RPA can handle routine administrative tasks with greater speed and accuracy than human workers, minimizing errors and accelerating business processes. In manufacturing, AI-driven quality control systems can detect defects more quickly and accurately than traditional methods, reducing waste and improving product quality (Arranz et al., 2023).

The integration of these technologies requires a strategic approach that considers the unique challenges and opportunities facing Latin American SMEs. Limited access to capital, skills shortages, and infrastructure gaps can impede the adoption of advanced technologies. However, innovative financing models, such as pay-as-you-go AI services and government-backed technology funds, can help overcome financial barriers. Collaborations with universities and technology providers can address skills gaps through targeted training programs and knowledge transfer initiatives (Banco Interamericano de Desarrollo, 2022).

It's important to note that the benefits of technology adoption are influenced by various factors, including the size of the SME, its sector, and its current level of digital maturity. For some businesses, simple digital tools like cloud-based accounting software or e-commerce platforms may yield significant productivity and efficiency gains. For others, more advanced AI applications might be necessary to achieve a competitive edge. A careful assessment of an SME's specific needs and capabilities is essential to determine the most appropriate technological investments.

The role of leadership in driving technology-led improvements cannot be overstated. SME owners and managers must foster a culture of continuous improvement and innovation, encouraging employees to embrace new technologies and ways of working. This may involve restructuring teams, redefining roles, and investing in ongoing training and development to ensure that staff can effectively leverage new tools and systems.

As Latin American SMEs navigate the path towards greater productivity, cost-effectiveness, competitiveness, and efficiency through technology adoption, they must remain agile and responsive to changing market conditions. The rapid pace of technological advancement means that today's cutting-edge solution may become obsolete tomorrow. Therefore, SMEs should aim to build a flexible technological foundation that can adapt to new innovations and evolving business needs (Melo et al., 2023).

By strategically leveraging AI and other emerging technologies to enhance these key business metrics, Latin American SMEs can position themselves for long-term success in the global marketplace. The resulting improvements in productivity, cost structure, competitiveness, and efficiency can drive sustainable growth, create new employment opportunities, and contribute to the overall economic development of the region.

## Internal Information Management and Decision Making

Effective internal information management and decision-making processes form the foundation of successful SMEs in Latin America. The integration of AI and advanced analytics tools has revolutionized how businesses collect, process, and utilize data to drive strategic decisions. This technological shift presents both opportunities and challenges for SMEs seeking to enhance their operational efficiency and competitive edge (Karuppiah et al., 2023).

AI-powered data analytics platforms enable SMEs to transform raw data into actionable insights. These systems can process vast amounts of information from various sources, including sales records, customer interactions, and market trends. By identifying patterns and correlations that might be invisible to human analysts, AI algorithms provide SMEs with a deeper understanding of their business operations and market dynamics (Hansen & Bøgh, 2021).

The implementation of Enterprise Resource Planning (ERP) systems, enhanced by AI capabilities, allows Latin American SMEs to centralize their data management. These integrated platforms streamline information flow across different departments, from finance and human resources to inventory management and customer relations. AI-driven ERP systems can automate data entry, reduce errors, and provide real-time updates, ensuring that decision-makers have access to accurate and up-to-date information at all times (Rojas-Berrio et al., 2022).

Predictive analytics, a key application of AI in business intelligence, empowers SMEs to anticipate future trends and challenges. By analyzing historical data and external factors, these tools can forecast demand, identify potential supply chain disruptions, and predict customer behavior. This foresight enables SMEs to make proactive decisions, allocating resources more effectively and mitigating risks before they materialize (Pigola et al., 2021).

NLP technologies are transforming how SMEs handle unstructured data. These AI-powered tools can analyze customer feedback, social media comments, and other text-based information to extract valuable insights. For Latin American SMEs, this capability is particularly valuable in understanding customers, identifying emerging market trends, and tailoring products or services to meet local preferences (Bhuiyan et al., 2024).

The adoption of AI in decision-making processes introduces the concept of augmented intelligence, where AI systems work in tandem with human expertise. This approach combines the analytical power of AI with human judgment and contextual understanding. For SMEs, this means leveraging AI recommendations while still relying on the experience and intuition of their leadership team to make final decisions (Schwaeke et al., 2024).

Cloud-based business intelligence platforms have democratized access to advanced analytics tools for Latin American SMEs. These services offer scalable, cost-effective solutions that allow smaller businesses to benefit from sophisticated data analysis without significant upfront investments in IT infrastructure. As a result, even SMEs with limited resources can now make data-driven decisions on par with larger competitors.

The implementation of AI-driven information management systems requires a shift in organizational culture. SMEs must foster a data-centric mindset, encouraging employees at all levels to base their decisions on empirical evidence rather than gut feelings. This cultural transformation often necessitates training programs to enhance data literacy and analytical skills across the organization.

Data security and privacy concerns are paramount as SMEs increasingly rely on digital information management systems. The sensitive nature of business data, combined with stringent data protection regulations, requires SMEs to implement robust cybersecurity measures. AI-powered security solutions can help by detecting anomalies, preventing unauthorized access, and ensuring compliance with data protection laws.

The ethical implications of AI in decision-making processes present a new frontier for Latin American SMEs. As AI systems become more involved in critical business decisions, issues of transparency, bias, and accountability come to the forefront. SMEs must establish clear guidelines for the use of AI in decision-making, ensuring that these systems align with the company's values and ethical standards (Dittmar, 2020).

Collaborative decision-making platforms, enhanced by AI, are emerging as valuable tools for SMEs with geographically dispersed teams. These systems facilitate real-time information sharing, virtual brainstorming sessions, and collective problem-solving. For Latin American SMEs expanding their regional or global presence, such tools can significantly improve coordination and decision-making across different locations and time zones.

As Latin American SMEs continue to embrace AI and advanced analytics in their internal information management and decision-making processes, they position themselves for greater agility and competitiveness. A country-level comparative study on AI technology development highlights the importance of strategic patent analysis in guiding innovation efforts for SMEs (Tseng & Ting, 2013). By leveraging these technologies effectively, SMEs can make more informed decisions, respond quickly to market changes, and drive innovation in their respective industries. The key lies in balancing technological capabilities with human insight, ensuring that AI serves as a powerful tool to augment, rather than replace, the decision-making skills of SME leaders.

## Collaboration Between Employees

The advent of digital technologies and AI has significantly transformed the landscape of employee collaboration in Latin American SMEs. These advancements have introduced new ways for team members to communicate, share information, and work together, regardless of physical location or time zones. The impact of these technologies extends beyond mere convenience, fundamentally altering work processes and organizational structures.

Cloud-based collaboration platforms have become indispensable tools for SMEs in the region. These platforms integrate various functionalities such as document sharing, real-time editing, project management, and instant messaging into a single ecosystem. By providing a centralized space for teamwork, these tools enhance transparency, reduce information silos, and streamline workflows. AI-powered features within these platforms, such as smart notifications and automated task assignments, further optimize team coordination and productivity (Bhuiyan et al., 2024).

VR and AR technologies are emerging as innovative solutions for remote collaboration in Latin American SMEs. These immersive technologies enable employees to participate in virtual meetings, training sessions, and collaborative design processes as if they were physically present. For SMEs with distributed teams across different countries or regions, VR and AR can foster a sense of presence and connection that traditional video conferencing may lack (Atieh et al., 2023).

AI-driven project management tools are revolutionizing how teams plan, execute, and monitor collaborative work. These systems can analyze historical project data, team performance metrics, and resource allocation patterns to provide intelligent recommendations for task distribution and deadline setting. By automating routine project management tasks, AI allows team leaders to focus on strategic decision-making and team development (Arranz et al., 2023).

NLP technologies are breaking down language barriers in multicultural teams, a common scenario in Latin American SMEs operating across borders. AI-powered translation tools enable real-time communication between employees speaking different languages, facilitating seamless collaboration in diverse work environments. This capability is particularly valuable for SMEs expanding their operations into new markets or engaging with international partners (Pigola et al., 2021).

The integration of AI in knowledge management systems has enhanced information sharing and collective learning within SMEs. These intelligent systems can categorize and tag information automatically, making it easier for employees to find relevant resources. AI algorithms can also analyze usage patterns to recommend pertinent information to team members based on their roles and current projects, fostering a culture of continuous learning and knowledge exchange (Schwaeke et al., 2024).

Gamification techniques, powered by AI, are being employed to boost engagement and motivation in collaborative activities. By introducing game-like elements such as points, leaderboards, and virtual rewards into work processes, SMEs can encourage healthy competition and teamwork. AI algorithms can personalize these gamified experiences, adapting challenges and rewards to individual employee preferences and performance levels (Karuppiah et al., 2023).

The rise of AI-assisted decision-making tools has introduced new dynamics in team collaboration. These systems can provide data-driven insights and recommendations, serving as an additional "team member" in collaborative problem-solving sessions. However, the integration of AI in decision-making processes also necessitates new skills among employees, such as the ability to interpret AI-generated insights and balance them with human judgment and creativity (Rojas-Berrio et al., 2022).

Remote work technologies, accelerated by recent global events, have become a cornerstone of employee collaboration in Latin American SMEs. AI-powered tools for time tracking, productivity monitoring, and virtual team building are helping businesses maintain cohesion and efficiency in distributed work environments. These technologies enable SMEs to tap into talent pools beyond their immediate geographical area, potentially leading to more diverse and skilled teams. Web platforms designed to develop collective intelligence in specific sectors, such as logistics, are emerging as valuable tools for Latin American SMEs to enhance collaboration and competitiveness (Cedillo-Campos, 2020).

The implementation of collaborative AI systems in SMEs raises important considerations about data privacy and security. As employees share more information through digital platforms, businesses must ensure robust measures to protect sensitive data. This includes implementing AI-driven security protocols, educating employees about cybersecurity best practices, and establishing clear policies for data handling in collaborative environments.

The shift towards AI-enhanced collaboration tools also necessitates ongoing training and development programs for employees. SMEs must invest in upskilling initiatives to ensure their workforce can effectively leverage these new technologies. This might include training on digital literacy, data interpretation, and AI-human collaboration strategies.

As Latin American SMEs continue to adopt these advanced collaboration technologies, they stand to gain significant advantages in terms of efficiency, innovation, and employee satisfaction. However, the successful implementation of these tools requires a balanced approach that combines technological capabilities with human-centered strategies. By fostering a culture that values both technological proficiency and interpersonal skills, SMEs can create collaborative environments that drive growth and competitiveness in the digital age.

## Customer Retention

For Latin American SMEs, maintaining a loyal customer base is essential for sustainable growth and long-term success. The integration of AI and advanced technologies has revolutionized customer retention strategies, providing businesses with powerful tools to understand, engage, and satisfy their clientele.

AI-driven Customer Relationship Management (CRM) systems serve as the cornerstone of modern retention efforts. These platforms collect and analyze vast amounts of customer data, including purchase history, preferences, and interactions across various touchpoints. By leveraging machine learning algorithms, CRM systems can identify patterns and trends, enabling SMEs to personalize their offerings and communications at scale (Hansen & Bøgh, 2021).

Predictive analytics play a pivotal role in proactive customer retention. By analyzing historical data and current behavior, AI models can forecast customer churn risk. This foresight allows SMEs to implement targeted retention strategies before customers consider switching to competitors. For instance, the system might trigger personalized offers or outreach to high-risk customers, potentially averting their departure (Pigola et al., 2021).

Chatbots and virtual assistants, powered by NLP, have transformed customer service for Latin American SMEs. These AI-driven tools provide instant, 24/7 support, addressing common queries and issues promptly. Understanding the factors that drive SMEs to adopt AI-based chatbots is crucial for successful implementation and maximizing their benefits in customer service (Sharma et al., 2022). By handling routine inquiries, chatbots free up human agents to focus on more complex customer needs, enhancing overall service quality. The ability to communicate in multiple languages makes these tools particularly valuable in the diverse Latin American market.

Personalization engines, fueled by AI, enable SMEs to create tailored experiences for each customer. These systems analyze individual preferences, browsing history, and purchase patterns to recommend products, content, or services most likely to resonate with each user. This level of personalization can significantly enhance customer satisfaction and loyalty, as clients feel understood and valued by the business (Ramírez-Solis et al., 2022).

Social media listening tools, enhanced by sentiment analysis algorithms, allow SMEs to monitor and respond to customer feedback in real-time. By analyzing comments, mentions, and reviews across various platforms, these tools provide valuable insights into customer sentiment and potential issues. This enables businesses to address concerns promptly, demonstrate responsiveness, and maintain a positive brand image (Bhuiyan et al., 2024).

Loyalty programs, reimagined through AI, offer more engaging and personalized rewards to customers. AI algorithms can analyze individual customer behavior to suggest relevant rewards, optimize point systems, and create targeted promotions. This data-driven approach ensures that loyalty initiatives remain compelling and effective, encouraging repeat business and long-term customer relationships (Van & Gómez, 2015).

Voice of Customer (VoC) programs, powered by text analytics and machine learning, help SMEs gather and interpret customer feedback at scale. These systems can analyze open-ended survey responses, customer emails, and support tickets to identify common themes, pain points, and areas for improvement. This deep understanding of customer needs and preferences enables SMEs to make informed decisions about product development, service enhancements, and overall business strategy (Karuppiah et al., 2023).

Predictive lead scoring, an AI application in sales and marketing, helps SMEs identify and prioritize high-value customers. By analyzing various data points, including demographic information, engagement metrics, and purchase history, these systems can predict which customers are most likely to make repeat purchases or upgrade their services. This allows businesses to allocate their retention efforts more efficiently, focusing on the most promising opportunities.

Customer journey mapping, enhanced by AI analytics, provides SMEs with a holistic view of the customer experience across all touchpoints. These tools can identify critical moments in the customer journey where intervention or support might be necessary to prevent churn. By understanding the entire customer lifecycle, businesses can design more effective retention strategies that address pain points and enhance satisfaction at every stage (Rojas-Berrio et al., 2022).

Privacy concerns and data protection regulations present important considerations in AI-driven customer retention efforts. Latin American SMEs must balance the benefits of data-driven personalization with respect for customer privacy. Implementing transparent data policies, obtaining proper consent, and ensuring secure data handling practices are essential for maintaining customer trust in the digital age.

As Latin American SMEs continue to adopt these AI-powered retention strategies, they position themselves to build stronger, more enduring relationships with their customers. The key lies in leveraging technology to enhance, rather than replace, the human touch in customer interactions. By combining AI-driven insights with empathy and personal attention, SMEs can create a customer experience that fosters loyalty and drives long-term business success in the competitive Latin American market.

## Security and Privacy

The digital transformation of Latin American SMEs, accelerated by the adoption of AI and emerging technologies, has brought security and privacy concerns to the forefront of business operations. As these enterprises increasingly rely on digital platforms and data-driven decision-making, they face a complex landscape of cyber threats, regulatory requirements, and customer expectations regarding data protection. The integration of robust security measures and privacy protocols has become not just a technical necessity but a fundamental business imperative for SMEs seeking to build trust and maintain competitiveness in the digital marketplace.

AI-powered cybersecurity solutions offer SMEs advanced capabilities to detect and respond to threats in real-time. Machine learning algorithms can analyze network traffic patterns, identify anomalies, and flag potential security breaches faster and more accurately than traditional rule-based systems. These AI-driven tools continuously learn from new data, adapting to evolving threat landscapes and providing SMEs with a dynamic defense against cyber attacks. For resource-constrained SMEs, such systems offer enterprise-grade security capabilities without the need for large, specialized IT teams (Hansen & Bøgh, 2021).

Blockchain technology is emerging as a powerful tool for enhancing data integrity and transparency in SME operations. By creating immutable, decentralized records of transactions and data exchanges, blockchain can significantly reduce the risk of data tampering and unauthorized access. This technology is particularly valuable for SMEs involved in supply chain management, financial transactions, or handling sensitive customer information. Blockchain's inherent security features can help SMEs comply with data protection regulations and build trust with partners and customers (Bican & Brem, 2020). Moreover, the combination of AI and blockchain technology can enhance transparency in governance, which is particularly valuable for SMEs navigating complex regulatory environments (AlShamsi et al., 2020).

The implementation of AI in privacy management systems enables SMEs to automate and streamline compliance with data protection regulations. These intelligent systems can categorize data based on sensitivity, track data flows across the organization, and enforce access controls automatically. AI algorithms can also assist in conducting privacy impact assessments, identifying potential risks in data processing activities, and suggesting mitigation measures. This capability is particularly valuable for SMEs navigating complex regulatory environments such as the General Data Protection Regulation (GDPR) or local data protection laws in Latin American countries (López Jiménez et al., 2023).

Cloud security posture management (CSPM) tools, enhanced by AI, provide SMEs with comprehensive visibility and control over their cloud environments. As more businesses migrate their operations to the cloud, ensuring the security of these distributed systems becomes increasingly challenging. AI-driven CSPM solutions can continuously monitor cloud configurations, detect misconfigurations or compliance violations, and even automate remediation actions. This proactive approach to cloud security helps SMEs maintain a robust security posture while leveraging the scalability and cost-effectiveness of cloud services (Atieh et al., 2023).

The rise of remote work and bring-your-own-device (BYOD) policies has expanded the attack surface for many SMEs, necessitating new approaches to endpoint security. AI-powered endpoint detection and response (EDR) systems offer advanced protection for diverse device ecosystems. These tools use behavioral analysis to identify suspicious activities on individual devices, providing real-time threat detection and response capabilities. For Latin American SMEs with distributed workforces, EDR solutions offer a scalable way to maintain security across various locations and device types.

Data encryption, bolstered by quantum-resistant algorithms, is becoming increasingly important for SMEs handling sensitive information. As quantum computing advances threaten to break traditional encryption methods, forward-thinking SMEs are exploring post-quantum cryptography to future-proof their data protection strategies. While still emerging, these advanced encryption techniques offer a path for SMEs to safeguard their data against both current and future threats, ensuring long-term data confidentiality and integrity (Bhuiyan et al., 2024).

The human factor remains a critical component of security and privacy in the digital age. AI-driven security awareness training platforms can help SMEs educate their employees about cybersecurity best practices and privacy regulations. These systems can personalize training content based on individual roles and risk profiles, simulate phishing attacks to test employee vigilance, and provide real-time feedback on security behaviors. By fostering a culture of security awareness, SMEs can significantly reduce the risk of human error-induced breaches and privacy violations.

As Latin American SMEs increasingly engage in cross-border data transfers and international business operations, navigating the complex landscape of global data protection regulations becomes relevant. AI-powered compliance management systems can help SMEs track and adhere to various international standards and regulations. These tools can automatically update policies and procedures in response to regulatory changes, conduct compliance audits, and generate necessary documentation for regulatory reporting. This capability is particularly valuable for SMEs looking to expand their operations beyond local markets while maintaining compliance with diverse regulatory requirements (Gonzalez-Tamayo et al., 2023).

The ethical implications of AI in security and privacy present new challenges for SMEs. As AI systems become more involved in data handling and decision-making processes, issues of algorithmic bias, transparency, and accountability come to the fore. SMEs must develop clear guidelines for the ethical use of AI in security and privacy applications, ensuring that these systems align with company values and respect individual rights. This may involve regular audits of AI systems, establishing oversight mechanisms, and maintaining human involvement in critical security and privacy decisions.

For Latin American SMEs, balancing the benefits of data-driven innovation with robust security and privacy practices is key to building trust and maintaining competitiveness in the digital economy. By leveraging AI and emerging technologies in their security and privacy strategies, these businesses can create resilient, compliant, and trustworthy digital environments. This approach protects against threats and regulatory risks and also positions SMEs as responsible stewards of data, enhancing their reputation and fostering long-term relationships with customers and partners in an increasingly interconnected business landscape.

## Resistance to Change

The integration of AI and emerging technologies in Latin American SMEs often encounters a significant hurdle: resistance to change. This phenomenon, deeply rooted in organizational culture and individual psychology, can substantially impede the digital transformation process. As SMEs in the region strive to adopt new technologies and innovative practices, understanding and addressing resistance to change becomes paramount. The complex interplay of factors contributing to this resistance, ranging from fear of job displacement to cultural norms and established business practices, necessitates a multifaceted approach to overcome these barriers and foster a culture of innovation and adaptability (Akpan et al., 2022).

Fear of job displacement stands as a primary driver of resistance to AI adoption in many SMEs. Employees across various levels of the organization may perceive AI and automation as threats to their job security, leading to reluctance or outright opposition to new technologies. This fear is often exacerbated by misconceptions about the capabilities and limitations of AI systems. To address this, SMEs must engage in transparent communication about the role of AI in augmenting human capabilities rather than replacing them. Implementing reskilling and upskilling programs can demonstrate a commitment to employee growth and adaptation in the face of technological change.

Cultural factors play a significant role in shaping attitudes towards technological change in Latin American SMEs. In some organizational cultures, there may be a strong emphasis on tradition and established ways of doing business, making it challenging to introduce new technologies and processes. The hierarchical structure common in many Latin American businesses can also slow down the adoption of new technologies if top management is resistant to change. Overcoming these cultural barriers requires a shift in organizational mindset, fostering a culture that values innovation, continuous learning, and adaptability. This may involve leadership development programs that emphasize change management and innovation-driven strategies (Dini & Stumpo, 2018; Sposato, 2025).

The financial investment required for AI and technology adoption can be a source of resistance, particularly for resource-constrained SMEs. The perceived high costs of implementation, coupled with uncertainty about return on investment, may lead business owners and managers to hesitate in embracing new technologies. To address this, SMEs can explore phased implementation strategies, starting with small-scale pilot projects to demonstrate value before scaling up. Additionally, leveraging cloud-based AI solutions and software-as-a-service (SaaS) models can provide more cost-effective entry points for SMEs to adopt advanced technologies without significant upfront investments (Heredia Zurita & Dini, 2021).

Lack of technical expertise within the organization often contributes to resistance to technological change. Employees may feel overwhelmed by the prospect of learning new systems or fear appearing incompetent when faced with unfamiliar technologies. This resistance can be mitigated through comprehensive training programs tailored to different skill levels and roles within the organization. Partnering with technology providers or educational institutions to offer ongoing learning opportunities can help build confidence and competence among employees. Furthermore, identifying and nurturing "technology champions" within the organization can create a support network for employees navigating the digital transformation process (Mishrif & Khan, 2023).

Regulatory uncertainty and concerns about compliance can fuel resistance to AI adoption in Latin American SMEs. The rapidly evolving landscape of data protection laws, AI regulations, and industry-specific requirements can create apprehension about the legal implications of implementing new technologies. To address these concerns, SMEs should prioritize staying informed about relevant regulations and consider engaging legal experts specializing in technology and data protection. Implementing robust governance frameworks for AI and data usage can help ensure compliance while building trust among employees and stakeholders in the ethical use of new technologies.

The comfort of established routines and processes poses another barrier to change in many SMEs. Employees and managers who have become accustomed to certain ways of working may resist new technologies that disrupt these familiar patterns. This inertia can be particularly strong in organizations that have experienced past success with traditional methods. Overcoming this resistance requires demonstrating the tangible benefits of new technologies in enhancing productivity, efficiency, and job satisfaction. Creating opportunities for employees to experiment with new tools in low-risk environments can help build comfort and confidence with technological changes (Molina-Ycaza & Sánchez-Riofrío, 2016).

Resistance to change can also stem from past experiences with failed technology implementations or poorly managed change initiatives. These negative experiences can create skepticism and cynicism towards new technological proposals. To overcome this, SMEs must approach change management with careful planning and execution. This includes setting realistic expectations, providing adequate resources and support throughout the implementation process, and celebrating early wins to build momentum and trust in the change initiative (Mancini & González, 2021).

The interconnected nature of business processes in SMEs can amplify resistance to change, as alterations in one area may have ripple effects across the organization. Employees may resist changes that affect established workflows or collaborations with other departments. Addressing this requires a holistic approach to technology implementation, considering the broader organizational impact of new systems. Cross-functional teams and collaborative planning processes can help ensure that technological changes are implemented in a way that aligns with overall business objectives and minimizes disruption to existing workflows (Bhuiyan et al., 2024).

Leadership plays a critical role in overcoming resistance to change in Latin American SMEs. When leaders themselves are resistant or ambivalent about new technologies, it can permeate throughout the organization. Conversely, leaders who champion innovation and demonstrate a commitment to digital transformation can inspire confidence and enthusiasm among employees. Developing change leadership capabilities among managers and executives is essential for driving successful technology adoption. This may involve leadership training programs focused on digital transformation, exposure to industry best practices, and opportunities for leaders to engage directly with new technologies (Sposato, 2024b).

As Latin American SMEs navigate the challenges of resistance to change in their digital transformation journeys, a strategic and empathetic approach is essential. By addressing the underlying fears and concerns, providing comprehensive support and education, and fostering a culture of innovation and adaptability, these organizations can overcome resistance and unlock the full potential of AI and emerging technologies. The successful management of change facilitates technological adoption and also positions SMEs for greater resilience and competitiveness in an increasingly digital business landscape.

## Skills Gap

The rapid advancement of AI and emerging technologies has created a significant skills gap within Latin American SMEs, posing a substantial challenge to their digital transformation efforts. This disparity between the skills possessed by the current workforce and those required to effectively leverage new technologies has become a critical issue for businesses across the region. The multifaceted nature of this skills gap, encompassing technical expertise, digital literacy, and adaptive capabilities, necessitates a comprehensive approach to workforce development and talent management. As SMEs strive to remain competitive in an increasingly technology-driven marketplace, addressing this skills gap has become not just a human resources concern, but a strategic imperative for sustainable growth and innovation (Akpan et al., 2022).

The technical skills gap is perhaps the most apparent challenge facing Latin American SMEs in their AI adoption journey. There is a shortage of professionals with expertise in areas such as machine learning, data science, cloud computing, and AI engineering. This scarcity of technical talent can significantly hinder an SME's ability to implement and maintain advanced AI systems. To address this, some SMEs are partnering with universities and technical institutions to develop tailored training programs that align with their specific technological needs. Others are exploring innovative recruitment strategies, such as hackathons or coding challenges, to identify and attract tech talent from non-traditional backgrounds (Rojas-Berrio et al., 2022).

Digital literacy, extending beyond specialized technical skills, represents another relevant aspect of the skills gap. Many employees in Latin American SMEs may lack the basic digital competencies necessary to work effectively with AI-enhanced tools and systems. This gap in digital literacy can lead to reduced productivity, errors in data handling, and resistance to new technologies. To combat this, SMEs are implementing comprehensive digital literacy programs that cover a range of skills from basic computer operations to data interpretation and digital collaboration tools. Some organizations are also adopting gamification techniques to make the learning process more engaging and effective for employees across different age groups and backgrounds (Hansen & Bøgh, 2021).

The rapid pace of technological change necessitates a workforce capable of continuous learning and adaptation. However, many employees in Latin American SMEs may lack the adaptive skills and learning mindset required to keep pace with evolving technologies. This adaptability gap can impede the organization's ability to innovate and respond to market changes. To foster a culture of continuous learning, some SMEs are implementing mentorship programs, creating internal knowledge-sharing platforms, and offering incentives for self-directed learning and skill development. Leadership training programs that emphasize change management and innovation are also being deployed to equip managers with the skills to guide their teams through technological transitions (Sposato, 2024a).

Data literacy has emerged as a critical skill in the age of AI and big data analytics. Many employees in Latin American SMEs may struggle to effectively interpret, analyze, and make decisions based on data-driven insights. This data literacy gap can lead to underutilization of AI capabilities and missed opportunities for data-driven innovation. To address this, some SMEs are implementing data literacy boot camps and workshops that teach employees how to read, interpret, and communicate data effectively. Collaborative projects that involve cross-functional teams working with data can also help embed data literacy skills across different departments of the organization (Pigola et al., 2021).

The shortage of AI ethics and governance expertise presents another dimension of the skills gap. As AI systems become more prevalent in business operations, there is a growing need for professionals who understand the ethical implications of AI and can develop appropriate governance frameworks. This skills gap can expose SMEs to reputational and regulatory risks associated with AI deployment. To mitigate this, some organizations are investing in specialized training programs on AI ethics and collaborating with ethics consultants to develop robust AI governance policies. Integrating ethical considerations into existing tech training programs can also help build a workforce that is both technically proficient and ethically aware.

Soft skills, often overlooked in discussions of technological skills gaps, play a significant role in the effective implementation and use of AI systems. Skills such as critical thinking, problem-solving, creativity, and emotional intelligence become even more valuable as routine tasks are increasingly automated. Many Latin American SMEs are finding that their workforce may lack the advanced soft skills necessary to fully leverage AI capabilities. To address this, some organizations are redesigning their training programs to place greater emphasis on soft skills development, using AI-powered assessment tools to identify skill gaps, and implementing experiential learning approaches to enhance these competencies.

The language barrier presents a unique challenge in the context of AI adoption for many Latin American SMEs. Much of the cutting-edge AI research, documentation, and training materials are primarily available in English, which can be a significant hurdle for non-English speaking employees. This language gap can slow down the adoption of new technologies and limit access to global knowledge resources. To overcome this, some SMEs are investing in language training programs for key technical staff, partnering with translation services to localize important technical documents, and fostering connections with international tech communities to facilitate knowledge exchange (Bianchi et al., 2017).

The management skills gap is another critical area affecting AI adoption in Latin American SMEs. Many managers may lack the necessary skills to lead AI-driven projects, integrate AI systems into existing business processes, or manage teams with diverse technical backgrounds. This leadership gap can result in poorly executed AI initiatives and missed opportunities for innovation. To address this, some organizations are implementing leadership development programs focused on digital transformation, sponsoring managers to attend AI strategy workshops, and creating opportunities for hands-on experience with AI projects (Karuppiah et al., 2023).

The gig economy and freelance marketplaces offer a potential solution to some aspects of the skills gap, allowing SMEs to access specialized AI talent on a project basis. However, effectively managing and integrating freelance or remote AI professionals presents its own set of challenges. Many Latin American SMEs may lack the project management and virtual collaboration skills necessary to fully leverage these flexible talent pools. To build these capabilities, some organizations are investing in project management training, implementing robust digital collaboration tools, and developing protocols for effective remote work and freelance integration.

As Latin American SMEs navigate the complexities of the AI-driven skills gap, a multifaceted and forward-looking approach to talent development is essential. By investing in comprehensive training programs, fostering a culture of continuous learning, and exploring innovative talent acquisition strategies, these organizations can build a workforce capable of driving AI adoption and digital innovation. Addressing the skills gap is not just about filling current needs, but about creating a resilient and adaptable workforce ready to meet the evolving demands of an AI-powered business landscape. The success of SMEs in bridging this skills gap will play a significant role in determining their competitiveness and growth potential in the rapidly evolving digital economy of Latin America.

## Keys to the Digitalization of Companies

The digitalization of Latin American SMEs represents a transformative journey that encompasses technological adoption, organizational change, and strategic realignment. As these businesses navigate the complexities of the digital landscape, several key factors emerge as critical to successful digitalization efforts. Understanding and implementing these key elements can significantly enhance an SME's ability to leverage AI and emerging technologies effectively, driving innovation, competitiveness, and sustainable growth in the digital era. This multifaceted approach to digitalization considers the technical aspects of implementation and also the human, cultural, and strategic dimensions that are essential for long-term success (Melo et al., 2023).

Strategic alignment stands as a cornerstone of effective digitalization. SMEs must ensure that their digital initiatives are closely aligned with general business objectives and market positioning. This alignment involves a comprehensive assessment of how digital technologies, particularly AI, can enhance core business processes, create new value propositions, and drive competitive advantage. Successful SMEs often establish clear digital roadmaps that outline short-term and long-term goals, prioritize initiatives based on potential impact and feasibility, and regularly review and adjust these strategies in response to technological advancements and market changes. By maintaining this strategic focus, SMEs can avoid the pitfall of adopting technology for its own sake and instead ensure that digital investments deliver tangible business value (Bhuiyan et al., 2024).

Leadership commitment and vision play a pivotal role in driving successful digitalization efforts. Leaders of Latin American SMEs must champion digital initiatives and demonstrate a deep understanding of the transformative potential of AI and emerging technologies. This involves cultivating a forward-thinking mindset, staying informed about technological trends, and being willing to challenge established business models. Effective digital leaders foster a culture of innovation, encourage experimentation, and provide the necessary resources and support for digital projects. They also play an important role in communicating the vision for digitalization across the organization, aligning teams around common goals, and addressing concerns and resistance to change. By embodying a commitment to digital transformation, leaders can inspire and mobilize their organizations to embrace the opportunities presented by the digital age.

Building a robust digital infrastructure forms the foundation for successful AI adoption and digitalization. This infrastructure encompasses hardware and software systems and also data management capabilities, connectivity solutions, and cybersecurity measures. For Latin American SMEs, this may involve investments in cloud computing platforms, which offer scalable and cost-effective access to advanced computing resources. Establishing robust data governance frameworks is equally critical, ensuring that data is collected, stored, and utilized ethically and efficiently. Additionally, implementing strong cybersecurity protocols is essential to protect digital assets and maintain customer trust. SMEs that prioritize the development of a comprehensive digital infrastructure position themselves to leverage AI and other emerging technologies more effectively, enabling faster innovation and more agile responses to market changes (Hansen & Bøgh, 2021).

Fostering a culture of continuous learning and adaptability is essential for SMEs navigating the rapidly evolving digital landscape. This involves creating an environment where employees are encouraged to acquire new skills, experiment with new technologies, and share knowledge across the organization. Successful SMEs often implement comprehensive training programs that cover both technical skills and digital literacy. They may also establish innovation labs or sandboxes where employees can explore new technologies and ideas in a low-risk environment. Encouraging a growth mindset among employees, where challenges are viewed as opportunities for learning and improvement, can significantly enhance an organization's ability to adapt to technological changes and drive innovation (Akpan et al., 2022).

Effective change management strategies are relevant for overcoming resistance and ensuring smooth adoption of digital technologies. This involves clear communication about the reasons for and benefits of digitalization, addressing employee concerns, and providing support throughout the transition process. Successful SMEs often adopt a phased approach to digital implementation, starting with pilot projects to demonstrate value and build confidence before scaling up. They also identify and empower "digital champions" within the organization who can advocate for new technologies and support their colleagues through the change process. By prioritizing the human aspect of digital transformation, SMEs can foster greater buy-in and engagement from employees, ultimately leading to more successful digitalization outcomes (Karuppiah et al., 2023).

Leveraging partnerships and ecosystems can significantly accelerate the digitalization process for Latin American SMEs. This may involve collaborations with technology providers, academic institutions, or other businesses to access expertise, share resources, and drive innovation. Participating in digital innovation hubs or industry consortiums can provide SMEs with valuable insights, best practices, and networking opportunities. Additionally, engaging with startup ecosystems can expose SMEs to cutting-edge technologies and innovative business models. Some SMEs are also exploring open innovation approaches, collaborating with external partners to solve complex challenges or develop new products and services. By strategically leveraging these partnerships and ecosystems, SMEs can overcome resource constraints and accelerate their digital transformation journeys.

Customer-centricity must remain at the heart of digitalization efforts. Successful SMEs use digital technologies, particularly AI, to gain deeper insights into customer needs, preferences, and behaviors. This may involve implementing advanced analytics tools to analyze customer data, using AI-powered personalization engines to tailor products and services, or leveraging chatbots and virtual assistants to enhance customer support. However, it's important to balance technological capabilities with the human touch, ensuring that digital interactions enhance rather than detract from the customer experience. SMEs that maintain a strong focus on customer value throughout their digitalization efforts are better positioned to build loyalty, drive growth, and differentiate themselves in competitive markets (Schnarch, 2013).

Agile and iterative approaches to digitalization can help SMEs navigate uncertainty and rapidly evolving technological landscapes. This involves breaking down large digital initiatives into smaller, manageable projects that can deliver quick wins and provide opportunities for learning and adjustment. Adopting agile methodologies in digital project management can enhance flexibility, speed up time-to-market for new digital products or services, and allow for continuous improvement based on feedback and results. This approach is particularly valuable in the context of AI implementation, where systems often require ongoing refinement and adaptation. By embracing agility in their digitalization efforts, SMEs can reduce risks, accelerate learning, and more effectively respond to changing market conditions and technological advancements (Schnarch, 2013).

Measuring and communicating the impact of digital initiatives is relevant for maintaining momentum and securing ongoing support for digitalization efforts. This involves establishing clear key performance indicators (KPIs) that align with business objectives and regularly tracking and reporting on progress. Successful SMEs often use data visualization tools to make this information accessible and actionable for decision-makers across the organization. They also celebrate digital successes and share lessons learned from challenges, fostering a culture of transparency and continuous improvement. By demonstrating the tangible benefits of digitalization, SMEs can build confidence in their digital strategies and justify further investments in AI and emerging technologies.

As Latin American SMEs embark on their digitalization journeys, a holistic and strategic approach that addresses these key elements can significantly enhance their chances of success. By aligning digital initiatives with business strategy, fostering a culture of innovation and learning, leveraging partnerships, and maintaining a strong customer focus, these organizations can harness the full potential of AI and emerging technologies. The path to digitalization may be challenging, but for SMEs that navigate it successfully, it offers unprecedented opportunities for growth, innovation, and competitiveness in the global digital economy.

## METHODOLOGY

This research utilized a quantitative approach based on a cross-sectional design to investigate the adoption of new technologies, particularly AI, in Latin American SMEs. This methodology was selected for its ability to capture a snapshot of current technology implementation practices and explore relationships between various factors influencing adoption. The cross-sectional approach is particularly relevant for examining the rapidly evolving landscape of technology adoption among SMEs in Latin America.

The sample consisted of 306 directors of SMEs in Latin America, chosen through stratified sampling by country and industry sector. This sampling strategy ensured adequate representation of the diverse national and sectoral contexts within the region. The study encompassed Argentina, Brazil, Chile, Colombia, Mexico, and Peru, representing the largest economies in Latin America. These countries were selected for their economic significance and because they offer varying levels of technological infrastructure and digital transformation stages, providing a comprehensive view of the region's technology adoption landscape.

A structured questionnaire served as the primary data collection instrument. The questionnaire was developed based on existing literature on technology adoption in SMEs, with careful adaptation to the Latin American context. This adaptation process involved consultation with regional technology experts and conducting pilot tests to ensure the relevance and clarity of questions in the local business environment. The questionnaire addressed several key dimensions including company characteristics, knowledge and perception of AI and emerging technologies, current technology adoption practices, motivations for implementing new technologies, perceived barriers to technology adoption, perceived benefits of technology implementation, the relationship between innovation and technology adoption, the impact of digital transformation on business processes, and skills development and training practices.

The questionnaire predominantly employed closed questions with 5-point Likert scales to facilitate quantitative analysis. This format was chosen for its ability to capture nuanced responses while enabling statistical analysis. Additionally, open-ended questions were included to gather qualitative insights that might not be fully addressed by the structured responses. This mixed approach allowed for a richer dataset, combining the benefits of quantitative measurement with the depth of qualitative insights.

Data collection was conducted through a combination of online surveys and video conference interviews. This dual approach was adopted to maximize response rates and accommodate the varying technological capacities and preferences of SMEs across the region. Online surveys offered efficiency and reach, while video conference interviews provided an opportunity for clarification and more detailed responses on complex technological topics.

For data analysis, SPSS statistical software was employed due to its robust capabilities in handling complex quantitative data and its suitability for analyzing technology-related datasets. The analysis encompassed several techniques to provide a comprehensive understanding of the data. Descriptive analysis was used to offer an overview of technology adoption practices in Latin American SMEs, providing baseline information on the current state of AI and emerging technology implementation. Correlation analysis explored relationships between variables, such as company size and level of technology adoption, offering insights into factors that might influence implementation practices. Multiple regression analysis was conducted to identify the factors that influence the adoption of new technologies, allowing for a more nuanced understanding of the drivers of digital transformation in the region. Analysis of variance (ANOVA) was employed to compare differences in technology adoption practices across countries and sectors, highlighting regional and industry-specific trends. Lastly, cluster analysis was used to identify groups of SMEs with similar technology adoption patterns, providing a deeper understanding of how different aspects of digital transformation are conceptualized and implemented in the region.

It is important to acknowledge the potential limitations of this study. The cross-sectional nature of the design, while providing valuable insights into the current state of technology adoption practices, does not allow for the establishment of causal relationships or the tracking of changes over time. This limitation suggests the potential value of future longitudinal studies in this area. Additionally, while the stratified sampling technique aimed to ensure representation, the sample may not be fully representative of all SMEs in Latin America, particularly given the vast diversity of businesses in the region. Furthermore, the reliance on self-reported responses introduces the possibility of response bias, where respondents may overreport their technology adoption levels. To mitigate this, the questionnaire was designed with carefully worded questions and assurances of anonymity, but the potential for bias should still be considered when interpreting the results. Despite these limitations, this methodology provides a robust framework for examining technology adoption practices among SMEs in Latin America, offering valuable insights into this critical and rapidly evolving area of business practice in the region.

## RESULTS

The study on the adoption of new technologies in Latin American SMEs yielded significant insights into the perceived benefits, barriers, and areas of application for these technologies. The results presented here are based on the responses from 306 SME directors across Argentina, Brazil, Chile, Colombia, Mexico, and Peru.

*Figure 1. Main benefits perceived when implementing new technologies in Latin American SMEs*

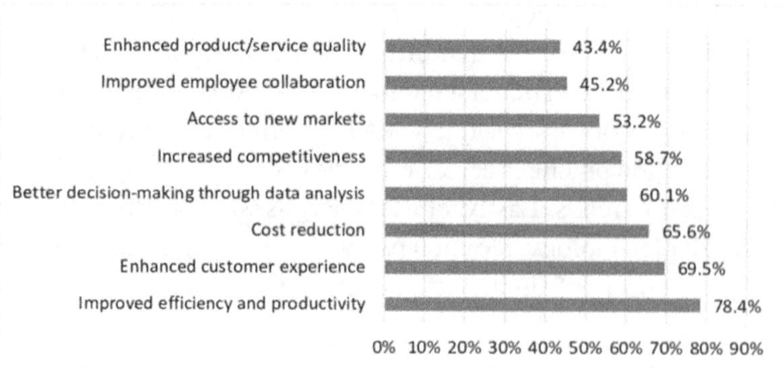


*Source: Authors' own work*

In figure 1 it is shown the main benefits perceived by SME directors when implementing new technologies in their organizations. The results indicate that improved efficiency and productivity is the most widely recognized benefit, with 78.4% of SMEs identifying it as a key advantage of new technology adoption. Then we can find the enhanced customer experience and cost reduction, recognized by 69.5% and 65.6% of SMEs respectively. It's noteworthy that 60.1% of the surveyed SMEs acknowledge the role of new technologies in enabling better decision-making through data analysis. Increased competitiveness and access to new markets, were recognized by 58.7% and 53.2% of SMEs respectively. The last two benefits were improved employee collaboration and enhanced product/service quality.

*Figure 2. Main barriers perceived towards technology adoption in Latin American SMEs (scale of 1 to 5)*

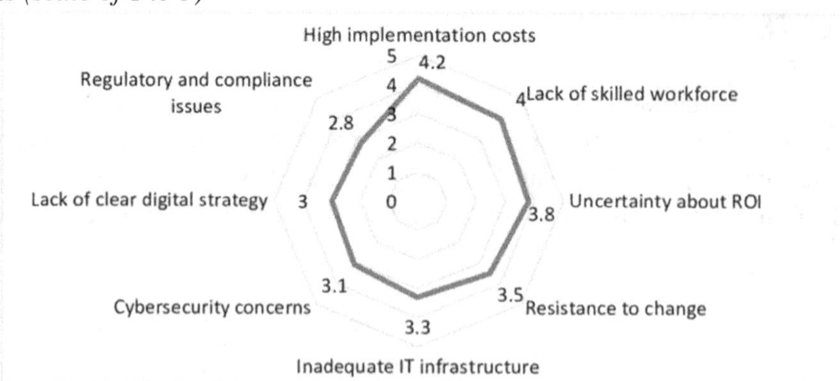


*Source: Authors' own work*

In figure 2 it is outlined the primary barriers that SMEs face when considering or implementing new technologies, rated on a scale of 1 to 5, where 1 represents the lowest level of concern and 5 represents the highest level of concern. The data reveals a hierarchy of barriers to technology adoption faced by Latin American SMEs, with financial concerns topping the list. High implementation costs emerge as the most significant obstacle, scoring 4.2 out of 5, closely followed by the lack of a skilled workforce at 4.0. This underscores the dual challenge of financial constraints and skills shortages in the region. Uncertainty about ROI (3.8) and resistance to change (3.5) represent the next tier of concerns, highlighting the need for clearer demonstration of technology benefits and change management strategies. The middle range of barriers includes inadequate IT infrastructure (3.3), cybersecurity concerns (3.1), and lack of clear digital strategy (3.0), suggesting that while these are significant issues, they are perceived as somewhat less pressing than the top-ranked barriers. Regulatory and compliance issues, while still noteworthy at 2.8, appear to be the least concerning among the listed barriers. Notably, all barriers score above the midpoint of 2.5, indicating that each presents a meaningful challenge to technology adoption among Latin American SMEs.

*Figure 3. Areas of business where new technologies are most applied in Latin American SMEs*

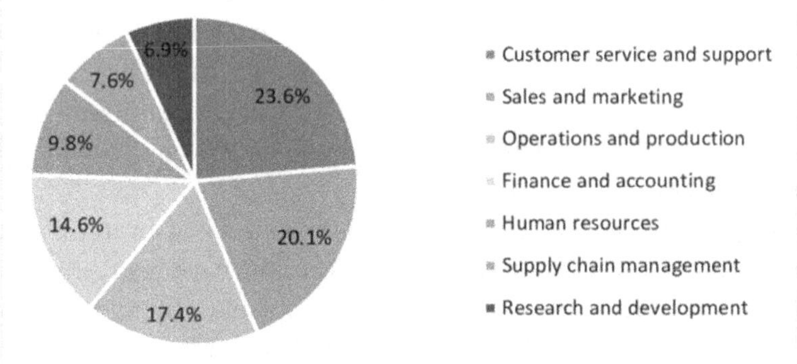


*Source: Authors' own work*

Figure 3 shows the distribution of new technology applications across different business areas. The results indicate that customer-facing operations are the primary focus for new technology adoption among Latin American SMEs. Customer service and support lead with 23.6% of SMEs applying new technologies in this area, closely followed by sales and marketing at 20.1%. Operations and production also show significant adoption at 17.4%. It's notable that back-office functions like finance and accounting (14.6%) and human resources (9.8%) are also seeing considerable technology implementation, suggesting a holistic approach to digital transformation among many SMEs in the region. With less than 15% we find the supply chain management and the research and development.

These findings provide valuable insights into the current state of technology adoption among Latin American SMEs, highlighting both the opportunities and challenges these businesses face in their digital transformation journeys. The results underscore the need for targeted strategies to address the identified barriers and leverage the recognized benefits of new technologies across various business functions.

## DISCUSSION AND CONCLUSIONS

The digital transformation of Latin American SMEs represents a critical juncture in the region's economic development. As emerging technologies, particularly AI, continue to reshape global markets, the ability of these businesses to adapt and innovate becomes increasingly vital. This study has shed light on the complex landscape of technology adoption among Latin American SMEs, revealing both promising trends and significant challenges that lie ahead.

The adoption of new technologies by SMEs in Latin America is driven by a compelling need to remain competitive in an increasingly digital marketplace. This process extends far beyond the mere acquisition of new tools; it encompasses a holistic integration of these technologies into existing business processes and the cultivation of novel capabilities within organizations. AI, in particular, emerges as a transformative force, offering SMEs unprecedented opportunities to enhance decision-making, automate routine tasks, and unlock new avenues for innovation across various business functions.

The conceptual framework guiding this study encompasses several interconnected components that shape technology adoption in Latin American SMEs. It begins by examining the diverse array of technologies available, including AI, IoT, cloud computing, and blockchain, and their potential applications across different business contexts. The framework also considers the dimensions of innovation capacity, productivity, competitiveness, and efficiency as key factors influencing adoption. Internal information management and decision-making processes are highlighted as critical areas where new technologies can significantly impact SME operations. The human element, including aspects such as employee collaboration and the challenges of resistance to change, forms another significant component of the framework. Additionally, the framework addresses the importance of customer retention and the considerations of security and privacy in the digital age. This comprehensive approach allows for a nuanced understanding of the complex interplay of factors affecting technology adoption among Latin American SMEs.

However, the path to technological adoption presents challenges for these businesses. Limited resources, both financial and human, often constrain the ability of SMEs to invest in and implement new technologies. The rapid pace of technological change can be overwhelming, making it difficult for smaller enterprises to keep up with the latest innovations and integrate them effectively into their operations. Despite these challenges, the potential benefits of technological adoption for Latin American SMEs are immense, ranging from enhanced productivity and improved operational efficiency to increased competitiveness in global markets.

Our empirical study, based on responses from 306 SME directors across major Latin American economies, provides valuable insights into the current state of technology adoption. The findings reveal a strong focus on customer-facing technologies, with customer service and support leading the areas of implementation. This suggests that SMEs are prioritizing technologies that offer immediate, tangible benefits in their customer interactions. However, it also highlights a potential gap in the strategic implementation of technologies across other critical business functions.

The study is not without its limitations. The cross-sectional nature of the research provides a snapshot of technology adoption practices at a specific point in time but doesn't capture their dynamic evolution. Additionally, while the study covered major Latin American economies, the diversity of the region means that practices may vary in countries not included in the sample. Future research could benefit from longitudinal approaches to track the evolution of technology adoption practices over time, as well as more focused studies on specific industries or technologies. Comparative studies with SMEs in other developing regions could also provide valuable insights into the unique aspects of the Latin American approach to digital transformation.

As we look to the future, it is clear that the ability of Latin American SMEs to effectively adopt and leverage new technologies will be a critical determinant of their success and the region's economic growth. This study serves as a call to action for policymakers, technology providers, educational institutions, and SME leaders to collaborate in creating an ecosystem that supports and accelerates digital transformation. By addressing the identified barriers, such as high implementation costs and skills shortages, and leveraging the recognized benefits of improved efficiency and productivity, stakeholders can work towards a more technologically advanced and competitive SME sector in Latin America. This has implications for individual businesses and for the broader economic development and global competitiveness of the region. The journey towards digital transformation may be challenging, but for Latin American SMEs that navigate it successfully, it offers unprecedented opportunities for growth, innovation, and sustainable development in the global digital economy.

## REFERENCES


Agbonyin, A., Reddy, P., & Jakkani, A. K. (2024). Utilizing Internet of Things (IoT), Artificial Intelligence, and vehicle telematics for sustainable growth in small, and medium firms (SMEs). [IJCET]. *International Journal of Computer Engineering and Technology*, 15(2), 182–191. DOI: 10.17605/OSF.IO/QX3DP

Akpan, I. J., Udoh, E. A. P., & Adebisi, B. (2022). Small business awareness and adoption of state-of-the-art technologies in emerging and developing markets, and lessons from the COVID-19 pandemic. *Journal of Small Business and Entrepreneurship*, 34(2), 123–140. DOI: 10.1080/08276331.2020.1820185

AlShamsi, M., Salloum, S. A., Alshurideh, M., & Abdallah, S. (2020). Artificial intelligence and blockchain for transparency in governance. In *Artificial intelligence for sustainable development: Theory, practice and future applications* (pp. 219–230). Springer International Publishing.

Arranz, C. F., Arroyabe, M. F., Arranz, N., & de Arroyabe, J. C. F. (2023). Digitalisation dynamics in SMEs: An approach from systems dynamics and artificial intelligence. *Technological Forecasting and Social Change*, 196, 122880. DOI: 10.1016/j.techfore.2023.122880

Atieh, A. M., Cooke, K. O., & Osiyevskyy, O. (2023). The role of intelligent manufacturing systems in the implementation of Industry 4.0 by small and medium enterprises in developing countries. *Engineering Reports*, 5(3), e12578. DOI: 10.1002/eng2.12578

Banco Interamericano de Desarrollo (BID). (2022). *Guía operativa para programas de competitividad para la pequeña y mediana empresa.*

Bhuiyan, M. R. I., Faraji, M. R., Rashid, M., Bhuyan, M. K., Hossain, R., & Ghose, P. (2024). Digital Transformation in SMEs Emerging Technological Tools and Technologies for Enhancing the SME's Strategies and Outcomes. *Journal of Ecohumanism*, 3(4), 211–224. DOI: 10.62754/joe.v3i4.3594

Bianchi, C., Glavas, C., & Mathews, S. (2017). SME international performance in Latin America: The role of entrepreneurial and technological capabilities. *Journal of Small Business and Enterprise Development*, 24(1), 176–195. DOI: 10.1108/JSBED-09-2016-0142

Bican, P. M., & Brem, A. (2020). Digital Business Model, Digital Transformation, Digital Entrepreneurship: Is There A Sustainable "Digital"? *Sustainability (Basel)*, 12(13), 5239. DOI: 10.3390/su12135239

Cedillo-Campos, M. G. (2020). Web platform to develop collective intelligence in logistics for Latin American SMEs: The case of SmartLogistiX3. com. *Nova Scientia*, 12(25). Advance online publication. DOI: 10.21640/ns.v12i25.2452

CEPAL. (2021). Mipymes y el COVID-19. https://www.cepal.org/es/euromipyme/mipymes-covid-19

Damioli, G., Van Roy, V., & Vertesy, D. (2021). The impact of artificial intelligence on labor productivity. *Eurasian Business Review*, 11(1), 1–25. DOI: 10.1007/s40821-020-00172-8

Dini, M., & Stumpo, G. (2018). *Mipymes en América Latina: un frágil desempeño y nuevos desafíos para las políticas de fomento*. CEPAL.

Dittmar, E. C. (2020). Evolución, tendencias e iniciativas en materia de RSC. In Dittmar, E. C. (Ed.), *Tendencias y organización empresarial frente al nuevo entorno tecnológico: Una perspectiva multidisciplinar*. Thomson Reuters Aranzadi.

Ferraro, C., & Rojo, S. (2018). Las MIPYMES en América Latina y el Caribe: Una agenda integrada para promover la productividad y la formalización. *OIT Américas, Informes Técnicos, 7.*

Gonzalez-Tamayo, L. A., Maheshwari, G., Bonomo-Odizzio, A., Herrera-Avilés, M., & Krauss-Delorme, C. (2023). Factors influencing small and medium size enterprises development and digital maturity in Latin America. *Journal of Open Innovation*, 9(2), 100069. DOI: 10.1016/j.joitmc.2023.100069

Hansen, E. B., & Bøgh, S. (2021). Artificial intelligence and internet of things in small and medium-sized enterprises: A survey. *Journal of Manufacturing Systems*, 58, 362–372. DOI: 10.1016/j.jmsy.2020.08.009

Heredia Zurita, A., & Dini, M. (2021). *Análisis de las políticas de apoyo a las pymes para enfrentar la pandemia de COVID-19 en América Latina*. CEPAL.

Karuppiah, K., Sankaranarayanan, B., D'Adamo, I., & Ali, S. M. (2023). Evaluation of key factors for industry 4.0 technologies adoption in small and medium enterprises (SMEs): An emerging economy context. *Journal of Asia Business Studies*, 17(2), 347–370. DOI: 10.1108/JABS-05-2021-0202

Kulkov, I., Kulkova, J., Leone, D., Rohrbeck, R., & Menvielle, L. (2024). Stand-alone or run together: Artificial intelligence as an enabler for other technologies. *International Journal of Entrepreneurial Behaviour & Research*, 30(8), 2082–2105. DOI: 10.1108/IJEBR-02-2023-0169

Liñán, F., Paul, J., & Fayolle, A. (2020). SMEs and entrepreneurship in the era of globalization: Advances and theoretical approaches. *Small Business Economics*, 55(3), 695–703. DOI: 10.1007/s11187-019-00180-7

López Jiménez, D., Dittmar, E. C., & Vargas Portillo, J. P. (2021). Cooperation and relationship in the triple helix model of innovation. *International Journal of Knowledge and Learning*, 14(1), 1–9. DOI: 10.1504/IJKL.2021.115025

López Jiménez, D., Dittmar, E. C., & Vargas Portillo, J. P. (2022). Nuevas estrategias publicitarias con influencers: Un examen multidisciplinar. *Revista de Ciencias Sociales*, 28(4), 63–78. DOI: 10.31876/rcs.v28i4.39117

López Jiménez, D., Dittmar, E. C., & Vargas Portillo, J. P. (2023). The Self-Regulating Jury in the Field of Interactive Advertising. *Revista de Direito. Estado e Telecomunicacoes*, 15(1), 1–30. DOI: 10.26512/lstr.v15i1.42146

Mancini, S., & González, J. L. C. (2021). Role of technology transfer, innovation strategy and network: A conceptual model of innovation network to facilitate the internationalization process of SMEs. *Technology and Investment*, 12(2), 82–128. DOI: 10.4236/ti.2021.122006

Melo, I. C., Queiroz, G. A., Junior, P. N. A., de Sousa, T. B., Yushimito, W. F., & Pereira, J. (2023). Sustainable digital transformation in small and medium enterprises (SMEs): A review on performance. *Heliyon*, 9(3), e13908. Advance online publication. DOI: 10.1016/j.heliyon.2023.e13908 PMID: 36915489

Mishrif, A., & Khan, A. (2023). Technology adoption as survival strategy for small and medium enterprises during COVID-19. *Journal of Innovation and Entrepreneurship*, 12(1), 53. DOI: 10.1186/s13731-023-00317-9

Molina-Ycaza, D., & Sánchez-Riofrío, A. (2016). Obstáculos para la micro, pequeña y mediana empresa en América Latina. *Pymes. Innovación y Desarrollo*, 4(2), 21–36.

Peter, O., Pradhan, A., & Mbohwa, C. (2023). Industrial internet of things (IIoT): Opportunities, challenges, and requirements in manufacturing businesses in emerging economies. *Procedia Computer Science*, 217, 856–865. DOI: 10.1016/j.procs.2022.12.282

Pigola, A., da Costa, P. R., Carvalho, L. C., Silva, L. F. D., Kniess, C. T., & Maccari, E. A. (2021). Artificial intelligence-driven digital technologies to the implementation of the sustainable development goals: A perspective from Brazil and Portugal. *Sustainability (Basel)*, 13(24), 13669. DOI: 10.3390/su132413669

Ramírez-Solis, E. R., Llonch-Andreu, J., & Malpica-Romero, A. D. (2022). How beneficial are relational capital and technology orientation for innovation? Evidence from Mexican SMEs. *International Journal of Innovation Studies*, 6(1), 1–10. DOI: 10.1016/j.ijis.2022.02.001

Rojas-Berrio, S., Rincon-Novoa, J., Sánchez-Monrroy, M., Ascúa, R., & Montoya-Restrepo, L. A. (2022). Factors influencing 4.0 technology adoption in manufacturing SMEs in an emerging country. *Journal of Small Business Strategy*, 32(3), 67–83. DOI: 10.53703/001c.34608

Schnarch, A. (2013). *Marketing para Pymes: un enfoque para Latinoamérica.* Alfaomega.

Schwaeke, J., Peters, A., Kanbach, D. K., Kraus, S., & Jones, P. (2024). The new normal: The status quo of AI adoption in SMEs. *Journal of Small Business Management*, •••, 1–35. DOI: 10.1080/00472778.2024.2379999

Sharma, S., Singh, G., Islam, N., & Dhir, A. (2022). Why do SMEs adopt artificial intelligence-based chatbots? *IEEE Transactions on Engineering Management*, 71, 1773–1786. DOI: 10.1109/TEM.2022.3203469

Sposato, M. (2024a). Are leaders born or made? Asking the right question. *Development and Learning in Organizations*, 38(3), 1–3. DOI: 10.1108/DLO-05-2023-0123

Sposato, M. (2024b). Leadership training and development in the age of artificial intelligence. *Development and Learning in Organizations*, 38(4), 4–7. DOI: 10.1108/DLO-12-2023-0256

Sposato, M. (2025). Developing Digital Leadership Skills for AI-Driven Research Environments. In *Impacts of Generative AI on the Future of Research and Education* (pp. 235–254). IGI Global., DOI: 10.4018/979-8-3693-0884-4.ch010

Tseng, C. Y., & Ting, P. H. (2013). Patent analysis for technology development of artificial intelligence: A country-level comparative study. *Innovation (North Sydney, N.S.W.)*, 15(4), 463–475. DOI: 10.5172/impp.2013.15.4.463

Van, B., & Gómez, H. (2015). *Pyme de avanzada: Motor del desarrollo en América Latina*. Universidad de los. *Andes (Salta)*.

Vermesan, O., & Friess, P. (2014). *Internet of things applications-from research and innovation to market deployment.* Taylor & Francis.

# Chapter 11
# Barriers and Opportunities in CSR Adoption Among Latin American SMEs in the AI Age

**Eduardo Carlos Dittmar**
https://orcid.org/0000-0002-8087-2444
*Universidad Rey Juan Carlos, Spain*

**Víctor Manuel Castillo Girón**
https://orcid.org/0000-0002-8307-2952
*Universidad de Guadalajara, Mexico*

## ABSTRACT

*In the era of Artificial Intelligence (AI), this study examines Corporate Social Responsibility (CSR) adoption among Small and Medium-sized Enterprises (SMEs) in Latin America. CSR in Latin American SMEs represents a complex interplay of global standards and local realities, shaped by unique socio-economic contexts and developmental challenges. The literature reveals a significant gap in understanding CSR practices among SMEs in developing regions. The empirical study, using a quantitative approach with 306 SME directors from six countries, reveals increasing CSR engagement, primarily focused on environmental practices and driven by ethical and reputational concerns. Key barriers include implementation costs and lack of knowledge. Findings highlight the need for tailored CSR approaches in Latin America, considering SMEs' unique motivations, barriers, and operational realities, offering insights for policymakers, business support organizations, and*

DOI: 10.4018/979-8-3693-9894-4.ch011

*SME leaders as they navigate CSR adoption in the AI age.*

## INTRODUCTION

In the evolving landscape of global business, Corporate Social Responsibility (CSR) has emerged as a pivotal concept, fundamentally altering the relationship between organizations, society, and the environment. This paradigm shift extends beyond large corporations to encompass Small and Medium-sized Enterprises (SMEs), which constitute the backbone of numerous economies worldwide. The Latin American context presents a unique and multifaceted terrain for the adoption and implementation of CSR practices, particularly among SMEs, which encounter distinct challenges and opportunities in embracing socially responsible business models.

Over recent decades, the concept of CSR has undergone significant evolution, transitioning from a peripheral concern to a core tenet of business strategy (Carroll, 1999). It now encompasses a broad spectrum of practices through which companies integrate social, environmental, ethical, and human rights concerns into their fundamental business operations. For SMEs in Latin America, the adoption of CSR represents not merely a moral imperative but a strategic necessity in an increasingly competitive and globally interconnected marketplace.

Latin America, with its rich tapestry of cultures, economies, and social structures, provides a compelling backdrop for examining the dynamics of CSR adoption among SMEs. The region's economic landscape is characterized by a predominance of small and medium-sized businesses, which contribute significantly to employment, innovation, and economic growth (Ferraro & Rojo, 2018). However, these enterprises often operate within constraints of limited resources, informal structures, and challenging market conditions, doing the implementation of CSR initiatives particularly complex (Jamali et al., 2017).

Globally, there is mounting pressure from consumers, investors, and regulatory bodies for businesses of all sizes to demonstrate ethical and sustainable practices. The United Nations' Sustainable Development Goals (SDGs) and the principles of the United Nations (UN) Global Compact have established a global agenda for responsible business conduct, influencing policy and practice across the region (Kolk & van den Buuse, 2012). Additionally, the growing awareness of environmental challenges, social inequalities, and governance issues specific to Latin America has enhanced the relevance of CSR for local businesses (Casanova & Dumas, 2010; Cezarino et al., 2022).

In this context, the advent of Artificial Intelligence (AI) presents both opportunities and challenges for CSR adoption among Latin American SMEs. AI technologies are emerging as powerful tools that can potentially aid these enterprises in implementing and managing their CSR initiatives more effectively. For instance, AI-powered data analysis can enhance CSR reporting and impact measurement, allowing SMEs to better understand and communicate their social and environmental contributions. AI can also optimize resource allocation for CSR projects, a crucial advantage for SMEs operating with limited means. Moreover, AI-driven customer insights can help align CSR initiatives more closely with stakeholder expectations, increasing their effectiveness and relevance.

However, the integration of AI in CSR practices is not without its complexities, particularly for Latin American SMEs. These businesses must navigate the ethical considerations of AI deployment, ensure data privacy and security, and bridge potential technological gaps. The challenge lies in harnessing the benefits of AI for CSR while addressing these concerns within the unique socio-economic context of Latin America (Sposato, 2025).

Despite the recognized importance of CSR and the potential of AI to facilitate its implementation, the path to adoption for Latin American SMEs is fraught with obstacles. The path to CSR adoption for Latin American SMEs is full of obstacles. Many of these enterprises grapple with financial limitations, lack of expertise, and inadequate access to information and technology necessary for implementing comprehensive CSR strategies (Vives, 2014). Cultural factors, including traditional business practices and varying perceptions of corporate responsibility across different Latin American countries, also play a significant role in shaping the CSR landscape for SMEs in the region.

Despite these challenges, the potential benefits of CSR adoption for Latin American SMEs are substantial. Embracing socially responsible practices can enhance brand reputation, improve customer loyalty, attract and retain talented employees, and potentially open new market opportunities (Turyakira et al., 2014). Moreover, CSR can serve as a catalyst for innovation and efficiency, driving long-term sustainability and competitiveness in an increasingly globalized economy (Martínez-Conesa et al., 2017).

This study aims to explore the multifaceted process of CSR adoption among Latin American SMEs, focusing on the barriers they face and the strategies employed to overcome these obstacles. By examining the unique context of Latin American business environments, we seek to contribute to the broader understanding of CSR implementation in developing economies and among smaller enterprises.

The significance of this research lies in its potential to inform policy, practice, and academic discourse on CSR in the context of developing economies and SMEs. By identifying successful strategies and actions in CSR adoption, this study aims to provide practical insights for SME owners, managers, and policymakers in Latin America and beyond.

As we deepen into the complexities of CSR adoption among Latin American SMEs, this study highlights the challenges faced and celebrates the innovative approaches and resilience demonstrated by these enterprises in their journey towards more sustainable and responsible business practices. Through this exploration, we aim to pave the way for a more nuanced understanding of CSR implementation in diverse economic and cultural contexts, ultimately contributing to the development of more effective and inclusive CSR strategies for SMEs in Latin America and other regions.

## CONCEPTUAL FRAMEWORK

In Latin American SMEs, CSR operates within a complex interplay of global standards and local realities. This framework encompasses ethical, social, and environmental responsibilities that extend beyond profit-making. In Latin America, CSR is uniquely shaped by historical paternalism, strong community ties, and pressing socio-economic challenges that characterize the region (Peinado-Vara, 2011).

Global initiatives provide overarching principles for CSR, which Latin American SMEs often adapt to address local issues (Kowszyk et al., 2011). These principles serve as a guide for businesses to integrate social and environmental considerations into their operations. However, the application of these principles varies significantly based on the local context and specific challenges faced by SMEs in different Latin American countries.

The United Nations' 2030 Agenda and its 17 Sustainable Development Goals offer a comprehensive framework for aligning business operations with global sustainability objectives (Bican & Brem, 2020). For Latin American SMEs, this presents both significant challenges and unique opportunities. While resource constraints can hinder full adoption, the SDGs also open new markets and enhance competitiveness for those able to align their practices with these goals (Herrera, 2016).

In this context, CSR extends far beyond ethical considerations, encompassing important aspects of business operations. It includes risk management, reputation enhancement, innovation, and stakeholder relationships (Surroca et al., 2010). As markets in Latin America continue to evolve and consumer awareness of social and environmental issues grows, CSR is becoming increasingly relevant for the long-term success and sustainability of SMEs in the region.

## Literature Review and Context of CSR

The evolution of CSR reflects the dynamic interplay between changing societal expectations and global challenges (Agudelo et al., 2019). From its initial conceptualization as primarily philanthropic endeavors, CSR has expanded to encompass a broad spectrum of social, environmental, and ethical responsibilities. This shift represents a fundamental change in how businesses are perceived to interact with and impact their surrounding communities and environments (Carroll, 1999).

Global events, particularly the 2008 financial crisis, have played a pivotal role in highlighting the inextricable link between business practices and societal well-being (Forcadell & Aracil, 2017). These events have underscored the need for more responsible and sustainable business models, pushing CSR from the periphery to the center of corporate strategy. As a result, businesses of all sizes are now expected to consider their broader impact on society and the environment (Muñoz-Martín, 2013).

International organizations have been instrumental in shaping and standardizing CSR practices across different regions and industries. Initiatives like the UN Global Compact provide principle-based frameworks that promote universal sustainability principles (Comisión Europea, 2011). These frameworks have helped create a common language and set of expectations for CSR practices globally, influencing how businesses approach their social and environmental responsibilities.

In Latin America, the development of CSR has been influenced by a unique set of regional factors that distinguish it from CSR practices in other parts of the world (Vives & Peinado-Vara, 2011). Historical patterns of paternalism in business practices and strong philanthropic traditions have significantly shaped local interpretations of corporate responsibility. These cultural and historical factors continue to influence how CSR is understood and implemented across the region.

## Background and Environment of CSR

Over the past few decades CSR has evolved from a peripheral concern to a central tenet of business strategy (Carroll, 1999). This evolution reflects a growing recognition of the role businesses play in addressing social and environmental challenges. As global issues such as climate change, inequality, and human rights violations have gained prominence, the expectations placed on businesses to contribute to solutions have increased (Crane et al., 2019; Khan et al., 2021).

The UN has been instrumental in shaping the global understanding of CSR. Through its Global Compact initiative, the UN defines CSR as a principle-based approach to doing business (Kolk & van den Buuse, 2012). It outlines ten principles in the areas of human rights, labor, environment, and anti-corruption. According to the UN, corporate sustainability starts with a company's value system and a principled approach to doing business, emphasizing the need to operate in ways that meet fundamental responsibilities in key areas of social and environmental concern (Agudelo et al., 2019).

The European Union (EU) offers another influential perspective on CSR. In its renewed EU strategy for CSR, the EU defines CSR as "the responsibility of enterprises for their impacts on society" (European Commission, 2011). This definition broadens the scope of CSR beyond voluntary actions, emphasizing the need for businesses to consider and address their overall impact on society. The EU emphasizes that to fully meet their social responsibility, enterprises should integrate social, environmental, ethical, human rights, and consumer concerns into their business operations and core strategy (Alonso-Almeida et al., 2015).

In Latin America, the development of CSR has been influenced by unique regional factors. The legacy of paternalistic business practices and strong philanthropic traditions in many Latin American countries has shaped how CSR is understood and implemented. The region's experiences with economic liberalization and privatization in the 1990s increased the role and visibility of the private sector in addressing social issues (Casanova & Dumas, 2010).

The adoption of CSR in Latin America has also been influenced by the growing presence of multinational corporations and the integration of local businesses into global supply chains (Bianchi et al., 2017). These factors have introduced international CSR standards and practices to the region, often requiring local adaptations to fit the specific contexts of Latin American countries.

Furthermore, the pressing social and environmental challenges faced by many Latin American countries have shaped a regional understanding of CSR that often places strong emphasis on community development and social issues. This has resulted in CSR practices that are deeply rooted in local contexts and relationships, particularly among SMEs (Jamali et al., 2017).

The evolution of CSR in Latin America also reflects the region's increasing awareness of environmental issues and sustainable development challenges. Climate change, deforestation, and biodiversity loss have become critical concerns, influencing how businesses approach their environmental responsibilities. As CSR has evolved globally and regionally, so too has the way it is measured and reported. The development of international standards and reporting frameworks has provided tools for businesses to assess and communicate their CSR efforts. However, the adoption of these frameworks among Latin American SMEs remains limited, often due to resource constraints and the informal nature of many small businesses in the region (Vives, 2014).

The CSR landscape in Latin America is thus characterized by a blend of global standards and local realities. While influenced by international trends and frameworks, CSR practices in the region often reflect a more informal, community-oriented approach, particularly among SMEs. This context-specific nature of CSR in Latin America presents both challenges and opportunities for businesses seeking to implement socially responsible practices.

## CSR and Agenda 2030

The United Nations' 2030 Agenda for Sustainable Development, adopted in 2015, has significantly influenced the global approach to CSR (Bican & Brem, 2020). This agenda, which outlines 17 Sustainable Development Goals (SDGs), provides a comprehensive framework for addressing global challenges such as poverty, inequality, climate change, environmental degradation, peace, and justice. The SDGs have become a common language for discussing sustainable development across sectors and regions (Herrera, 2016).

For businesses, particularly SMEs, the SDGs provide a framework to align their strategies and operations with global priorities (Cantele & Zardini, 2018). This alignment can potentially create new business opportunities while contributing to societal progress. The integration of SDGs into CSR strategies represents a shift from a risk-management approach to one that emphasizes creating shared value and positive impact (Molteni & Pedrini, 2010). It encourages businesses to view social and environmental challenges as opportunities for innovation and growth (Martínez-Conesa et al., 2017; López Jiménez et al., 2021).

In the context of Latin American SMEs, the alignment of CSR with the SDGs presents both opportunities and challenges. On one hand, the SDGs offer a pathway for SMEs to contribute to national development priorities. Many Latin American countries have aligned their national development plans with the SDGs, creating an enabling environment for businesses to engage in sustainable practices (OCDE, 2021). This alignment can facilitate access to support mechanisms, including funding, capacity building, and policy incentives for SMEs engaging in SDG-aligned CSR initiatives (Hernández-Perlines & Rung-Hoch, 2017).

However, aligning with the SDGs also presents challenges for Latin American SMEs. The comprehensive nature of the SDGs can be overwhelming for small businesses with limited resources. Measuring and reporting progress towards the SDGs often requires sophisticated data collection and analysis capabilities, which many SMEs lack (Vives, 2014). Additionally, while the SDGs are interconnected, SMEs may need to prioritize certain goals based on their core competencies and local contexts, requiring strategic decision-making to balance various sustainability objectives with business realities (Choongo, 2017).

The SDGs also emphasize the importance of partnerships, encouraging collaboration between businesses, governments, and civil society. For Latin American SMEs, this focus on partnerships can open doors to new resources and expertise.

Collaborative efforts can help SMEs overcome resource limitations and scale up their positive impacts. By engaging in multi-stakeholder partnerships, SMEs can contribute to and benefit from collective efforts to address complex sustainability challenges in their local contexts.

Indeed, the alignment of CSR with the SDGs can enhance the competitiveness of Latin American SMEs in global markets. As international buyers and consumers increasingly prioritize sustainability, SMEs that can demonstrate their contribution to the SDGs may find new opportunities in global value chains. This alignment can serve as a differentiator, potentially opening access to new markets and customers who value sustainable and socially responsible business practices. For Latin American SMEs, this represents an opportunity to leverage their CSR efforts for business growth and international expansion.

## CSR in SMEs as a Business Strategy

The adoption of CSR by SMEs in Latin America is increasingly recognized not just as an ethical obligation, but as a strategic business imperative. This shift in perspective is driven by changing market dynamics, stakeholder expectations, and the realization that CSR can contribute to long-term business success and competitiveness. For Latin American SMEs, integrating CSR into their business strategy offers several potential benefits.

One of the primary benefits of CSR for SMEs is the enhancement of reputation and brand value. In markets where trust is a critical factor, CSR initiatives can significantly improve an SME's standing in the community. This is particularly important in Latin America, where personal relationships and community standing often play a significant role in business success. By demonstrating a commitment to social and environmental responsibility, SMEs can differentiate themselves from competitors and build stronger connections with customers and other stakeholders.

Moreover, CSR initiatives can drive innovation in products, services, and processes (Martínez-Conesa et al., 2017). Efforts to reduce environmental impact, for instance, can lead to more efficient resource use, resulting in cost savings and new product developments. This innovation can be a key differentiator for SMEs in competitive markets (Revell et al., 2010). By viewing social and environmental challenges as opportunities for innovation, SMEs can develop unique solutions that address local needs while creating new business opportunities.

In terms of market access, as larger corporations increasingly prioritize sustainability in their supply chains, SMEs with strong CSR practices are better positioned to secure contracts and partnerships (Bianchi et al., 2017). This is particularly important for Latin American SMEs looking to integrate into global value chains. By adopting CSR practices, these businesses can meet the increasingly stringent social and environmental criteria set by multinational corporations and international buyers (Perrini et al., 2007).

By demonstrating a commitment to social and environmental responsibility, SMEs can become more attractive employers, potentially reducing turnover and associated costs while fostering a more engaged and productive workforce (Baumann-Pauly et al., 2013). Employees, especially younger generations, often seek purpose-driven work environments (Siddiqui & Sposato, 2021; Khokhar et al., 2023). So, in this sense, SMEs could attract workers to stay in the company.

Effective CSR strategies can improve relationships with various stakeholders, including local communities, government entities, and Non-Governmental Organizations (NGOs) (Murillo & Lozano, 2006). This can lead to more supportive operating environments and potential collaborations, which can be particularly valuable for SMEs with limited resources. Strong community relationships can translate into customer loyalty, while positive engagement with government entities may result in more favorable policy environments or access to public sector opportunities (Vives, 2014).

While the relationship between CSR and financial performance is complex, evidence suggests that strategic CSR can contribute to long-term financial sustainability through enhanced efficiency, reputation, and market opportunities (Surroca et al., 2010). For SMEs, this can mean improved access to capital, as investors and financial institutions increasingly consider ESG (Environmental, Social, and Governance) factors in their decision-making processes (Cantele & Zardini, 2018).

However, the implementation of CSR as a business strategy in Latin American SMEs faces several challenges. Many SMEs struggle with limited financial and human resources to dedicate to CSR initiatives (Jamali et al., 2017). There's often a lack of awareness and understanding of how to effectively implement and benefit from CSR strategies among SME owners and managers (Vives, 2014). The immediate pressures of day-to-day operations and survival can overshadow long-term strategic CSR considerations (Jenkins, 2006).

SMEs often find it challenging to measure the impact of their CSR initiatives and effectively communicate these efforts to stakeholders (Choongo, 2017). The high level of informality in Latin American economies can make it difficult to implement and document formal CSR practices. Additionally, the diverse nature of SMEs means that there is no one-size-fits-all approach to CSR, requiring each business to tailor its strategy to its specific context and capabilities (Spence, 2016).

Despite these challenges, there's growing recognition among Latin American SMEs of the strategic value of CSR (Pastrana & Sriramesh, 2014). Many are finding innovative ways to integrate social and environmental considerations into their business models, often leveraging their agility and close community ties (Hernández-Perlines & Rung-Hoch, 2017). The strategic approach to CSR in Latin American

SMEs often differs from that of larger corporations. It tends to be more informal, deeply rooted in the personal values of business owners, and closely tied to local community needs (López Jiménez et al., 2022).

This context-specific approach can be a strength, allowing for more authentic and impactful CSR initiatives. SMEs are often able to respond more quickly to local needs and can create highly tailored solutions to social and environmental challenges in their communities. This agility and local focus can result in CSR initiatives that are particularly effective and well-received by stakeholders.

As the business landscape in Latin America continues to evolve, with increasing emphasis on sustainability and social responsibility, SMEs that strategically integrate CSR into their core business practices are likely to find themselves better positioned for long-term success (Stoian & Gilman, 2017). The challenge lies in developing approaches that are both strategically beneficial for the business and meaningfully impactful for society and the environment (Soundararajan et al., 2018).

## Challenges in the Incorporation of CSR Inside SMEs

The incorporation of CSR into SMEs presents a unique set of challenges, particularly in the Latin American context. While larger corporations often have dedicated resources and departments for CSR initiatives, SMEs typically operate with limited financial and human resources, making the integration of comprehensive CSR strategies more challenging (Jenkins, 2006; Baumann-Pauly et al., 2013).

One of the primary obstacles is the lack of awareness and understanding of CSR concepts and practices among SME owners and managers (Vives, 2014). Many may perceive CSR as a luxury reserved for larger companies or as an additional cost rather than a strategic investment. This misconception can lead to reluctance in adopting CSR practices, even when they could potentially benefit the business in the long term (Jamali et al., 2017).

The informal nature of many SMEs in Latin America further complicates the implementation of structured CSR programs (Ferraro & Rojo, 2018; Mahmood et al., 2021). With less formalized management systems and reporting processes, these businesses may struggle to systematically integrate CSR into their operations and effectively measure and communicate their social and environmental impacts (Choongo, 2017).

Moreover, SMEs often face more immediate pressures related to day-to-day operations and financial survival, which can overshadow long-term strategic considerations like CSR (Spence, 2016). The perceived trade-off between short-term profitability and long-term sustainability can discourage SMEs from investing time and resources in CSR initiatives, even when such initiatives could ultimately contribute to their competitiveness and resilience (Stoian & Gilman, 2017).

Despite these challenges, many SMEs in Latin America are finding innovative ways to incorporate CSR into their business models. By leveraging their agility, close community ties, and intimate knowledge of local contexts, these enterprises are developing unique approaches to social responsibility that are both impactful and aligned with their business objectives (Pastrana & Sriramesh, 2014; Hernández-Perlines & Rung-Hoch, 2017). As with many aspects of business in the 21st century, these CSR efforts are unfolding against the backdrop of the AI revolution.

## Advantages and Opportunities for SMEs to be Socially Responsible

Despite the challenges, there are numerous advantages and opportunities for SMEs in Latin America to embrace social responsibility. These benefits can contribute significantly to their long-term success and competitiveness in an increasingly conscious marketplace (Turyakira et al., 2014; Cantele & Zardini, 2018).

One of the primary advantages is enhanced reputation and brand value (Surroca et al., 2010). In the close-knit communities where many Latin American SMEs operate, a strong reputation for social responsibility can translate directly into customer loyalty and business opportunities. By demonstrating commitment to local social and environmental issues, SMEs can differentiate themselves from competitors and build stronger, more trusting relationships with their stakeholders (Jenkins, 2006; Murillo & Lozano, 2006).

CSR can also drive innovation within SMEs (Martínez-Conesa et al., 2017). By considering social and environmental factors in their operations, these businesses often discover new, more efficient ways of working. This can lead to cost savings, for example through reduced energy consumption or waste reduction, as well as the development of new products or services that address social or environmental needs (Revell et al., 2010). Such innovation can open up new market opportunities and revenue streams (Herrera, 2016).

Improved access to markets is another significant opportunity (Bianchi et al., 2017). As larger corporations increasingly prioritize sustainability in their supply chains, SMEs with strong CSR practices are better positioned to secure contracts and partnerships. This is particularly relevant for Latin American SMEs looking to integrate into global value chains, where meeting international social and environmental standards can be a key differentiator (Perrini et al., 2007).

In the competitive Latin American labor market, demonstrating a commitment to social and environmental responsibility can make an SME a more attractive employer, particularly to younger generations who often prioritize purpose-driven work environments. This can lead to reduced turnover, increased employee engagement, and ultimately, improved productivity (Baumann-Pauly et al., 2013).

Furthermore, strong CSR practices can improve relationships with various stakeholders, including local communities, government entities, and NGOs. These improved relationships can translate into a more supportive operating environment, potential collaborations, and even preferential treatment in terms of licenses or permits. For SMEs operating in challenging business environments, such positive relationships can be important for long-term success.

Another advantage is the potential for improved risk management (Bernal-Conesa et al., 2017). By proactively addressing social and environmental issues, SMEs can mitigate risks associated with regulatory non-compliance, environmental incidents, or labor disputes (López Jiménez et al., 2023). This is particularly relevant in the context of evolving regulatory landscapes across Latin American countries, where environmental and social regulations are becoming increasingly stringent (Forcadell & Aracil, 2017). This risk mitigation can be particularly valuable for SMEs, which may have less capacity to absorb the impacts of unforeseen challenges or crises.

While the relationship between CSR and financial performance is complex, there is growing evidence that strategic CSR can contribute to long-term financial sustainability. For SMEs, this can mean improved access to capital, as investors and financial institutions increasingly consider ESG (Environmental, Social, and Governance) factors in their decision-making processes.

## Obstacles and Risks for SMEs in the Application of CSR

While the potential benefits of CSR for SMEs are significant, there are also numerous obstacles and risks that these businesses face in implementing social responsibility practices, particularly in the Latin American context. One of the primary obstacles is the limited financial and human resources typically available to SMEs (Jenkins, 2006). Unlike larger corporations, small businesses often operate with tight budgets and lean teams, making it challenging to allocate resources specifically to CSR initiatives. The perceived high costs of implementing CSR programs, especially in the short term, can discourage SME owners from taking action, even when they recognize the potential long-term benefits.

Another significant challenge is the lack of knowledge and expertise in CSR practices among SME owners and managers (Spence, 2016). Many may not fully understand what CSR entails or how to effectively implement it within their business context. This knowledge gap can lead to ineffective or superficial CSR efforts that fail to deliver meaningful impact or business benefits. Additionally, the absence of clear guidelines or standards specifically tailored to SMEs in Latin America can make it difficult for these businesses to know where to start or how to measure their progress in CSR implementation (Kowszyk et al., 2011).

The informal nature of many SMEs in Latin America presents another obstacle to CSR adoption. With less structured management systems and reporting processes, these businesses may struggle to systematically integrate CSR into their operations. This informality can also make it difficult to measure and communicate the impacts of CSR initiatives, which is significant for realizing many of the potential benefits. Furthermore, the high level of informality in some sectors can create challenges in ensuring compliance with labor and environmental standards, which are often key components of CSR programs (Pastrana & Sriramesh, 2014).

Short-term thinking and the pressure of immediate business needs can also hinder CSR adoption (Stoian & Gilman, 2017). SMEs often face day-to-day challenges related to cash flow, market competition, and operational issues. In this context, long-term investments in CSR may be seen as a luxury they cannot afford, even if such investments could ultimately contribute to their resilience and competitiveness. This focus on short-term survival can make it difficult for SMEs to prioritize CSR initiatives that may not show immediate financial returns (Choongo, 2017).

There's also a risk of greenwashing, where businesses may be tempted to overstate their CSR efforts for marketing purposes without making substantive changes (Berger & Nakata, 2013). This can backfire, damaging the company's reputation if stakeholders perceive the CSR claims as insincere or misleading. In the age of social media and increased transparency, such reputational risks can be particularly damaging for SMEs that often rely heavily on local community trust and relationships (Jamali et al., 2017).

Another potential risk is the misalignment of CSR initiatives with the core business strategy (Martínez-Conesa et al., 2017). If CSR efforts are not well-integrated with the company's overall objectives and operations, they may become a distraction or drain on resources rather than a source of value creation. This misalignment can occur when CSR is viewed as a separate "add-on" rather than an integral part of the business model, leading to inefficiencies and reduced impact (Spence, 2016).

Another challenge important to mention is measuring and demonstrating the impact of CSR initiatives (Choongo, 2017). Without clear metrics and reporting mechanisms, it can be difficult for SMEs to quantify the benefits of their CSR efforts, both internally and to external stakeholders. This can make it hard to justify continued investment in CSR, especially in the face of competing business priorities. The lack of standardized measurement tools specifically designed for SMEs can further complicate this process, making it challenging for these businesses to effectively communicate their CSR performance to stakeholders.

## Practical Approaches in the Integration of CSR in SMEs

Despite the challenges, there are several practical approaches that SMEs in Latin America can adopt to effectively integrate CSR into their operations. These approaches can help SMEs overcome resource constraints and realize the benefits of social responsibility (Jamali et al., 2017). Firstly, SMEs can start small and focus on incremental changes (Jenkins, 2006). Rather than trying to implement a comprehensive CSR program all at once, businesses can identify one or two key areas where they can make a meaningful impact. This could be related to their core business activities, such as improving energy efficiency in their operations or ensuring fair labor practices in their supply chain. By starting with manageable initiatives, SMEs can build momentum and gradually expand their CSR efforts over time (Murillo & Lozano, 2006).

Collaboration and partnerships can be a powerful approach for SMEs with limited resources (Bianchi et al., 2017). By joining forces with other local businesses, industry associations, or NGOs, SMEs can pool resources, share knowledge, and amplify their impact. Such collaborations can also help SMEs access expertise and resources they might not have internally. For example, a group of SMEs in the same industry could work together to develop shared supplier auditing processes, reducing the cost and complexity for each individual business while improving overall supply chain sustainability (Perrini et al., 2007).

Leveraging existing community connections is another effective strategy for Latin American SMEs (Pastrana & Sriramesh, 2014). Many small businesses already have strong ties to their local communities. By formalizing and expanding these existing relationships into CSR initiatives, SMEs can create impactful programs that are well-aligned with local needs and expectations. This approach enhances the effectiveness of CSR efforts and strengthens the business's local reputation and relationships, which can be essencial for long-term success.

Integrating CSR into core business processes, rather than treating it as a separate activity, can help SMEs maximize the impact of their efforts (Martínez-Conesa et al., 2017). This could involve considering social and environmental factors in product design, procurement decisions, or marketing strategies. By embedding CSR principles into day-to-day operations, SMEs can ensure that social responsibility becomes a natural part of how they do business. This integration can lead to more sustainable and impactful CSR initiatives that are closely aligned with the company's overall objectives and capabilities (Spence, 2016).

Another factor which is important to mention is the employee engagement, which is relevant for successful CSR integration in SMEs. By involving employees in the planning and implementation of CSR initiatives, businesses can tap into their team's creativity and local knowledge. This approach can also enhance employee satisfaction and loyalty, contributing to the overall success of the CSR efforts. Moreover, engaged employees can become powerful advocates for the company's CSR initiatives, both within the organization and in their interactions with customers and the broader community (Celma et al., 2014).

Utilizing digital tools and platforms can help SMEs overcome resource constraints in implementing and communicating their CSR efforts (Bican & Brem, 2020; Díaz-Arancibia et al., 2024). Social media, for instance, can be an effective and low-cost way to engage with stakeholders and showcase CSR initiatives. Various online tools are also available to help SMEs measure and report on their social and environmental impacts. These digital solutions can help level the playing field, allowing smaller businesses to implement and communicate their CSR efforts effectively, even with limited resources.

SMEs can also benefit from adopting a learning mindset towards CSR. By starting with pilot projects, measuring outcomes, and continuously refining their approach, SMEs can develop CSR strategies that are both impactful and sustainable in the long term. This iterative approach allows for flexibility and adaptation, which is particularly valuable in the dynamic business environments of Latin America. It also helps SMEs to build their CSR capabilities over time, gradually increasing the sophistication and impact of their initiatives as they gain experience and resources (Jamali et al., 2017).

Another practical approach is for SMEs to focus on CSR initiatives that are closely aligned with their core competencies and business objectives (Stoian & Gilman, 2017). By identifying areas where their business activities naturally intersect with social or environmental issues, SMEs can develop CSR programs that contribute to societal goals and enhance their competitive advantage. For example, a small food producer might focus on sustainable agriculture practices, which can both address environmental concerns and improve the quality and marketability of their products (Revell et al., 2010).

Another interesting point to consider is that SMEs can leverage industry-specific guidelines and standards to guide their CSR efforts (Kowszyk et al., 2011). While comprehensive CSR frameworks might be overwhelming, many industries have developed sector-specific guidelines that are more accessible to smaller businesses. By aligning with these standards, SMEs can ensure their CSR efforts are relevant and recognized within their industry, potentially opening up new business opportunities and partnerships.

## Effects of the Application of CSR Within SMEs

The application of CSR within SMEs can have far-reaching effects on various aspects of the business. These impacts extend beyond mere compliance with ethical standards, influencing the company's operations, stakeholder relationships, and overall performance in significant ways (Turyakira et al., 2014).

One of the primary effects is the enhancement of the company's reputation and brand image. SMEs that actively engage in CSR often experience improved perception among customers, employees, and the broader community. This positive reputation can translate into increased customer loyalty, better employee retention, and stronger community support, all of which contribute to the long-term sustainability of the business (Jenkins, 2006).

CSR initiatives can also drive innovation within SMEs (Martínez-Conesa et al., 2017). By considering social and environmental factors in their operations, these businesses often discover new, more efficient ways of working. This can lead to the development of innovative products or services that address societal needs while opening new market opportunities. Such innovation can be a key differentiator for SMEs in competitive markets. Additionally, CSR practices can position SMEs to better leverage emerging technologies. For instance, companies with strong ethical frameworks and CSR policies may find it easier to responsibly integrate AI technologies, aligning their use with societal values and expectations.

Furthermore, the implementation of CSR practices often results in improved operational efficiency (Revell et al., 2010). Initiatives aimed at reducing energy consumption, minimizing waste, or optimizing resource use can lead to significant cost savings over time. These efficiencies benefit the final result and contribute to the company's environmental sustainability goals (Cantele & Zardini, 2018).

The adoption of CSR can also enhance an SME's ability to attract and retain talent (Celma et al., 2014). In today's job market, particularly among younger generations, there is a growing preference for employers who demonstrate a commitment to social and environmental responsibility. By engaging in meaningful CSR initiatives, SMEs can position themselves as attractive employers, potentially gaining access to a wider pool of skilled workers.

## Importance of CSR for SMEs With Customers and Society

The importance of CSR for SMEs in their relationships with customers and society cannot be overstated. In an era of increased social consciousness and transparency, CSR has become an essential factor in shaping consumer perceptions and purchasing decisions. For SMEs, effective CSR practices can be a powerful tool for building strong, lasting relationships with customers and the broader community (Murillo & Lozano, 2006).

One of the primary ways CSR impacts customer relationships is through enhanced brand reputation (Surroca et al., 2010). Consumers are increasingly looking to support businesses that align with their values and demonstrate a commitment to social and environmental responsibility. SMEs that actively engage in CSR initiatives can differentiate themselves in the marketplace, attracting customers who prioritize ethical and sustainable business practices. This alignment of values can lead to increased customer loyalty and advocacy, with satisfied customers more likely to recommend the business to others (Jenkins, 2006).

Moreover, CSR can play a significant role in building trust with customers. In the age of social media and instant information sharing, consumers are more aware than ever of business practices and their impacts. SMEs that are transparent about their CSR efforts and can demonstrate genuine commitment to social and environmental causes are more likely to earn the trust of their customers. This trust is particularly important for SMEs, which often rely heavily on repeat business and word-of-mouth recommendations.

CSR initiatives can also provide opportunities for direct engagement with customers and the community (Murillo & Lozano, 2006). For example, SMEs might involve customers in charitable initiatives, sustainability programs, or local community projects. This engagement strengthens the bond between the business and its customers and creates a sense of shared purpose and community impact. Such initiatives can transform customers from mere consumers into engaged stakeholders who feel a personal connection to the business and its values.

From a societal perspective, CSR practices of SMEs can have a significant cumulative impact (Spence, 2016). While individual SMEs may have a smaller footprint compared to large corporations, collectively they represent a substantial portion of the business landscape in most economies. When SMEs embrace CSR, they contribute to addressing broader societal challenges, from environmental sustainability to social equity. This collective impact can be particularly significant in local communities, where SMEs often play a central role in the economic and social fabric (Ferraro & Rojo, 2018).

Furthermore, CSR initiatives by SMEs can inspire broader societal change (Herrera, 2016). As SMEs are often closely connected to their local communities, their CSR efforts can have a ripple effect, inspiring other businesses, community members, and even local policymakers to take action on social and environmental issues. This can lead to a virtuous cycle of positive change, with SMEs serving as catalysts for broader community development and sustainability initiatives (Bianchi et al., 2017).

CSR can also help SMEs navigate the complex regulatory landscape and societal expectations (Bernal-Conesa et al., 2017). As governments and societies increasingly prioritize sustainable development, businesses that proactively embrace CSR are better positioned to adapt to new regulations and societal norms. This forward-thinking approach can help SMEs stay ahead of compliance requirements and avoid potential penalties or reputational damage associated with non-compliance (Forcadell & Aracil, 2017).

We can affirm that the importance of CSR for SMEs in their relationship with customers and society is reflected in its potential to drive innovation and market opportunities (Martínez-Conesa et al., 2017). By engaging with societal challenges through CSR initiatives, SMEs can identify unmet needs and develop innovative products or services that address these issues. This contributes to solving societal problems and open up new market segments and revenue streams for the business (Revell et al., 2010).

## Improving the Growth and Competitiveness of Socially Responsible SMEs

The adoption of CSR practices can significantly enhance the growth and competitiveness of SMEs (Turyakira et al., 2014). By integrating social and environmental considerations into their business strategies, SMEs can unlock new opportunities for growth while strengthening their market position (Stoian & Gilman, 2017).

One of the primary ways CSR improves competitiveness is through differentiation. In increasingly crowded markets, CSR can be a key differentiator that sets an SME apart from its competitors. Consumers, particularly in younger demographics, are showing a growing preference for brands that demonstrate social and environmental responsibility. By effectively communicating their CSR initiatives, SMEs can attract these conscious consumers, potentially commanding premium prices for products or services perceived as more ethical or sustainable (Surroca et al., 2010).

CSR can also drive innovation within SMEs, leading to improved competitiveness (Martínez-Conesa et al., 2017). By considering social and environmental factors in their operations, businesses often discover new, more efficient ways of working or identify opportunities for innovative products and services. For example, efforts to reduce environmental impact might lead to the development of eco-friendly products that meet emerging market demands. This innovation can open up new market segments and revenue streams, fueling growth and enhancing the SME's competitive position (Revell et al., 2010).

Furthermore, CSR practices can lead to significant cost savings and operational efficiencies, directly impacting an SME's bottom line and competitiveness (Cantele & Zardini, 2018). Initiatives aimed at reducing energy consumption, minimizing waste, or optimizing resource use can result in substantial cost reductions over time. These savings can be reinvested in the business, funding growth initiatives or allowing the SME to offer more competitive pricing (Bernal-Conesa et al., 2017).

The adoption of CSR can also enhance an SME's ability to attract and retain talent, which is important for growth and competitiveness (Celma et al., 2014). In today's job market, many skilled professionals, especially among younger generations, prioritize working for companies that demonstrate a commitment to social and environmental responsibility. By engaging in meaningful CSR initiatives, SMEs can position themselves as attractive employers, potentially gaining access to a wider pool of talented employees who can drive the business forward.

CSR can play a significant role in improving an SME's access to capital and partnerships (Surroca et al., 2010). As investors and larger corporations increasingly consider Environmental, Social, and Governance (ESG) factors in their decision-making, SMEs with strong CSR practices may find it easier to secure funding or enter into strategic partnerships. This improved access to resources and networks can be a significant driver of growth and competitiveness.

Moreover, CSR can help SMEs build stronger, more resilient supply chains (Perrini et al., 2007). By engaging suppliers on social and environmental issues, SMEs can reduce risks associated with supply chain disruptions, reputational damage, or regulatory non-compliance. This enhanced supply chain resilience can be a significant competitive advantage, particularly in times of crisis or rapid market changes (Bianchi et al., 2017). In the case of the internationalization efforts of SMEs, global markets increasingly demand sustainable and socially responsible business practices, and SMEs with strong CSR credentials may find it easier to enter new markets or integrate into global value chains. This can open up significant growth opportunities and enhance the SME's competitiveness on an international scale.

## Involvement of CSR in the Responses of Latin American SMEs to the Demands of Different Interest Groups

Latin American SMEs have been increasingly using CSR as a strategic tool to respond to the diverse demands of various stakeholder groups (Vives & Peinado-Vara, 2011). These responses reflect the unique socio-economic context of the region and demonstrate how SMEs are adapting global CSR principles to address local challenges and expectations (Haslam, 2007).

In response to environmental concerns raised by local communities and NGOs, many Latin American SMEs have implemented resource conservation initiatives (Revell et al., 2010). These often include water recycling systems, energy efficiency measures, and waste reduction programs. Some agricultural SMEs have transitioned to organic farming practices or obtained sustainability certifications to meet the growing demand for environmentally responsible products (Aninat, 2015). These efforts can address ecological concerns and often result in cost savings and improved relationships with local stakeholders (Bernal-Conesa et al., 2017).

To address social issues raised by employees and labor advocacy groups, numerous SMEs in the region have focused on improving working conditions and employee welfare (Celma et al., 2014). This includes implementing fair wage policies, offering profit-sharing schemes, and providing additional benefits such as health insurance or educational support. Some companies have also established vocational training programs, particularly for disadvantaged youth, as part of their commitment to community development and social inclusion (Jamali et al., 2017).

In response to government initiatives promoting innovation and social inclusion, some technology-focused SMEs have developed products and services aimed at addressing societal needs (Herrera, 2016). This includes creating affordable solutions for rural connectivity, developing educational technology for underserved communities, or innovating in areas such as renewable energy and sustainable agriculture. These efforts often align with national development priorities, leading to potential partnerships with public sector entities and expanded market opportunities (Bianchi et al., 2017).

To meet the growing demands of international markets and conscious consumers for sustainable and ethically sourced products, many export-oriented SMEs in Latin America have adopted fair trade practices and obtained various sustainability certifications (Perrini et al., 2007). This is particularly evident in sectors such as agriculture, textiles, and handicrafts. Some companies have gone further by implementing traceability systems or partnering with indigenous communities to ensure ethical sourcing and benefit-sharing (Pastrana & Sriramesh, 2014).

In response to increasing pressure for transparency and ethical practices from customers and regulatory bodies, a growing number of Latin American SMEs have implemented comprehensive codes of conduct and established reporting systems for their social and environmental impacts (Forcadell & Aracil, 2017). Many have also initiated regular stakeholder dialogues to better understand and address community concerns. This proactive approach to transparency and stakeholder engagement has helped these SMEs build trust and navigate increasingly complex regulatory environments (Vives, 2014).

The tourism sector in Latin America has seen SMEs responding to the demand for sustainable and culturally sensitive travel experiences (Bianchi et al., 2017). Many small tourism operators have developed eco-friendly tour packages that minimize environmental impact and contribute to local conservation efforts. There's also a trend towards community-based tourism initiatives that ensure economic benefits are shared with local and indigenous populations (Kowszyk et al., 2011).

Across various sectors, Latin American SMEs are increasingly integrating CSR into their core business strategies rather than treating it as a separate initiative (Martínez-Conesa et al., 2017). This integration is often driven by a recognition that addressing social and environmental concerns can also create business value through innovation, improved efficiency, enhanced reputation, and access to new markets (Cantele & Zardini, 2018).

Collaboration has emerged as a key feature of CSR responses among Latin American SMEs (Jamali et al., 2017). Many companies are partnering with NGOs, academic institutions, government agencies, and even other businesses to enhance the impact of their CSR initiatives. These collaborations often allow SMEs to overcome resource limitations and access specialized expertise in addressing complex social or environmental challenges (Bianchi et al., 2017).

The responses of Latin American SMEs to stakeholder demands through CSR initiatives are characterized by a strong focus on local context and community needs (Spence, 2016). While global CSR principles and frameworks inform these efforts, successful strategies are typically tailored to address specific regional or local challenges and opportunities. This localized approach allows SMEs to create more meaningful impact and build stronger relationships with their immediate stakeholders (Murillo & Lozano, 2006).

In other words, the involvement of CSR in the responses of Latin American SMEs to stakeholder demands reflects a growing recognition of the strategic importance of social and environmental responsibility (Stoian & Gilman, 2017). By aligning their CSR efforts with both stakeholder expectations and business objectives, these SMEs are addressing societal challenges and enhancing their competitiveness and resilience in an increasingly conscious marketplace. This trend suggests a promising trajectory for the future of sustainable and responsible business practices among SMEs in Latin America.

## METHODOLOGY

This study employed a quantitative approach based on a cross-sectional research design to examine the implementation of CSR practices in Latin American SMEs. This method was chosen as it allows for data collection at a specific point in time, providing a snapshot of current CSR practices and enabling the exploration of relationships between different variables. The cross-sectional design is particularly suitable for this study as it offers insights into the current state of CSR adoption among SMEs in Latin America, a region where such practices are still evolving.

The sample consisted of 306 directors of SMEs in Latin America, selected through stratified sampling by country and industry sector. This sampling technique was chosen to ensure adequate representation of the diverse national and sectoral contexts in the region. The study included Argentina, Brazil, Chile, Colombia, Mexico, and Peru, representing the largest economies in Latin America. These countries were selected not only for their economic significance but also because they offer a variety of regulatory environments and stages of CSR development, providing a comprehensive view of the region.

A structured questionnaire was developed as the primary data collection instrument. The questionnaire was designed based on existing literature on CSR and SMEs, with careful adaptation to the Latin American context. This adaptation process involved consulting with regional experts and conducting pilot tests to ensure the relevance and clarity of questions in the local business environment. The questionnaire addressed several key dimensions including company characteristics, knowledge and perception of CSR, current CSR practices (encompassing environmental, social, labor, and ethical aspects), motivations for implementing CSR practices, perceived barriers to CSR implementation, perceived benefits of CSR practices, the relationship between innovation and CSR, the impact of digital transformation on CSR, and equality and diversity practices.

The questionnaire primarily used closed questions with 5-point Likert scales to facilitate quantitative analysis. This format was chosen for its ability to capture nuanced responses while still allowing for statistical analysis. Additionally, open-ended questions were included to capture qualitative insights that might not be fully addressed by the structured responses. This mixed approach allowed for a richer dataset, combining the benefits of quantitative measurement with the depth of qualitative insights.

Data collection was conducted through a combination of online surveys and telephone interviews. This dual approach was adopted to maximize response rates and to accommodate the varying technological capacities and preferences of SMEs across the region. Online surveys offered efficiency and reach, while telephone interviews provided an opportunity for clarification and more detailed responses.

For data analysis, SPSS statistical software was employed due to its robust capabilities in handling complex quantitative data. The analysis encompassed several techniques to provide a comprehensive understanding of the data. Descriptive analysis was used to offer an overview of CSR practices in Latin American SMEs, providing baseline information on the current state of CSR adoption. Correlation analysis explored relationships between variables, such as company size and level of CSR implementation, offering insights into factors that might influence CSR practices. Multiple regression analysis was conducted to identify the factors that influence the adoption of CSR practices, allowing for a more nuanced understanding of the drivers of CSR in the region. Analysis of variance (ANOVA) was employed to compare differences in CSR practices across countries and sectors, highlighting regional and industry-specific trends. Lastly, factor analysis was used to identify the underlying dimensions of CSR practices in Latin American SMEs and micro-enterprises, providing a deeper understanding of how different aspects of CSR are conceptualized and implemented in the region.

It is important to acknowledge the potential limitations of this study. The cross-sectional nature of the design, while providing valuable insights into the current state of CSR practices, does not allow for the establishment of causal relationships or the tracking of changes over time. This limitation suggests the potential value of future longitudinal studies in this area. Additionally, while the stratified sampling technique aimed to ensure representation, the sample may not be fully representative of all SMEs in Latin America, particularly given the vast diversity of businesses in the region. Furthermore, the reliance on self-reported responses introduces the possibility of social desirability bias, where respondents may overreport positive CSR practices. To mitigate this, the questionnaire was designed with carefully worded questions and assurances of anonymity, but the potential for bias should still be considered when interpreting the results. Despite these limitations, this methodology provides a robust framework for examining CSR practices among SMEs in Latin America, offering valuable insights into this important and evolving area of business practice in the region.

## RESULTS

The analysis of surveys conducted with directors of SMEs in Latin America reveals significant findings about the implementation of CSR practices in these companies. The following results, organized into different thematic categories, provide insights into the most common CSR practices, barriers to implementation, perceived benefits, and motivations for adopting CSR among Latin American SMEs. These findings provide valuable insights into the current state of CSR implementation among Latin American SMEs, highlighting both progress and areas for potential growth and support.

In figure 1 it is shown the percentage of SMEs implementing various CSR practices, highlighting the most common initiatives among Latin American companies. Environmental practices such as recycling (47.4%) and energy saving (41.3%) are considered the most widely implemented CSR initiatives among Latin American SMEs. These are followed by labor policies like non-discrimination (39.1%) and employee training programs (35.7%). Community support initiatives (28.5%) and ethical codes (16.9%) are less frequently adopted. This distribution suggests that SMEs may be prioritizing practices that offer more immediate tangible benefits or are easier to implement within their operational constraints.

*Figure 1. Most implemented CSR practices in Latin American SMEs*

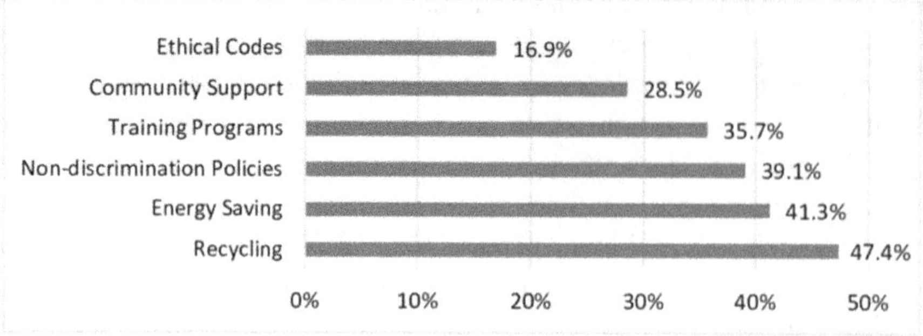


*Source: Authors' own work*

This radar chart (figure 2) illustrates the main obstacles to CSR implementation, as perceived by SME directors, rated on a scale of 1 to 5, with 5 being the most significant barrier. The most significant barriers to CSR implementation, as reported by SME directors, are implementation costs (3.6) and lack of knowledge (3.4). These are followed by lack of time (3.1) and lack of government support (2.8). The difficulty in measuring CSR impact is also a considerable barrier (2.8). These ratings indicate that financial and knowledge-related constraints are the primary challenges SMEs face in implementing CSR practices, suggesting a need for more accessible resources and support in these areas.

*Figure 2. Barriers to CSR implementation in Latin American SMEs (scale of 1 to 5)*

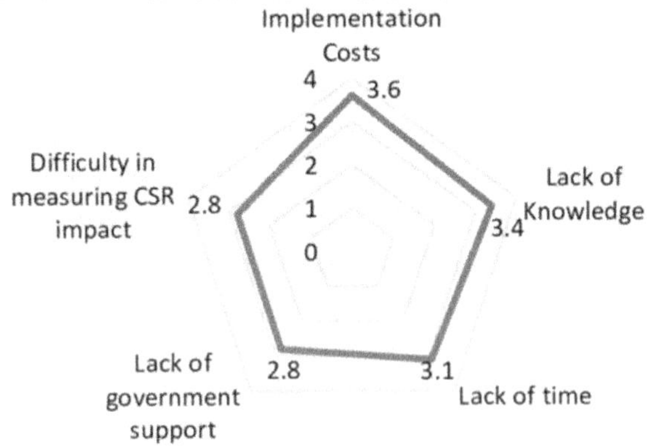


*Source: Authors' own work*

Figure 3 shows the distribution of perceived benefits from CSR practices among Latin American SMEs, as reported by their directors. Improved reputation (33.2%) and increased employee satisfaction (24.1%) are the most recognized benefits of CSR practices among SME directors. Operational efficiency is also a significant perceived benefit (18.3%). Access to new markets (13.4%) and long-term cost reduction (11%) are recognized as benefits, although to a lesser extent. This distribution suggests that SME directors primarily view CSR as a tool for enhancing company image and employee relations, with less emphasis on its potential for market expansion and cost savings.

*Figure 3. Benefits of CSR practices in Latin American SMEs*

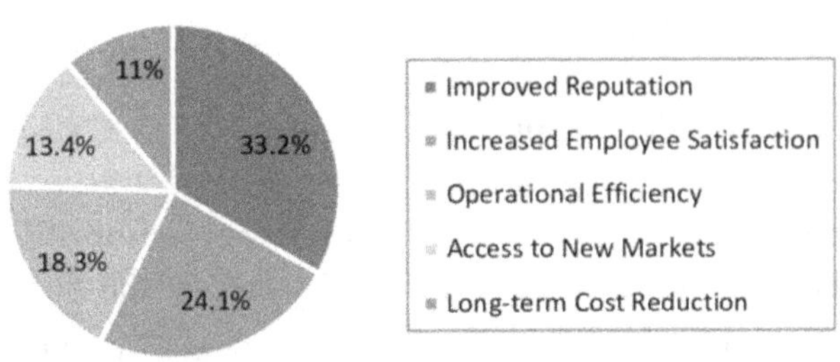


*Source: Authors' own work*

Figure 4 shows the primary motivations for SMEs to implement CSR practices in Latin America, as reported by their directors. Ethical considerations (4.5) and improving company image (4.2) are the strongest motivators for implementing CSR among Latin American SMEs. Attracting and retaining employees (3.8) and meeting customer expectations (3.6) are also significant motivators. Regulatory compliance (3.4), cost savings (3), and accessing new markets (2.8) are rated as less important motivators. This ranking suggests that SME directors are primarily driven by moral and reputational factors in their CSR decisions, with less emphasis on potential business advantages such as cost reduction or market expansion.

*Figure 4. Motivations for implementing CSR in Latin American SMEs (scale of 1 to 5)*

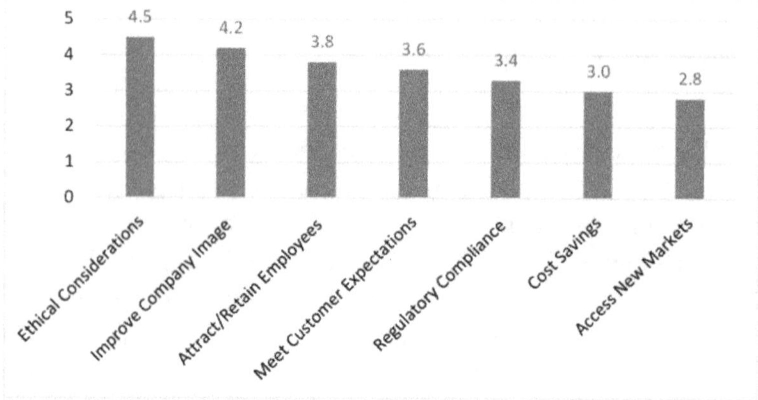


*Source: Authors' own work*

## DISCUSSION AND CONCLUSIONS

This study has provided a comprehensive exploration of CSR among SMEs in Latin America, offering valuable insights into the current state, challenges, and opportunities for CSR implementation in this relevant sector of the Latin American economy. The theoretical framework established at the outset of this study highlighted the evolving nature of CSR and its growing importance in the global business environment. There is an important need to consider CSR not just as a set of practices, but as a strategic approach that integrates social, environmental, and ethical concerns into core business operations.

Our literature review revealed a significant gap in understanding CSR practices among SMEs in Latin America. While CSR has gained traction among larger corporations globally, its adoption and implementation among SMEs have been less studied. This research gap underscored the importance of empirical investigation into CSR practices in this significant yet often overlooked segment of the business community. For Latin American SMEs, CSR represents a complex interplay of global standards and local realities, shaped by the region's unique socio-economic context, historical patterns of business engagement with society, and pressing developmental challenges.

The empirical study, conducted through a survey of SME directors across major Latin American economies, provided evidence to support and expand upon the theoretical foundations. The findings confirmed some existing understandings of CSR in SMEs while revealing new patterns specific to the Latin American context. The prevalence of environmental practices as the primary form of CSR implementation suggests that SMEs prioritize tangible, operational benefits in their CSR efforts. This presents an opportunity to use environmental CSR as a gateway to broader CSR implementation.

A key finding from the empirical study was the strong ethical motivations driving CSR adoption among Latin American SME directors. This ethical foundation provides a solid basis for expanding CSR practices. However, it also highlights a potential limitation: the predominantly philanthropic view of CSR may hinder its full integration into core business strategies. An inconclusive result emerged regarding the perceived benefits of CSR. While improved reputation and increased employee satisfaction were widely recognized, the strategic benefits such as access to new markets and long-term cost reduction were less acknowledged. This ambiguity may stem from the difficulty in measuring and attributing these long-term strategic outcomes directly to CSR initiatives. The lack of clear consensus on these strategic benefits suggests a need for further research to clarify the relationship between CSR implementation and long-term business advantages in the context of Latin American SMEs.

It's important to acknowledge the limitations of this study. The cross-sectional nature of the research provides a snapshot of CSR practices at a specific point in time but doesn't capture their dynamic evolution. Additionally, while the study covered major Latin American economies, the diversity of the region means that practices may vary in countries not included in the sample. The reliance on self-reported data from SME directors also introduces the potential for social desirability bias. Future studies should consider longitudinal approaches to track the evolution of CSR practices in Latin American SMEs over time. Sector-specific studies could offer more nuanced understanding of how CSR manifests in different industries. Additionally, comparative studies with SMEs in other developing regions could highlight unique aspects of the Latin American approach to CSR.

For researchers, these results highlight several important areas for future investigation. The unique pattern of CSR adoption among Latin American SMEs underscores the need for context-specific CSR models that account for local economic, social, and cultural factors. The gap between ethical motivations and strategic implementation of CSR also presents an interesting avenue for research into how SMEs can better align their CSR efforts with business objectives. Furthermore, the inconclusive results regarding strategic benefits of CSR call for more in-depth studies on the long-term impacts of CSR on SME performance and competitiveness. Additionally, the potential role of AI in facilitating CSR implementation and measurement among Latin American SMEs emerges as a promising area for future research, particularly in addressing resource constraints and enhancing strategic alignment of CSR initiatives.

Finally, we can affirm that this study reveals that while Latin American SMEs show growing engagement with CSR, there remains significant potential for more strategic and comprehensive implementation. The strong ethical foundation and focus on environmental practices provide a solid starting point, but there is a clear need for increased knowledge, resources, and support to help SMEs fully leverage CSR for both social impact and business success. The empirical findings underscore the importance of tailored approaches to CSR promotion and implementation in the Latin American context, taking into account the unique motivations, barriers, and operational realities of SMEs in the region. By addressing these challenges and leveraging the opportunities identified, stakeholders can work towards a more socially responsible and sustainable business environment in Latin America, contributing significantly to the region's sustainable development and global competitiveness.

## REFERENCES


Agudelo, M. A. L., Jóhannsdóttir, L., & Davídsdóttir, B. (2019). A literature review of the history and evolution of corporate social responsibility. *International Journal of Corporate Social Responsibility*, 4(1), 1–23. DOI: 10.1186/s40991-018-0039-y

Alonso-Almeida, M. D. M., Perramon, J., & Bagur-Femenías, L. (2015). Women managers and corporate social responsibility in Spain: Perceptions and drivers. *Women's Studies International Forum*, 50, 47–56. DOI: 10.1016/j.wsif.2015.02.007

Aninat, M. (2015). *Estudio sobre prácticas de responsabilidad social empresarial de las empresas en Chile*. Fundación ProHumana.

Baumann-Pauly, D., Wickert, C., Spence, L. J., & Scherer, A. G. (2013). Organizing corporate social responsibility in small and large firms: Size matters. *Journal of Business Ethics*, 115(4), 693–705. DOI: 10.1007/s10551-013-1827-7

Berger, E., & Nakata, C. (2013). Implementing technologies for financial service innovations in base of the pyramid markets. *Journal of Product Innovation Management*, 30(6), 1199–1211. DOI: 10.1111/jpim.12054

Bernal-Conesa, J. A., de Nieves Nieto, C., & Briones-Peñalver, A. J. (2017). CSR strategy in technology companies: Its influence on performance, competitiveness and sustainability. *Corporate Social Responsibility and Environmental Management*, 24(2), 96–107. DOI: 10.1002/csr.1393

Bianchi, C., Glavas, C., & Mathews, S. (2017). SME international performance in Latin America: The role of entrepreneurial and technological capabilities. *Journal of Small Business and Enterprise Development*, 24(1), 176–195. DOI: 10.1108/JSBED-09-2016-0142

Bican, P. M., & Brem, A. (2020). Digital Business Model, Digital Transformation, Digital Entrepreneurship: Is There A Sustainable "Digital"? *Sustainability (Basel)*, 12(13), 5239. DOI: 10.3390/su12135239

Cantele, S., & Zardini, A. (2018). Is sustainability a competitive advantage for small businesses? An empirical analysis of possible mediators in the sustainability–financial performance relationship. *Journal of Cleaner Production*, 182, 166–176. DOI: 10.1016/j.jclepro.2018.02.016

Carroll, A. B. (1999). Corporate social responsibility: Evolution of a definitional construct. *Business & Society*, 38(3), 268–295. DOI: 10.1177/000765039903800303

Casanova, L., & Dumas, A. (2010). Corporate social responsibility and Latin American multinationals: Is poverty a business issue? *Universia Business Review*, 25, 132–145.

Celma, D., Martínez-Garcia, E., & Coenders, G. (2014). Corporate social responsibility in human resource management: An analysis of common practices and their determinants in Spain. *Corporate Social Responsibility and Environmental Management*, 21(2), 82–99. DOI: 10.1002/csr.1301

Cezarino, L. O., Liboni, L. B., Hunter, T., Pacheco, L. M., & Martins, F. P. (2022). Corporate social responsibility in emerging markets: Opportunities and challenges for sustainability integration. *Journal of Cleaner Production*, 362, 132224. DOI: 10.1016/j.jclepro.2022.132224

Choongo, P. (2017). A longitudinal study of the impact of corporate social responsibility on firm performance in SMEs in Zambia. *Sustainability (Basel)*, 9(8), 1300. DOI: 10.3390/su9081300

Comisión Europea. (2011). Comunicación de la Comisión al Parlamento Europeo, al Consejo, al Comité Económico y Social Europeo y al Comité de las Regiones: Estrategia renovada de la UE para 2011-2014 sobre la responsabilidad social de las empresas. https://www.europarl.europa.eu/meetdocs/2009_2014/documents/com/com_com(2011)0681_/com_com(2011)0681_es.pdf

Crane, A., Matten, D., & Spence, L. (2019). *Corporate social responsibility: Readings and cases in a global context*. Routledge. DOI: 10.4324/9780429294273

Díaz-Arancibia, J., Hochstetter-Diez, J., Bustamante-Mora, A., Sepúlveda-Cuevas, S., Albayay, I., & Arango-López, J. (2024). Navigating Digital Transformation and Technology Adoption: A Literature Review from Small and Medium-Sized Enterprises in Developing Countries. *Sustainability (Basel)*, 16(14), 5946. DOI: 10.3390/su16145946

European Commission. (2011). *A renewed EU strategy 2011-14 for Corporate Social Responsibility*. European Commission.

Ferraro, C., & Rojo, S. (2018). Las MIPYMES en América Latina y el Caribe: Una agenda integrada para promover la productividad y la formalización. *OIT Américas, Informes Técnicos*, 7.

Forcadell, F. J., & Aracil, E. (2017). European banks' reputation for corporate social responsibility. *Corporate Social Responsibility and Environmental Management*, 24(1), 1–14. DOI: 10.1002/csr.1402

Haslam, P. A. (2007). *The corporate social responsibility system in Latin America and the Caribbean. Policy Paper.* Canadian Foundation for the Americas.

Hernández-Perlines, F., & Rung-Hoch, N. (2017). Sustainable entrepreneurial orientation in family firms. *Sustainability (Basel)*, 9(7), 1212. DOI: 10.3390/su9071212

Herrera, M. E. B. (2016). Innovation for impact: Business innovation for inclusive growth. *Journal of Business Research*, 69(5), 1725–1730. DOI: 10.1016/j.jbusres.2015.10.045

Jamali, D., Lund-Thomsen, P., & Jeppesen, S. (2017). SMEs and CSR in developing countries. *Business & Society*, 56(1), 11–22. DOI: 10.1177/0007650315571258

Jenkins, H. (2006). Small business champions for corporate social responsibility. *Journal of Business Ethics*, 67(3), 241–256. DOI: 10.1007/s10551-006-9182-6

Khan, S. A. R., Yu, Z., Panait, M., Janjua, L. R., & Shah, A. (Eds.). (2021). *Global corporate social responsibility initiatives for reluctant businesses*. IGI Global. DOI: 10.4018/978-1-7998-3988-0

Khokhar, M. S., Agashe, A., Deogaonkar, A., & Paralkar, T. A. (2023). Ethical Leadership and Corporate Social Responsibility in Diversified Business Groups: A Conceptual Model of Asian and Latin America. *International Journal of Professional Business Review: Int.J. Prof. Bus. Rev.*, 8(6), 19.

Kolk, A., & van den Buuse, D. (2012). In search of viable business models for development: Sustainable energy in developing countries. *Corporate Governance (Bradford)*, 12(4), 551–567. DOI: 10.1108/14720701211267865

Kowszyk, Y., Covarrubias, A., & García, L. (2011). *El estado de la responsabilidad social empresarial en América Latina 2011*. Red Forum Empresa.

López Jiménez, D., Dittmar, E. C., & Vargas Portillo, J. P. (2021). Cooperation and relationship in the triple helix model of innovation. *International Journal of Knowledge and Learning*, 14(1), 1–9. DOI: 10.1504/IJKL.2021.115025

López Jiménez, D., Dittmar, E. C., & Vargas Portillo, J. P. (2022). Nuevas estrategias publicitarias con influencers: Un examen multidisciplinar. *Revista de Ciencias Sociales*, 28(4), 63–78. DOI: 10.31876/rcs.v28i4.39117

López Jiménez, D., Dittmar, E. C., & Vargas Portillo, J. P. (2023). The Self-Regulating Jury in the Field of Interactive Advertising. Revista de Direito. *Estado e Telecomunicacoes*, 15(1), 1–30. DOI: 10.26512/lstr.v15i1.42146

Mahmood, A., Naveed, R. T., Ahmad, N., Scholz, M., Khalique, M., & Adnan, M. (2021). Unleashing the barriers to CSR implementation in the sme sector of a developing economy: A thematic analysis approach. *Sustainability (Basel)*, 13(22), 12710. DOI: 10.3390/su132212710

Martínez-Conesa, I., Soto-Acosta, P., & Palacios-Manzano, M. (2017). Corporate social responsibility and its effect on innovation and firm performance: An empirical research in SMEs. *Journal of Cleaner Production*, 142, 2374–2383. DOI: 10.1016/j.jclepro.2016.11.038

Molteni, M., & Pedrini, M. (2010). In search of socio-economic syntheses. *Journal of Management Development*, 29(7/8), 626–636. DOI: 10.1108/02621711011059059

Muñoz-Martín, J. (2013). Ética empresarial, Responsabilidad Social Corporativa (RSC) y Creación de Valor Compartido (CVC). *Journal of Globalization, Competitiveness & Governability, 7*(3).

Murillo, D., & Lozano, J. M. (2006). SMEs and CSR: An approach to CSR in their own words. *Journal of Business Ethics*, 67(3), 227–240. DOI: 10.1007/s10551-006-9181-7

OCDE. (2021). *Perspectivas económicas de América Latina 2021: Avanzando juntos hacia una mejor recuperación*. OECD Publishing.

Pastrana, N. A., & Sriramesh, K. (2014). Corporate social responsibility: Perceptions and practices among SMEs in Colombia. *Public Relations Review*, 40(1), 14–24. DOI: 10.1016/j.pubrev.2013.10.002

Peinado-Vara, E. (2011). RSE en América Latina. In Vives, A., & Peinado-Vara, E. (Eds.), *La responsabilidad social de la empresa en América Latina* (pp. 65–82). Banco Interamericano de Desarrollo.

Perrini, F., Russo, A., & Tencati, A. (2007). CSR strategies of SMEs and large firms. Evidence from Italy. *Journal of Business Ethics*, 74(3), 285–300. DOI: 10.1007/s10551-006-9235-x

Revell, A., Stokes, D., & Chen, H. (2010). Small businesses and the environment: Turning over a new leaf? *Business Strategy and the Environment*, 19(5), 273–288. DOI: 10.1002/bse.628

Siddiqui, S., & Sposato, M. (2021). Influential factors in physician burnout in the United Arab Emirates. *International Journal of Work Organisation and Emotion*, 12(3), 249–267. DOI: 10.1504/IJWOE.2021.118994

Soundararajan, V., Jamali, D., & Spence, L. J. (2018). Small business social responsibility: A critical multilevel review, synthesis and research agenda. *International Journal of Management Reviews*, 20(4), 934–956. DOI: 10.1111/ijmr.12171

Spence, L. J. (2016). Small business social responsibility: Expanding core CSR theory. *Business & Society*, 55(1), 23–55. DOI: 10.1177/0007650314523256

Sposato, M. (2025). Developing Digital Leadership Skills for AI-Driven Research Environments. In *Impacts of Generative AI on the Future of Research and Education* (pp. 235–254). IGI Global.

Stoian, C., & Gilman, M. (2017). Corporate social responsibility that "pays": A strategic approach to CSR for SMEs. *Journal of Small Business Management*, 55(1), 5–31. DOI: 10.1111/jsbm.12224

Surroca, J., Tribó, J. A., & Waddock, S. (2010). Corporate responsibility and financial performance: The role of intangible resources. *Strategic Management Journal*, 31(5), 463–490. DOI: 10.1002/smj.820

Turyakira, P., Venter, E., & Smith, E. (2014). The impact of corporate social responsibility factors on the competitiveness of small and medium-sized enterprises. *Suid-Afrikaanse Tydskrif vir Ekonomiese en Bestuurswetenskappe*, 17(2), 157–172. DOI: 10.4102/sajems.v17i2.443

Vives, A. (2014). Guías para la responsabilidad social en las PyMEs: Efectividad de herramientas de autoevaluación. *Journal of Globalization. Competitiveness and Governability*, 8(2), 29–54. DOI: 10.3232/GCG.2014.V8.N2.02

Vives, A., & Peinado-Vara, E. (Eds.). (2011). *La responsabilidad social de la empresa en América Latina*. Banco Interamericano de Desarrollo.

# Chapter 12
# The Twilight of CSR (Corporate Social Responsibility) in the Tourism and Hospitality Industries:
## The Case of Argentina, South America

**Maximiliano Emanuel Korstanje**
https://orcid.org/0000-0002-5149-1669
*University of Palermo, Argentina*

## ABSTRACT

*The recent ecological crisis is wreaking havoc not only in the tourist system but also in the global trade. This point doubtless has occupied a central position in many academic circles and conferences. The future of tourism seems to be grim. Some voices have alerted on the urgency to adopt new sustainable forms of consumption and practices applied to the service industry while others have questioned the nature of the tourism industry dominated by an economic-centered paradigm. Recently, shared economy as well as the figure of corporate social responsibility (CSR) have has played a leading role in the configuration of a new green tourism. This chapter focuses on some Argentinian study cases based on the application of CSR programs in the fields of tourism and hospitality.*

DOI: 10.4018/979-8-3693-9894-4.ch012

## INTRODUCTION

Sustainability has become more complex than a buzzword in recent years. Sustainability is urgent for policymakers and professionals in the tourism and hospitality industries. As a consequence, scholars have hotly debated the role of sustainability in the future of tourism (Brammwell & Lane, 2011; Ivars-Baidal et al 2023). The current ecological crisis, without mentioning the recent COVID-19 pandemic, has negatively impacted the tourist system as never before (Higgins-Desbiolles, 2020; Pham et al. 2021). Expressed in these terms, the problem of sustainability is mainly based on a type of incompatibility between profits and logic preservation. While tourism tends to expand, to gain further profits, the environment is ultimately degraded (Gossling 2000; Sharpley 2020). To what extent is tourism sustainable or not seems to be a question very hard to answer. In this context, some studies have focused their attention on the role played by corporate social responsibility (CSR) to achieve sustainable growth (Lund-Durlacher, 2015; Font & Lynes 2018). Coles, Fenclova & Dinan (2013) argue that CSR has been limited to a few cases or studies in the former decades but the interest in this field has been notably increased. CSR gravitates toward the terrain of governance and good practices in tourism. Despite the abundance of CSR literature in the global North, few studies have seen the light of publicity in Argentina. To fill the gap, the present book chapter centers effort in discussing the role and future of CSR for the tourism industry in Argentina. At the same time, it brings some reflection to what extent sustainable tourism is possible in the region.

## DETACHING SOCIAL RESPONSIBILITY AND CAPITALISM

Although philosophy and humanism avoided discussing the potential of CSR to better daily life, interesting philosophical discussions are mainly given in recent decades. This section offers a robust conceptual background to what extent CSR follows the ethical lines towards a safer and better society. Over the years, humanism never trusted that businesses can potentiate human performance. Most certainly, this imprint is based on the influence of French philosophy, which was systematically reluctant to the economic-based paradigms. This happens because economic gains, profits, and consumption have been historically ridiculed by classic philosophy. Economic profits have been depicted as the origins of eagerness and social injustice –in a whole part of classic philosophical texts originated in the Middle Ages- (Donohue, 2003; Heilbronner 2011). Whatever the case may be, British and American philosophies (pragmatism above all) have incurred in pungent approaches that placed the topic into the foreground. As Dirk Matten & Jeremy Moon (2004) put it, CSR departs from the urgency for the anticipation of institutional drivers that legitimate future gains. Business Schools today are educating their students in good practices and business ethics. As a result of this CSR has situated as a fertile ground for higher education curricula. In the Anglo-Saxon world, the curricula are dominated by subfields such as sustainability, followed by business and marketing ethics.

As the previous backdrop, one of the authoritative voices in the philosophy of CSR, Archie Carroll, says CSR was a term that originated in the 1960s and was systematically replicated during the 1970s. In this vein, in the 1980s scholars devoted their time and efforts to testing empirically how CSR adjusts to society and economic development. In its varied history, the term has taken different forms and shapes. CSR originated in an age of expansion for Modern Corporation. It is intended to mitigate the negative effects of corporations in society. The lesson is mainly given to businessmen or young managers. Their decisions had a substantial weight in the lives of lay citizens. Originally the term was based on *the obligations of businessmen to offer policies desirable for the values of society*. CSR also appealed to create a type of *social consciousness* that wakes up responsibility for the "Other". This responsibility will invariably lead the corporation to new business opportunities and profits. It is the time of Bowen´s seminal book *entitled Social Reasonability of the Businessmen.* Having said this, the proliferation of specialized literature in the successive decades not only reminds Bowen´s ideas but also the impact of the decision-making process in society (most certainly beyond the spheres of obligations). A third stage of research applies previous theories to practical study cases. Here some voices alert that CSR is entering an unparalleled crisis because of the impossibility of governments and the corporate world to reverse climate change as well as the ecological crisis. The US and China have denied systematically their engagement with the reduction of greenhouse gas emissions. This begs a more than interesting question: how can we imagine CSR after Hiroshima and Nagasaki? This suggests that governments and corporations pursue specific individual interests to maximize their gains that ultimately collide with social responsibility (Allen & Craig, 2016; Hossain & Massum, 2022; Jaworska 2018; Mcintyre, Ivanaj & Ivanaj 2018). As Helled Jenkins (2004) eloquently noted, CSR departs from the premise that global business crystalizes a superior stage of civility that should replace public interventions to make people´s lives safer and happier. This discourse enmeshes precisely in a panacea that supports selfish behavior. Bobby Banerjee (2014) laments how CSR enthralls semantically the modern corporation as a significant agent for social change. In its current form, the corporation seems to be inappropriate to achieve sustainable social change. The symbolic barriers and limitations of firms to a more sustainable society are mainly given by their rationality. This starts from the idea that the nature of a corporation should be replicated in the environment or the rest of society. The opposite is equally true, the managerial logic of the market would somehow organize human relations and power relationships in favor of corporate rationality. An interesting set of critiques is posed over the role of CSR strategies as well as the win-win assumptions based on modern rationality. The stakeholders´ cooperation is often determined by the urgency to control conflict, which is vital to amass further wealth.

Last but not least, Slavoj Zizek has exerted a lucid critique of CSR and ethical business. In his texts, Zizek traces back to psychoanalysis to detach the ideological inconsistencies of global capitalism. Centered on a schizoid hysteria, capitalism desires to do what at the bottom it hates. He provides the example of philosophers and social thinkers who applaud illegal migration while at the bottom they know what they propose is impossible to apply. In fact, social responsibility is touched as a narcissistic disposition aimed at marketing new products. In a bipolar world, the US conducted a symbolic war with the Soviet Union. After the collapse of the Soviets, left-wing scholars have fallen into a strange cynic position in which although they criticize the effects of capitalism, they did not the minimum effort to change their zone of comfort. At the same time, it marks a clear dissociation between the subject of enunciated and the resulting subject of enunciation. The modern politics, even CSR, are not pretty different than modern terrorism messages which punctuate I want you not only to do what I want, but I want you to do it as you really want to do it! Zizek acknowledges that lay citizens are often trapped in *extreme civility* that is aimed at expanding the belief people move freely while at the bottom they are firmly grounded by the "Big Other". The concept of "Big Other" is related to the grammatical implicit norms and conventions that regulate social behavior. The Big Other legitimates covert conditions for worker exploitation under the auspices of capitalism (Zizek 2003; 2015).

> *"The role of civility in modern societies to the rise of autonomous free individual – not only in the sense that civility is the practice of treating others as equal, free and autonomous subjects but, in a much more refined way, the fragile web of civility is the social substance of free independent individuals" (Zizek 2015: preface, xv)*

Echoing this, the extreme civility represents the opposite making people believe they are free when they are not. This extreme civility aligns with *the obscene superego* which affirms a hidden law. To set a clear example, Zizek mentions the case based on the legal actions of KKK in the Southern America. While formal punishment against blacks was prohibited in the US, the KKK imposed a disciplinary mechanism legitimated in the formal juridical background. Any KKK member was a renowned member of the community by the day, but a killer by the night when he mutilated or lynched blacks. Per Zizek, this happens because the system keeps two sides. Lay-persons are unable to break the covert (hidden) laws even if they are considered crimes. Lastly, Zizek considers CSR as a part of an ideological background that shows capitalism and corporate culture are the best possible realities. While corporations appeal to social responsibility (helping others) they do nothing to reduce the asymmetrical inter-class inequalities. Since corporations want to amass further profits and appeal to solidarity to enhance consumption, as Zizek infers, paradoxically they create more poverty (Zizek 2003; 2015; Korstanje 2018).

## Corporate Social Responsibility in Tourism

It is important to mention that CSR (Corporate Social Responsibility) can involve a set of complex factors and stakeholders. Basically, the term denotes the responsibility of the company or the corporation for environmental protection as well as the well-being of the local population. This includes not only sustainable goals but also an ethical compromise not to harm local resources (if not fair working conditions for locals). In the constellations of tourism, the word has been widely utilized to serve as a guideline for good practice and sustainable programs. The correct interaction among all stakeholders occupies a central position in CSR (Lund-Lurlacher 2015; Font & Lynes 2018). At a closer look, Emma Hugues & Regina Scheyvens (2016) hold that as a guiding concept, CSR has revolutionized the central planning model. The private sector has historically cooperated with international bodies to achieve sustainable practices at the destinations. However, after 2015 the acceleration of climate change not only called for new urgent but also more thought-provoking strategies to revert the ecological crisis. Businesses are now conceptualized as an integral part of ethics and sustainability. As the authors infer, since the literature suggests companies working in different cultural contexts keep different interests and aims, an integrated (mixed-balanced) approach of synergy and cooperation is at least necessary. One might speculate that policymakers should adopt development-first Planning as a main strategy or model. Based on Burns´ contributions, Hugues & Scheyvens remind us that sustainable mass tourism is always possible whether the interests of locals and the community are heard. Hatipoglu, Ertuna & Salman (2019) review the CSR programs applied in the tourism industry in Turkey. The obtained outcome reveals that even if all stakeholders´ interests can be met, CSR programs can fall short simply because the capabilities of partners differ. At the same time, the impacts of tourism in long-term contexts are almost impossible to predict. What is more important, under some conditions though the effects of tourism on the local community are positive, they are negated or perceived as pernicious by local voices (Yilmazdogan, Seclimis & Cicek 2015; Volgger & Huang 2019). In addition, Horng, Hsu & Tsai (2018) alert that at the first stage of investment, tourism exhibits a notable growth for local economies but in the threshold of time, some negative effects come to stay. The literature suggests that sooner than later the negative effects of tourism (like over-tourism) affect the destination while declining the consumers´ interest.

At the present time, corporations´ behavior plays a leading role in the configuration of a sustainable product that keeps the consumers´ loyalty. In fact, CSR seems to be something more complex than a matter of perception socially constructed. CSR speaks to us of how a corporation implements social and environmental projects to boost profits. Whenever CSR is successfully orchestrated the competitive edge of the destination is notably higher. CSR, so to say, has serious practical implications in tourism management, overlooked by scholars. Those companies or corporations that engage in CSR activity not only gain further competitive strengths but also contribute positively to society, culture, and the environment. Echoing this, Joan Henderson (2007) acknowledges that CSR can be seen as a useful instrument to placate the devastating consequences of natural disasters but it keeps some tensions between philanthropic activity and profits. Defined as any set of actions oriented to social good or well-being beyond the hegemony of the market or the interests of corporations, CSR generates new business that unless regulated can push out some actors into a peripheral position or area of the city. Some studies have shown how the recovery facet, supported by post-disaster tourism, debars some local actors to a peripheral area of the city in favor of new businesses for foreign investment. Paradoxically, post-disaster tourism offers a fertile ground for fresh investment that ultimately accelerates a long-dormant gentrification process in the affected zone. This process aligns with some scholars dubbed corporate extractivist (Korstanje, Seraphin & Gowreesunkar, 2020; Azcárate 2020; Rossi 2022).

As the previous argument is given, Coles, Fenclova & Dinan (2013) exert an interesting critique on CSR and its real (durable) applications in the destination. Per their stance, CSR is monopolized invariably by the corporate vision (which is cemented by economic-centered paradigm). The opposite is equally true, in the academic domain, CSR turns a selective tone based on profits and business. Lovelock & Lovelock (2013) call attention to how tourism, which should be seen as the world´s largest industry, incorporates ethics in tourism consumption. There are ethical problems in how the great players (in the tourist system) interact with local people, even indigenous cultures. Corporate responsibility in tourism faces some methodological tensions (cleavages) even in academic circles. Lastly, Bramwell et al. (2008) recognize that tourism research in CSR takes ultimately four clear-cut directions. Firstly, some studies toy with the belief that CSR or ethical tourism operates beyond self-interest and there is a possibility that it alters the current tourism practices towards a more sustainable paradigm. Secondly, other sets of works emphasize how responsibility impacts different cultures and communities. The question of ethics cannot be universally extrapolated. Other voices advocate for global ethical codes applicable to almost all cases worldwide. Lastly, other studies concentrate efforts to create a liable measurement instrument to understand to what extent corporate responsibility encourages good practices in sustainable tourism

(Martinez-Perez & Rodriguez del Bosque 2013; Fatma, Rahman & Khan 2016; Latif & Sajjad, 2018; Paskova & Zelenka, 2019). Beyond any discrepancy, CSR needs cooperation between Academia and the private sector while giving valuable instruments to authorities and policymakers (Camillieri, 2012; de Grosbois, 2016).

## Measurable Questions of CSR in the Tourism Sector

The literature has ignited a hot debate revolving not only around the ethical question of CSR applied in tourism but also how efficient the established methods are in creating predictable models. It is not simplistic to say that some studies have valorized the role of quantitative techniques in measuring the positive impacts of CSR in the tourism sector (Madanaguli, et al. 2022; Horng, Hsu & Tsai 2018; Martinez, Perez & Rodriguez del Bosque 2013). In this context, Fatma, Rahman & Khan (2016) offer a valid scale to measure consumer perception of corporate social responsibility in tourism activities. Per their viewpoint, qualitative-led methodologies complement the creation of new items and scales to better the current understanding of the phenomenon. CSR reminds –at least in tourism- how firms should adopt efficient and responsible steps to articulate sustainable and competitive strategies for businesses. The fast expansion of tourism and hospitality has created some problems in the calibration of measurable techniques that describe the real impact of CSR in the local community. The applied model –no matter its nature- should construct a criterion of reliability to be extrapolated to other cases and universes. This seems to be particularly difficult in view of the different types and scales of perception each consumer has developed. In sum, the perception of consumers on CSR in tourism varies on demographic, economic, socio-cultural, and contextual variables. By the way, Liburd, Beckendorff & Carlsen (2011) call attention to the methodological issues of CSR in service sectors. As a socio-economic phenomenon, tourism contributes positively not only to CSR but to quality of life. Corporate Social responsibility appears to be often applied to describe the convergence of profitable businesses in the context of sustainable development. The involved companies should integrate environmental worries into the interactions with local agents. CSR activates obligations for businesses to adopt politics that contribute positively to society. The question is many given to what extent is CSR desirable for society or community members. CSR offers good opportunities for good jobs while producing high-quality products for consumers. Arguably, CSR practices should be not only coded into a legal background but also subordinated to an ethical code commonly negotiated with all stakeholders. Although innovative suppliers can guide sustainable practices no less true is that the responsibility of CSR should be driven by government regulators. Last but not least, the authors introduce readers to a new technique (importance-performance analysis) to understand how consumers perceive the effects of CSR in tourism. The authors go on to write: "*Importance-performance analysis is a technique which has been predominantly used in marketing and consumer research to gauge customer acceptance and satisfaction with products and services. The technique is based on the notion that the importance of different product or service attributes varies and that customer satisfaction is mediated by the importance of each attribute and how well these attributes meet expectations" (p. 10)*. With the benefits of hindsight, this technique distinguishes key informants from interviewees stressing how information about others is ultimately obtained. The technique articulates different measurement tools to map the consequences, trends, and potential intricacies of decision-making processes. Whatever the case may be, experts –in the field- valorize the triangulation of qualitative–quantitative methods in the study of CSR globally.

## Case Studies in Tourism for South America

This section reflects successful and unsuccessful case studies in tourism in South America. At a closer look, Luis Garay Tamajon & Xavier Font (2013) analyze different cases in Europe (Catalonia-Spain) and South America (Chile). Even though the literature on CSR is extensive, as the authors alert, less attention was given to medium or small enterprises (SMEs). In normal conditions, government policies facilitate the rise of market-based mechanisms to regulate those glitches that may very well affect economic growth. These market-centered instruments allude to corporate transparency as a vehicle to improve the quality of life. Farfetched as it may sound, CSR in medium or small firms has different dynamics than larger corporations. Secondly, CSR should be considered as a voluntary practice, not all firms adopt. Some agents introduce CSR for altruistic reasons while others preferably do it in the quest for new competitive opportunities. Third, one of the most important limitations is given by the complex interests of all involved actors. The current ecological crisis –accelerated by the proliferation of new global risks- has led policymakers to consider CSR as a valid instrument to protect the tourism industry. Per the obtained results, both study cases have shown similarities. CSR is pondered because of economic reasons and cost reduction. At the same time, CSR opens the doors to introduce new models that help in reducing the risk of environmental degradation. Among the barriers to adopting successful CSR-based strategies, the authors enumerate the lack of budget, legal background, or simply the lack of interest of stakeholders or firms in sustainable practices. In consonance with this, Ralph Buckley & Fernand de Vasconcellos Pega (2012) lament that CSR is shown as something firms actually do, or something they pretend to do. These actions cannot be unfortunately dissociated from politics. Different study cases should take into consideration consumers drives, staff working conditions, and legal frameworks.

In Latin American countries, the lack of interest in local authorities has invariably led to legal chaos where players move strategically according to corporate goals instead of an intra-systemic synergy. This means that each corporation, player, or firm evaluates its own risks and opportunities to adopt CSR-based practices. In the fields of tourism and hospitality industry, there is a legal vacuum that in fact impedes cooperation among states, provinces, or nations. Given the problem in these terms, CSR depends on the political action contextually performed and negotiated with locals.

## CSR in Argentina

The CSR interests in scholars have been started since 2007. In fact, it relates to the acceleration of climate change and the urgency to adopt sustainable practices in the tourism industry (Zanfardini, Aguirre & Tamagni, 2016). Doubtless, one of the most challenging cases in Argentina is not only the lack of interest for the Tourism Ministry beyond the management of local government but also the juridical deficiency to regulate legally the CSR and its impact in the territory (Ubeda et al 2016; Tamajon & Font, 2013; Reinert Lyra, Barbosa de Souza, 2015). What is more important, interesting literature reviews the existent CSR applications in different provinces, but invariably it escapes to the control of central administration. CSR is applied, discarded, or ignored by local governments according to their interests and discretion. A second problem or limitations rests on the fact CSR has not liable forms of measurement or simply is distorted by local government to entice further foreign investment. As Peña Miranda (2012) observes, beyond the interest ignited by CSR in the world, in tandem with an ecological crisis, there are serious deficiencies in developing valid indicators to be measured in South America. At the same time, what experts dubbed "good practices" vary from country to country and culture to culture without mentioning the sub-service sectors within the same country. To resolve this problem, Mtapuri & Giampiccolli (2021) hold the thesis that Community-based diffused tourism (CBDT) situates as an alternative patchy answer to the capital concentration. The model consists of the development of dispersed communities to assemble into a coherent corpus of stakeholders. Framed within what scholars named a shared economy this model opens doors to describe the economy through a local lens. The resource control is also left in the local hands. It allows also access to locally generated knowledge that avoids capital repatriation. Florez-Ruiz, Bino Raya & Barroso-Gonzalez (2016) review a successful case of CSR with a basis in Cordoba, Argentina. Within the hotel chain, as authors infer, CSR contributed notably to boosting good practices in the hospitality industry. Having said this, transparency played a leading role in organizing harmonized cooperation among stakeholders. These good practices should not be limited to the tourism industry or government but also coordinated efforts involving other subsectors. Additionally, the lack of systematized information monopolized by the public sector impedes in some cases the correct functioning of CSR-related programs. A second barrier is given by the lack of applicable jurisprudence to control the private sector interventions in questions of ecology. Gallo (2019) puts CSR as an integrative opportunity to enhance higher tourism education in the fields of tourism management, development, and rural marketing. Based on Zarate, Buenos Aires, as a main study case, the author offers a model that combines service-learning approaches as well as its derived theoretical imprint with community-based tourism. In the experiment, all involved participants showed higher levels of engagement with community-based tourism representing a positive change in the relation with their peers. The author values CSR as a good opportunity to potentiate professional skills, and competence, as well as self-management and problem-solving capacities. Other voices called for CSR as goodwill of impossible application in Latin America because of the following reasons: a) lack of necessary budget in the public sector to regulate the activity, b) deficiencies in the legal background to control the stakeholders´ synergy, c) political issues derived from long-dormant inter-ethnic discrepancies, d) economic monopolies that repatriates invested capital, e) lack of standardized forms of measurement, and bureaucratic demands or steps almost impossible to fulfill (Tamajon & Font, 2013). To this one must add the lack of interest of an Academia (Academia Argentina de Turismo) to produce guanine (scientific) knowledge on the impact and future of CSR in the tourism and hospitality industries. As discussed in earlier sections, the successful implementation of CSR not only depends on the synergy between the public and private sectors but also on the cooperation of Academia and the market. The Academia is unfortunately inspired by old-fashioned topics related to the history of classic destinations development (i.e. Mar del Plata) during the 50s decade or simply interested in old-fashioned themes. This lack of updating has certainly created two negative consequences for the higher education curricula. At a first glimpse, higher education curricula seem to be far from updated regarding the new (challenging) topics discussed worldwide. Secondly and most importantly, the private sector is not provided with academic publications or empirical studies to improve CSR policies. As a result of this, the Tourism Ministry shows certain indifference regarding CSR policy applications in Argentina.

## Implication of CSR after the Pandemic

For sure, the devastating and long-lasting effects of the pandemic on the tourism industry have accelerated radical shifts in the question of sustainability. The pandemic not only has wreaked havoc in global trade (as well as other sub-service sectors) but also changed the managerial viewpoint around the environment. What seems to be equally important, the lockdown accompanied by other restrictive measures generated an unparalleled stock and market crisis that whipped developed and developing economies globally (Bae, et al. 2021; Carroll 2021). In the constellations of tourism and hospitality, this crisis was certainly applauded towards a new green stage centered on environmental preservation (Higgins-Desbiolles 2020; Johann 2022). Seoki Lee (2022) argues convincingly that we need to think about CSR before and after the pandemic. The crisis prompted by the pandemic has confronted the ways top managers think of CSR in the service sectors. A whole part of service sectors have been funded by local government to stave off an irreversible stagnation. This event evinced the material asymmetries, culturally enrooted in global capitalism, between rich and poor countries. At the same time, the inter-class income inequality still remains far from being resolved. Hence it is important to discuss the CSR practices in pre and post-pandemic contexts. In the pre-pandemic days, employees´ relationships appeared not to be important for firm performance whereas investment in working conditions was particularly uncanny because of the possible instability of jobs after the COVID-19 pandemic. In other cases, the crisis not only updated the access of workers and consumers to new digital technologies but also to more sustainable travel behavior. Thus, it is time to reconsider all the existing specialized literature in the field of CSR. Some of the innovative steps and strategies implemented to recover the industry have come to stay. Doubtless, there were important advances in philanthropic tourism as well as CSR activities that need to be discussed. However, the ethical dilemma lies in the fact that firms adhere voluntarily to CSR programs (Abas et al 2023). Choi & Choi (2023) incorporate a qualitative approach to measuring Carroll´s corporate social responsibility pyramid in hotels during the pandemic in South Korea. The findings evolve in two clear-cut dimensions. On one hand, the pandemic changed the interaction of hotels´ employees, and of course, their perspective about a grim future (job instability). On another, strategic partnership very well protects local communities while alleviating the economic difficulties toward a faster recovery stage. In sum, as the experts agree, tourism higher education curricula should be updated according to the new challenges posed by the COVID-19 pandemic. In the case of Argentina, as we have discussed, the lack of updating is a serious barrier to a revolution in higher education. Argentina –in comparison with other Latin American countries- showed a clear indifference respecting CSR and the future implications of the tourism industry. Although this indifference depends upon many factors, the lack of interest of Academia as well as local authorities in CSR philosophy still is part of the setbacks for more sustainable practices in the country. To cut the long story short, the scientific and business sectors move around independently while disengaging from cooperation. This moot point increases the risk dominant tourism-led corporations take CSR as an advantage to amass fresh profits instead of following altruistic goals.

## CONCLUSION

The current ecological crisis is affecting not only the tourist system but also in the global trade. This moot point invariably has been situated as a main concern for many academic circles as well as a point of debate for academicians. The recent COVID-19 pandemic has shown how the future of tourism seems to be grim. Some voices have alerted on the urgency to adopt new sustainable forms of consumption and practices applied to the service industry while others have questioned the nature of the tourism industry monopolized by an economic-centered paradigm. Other works have applauded the arrival of new concepts such as shared economy or CSR in the tourism industry. In fact, the shared economy as well as the figure of corporate social responsibility (CSR) have has played a leading role in the configuration of a new green tourism. This chapter focuses on some Argentinian study cases based on the application of CSR programs in the fields of tourism and hospitality. Contextualized in Argentina as a main study case, the chapter discusses critically the synergy between the private and public sectors as well as the shortcoming between Academia and the market. Unlike the rest of Latin American countries, in Argentina, the Academia shows certain indifference regarding CSR and its applications in the industry. Based on the critical contributions left by philosophy, the present book chapter brings some reflection on the future of the tourism industry and CSR to shape more sustainable practices.

## REFERENCES


Abbas, J., Al-Sulaiti, K., Lorente, D. B., Shah, S. A. R., & Shahzad, U. (2023). Reset the industry redux through corporate social responsibility: The COVID-19 tourism impact on hospitality firms through business model innovation. In *Economic growth and environmental quality in a post-pandemic world* (pp. 177–201). Routledge. DOI: 10.4324/9781003336563-9

Allen, M. W., & Craig, C. A. (2016). Rethinking corporate social responsibility in the age of climate change: A communication perspective. *International Journal of Corporate Social Responsibility*, 1(1), 1–11. DOI: 10.1186/s40991-016-0002-8

Azcárate, M. C. (2020). *Stuck with tourism: Space, power, and labor in contemporary Yucatán*. University of California Press. DOI: 10.2307/j.ctv17db304

Bae, K. H., El Ghoul, S., Gong, Z. J., & Guedhami, O. (2021). Does CSR matter in times of crisis? Evidence from the COVID-19 pandemic. *Journal of Corporate Finance*, 67, 101876. DOI: 10.1016/j.jcorpfin.2020.101876

Bobby Banerjee, S. (2014). A critical perspective on corporate social responsibility: Towards a global governance framework. *Critical Perspectives on International Business*, 10(1/2), 84–95. DOI: 10.1108/cpoib-06-2013-0021

Bramwell, B., & Lane, B. (2011). Critical research on the governance of tourism and sustainability. *Journal of Sustainable Tourism*, 19(4-5), 411–421. DOI: 10.1080/09669582.2011.580586

Bramwell, B., Lane, B., McCabe, S., Mosedale, J., & Scarles, C. (2008). Research perspectives on responsible tourism. *Journal of Sustainable Tourism*, 16(3), 253–257. DOI: 10.1080/09669580802208201

Buckley, R., & de Vasconcellos Pegas, F. (2012). Tourism and CSR. In *The Routledge Handbook of Tourism and the Environment* (pp. 521–530). Routledge.

Camilleri, M. A. (2012). Creating shared value through strategic CSR in tourism. *Camilleri, MA (2012). Creating shared value through strategic CSR in tourism. Ph. D. Dissertation University of Edinburgh, Edinburgh, UK.*https://era. ed. *ac. uk/ bitstream/handle/1842/6564/Camilleri2012. pdf.*

Carroll, A. B. (1999). Corporate social responsibility: Evolution of a definitional construct. *Business & Society*, 38(3), 268–295. DOI: 10.1177/000765039903800303

Carroll, A. B. (2021). Corporate social responsibility (CSR) and the COVID-19 pandemic: Organizational and managerial implications. *Journal of Strategy and Management*, 14(3), 315–330. DOI: 10.1108/JSMA-07-2021-0145

Choi, M., & Choi, Y. (2021). Employee perceptions of hotel CSR activities during the COVID-19 pandemic. *International Journal of Contemporary Hospitality Management*, 33(10), 3355–3378. DOI: 10.1108/IJCHM-03-2021-0289

Coles, T., Fenclova, E., & Dinan, C. (2013). Tourism and corporate social responsibility: A critical review and research agenda. *Tourism Management Perspectives*, 6, 122–141. DOI: 10.1016/j.tmp.2013.02.001

De Grosbois, D. (2016). Corporate social responsibility reporting in the cruise tourism industry: A performance evaluation using a new institutional theory based model. *Journal of Sustainable Tourism*, 24(2), 245–269. DOI: 10.1080/09669582.2015.1076827

Donohue, K. G. (2003). *Freedom from want: American liberalism and the idea of the consumer*. JHU Press.

Fatma, M., Rahman, Z., & Khan, I. (2016). Measuring consumer perception of CSR in tourism industry: Scale development and validation. *Journal of Hospitality and Tourism Management*, 27, 39–48. DOI: 10.1016/j.jhtm.2016.03.002

Flores-Ruiz, D., & Bino-Raya, R. E., & de la O Barroso-González, M. (2016). Responsabilidad social en el sector hotelero. Análisis de caso en Córdoba (Argentina). *Journal of Globalization, Competitiveness & Governability/Revista de Globalización, Competitividad y Gobernabilidad/Revista de Globalização. Competitividade e Governabilidade*, 10(3), 116–135.

Font, X., & Lynes, J. (2018). Corporate social responsibility in tourism and hospitality. *Journal of Sustainable Tourism*, 26(7), 1027–1042. DOI: 10.1080/09669582.2018.1488856

Gallo, G. (2019). Desarrollo rural comunitario: Experiencia de la Escuela Argentina de Negocios en Zárate, Buenos Aires. *RIDAS. Revista Iberoamericana de Aprendizaje-Servicio*, (8), 162–173. DOI: 10.1344/RIDAS2019.8.11

Gössling, S. (2000). Tourism–sustainable development option? *Environmental Conservation*, 27(3), 223–224. DOI: 10.1017/S0376892900000242

Hatipoglu, B., Ertuna, B., & Salman, D. (2019). Corporate social responsibility in tourism as a tool for sustainable development: An evaluation from a community perspective. *International Journal of Contemporary Hospitality Management*, 31(6), 2358–2375. DOI: 10.1108/IJCHM-05-2018-0448

Heilbronner, R. L. (2011). *The worldly philosophers: The lives, times and ideas of the great economic thinkers*. Simon and Schuster.

Higgins-Desbiolles, F. (2020). The "war over tourism": Challenges to sustainable tourism in the tourism academy after COVID-19. *Journal of Sustainable Tourism*, 29(4), 551–569. DOI: 10.1080/09669582.2020.1803334

Horng, J. S., Hsu, H., & Tsai, C. Y. (2018). An assessment model of corporate social responsibility practice in the tourism industry. *Journal of Sustainable Tourism*, 26(7), 1085–1104. DOI: 10.1080/09669582.2017.1388384

Hossain, A. T., & Masum, A. A. (2022). Does corporate social responsibility help mitigate firm-level climate change risk? *Finance Research Letters*, 47, 102791. DOI: 10.1016/j.frl.2022.102791

Hughes, E., & Scheyvens, R. (2016). Corporate social responsibility in tourism post-2015: A development first approach. *Tourism Geographies*, 18(5), 469–482. DOI: 10.1080/14616688.2016.1208678

Ivars-Baidal, J. A., Vera-Rebollo, J. F., Perles-Ribes, J., Femenia-Serra, F., & Celdrán-Bernabeu, M. A. (2023). Sustainable tourism indicators: What's new within the smart city/destination approach? *Journal of Sustainable Tourism*, 31(7), 1556–1582. DOI: 10.1080/09669582.2021.1876075

Jaworska, S. (2018). Change but no climate change: Discourses of climate change in corporate social responsibility reporting in the oil industry. *International Journal of Business Communication*, 55(2), 194–219. DOI: 10.1177/2329488417753951

Jenkins, H. (2004). A critique of conventional CSR theory: An SME perspective. *Journal of General Management*, 29(4), 37–57. DOI: 10.1177/030630700402900403

Johann, M. (2022). CSR Strategy in Tourism during the COVID-19 Pandemic. *Sustainability (Basel)*, 14(7), 3773. DOI: 10.3390/su14073773

Korstanje, M. E. (2018). Dialogues with Slavoj Zizek: Placing the role of torture in context. *International Journal of Žižek Studies*, 12(2), 1–15.

Korstanje, M. E., Séraphin, H., & Gowreesunkar, V. G. (Eds.). (2020). *Post-disaster and post-conflict tourism: Toward a new management approach*. CRC Press.

Latif, K. F., & Sajjad, A. (2018). Measuring corporate social responsibility: A critical review of survey instruments. *Corporate Social Responsibility and Environmental Management*, 25(6), 1174–1197. DOI: 10.1002/csr.1630

Lee, S. (2022). Corporate social responsibility and COVID-19: Research implications. *Tourism Economics*, 28(4), 863–869. DOI: 10.1177/1354816620978136

Liburd, J. J., Benckendorff, P., & Carlsen, J. (2011). Tourism and quality-of-life: How does tourism measure up? *Handbook of tourism and quality-of-life research: Enhancing the lives of tourists and residents of host communities*, 105-132.

Lovelock, B., & Lovelock, K. (2013). *The ethics of tourism: Critical and applied perspectives*. Routledge. DOI: 10.4324/9780203854532

Lund-Durlacher, D. (2015). *Corporate social responsibility and tourism. Education for sustainability in tourism: A handbook of processes, resources, and strategies*. Springer.

Madanaguli, A., Srivastava, S., Ferraris, A., & Dhir, A. (2022). Corporate social responsibility and sustainability in the tourism sector: A systematic literature review and future outlook. *Sustainable Development (Bradford)*, 30(3), 447–461. DOI: 10.1002/sd.2258

Martínez, P., Pérez, A., & Rodriguez del Bosque, I. (2013). Measuring corporate social responsibility in tourism: Development and validation of an efficient measurement scale in the hospitality industry. *Journal of Travel & Tourism Marketing*, 30(4), 365–385. DOI: 10.1080/10548408.2013.784154

Matten, D., & Moon, J. (2004). Corporate social responsibility. *Journal of Business Ethics*, 54, 323–337.

McIntyre, J. R., Ivanaj, S., & Ivanaj, V. (Eds.). (2018). *CSR and climate change implications for Multinational Enterprises*. Edward Elgar Publishing. DOI: 10.4337/9781786437761

Mtapuri, O., & Giampiccoli, A. (2021). Contextualing a tourism development alternative for Argentina: A proposal for community based diffused tourism. *Journal of Spatial and Organizational Dynamics*, 9(2), 138–155.

Paskova, M., & Zelenka, J. (2019). How crucial is the social responsibility for tourism sustainability? *Social Responsibility Journal*, 15(4), 534–552. DOI: 10.1108/SRJ-03-2018-0057

Peña Miranda, D. D., & Serra Cantallops, A. (2012). Responsabilidad social empresarial en el sector turístico: Estudio de caso en empresa de alojamiento de la ciudad de Santa Marta, Colombia. *Estudios y perspectivas en turismo, 21*(6), 0-0.

Pham, T. D., Dwyer, L., Su, J. J., & Ngo, T. (2021). COVID-19 impacts of inbound tourism on Australian economy. *Annals of Tourism Research*, 88, 103179. DOI: 10.1016/j.annals.2021.103179 PMID: 36540369

Reinert Lyra, F., & Barbosa de Souza, M. J. (2015). Responsabilidad social corporativa en el sector turístico: Un estudio de caso en el Parque Temático Beto Carrero World (Santa Catarina-Brasil). *Estudios y Perspectivas en Turismo*, 24(2), 264–278.

Rossi, U. (2022). The existential threat of urban social extractivism: Urban revival and the extinction crisis in the European South. *Antipode*, 54(3), 892–913. DOI: 10.1111/anti.12802

Sharpley, R. (2020). Tourism, sustainable development and the theoretical divide: 20 years on. *Journal of Sustainable Tourism*, 28(11), 1932–1946. DOI: 10.1080/09669582.2020.1779732

Tamajón, L. G., & Font, X. (2013). Corporate social responsibility in tourism small and medium enterprises evidence from Europe and Latin America. *Tourism Management Perspectives*, 7, 38–46. DOI: 10.1016/j.tmp.2013.03.002

Ubeda, M. A. S., Cerna, Y. A. H., Hurtado, M. J., del Socorro Villanueva, J., & Castro, C. M. (2024). Turismo sostenible desde la responsabilidad social de las empresas turísticas. *Revista Torreón Universitario, 13*(36).

Volgger, M., & Huang, S. S. (2019). Scoping irresponsible behaviour in hospitality and tourism: Widening the perspective of CSR. *International Journal of Contemporary Hospitality Management*, 31(6), 2526–2543. DOI: 10.1108/IJCHM-05-2018-0367

Yılmazdogan, O. C., Secilmis, C., & Cicek, D. (2015). The effect of corporate social responsibility (CSR) perception on tourism students' intention to work in sector. *Procedia Economics and Finance*, 23, 1340–1346. DOI: 10.1016/S2212-5671(15)00321-4

Zanfardini, M., Aguirre, P., & Tamagni, L. (2016). The evolution of CSR's research in tourism context: A review from 1992 to 2012. *Anatolia*, 27(1), 38–46. DOI: 10.1080/13032917.2015.1083207

Zizek, S. (2003). *The puppet and the dwarf: the perverse core of Christianity*. Verso. DOI: 10.7551/mitpress/5706.001.0001

Zizek, S. (2015). *The Universal Excemption*. Bloomsbury.

## ADDITIONAL READING

Camilleri, M. (2014). Advancing the sustainable tourism agenda through strategic CSR perspectives. *Tourism Planning & Development*, 11(1), 42–56. DOI: 10.1080/21568316.2013.839470

Campos, M. J. Z., Hall, C. M., & Backlund, S. (2020). Can MNCs promote more inclusive tourism? Apollo tour operator's sustainability work. In *Tourism and Sustainable Development Goals* (pp. 88–110). Routledge. DOI: 10.1201/9780429324253-7

Chettiparamb, A., & Kokkranikal, J. (2012). Responsible tourism and sustainability: The case of Kumarakom in Kerala, India. *Journal of Policy Research in Tourism, Leisure & Events*, 4(3), 302–326. DOI: 10.1080/19407963.2012.711088

Chilufya, A., Hughes, E., & Scheyvens, R. (2019). Tourists and community development: Corporate social responsibility or tourist social responsibility? *Journal of Sustainable Tourism*, 27(10), 1513–1529. DOI: 10.1080/09669582.2019.1643871

Dodds, R., & Kuehnel, J. (2010). CSR among Canadian mass tour operators: Good awareness but little action. *International Journal of Contemporary Hospitality Management*, 22(2), 221–244. DOI: 10.1108/09596111011018205

González-Morales, O., Álvarez-González, J. A., Sanfiel-Fumero, M. Á., & Armas-Cruz, Y. (2016). Governance, corporate social responsibility and cooperation in sustainable tourist destinations: The case of the island of Fuerteventura. *Island Studies Journal*, 11(2), 561–584. DOI: 10.24043/isj.367

Martínez, P., Pérez, A., & Rodríguez del Bosque, I. (2014). Exploring the role of CSR in the organizational identity of hospitality companies: A case from the Spanish tourism industry. *Journal of Business Ethics*, 124(1), 47–66. DOI: 10.1007/s10551-013-1857-1

Meyer, D. (2013). Pro-poor tourism: From leakages to linkages. A conceptual framework for creating linkages between the accommodation sector and 'poor'neighbouring communities. *Tourism and the millennium development goals*, 123-148.

Smith, R. A., & Ong, J. L. T. (2015). Corporate social responsibility and the operationalization challenge for global tourism organizations. *Asia Pacific Journal of Tourism Research*, 20(5), 487–499. DOI: 10.1080/10941665.2014.918555

Snyman, S., & Spenceley, A. (2019). *Private sector tourism in conservation areas in Africa*. CABI. DOI: 10.1079/9781786393555.0000

Whitfield, J., & Dioko, L. A. (2012). Measuring and examining the relevance of discretionary corporate social responsibility in tourism: Some preliminary evidence from the UK conference sector. *Journal of Travel Research*, 51(3), 289–302. DOI: 10.1177/0047287511418369

## KEY TERMS AND DEFINITIONS

**Climate Change:** The concept refers to the radical changes suffered in the environment because of greenhouse emissions.

**Consumption:** It is the act of consuming resources to meet human needs and wants.

**CSR (Corporate Social Responsibility):** It is a form of international cooperation to regulate private activity during a code of ethics.

**Ethics:** It refers to the disposition of moral code oriented to harmonize human relations and the impacts of human activity in the environment.

**Tourism:** A leisure industry dedicated to travel and commercial activity.

# Chapter 13
# Integrating Artificial Intelligence and Public Educational Reforms:
## Advancing Education 4.0 in Costa Rica

**Tom Okot**
https://orcid.org/0000-0002-4402-2127
*Universidad Latinoamericana de Ciencia y Tecnología, Costa Rica*

## ABSTRACT

*This chapter explores the synergy between public educational reforms and artificial intelligence within the context of Education 4.0 and the Fourth Industrial Revolution, with a focus on Costa Rica. It highlights how public initiatives, including the Bicentennial Educational Network and the Ministerial Platform, address structural challenges such as connectivity, digital infrastructure, and educational management. The analysis reveals that AI plays a critical role in enhancing both learning and administrative processes, creating more personalized and efficient education systems. Moreover, it discusses how these reforms and AI can reduce educational inequality by improving access and tailoring education to diverse student needs. The study offers insights into the transformative potential of AI-driven education systems and emphasizes the importance of integrating technology to support sustainable, inclusive development in Costa Rica's education system. The findings can serve as a model for other developing nations seeking to adapt to the demands of the Fourth Industrial Revolution.*

DOI: 10.4018/979-8-3693-9894-4.ch013

## 1 INTRODUCTION

Since the late 1980s, Costa Rica has actively sought to incorporate digital technologies into its public education system. These policy efforts directly responded to the technological advances that defined the Third Industrial Revolution, which introduced sweeping changes across economic, social, and productive sectors globally. This revolution, characterized by the rapid development of electronics, information technology, and telecommunications infrastructure, required nations to rethink how education could prepare their citizens for increasingly automated and interconnected workplaces (Schwab, 2017). Costa Rica's response has evolved into a long-term, consistent policy framework, built through public-private partnerships, most notably the collaboration between the Ministry of Public Education (MEP) and the Omar Dengo Foundation (FOD). This framework is still evolving but faces significant challenges, including the need to compete for limited public resources and attention amidst a broader landscape of public policy priorities.

Costa Rica's public education policy framework, developed during the Third Industrial Revolution, has recently expanded its scope to address the rapid technological changes brought about by the Fourth Industrial Revolution, also referred to as Industry 4.0. This revolution represents a significant departure from previous industrial transformations, as it builds upon the advancements made during the Third Industrial Revolution, but at an exponentially faster pace and with far-reaching consequences (Lee, & Lee, 2021) The Fourth Industrial Revolution is not merely about increased automation; it fuses the digital, physical, and biological worlds, enabling unprecedented levels of interconnectivity and interaction between virtual and real systems (Li, 2020).

Central to this revolution is artificial intelligence (AI), a transformative force that is driving innovations and reshaping economic sectors across the globe. According to Dingli et al. (2021), AI plays a critical role in Industry 4.0 by enabling automation, optimizing supply chains, supporting predictive maintenance, and fostering the development of intelligent robotics. These AI-driven advancements have far-reaching implications, not just for industries but for educational systems as well. As AI continues to permeate various sectors, the challenge for education becomes clear: how can we prepare future generations to navigate a world where humans and machines work together, and where data literacy, technological fluency, and critical thinking skills are indispensable?

Costa Rica's public education system, with its established focus on integrating digital technologies, is uniquely positioned to address this challenge. However, as this chapter will demonstrate, there is still much work to be done. The transition from the Third to the Fourth Industrial Revolution presents new and complex demands that Costa Rica's education system must meet if it is to continue fostering innovation, competitiveness, and economic resilience (Kalolo, 2019). In this context, AI is not just another technological tool to be integrated into the classroom; it represents a paradigm shift that will redefine the nature of education itself.

## 1.1 Bridging the Gap Between Industrial Revolutions

The Third Industrial Revolution brought with it the massification of personal computers, the rise of the internet, and the gradual digitalization of social platforms such as news outlets and social networks. These changes, often referred to as "simple digitalization," significantly impacted education, requiring new models to develop digital literacy and skills for a rapidly changing world. However, the Fourth Industrial Revolution (4IR), driven by AI, poses a much greater challenge (Derici, 2024). AI is accelerating the pace of technological change and transforming industries at an exponential rate, creating pressure to adapt educational models not only to current demands but also to anticipate future needs.

One of the most critical tasks for educators and policymakers is to ensure that AI-driven technological advancements enhance human labor and cognition, rather than replace it. According to Licardo et al. (2024), the fusion of digital, physical, and biological technologies will largely serve to augment human capabilities, meaning that leaders must develop education models that teach individuals how to work with and alongside intelligent machines. This is no small task, as it involves rethinking everything from curriculum content to classroom methodologies and the role of teachers themselves.

If the Third Industrial Revolution required education systems to develop basic digital literacy, the 4IR demanded far more sophisticated skills. These include data analytics, artificial intelligence literacy, cybersecurity awareness, and the ability to navigate complex digital ecosystems where humans and machines collaborate (Haleem et al., 2022). Additionally, students must learn how to apply critical thinking and critical thinking skills in increasingly virtual and hybrid environments.

The integration of AI into education, therefore, is not just a matter of adding a new subject or technology to the existing framework; it represents a fundamental reimagining of what education should be. AI is rapidly evolving from a technological tool to a central force that will shape how individuals learn, how teachers teach, and how educational systems operate. According to Holmes & Tuomi (2022), the synergy between AI and education is critical in preparing future generations to thrive in a world where the line between physical and virtual reality is increasingly blurred.

## 1.2 The Role of AI in Public Education

In Costa Rica, the use of AI in public education remains in its initial stages, but significant strides have been made in integrating Information and Communication Technologies (ICT) into the national education system. The National Educational Informatics Program (PRONIE), established in 1987 through a public-private partnership between MEP and FOD, was one of the first programs of its kind in Latin America. PRONIE was designed to strengthen technical, digital, and scientific education by providing students and teachers with the necessary technological infrastructure and equipment.

Since its inception, PRONIE has expanded significantly. As of December 2014, the program serves 1,752 public schools and 370 high schools across the country. Of these, 818 primary schools operate using mobile technology, while 934 primary schools and 227 high schools are equipped with computer labs for educational purposes (Calvo-Rodriguez, 2021). This widespread technological infrastructure has laid the foundation for further advancements, including the integration of AI technologies into teaching and learning practices.

In 2018, MEP assigned FOD a new project focused on expanding connectivity across all public schools and high schools in the country. This initiative aims to provide reliable internet access, thereby enabling the use of AI-driven educational tools, such as adaptive learning platforms, intelligent tutoring systems, and automated administrative processes. These technologies have the potential to personalize education, reduce teacher workloads, and improve student engagement and outcomes (Zhai et al., 2021).

However, despite these efforts, significant challenges remain. Many of Costa Rica's educational policies and plans are still designed to meet the demands of the Third Industrial Revolution, leaving the education system underprepared to face the more complex demands of AI and Industry 4.0. As Zhai et al. (2021) point out, integrating AI into education is not merely about providing students with access to digital tools; it requires a complete overhaul of how education is structured, delivered, and assessed.

For instance, traditional curricula, which focus on rote learning and standardized testing, are ill-suited to the kinds of skills that will be required in the future. Instead, education systems need to focus on fostering creativity, collaboration, critical thinking, and digital fluency. AI can play a crucial role in this transformation by enabling personalized learning experiences that cater to individual student's strengths and weaknesses, thus promoting deeper learning and engagement.

Moreover, AI can support teachers by automating administrative tasks such as grading and attendance, allowing them to focus on more meaningful interactions with students. AI-powered intelligent tutoring systems can provide students with instant feedback, guiding them through complex problems and helping them learn at their own pace. This individualized approach to learning is essential in preparing students for a world where lifelong learning and adaptability are crucial to success (Holmes & Tuomi, 2022).

## 1.3 The Importance of Public-Private Partnerships

The role of public-private partnerships in advancing Costa Rica's education system cannot be overstated. The PRONIE MEP-FOD collaboration has been instrumental in expanding access to digital technologies in public schools and high schools, helping to bridge the digital divide and ensure that students in rural and underserved areas have access to the same opportunities as those in urban centers. This partnership has also been critical in providing teachers with the training and resources they need to effectively integrate digital tools into their teaching practices (Calvo-Rodriguez, 2021).

However, as Costa Rica transitions into the era of the 4IR, new and expanded partnerships will be required to meet the demands of AI and Industry 4.0. These partnerships must go beyond providing technological infrastructure and focus on fostering innovation in curriculum design, teacher training, and the development of AI-driven educational tools. They should also aim to create opportunities for students to gain firsthand experience with emerging technologies, such as robotics, machine learning, and big data analytics.

One area where public-private partnerships can play a significant role is in supporting continuous professional development for teachers. As AI and other technologies continue to evolve, teachers must receive ongoing training to stay current with the latest advancements. This will require not only investment in teacher education programs but also the creation of networks and platforms where teachers can share best practices and learn from one another.

As Costa Rica continues to navigate the challenges and opportunities presented by the 4IR, the synergy between public educational reforms and AI will be critical to the country's success. AI has the potential to revolutionize education, providing personalized learning experiences, automating administrative tasks, and fostering the development of critical skills that will be essential in the future workforce. However, achieving these outcomes will require a concerted effort from educators, policymakers, and private sector partners to ensure that Costa Rica's education system is prepared to meet the demands of this rapidly evolving technological landscape.

## 1.4 Background Information: Ethical Considerations in AI-Driven Education Reforms

Ethical Considerations in AI Integration in Education

The integration of artificial intelligence (AI) into education systems, particularly within the context of the Fourth Industrial Revolution, has the potential to transform learning experiences and administrative processes significantly. However, these advancements are accompanied by critical ethical considerations that must be addressed to ensure equitable, responsible, and inclusive implementation (Elayyan, 2021).

Issues in AI-Driven Education Systems

- Equity and Accessibility: AI technologies in education often require robust infrastructure and connectivity. This raises concerns about equitable access, especially in regions where digital divides persist. According to the World Economic Forum (2020), unequal access to AI-driven tools can exacerbate existing inequalities, leaving marginalized populations further behind in acquiring essential skills.
- Privacy and Data Protection: AI systems rely heavily on collecting and analyzing large volumes of student data. This reliance introduces risks related to privacy, data security, and potential misuse of information. For instance, sensitive student information could be exposed if robust data governance policies are not implemented (UNESCO, 2021).
- Algorithmic Bias and Fairness: Algorithms used in AI systems can unintentionally perpetuate biases present in their training data. This can lead to discriminatory outcomes, such as unequal learning opportunities or misrepresentation of student capabilities (Binns, 2018). Ensuring fairness in AI decision-making is essential to uphold the integrity of education systems.
- Transparency and Accountability: The complexity of AI models often renders their decision-making processes opaque. This lack of transparency challenges accountability and raises questions about who is responsible for decisions made by AI in educational contexts (Cath et al., 2018).
- Case-Based Discussion: Costa Rica's PRONIE MEP-FOD and AI Integration
- Costa Rica's efforts to integrate AI into its education system, particularly through programs such as PRONIE MEP-FOD, provide a valuable case study to examine ethical challenges and opportunities. These programs aim to bridge the digital divide, enhance educational quality, and

prepare students for the demands of the Fourth Industrial Revolution. However, their implementation highlights several ethical dilemmas:

- Connectivity Challenges: Despite initiatives to expand broadband infrastructure, many rural and underserved communities remain disconnected. This creates a two-tier education system where only digitally connected students benefit from AI-driven tools, further entrenching socio-economic disparities (Cerdas, 2021).
- Data Privacy Concerns: PRONIE MEP-FOD's reliance on AI-based Management Information Systems (MIS) involves the collection of student data to optimize administrative processes. Without stringent data protection laws, there is a risk of data breaches and unauthorized access, jeopardizing student privacy.
- Bias in AI Applications: The adoption of AI in adaptive learning platforms has the potential to customize education, yet there is a risk of reinforcing biases if the algorithms are not carefully monitored. For instance, students from low-performing schools may be unfairly categorized, limiting their access to advanced learning opportunities (Schwab, 2017).

Ethical Frameworks for Responsible AI in Education

To address these issues, several ethical frameworks and principles can guide the integration of AI in education:

- Inclusive Design: AI systems should be designed to cater to diverse student populations, ensuring equitable access regardless of socio-economic background (Floridi et al., 2018).
- Data Governance: Implementing robust data protection regulations, such as anonymization and secure storage practices, can mitigate privacy concerns (UNESCO, 2021).
- Algorithmic Fairness: Regular audits of AI algorithms can help identify and correct biases, ensuring fair treatment of all students (Binns, 2018).
- Transparency and Stakeholder Engagement: Transparent AI systems that allow stakeholders, including educators, students, and policymakers, to understand and question AI decisions can foster accountability (Cath et al., 2018).

The integration of AI into education systems offers transformative potential but requires careful consideration of ethical implications. Costa Rica's efforts under PRONIE MEP-FOD illustrate both the opportunities and challenges in leveraging AI for Education 4.0 (Xu et al., 2018). By adopting inclusive, transparent, and accountable practices, education systems can harness AI's benefits while mitigating its risks, fostering a more equitable and effective learning environment.

## 2 THEORETICAL BACKGROUND

The literature surrounding the concept of the 4IR and its implications for education offers a comprehensive understanding of the profound shifts that are underway. Klaus Schwab, Founder and Executive Chair of the World Economic Forum (WEF) has been instrumental in framing the discourse. Schwab argues that the 4IR was built upon the Third Industrial Revolution, which introduced the digital era through the development of electronics, information technology, and telecommunications. However, unlike its predecessor, this new revolution is characterized by a fusion of technologies that blur the boundaries between the physical, digital, and biological spheres (Schwab, 2024). This new phase represents a paradigmatic shift, not merely an extension of the digital era but a transformation that challenges the fundamental way society operates.

### 2.1 The Industrial Revolutions: Historical Context

The term "4IR" is part of a broader historical framework identifying four key industrial revolutions, each marked by significant technological and social transformations. According to Stearns (2020), the First Industrial Revolution began in the late 18th century with mechanization powered by steam and water, fundamentally altering production processes and labor systems. The Second Industrial Revolution, commencing in the late 19th century, introduced electricity and mass production techniques, creating new industrial sectors and labor patterns.

The Third Industrial Revolution, beginning in the mid-20th century, marked the transition into the digital age, driven by the advent of semiconductors, mainframe computing, personal computing, and the internet (Schwab, 2024). This revolution brought about a digital transformation in almost every industry, emphasizing data processing, automation, and the initial stages of globalization through interconnected systems. It fundamentally altered the ways economies operated by transitioning from mechanical to digital processes.

However, the 4IR is distinctive not because of the emergence of innovative technologies per se, but because of the way these technologies integrate and enhance each other, forming new systems of interaction between the digital, biological, and physical worlds (Li, 2020). Schwab (2024) suggests that this revolution's transformative potential lies in its capacity to connect systems, enabling real-time interaction and decision-making across multiple platforms—whether in industry, healthcare, or education. This integration fundamentally shifts societal and economic paradigms, particularly as technologies such as AI, robotics, and biotechnology converge.

A central concern in discussions about the 4IR is the question of labor and productivity. Schwab (2024) notes that automation, a key feature of this new era, could either exacerbate inequality by displacing workers or create new jobs and opportunities for growth. The transformative nature of this revolution calls for educational systems that are agile and capable of reskilling and upskilling workers to adapt to these changes.

Carl Benedikt Frey, a prominent researcher from the University of Oxford, highlights the role of technology in shaping labor markets. In his work "The Technology Trap: Capital, Labor, and Power in the Age of Automation," Frey (2019) makes an essential distinction between technologies that replace human labor and those that enable it. Replacing technologies leads to job displacement, whereas enabling technologies increase workers' productivity by complementing human skills. According to Frey 2019), educational systems must focus on fostering skills that enable workers to remain relevant in an increasingly automated world.

The potential displacement of workers has been a concern since the early industrial revolutions. Frey & Osborne (2017) examined the susceptibility of various job categories to automation and concluded that many jobs traditionally performed by low- or middle-skilled workers are at considerable risk of being replaced by machines. In this context, the ability of workers to adapt by acquiring new skills through education is critical. However, their research also points to a worrying trend: the demand for high-skilled workers has plateaued in recent years, even as the supply of educated workers has increased. This mismatch highlights the inadequacy of current educational models in addressing the rapidly evolving skill requirements driven by technological advancement.

## 2.2 Education's Strategic Role in the Fourth Industrial Revolution

Both Schwab (2024) and Frey (2019) emphasize the need for education systems to evolve to meet the demands of the 4IR. Schwab (2024) notes that educational institutions must shift away from traditional methods that prioritize rote learning and memorization, toward models that promote critical thinking, creativity, and adaptability. The capacity to learn continuously and apply new skills quickly will become more important than ever as technological advancements reshape industries.

According to the WEF, these challenges present unique opportunities and risks for education systems worldwide. The standard educational model that has been in place since the First and Second Industrial Revolutions, which focused on mass-producing uniform talent for repetitive, process-oriented manufacturing jobs, is no longer sufficient. In contrast, the Fourth Industrial Revolution requires a workforce that is adaptable, technologically literate, and capable of complex problem-solving, Scepanovič (2019). The transition from this outdated model to an "Education 4.0" framework, designed for the current technological age, is essential to ensure that students are adequately prepared for the future workforce.

However, Qureshi et al. (2021) argue that the 4IR has already prompted significant reforms in educational policies, particularly in developed nations where the infrastructure and political will exist to adopt innovative technologies. However, for many developing nations, the challenges are more pronounced due to limited access to technology, insufficient funding, and inadequate policy implementation. In these contexts, bridge the gap between education systems and technological advancements becomes even more critical.

## 2.3 The Importance of Reskilling and Upskilling

One of the most pressing challenges for educational systems in the 4IR is the need for rapid reskilling and upskilling. Schwab (2017) suggests that traditional educational models are not equipped to keep pace with the rapid technological changes that characterize this era. New digital tools, AI, and data analytics must be integrated into the curriculum to train students for jobs that may not yet exist. Similarly, education systems must emphasize flexibility, adaptability, and the ability to learn new skills quickly.

Frey (2019) supports this argument by highlighting the importance of distinguishing between technologies that replace labor and those that enable it. While the displacement of certain jobs by automation is inevitable, education systems can mitigate these effects by ensuring that workers are equipped with the skills necessary to thrive in new roles created by technological advancements. These skills include not only technical competencies but also soft skills such as creativity, critical thinking, and emotional intelligence.

The rise of AI is expected to transform education by enabling personalized learning experiences. AI-driven tools can analyze vast amounts of data to identify individual students' strengths and weaknesses, enabling teachers to tailor instruction accordingly. Moreover, AI can help automate administrative tasks, freeing up time for teachers to focus on more meaningful interactions with students (Holmes & Tuomi, 2022). However, for these innovations to be successfully integrated into educational systems, there must be a concerted effort to provide the necessary infrastructure and training.

## 2.4 The Digital Divide and Global Disparities in Education

While the 4IR offers significant opportunities for educational reform, it also has the potential to exacerbate global inequalities. As the World Economic Forum (2020) notes, many education systems, particularly in developing countries, still lack the basic infrastructure needed to support digital learning. Access to the internet, computers, and other digital tools is unevenly distributed, meaning that students in these regions may be left behind as the rest of the world advances technologically.

The digital divide is not just a problem for individual countries but for the global economy. If significant portions of the world's population are unable to participate in the digital economy, global productivity will suffer. The World Economic Forum estimates that US$11.5 trillion could be added to global GDP by 2028 if countries succeed in better preparing their populations for the needs of the Fourth Industrial Revolution (WEF, 2020).

The 4IR represents a fundamental shift in the way societies and economy's function, driven by the fusion of digital, biological, and physical systems. Its impact on labor markets is profound, raising critical questions about the role of education in preparing the workforce for the future. Educational systems must adapt rapidly to keep pace with technological changes, emphasizing the development of both technical skills and soft skills such as creativity, critical thinking, and adaptability.

To achieve this, a new "Education 4.0" model is needed—one that moves beyond traditional, passive forms of learning to embrace interactive, personalized, and technology-driven methods. At the same time, policymakers must address the global disparities in access to digital tools and infrastructure to ensure that no one is left behind in the transition to this new era.

In general, the synergy between AI, technology, and education is crucial in shaping a future workforce capable of thriving in the dynamic environment created by the 4IR. Through strategic investment in educational reform and infrastructure, countries can harness the potential of these innovative technologies to create more equitable, productive, and prosperous societies.

# 3 METHODOLOGY

This research employed an explanatory case study methodology, which is particularly suited for answering questions that explore the causal relationships between complex real-life interventions and their effects, making it an appropriate method for evaluating policy outcomes. According to Yin (2009), explanatory case studies are ideal when "how" and "why" questions are involved, as these questions deal with operational links that need to be traced over time. This method offers flexibility to examine both the process and outcome of the initiatives under study, providing a comprehensive understanding of the interactions and dynamics involved in policy implementation (Fisher & Ziviani, 2004).

In this study, we utilized Yin's (2009) explanatory case study approach to analyze the intersection of technological and educational reforms in Costa Rica. Specifically, the research focuses on how the integration of Education 4.0 technologies has shaped public educational reform in response to the demands of the 4IR. The goal is to understand the causal links between policy design and its intended outcomes, exploring how new educational models are being developed to equip students with the skills necessary for a technology-driven economy. The case study method is appropriate for this analysis because it allows for in-depth investigation into the specific public policy initiatives and their broader implications for national education reform (Baškarada, 2014).

To ensure rigor and validity in the research design, this study followed the construct validity test outlined by Yin (2009). This involves three essential tactics:

- Use of multiple sources of evidence: By collecting data from various sources, the study ensures that different perspectives are considered. This includes both documentary analysis and interviews with key informants, creating a robust dataset that captures the complexity of the case.
- Establishing a chain of evidence: All data collected will be systematically linked to the research questions, ensuring transparency, and allowing for replication or further examination by other researchers.
- Key informant interviews: Interviews with individuals directly involved in the policymaking and implementation process are essential to capture insights that might not be reflected in the documentation.

The research focused on a particular case study design, chosen due to the unique circumstances in Costa Rica, where technological reforms in education have been centrally driven by two major public policy projects during the period of analysis (2018–2021). These projects aimed to transform the Ministry of Education's capacity to implement systematic changes to the educational model in response to the needs of the Fourth Industrial Revolution. The case is unique in that it involves the convergence of technological and educational reforms in a country where the public education system is a key pillar of national development.

The data collection process involved two primary sources of evidence: document review and interviews with key informants.

- The documentary review involved two sets of bibliographic materials: Academic and policy papers: These will include articles published in scholarly journals and policy white papers from international organizations that focus on global education trends and the impacts of the Fourth Industrial Revolution on education systems. These sources will provide a theoretical and contextual foundation for understanding the broader global forces at play. Local media and institutional reports: Costa Rican news articles, government press releases, project presentations, and official reports from the Ministry of Education will be analyzed to provide insights into the specific actions taken at the national level. This will help establish a timeline and narrative for the reforms, as well as provide empirical evidence of their implementation and status.

- To deepen the understanding of the case, the study conducted unstructured interviews with open-ended questions. This approach allows for flexibility in exploring the perspectives and insights of key decision-makers who were directly involved in the policy initiatives. The interviews will focus on identifying the motivations, objectives, and expected outcomes of the public policy projects, as well as the challenges faced during their implementation. The following individuals have been identified as key informants: Edgar Mora: Minister of Education (2018–2020), who played a significant role in the policy initiatives during the period under analysis. Amparo Pacheco: Vice Minister of Institutional Planning (2018–2020), involved in coordinating strategic reforms. Andrés Fernández Arauz: Project coordinator for the Bicentennial Education Network, who oversaw the technical aspects of the educational reform projects. These interviews provided first-hand insights into the policymaking process, highlighting the strategic goals and obstacles encountered in implementing Education 4.0 initiatives in Costa Rica.

This case study seeks to achieve the following objectives:

- Examine the relationship between AI and educational reform: This will include a review of how AI concepts have influenced educational policy in Costa Rica and globally, particularly the shift towards digitalization and technology integration in education.
- Analyze Costa Rican public policy proposals aimed at transforming education through technology: The study will identify and review key policy documents and initiatives implemented between 2018 and 2021 that sought to integrate digital technologies into the public education system.
- Classify the intended impacts of these policies: The research will categorize the desired outcomes of the reforms, focusing on how they aim to enhance digital skills and prepare students for participation in a technology-driven economy.

- Assess current challenges and gaps in the implementation of these policies: The study will describe the obstacles that have hindered the full realization of the policy goals, particularly in terms of infrastructure, resources, and systemic change.

It is important to note that this research does not aim to evaluate the current state of the reforms or their ultimate success or failure. Rather, it focuses on the motivations behind the policies, their design, and their expected outcomes as expressed by key decision-makers during the period of analysis. The results will thus provide a snapshot of the policy landscape and its intended trajectory but will not offer a comprehensive evaluation of their long-term impact.

By focusing on a specific period and set of initiatives, this case study provides a detailed exploration of how educational reforms in Costa Rica have been shaped by the demands of the Fourth Industrial Revolution, and how policymakers are attempting to navigate these challenges through strategic, technology-driven interventions.

## 4 RESULTS

### 4.1 Fourth Industrial Revolution and Its Impact on Education Reform

The 4IR represents a period of unprecedented technological convergence, where advancements in fields such as the Internet of Things (IoT), integrated sensors, Cloud Computing, Big Data, and AI are revolutionizing various aspects of human life (Okot et al, 2023). These innovations build upon foundational skills such as literacy, numeracy, and writing, enhancing them with new technological capabilities that redefine the way industries, governments, and individuals operate.

In this revolution, "physical, digital, and biological systems are fused," creating an interconnected world where these distinctions are increasingly blurred. 4IR is now deeply embedded in key sectors such as industry, agriculture, healthcare, and economics, and education is no exception. Educational systems worldwide are expected to integrate these technologies, significantly impacting learning opportunities, educational policies, and instructional methodologies (Eleyyan, 2021).

The WEF (2020) report by Schwab & Zahidi (2018) highlighted that 65% of students currently in primary school will eventually work in jobs that do not yet exist. By the end of this decade, it is predicted that 47% of all existing jobs will be replaced by automation, and nearly half of the content of university degrees will be outdated and no longer aligned with the economy's evolving needs (Schwab & Zahidi, 2018).

Recognizing the urgency for change, the WEF introduced Education 4.0, a concept that aligns education systems with the demands of the 4IR. Education 4.0 is aimed at preparing students for the future of work, improving productivity, and enhancing social cohesion by equipping individuals with the skills needed to thrive in a rapidly changing labor market. The WEF asserts that transitioning global education systems to an Education 4.0 framework is essential for reviving pathways to social mobility and ensuring that education remains relevant (WEF, 2020).

## 4.2 Education 4.0 Framework: Critical Characteristics

The WEF proposed a Global Framework for Shifting Learning Content and Experiences, which outlines eight critical characteristics of Education 4.0, divided into two main categories: Content and Experience.

- Content (Skills Adaptation)
  - The focus here is on evolving educational content to build upon and enhance basic foundational skills while also developing future-oriented skills:
  - Global Citizenship Skills: Education must focus on creating global awareness, promoting sustainability, and encouraging active participation in the global community.
  - Innovation and Creativity Skills: The curriculum should nurture skills like complex problem-solving, analytical thinking, creativity, and systems analysis to foster innovation.
  - Technology Skills: A priority is placed on digital literacy, including programming, understanding digital responsibility, and navigating emerging technologies.
  - Interpersonal Skills: Emotional intelligence, cooperation, empathy, leadership, and social awareness are critical to navigating increasingly interconnected and collaborative workplaces.
- Experiences (Learning Mechanisms)
  - Education systems must also adapt the learning experience to mirror the evolving nature of work and to leverage new learning technologies:
  - Personalized and Self-Paced Learning: Education should be tailored to individual learners, allowing them to progress at their own pace.
  - Accessible and Inclusive Learning: Learning opportunities should be available to all, regardless of location or socio-economic status, ensuring inclusivity.

- o Problem-Based and Collaborative Learning: Learning should move towards project- and problem-based approaches, requiring teamwork and collaboration, reflective of future workplace environments.
- o Lifelong and Student-Driven Learning: Education should become a continuous, lifelong process, allowing learners to continuously update their skills as needed.

This comprehensive framework is designed to ensure that education systems not only adapt to but also lead in equipping learners with the skills necessary to succeed in the rapidly evolving labor markets of the 4IR (Xing et al., 2018).

Other international organizations also emphasize the importance of adapting education systems to meet the demands of the 4IR. The World Bank (2018) notes that the future of work will increasingly depend on continuous learning and that rapid technological changes necessitate educational reforms that prioritize skill adaptation and technological integration.

The World Bank's vision for educational reform in the context of the 4IR identifies eight key dynamics of change:

- Transformation of pedagogical processes: Incorporating online platforms and virtual education into teaching methods.
- Reimagining assessment: Transitioning towards results-based assessment and certification systems, such as micro-credentials for skills.
- Enhanced management and governance: Improving technological capacity within education systems.
- Technology-aligned curricula: Incorporating relevant technology skills into learning content.
- Personalized digital learning: Providing access to digital resources that build both technical and administrative skills.
- Curricular updates: Aligning educational programs with current and future job market demands.
- Building digital infrastructure: Creating the necessary technological foundation for efficient education systems.
- Job placement for graduates: Focusing on immediate employment prospects for postgraduation.

The World Bank (2018) also highlights that effective school management and governance are crucial to maintaining educational quality, especially in low-income countries where school management capacities are often limited (Díez et al., 2020).

Sharma (2019) further supports the importance of Education 4.0 by emphasizing its transformative potential in promoting technology-based learning. Education 4.0 encourages the use of Internet technologies, open online courses, and collaborative tools that foster dynamic, student-driven learning experiences. This shift moves away from traditional classroom settings, enabling students to learn remotely, which is particularly relevant in the context of increasing digital connectivity.

However, connectivity remains a fundamental prerequisite for the successful implementation of Education 4.0. According to CEPAL (2020), connectivity is crucial not only for accessing educational opportunities but also for reducing socio-economic inequalities. In Latin America, limited access to digital technologies continues to pose a significant barrier to fully leveraging the benefits of digital learning tools. Improving connectivity, particularly broadband access, is essential to ensuring that all students have equitable access to quality education.

## 4.3 Education Reform in Costa Rica: Promoting Digital Technology Transformations

Costa Rica's efforts to integrate digital technology into its education system can be traced back to 1987, with the establishment of the FOD. This non-profit organization, created through a public-private partnership with the MEP, aims to promote access to digital technologies within the public education system. The foundation focuses on empowering students to use technology as a learning and capacity-building tool (Calvo-Rodriguez, 2021).

In 1988, the National Educational Informatics Program (PRONIE MEP-FOD) was launched, formalizing this partnership between the MEP and FOD. The program was developed as a public policy platform designed to implement information technology projects in Costa Rican public schools. The legislative assembly further supported the program by passing Law No. 8207 in 2002, which declared PRONIE to be of public utility, allowing the transfer of state funds to FOD for its initiatives.

PRONIE MEP-FOD was Costa Rica's first comprehensive public policy effort to address the digital divide in education, recognizing that access to technology alone was insufficient. The program's mission has evolved to address both the access gap (ensuring students have the necessary devices and connectivity) and the knowledge gap (ensuring students know how to use these technologies effectively).

In line with the demands of the 4IR, PRONIE MEP-FOD has adapted its mission to focus on fostering the skills needed to navigate technological innovations. It continues to receive public funding and international cooperation support to run a variety of projects aimed at integrating digital tools into the public education system.

Some of PRONIE MEP-FOD's current initiatives include:

- Bicentennial Educational Network (BEN): A nationwide initiative to enhance digital connectivity in schools.
- Educational Informatics (LIE++): A project designed to introduce students to information technology as a learning tool.
- Learning with Mobile Technologies (ATM): An initiative focused on incorporating mobile devices into the learning environment.
- Entrepreneurship and Employability Capabilities (CEE): A program aimed at fostering entrepreneurial skills and enhancing employability among students.

These projects underscore Costa Rica's ongoing commitment to leveraging digital technology to improve educational outcomes and ensure that the country's students are prepared for the challenges and opportunities presented by the 4IR.

The results from Costa Rica's efforts to align its education system with the principles of Education 4.0 illustrate both the progress made and the challenges that remain, particularly in terms of infrastructure development and equitable access to digital technologies (Table 1).

*Table 1. PRONIE MEP-FOD projects status*

| Project Name | Project Description | CCurrent Status |
|---|---|---|
| Bicentennial Educational Network (BEN) | A governmental project introduced in August 2018, led by the Ministry of Public Education (MEP) and FOD, with financing from a fund administered by the telecommunications regulator SUTEL, aims to interconnect all educational centers in the country through an integrated internet infrastructure. This network provides sufficient bandwidth, with speeds of up to 500 Mbps, making connectivity a central pillar of the educational process, fully integrated into the curriculum.<br><br>This is the latest project under FOD's supervision. | The current plans are set to benefit more than 700,000 students, representing 73% of MEP's total student population, and will reach 2,139 educational centers, selected by the available budget.<br><br>In 2020, FOD designed the BEN and defined the technical specifications and contractual framework, which led to the publication of a tender to select the company that would provide connectivity services. The plan includes an installation rate of 300 institutions per month. |
| Educational Informatics (LIE ++) | Educational computer labs are designed to implement programs that create creative and playful learning spaces for public education students to acquire skills in programming, computational thinking, robotics, big data, problem-solving, and critical thinking. | Ten educational proposals promote computational thinking for students from preschool through ninth grade. In 2020, these programs reached 1,281 educational centers, benefiting a total of 512,995 students. |
| Learning with Mobile Technologies (ATM) | The initiative promotes the use of mobile technologies in the pedagogical work of teachers and the learning experiences of students. | It benefited 222,373 students from 2,703 educational centers, representing 67.8% of the total institutions served by PRONIE MEP-FOD. In single-teacher schools or schools with fewer than 90 students, the program provides one computer per student, while for educational centers with more than 90 students, it supplies mobile carts containing 30 computers. |
| Entrepreneurship and Employability Capabilities (CEE) | The program promotes the development of skills to diversify and specialize the educational offerings in emerging technological fields associated with Industry 4.0. This is achieved through student certifications in technical high schools (CTPs) across areas such as programming, computer maintenance, virtual competencies, the Internet of Things (IoT), connectivity, data analysis and visualization, cybersecurity, electronics fundamentals, entrepreneurship, and innovation, all supported by digital technologies. | In 2020, 5,124 students from 134 CTPs were certified in internet networking and computer maintenance. Additionally, 800 computer science teachers received training and certification.<br><br>The CISCO FOD Academy certified 2,156 students in various certifications, including Cisco Certified Networks, Linux, CompTIA, A+ 902, VMware, SQL, WS, and Python. |
| Technology training for teachers | Training is provided to enhance teaching competencies in technological integration, innovation, and the strengthening of pedagogical practices. | In 2020, 8,944 teachers received training, including 1,509 who were specifically trained to implement the LIE++ proposal. |

Source: adapted from (Calvo-Rodriguez, 2021).

The BEN marks a pivotal moment in Costa Rica's efforts to integrate digital technology into public education, recognizing the critical role connectivity plays in broader educational reform. The BEN initiative aims to address long-standing disparities in internet access across the nation's public schools and high schools, providing the necessary infrastructure for more efficient education management and dynamic learning experiences. Its purpose extends beyond mere connectivity—it serves as a tool to transform how education is delivered and managed within the framework of the Fourth Industrial Revolution.

## 4.4 The Role of Artificial Intelligence in the Educational Transformation

AI plays an increasingly significant role in reshaping education systems globally, and BEN could function as a platform for integrating AI-driven solutions into Costa Rica's public education system. With the enhanced connectivity that BEN promises, AI-powered tools and platforms can significantly improve both administrative efficiency and pedagogical outcomes.

AI has the potential to transform how students interact with learning materials. With the use of machine learning algorithms, educational platforms can offer personalized learning experiences, adjusting content delivery to match a student's unique learning style and pace, Jaiswal & Arun (2021). This aligns with the global push towards Education 4.0, where learning experiences are increasingly personalized, self-paced, and accessible to everyone. AI-driven assessments can provide real-time feedback to students and teachers, helping to identify gaps in understanding and allowing for more targeted interventions. Moreover, automated grading systems could reduce the administrative burden on teachers, freeing them to focus more on instructional quality.

Additionally, according to Chen et al. (2020) for the teachers, AI can offer sophisticated tools for tracking student performance, helping to identify students who may need additional support or those who are ready for more advanced challenges. Additionally, AI can support professional development by recommending personalized training programs based on teachers' past performance, feedback, and the evolving needs of their students.

The integration of IoT devices into the classroom is another area where BEN could facilitate significant advancements. IoT can help gather data on student engagement and classroom environments, offering insights that can be used to optimize learning spaces and improve instructional strategies. For instance, smart devices such as sensors can monitor air quality, lighting, and noise levels in classrooms, providing feedback on how to create optimal conditions for learning (Ali & Nihad (2021) IoT could also enable adaptive learning environments, where classroom settings are automatically adjusted to meet the specific needs of a lesson or group of students.

In addition to IoT, the potential for Big Data analytics to reshape education should not be overlooked. With thousands of schools and students connected through BEN, the MEP can harness data analytics to monitor student performance at scale, track educational outcomes, and make data-driven decisions. Predictive analytics could also help policymakers identify trends in student achievement, drop-out rates, and resource allocation needs, thus enabling more responsive and effective interventions.

AI combined with big data also holds promise in administrative efficiency. AI algorithms could streamline the management of teacher assignments, student enrollments, and resource distributions, improving the overall operational effectiveness of schools (Rabah, 2018). For example, AI could be used to optimize the distribution of teachers to areas where they are most needed or to predict future enrollment trends based on demographic data, allowing for better long-term planning.

While the potential of AI and IoT in education is substantial, several challenges remain in the Costa Rican context. The first is ensuring that the necessary digital infrastructure is in place. Despite the progress that BEN represents, as of 2021, over 67% of public schools had internet speeds below 10 Mbps, which is insufficient for supporting advanced technological solutions like AI-driven platforms and IoT integration. High-speed internet is a prerequisite for these technologies to function effectively (Gómez-García et al., 2024) The BEN initiative's goal of delivering broadband internet to all public schools must be realized before AI and IoT can be fully deployed.

Another challenge is digital literacy among both students and teachers. AI tools and IoT devices require users to have a certain level of technical competency to operate them effectively (Sánchez-Cruzado et al., 2021). This highlights the importance of incorporating training programs for educators that not only focus on basic digital skills but also the use of AI in educational contexts. Moreover, students must be trained not just in the use of these tools, but also in critical digital skills like coding, cybersecurity awareness, and responsible internet use.

Costa Rica's approach to integrating technology into education, particularly through public-private partnerships like the one between MEP and FOD, sets a strong precedent for continued collaboration on AI-driven initiatives. These partnerships can play a crucial role in ensuring that the necessary resources, expertise, and innovation are available to support BEN's successful implementation. For instance, the FOD has already been involved in projects like Innovation Laboratories for Training and Certification in Industry 4.0, which could serve as pilot programs for broader AI integration across schools.

Furthermore, global tech companies such as Microsoft and Intel, which have been involved in past initiatives, could be instrumental in bringing AI-powered educational tools to Costa Rican classrooms. Their expertise in cloud computing and AI applications could facilitate the development of customized learning platforms that cater to the needs of Costa Rica's students and teachers.

An essential aspect of AI integration into education is its potential to promote equity and inclusivity. One of the core goals of BEN is to ensure that all students, regardless of geographic location or socio-economic background, have equal access to high-quality educational resources. AI can play a pivotal role in achieving this goal. By offering personalized learning paths, AI can help close achievement gaps between students from diverse backgrounds. AI tools can be particularly beneficial for students with learning disabilities or those who require specialized instruction, as these tools can be adapted to meet individual needs more effectively than traditional classroom instruction.

However, care must be taken to ensure that AI does not inadvertently widen the digital divide. Students in schools with lower internet speeds or outdated infrastructure may not be able to access the same AI-driven resources as their peers in more technologically advanced schools. This is why the successful implementation of BEN's broadband connectivity goals is so crucial to the equitable rollout of AI technologies.

BEN is a foundational step toward transforming Costa Rica's education system to meet the demands of the 4IR. With enhanced broadband infrastructure, the integration of AI, IoT, and data analytics will become increasingly feasible, allowing for personalized, efficient, and data-driven educational experiences. However, the success of these initiatives will depend on addressing challenges related to infrastructure, digital literacy, and ensuring equity across all schools. Through continued collaboration between the government, private sector, and educational institutions, Costa Rica can pave the way for a future-ready education system.

BEN is poised to have a transformative impact on the educational and administrative infrastructure of Costa Rica's public education system. To establish comprehensive broadband connectivity across all public educational institutions, the network's influence extends beyond mere internet access. It promises to reshape institutional planning, human resource management, and budgetary control while fostering innovation in pedagogical practices.

According to Andrés Fernández Arauz, the project coordinator of BEN at the Ministry of Public Education (MEP), BEN is constructed in four distinct layers. Each layer is designed to add value to the previous one. The first layer focuses on broadband infrastructure, funded by MEP and FONATEL, with the support of FOD. The subsequent layers progressively integrate internal connectivity, device management, cloud-based administrative tools, and technical support, forming the backbone of a fully interconnected education system. Fernández underscores that the current internet speeds in many schools—often as low as 6 Mbps—are inadequate for the demands of modern education. BEN seeks to resolve these bottlenecks, facilitating the adoption of digital learning tools and the use of AI in educational settings.

The implementation of AI technologies could provide tailored learning experiences, improve administrative efficiencies, and offer real-time data analysis for decision-making. For instance, AI-powered platforms can analyze student performance data to recommend personalized learning paths, identify students at risk of falling behind, and suggest interventions. In administrative contexts, AI could streamline tasks such as grading, attendance tracking, and human resources management, reducing the workload on educators and allowing them to focus on more impactful activities.

Despite the ambitious goals, the project faces delay due to procurement issues and legal challenges. The bidding process for the first phase of the broadband infrastructure, initially won by Ufinet, has been delayed by appeals from competing bidders, such as Grupo ICE and Tigo. These delays highlight the complexities of public-private collaborations in large-scale national projects. Nevertheless, MEP continues to pursue innovative strategies, such as a public-public partnership between the Costa Rican Institute of Electricity (ICE) and FONATEL, to bring internet access to 3,589 educational centers. This collaboration seeks to leverage the strengths of both the public and private sectors to implement and sustain the network in the long term.

The completion of BEN is critical not only for enhancing internet access but also for positioning Costa Rica as a leader in Education 4.0—a model that integrates emerging technologies such as AI, big data, and the IoT into the education system. AI is expected to play a pivotal role in managing the vast amounts of data generated by interconnected schools, facilitating predictive analytics that could improve educational outcomes and resource allocation. For instance, AI can be used to monitor student engagement in real-time, flagging potential issues before they escalate and providing targeted interventions to support learning.

AI's integration into the educational system is a key feature of BEN's long-term vision. AI-driven systems could revolutionize the way Costa Rica manages its public education system by enabling data-informed decisions. For example, predictive analytics could help identify patterns in student attendance, academic performance, and dropout rates, allowing administrators to intervene proactively. Additionally, AI tools could help manage the logistical challenges of maintaining an interconnected network of schools by automating tasks such as network diagnostics, bandwidth allocation, and cybersecurity monitoring.

The integration of AI into the educational framework also opens opportunities for teachers to use data-driven insights to enhance pedagogical practices. AI can analyze student learning behaviors, providing teachers with recommendations on how to adjust lesson plans or identify areas where students may need additional support. This personalized learning approach can foster a more inclusive and effective education system, catering to the unique needs of each student.

## 4.5 Ministerial Platform (MP)

Parallel to BEN, the MP represents another critical initiative aimed at modernizing the educational and administrative processes in Costa Rica's public education system. Officialized in November 2018, the MP seeks to integrate multiple Management Information Systems (MIS) into a unified platform. This digital system would support various functions, from human resource planning and budget management to academic performance tracking and student enrollment processes.

Before MP, the MEP's administrative processes were fragmented, with each educational center managing its records independently. As a result, basic administrative tasks, such as student enrollment, were often performed manually, creating inefficiencies and data inconsistencies. For instance, an internal audit in March 2019 highlighted that MEP lacked a centralized database for managing student records. The audit revealed that 40% of educational centers were still using their registration systems, making it difficult to maintain accurate and up-to-date information across the system, figure 1 demonstrates the project scope.

*Figure 1. Scope of the MP project.*

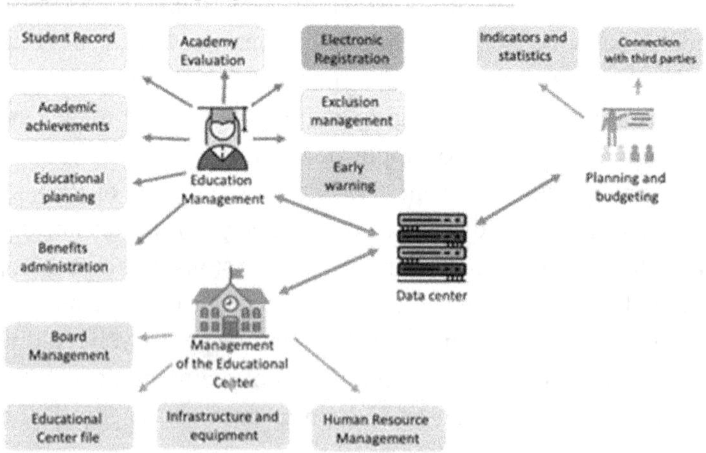


*Source: MEP, Circular, DVM-PICR-0053-10-2018*

The MP aims to resolve these issues by leveraging the enhanced connectivity provided by BEN. By creating a centralized system that integrates all educational centers, the MP seeks to streamline administrative tasks, improve data accuracy, and enhance decision-making processes. The platform would allow real-time access to student records, enabling administrators to track enrollment, performance, and other key metrics more efficiently. Moreover, the system would be able to generate reports and statistical analyses, providing valuable insights for institutional planning and policy development.

The integration of AI into the MP could further enhance the platform's capabilities by automating administrative tasks, improving data analysis, and providing actionable insights. For example, AI could be used to monitor school performance metrics in real time, alerting administrators to potential issues before they become systemic problems. AI algorithms could also assist in human resource planning by analyzing workforce trends, such as teacher turnover rates or the distribution of qualified staff across educational centers, to optimize resource allocation.

In addition to administrative efficiencies, the MP is expected to improve communication between schools, teachers, students, and parents. AI-powered platforms could facilitate more dynamic interactions, allowing for real-time updates on student progress and enabling collaborative learning environments. For instance, AI-driven chatbots could be used to answer frequently asked questions, reducing the administrative burden on school staff and ensuring that parents and students have access to timely information.

As Costa Rica transitions toward Education 4.0, AI will be a critical component of the new educational paradigm. In addition to improving administrative processes, AI can support innovative teaching methods by providing teachers with real-time data on student engagement and performance. This information can be used to adjust instructional strategies, ensuring that each student receives the support they need to succeed. Moreover, AI-powered tools can help students develop critical skills for the 21st-century workforce, such as problem-solving, critical thinking, and collaboration.

For example, AI-driven learning platforms can adapt to individual student needs, providing personalized learning experiences that cater to different learning styles and paces. These platforms can analyze student interactions with digital content, offering insights into how well students understand the material and where they may need additional support. Teachers can then use this data to tailor their instruction, helping students stay engaged and motivated in their learning journey.

The development of BEN and the MP represents a significant step toward modernizing Costa Rica's public education system. By leveraging AI and advanced digital technologies, these initiatives aim to enhance both administrative efficiency and educational quality. The integration of AI into these systems is expected to revolutionize how data is collected, analyzed, and utilized, enabling data-driven decision-making that can improve student outcomes and resource management. As Costa Rica continues to build its Education 4.0 model, the role of AI will become increasingly important in shaping a more inclusive, efficient, and innovative education system.

The MP would be developed in two stages. The first stage would design the mainframe with the central software architecture for the complete platform, the second stage would develop the education management platform, the first phase for student enrollment processes, the second phase for Administrative Assessment and Evaluation, and a third phase for teacher management services (Figure 2).

*Figure 2. Stages of implementation of the MP project*

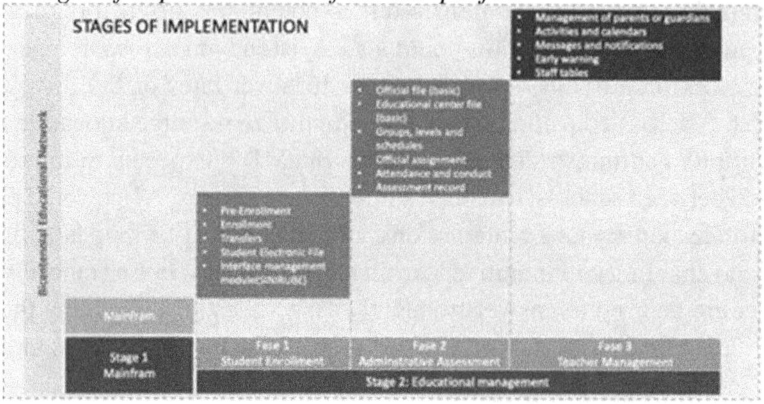


*Source: MEP, Circular, DVM-PICR-0053-10-2018*

## 5 DISCUSSION

### 5.1 Education 4.0 and Its Impact on the Fourth Industrial Revolution

Education is not just a response to the present but also a preparation for the future, placing it at the center of every industrial revolution. As the world maneuvers into the 4IR, Education 4.0 emerges as an essential model to meet the demands of this new era. The fusion of digital, physical, and biological technologies is fundamentally reshaping industries and society, requiring education systems to adapt quickly to these changes. Our analysis of the BEN and related educational reforms in Costa Rica yields three key lessons for understanding the synergy between Education 4.0,

AI, and digital technology within this context as indicated by internet connectivity in the country (Table 2).

*Table 2. Internet connectivity in Costa Rican schools (2018-2024)*

| Year | Schools with Broadband Connectivity (%) | Schools with No Connectivity (%) |
|---|---|---|
| 2018 | 35 | 65 |
| 2020 | 50 | 48 |
| 2022 | 70 | 30 |
| 2024 | 85 | 15 |

Source: data survey from the study

Connectivity improvements directly correlate with implementing PRONIE MEP-FOD projects, demonstrating a 50% reduction in schools without connectivity over six years.

Yet, rural schools still lag as regards AI and pedagogical innovations and their adoption as shown in Figure 3, representing 60% of non-connected institutions in 2024 (Cerdas, 2021).

*Figure 3. Adoption of AI in educational practices by region (2024)*

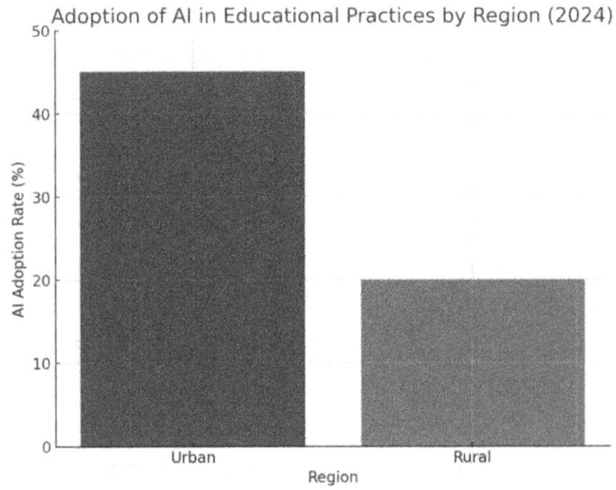


*Source: data survey from the study*

Urban areas show a 45% adoption rate of AI-driven platforms (e.g., personalized learning tools), while rural regions remain at 20%. However, a pilot program using AI-driven virtual tutors in urban areas improved student performance in mathematics by 35% (UNESCO, 2021).

The study also highlighted a direct relationship between technological accessibility and equity, suggesting a positive impact of connectivity on student learning outcomes (Table 3).

*Table 3. Comparative data from connected vs. non-connected schools (2023-2024).*

| Metric | Connected Schools (Avg.) | Non-Connected Schools (Avg.) |
|---|---|---|
| Math Proficiency (%) | 78 | 54 |
| Digital Literacy (%) | 82 | 40 |
| Retention Rates (%) | 95 | 70 |

Source: data survey from the study

Students in connected schools consistently outperform their peers in non-connected settings, underscoring the critical role of broadband in educational equity (UNESCO, 2021).

Ethical consideration, the digital divide risks exacerbating societal inequalities if left unaddressed. Below are key takeaways from the data:

### First Lesson: Broadband Connectivity is Both a Fundamental Requisite for Education 4.0 and a Basic Requirement for the Continuity of Education Services

Connectivity is no longer a luxury but a fundamental prerequisite for enabling Education 4.0. The WEF emphasizes that technology must be used to "move from a system where learning is confined to those with access to school buildings to one in which everyone has access to learning, making education more inclusive" (WEF, 2020). BEN's ambitious goals of establishing broadband internet in every public school in Costa Rica underscore this point.

In Costa Rica, the development of BEN seeks to address the current limitations in internet connectivity, ensuring that students, teachers, and administrators have access to robust digital infrastructure. With broadband at the core, BEN enables the use of AI and other advanced technologies to enhance teaching, learning, and educational management. AI-powered systems, for example, can analyze vast datasets to personalize learning experiences, improve administrative efficiencies, and predict student performance trends. By leveraging broadband connectivity, AI-driven tools can make learning adaptive, student-centered, and more effective in real time.

The interconnectivity offered by BEN is not only a technical requirement but also a socio-economic one. As Costa Rica navigates the 4IR, the nation must prepare its workforce for jobs that demand both technical and soft skills, such as problem-solving, collaboration, and creativity. These skills are nurtured by modern educational models that integrate AI and other emerging technologies, positioning students for success in a hyperconnected world.

### Second Lesson: Societies Must Embed Education 4.0 Models Within the Context of the 4IR.

The 4IR brings significant challenges and opportunities, and education is a critical lever to address these. The integration of AI, robotics, big data, and IoT into everyday life underscores the importance of reforming educational models. As Klaus Schwab (2017) notes, "The great beneficiaries of the 4IR are the providers of intellectual or physical capital—the innovators, the investors, and the shareholders."

For Costa Rica, ensuring access to quality education means aligning its systems with the demands of the 4IR. This requires more than just equipping students with technical skills; it also involves fostering human-centric skills such as empathy, social awareness, and global citizenship, which are critical for navigating a rapidly changing world. The BEN and MEP's MP represent the foundational infrastructure necessary for these reforms. With AI playing a key role in transforming both learning environments and administrative systems, these reforms aim to make education more relevant, accessible, and impactful.

For example, AI-driven systems can streamline administrative tasks, reducing workloads and improving efficiency. This allows teachers to focus more on instruction and student engagement, while AI-powered data analytics can provide real-time insights into student performance, helping educators tailor their teaching methods to individual needs. Furthermore, AI can support institutional planning, human resources, and budget management, ensuring that education systems operate more efficiently and are better aligned with the needs of the Fourth Industrial Revolution.

### Third Lesson: MIS are Key Component of Education Systems in the Fourth Industrial Revolution

MIS is critical in enabling education systems to function effectively in an increasingly complex and interconnected world. The 4IR has brought about a greater reliance on data-driven decision-making, and education systems must keep pace with these developments. MIS technologies, underpinned by AI, can automate administrative tasks, enhance resource allocation, and provide insights for data-driven educational policies. Regarding MIS and AI Integration, it is observed that schools with MIS reported a 60% reduction in administrative errors and a 30% increase in resource allocation efficiency (Figure 4).

*Figure 4. Efficiency gains from management information systems (2021-2024)*

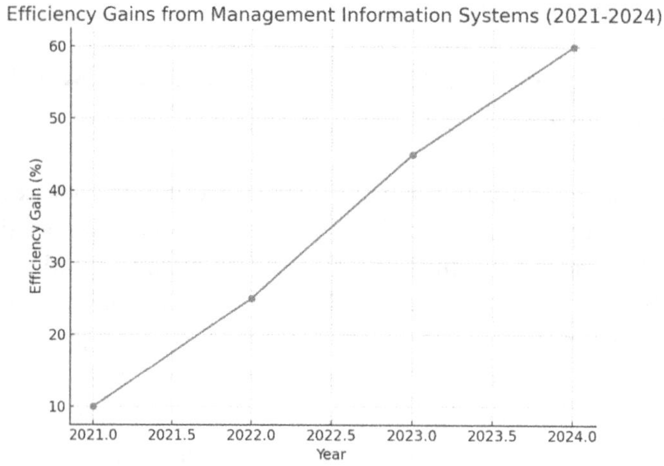


*Source: data survey from the study*

This trend affirms the World Bank report that shows that the integration of MIS at a regional level led to a 25% improvement in teacher-student ratios (World Bank, 2018).

Costa Rica's MP exemplifies the role of MIS in modernizing education. MP aims to integrate diverse management activities, from human resource planning to student academic records, into a single, streamlined system. This initiative will rely heavily on AI to manage and process the vast amounts of data generated by public schools, improving both operational efficiency and decision-making. AI can analyze trends in student performance, identify potential areas for improvement, and provide real-time data to policymakers, allowing them to make more informed decisions about resource allocation and educational priorities.

By integrating AI into its MIS, Costa Rica is taking a proactive approach to managing the complexities of its education system. The result is a more agile and responsive system that can adapt to the changing needs of students, educators, and administrators in real-time.

## 5.2 Education Reform in Costa Rica: Promoting Digital Technology Transformations and Changes in Education Services

Costa Rica's educational reforms, particularly through initiatives such as BEN and MP, reflect the country's commitment to leveraging digital technology to transform its education system. These reforms fall under two categories: education-yielding projects and education-enabling projects, both of which are critical for the future of education in the country.

- Education-Yielding Projects: Promoting Technological Skills and Competencies.
    - o Education-yielding projects in Costa Rica, such as Educational Informatics (LIE++) and CEE, focus on equipping students with the technical skills necessary for the Fourth Industrial Revolution. These projects introduce new learning environments and pedagogies, encouraging students to develop competencies in areas such as AI, robotics, and data analysis. Moreover, programs like Technopreneur emphasize the integration of mobile digital technologies into classroom learning, allowing students to engage with digital tools in a meaningful way. By providing students with access to innovative technology and promoting the development of both technical and soft skills, Costa Rica's education-yielding projects align closely with the goals of Education 4.0. These initiatives foster creativity, critical thinking, and problem-solving—skills that are essential for navigating the complexities of the modern world.
- Education-Enabling Projects: Ensuring Access to Digital Infrastructure.
    - o Education-enabling projects, such as BEN and MP, are foundational to Costa Rica's ability to provide high-quality education in the digital age. BEN's focus on broadband connectivity and MP's role in integrating administrative processes are critical components of this effort. By providing schools with the necessary digital infrastructure, Costa Rica is ensuring that students and educators have access to the tools they need to succeed in a rapidly changing world. AI will play an increasingly significant role in these education-enabling projects. For instance, AI can be used to manage and analyze the vast amounts of data generated by BEN's connectivity network, optimizing resource allocation, and ensuring that educational services are delivered efficiently. Additionally, AI-driven tools can help monitor and maintain the security of the network, ensuring that students and educators can use digital technologies safely and effectively.

The integration of AI into Costa Rica's education system, supported by BEN and MP, represents a significant step toward achieving the goals of Education 4.0. By providing students, educators, and administrators with access to AI-driven tools, Costa Rica is positioning itself as a leader in digital education. AI has the potential to revolutionize teaching and learning, making education more personalized, accessible, and effective.

Moreover, AI can support the development of new pedagogical models that emphasize collaboration, creativity, and critical thinking (George, 2023). These models will be essential for preparing students for the challenges of the 4IR, ensuring that they have the skills and knowledge they need to succeed in a rapidly changing world.

Costa Rica's education reforms, particularly through the development of BEN and MP, demonstrate the country's commitment to leveraging digital technologies to transform its education system. The integration of AI and broadband connectivity will play a critical role in ensuring that Costa Rica's students are prepared for the challenges and opportunities of the 4IR. By prioritizing Education 4.0 and embracing AI-driven innovations, Costa Rica is laying the foundation for a more inclusive, equitable, and effective education system in the digital age (Okot & Zuñiga Castro, 2023).

## 6 IMPLICATIONS AND RECOMMENDATIONS

The findings from this study emphasize the transformative role of AI and digital infrastructure in redefining educational landscapes, particularly in Costa Rica. By integrating AI-driven solutions, such as adaptive learning platforms and MIS, public education systems can address challenges related to accessibility, equity, and quality of education. However, the disparities in broadband connectivity and the unequal adoption of AI tools underscore the digital divide, which remains a significant barrier to achieving Education 4.0 objectives. Furthermore, the study highlights the ethical considerations in implementing AI technologies, such as data privacy, algorithmic biases, and inclusivity, which require deliberate policy frameworks to safeguard stakeholders.

The implications extend to policymakers, educators, and stakeholders in the technology sector, advocating for collaborative efforts to bridge technological gaps, enhance teacher training, and promote sustainable investments in digital infrastructure. The research also demonstrates that effective integration of AI and education reforms can support broader societal goals, such as reducing inequality and fostering economic resilience.

Based on the findings, the following solutions and recommendations are proposed:

- Enhancing Connectivity: Investments in broadband infrastructure must be prioritized to ensure equitable access to digital learning tools, particularly in underserved rural areas. Public-private partnerships can play a pivotal role in expanding coverage and reducing costs.

- AI Integration in Curriculum: Governments should collaborate with educational institutions and tech companies to design curricula that incorporate AI-driven tools, emphasizing critical thinking, problem-solving, and digital literacy skills.
- Teacher Training Programs: Comprehensive training programs are essential to equip educators with the skills to use AI and digital tools effectively. This includes workshops, certifications, and ongoing professional development opportunities.
- Addressing Ethical Concerns: Policymakers must establish guidelines to manage data privacy, mitigate biases in AI algorithms, and ensure transparency in the deployment of AI technologies in education.
- Monitoring and Evaluation: Continuous monitoring and evaluation mechanisms are necessary to measure the impact of AI and technological interventions on learning outcomes and administrative efficiency.

Encouraging Research and Innovation: Funding and support should be directed toward research initiatives that explore innovative applications of AI in education, including personalized learning, predictive analytics, and virtual reality-based training.

## 7 CONCLUSION

The review and analysis of Costa Rica's educational reforms in the context of the 4IR highlights a profound synergy between public educational initiatives and AI as key drivers of Education 4.0. The successful adaptation of education systems to the demands of this new industrial era hinges on resolving structural factors, particularly the enhancement of digital management infrastructure, connectivity, and equitable access. These structural changes lay the foundation for the effective use of AI in transforming both learning and administrative processes within public education.

### Connectivity and Digital Infrastructure: The Backbone of Education 4.0

As a prerequisite for Education 4.0, the development of robust digital infrastructure, particularly broadband connectivity, is indispensable. Costa Rica's BEN is a pivotal public reform aimed at addressing this foundational requirement. BEN is designed to ensure that every public school is equipped with broadband connectivity, thereby enabling the integration of AI-powered educational tools, personalized learning platforms, and administrative systems. This reform is crucial not only for advancing technological learning environments but also for the continuity of education services in the face of disruptions like the COVID-19 pandemic.

AI and digital connectivity form a mutually reinforcing cycle. Broadband access allows for the deployment of AI systems that personalize learning, automate administrative tasks, and provide real-time feedback to both students and educators. At the same time, AI enhances the efficiency and effectiveness of digital infrastructure by managing data flows, optimizing connectivity, and predicting network demands. The deployment of AI in Costa Rica's education sector would enable the education system to become more adaptable, scalable, and responsive to the evolving needs of students and educators.

### AI-Driven Education Management: Transforming Administrative Systems

The role of AI extends beyond classrooms and into the broader administration of education systems through MIS. Costa Rica's MP exemplifies the integration of AI into educational administration. AI-driven MIS solutions streamline operations such as human resource planning, resource allocation, and student performance monitoring. This innovation ensures that educational institutions can operate more efficiently, directing resources where they are needed most and supporting data-driven policy decisions.

The synergy between public reforms like the MP and AI-driven technologies ensures that Costa Rica's education system can overcome challenges such as limited management capacity and complex administrative structures. AI-powered tools can provide actionable insights from large datasets, making it easier for policymakers and administrators to align educational resources and priorities with the demands of the Fourth Industrial Revolution.

### Addressing Inequality Through AI and Educational Reform

One of the most pressing concerns of the 4IR is the potential for exacerbated inequality, especially in education. Costa Rica's educational system has been under pressure, particularly due to the COVID-19 pandemic, which has highlighted the gaps in connectivity and digital access. AI can play a crucial role in mitigating these inequalities by facilitating more inclusive learning experiences. Personalized learning platforms powered by AI can cater to individual student needs, ensuring that even students in remote areas or those from disadvantaged backgrounds have access to quality education.

Costa Rica's public educational reforms, including programs like Technopreneur, which promotes the use of mobile digital technologies, and AI integration into learning environments, work in tandem to reduce educational exclusion. These reforms aim to bridge the digital divide by providing students with the tools and resources needed to succeed in a digital-first world, thereby reducing the risk of poverty associated with a lack of access to education.

### New Knowledge: AI and Public Reforms as Catalysts for Educational Transformation

The convergence of AI and public educational reforms in Costa Rica presents new knowledge and insights into the potential for Education 4.0 to drive both social and economic progress. AI enables education systems to become more agile and personalized, offering tailored learning experiences that adapt to the evolving needs of students. Public educational reforms, such as BEN and MP, provide the necessary infrastructure and policy frameworks to ensure the successful integration of AI into both pedagogical and administrative processes.

This synergy between AI and public educational initiatives demonstrates a forward-thinking approach to education that can serve as a model for other developing nations. Costa Rica's experience shows that the key to unlocking the full potential of Education 4.0 lies in addressing structural barriers—such as connectivity and digital infrastructure—while leveraging the transformative power of AI to create more inclusive, efficient, and responsive education systems.

In conclusion, Costa Rica's efforts to align its education system with the 4IR through AI and public educational reforms offer a roadmap for how technology can be harnessed to create a more equitable and effective learning environment. The integration of AI not only enhances the quality of education but also ensures that the nation's students are prepared for the challenges and opportunities of the future. This synergy represents a significant step forward in realizing the full potential of Education 4.0.

## REFERENCES


Ali, S. I. M., & Nihad, M. (2021, May). Internet of Things for education field. In *Journal of physics: conference series* (Vol. 1897, No. 1, p. 012076). IOP Publishing. https://iopscience.iop.org/article/10.1088/1742-6596/1897/1/012076/meta

Baškarada, S. (2014). Qualitative case studies guidelines. *The Qualitative Report*, 19(40), 1–25.

Binns, R. (2018). Fairness in machine learning: Lessons from political philosophy. *Proceedings of the 2018 Conference on Fairness, Accountability, and Transparency*. 81:149-159

Calvo-Rodriguez, A. (2021). Learning with Mobile Technologies at Public Primary Schools in Costa Rica: The case of the National Program of Educational Informatics of the Ministry of Public Education and the Omar Dengo Foundation. *Journal of Universality of Global Education Issues*, 7(1).

Cath, C., Wachter, S., Mittelstadt, B., Taddeo, M., & Floridi, L. (2018). Artificial Intelligence and the 'Good Society': The US, EU, and UK approach. *Science and Engineering Ethics*, 24(5), 505–528. PMID: 28353045

CEPAL. N. (2020). Universalizing access to digital technologies to address the consequences of COVID-19. *CEPAL*. https://hdl.handle.net/11362/45939

Cerdas, E. (2021). Costa Rica's educational challenges in the digital era. *La Nación*. Retrieved from https://www.nacion.com

Chen, L., Chen, P., & Lin, Z. (2020). Artificial intelligence in education: A review. *IEEE Access : Practical Innovations, Open Solutions*, 8, 75264–75278. DOI: 10.1109/ACCESS.2020.2988510

Derici, S. (2024). Digitalization Concept and the Historical Evolution of Digitalization. In *Developing Digital Inclusion Through Globalization and Digitalization* (pp. 90–106). IGI Global. DOI: 10.4018/979-8-3693-4111-7.ch006

Díez, F., Villa, A., López, A. L., & Iraurgi, I. (2020). Impact of quality management systems in the performance of educational centers: Educational policies and management processes. *Heliyon*, 6(4), e03824. Advance online publication. DOI: 10.1016/j.heliyon.2020.e03824 PMID: 32373736

Dingli, A., Haddod, F., & Klüver, C. (2021). *Artificial intelligence in industry 4.0* (Vol. 928). Springer International Publishing. DOI: 10.1007/978-3-030-61045-6

Elayyan, S. (2021). The future of education according to the fourth industrial revolution. *Journal of Educational Technology and Online Learning*, 4(1), 23–30. DOI: 10.31681/jetol.737193

Fisher, I., & Ziviani, J. (2004). Explanatory case studies: Implications and applications for clinical research. *Australian Occupational Therapy Journal*, 51(4), 185–191. DOI: 10.1111/j.1440-1630.2004.00446.x

Floridi, L., Cowls, J., Beltrametti, M., Chatila, R., Chazerand, P., Dignum, V., Luetge, C., Madelin, R., Pagallo, U., Rossi, F., Schafer, B., Valcke, P., & Vayena, E. (2018). AI4People's ethical framework for a good AI society: Opportunities, risks, principles, and recommendations. *Minds and Machines*, 28(4), 689–707. DOI: 10.1007/s11023-018-9482-5 PMID: 30930541

Frey, C. B. (2019). The technology trap: Capital, labor, and power in the age of automation. In *The technology trap*. Princeton University Press., DOI: 10.1515/9780691191959

Frey, C. B., & Osborne, M. A. (2017). The future of employment: How susceptible are jobs to computerisation? *Technological Forecasting and Social Change*, 114, 254–280. DOI: 10.1016/j.techfore.2016.08.019

George, A. S. (2023). Preparing students for an AI-driven world: Rethinking curriculum and pedagogy in the age of artificial intelligence. *Partners Universal Innovative Research Publication*, 1(2), 112–136. DOI: 10.5281/zenodo.10245675

Gómez-García, M., Soto-Varela, R., Umaña-Mata, A. C., & Pérez-Pérez, E. (2024). Digital Transformation Training and Digital Inclusion in Costa Rica. In *From Digital Divide to Digital Inclusion: Challenges, Perspectives and Trends in the Development of Digital Competences* (pp. 149-166). Singapore: Springer Nature Singapore. https://doi.org/DOI: 10.1007/978-981-99-7645-4_7

Haleem, A., Javaid, M., Qadri, M. A., & Suman, R. (2022). Understanding the role of digital technologies in education: A review. *Sustainable operations and computers*, 3, 275-285. https://doi.org/DOI: 10.1016/j.susoc.2022.05.004

Holmes, W., & Tuomi, I. (2022). State of the art and practice in AI in education. *European Journal of Education*, 57(4), 542–570. DOI: 10.1111/ejed.12533

Jaiswal, A., & Arun, C. J. (2021). Potential of Artificial Intelligence for transformation of the education system in India. *International Journal of Education and Development Using Information and Communication Technology*, 17(1), 142–158.

Kalolo, J. F. (2019). Digital revolution and its impact on education systems in developing countries. *Education and Information Technologies*, 24(1), 345–358. DOI: 10.1007/s10639-018-9778-3

Lee, J., & Lee, K. (2021). Is the fourth industrial revolution a continuation of the third industrial revolution or something new under the sun? Analyzing technological regimes using US patent data. *Industrial and Corporate Change, 30*(1), 137-159. https://doi.org/DOI: 10.1093/icc/dtaa059

Li, L. (2020). Education supply chain in the era of Industry 4.0. *Systems Research and Behavioral Science*, 37(4), 579–592. DOI: 10.1002/sres.2702

Licardo, J. T., Domjan, M., & Orehovački, T. (2024). Intelligent robotics—A systematic review of emerging technologies and trends. *Electronics (Basel)*, 13(3), 542. DOI: 10.3390/electronics13030542

Okot, T., Madrigal-Mendez, P., & Solorzano-Arias, D. (2023). The internet of things (IoT) for sustainability: A framework for Costa Rica. *Journal of Technology Management & Innovation*, 18(4), 3–17. DOI: 10.4067/S0718-27242023000400003

Okot, T., & Zuñiga Castro, M. (2023). Desigualdad Digital en el Sistema de Educación Pública: Estudio de Caso Fuera del Área Metropolitana de Costa Rica. *Revista De Educación Y Derecho*, (28). https://doi.org/DOI: 10.1344/REYD2023.28.41707

Qureshi, M. I., Khan, N., Raza, H., Imran, A., & Ismail, F. (2021). *Digital technologies in education 4.0. Does it enhance the effectiveness of learning?* http://hdl.handle.net/123456789/25661

Rabah, K. (2018). Convergence of AI, IoT, big data and blockchain: a review. *The lake institute Journal, 1*(1), 1-18.

Sánchez-Cruzado, C., Santiago Campión, R., & Sánchez-Compaña, M. T. (2021). Teacher digital literacy: The indisputable challenge after COVID-19. *Sustainability (Basel)*, 13(4), 1858. DOI: 10.3390/su13041858

Scepanovič, S. (2019, June). The fourth industrial revolution and education. *In 2019 8th Mediterranean Conference on Embedded Computing (MECO)* (pp. 1-4). IEEE. DOI: 10.1109/MECO.2019.8760114

Schwab, K. (2017). *The fourth industrial revolution*. Crown Currency.

Schwab, K. (2024). The Fourth Industrial Revolution: what it means, how to respond1. In *Handbook of Research on Strategic Leadership in the Fourth Industrial Revolution* (pp. 29-34). Edward Elgar Publishing. https://doi.org/DOI: 10.4337/9781802208818.00008

Schwab, K., & Zahidi, S. (2018). The future of jobs report. In *World Economic Forum* (pp. 1-133).

Sharma, P. (2019). Digital revolution of education 4.0. *International Journal of Engineering and Advanced Technology*, 9(2), 3558–3564. DOI: 10.35940/ijeat.A1293.129219

Stearns, P. N. (2020). *The industrial revolution in world history*. Routledge., DOI: 10.4324/9781003050186

UNESCO. (2021). Artificial Intelligence in education: Challenges and opportunities. Retrieved from https://www.unesco.org

World Bank. (2018). World Development Report 2018: Learning to Realize Education's Promise. *Washington, DC: World Bank*. https://hdl.handle.net/10986/28340

World Economic Forum. (2020, August), *Schools of the Future Defining New Models of Education for the Fourth Industrial Revolution*. Geneva: World Economic Forum. https://www.weforum.org/publications/schools-of-the-future-defining-new-models-of-education-for-the-fourth-industrial-revolution/

Xing, B., Marwala, L., & Marwala, T. (2018). *Adopt fast, adapt quick: Adaptive approaches in the South African context*. Springer Singapore., DOI: 10.1007/978-981-13-0194-0

Xu, M., David, J. M., & Kim, S. H. (2018). The fourth industrial revolution: Opportunities and challenges. *International journal of financial research, 9*(2), 90-95. https://doi.org/DOI: 10.5430/ijfr.v9n2p90

Yin, R. K. (2009). *Case study research: Design and methods* (Vol. 5). sage.

Zhai, X., Chu, X., Chai, C. S., Jong, M. S. Y., Istenic, A., Spector, M., Liu, J.-B., Yuan, J., & Li, Y. (2021). A Review of Artificial Intelligence (AI) in Education from 2010 to 2020. *Complexity*, 2021(1), 8812542. DOI: 10.1155/2021/8812542

## KEY TERMS AND DEFINITIONS

**Artificial Intelligence (AI):** Computer systems designed to simulate human intelligence, enabling tasks such as learning, reasoning, problem-solving, and decision-making.

**Connectivity:** The availability and capability of technological infrastructure to provide internet access, enabling communication, collaboration, and access to digital resources.

**Digital Divide:** The gap between individuals, groups, or countries in terms of access to and use of information and communication technologies (ICTs), often influenced by socio-economic factors.

**Education 4.0:** A transformative approach to learning that integrates advanced digital technologies, such as artificial intelligence, virtual reality, and data analytics, to prepare students for the demands of the Fourth Industrial Revolution.

**Fourth Industrial Revolution:** A global shift characterized by the convergence of digital, biological, and physical technologies, including artificial intelligence, robotics, and the Internet of Things, which fundamentally transforms industries and societies.

**Management Information Systems (MIS):** Tools and systems that manage, analyze, and process data within organizations to enhance decision-making and operational efficiency.

**Public Educational Reform:** Systematic changes in education policies, curricula, and technologies aimed at improving access, quality, and equity in education systems.

Section 4

# Emerging Applications and Future Directions

# Chapter 14
# Corporate Social Responsibility and AI and Their Impact on Smart Cities

**Matthew Brown**
https://orcid.org/0009-0000-1447-1944
*Middlesex University, Dubai, UAE*

## ABSTRACT

*Due to increasing urbanization, smart cities have developed rapidly, and they focus on technology driven infrastructure and sustainable development. With cities becoming more digital, Corporate Social Responsibility (CSR) and Artificial Intelligence (AI) are key issues in determining the urban habitat of the future. This work investigates the relationship between CSR, AI and smart cities, and their implications for urban development. Aiming from the perspective of the role of AI in smart city making and the responsibility of corporations in enhancing sustainable city environment, this chapter discusses the opportunities and difficulties in combining CSR and AI in building more liveable, efficient, and sustainable cities. More specifically, this study aims to help extend understanding of entanglement between corporate responsibility, technological innovation, and urban sustainability to guide the development of more resilient and just cities of the future.*

DOI: 10.4018/979-8-3693-9894-4.ch014

## INTRODUCTION

City living has changed dramatically in recent years and is predicted to change even more in the future with the UN predicting that over 2 billion people will be living in urban areas by 2050 (United Nations, 2021). The UN considers development in urban or city environments to directly link to eight of their sustainability goals. These urban centres are increasingly being referred to as smart cities (De Falco, 2019). There are many definitions as to what constitutes a smart city. A definition from Ranchordás (2020, p261) is perhaps one of the most useful to this discussion; "Smart cities are defined as urban centers where local institutions implement smart technologies (IoT, big data, AI or ML, blockchain, virtual reality) to advance the innovative character of the city and improve the inclusion, participation, and well-being of citizens." This rise in urbanization presents challenges for city planners and citizens (Tan and Taeihagh, 2020), with cities around the world harnessing technological capabilities in the urban sphere to deal with the trend toward greater 'smartness' in cities, with AI being at the forefront of this endeavour (Okai, Feng and Sant, 2019).

The constituent building blocks of smart cities are defined by Giffinger *et al.* (2007) into six domains, these are smart economy, smart people, smart governance, smart mobility, smart environment and smart living. These domains are widely agreed on by scholars (Bifulco *et al.*, 2016; Nieto, Yelpo and Guzmán, 2021) as the building blocks of smart cities and while they were established almost two decades ago, they are still relevant today. As illustrated in Table 1 the smart city construct details much of what will be discussed in this chapter. Smart cities are built on many of the aspects recognized in CSR, such as responsible use of resources, sustainability and community. While ethics are not explicitly detailed here an ethical approach is implied throughout the domains (Chang, 2021; Ziosi *et al.*, 2024), nor is AI explicitly detailed here, this is perhaps unsurprising given that developments in this area leapfrogged in the last ten years, smart cites are very much built around ICT and its potential. Developments in digital technology have driven smart urbanization (Bunders and Varró, 2019; Han and Kim, 2021). The use of Artificial Intelligence (AI) has very much taken hold (Luusua *et al.*, 2023), providing scope for greater efficiency and additional city services.

*Table 1. Domains of a smart city with detailed aspects for each smart domain. Adapted from Giffinger et al. (2007)*

| Economy | People | Governance |
|---|---|---|
| Innovative spirit<br>Entrepreneurship<br>Economic image & trademarks<br>Productivity<br>Labour Flexibility<br>Ability to transform | Level of qualification<br>Affinity to lifelong learning<br>Social and ethnic plurality<br>Flexibility<br>Creativity<br>Cosmopolitanism<br>Participation | Participation in decision-making<br>Public and social services<br>Transparent governance<br>Political strategies & perspectives |
| **Mobility** | **Environment** | **Living** |
| Local accessibility<br>International accessibility<br>Availability of ICT- infrastructure<br>Sustainable, innovative and safe transport systems | Lack of pollution of natural conditions<br>Pollution<br>Environmental protection<br>Sustainable resource management | Cultural facilities<br>Health facilities<br>Individual safety<br>Housing quality<br>Education facilities<br>Social cohesion |

Cities that are deemed to be 'smart' are those in which actors (both human and AI) or objects (Internet of Things (IoT)) are connected through Information Communication Technology (ICT), enabling the sharing of information across a range of areas to enhance the living experience of citizens (Oke *et al.*, 2020). This use of on and offline channels has been seen to dominate the public sector agenda in recent years (Wang and Teo, 2020), supported by the idea that the two principal activities of governments are policymaking and service delivery (Hansen and Fuglsang, 2020). These two activities are greatly improved by higher levels of citizen participation (de Jong, Neulen and Jansma, 2019), while AI applications are also greatly improved by user engagement (Abdulqadir *et al.*, 2024).

The interconnected nature of this smart city concept is built around the sharing of information, sharing economy and creation through multiple actors (both human and artificial); therefore, co-creation begins to become relevant to the study of smart cities. Actors in a smart city context are seen to be those stakeholders that have some function within the city such as citizens, suppliers, city workforce and private sector. Some authors even recognise the overlap between the sharing economy and smart cities (Šiuškaitė, Pilinkienė and Zvirdauskas, 2019; Ranchordás and Goanta, 2020; Palgan, Mont and Sulkakoski, 2021; Sánchez Vergara, Papaoikonomou and Ginieis, 2021).

The concept of corporate social responsibility (CSR) in its most basic form is to recognize that an organization is part of the community within which it operates (Wan-Jan, 2006). This view proposes that organizations are not solely in existence to make money via transactions of goods or services, but also to behave like other members of society, not just exploiting resources for profit, but also giving back to the community in other ways. This is conceptualized through the triple bottom line concept (Elkington, 1998), where organizations must judge success not only through growing profits, but improvements in the planet (wider environment) and people (giving back to the community). While this concept has been originally focused on for-profit organizations, it can also be applied to not-for-profit organizations, charities are often set up to make money and dispense it in activities designed to develop the community and/or the environment. This can also be said of the public sector, which encompasses cities that many people live in; money is generated normally through some form of taxation and allocated to both environmental and community development. Research from Dahlsrud (2008), refines the scope of CSR further into five dimensions; environmental, social, economic, stakeholder and voluntariness.

The following chapter explores the concept of AI, smart cities and CSR in more detail, looking at the applications of AI within smart cities and its ability to develop CRS goals and activities further. The chapter goes on to examine these concepts in relation to safety and well-being and the related ethical issues. The chapter goes on to a critique of much of the development within the fields of AI, smart cites and CSR, before concluding and outlining some limitations.

## ARTIFICIAL INTELLIGENCE

Artificial intelligence (AI), so long the trope of science fiction, is increasingly becoming science fact. The concept holds that machines using software can replicate or even exceed what humans are able to do with their natural intelligence i.e. to think and reason. Put another way artificial intelligence enables machines to perceive their environment, learn from experience and undertake actions to achieve an objective, without the need to be preprogrammed for the task or request further instruction (Russell and Norvig, 2020). This has given rise to an acceleration in scientific research with AI being able to generate hypotheses, collect, examine and interpret huge datasets with little or no human involvement, in much shorter timescales than before (Wang *et al.*, 2023). AI is also being harnessed to identify and act for greater efficiency and effectiveness in areas such as energy and resource usage (Li *et al.*, 2023), customer service (Buhalis and Moldavska, 2022), customer relationship management (CRM) (Kumar, Sharma and Dutot, 2023) to name but a few, as well of course its application to the smart city phenomenon (Ahmed, Jeon and Piccialli, 2022). In recent years machine learning and deep learning have taken the AI concept much further. Machine learning concerns itself with algorithms that enable machines to learn from big data and make generalization whereas deep learning relies on neural networks to learn from networks of large datasets often with unstructured data (Sharifani and Amini, 2023). The scope of AI usage is perhaps best highlighted by Alahakoon *et al.* (2023) who suggest that AI can be used to manage smart city activities such as traffic, police and other emergency service deployment, the spread of epidemics within a community, infrastructure repair and utilities such as water and electricity.

Brem, Giones and Werle (2023) look at AI from two perspectives firstly as the originator of activity, secondly as the facilitator. Essentially this is saying that an originator invents or creates, whereas the facilitator uses what is already creative to look at efficiencies and improvements. While Papagiannidis *et al.* (2021) discuss the benefits of AI in terms of resources, suggesting that AI can be used to create value, building on the concept of resource orchestrated value (Sirmon, Hitt and Ireland, 2007) which aims to replace resource-based view (RBV). By using AI an organisation can better co-ordinate its resources to create greater value in a more efficient way. Measuring AI output is important organisations need to understand what they need to achieve and set KPI's to measure the performance of AI to ensure that the software is delivering on what the organisation needs (Mikalef and Gupta, 2021).

## Artificial Intelligence's Role in Smart City Development and Operations

Technology has always been considered to be at the centre of the smart city phenomena (Han and Kim, 2021; Kumari, Gupta and Tanwar, 2021), so it is perhaps unsurprising that many smart cities have embraced AI to help improve current services and support development of new services.

While perhaps, not the most glamorous of smart city applications, smart bins are playing a key role in city waste management. These are refuse bins that have been fitted with sensors to determine not only how full a bin is, but what type of waste is present in it based on factors such as heat, type of gas found in the bin and humidity. These enable the dispatch of collection trucks in a timely and efficient manner but also with the correct equipment to collect and then recycle the type of waste that has been deposited (Fang *et al.*, 2023). All of these activities ensure that not only are the optimum amount of resources used to collect the waste, but also that it is recycled or repurposed in the most effective way. Application of smart bins can be seen in cities such as Najran (KSA) (Ali *et al.*, 2020), Milton Keynes (UK) (Kumar *et al.*, 2024) and Klang Valley (Malaysia) (Josephng *et al.*, 2024). Smart bins are not the only area of waste that AI is used in. It is also applied to sewage management, to improve sanitation and general public health, as well as to protect the environment (Madhavi *et al.*, 2024). Using senor, AI can detect sewage levels, warning of potential overflows and blockages, as well as detecting gas anomalies. AI systems are also linked to water pumps and control valves in order that they can take corrective action where necessary, which enables flood prevention and sewage spillage (Alprol *et al.*, 2024). These systems are also able to predict potential usage and operate accordingly, often triangulating with weather reporting that could also impact on the volume of water in the sewage system (Ma *et al.*, 2024).

The application of AI in smart cities activities does not stop at smart bins and sewage management, power grids in many cities use AI to anticipate demand, reduce waste, increasing generation of power as needed to avoid unnecessary surplus (Sulaiman *et al.*, 2023). AI uses a range of data sets both historic and real-time to both analyse consumption (Pandiyan *et al.*, 2023) and predict need (Selvaraj, Kuthadi and Baskar, 2023) which enhances sustainable and efficient generation, with consideration toward the most effective use of resources. These approaches are used throughout the world in cities such as Boulder (Colorado US) (Levenda, 2019), which was the first US city to implement a complete smart grid termed 'SmartGridCity', while in Europe the city of Copenhagen has a similar system named 'EnergyLab Nordhavn' (Wang *et al.*, 2017). It should also be noted that AI is not just providing benefits in the generation and management of smart grids, but also in relation to examining faults in the grid, through fault prediction, identification and resolution (De La Cruz *et al.*, 2023). By predicting potential faults through understanding component lifecycles, to identifying where faults have occurred and directing swift maintenance, AI smart grids can reduce outages and aid in more efficient maintenance routines and procedures.

Not only energy grids can be seen to flourish with AI but transportation grids too. Smart cities around the world are increasingly using AI to manage transportation. Whether it is the city of Barcelona who use AI to ease traffic flow and the development of autonomous vehicles, to the cities using AI to operate metro networks such as Seoul (South Korea), Doha (Qatar) and Kobe (Japan). By leveraging AI, train journeys can be scheduled more efficiently to match peak usage times improving service provision for citizens (Lukic Vujadinovic *et al.*, 2024), while also improving journey times (Lin *et al.*, 2024). Equally journey times can be improved when AI is applied to traffic management aiding with greater efficiencies in flow and predicting potential choke points (Hasanujjaman, Chowdhury and Jang, 2023; Mushtaq *et al.*, 2023).

AI is also enabling development of autonomous vehicles on the road, providing greater road safety and public transport opportunities such as autonomous taxis. Autonomous vehicles are not confined to public transportation as there are increasing opportunities for automated road haulage (Sindi and Woodman, 2021), where automated lorries can transport large quantities via roads without the need for drivers who need regular rest periods, so companies can provide longer service periods more safely. It appears clear that AI can not only provide efficiencies in the use of resources and a better service for users but also a reduction in the use of expensive human resources.

The smart city of Dubai is currently developing a new airport which will be controlled by AI to ensure a smooth and efficient passenger experience while maintaining all the appropriate checks for security, immigration and passenger transit (Kamel, 2024). AI in public service has not only improved efficiency, making the process of public service seamless (Kulal *et al.*, 2024), but it has reduced corruption as it provides greater transparency (Mistry, 2012). Improvement in efficiency and reduction of corruption ensures that resources are used more effectively in keeping with the principles of CSR.

AI application can also be applied in building management, in what is unsurprisingly termed smart buildings. In practice AI is used to regulate things like heating, lighting, ventilation and building access (Javed *et al.*, 2023), even automating the use of windows to control the temperature of a building naturally, limiting the need for using energy to either heat or cool the interior environment. Having AI control some or all of these smart building elements can have benefits such as targeted energy consumption savings and providing greater comfort (Parekh, 2024). Adding solar panel co-ordination into the mix (Okiye, 2024) AI can really start to manage the building and provide efficiencies, with the potential cost benefit of selling excess electricity back to the national grid.

## CSR in the AI-Enabled Smart City: Examples of Best Practice

The development of smart cities and urban development in general is dependent on CSR concept, enabling public policy makers to develop sustainable urban living spaces (Singh *et al.*, 2024) citing technologies such as IoT and AI as key to that development. Adding to this Jain, Gue and Jain (2023) point out that AI can be particularly helpful in UN sustainability goals in areas such as; Housing, Transport Systems, Urbanization, Natural Disaster management, Environmental Impact and Green and Public Spaces. Pérez-del Hoyo *et al.* (2021) relate the smart city paradigm to the UN 2030 Agenda on sustainability (Goal 13 – Target 11.3) (United Nations, 2015), which also requires smart public participation, while bottom-up governed cities remain a challenge.

Corporate social responsibility is viewed as being at the core of smart cities. Pašalić, Ćukušić and Jadrić (2021) view smart cities as urban centres built around the three pillars of technology, people and community. Building on this Sun and Zhang (2020) state that within smart cities technologies create value for society, community autonomy, service efficiency and social collaboration. Evidence from China (Kong and Liu, 2023) suggests that digital transformation (through mechanisms such as smart cities) has shown positive effects on organisations being more socially response and improving the CSR performance of enterprises.

Any digital transformation implementation and improvement is in part dependent on benchmarking and measurement (Ahmad *et al.*, 2021; Orbik, 2022). To support this there are some standards in place to help guide development in the area of CSR such as International Standard ISO 26000 Guidance on Social Responsibility (Söderberg, 2017) and for smart cities standards by which they are developed and measured exist in the form of International Organization for Standardization (ISO); ISO 37120 (Heaton and Parlikad, 2019; Bencke, Cechinel and Munoz, 2020). Both of these standards have aspects of alignment with the fundamental aspects of CSR outlined by scholars above (Elkington, 1998; Wan-Jan, 2006), around ethical behaviour, governance and community, continual improvement. Organisations need to decide on the metrics that are suitable to measure their activities, however the key areas of CSR need to be the focal point of measurement; community, diversity, employee relations, environment, product, and human rights (Koh, Li and Tong, 2023).

Frameworks for managing quality such as SERVQUAL (Parasuraman, Zeithaml and Berry, 1988) have existed long before AI and the rise of smart cities. The European Quality Framework Model (EQFM) was designed to improve business results, drawing on resources and staff at the organisation's disposal to provide results, which are viewed not only in terms of business results (profit), but also results in terms of staff, customers and society ensuring continual improvement through innovation. This model draws on ideas of the triple bottom line (Elkington, 1998), accordingly this model lends itself well to smart city services operating in line within CSR values and EQFM is being widely used. For example, the Abu Dhabi (UAE) police have been using the EQFM to transform how they deal with digital information, integrating databases providing greater efficiencies and productivity (EQFM, 2024) providing greater value to the community. Writing extensively on the subject of smart cities Yigitcanlar *et al.* (2021) offer a framework for responsible urban innovation, which includes the three pillars of governance, policy and community and technology (including AI), all of which need to be considered in terms of cost, benefit, risk and impact. This is somewhat akin to the EQFM outlined earlier. Underpinning all of this are CSR considerations of explainable (transparent), ethical, trustworthy and frugal (efficient use of minimal resources). While another framework devised by Bokhari and Myeong (2023) provides guidance to city managers and planners in the application AI and IoT to deliver and enhance a range of city services such as healthcare, transportation and education.

## AI for Public Safety and Community Well-Being and Ethical Approaches

Well-being and public safety has always been at the heart of both smart cities (Giffinger and Gudrun, 2010) and CSR (Macassa *et al.*, 2021), with human well-being forming the cornerstone of many economic and green policy-makers around the world (Szpilko *et al.*, 2023). However, the role of AI in these areas has been less clear. In relation to public safety AI chatbots are providing secure platforms to support women's safety, enabling reporting and crowdsourcing data to provide greater safety with the community enabling faster responses to safety issues (Jewani *et al.*, 2023). While Sandoval *et al.* (2023) highlight the benefits of AI controlling street lighting from both a public safety perspective by ensuring that public areas are well lit, but also from an energy consumption point of view with lighting turned off where it is not being used. AI is also being deployed to tackle crime (Ejjami, 2024), with systems such as CCTV being linked to AI to deter crime more swiftly and effectively, deploying resources (such as police) in real-time, while also building up database modelling to plan better responses and predict future incidents (Sung and Park, 2021).

Turning to public safety and in particular pandemics Alrashdi and Alqazzaz (2024), highlight that the integration of smart cities aspects enables potential early detection of outbreak, effective and efficient tracing, and optimised allocation of necessary healthcare and other resources. Leveraging off smart city big data it is possible to be more proactive in terms of preventative interventions.

## Critique

Despite the benefits AI offers to both smart cities and corporate social responsibility goals, these three facets are not without criticism, and it would be foolish to treat them as a panacea. To suitably harness the benefits outlined above, it is important to understand the drawbacks.

Bibri *et al.* (2023) acknowledge that AI provides smart cities with opportunities to provide better services and sustainability, particularly in line with SDG 11 (United Nations, 2016), however the concept of smart cities has fragmentated in recent years with different cities taking different approaches some of which undermine the sustainability values within. Cugurullo *et al.* (2024) go further suggesting that urban AI may not be sustainable given the expense of new technology and the energy and raw material it consumes.

The topic of surveillance of citizens has long been an area of controversy in the public sphere, this has been intensified with the introduction of AI within digital surveillance. There have been many reports of facial recognition systems used in surveillance and crime detection that is unfairly biased against non-westerners (Henman, 2020), as well as have a gender bias (O'Connor and Liu, 2024) and exhibiting ageism (Diaz, 2020) and ablism (Van Leeuwen, Smets and Jacobs, 2021).

While for many advances in AI, smart cities technologies and CRS practice are welcome and beneficial, it is important to remember that not all benefit from or have access to these developments (Lipuma and Leon, 2024). Some sections of the community don't have the necessary access to wifi-enabled devices and good internet access, creating a digital divide between those how have and those who do not. These groups can begin to miss out on the opportunities created by new development and risk falling behind the rest of society creating an underclass (Božić, 2023). Others may have access to these technologies but lack the skills, understanding and training to effectively use AI and smart devices and services and benefit from them (Luttrell *et al.*, 2020). Finally, people with physical disabilities are often overlooked within the literature, they should not be left out of AI and other smart developments (Makkonen and Inkinen, 2024). CSR cannot truly be achieved while members of the community are disenfranchised. Further criticism is levelled at AI in terms of its lack of transparency (Barredo Arrieta *et al.*, 2020), not only in the data it collects on the citizen, but also how it is used to arrive at particular AI generated decisions and action. Transparency is key not only for generating trust, but also for accountability which is vital to both smart city operations and CSR reporting (Larsson and Heintz, 2020). To help combat this lack of transparency regulation needs to be considered; as is often the case with new technologies, regulation of AI is somewhat lagging behind developments (Smuha, 2021; Hinojosa and González-Cacho, 2023), with laws such as GDPR providing some protection around use of personal data, this is focused more towards private sector use of an individual's data. Data collected in the public space by government entities is somewhat murkier and the application of that data by AI and the decisions made by AI systems in relation to the individual murkier still.

With AI, CSR and smart cities dependent on data for efficiency, effectiveness and improvement, it raises a major problem in terms of privacy. Much of the data that is collected by these activities is private and personal to both individuals and organizations (Yaraziz *et al.*, 2023). While there is a recognition that data does aid in the development of AI, CSR and smart cities, there are concerns over how individual privacy is maintained and how security the data is with cyber security and cyber attacked on the rise (Zhu and Yu, 2019). However, elements such as AI are not just a cause of a privacy problem, they can be the solution, identifying weaknesses in the current systems and responding to cyber-attacks and the like (Vegesna, 2023).

There is some criticism related to AI and its use in smart cities, firstly the need in most smart cities to have digital access can be prohibitive to some community groups (Taylor, 2021), running the risk of creating a digital underclass. Many parts of the developing world still have limited access to the internet, let alone AI and smart city services (Okolo, 2021) Given the autonomous nature of AI, Cugurullo (2024) feels that many individuals have lost power over their environment to AI, pointing out that the smart city of Barcelona has successfully used a bottom-up approach to city management, whereas AI, by its very nature, is top-down.

Criticism of smart cites themselves have often come from their top-down approach (Porto and Oliveira, 2020; Zandbergen and Uitermark, 2020), this is often seen as a Western and capitalist approach to smart cites and not necessarily in keeping with all the foundations of a smart city laid out by Giffinger and Gudrun (2010).

Many smart cities models are global North and Western based (Miller *et al.*, 2021; Hoefsloot *et al.*, 2022) and they favour economic and industry growth over community needs. Png (2022) suggests that the global North approach to smart cities, which appears to be the prevailing one, is also reflected in the use of AI, being top-down in nature, arguing that this its not the only template for AI governance in smart cites and that community led bottom-up approaches need to be explored much more for their potential benefits to the community rather than exclusively industry.

On a human level some research found that individual perceived AI and AI delivered services to be impersonal (Parekh, 2024), from a service perspective this can foster value destruction (Järvi, Kähkönen and Torvinen, 2018).

## CONCLUSION

Having explored AI, CSR and smart cities in some detail, it is we are now possible perhaps to more critically understand what benefits all three of these have to offer and what pitfalls should be avoided to gain the most of these emerging entities.

As we have seen, various different types of AI algorithms can be used in smart cities to improve efficiency, sustainability, and quality of life (Alahi *et al.*, 2023), while meeting CSR requirements and link back to the six pillars defined by Giffinger and Gudrun (2010) upon which smart cities have their foundations. The AI concepts continue to be employed in terms of autonomous cities in experimental urban projects like Neom in Saudi Arabia and Beiyang AI Town in China (Cugurullo *et al.*, 2024). While ethical concerns around the use of data and the application of AI with limited transparency and oversight should not be trivialized, the benefits and processes AI provides to city managers in their work to provide better services in a socially responsible way should not be ignored and all three disciplines (CSR, AI and smart cities) should be explored simultaneously and in conjunction with one another, rather than the consideration of ethics imperatives being relegated to an afterthought. With this in mind, further areas that potentially need to be explored. Clarity around intellectual property in relation to AI; where does the ownership lie

(Chesterman, 2024). The ability of AI to help examine and improve organizational capabilities, as well as performance efficiencies and effectiveness continues to be needed (Mariani *et al.*, 2023). Additionally, while the IoT has been widely explored, the emerging concept of AI controlled IoT or AI-IoT needs much further study (Popescu *et al.*, 2024).

In terms of corporate social responsibility, the concept of stakeholder wealth, where organizations voluntarily develop environmental initiatives and social networks, achieving high corporate reputation, fosters greater CSR engagement (Zhao *et al.*, 2023). Cross-sector social partnerships, where groups from different sectors of the community work together, also need to be examined further in relation, not only to CSR but also to smart cities and how AI can support these activities (Sadabadi, Rahimirad and Nikijoo, 2024).

This chapter is not without its limitations, firstly the chapter has mainly focused on examples from the Western approach and from the Global North, this is largely because much of the work in these domains is from this background. The chapter has also focused on a management perspective and perhaps overlooks the perspective of other stakeholders such as customers and users. The longer-term benefits and drawbacks of AI, CRS and smart cities, have not been looked at fully. Emerging themes such as AI controls devices or AI-IoT is lacking, partly due to the very contemporary nature of these devices.

This chapter has drawn together three important areas, artificial intelligence, smart cities and corporate social responsibility. These areas have not been widely explored in connection to one and other. This chapter has attempted to go some way to redress this imbalance and enable academics, citizens and city smart city managers to consider how best to approach city activities and AI developments in conjunction while maintaining a firm commitment to corporate social responsibility. The chapter also recognizes that these concepts are ever evolving and suggests some, but not all areas where development needs to be examined and applied in an ethical and sustainable way.

## REFERENCES


Abdulqadir, Z., Abdulqader, D., Ahmed, O., Ismael, H. R., Ahmed, S. H., & Haji, L. (2024). Responsible AI Development for Sustainable Enterprises A Review of Integrating Ethical AI with IoT and Enterprise Systems. *Journal of Information Technology and Informatics*, 3(2). https://qabasjournals.com/index.php/jiti/

Ahmad, A., Alshurideh, M., Al Kurdi, B., Aburayya, A. and Hamadneh, S. (2021) *Digital transformation metrics: a conceptual view, Journal of Management Information and Decision Sciences.*

Ahmed, I., Jeon, G., & Piccialli, F. (2022). From Artificial Intelligence to Explainable Artificial Intelligence in Industry 4.0: A Survey on What, How, and Where. *IEEE Transactions on Industrial Informatics*, 18(8), 5031–5042. DOI: 10.1109/TII.2022.3146552

Alahakoon, D., Nawaratne, R., Xu, Y., De Silva, D., Sivarajah, U., & Gupta, B. (2023). Self-Building Artificial Intelligence and Machine Learning to Empower Big Data Analytics in Smart Cities. *Information Systems Frontiers*, 25(1), 221–240. DOI: 10.1007/s10796-020-10056-x

Alahi, M. E. E., Sukkuea, A., Tina, F. W., Nag, A., Kurdthongmee, W., Suwannarat, K., & Mukhopadhyay, S. C. (2023). *'Integration of IoT-Enabled Technologies and Artificial Intelligence (AI) for Smart City Scenario: Recent Advancements and Future Trends', Sensors*. MDPI., DOI: 10.3390/s23115206

Ali, T., Irfan, M., Alwadie, A. S., & Glowacz, A. (2020). IoT-Based Smart Waste Bin Monitoring and Municipal Solid Waste Management System for Smart Cities. *Arabian Journal for Science and Engineering*, 45(12), 10185–10198. DOI: 10.1007/s13369-020-04637-w

Alprol, A. E., Mansour, A. T., Ibrahim, M. E. E. D., & Ashour, M. (2024) 'Artificial Intelligence Technologies Revolutionizing Wastewater Treatment: Current Trends and Future Prospective', *Water (Switzerland)*. Multidisciplinary Digital Publishing Institute (MDPI). Available at: DOI: 10.3390/w16020314

Alrashdi, I., & Alqazzaz, A. (2024). Synergizing AI, IoT, and Blockchain for Diagnosing Pandemic Diseases in Smart Cities: Challenges and Opportunities. *Sustainable Machine Intelligence Journal*, 7. Advance online publication. DOI: 10.61356/SMIJ.2024.77106

Barredo Arrieta, A., Díaz-Rodríguez, N., Del Ser, J., Bennetot, A., Tabik, S., Barbado, A., Garcia, S., Gil-Lopez, S., Molina, D., Benjamins, R., Chatila, R., & Herrera, F. (2020). Explainable Artificial Intelligence (XAI): Concepts, taxonomies, opportunities and challenges toward responsible AI. *Information Fusion*, 58, 82–115. DOI: 10.1016/j.inffus.2019.12.012

Bencke, L., Cechinel, C., & Munoz, R. (2020). Automated classification of social network messages into Smart Cities dimensions. *Future Generation Computer Systems*, 109, 218–237. DOI: 10.1016/j.future.2020.03.057

Bibri, S. E., Alexandre, A., Sharifi, A., & Krogstie, J. (2023). *'Environmentally sustainable smart cities and their converging AI, IoT, and big data technologies and solutions: an integrated approach to an extensive literature review', Energy Informatics*. Springer Nature., DOI: 10.1186/s42162-023-00259-2

Bifulco, F., Tregua, M., Amitrano, C. C., & D'Auria, A. (2016). ICT and sustainability in smart cities management. *International Journal of Public Sector Management*, 29(2), 132–147. DOI: 10.1108/IJPSM-07-2015-0132

Bokhari, S. A. A., & Myeong, S. (2023). The Impact of AI Applications on Smart Decision-Making in Smart Cities as Mediated by the Internet of Things and Smart Governance. *IEEE Access : Practical Innovations, Open Solutions*, 11, 120827–120844. DOI: 10.1109/ACCESS.2023.3327174

Božić, V. (2023) 'Encouragement and Engagement in Technology-Based Language Learning', *Language Education & Technology (LET Journal)*, 3(2), pp. 96–109. Available at: http://langedutech.com

Brem, A., Giones, F., & Werle, M. (2023). The AI Digital Revolution in Innovation: A Conceptual Framework of Artificial Intelligence Technologies for the Management of Innovation. *IEEE Transactions on Engineering Management*, 70(2), 770–776. DOI: 10.1109/TEM.2021.3109983

Buhalis, D., & Moldavska, I. (2022). Voice Assistants in Hospitality: Using Artificial Intelligence for customer service. *Journal of Hospitality and Tourism Technology*, 13(3), 386–403. DOI: 10.1108/JHTT-03-2021-0104

Bunders, D. J., & Varró, K. (2019). Problematizing data-driven urban practices: Insights from five Dutch "smart cities". *Cities (London, England)*, 93, 145–152. DOI: 10.1016/j.cities.2019.05.004

Chang, V. (2021). An ethical framework for big data and smart cities. *Technological Forecasting and Social Change*, 165(January), 120559. DOI: 10.1016/j.techfore.2020.120559

Chesterman, S. (2024). Good models borrow, great models steal: Intellectual property rights and generative AI [Preprint]. *Policy and Society*, puae006. Advance online publication. DOI: 10.1093/polsoc/puae006

Cugurullo, F. (2024) 'The obscure politics of artificial intelligence: a Marxian socio-technical critique of the AI alignment problem thesis', *AI and Ethics* [Preprint]. Available at: DOI: 10.1007/s43681-024-00476-9

Cugurullo, F., Caprotti, F., Cook, M., & Karvonen, A. M Guirk, P. and Marvin, S. (2024) 'The rise of AI urbanism in post-smart cities: A critical commentary on urban artificial intelligence', *Urban Studies*. SAGE Publications Ltd, pp. 1168–1182. Available at: DOI: 10.1177/00420980231203386

Dahlsrud, A. (2008). How corporate social responsibility is defined: An analysis of 37 definitions. *Corporate Social Responsibility and Environmental Management*, 15(1), 1–13. DOI: 10.1002/csr.132

De Falco, S. (2019). Are smart cities global cities? A European perspective. *European Planning Studies*, 27(4), 759–783. DOI: 10.1080/09654313.2019.1568396

de Jong, M. D. T., Neulen, S., & Jansma, S. R. (2019). 'Citizens' intentions to participate in governmental co-creation initiatives: Comparing three co-creation configurations'. *Government Information Quarterly*, 36(3), 490–500. DOI: 10.1016/j.giq.2019.04.003

De La Cruz, J., Gómez-Luna, E., Ali, M., Vasquez, J. C., & Guerrero, J. M. (2023). *'Fault Location for Distribution Smart Grids: Literature Overview, Challenges, Solutions, and Future Trends', Energies*. MDPI., DOI: 10.3390/en16052280

Diaz, M. (2020) *Biases as Values: Evaluating Algorithms in Context*. Northwestern University. Available at: https://dataverse.harvard.edu/dataverse/algorithm-age-bias/

Ejjami, R. (2024). AI-Driven Smart Cities in France. *International Journal For Multidisciplinary Research*, 6(3), 21920. Advance online publication. DOI: 10.36948/ijfmr.2024.v06i03.21920

Elkington, J. (1998). Partnerships from cannibals with forks: The triple bottom line of 21st-century business. *Environmental Quality Management*, 8(1), 37–51. DOI: 10.1002/tqem.3310080106

EQFM. (2024) *Abu Dhabi Police Becoming a Stakeholder-Centric Organisation*. Available at: https://efqm.org/case-studies/abu-dhabi-police/ (Accessed: 26 October 2024).

Fang, B., Yu, J., Chen, Z., Osman, A. I., Farghali, M., Ihara, I., Hamza, E. H., Rooney, D. W., & Yap, P. S. (2023). *'Artificial intelligence for waste management in smart cities: a review', Environmental Chemistry Letters*. Springer Science and Business Media Deutschland GmbH., DOI: 10.1007/s10311-023-01604-3

Giffinger, R., Fertner, C., Kramar, H., & Meijers, E. (2007) 'City-ranking of European medium-sized cities', *Centre of Regional Science* [Preprint]. Available at: https://www.smart-cities.eu/download/smart_cities_final_report.pdf

Giffinger, R. and Gudrun, H. (2010) 'Smart cities ranking: an effective instrument for the positioning of the cities?', *ACE: architecture, city and environment*, 4(12), pp. 7–26. Available at: .DOI: 10.1007/BF02992681

Han, M. J. N., & Kim, M. J. (2021). A critical review of the smart city in relation to citizen adoption towards sustainable smart living. *Habitat International*, 108, 102312. DOI: 10.1016/j.habitatint.2021.102312

Hansen, A. V., & Fuglsang, L. (2020). Living Labs as an Innovation Tool for Public Value Creation: Possibilities and Pitfalls. *The Innovation Journal*, 25(3), 1–21.

Hasanujjaman, M., Chowdhury, M. Z., & Jang, Y. M. (2023). Sensor Fusion in Autonomous Vehicle with Traffic Surveillance Camera System: Detection, Localization, and AI Networking. *Sensors (Basel)*, 23(6), 3335. Advance online publication. DOI: 10.3390/s23063335 PMID: 36992043

Heaton, J., & Parlikad, A. K. (2019) 'A conceptual framework for the alignment of infrastructure assets to citizen requirements within a Smart Cities framework', *Cities*, 90(April 2018), pp. 32–41. Available at: DOI: 10.1016/j.cities.2019.01.041

Henman, P. (2020). Improving public services using artificial intelligence: Possibilities, pitfalls, governance. *Asia Pacific Journal of Public Administration*, 42(4), 209–221. DOI: 10.1080/23276665.2020.1816188

Hinojosa, H., & González-Cacho, T. (2023). The dark side of smart cities. In Cebral-Loureda, M., Rincón-Flores, E. G., & Sanchez-Ante, G. (Eds.), *What AI Can Do*. Taylor and Francis Group, LLC. DOI: 10.1201/b23345-13

Hoefsloot, F. I., Jimenez, A., Martinez, J., Miranda Sara, L., & Pfeffer, K. (2022). Eliciting design principles using a data justice framework for participatory urban water governance observatories. *Information Technology for Development*, 28(3), 617–638. DOI: 10.1080/02681102.2022.2091505

Jain, A., Gue, I. H., & Jain, P. (2023). Research trends, themes, and insights on artificial neural networks for smart cities towards SDG-11. *Journal of Cleaner Production*, 412, 137300. Advance online publication. DOI: 10.1016/j.jclepro.2023.137300

Järvi, H., Kähkönen, A. K., & Torvinen, H. (2018). When value co-creation fails: Reasons that lead to value co-destruction. *Scandinavian Journal of Management*, 34(1), 63–77. DOI: 10.1016/j.scaman.2018.01.002

Javed, A. R., Ahmed, W., Pandya, S., Maddikunta, P. K. R., Alazab, M., & Gadekallu, T. R. (2023). *'A Survey of Explainable Artificial Intelligence for Smart Cities', Electronics*. MDPI., DOI: 10.3390/electronics12041020

Jewani, V. K., Ajmire, P. E., Chaurasia, S., & Brijwani, G. N. (2023). Artificial Intelligence: A Smart and Empowering Approach to Women's Safety. In Ponnusamy, S., Bora, V., Daigavane, P. M., & Wazalwar, S. S. (Eds.), *Impact of AI on Advancing Women's Safety* (pp. 121–138). IGI Global., DOI: 10.4018/979-8-3693-2679-4.ch008

Josephng, P. S., Vasu, K. P., Phan, K. Y., Sun, J., & Wei, Z. (2024). Managing Sustainable E-Waste Resilient Infrastructure with Smart Bin. *Journal of Advanced Research in Applied Mechanics*, 118(1), 108–130. DOI: 10.37934/aram.118.1.108130

Kamel, D. (2024) *Dubai's new airport terminal promises easier and faster check-in enabled by AI, The National*. Available at: https://www.thenationalnews.com/business/aviation/2024/10/24/dubais-new-airport-terminal-promises-easier-and-faster-check-in-enabled-by-ai/ (Accessed: 26 October 2024).

Koh, K., Li, H., & Tong, Y. H. (2023). Corporate social responsibility (CSR) performance and stakeholder engagement: Evidence from the quantity and quality of CSR disclosures. *Corporate Social Responsibility and Environmental Management*, 30(2), 504–517. DOI: 10.1002/csr.2370

Kong, D., & Liu, B. (2023). Digital Technology and Corporate Social Responsibility: Evidence from China. *Emerging Markets Finance & Trade*, 59(9), 2967–2993. DOI: 10.1080/1540496X.2023.2199122

Kulal, A., Rahiman, H. U., Suvarna, H., Abhishek, N., & Dinesh, S. (2024). Enhancing public service delivery efficiency: Exploring the impact of AI. *Journal of Open Innovation*, 10(3), 100329. Advance online publication. DOI: 10.1016/j.joitmc.2024.100329

Kumar, P., Sharma, S. K., & Dutot, V. (2023). Artificial intelligence (AI)-enabled CRM capability in healthcare: The impact on service innovation. *International Journal of Information Management*, 69, 102598. Advance online publication. DOI: 10.1016/j.ijinfomgt.2022.102598

Kumar, V., Gunner, S., Pregnolato, M., Tully, P., Georgalas, N., Oikonomou, G., Karatzas, S. and Tryfonas, T. (2024) 'Sense (and) the city: From Internet of Things sensors and open data platforms to urban observatories', *IET Smart Cities* [Preprint]. John Wiley and Sons Inc. Available at: .DOI: 10.1049/smc2.12081

Kumari, A., Gupta, R., & Tanwar, S. (2021). Amalgamation of blockchain and IoT for smart cities underlying 6G communication: A comprehensive review. *Computer Communications*, 172, 102–118. DOI: 10.1016/j.comcom.2021.03.005

Larsson, S., & Heintz, F. (2020). Transparency in artificial intelligence. *Internet Policy Review*, 9(2), 1–16. DOI: 10.14763/2020.2.1469

Levenda, A. M. (2019). 'Mobilizing smart grid experiments: Policy mobilities and urban energy governance', *Environment and Planning C. Politics and Space*, 37(4), 634–651. DOI: 10.1177/2399654418797127

Li, J., Ma, S., Qu, Y., & Wang, J. (2023). 'The impact of artificial intelligence on firms' energy and resource efficiency: Empirical evidence from China'. *Resources Policy*, 82, 103507. Advance online publication. DOI: 10.1016/j.resourpol.2023.103507

Lin, D., Zhou, Z., Weng, M., Broere, W., & Cui, J. (2024). Metro systems: Construction, operation and impacts. *Tunnelling and Underground Space Technology*, 143, 105373. Advance online publication. DOI: 10.1016/j.tust.2023.105373

Lipuma, J., & Leon, C. (2024) 'Minorities and the AI Revolution: Examining the Literature on Equity and the Digital Divide Equity', *Academia Journals*, 16(6). Available at: https://orcid.org/0000-0002-9778-3843

Lukic Vujadinovic, V., Damnjanovic, A., Cakic, A., Petkovic, D. R., Prelevic, M., Pantovic, V., Stojanovic, M., Vidojevic, D., Vranjes, D., & Bodolo, I. (2024). AI-Driven Approach for Enhancing Sustainability in Urban Public Transportation. *Sustainability (Basel)*, 16(17), 7763. DOI: 10.3390/su16177763

Luttrell, R., Wallace, A., McCollough, C., & Lee, J. (2020). The Digital Divide: Addressing Artificial Intelligence in Communication Education. *Journalism and Mass Communication Educator*, 75(4), 470–482. DOI: 10.1177/1077695820925286

Luusua, A., Ylipulli, J., Foth, M., & Aurigi, A. (2023). *'Urban AI: understanding the emerging role of artificial intelligence in smart cities', AI and Society*. Springer Science and Business Media Deutschland GmbH., DOI: 10.1007/s00146-022-01537-5

Ma, S., Zhu, Z., Liu, Y., Zheng, Y., Lu, J., & Xu, J. (2024). Artificial intelligence-enabled predictive planning for sewage treatment based on improved DNN and LSTM. *Computers & Industrial Engineering*, 198, 110636. Advance online publication. DOI: 10.1016/j.cie.2024.110636

Macassa, G., McGrath, C., Tomaselli, G., & Buttigieg, S. C. (2021). *'Corporate social responsibility and internal stakeholders' health and well-being in Europe: A systematic descriptive review', Health Promotion International.* Oxford University Press., DOI: 10.1093/heapro/daaa071

Madhavi, S., Ashmita, R. S., Dakshatha, E. S., & Dhinakar, T. (2024) 'Smart Sewage System with Advanced Remote Monitoring for Efficient Urban Infrastructure Management', in *2nd International Conference on Artificial Intelligence and Machine Learning Applications: Healthcare and Internet of Things, AIMLA 2024.* Institute of Electrical and Electronics Engineers Inc. Available at: DOI: 10.1109/AIMLA59606.2024.10531479

Makkonen, T., & Inkinen, T. (2024). Inclusive smart cities? Technology-driven urban development and disabilities. *Cities (London, England)*, 154, 105334. Advance online publication. DOI: 10.1016/j.cities.2024.105334

Mariani, M. M., Machado, I., Magrelli, V., & Dwivedi, Y. K. (2023). Artificial intelligence in innovation research: A systematic review, conceptual framework, and future research directions. *Technovation*, 122, 102623. Advance online publication. DOI: 10.1016/j.technovation.2022.102623

Mikalef, P., & Gupta, M. (2021). Artificial intelligence capability: Conceptualization, measurement calibration, and empirical study on its impact on organizational creativity and firm performance. *Information & Management*, 58(3), 103434. Advance online publication. DOI: 10.1016/j.im.2021.103434

Miller, B., Ward, K., Burns, R., Fast, V., & Levenda, A. (2021). Worlding and provincialising smart cities: From individual case studies to a global comparative research agenda. *Urban Studies (Edinburgh, Scotland)*, 58(3), 655–673. DOI: 10.1177/0042098020976086

Mistry, J. J. (2012). The role of egovernance in mitigating corruption. *Accounting and the Public Interest*, 12(1), 137–159. DOI: 10.2308/apin-10287

Mushtaq, A., Haq, I. U., Sarwar, M. A., Khan, A., Khalil, W., & Mughal, M. A. (2023). Multi-Agent Reinforcement Learning for Traffic Flow Management of Autonomous Vehicles. *Sensors (Basel)*, 23(5), 2373. Advance online publication. DOI: 10.3390/s23052373 PMID: 36904577

Nieto, S. G., Yelpo, P. C., & Guzmán, K. P. (2021). Smart City Puebla: Measuring smartness. *Revista Ibero-Americana de Estratégia*, 20(1), e15793. DOI: 10.5585/riae.v20i1.15793

O'Connor, S., & Liu, H. (2024). Gender bias perpetuation and mitigation in AI technologies: Challenges and opportunities. *AI & Society*, 39(4), 2045–2057. DOI: 10.1007/s00146-023-01675-4

Okai, E., Feng, X., & Sant, P. (2019) 'Smart Cities Survey', in *Proceedings - 20th International Conference on High Performance Computing and Communications, 16th International Conference on Smart City and 4th International Conference on Data Science and Systems, HPCC/SmartCity/DSS 2018*. IEEE, pp. 1726–1730. Available at: DOI: 10.1109/HPCC/SmartCity/DSS.2018.00282

Oke, A. E., Aghimien, D. O., Aigbavboa, C. O., & Akinradewo, O. I. (2020). Appraisal of the drivers of smart city development in South Africa. *Construction Economics and Building*, 20(2), 109–126. DOI: 10.5130/AJCEB.v20i2.6632

Okiye, S. E. (2024). Renewable energy construction: Role of AI for smart building infrastructures. *Journal of Inventive Engineering and Technology*, 5(3), 40–48. www.jiengtech.com

Okolo, C.T. (2021) 'AI in the Global South: Opportunities and Challenges Towards More Inclusive Governance', *International Journal of Innovative Research in Arts, Education and Technology | IJIRAET*, 2(1). Available at: https://doi.org/.DOI: 10.48028/iiprds/ijiraet.v2.i1.09

Orbik, Z. (2022). 'CORPORATE SOCIAL RESPONSIBILITY AND THE SMART CITY CONCEPT', *Scientific Papers of Silesian University of Technology. Organization and Management Series*, 2022(165), 245–257. DOI: 10.29119/1641-3466.2022.165.18

Palgan, Y. V., Mont, O., & Sulkakoski, S. (2021). Governing the sharing economy: Towards a comprehensive analytical framework of municipal governance. *Cities (London, England)*, 108, 102994. DOI: 10.1016/j.cities.2020.102994

Pandiyan, P., Saravanan, S., Usha, K., Kannadasan, R., Alsharif, M. H., & Kim, M. K. (2023). Technological advancements toward smart energy management in smart cities. *Energy Reports*, 10, 648–677. DOI: 10.1016/j.egyr.2023.07.021

Papagiannidis, E., Enholm, I. M., Mikalef, P., & Krogstie, J. (2021) 'Structuring AI resources to build an AI capability: A conceptual framework', in *ECIS*. Available at: https://www.researchgate.net/publication/351069404

Parasuraman, A., Zeithaml, V. A., & Berry, L. L. (1988). SERVQUAL: A multiple-item scale for measuring consumer perceptions of service quality. *Electronics Letters*, 64(1), 12–40. DOI: 10.1049/el:19850169

Parekh, R. (2024). Automating the design process for smart building technologies. *World Journal of Advanced Research and Reviews*, 23(2), 1213–1234. DOI: 10.30574/wjarr.2024.23.2.2461

Pašalić, I., Ćukušić, M., & Jadrić, M. (2021). Smart city research advances in Southeast Europe. *International Journal of Information Management*, 58, 102127. Advance online publication. DOI: 10.1016/j.ijinfomgt.2020.102127

Pérez-delHoyo, R., Mora, H., Nolasco-Vidal, J. M., Abad-Ortiz, R., & Mollá-Sirvent, R. A. (2021). Addressing new challenges in smart urban planning using Information and Communication Technologies. *Systems Research and Behavioral Science*, 38(3), 342–354. DOI: 10.1002/sres.2787

Png, M. T. (2022) 'At the Tensions of South and North: Critical Roles of Global South Stakeholders in AI Governance', in *ACM International Conference Proceeding Series*. Association for Computing Machinery, pp. 1434–1445. Available at: DOI: 10.1145/3531146.3533200

Popescu, S.M., Mansoor, S., Wani, O.A., Kumar, S.S., Sharma, V., Sharma, A., Arya, V.M., Kirkham, M.B., Hou, D., Bolan, N. and Chung, Y.S. (2024) 'Artificial intelligence and IoT driven technologies for environmental pollution monitoring and management', *Frontiers in Environmental Science*. Frontiers Media SA. Available at: .DOI: 10.3389/fenvs.2024.1336088

Porto, J. B., & Oliveira, M. (2020). The smart cities methodology based on public value: The first evaluation cycle. *BAR - Brazilian Administration Review*, 17(1), e190048. Advance online publication. DOI: 10.1590/1807-7692bar2020190048

Ranchordás, S. (2020). Nudging citizens through technology in smart cities. *International Review of Law Computers & Technology*, 34(3), 254–276. DOI: 10.1080/13600869.2019.1590928

Ranchordás, S., & Goanta, C. (2020). The New City Regulators: Platform and Public Values in Smart and Sharing Cities. *Computer Law & Security Report*, 36, 105375. Advance online publication. DOI: 10.1016/j.clsr.2019.105375

Russell, S., & Norvig, P. (2020). *Artificial Intelligence: A Modern Approach* (4th ed.). Pearson.

Sadabadi, A. A., Rahimirad, Z., & Nikijoo, I. (2024). Enhancing cross-sector partnerships in energy saving through social entrepreneurship: A social network analysis approach. *Energy Research & Social Science*, 109, 103412. Advance online publication. DOI: 10.1016/j.erss.2024.103412

Sánchez Vergara, J. I., Papaoikonomou, E., & Ginieis, M. (2021). Exploring the strategic communication of the sharing city project through frame analysis: The case of Barcelona sharing city. *Cities (London, England)*, 110, 103082. DOI: 10.1016/j.cities.2020.103082

Sandoval, J. D. P., Arciniega-Nevárez, J. A., Delgado-Galván, X., Ramos, H. M., Pérez-Sánchez, M., López-Jiménez, P. A., & Mora Rodríguez, J. (2023). Street Lighting and Charging Stations with PATs Location Applying Artificial Intelligence. *Water (Basel)*, 15(4), 616. Advance online publication. DOI: 10.3390/w15040616

Selvaraj, R., Kuthadi, V. M., & Baskar, S. (2023). Smart building energy management and monitoring system based on artificial intelligence in smart city. *Sustainable Energy Technologies and Assessments*, 56, 103090. Advance online publication. DOI: 10.1016/j.seta.2023.103090

Sharifani, K., & Amini, M. (2023) 'Machine Learning and Deep Learning: A Review of Methods and Applications', *World Information Technology and Engineering Journal*, 10(7), pp. 3897–3904. Available at: https://www.researchgate.net/publication/371011515

Sindi, S., & Woodman, R. (2021). Implementing commercial autonomous road haulage in freight operations: An industry perspective. *Transportation Research Part A, Policy and Practice*, 152, 235–253. DOI: 10.1016/j.tra.2021.08.003

Singh, K., Kolar, P., Nanduri, S., Seetha Ram, V., & Kumar, D. (2024). CSR and smart city progress: A proposed model for urban development. *Letters in Spatial and Resource Sciences*, 17(1), 3. Advance online publication. DOI: 10.1007/s12076-023-00367-3

Sirmon, D. G., Hitt, M. A., & Ireland, R. D. (2007). Managing Firm Resources in Dynamic Environments to Create Value: Looking inside the Black Box. *Academy of Management Review*, 32(1), 273–292. DOI: 10.5465/amr.2007.23466005

Šiuškaitė, D., Pilinkienė, V., & Zvirdauskas, D. (2019). The conceptualization of the sharing economy as a business model. *The Engineering Economist*, 30(3), 373–381. DOI: 10.5755/j01.ee.30.3.21253

Smuha, N. A. (2021) *FROM A 'RACE TO AI' TO A 'RACE TO AI REGULATION': REGULATORY COMPETITION FOR ARTIFICIAL INTELLIGENCE, Innovation & Technology*. Available at: www.cifar.ca/ai/pan-canadian-

Söderberg, S. (2017) *ISO 26000 and OECD Guidelines*.

Sulaiman, A., Nagu, B., Kaur, G., Karuppaiah, P., Alshahrani, H., Al Reshan, M. S., AlYami, S., & Shaikh, A. (2023). Artificial Intelligence-Based Secured Power Grid Protocol for Smart City. *Sensors (Basel)*, 23(19), 8016. Advance online publication. DOI: 10.3390/s23198016 PMID: 37836846

Sun, M., & Zhang, J. (2020). Research on the application of block chain big data platform in the construction of new smart city for low carbon emission and green environment. *Computer Communications*, 149, 332–342. DOI: 10.1016/j.comcom.2019.10.031

Sung, C. S., & Park, J. Y. (2021). Design of an intelligent video surveillance system for crime prevention: Applying deep learning technology. *Multimedia Tools and Applications*, 80(26–27), 34297–34309. DOI: 10.1007/s11042-021-10809-z

Szpilko, D., Naharro, F. J., Lăzăroiu, G., Nica, E., & de la Torre Gallegos, A. (2023). Artificial intelligence in the smart city - a literature review. *Engineering Management in Production and Services*, 15(4), 53–75. DOI: 10.2478/emj-2023-0028

Tan, S. Y., & Taeihagh, A. (2020). Smart city governance in developing countries: A systematic literature review. *Sustainability (Basel)*, 12(3), 1–29. DOI: 10.3390/su12030899

Taylor, L. (2021). The taming of chaos: Optimal cities and the state of the art in urban systems research. *Urban Studies (Edinburgh, Scotland)*, 58(15), 3196–3202. DOI: 10.1177/00420980211012838

United Nations (2015) *TRANSFORMING OUR WORLD: THE 2030 AGENDA FOR SUSTAINABLE DEVELOPMENT.*

United Nations. (2016) *United Nations Sustainability Goals.* Available at: https://sdgs.un.org/goals (Accessed: 11 October 2024).

United Nations. (2021). *People-Smart Sustainable Cities.* People-Smart Sustainable Cities., DOI: 10.18356/9789210052658

Van Leeuwen, C., Smets, A., Jacobs, A., & Ballon, P. (2021). Blind Spots in AI: The Role of Serendipity and Equity in Algorithm-Based Decision-Making. *SIGKDD Explorations*, 23(1), 42–49. DOI: 10.1145/3468507.3468514

Vegesna, V. V. (2023). Privacy-Preserving Techniques in AI-Powered Cyber Security: Challenges and Opportunities. *International Journal of Machine Learning for Sustainable Development*, 5, 1–8.

Wan-Jan, W. S. (2006). Defining corporate social responsibility. *Journal of Public Affairs*, 6(3–4), 176–184. DOI: 10.1002/pa.227

Wang, C., & Teo, T. S. H. (2020). Online service quality and perceived value in mobile government success: An empirical study of mobile police in China. *International Journal of Information Management*, 52, 102076. DOI: 10.1016/j.ijinfomgt.2020.102076

Wang, H., Fu, T., Du, Y., Gao, W., Huang, K., Liu, Z., Chandak, P., Liu, S., Van Katwyk, P., Deac, A., Anandkumar, A., Bergen, K., Gomes, C. P., Ho, S., Kohli, P., Lasenby, J., Leskovec, J., Liu, T. Y., Manrai, A., & Zitnik, M. (2023). *'Scientific discovery in the age of artificial intelligence', Nature*. Nature Research., DOI: 10.1038/s41586-023-06221-2

Wang, J., You, S., Zong, Y., & Træholt, C. (2017) 'EnergyLab Nordhavn: An integrated community energy system towards green heating and e-mobility', in *IEEE Transportation Electrification Conference and Expo, Asia Pacific (ITEC Asia Pacific)*. IEEE. DOI: 10.1109/ITEC-AP.2017.8080846

Yaraziz, M. S., Jalili, A., Gheisari, M., & Liu, Y. (2023). Recent trends towards privacy-preservation in Internet of Things, its challenges and future directions. *IET Circuits, Devices & Systems*, 17(2), 53–61. DOI: 10.1049/cds2.12138

Yigitcanlar, T., Corchado, J. M., Mehmood, R., Li, R. Y. M., Mossberger, K., & Desouza, K. (2021). Responsible urban innovation with local government artificial intelligence (Ai): A conceptual framework and research agenda. *Journal of Open Innovation*, 7(1), 1–16. DOI: 10.3390/joitmc7010071

Zandbergen, D., & Uitermark, J. (2020). In search of the Smart Citizen: Republican and cybernetic citizenship in the smart city. *Urban Studies (Edinburgh, Scotland)*, 57(8), 1733–1748. DOI: 10.1177/0042098019847410

Zhao, L., Yang, M. M., Wang, Z., & Michelson, G. (2023). Trends in the Dynamic Evolution of Corporate Social Responsibility and Leadership: A Literature Review and Bibliometric Analysis. *Journal of Business Ethics*, 182(1), 135–157. DOI: 10.1007/s10551-022-05035-y

Zhu, T., & Yu, P. S. (2019). 'Applying differential privacy mechanism in artificial intelligence', in *Proceedings - International Conference on Distributed Computing Systems*. Institute of Electrical and Electronics Engineers Inc., pp. 1601–1609. Available at: DOI: 10.1109/ICDCS.2019.00159

Ziosi, M., Hewitt, B., Juneja, P., Taddeo, M., & Floridi, L. (2024). Smart cities: Reviewing the debate about their ethical implications. *AI & Society*, 39(3), 1185–1200. DOI: 10.1007/s00146-022-01558-0 PMID: 36212227

## ADDITIONAL READING


Baccarne, B., & De Marez, L. (2021). Co-shaping smart cities: Participation inequalities in civic crowdsourcing. [IJUPSC]. *International Journal of Urban Planning and Smart Cities*, 2(2), 34–47. DOI: 10.4018/IJUPSC.2021070103

Dawar, I., & Kumar, N. (2024). Making Smart Cities Smarter: Role of AI in Smart Cities Application. In Exploring Ethical Dimensions of Environmental Sustainability and Use of AI (pp. 240-262). IGI Global.

Deakin, M. (2010). The IntelCities community of practice: the eGov services model for socially inclusive and participatory urban regeneration programs. In *Web-based learning solutions for communities of practice: developing virtual environments for social and pedagogical advancement* (pp. 263–284). IGI Global. DOI: 10.4018/978-1-60566-711-9.ch018

Karthikeyan, C. (2025). Smart Governance With AI for Transformative Urban Development in India: Harnessing Data-Driven Insights to Shape the Future of Indian Cities. In Nexus of AI, Climatology, and Urbanism for Smart Cities (pp. 217-246). IGI Global Scientific Publishing.

Lombardi, P., Giordano, S., Caragliu, A., Del Bo, C., Deakin, M., Nijkamp, P., & Farouh, H. (2012). An advanced triple-helix network model for smart cities performance. In *Regional development: concepts, methodologies, tools, and applications* (pp. 1548–1562). IGI Global. DOI: 10.4018/978-1-4666-0882-5.ch808

Manivannan, R., Rajakumaran, M., Ananth, A. D., Markkandeyan, S., Venkatesan, R., & Ghalib, M. R. (2024). The Intelligent Urban Nexus: AI-Driven Decision Making in Smart City Development. In Blockchain-Based Solutions for Accessibility in Smart Cities (pp. 29-42). IGI Global.

McKenna, H. P. (Ed.). (2022). *Urban life and the ambient in smart cities, learning cities, and future cities*. IGI Global. DOI: 10.4018/978-1-6684-4096-4

Padhiary, M., Roy, P., & Roy, D. (2025). The Future of Urban Connectivity: AI and IoT in Smart Cities. In Sustainable Smart Cities and the Future of Urban Development (pp. 33-66). IGI Global Scientific Publishing.

Sposato, M. (2025). Developing Digital Leadership Skills for AI-Driven Research Environments. In Impacts of Generative AI on the Future of Research and Education (pp. 235-254). IGI Global.

Sposato, M. (2025). Digital Leadership in Organizations for Digital Transformation. In Multidisciplinary Organizational Training of Human Capital in the Digital Age (pp. 77-96). IGI Global Scientific Publishing. DOI: 10.4018/979-8-3693-7086-5.ch004

## KEY TERMS AND DEFINITIONS

**Artificial Intelligence (AI):** A technology that enables machines to perceive their environment, learn from experience, and undertake actions to achieve objectives without being preprogrammed or requiring further instruction. In smart cities, AI is used for various applications including waste management, traffic control, power grid optimization, and public service delivery. The technology encompasses both machine learning (algorithms that learn from big data) and deep learning (neural networks that learn from large unstructured datasets).

**Corporate Social Responsibility (CSR):** A concept recognizing that organizations are part of the communities in which they operate and have responsibilities beyond profit-making. CSR encompasses five dimensions: environmental, social, economic, stakeholder engagement, and voluntariness. In smart cities, CSR principles guide sustainable urban development and the ethical implementation of technologies. It's often conceptualized through the "triple bottom line" approach, focusing on profits, planet (environment), and people (community).

**Internet of Things (IoT):** A network of interconnected physical objects embedded with sensors, software, and other technologies that enable them to collect and exchange data. In smart cities, IoT devices are crucial components that work alongside AI systems to manage various urban services. Examples include smart bins with sensors for waste management, traffic monitoring systems, and environmental monitoring devices. IoT enables real-time data collection and automated responses to urban challenges.

**Smart Cities:** Urban centers where local institutions implement smart technologies (IoT, big data, AI/ML, blockchain, virtual reality) to advance innovation and improve citizen inclusion, participation, and well-being. Smart cities are built on six key domains: smart economy, smart people, smart governance, smart mobility, smart environment, and smart living. These cities use Information Communication Technology (ICT) to connect human actors, AI systems, and Internet of Things (IoT) devices to enhance citizens' living experience.

**Smart Governance:** One of the six fundamental domains of smart cities, referring to the use of technology to enhance public participation in decision-making, improve public services, and ensure transparent governance. It involves digital transformation of public services, citizen engagement platforms, and data-driven policy-making. Smart governance aims to create more efficient, transparent, and responsive city administration through technology integration while maintaining ethical considerations and citizen privacy.

# Chapter 15
# Fostering Sustainable Development in Undergraduate Students' Entrepreneurial Mindsets:
## Integrating Digital and AI Ethics in General Education

**Areej ElSayary**
https://orcid.org/0000-0002-5554-0069
*Zayed University, UAE*

## ABSTRACT

*This chapter explores integrating digital and AI ethics into undergraduate general education as a vital approach for cultivating sustainable entrepreneurial mindsets. As AI and digital technologies reshape the entrepreneurial landscape, ethical concerns such as data privacy, algorithmic bias, and environmental sustainability must be addressed to ensure responsible innovation. By embedding ethical principles into entrepreneurship education, universities can guide students to develop ventures aligned with global frameworks like the United Nations' Sustainable Development Goals (SDGs). The chapter discusses the role of universities in shaping future business leaders, the challenges and opportunities of embedding ethics in education, and best practices for fostering ethical entrepreneurship. Through interdisciplinary collaboration, experiential learning, and established ethical frameworks, universities can prepare students to balance innovation with social and environmental responsibility, creating ventures that contribute positively to society and sustainable development.*

DOI: 10.4018/979-8-3693-9894-4.ch015

## INTRODUCTION

Breakthroughs like climate change, resource depletion and social inequality require new generations to address these challenges collaboratively and responsibly. Encouraging undergraduates toward sustainable entrepreneurial thinking is essential in developing a new generation of leaders who can address these global issues. It is more than just what we know as the traditional, profit-oriented way of thinking and emphasizes the ethical consequences of social, economic, and environmental results, respectively (Daddi et al., 2020; Hansen & Wyman, 2021; Mohapeloa, 2017).

No longer being positioned as an isolated target, sustainable development is closely related to the economic target. Global efforts such as the United Nations' Sustainable Development Goals (SDGs) advocate for a more balanced approach in which businesses operate responsibly, and economic growth coexists with the challenge of addressing poverty, inequality, and environmental sustainability. This paves the way for entrepreneurship to be a force for social good.

For example, countries like the United Arab Emirates (UAE) represent this mentality, with national strategies towards innovation and sustainability. The UAE's Vision 2021 calls for entrepreneurship to align with sustainability and requires both technical know-how and a commitment to ethical principles. Emphasizing the development of businesses that are financially viable, yet benefit the wellbeing of society, makes it crucial to impart a sustainable entrepreneurial mindset in students.

## THE ROLE OF UNIVERSITIES IN PROMOTING SUSTAINABILITY

Universities play an important role in educating future decision-makers who will lead global sustainable development. As key institutions that equip students with the skills needed to tackle global challenges, they can integrate sustainability and ethics into entrepreneurship education. This synergy primes students to smoothly adapt to a business environment that needs to balance the force of economic prosperity with aspects of societal responsibility and environmental management (Daddi et al., 2020; Voldsund et al., 2020).

Creating university programs in line with these frameworks, the approaches we call SDGs, provides students with the base to grow a venture tackling important global challenges.prepare These ethical constructs also extends their focus beyond profitability, so that students see their businesses as vehicles for positive social transformation, as building blocks of a better society, which are key value-added constructs to include into the curriculum. As Mohapeloa (2017) argues, this change can be seen as an increasing acceptance that sustainable development plays an integral part in modern business education.

In the United Arab Emirates (UAE), universities play a critical role in the national agenda for sustainability. Under the UAE's broader strategy, universities equip graduates to contribute to the country's sustainable development initiatives through a blend of technical expertise and the application of ethical business practices.

## IMPACT OF AI AND DIGITAL TECHNOLOGIES ON ENTREPRENEURSHIP

However, the previous workplace knew AI in its genesis and its place was not quite well understood and the receptivity towards the impact that it could have on entrepreneurship was still in the incubation stage. AI increases efficiency, creates new markets, and spurs economic development. These same technologies have important ethical concerns including data privacy, algorithmic bias, and the environmental impact of digital systems (Hansen & Wyman, 2021) As AI has evolved, so have the potential dangers behind it, and moving forward, those wishing to be future entrepreneurs must step in to the forefront of addressing these issues responsibly.

If not properly designed, AI systems can reinforce social inequities, for example in hiring, financial decisions, or criminal justice. AI "Ethics" Forces Students To Create Systems That Don't Reinforce Biases Data Privacy has also become a major concern as more and more businesses rely on personal data. Your usage of this data can result in leaving a scar on your reputation and legal troubles.

In addition, digital technologies also have a negative impulse on the environment, most notably in terms of energy use in data and cloud computing centers. By educating students on how their technological choices can affect the environment, they learn to make sustainable choices that are energy-efficient. Such ethical challenges underscore the need for an inclusion of digital and AI ethics in entrepreneurship education to ensure that innovation leads to a better society.

This chapter explores the incorporation of digital and AI ethics in undergraduate general education as a means of cultivating sustainable entrepreneurial mindsets. The central research question is: How does integration of digital and AI ethics in undergraduate general education shape entrepreneurial mindsets for sustainable development and what are the best practices of integration?

Against this background, the chapter discusses how financialization has infiltrated entrepreneurship education, the relevance of sustainability in a world where business has become only servitude, the disruption of AI and digital technologies, and the need for combat in the present and future spheres. It also addresses adding these ethical questions into general education systems and presents driving factors behind integrating ethics into entrepreneurship education systems. The purpose is to train them to become responsible entrepreneurs who add value to the society and environment through their business ventures. Accordingly, the guiding research question is: How can integrating digital and AI ethics in undergraduate general education foster entrepreneurial mindsets that prioritize sustainable development, and what are the best practices for implementing this integration?

## THE IMPORTANCE OF ETHICAL FRAMEWORKS IN ENTREPRENEURSHIP EDUCATION

### Global Sustainability Goals and Entrepreneurship

Each of the United Nations Sustainable Development Goals (SDGs) focus on challenges the world faces today ranging from poverty to inequality, from environmental degradation to sustainable economic growth; and entrepreneurship plays a critical role in addressing these challenges. Aligning with entrepreneurial thinking that considers broader societal impacts (Daddi et al., 2020; Hansen & Wyman, 2021), the SDGs focus on the inter-linkage of social, economic and environmental challenges.

Establishing the framework of entrepreneurship education around the SDGs can help ensure that students design ventures with sustainability in mind. Integrating ethical structures into curricula enables students to reflect on the far-off impacts of their initiatives, which in turn prepares them to partake in development initiatives both in their local and global environment.

Goal-oriented development, measured against the SDGs, provides both entrepreneurs and society with signposts to guide innovation into the mega-challenges faced by our society, including social inequalities and climate change. By aligning their business practices with these goals, enables entrepreneurs to take steps toward generating long-term value while contributing to global solutions.

### Aligning Entrepreneurial Ventures with the SDGs

Aligning ventures with the SDGs requires entrepreneurs to go beyond profit and market share, focusing on how their businesses can directly contribute to sustainable outcomes such as poverty reduction (SDG 1), gender equality (SDG 5), or responsible consumption (SDG 12). This approach fosters a more holistic understanding of responsible entrepreneurship (Hansen & Wyman, 2021; Voldsund et al., 2020).

For example, solar energy projects that offer accessible energy alternatives contribute to SDG 7 (Affordable and Clean Energy). In addition, businesses focused on equitable labor practices support SDG 8 (Decent Work and Economic Growth). This SDG-aligned line of thought prepares students for a long-term sustainable future, especially as accelerating consumers and investors are preferring social-responsible corporations.

Teaching entrepreneurship to include the SDGs shall develop the new generation of entrepreneurs, capable of creating sustainable businesses, whilst at the same time tackling global challenges, therefore increasing their marketability and social impact.

## Challenges in Achieving Sustainable Development Goals

While aligning entrepreneurship to the SDGs is beneficial, it poses challenges. According to the 2024 United Nations SDG progress report, only 17% of targets are on track, while the rest remain unmet due to factors including the COVID-19 pandemic, conflicts, and climate change (United Nations, 2024).

One of the biggest challenges around entrepreneurship education is figuring out how to teach students to balance them both, thriving businesses and sustainable development. Early-stage entrepreneurs may feel pressured to focus on profitability, while a limited understanding of how to integrate ethical practices into their businesses complicates efforts to achieve SDG targets. For instance, digital technologies can improve innovation, but if not properly adopted, come with risks such as algorithmic bias and skyrocketing energy consumption (Hansen & Wyman, 2021).

Moreover gaps in access to resources and education between developed and developing regions impose supplementary challenges. Entrepreneurship education needs to consider these differences and equip students with knowledge in their contexts on how to break the barriers to become sustainable in their settings.

# THE SIGNIFICANCE OF ETHICAL ENTREPRENEURSHIP EDUCATION AT THE NATIONAL LEVEL

The national level of ethical entrepreneurship education is imperative in advancing the agenda, especially those with lofty sustainability goals. In the UAE, the governing national agenda prioritizes an innovative, sustainable, and knowledge-based economy, which maintains economic growth while addressing environmental and social responsibilities (United Arab Emirates Government, 2023).

Universities increase the readiness of their students to establish their own ventures in a way that is aligned with local and global sustainability goals, through incorporating ethical frameworks into entrepreneurship education. The UAE's emphasis on energy, water conservation and waste management provides a golden opportunity for entrepreneurial solutions that are innovative and aligned with high ethical standards. Digital and AI ethics-trained students are better equipped to craft technologies complementing these sustainability endeavors, thereby minimizing the risk of data exploitation or harm to the environment.

## Ethics in the Era of Artificial Intelligence and Digital Technologies

The drive to AI and digital technologies has changed the way of business in the world as well as opened many ethical questions. These are the issues that need to be addressed including algorithmic bias, data privacy, environmental impact and social responsibility, to make sure that innovation does not ruin society. Universities must train tomorrow's entrepreneurs to address such complexities responsibly.

### Addressing Algorithmic Bias in AI Systems

Tackling algorithmic bias is a critical ethical challenge in AI, as algorithms can reinforce biases present in society if they are not designed and monitored correctly. Needless to say, artificial intelligence systems are built on data, and when that data reflects the status quo, the algorithm has the potential to replicate it, resulting in biased outcomes during hiring, credit scoring, judicial decisions, and many other areas (Hansen & Wyman, 2021).

This is important for entrepreneurs to avoid bias within their algorithms and keep their businesses fair and inclusive. AI bias can damage a company's brand, compromise consumer trust and invite legal challenges. Teaching students how to recognize and eliminate biases in datasets, how to create transparent processes and how to audit AI systems teaches them how to ensure a fair and ethical technology. It means teaching entrepreneurs how to navigate the ethical dilemmas presented by AI-powered companies.

### Data Privacy Issues in Digital Entrepreneurship

As businesses tap into huge quantities of personal data, data privacy presents another pressing ethical consideration. Failure to properly safeguard customer data may lead to issues either by losing the customers' trust, damaging company reputation or falling to legal action, particularly with rules such as General Data Protection Regulation (GDPR) (Obschonka & Audretsch, 2019).

Data privacy is not only a matter of legal compliance for entrepreneurs, but also essential to build and maintain a relationship based on trust with the customer. Startup education should cover privacy laws, crafting transparent data policies, and other best practices, like security by design that protects sensitive information. While it is important that businesses grow, it is equally as important that it is done without compromising individual privacy, as improper usage of personal data can seriously breach ethical boundaries.

## Environmental impact of information and communication technologies

Growing concern over the environmental impact of digital technologies, particularly AI and cloud computing, has arisen because of the significant energy use and carbon emissions from data centers and large-scale processing. Non-renewable energy sources power many digital systems, significantly boosting global emissions (Hansen & Wyman, 2021).

Entrepreneurs should bear in mind the environmental impact of their digital enterprises. Neglecting the energy and waste produced by these technologies undercuts larger sustainability initiatives. Entrepreneurship education needs to require students to assess the sustainability of their technological choices, and to consider energy-efficient alternatives, such as algorithm optimization or using renewable energy to run data centers. This practice cultivates a breed of entrepreneurs driven by environmental sustainability, a philosophy which resonates with international sustainability objectives.

## Social Responsibility and Technological Entrepreneurship

One major element that is becoming more important in technological entrepreneurship is social responsibility. As AI and other new technologies disrupt industries, innovators must ensure their tools do not have a negative impact on society. Automation, helpful as it may be, can lead to joblessness, and poorly developed platforms can perpetuate social inequities.

Tech entrepreneurs should the broader implications of their innovations, from disruption in the labor market to access bias." A focus solely on "Greenlighting" can lead to products that are alienating to targeted audiences. Universities should also show students how these inclusive technologies can benefit all stakeholders, particularly underserved communities. Universities promote socially responsible entrepreneurship to ensure that innovation enhances social good alongside business success (Voldsund et al., 2020).

## General Education Course in Digital and AI Ethics

Including digital and AI ethics as part of their general education will help aspiring entrepreneurs be innovative without being careless about the ethical, social, and environmental consequences of their entrepreneurship activity. AI and digital technologies are at the heart of modern business, and students must be armed with ethical frameworks to responsibly tackle these complexities. Achieving this integration will need a systematic effort, including dedicated ethics courses, interdisciplinary collaboration, experiential learning, and a response to the gaps in existing entrepreneurship education.

## Inclusion of Specialized Digital and AI Ethics Courses

An effective way to bring ethics into education is through courses specifically addressing ethical challenges raised by emerging technologies such as AI and digital systems. In these courses, students learn how to assess the ethical implications of technological innovation, with a special focus on topics including algorithmic bias, data privacy and the ecological impact of the digital infrastructure (Görur et al., 2020).

In doing so, when universities teach students about how biased data can produce unfair results in digital systems (and how these systems are adding to sustainability problems), they can make sure that the future movers and shakers understand what ethical pitfalls they may face in their endeavors, in which they will have tools to mitigate them. These courses make up an ethical foundation upon which business decisions can be based, and help students align the path of innovating toward a goal that benefits society in the long run.

## Integrating Ethics through Cross-Disciplinary Intervention

By employing a cross-disciplinary collaboration, students receive a broader context of the ethical implications surrounding digital technologies. Students gain both technical knowledge and ethical frameworks needed to address complex challenges in business through the intersection of computer science and ethics (Du Toit & Kempen, 2020).

For example, collaboration between business and environmental science departments can prepare students to create sustainable business models. Such a holistic approach provides students with the tools to think critically and solve problems from diverse perspectives and with an awareness of the ethical challenges that business may hold for them in the future, allowing them to tackle the normative issues they will likely encounter as entrepreneurs (Görur et al., 2020, Obschonka & Audretsch, 2019).

## Ethics Education Using Experiential Learning Strategies

Experiential learning, in the form of internships, service-learning projects and the capstone course, helps students translate ethical principles into practice in real-world business situations. By facing ethical issues and making decisions based on fairness, transparency and sustainability (Obschonka & Audretsch, 2019), these experiences give students the opportunity to grapple first-hand with ethical dilemmas.

Internships at companies that emphasize ethical practices reinforce what is learned in class, showing how ethics is put into practice in business. Oriented towards practical implementation of this knowledge is designed to eliminate the dichotomy between theory and practice, allowing students to apply their knowledge in a responsible way when embarking on an entrepreneurial career.

## Addressing Ethical Gaps in Current Entrepreneurship Education

Ethics is becoming increasingly important, but most entrepreneurship courses do not teach ethics in an integrated way when teaching what technology does. Recent curricula tend to emphasize professional ethics and overlook the effects of AI and digital systems on broader society (Stavrakakis et al., 2021).

Bridging these gaps requires more attention to macro-ethical issues, which seek to understand how phenomena such as technology influence society and the environmental crises we are facing. Furthermore, students need to be trained to evaluate whether their innovations might contribute to social inequities or environmental destruction. Curriculum updates are needed so students can prepare for the technological ethical obstacles ahead.

# SHAPING UP SUSTAINABLE ENTREPRENEURIAL MINDSETS

To prepare students for the challenges of today's business world, universities need to promote sustainable entrepreneurial mindsets. It combines technical skills and ethical thinking, connecting entrepreneurship with the United Nations Sustainable Development Goals and weighing the cut and thrust of innovation with social and environmental responsibility.

## Navigating the Link: Ethics in Entrepreneurship

While entrepreneurship legislation conveys the minimum levels of acceptable behaviour for ethical actions, ethics in entrepreneurship moves beyond this to build on fairness, equity and sustainability (Mohapeloa, 2017). Entrepreneurs often face decisions where profit conflicts with ethical considerations, such as the societal impacts of data privacy, algorithmic bias, and environmental degradation. Entrepreneurship education should prepare students for these dilemmas, encouraging them to think about ways in which their ventures can make a positive contribution to society. Universities have an opportunity to embed ethics in the curriculum to protect the mission of business as it relates to a profit-seeking force as well as one that leads to greater collective value creation in society (Voldsund et al., 2020).

## Starting Ventures in Line with the Sustainable Development Goals

It seeks to find solutions for humanity, especially when it comes to building 'better' cities, partnerships, achieving climate action, empowering equality and economic growth and promoting SDGs - Sustainable Development Goals. The Sustainable Development Goals (SDGs) are a set of 17 global goals aimed at addressing issues such as poverty, gender equality, and environmental sustainability, and they can serve as a framework for entrepreneurs to shape their business ventures to meet these challenges (Hansen & Wyman, 2021). SDG 7 (Affordable and Clean Energy): Clean Energy SolutionsSDG 6 (Clean Water and Sanitation): Water Conservation Ventures Adapting entrepreneurship education to the SDGs pushes students to develop ventures targeting long-term societal problems that ultimately support sustainability and marketability.

## Balancing Innovation with Social and Environmental Responsibility

Without a dedication to responsibility, entrepreneurial innovation can lead to negative consequences such as social inequity and environmental destruction. For instance, Industries built around AI are booming at an unprecedented pace, this leads to increase of energy consumption which leads to the emission of carbon (Hansen & Wyman, 2021). Hence, entrepreneurs should take the initiative to find solutions to minimize their impact on the environment, be they energy-efficient technologies or something else_SETTOPIC_2023-10-20. Moreover, companies should be inclusive, by ensuring their innovations benefit everyone—including underserved populations. Teaching students to align their goals with those that have long-lasting implications aids the development of responsible leaders who are dedicated to pursuing progress while maintaining societal well-being.

## Skills and Values for Sustainable Entrepreneurship

These skills include opportunity recognition, problem solving, risk management, and collaboration are all part of developing a sustainable mindset (Mohapeloa, 2017; Voldsund et al., 2020). Entrepreneurs need to spot opportunities in areas ranging from renewable energy to ethical AI, tackle societal challenges, and balance profit with ethics. A successful venture in such an arena requires effective collaboration with stakeholders in government, NGOs and others. With this, persistence and resilience also come into play, working on a sustainable idea and in a sustainable manner often needs more than one attempt. Universities play an important role in brining these values to students, which prepare them for current challenges and achieve long-term sustainable success (Daddi et al., 2020).

## Challenges and Opportunities in Embedding Ethics in Entrepreneurship Education

Ethics in Entrepreneurship Education To prepare leaders to solve social, environmental, and economic challenges, it is necessary to embed ethics in entrepreneurship education. On the flip side of this process are complications, such as weighing profit against an ethical commitment, little exposure to ethics via the curriculum, and the fast-moving world of technology itself. Digital technologies also provide an opportunity for ethical entrepreneurship development, and universities can contribute to building the ethical foundations of entrepreneurial leaders.

## Navigating the Profit vs. Ethics Dilemma in Entrepreneurship

Instilling ethics in entrepreneurship education on the other hand has the challenge of setting profit oriented goals against ethical responsibility. For example, traditional education is often focused on profitability and market share, which can come at the expense of a wider societal and environmental impact of the business decisions that they will make in the future. Entrepreneurs often find themselves facing such dilemmas where ethical considerations including sustainability or fair labor practices are at odds with economic objectives (Mohapeloa, 2017).

In particular, students need frameworks to help guide their decision-making so that they take into account not just the immediate financial benefits of the work they do, but also the long-term implications for society. More importantly, future entrepreneurs who can learn to weigh up these trade-offs will be better equipped to make decisions, which uphold their ethical responsibilities alongside the desire to generate a profit (Voldsund et al., 2020).

## Limited Exposure to Ethics in General Education Curricula

The exposure to ethical frameworks, if any, with entrepreneurship education is also limited in most general education curricula. Ethics training is often limited to defined areas, such as philosophy or professional conduct, without addressing the new challenges presented by technologies such as AI and digital platforms. As a result, students are emerging unprepared to confront issues such as algorithmic prejudice, data privacy and the ecological consequences of digital technologies (Pasricha, 2023).

Which means that to fill this gap, universities need to incorporate ethics into the entrepreneurship curriculum across disciplines. This is to guarantee that at students understand the ethics of which the innovations they create are about, in order to response to be able to present modern challenge (Görur et al., 2020).

## Opportunities for Ethical Entrepreneurship in the Digital Era

Digital technologies enable ethical entrepreneurship, and the potential for action on the most important social and environmental issues. Examples include AI, big data and digital platforms to improve access to healthcare, lower carbon emissions, and advance fair labor practices (Obschonka & Audretsch, 2019).

AI technology, for example, can be utilized to discover areas of the country that don't have access to healthcare services and address that unaddressed need. Increasing transparency in supply chains, digital platforms provide an opportunity for consumer to make sustainable choices. This will help entrepreneurs integrate ethical principles into the technologies for building their ventures that could directly impact sustainability goals, and making a profit. This is where universities can have a significant impact on the ethics of tomorrow's ethical business leaders. By integrating ethics into entrepreneurship education, they equip students with the means to ingrain ethics in their enterprises (Görur et al., 2020).

Some of the important ones are fostering thinking skills, promoting collaborative learning, and providing practical exposure. These methodologies guarantee that the students will be successful in business and also serve society as well as the business by means of ethical entrepreneurship. Academic libraries are also involved in broadening digital literacy in their respective higher education institutions, and have in recent years begun to extend their efforts to include discussion of ethics in digital and artificial intelligence (AI) practices.

## BEST PRACTICES FOR INTEGRATING DIGITAL AND AI ETHICS IN UNDERGRADUATE EDUCATION

Entrepreneurship education must move beyond the theory to empower students with best practices in digital and AI ethics, providing them with ethical frameworks and practical skills that will guide their future ventures. Examples of these practices are interdisciplinary collaboration, experiential learning, industry partnerships, leveraging existing frameworks, and a continuous assessment of the curriculum to capture the latest developments in technology.

### Collaboration Between Academic Divisions

Integrating ethics in entrepreneurship education requires interdisciplinary collaboration. Many models, such as those in business, computer science, ethics, environmental studies, are different for ethical challenges in digital technologies. Giving students a holistic understanding of the social, ethical, and economic implications of their decisions requires collaboration between these departments (Du Toit & Kempen, 2020).

Joint classes between business and computer science could look at the societal dynamics of algorithmic decision-making; environmentalstudies might examine the environmental impacts of digital technologies. This interdisciplinary focus allows students to not only develop technical skills but also acquire ethical perspectives, equipping them for work in complex technological environments (Obschonka & Audretsch, 2019).

### Real World Ethical Situations through Experiential Learning

While theory is undeniable a part of the ethical decision-making process, experiential learning provides students with the practical exposure necessary to bridge this gap between the concepts and their real-world application. Organizations can include interns, capstone projects, and service-learning opportunities to supplement classroom learning with practical experience, deepening understanding of the influence of ethics on business performance.

For example, students may model a business based on sustainability and data privacy in a senior project. These hands-on experiences help students build a framework for understanding the importance of ethics in running a successful business and prepare them for navigating the ethical grey areas they're likely to face (Obschonka & Audretsch, 2019).

## Industry Collaboration for Ethical Entrepreneurship

Industry collaborators provide real-world perspectives that can inspire students and advance ethical practices across business education through their shared insights in the classroom. Partnering with organizations that are striving towards ethical AI or responsible use of data also provides students with real-world examples of how ethics can play a role in decision-making in a business context (Zhang, 2021).

By establishing professional connections through guest lectures, internships, and mentorships with ethical companies, students gain hands-on experience and a practical understanding of tackling ethical issues. Such partnerships enhance the academic experience and serve as examples for students on how to maintain ethical practices in their future endeavors.

## Applying Established Ethical Frameworks on Curriculum Development

One proposed change is having universities introduce well-established ethical frameworks into the curriculum, which would give students structured approaches to both receiving an academic degree and dealing with ethical dilemmas. Specific frameworks like the IEEE's AI ethics guidelines or the OECD's principles for responsible business conduct provide tangible tools for assessing the ethical dimensions of business decisions (Pasricha, 2023).

Integrating these frameworks into entrepreneurship education prepares students to critically evaluate their business ideas in a systematic way to ensure adherence to global ethical norms. These tools also assist students in their navigation of the ethical complexities they will face in their professional lives.

## Ongoing Evaluation and Adaptation of Curricula

Curricula must adapt to current technology to remain relevant. The formal ethics education at universities needs to be continuously re-evaluated and revised to be relevant in the context of emerging technologies in the fields of AI, blockchain and others (Chen et al., 2021).

Feedback from students, faculty, and the industry is being used to adapt curriculum to meet the needs of the continually changing technological landscape. Ethics-centered entrepreneurship education should be continuously evaluated to ensure it remains relevant and effective, helping prepare students for the ethical challenges of the future.

## Developing Key Skills for Sustainable Entrepreneurship

Promoting a sustainable entrepreneurial mindset is based on acquiring particular skills that help students successfully navigate business challenges in the 21st century. These include identifying opportunities within global challenges, social and environmental problem-solving, ethical risk-taking, co-operation, persistence, and resilience and socially-responsible mindsets and behaviours. Developing these competencies allows for preparing students to lead ventures that align with sustainable development goals.

## Opportunity Recognition in the Context of Global Challenges

Opportunity is crucial to sustainable entrepreneurship. Entrepreneurs as a result must search for market gaps where new and innovative solutions can solve all of the determining global challenges including climate change poverty and inequality (Mohapeloa, 2017; Voldsund et al., 2020). Being aware of opportunities in sectors such as renewable energy, sustainable agriculture or ethical AI allows entrepreneurs to build ventures that serve societal needs and have a competitive advantage.

Universities should seek to instill the importance of aligning more profitable business opportunities with the goals of sustainability. Identifying new approaches that advance, or at least contribute to advancing, solutions to global problems is also an opportunity for students to uplift the generations of innovators who will take us on the 21st-century ride of complexity and uncertainty.

## How to Solve Problems for Social and Environmental Impact?

Such knowledge is important for sustainable entrepreneurship in complex social and environmental problems, which relies heavily on analytical skills, problem solving, and empowerment skills. Entrepreneurs need to develop creative, solutions-oriented approaches to balancing conflicting goals such as reducing impacts on the environment while ensuring the commercial viability of their businesses (Voldsund et al., 2020).

Universities should teach students to tackle real-world problems through case studies and project-based learning. It nurtures the capacity for critical thinking and innovation with an eye on the social and environmental impact.

## RiskTaking: Prioritizing Ethical Solutions

Entrepreneurship is inherently about risk-taking, but the risk must be tempered with ethics. Entrepreneurs should take calculated risks, considering the social and environmental impacts of their innovations. Ensuring the right balance is essential in order to promote new technologies and business models that do not harm either the society or the environment (Voldsund et al, 2020).

Universities should be training students in extensive impact assessments, enabling them to predict the outcomes of actions. Thus, allowing students to develop reasoned, moral choices that reflect innovation while upholding ethical responsibilities.

## The Importance of Collaboration and Teamwork for Sustainable Ventures

For tackling large issues related to sustainability that need multidisciplinary expertise, collaboration is key. Morris & Kuratko, 2020Entrepreneurs have to collaborate across sectors (governments, NGOs, businesses), but design solutions that do not leave any stakeholder behind (Morris & Kuratko, 2020).

Any Entrepreneurship education should promote working in teams, give students diverse teams to work in. This collaboration fosters the teams and students to stitch together ventures targeting intricate sustainability issues.

## Cultivating Persistence and Resilience in Entrepreneurship

Entrepreneurs must show persistence and resilience, especially in sustainable enterprises, where challenges related to regulatory and market frameworks are likely (Daddi et al., 2020). Entrepreneurs have to not only stay grounded on their long term objectives but also be flexible enough to adjust.

One way to encourage resilience in universities is to help students reframe challenges as potential growth opportunities. Learning how to bounce back and persevere is a lifetime skill that will serve students well in an uncertain and competitive business environment.

## Fostering a Sense of Social Responsibility

Sustainable entrepreneurship is all about social responsibility. Such entrepreneurs have a higher propensity to build enterprises that generate enduring positive change (Morris & Kuratko, 2020). Social responsibility is about how business decisions affect not just profits, but employees, communities and the environment.

Entrepreneurship education needs to move beyond sole pursuit of profit to become a force for social impact. Instilling accountability for broader consequences and emphasizing the significance of ethical decision-making encourages students to build ventures that foster a more just and sustainable world.

# CONCLUSION

In a rapidly evolving, hyperconnected, and digital business landscape, embracing sustainable entrepreneurial mindsets among undergraduate students is not just a need but a true opportunity for shaping the future generations of business leaders who are responsible and ethical in their approaches. The chapter has shown how incorporating digital and AI ethics within general education represents a key approach in preparing students for the challenges posed by modern entrepreneurship. Integrating ethical principles within the core of entrepreneurship education helps universities train an innovative generation of entrepreneurs who want to solve societal, environmental, and economic problems.

Such a position is further evidenced in the discussion throughout this chapter that depicts how universities in particular have a crucial role in the formation of future business leaders, and how the alignment of entrepreneurial ventures to a global sustainability agenda and, in particular, that of the United Nations' Sustainable Development Goals (SDGs), is an important aspect of this. By incorporating ethical frameworks into entrepreneurship education, these schools are providing students with the tools to build businesses that prioritize social responsibility, environmental stewardship, and long-term success.

The rise of AI and digital technologies has also brought about ethical challenges including algorithmic bias, data privacy, and the environmental impact of digital infrastructure, which highlight the need for responsible innovation. Hence, by incorporating these concepts in the management curriculum, the institutions would be equipped their students to make their choices appropriately and generate endeavors that can further create the better society.

There is also an opportunity as entrepreneurs adopt ethical practices. Investment in entrepreneurship education for sustainability may initiate productive but taking a step further through interdisciplinary collaboration, experiential learning and critical evaluation of curricula and content would foster sustainable entrepreneurship skills and values aligned with society harnessing and tall herding influence and skills into sustainable entrepreneurship education. Through this visionary approach, they are inspiring a new generation of entrepreneurs who will prioritize progress over profit, ensuring sustainable business models that contribute positively to society and the planet.

## Future Directions

In this future-looking work, embedding digital and AI ethics in undergraduate general education will reveal deep potential for cultivating sustainable entrepreneurial orienting strategies. To lead in sustainable development, universities can adopt several key pathways, driven by the fast-paced technological progress that is changing fast global challenges, providing tools for their solution.

The one key future direction would be the expansion of interdisciplinarity of education. Some argue that an effective approach to teaching ethics involves looking beyond frameworks to engage in deep collaboration around a shared problem set, such as the intersection of computer science, business, environmental studies, and ethics. For example, offering an environmental science course as part of an AI curriculum might better inform students of the environmental costs of technology use, while partnerships with social sciences can turn students' attention to the social consequences of digital innovation. From an academic perspective, this interdisciplinary approach means students will learn to think about complex ethical problems from many angles and be encouraged to find sustainable solutions that go beyond just economic, social or environmental dimensions.

One of the most important directions is the introduction of experiential learning in real time within the curriculum. As ethical dilemmas change with technology, students need to work on real-world problems to come up with insights that can be applied in practice. In the future [the programs] may expand on existing efforts through more collaboration with ethical businesses, NGOs and government bodies to marry students with projects that can provide real impact. Educational institutions might also incorporate virtual reality and AI-powered simulation technologies into these experiential learning opportunities, enabling students to engage with immersive programs designed to practice and hone their decision-making abilities within morally hazardous contexts. These approaches help students not only grasp what the ethical theories are but also facilitate their navigation of how to apply those principles quickly in fast-paced, real-world environments.

Additionally, it is crucial that universities take a more nimble and adaptive approach to creating curriculum. In light of the increasing speed of technological advancement, the implementation of continuous feedback from industry experts, faculty, and students can help to ensure that the educational material remains relevant and well-tackles the newest ethical challenges. For example, new curricula could be continuously updated to include case studies and examples that reflect current technologies, as they emerge, like new AI applications and digital tools. This adaptability ensures students' knowledge will be current and relevant, enabling them to engage thoughtfully with the ethical implications of emerging technologies as they join the workforce.

Another future direction, integrating industry partners, looks especially promising. Partnerships with industry leaders in ethical AI and digital innovation offer invaluable insights and allow students to learn from operational practitioners addressing real-world challenges. Such partnerships can also empower students to make ethical entrepreneurial choices, shaping them to build startups or innovations well suited to meet sustainability objectives. Industry mentorships, guest lectures, and internships all expose students to a wide range of strategies and decision-making processes that characterize ethical practices, which may inspire them to mimic or modify these models in their businesses.

With a broader global context, it will be crucial for universities to promote equity and inclusivity in their ethics education initiatives. Universities can shape this new generation of entrepreneurs, steeped in digital and AI ethics and aware of their part in the technological journey towards an equitable future, by making sure that students from different backgrounds have equal access to resources and opportunities. Specifically, bridging the digital divide and fostering inclusive entrepreneurship may alleviate inequities and help ensure that blossoms in innovation positively impact all members of society, particularly marginalized ones. To achieve this, we need to be integrating topics of digital inclusivity and equity into ethics education itself, emphasizing the necessity of crafting technologies that are usable, just, and advantageous for all.

Third, we need to emphasize environmental ethics and sustainability moving forward. As global environmental challenges grow, and digital technologies continue to aggravate them, we need students to start thinking about the long-term ecological consequences of their entrepreneurial choices. Future curricula can focus on teaching students to assess the carbon footprint of AI and digital systems and if they can explore energy-efficient alternatives, and how their new-age ventures can be aligned with the global goal for the environment like the United Nations' SDGs. Through a strong emphasis on ecological stewardship, universities can mentor students in developing entrepreneurship that reduces their environmental footprint and promotes long-term societal health.

By employing these methods, universities can continue to be leaders in responsible and sustainable entrepreneurship education, constantly keeping pace with the changing face of the digital world. Universities therefore contribute to meaningful change by training students to make responsible, innovative leaders, and encourage a new generation of forward-thinking entrepreneurs who are guided by ethical priorities and sustainability. The approach guarantees that the future of technology progresses on a trajectory that serves humanity and the ecosystem, paving the way towards an equitable and sustainable future.

## REFERENCES


Bautista-Puig, N., Aleixo, A. M., Leal, S., Azeiteiro, U., & Costas, R. (2020). Unveiling the research landscape of Sustainable Development Goals and their inclusion in Higher Education Institutions and Research Centers: major trends in 2000-2017. *arXiv (Cornell University)*. https://doi.org//arxiv.2002.04895DOI: 10.48550

Chen, Y., Albert, L. J., & Jensen, S. (2021). Innovation farm: Teaching artificial intelligence through gamified social entrepreneurship in an introductory MIS course*. *Decision Sciences Journal of Innovative Education*, 20(1), 43–56. DOI: 10.1111/dsji.12253

Daddi, D., Boffo, V., Buragohain, D., & Iyaomolere, T. (2020). Programmes and methods for developing entrepreneurial skills in higher education. *Andragoske Studije*, 2(2), 101–123. DOI: 10.5937/AndStud2001101D

Du Toit, A., & Kempen, E. L. (2020). Effectual Structuring of Entrepreneurship Education: Guidelines for Overcoming Inadequacies in the South African School curriculum. *Africa Education Review*, 17(4), 41–55. DOI: 10.1080/18146627.2020.1868074

Espaῃol, J. B., Barayuga, S. J. R., Tariga, J. N., Eraῃa, P. L. C., Bautista, R. G., & Mayoya, M. A. (2021). Enterprising skills of hospitality management students. *American Journal of Educational Research*, 9(2), 72–76. DOI: 10.12691/education-9-2-3

Filser, M., Kraus, S., Roig-Tierno, N., Kailer, N., & Fischer, U. (2019). Entrepreneurship as catalyst for sustainable development: Opening the black box. *Sustainability (Basel)*, 11(16), 4503. DOI: 10.3390/su11164503

Garrett, N., Beard, N., & Fiesler, C. (2020). *More Than "If Time Allows."* AIES '20: Proceedings of the AAAI/ACM Conference on AI, Ethics, and Society. DOI: 10.1145/3375627.3375868

Ghezali, F., & Boudi, A. (2020). The moderating effect of information technology capabilities on the relationship between marketing mix and corporate entrepreneurship. *PSU Research Review*, 5(2), 101–119. DOI: 10.1108/PRR-12-2019-0037

Gorur, R., Hoon, L., & Kowal, E. (2020). *Computer Science Ethics Education in Australia – A Work in Progress. 2020 IEEE International Conference on Teaching, Assessment, and Learning for Engineering (TALE)*. DOI: 10.1109/TALE48869.2020.9368375

Hamburg, I., O'brien, E., & Vladut, G. (2019). Entrepreneurial learning and AI literacy to support digital entrepreneurship. *Balkan Region Conference on Engineering and Business Education, 3*(1), 132–144. DOI: 10.2478/cplbu-2020-0016

Hansen, D. J., & Wyman, D. (2021). Beyond making a profit: Using the UN SDGs in entrepreneurship programs to help nurture sustainable entrepreneurs. *Journal of the International Council for Small Business*, 2(2), 125–133. DOI: 10.1080/26437015.2021.1881931

Islam, M., Rashid, M., & Nuruzzaman, M. (2021). Sustainable corporate entrepreneurship of publicly traded Commercial Banks: A Developing Country perspective. *Journal of International Business and Management*. DOI: 10.37227/jibm-2021-09-1498

Kariv, D., Matlay, H., & Fayolle, A. (2019). Introduction: entrepreneurial trends meet entrepreneurial education. In *Edward Elgar Publishing eBooks*. DOI: 10.4337/9781786438232.00006

Makhloufi, L., Laghouag, A. A., Sahli, A. A., & Belaid, F. (2021). Impact of entrepreneurial orientation on innovation capability: The mediating role of absorptive capability and organizational learning capabilities. *Sustainability (Basel)*, 13(10), 5399. DOI: 10.3390/su13105399

Michaeli, T., Romeike, R., & Seegerer, S. (2023). What Students Can Learn About Artificial intelligence – Recommendations for K-12 computing education. In *IFIP advances in information and communication technology* (pp. 196–208). DOI: 10.1007/978-3-031-43393-1_19

Mohapeloa, M. (2017). Developing an entrepreneurial mindset within the social sector: A review of the South African context. *African Journal of Science, Technology, Innovation and Development*, 9(5), 645–652. DOI: 10.1080/20421338.2017.1358917

Morris, M. H., & Kuratko, D. F. (2020). The entrepreneurial journey: intention versus emergence. In *Edward Elgar Publishing eBooks* (pp. 1–16). DOI: 10.4337/9781789900224.00009

Napal, M., Mendióroz-Lacambra, A. M., & Peñalva, A. (2020). Sustainability teaching tools in the digital age. *Sustainability (Basel)*, 12(8), 3366. DOI: 10.3390/su12083366

Ngah, R., Sarmidy, R., & Halil, N. H. A. (2020). Implications of generic skills on Innovative Behavior towards Opportunity Recognition in Youth. *Review of World Economics*, 11(1), 123. DOI: 10.5430/rwe.v11n1p123

Obschonka, M., & Audretsch, D. B. (2019). Artificial intelligence and big data in entrepreneurship: A new era has begun. *Small Business Economics*, 55(3), 529–539. DOI: 10.1007/s11187-019-00202-4

Ogunlela, O., & Tengeh, R. (2021). The fourth industrial revolution and the future of entrepreneurial university in South Africa. *International Journal of Research in Business and Social Science (2147-4478), 10*(3), 91–100. DOI: 10.20525/ijrbs.v10i3.1103

Pasricha, S. (2023). Ethics in Computing Education: Challenges and Experience with Embedded Ethics. *arXiv (Cornell University).* /arxiv.2303.12909DOI: 10.1145/3583781.3590240

Popescu, C. (2019). Adaptive Sustainable academic management practices. In *IntechOpen eBooks*. DOI: 10.5772/intechopen.87018

Stanford Institute for Human-Centered Artificial Intelligence (HAI). (2022). *Capstone projects on ethical AI solutions for nonprofits.* Stanford University. https://hai.stanford.edu

Stavrakakis, I., Gordon, D., Tierney, B., Becevel, A., Murphy, E., Dodig-Crnkovic, G., Dobrin, R., Schiaffonati, V., Pereira, C., Tikhonenko, S., Gibson, J. P., Maag, S., Agresta, F., Curley, A., Collins, M., & O'Sullivan, D. (2021). The teaching of computer ethics on computer science and related degree programmes. a European survey. *International Journal of Ethics Education*, 7(1), 101–129. DOI: 10.1007/s40889-021-00135-1

United Arab Emirates Government. (2023). *UAE Vision 2030 and National Agenda.* Retrieved from https://www.government.ae/en/about-the-uae/strategies-initiatives-and-awards/federal-governments-strategies-and-plans/uae-vision-2030

United Nations. (2015). *Sustainable Development Goals.* United Nations. https://sdgs.un.org/goals

United Nations. (2024). *Progress towards the Sustainable Development Goals: Report of the Secretary-General* (A/79/79-E/2024/54). United Nations. https://unstats.un.org/sdgs

Voldsund, K. H., Hasleberg, H., & Bragelien, J. J. (2020). *Entrepreneurship Education Through Sustainable Value Creation. 2020 IEEE Global Engineering Education Conference (EDUCON).* DOI: 10.1109/EDUCON45650.2020.9125171

Zhang, Z. (2021). The impact of digital technologies on entrepreneurship education. *Advances in Social Science, Education and Humanities Research. Advances in Social Science, Education and Humanities Research.* Advance online publication. DOI: 10.2991/assehr.k.210407.088

# Compilation of References


Abbas, J., Al-Sulaiti, K., Lorente, D. B., Shah, S. A. R., & Shahzad, U. (2023). Reset the industry redux through corporate social responsibility: The COVID-19 tourism impact on hospitality firms through business model innovation. In *Economic growth and environmental quality in a post-pandemic world* (pp. 177–201). Routledge. DOI: 10.4324/9781003336563-9

Abdulqadir, Z., Abdulqader, D., Ahmed, O., Ismael, H. R., Ahmed, S. H., & Haji, L. (2024). Responsible AI Development for Sustainable Enterprises A Review of Integrating Ethical AI with IoT and Enterprise Systems. *Journal of Information Technology and Informatics*, 3(2). https://qabasjournals.com/index.php/jiti/

Acosta-Enriquez, B. G., Arbulú Ballesteros, M. A., Arbulu Perez Vargas, C. G., Orellana Ulloa, M. N., Gutiérrez Ulloa, C. R., Pizarro Romero, J. M., Gutiérrez Jaramillo, N. D., Cuenca Orellana, H. U., Ayala Anzoátegui, D. X., & López Roca, C. (2024). Knowledge, attitudes, and perceived Ethics regarding the use of ChatGPT among generation Z university students. *International Journal for Educational Integrity*, 20(1), 10. DOI: 10.1007/s40979-024-00157-4

Adadi, A., & Berrada, M. (2018). Peeking Inside the Black-Box: A Survey on Explainable Artificial Intelligence (XAI). *IEEE Access : Practical Innovations, Open Solutions*, 6, 52138–52160. DOI: 10.1109/ACCESS.2018.2870052

Adams, J. (2023). Defending explicability as a principle for the ethics of artificial intelligence in medicine. *Medicine, Health Care, and Philosophy*, 26(4), 615–623. DOI: 10.1007/s11019-023-10175-7 PMID: 37642834

Adler, M., & Shavit, N. (2024). On the Complexity of Neural Computation in Superposition. CSAIL Technical Reports (July 1, 2003 - present). https://hdl.handle.net/1721.1/157073

Agarwal, S. (2021). Artificial Intelligence Techniques of Fraud Prevention. In Applications of Artificial Intelligence in Business and Finance (pp. 113-132). Apple Academic Press. DOI: 10.1201/9781003129639-6

Agbonyin, A., Reddy, P., & Jakkani, A. K. (2024). Utilizing Internet of Things (IoT), Artificial Intelligence, and vehicle telematics for sustainable growth in small, and medium firms (SMEs). [IJCET]. *International Journal of Computer Engineering and Technology*, 15(2), 182–191. DOI: 10.17605/OSF.IO/QX3DP

Agudelo, M. A. L., Jóhannsdóttir, L., & Davídsdóttir, B. (2019). A literature review of the history and evolution of corporate social responsibility. *International Journal of Corporate Social Responsibility*, 4(1), 1–23. DOI: 10.1186/s40991-018-0039-y

Ahdadou, M., Aajly, A., & Tahrouch, M. (2024). Enhancing corporate governance through AI: A systematic literature review. *Technology Analysis and Strategic Management*, •••, 1–14. DOI: 10.1080/09537325.2024.2326120

Ahmad, A., Alshurideh, M., Al Kurdi, B., Aburayya, A. and Hamadneh, S. (2021) *Digital transformation metrics: a conceptual view, Journal of Management Information and Decision Sciences.*

Ahmed, I., Jeon, G., & Piccialli, F. (2022). From Artificial Intelligence to Explainable Artificial Intelligence in Industry 4.0: A Survey on What, How, and Where. *IEEE Transactions on Industrial Informatics*, 18(8), 5031–5042. DOI: 10.1109/TII.2022.3146552

Ajunwa, I. (2020). The paradox of automation as anti-bias intervention. *Cardozo Law Review*, 41, 1671–1742. DOI: 10.2139/ssrn.2746078

Akpan, I. J., Udoh, E. A. P., & Adebisi, B. (2022). Small business awareness and adoption of state-of-the-art technologies in emerging and developing markets, and lessons from the COVID-19 pandemic. *Journal of Small Business and Entrepreneurship*, 34(2), 123–140. DOI: 10.1080/08276331.2020.1820185

Akter, S., Dwivedi, Y. K., Sajib, S., Biswas, K., Bandara, R. J., & Michael, K. (2022). Algorithmic bias in machine learning-based marketing models. *Journal of Business Research*, 144, 201–216. DOI: 10.1016/j.jbusres.2022.01.083

Alahakoon, D., Nawaratne, R., Xu, Y., De Silva, D., Sivarajah, U., & Gupta, B. (2023). Self-Building Artificial Intelligence and Machine Learning to Empower Big Data Analytics in Smart Cities. *Information Systems Frontiers*, 25(1), 221–240. DOI: 10.1007/s10796-020-10056-x

Alahi, M. E. E., Sukkuea, A., Tina, F. W., Nag, A., Kurdthongmee, W., Suwannarat, K., & Mukhopadhyay, S. C. (2023). *'Integration of IoT-Enabled Technologies and Artificial Intelligence (AI) for Smart City Scenario: Recent Advancements and Future Trends', Sensors*. MDPI., DOI: 10.3390/s23115206

Albayati, H., Kim, S. K., & Rho, J. J. (2020). Accepting financial transactions using blockchain technology and cryptocurrency: A customer perspective approach. *Technology in Society*, 62, 101320. DOI: 10.1016/j.techsoc.2020.101320

Aldaihani, F. M. F., & Asadul Islam, S. G. (2024). Harnessing Green Purchase Intention of Generation Z Consumers through Green Marketing Strategies. *Business Strategy & Development*, 7(3), e419. Advance online publication. DOI: 10.1002/bsd2.419

Aleman, E., & Martínez, R. (2024). 'It's Like They Are Using Our Data Against Us.' Counter-Cartographies of AI Literacy. *Reading Research Quarterly*, 59(4), 665–677. DOI: 10.1002/rrq.574

Ali, S. I. M., & Nihad, M. (2021, May). Internet of Things for education field. In *Journal of physics: conference series* (Vol. 1897, No. 1, p. 012076). IOP Publishing. https://iopscience.iop.org/article/10.1088/1742-6596/1897/1/012076/meta

Ali, A., Razak, S. A., Othman, S. H., Eisa, T. A. E., Al-Dhaqm, A., Nasser, M., Elhassan, T., Elshafie, H., & Saif, A. (2022). Financial Fraud Detection Based on Machine Learning: A Systematic Literature Review. *Applied Sciences (Basel, Switzerland)*, 12(19), 9637. DOI: 10.3390/app12199637

Ali, T., Irfan, M., Alwadie, A. S., & Glowacz, A. (2020). IoT-Based Smart Waste Bin Monitoring and Municipal Solid Waste Management System for Smart Cities. *Arabian Journal for Science and Engineering*, 45(12), 10185–10198. DOI: 10.1007/s13369-020-04637-w

Aljabri, M., Zagrouba, R., Shaahid, A., Alnasser, F., Saleh, A., & Alomari, D. M. (2023). Machine learning-based social media bot detection: A comprehensive literature review. *Social Network Analysis and Mining*, 13(1), 20. Advance online publication. DOI: 10.1007/s13278-022-01020-5

Aljarah, A., Ibrahim, B., & López, M. (2024). *AI, we do not trust! The nexus between awareness of falsity in AI-generated CSR ads and online brand engagement, Internet Research, Vol. ahead-of-print No. ahead-of-print*. DOI: 10.1108/INTR-12-2023-1156

Allen, M. W., & Craig, C. A. (2016). Rethinking corporate social responsibility in the age of climate change: A communication perspective. *International Journal of Corporate Social Responsibility*, 1(1), 1–11. DOI: 10.1186/s40991-016-0002-8

Almazroi, A. A., & Ayub, N. (2023). Online Payment fraud detection model using machine learning techniques. *IEEE Access : Practical Innovations, Open Solutions*, 11, 137188–137203. DOI: 10.1109/ACCESS.2023.3339226

Alonso-Almeida, M. D. M., Perramon, J., & Bagur-Femenías, L. (2015). Women managers and corporate social responsibility in Spain: Perceptions and drivers. *Women's Studies International Forum*, 50, 47–56. DOI: 10.1016/j.wsif.2015.02.007

Alprol, A. E., Mansour, A. T., Ibrahim, M. E. E. D., & Ashour, M. (2024) 'Artificial Intelligence Technologies Revolutionizing Wastewater Treatment: Current Trends and Future Prospective', *Water (Switzerland)*. Multidisciplinary Digital Publishing Institute (MDPI). Available at: DOI: 10.3390/w16020314

Alrashdi, I., & Alqazzaz, A. (2024). Synergizing AI, IoT, and Blockchain for Diagnosing Pandemic Diseases in Smart Cities: Challenges and Opportunities. *Sustainable Machine Intelligence Journal*, 7. Advance online publication. DOI: 10.61356/SMIJ.2024.77106

AlShamsi, M., Salloum, S. A., Alshurideh, M., & Abdallah, S. (2020). Artificial intelligence and blockchain for transparency in governance. In *Artificial intelligence for sustainable development: Theory, practice and future applications* (pp. 219–230). Springer International Publishing.

Amazon (17 de diciembre de 2021). *Amazon refuerza su compromiso con la igualdad de género.* https://www.aboutamazon.es/noticias/trabajar-en-amazon/amazon-refuerza-su-compromiso-con-la-igualdad-de-genero

Amazon Web Services. (n.d). *Inclusión, diversidad y equidad en AWS.* https://aws.amazon.com/es/diversity-inclusion/?nc1=f_cc

Amazon Web Services. (n.d.). *Inteligencia artificial› Servicios de IA.* https://aws.amazon.com/ai/services/?nc1=h_ls

Amerirad, B., Cattaneo, M., Kenett, R. S., & Luciano, E. (2023). Adversarial Artificial Intelligence in Insurance: From an Example to Some Potential Remedies. *Risks*, 11(1), 20. DOI: 10.3390/risks11010020

Anantrasirichai, N., & Bull, D. (2022). Artificial intelligence in the creative industries: A review. *Artificial Intelligence Review*, 55(1), 589–656. DOI: 10.1007/s10462-021-10039-7

Anderson, R. (2022). The dawn of credit scoring. In *Credit intelligence and modelling: many paths through the forest of credit rating and scoring* (pp. 281–314). Oxford University Press., DOI: 10.1093/oso/9780192844194.003.0008

Anderson, S., Allen, P., Peckham, S., & Goodwin, N. (2008). Asking the right questions: Scoping studies in the commissioning of research on the organisation and delivery of health services. *Health Research Policy and Systems*, 6(1), 7. Advance online publication. DOI: 10.1186/1478-4505-6-7 PMID: 18613961

Anderson, T., Schum, D., & Twining, W. (2005). *Analysis of Evidence* (2nd ed.). Cambridge University Press., DOI: 10.1017/CBO9780511610585

Aninat, M. (2015). *Estudio sobre prácticas de responsabilidad social empresarial de las empresas en Chile*. Fundación ProHumana.

Arksey, H., & O'Malley, L. (2005). Scoping studies: Towards a methodological framework. *International Journal of Social Research Methodology*, 8(1), 19–32. DOI: 10.1080/1364557032000119616

Arner, D. W., Barberis, J., & Buckley, R. P. (2017). FinTech, RegTech and the Reconceptualization of Financial Regulation. *Northwestern Journal of International Law & Business*, 37(3), 371–413.

Arranz, C. F., Arroyabe, M. F., Arranz, N., & de Arroyabe, J. C. F. (2023). Digitalisation dynamics in SMEs: An approach from systems dynamics and artificial intelligence. *Technological Forecasting and Social Change*, 196, 122880. DOI: 10.1016/j.techfore.2023.122880

Arrieta, A. B., Díaz-Rodríguez, N., Del Ser, J., Bennetot, A., Tabik, S., Barbado, A., Garcia, S., Gil-Lopez, S., Molina, D., Benjamins, R., Chatila, R., & Herrera, F. (2019). Explainable Artificial Intelligence (XAI): Concepts, taxonomies, opportunities and challenges toward responsible AI. *Information Fusion*, 58, 82–115. DOI: 10.1016/j.inffus.2019.12.012

Arrow, K. J. (1974). Limited Knowledge and Economic Analysis. *The American Economic Review*, 64(February), 1–10. https://papers.ssrn.com/sol3/papers.cfm?abstract_id=1506319

Ashtiani, M., & Abdollahi Azgomi, M. (2019). A novel trust evolution algorithm based on a quantum-like model of computational trust. *Cognition Technology and Work*, 21(2), 201–224. DOI: 10.1007/s10111-018-0496-9

Aslam, N., Khan, I. U., Mirza, S., AlOwayed, A., Anis, F. M., Aljuaid, R. M., & Baageel, R. (2022). Interpretable Machine Learning Models for Malicious Domains Detection Using Explainable Artificial Intelligence (XAI). *Sustainability (Basel)*, 14(12), 7375. DOI: 10.3390/su14127375

Atieh, A. M., Cooke, K. O., & Osiyevskyy, O. (2023). The role of intelligent manufacturing systems in the implementation of Industry 4.0 by small and medium enterprises in developing countries. *Engineering Reports*, 5(3), e12578. DOI: 10.1002/eng2.12578

Austin, W. G., & Worchel, S. (1979). *The social psychology of intergroup relations*. Brooks Cole Publishing.

Awan, U., Kraslawski, A., & Huiskonen, J. (2018). Governing interfirm relationships for social sustainability: The relationship between governance mechanisms, sustainable collaboration, and cultural intelligence. *Sustainability (Basel)*, 10(12), 4473. DOI: 10.3390/su10124473

Awosika, T., Shukla, R. M., & Pranggono, B. (2024). Transparency and Privacy: The Role of Explainable AI and Federated Learning in Financial Fraud Detection. *IEEE Access : Practical Innovations, Open Solutions*, 1, 64551–64560. Advance online publication. DOI: 10.1109/ACCESS.2024.3394528

Azcárate, M. C. (2020). *Stuck with tourism: Space, power, and labor in contemporary Yucatán*. University of California Press. DOI: 10.2307/j.ctv17db304

Azzutti, A. (2022). AI trading and the limits of EU law enforcement in deterring market manipulation. Computer Law And Security Report. *Computer Law & Security Report*, 45, 105690. DOI: 10.1016/j.clsr.2022.105690

Baabdullah, T., Alzahrani, A., Rawat, D. B., & Liu, C. (2024). Efficiency of Federated Learning and Blockchain in Preserving Privacy and Enhancing the Performance of Credit Card Fraud Detection (CCFD) Systems. *Future Internet*, 16(6), 196. DOI: 10.3390/fi16060196

Bae, K. H., El Ghoul, S., Gong, Z. J., & Guedhami, O. (2021). Does CSR matter in times of crisis? Evidence from the COVID-19 pandemic. *Journal of Corporate Finance*, 67, 101876. DOI: 10.1016/j.jcorpfin.2020.101876

Banco Interamericano de Desarrollo (BID). (2022). *Guía operativa para programas de competitividad para la pequeña y mediana empresa*.

Bansal, K., Paliwal, A. C., & Singh, A. K. (2024). *Analysis of the benefits of artificial intelligence and human personality study on online fraud detection*. International Journal Of Law And Management./International Journal Of Law And Management., DOI: 10.1108/IJLMA-08-2023-0198

Barocas, S., Hardt, M., & Narayanan, A. (2019). *Fairness and machine learning: Limitations and opportunities*. https://fairmlbook.org

Barocas, S., & Barocas, A. D. (2016). Big data's disparate impact. *California Law Review*, 104, 671–732. . doi: DOI: 10.2139/ssrn.2477899

Baškarada, S. (2014). Qualitative case studies guidelines. *The Qualitative Report*, 19(40), 1–25.

Baumann-Pauly, D., Wickert, C., Spence, L. J., & Scherer, A. G. (2013). Organizing corporate social responsibility in small and large firms: Size matters. *Journal of Business Ethics*, 115(4), 693–705. DOI: 10.1007/s10551-013-1827-7

Baum, S. (2018). Countering superintelligence misinformation. *Information (Basel)*, 9(10), 244. DOI: 10.3390/info9100244

Bautista-Puig, N., Aleixo, A. M., Leal, S., Azeiteiro, U., & Costas, R. (2020). Unveiling the research landscape of Sustainable Development Goals and their inclusion in Higher Education Institutions and Research Centers: major trends in 2000-2017. *arXiv (Cornell University)*. https://doi.org//arxiv.2002.04895DOI: 10.48550

Bawack, R. E., Wamba, S. F., Carillo, K. D. A., & Akter, S. (2022). Artificial intelligence in E-Commerce: A bibliometric study and literature review. *Electronic Markets*, 32(1), 297–338. DOI: 10.1007/s12525-022-00537-z PMID: 35600916

Bayazitov, D., Kozhakhmet, K., Omirali, A., & Zhumaliyeva, R. (2024). Leveraging Amazon Web Services for Cloud Storage and AI Algo*rithm Integration: A Comprehensive Analysis.Applied Mathematics & Information Sciences*, 18(6), 1235–1246. DOI: 10.18576/amis/180606

Beattie, J. R., & Esmonde-White, F. W. L. (2021). Exploration of Principal Component Analysis: Deriving Principal Component Analysis Visually Using Spectra. *Applied Spectroscopy*, 75(4), 361–375. DOI: 10.1177/0003702820987847 PMID: 33393349

Bécue, A., Praça, I., & Gama, J. (2021). Artificial intelligence, cyber-threats and Industry 4.0: Challenges and opportunities. *Artificial Intelligence Review*, 54(5), 3849–3886. DOI: 10.1007/s10462-020-09942-2

Belz, A. (2022). A Metrological Perspective on Reproducibility in NLP*. *Computational Linguistics*, 48(4), 1125–1135. DOI: 10.1162/coli_a_00448

Bencke, L., Cechinel, C., & Munoz, R. (2020). Automated classification of social network messages into Smart Cities dimensions. *Future Generation Computer Systems*, 109, 218–237. DOI: 10.1016/j.future.2020.03.057

Berger, E., & Nakata, C. (2013). Implementing technologies for financial service innovations in base of the pyramid markets. *Journal of Product Innovation Management*, 30(6), 1199–1211. DOI: 10.1111/jpim.12054

Berman, E. (2018). A government of laws and not of machines. *SSRN*, 98, 1277–1355. DOI: 10.2139/ssrn.3098995

Bernal-Conesa, J. A., de Nieves Nieto, C., & Briones-Peñalver, A. J. (2017). CSR strategy in technology companies: Its influence on performance, competitiveness and sustainability. *Corporate Social Responsibility and Environmental Management*, 24(2), 96–107. DOI: 10.1002/csr.1393

Bhuiyan, M. R. I., Faraji, M. R., Rashid, M., Bhuyan, M. K., Hossain, R., & Ghose, P. (2024). Digital Transformation in SMEs Emerging Technological Tools and Technologies for Enhancing the SME's Strategies and Outcomes. *Journal of Eco-humanism*, 3(4), 211–224. DOI: 10.62754/joe.v3i4.3594

Bianchi, C., Glavas, C., & Mathews, S. (2017). SME international performance in Latin America: The role of entrepreneurial and technological capabilities. *Journal of Small Business and Enterprise Development*, 24(1), 176–195. DOI: 10.1108/JSBED-09-2016-0142

Bibri, S. E., Alexandre, A., Sharifi, A., & Krogstie, J. (2023). *'Environmentally sustainable smart cities and their converging AI, IoT, and big data technologies and solutions: an integrated approach to an extensive literature review', Energy Informatics*. Springer Nature., DOI: 10.1186/s42162-023-00259-2

Bican, P. M., & Brem, A. (2020). Digital Business Model, Digital Transformation, Digital Entrepreneurship: Is There A Sustainable "Digital"? *Sustainability (Basel)*, 12(13), 5239. DOI: 10.3390/su12135239

Bifulco, F., Tregua, M., Amitrano, C. C., & D'Auria, A. (2016). ICT and sustainability in smart cities management. *International Journal of Public Sector Management*, 29(2), 132–147. DOI: 10.1108/IJPSM-07-2015-0132

Binns, R. (2018). Fairness in machine learning: Lessons from political philosophy. *Proceedings of the 2018 CHI Conference on Human Factors in Computing Systems*, 1-14. DOI: 10.1145/3173574.3173982

Binns, R. (2018). Fairness in machine learning: Lessons from political philosophy. *Proceedings of the 2018 Conference on Fairness, Accountability, and Transparency*. 81:149-159

Biondi, G., Cagnoni, S., Capobianco, R., Franzoni, V., Lisi, F. A., Milani, A., & Vallverdú, J. (2023). Editorial: Ethical design of artificial intelligence-based systems for decision making. *Frontiers in Artificial Intelligence*, 6, 1250209. Advance online publication. DOI: 10.3389/frai.2023.1250209 PMID: 37554695

Blau, P. (1964). *Power and exchange in social life*. J Wiley & Sons.

Boatwright, B. C., & White, C. (2020). Is Privacy Dead? Does It Matter? How Facebook Frames Its Data Policy Through Public Communication. *Journal of Public Interest Communications*, 4(1), 78–101. DOI: 10.32473/jpic.v4.i1.p78

Bobby Banerjee, S. (2014). A critical perspective on corporate social responsibility: Towards a global governance framework. *Critical Perspectives on International Business*, 10(1/2), 84–95. DOI: 10.1108/cpoib-06-2013-0021

Bode, C., Herzog, C., Hook, D., & McGrath, R. (2018). *A guide to the Dimensions data approach. Dimensions Report*. Digital Science.

Bokhari, S. A. A., & Myeong, S. (2023). The Impact of AI Applications on Smart Decision-Making in Smart Cities as Mediated by the Internet of Things and Smart Governance. *IEEE Access : Practical Innovations, Open Solutions*, 11, 120827–120844. DOI: 10.1109/ACCESS.2023.3327174

Borda, A., Molnar, A., Neesham, C., & Kostkova, P. (2022). Ethical Issues in AI-Enabled Disease Surveillance: Perspectives from Global Health. *Applied Sciences (Basel, Switzerland)*, 12(8), 3890. Advance online publication. DOI: 10.3390/app12083890

Borden, S.L., Codina, L. & Ufarte-Ruiz, M.-J. (2024). Introduction. Our Relationships with GenAI and the Media: Testing the Limits of Transparency, Trust and Moral Agency. *Communication and Society* 37 (4 Special), 217–21. .DOI: 10.15581/003.37.4.217-221

Borenstein, J., Grodzinsky, F. S., Howard, A., Miller, K. W., & Wolf, M. J. (2021). AI Ethics: A Long History and a Recent Burst of Attention. *Computer*, 54(1), 96–102. DOI: 10.1109/MC.2020.3034950

Bostrom, N. (2014). *Superintelligence: Paths, dangers, strategies*. Oxford University Press.

Boustani, N. M. (2021). Artificial intelligence impact on banks clients and employees in an Asian developing country. *Journal of Asia Business Studies*, 16(2), 267–278. DOI: 10.1108/JABS-09-2020-0376

Bowling, B., Marks, A., & Keenan, C. (2017). Automated justice? Technology, crime, and social control. In *The Oxford Handbook of Law, Regulation, and Technology* (pp. 705–730). Oxford University Press., DOI: 10.1093/oxfordhb/9780199680832.013.32

Božić, V. (2023) 'Encouragement and Engagement in Technology-Based Language Learning', *Language Education & Technology (LET Journal)*, 3(2), pp. 96–109. Available at: http://langedutech.com

Bramwell, B., & Lane, B. (2011). Critical research on the governance of tourism and sustainability. *Journal of Sustainable Tourism*, 19(4-5), 411–421. DOI: 10.1080/09669582.2011.580586

Bramwell, B., Lane, B., McCabe, S., Mosedale, J., & Scarles, C. (2008). Research perspectives on responsible tourism. *Journal of Sustainable Tourism*, 16(3), 253–257. DOI: 10.1080/09669580802208201

Braun, M., Bleher, H., & Hummel, P. (2021). A Leap of Faith: Is There a Formula for "Trustworthy" AI? *The Hastings Center Report*, 51(3), 17–22. DOI: 10.1002/hast.1207 PMID: 33606288

Brem, A., Giones, F., & Werle, M. (2023). The AI Digital Revolution in Innovation: A Conceptual Framework of Artificial Intelligence Technologies for the Management of Innovation. *IEEE Transactions on Engineering Management*, 70(2), 770–776. DOI: 10.1109/TEM.2021.3109983

Brundage, M., Avin, S., Clark, J., . . .. (2020). Toward Trustworthy AI Development: Mechanisms for Supporting Verifiable Claims. *arXiv preprint arXiv:2004.07213*.

Brundage, M. (2015). Taking superintelligence seriously. *Futures*, 72, 32–35. DOI: 10.1016/j.futures.2015.07.009

Brynjolfsson, E., & McAfee, A. (2014). *The second machine age: Work, progress, and prosperity in a time of brilliant technologies*. W.W. Norton & Company.

Buchanan, L., & O'Connell, A. (2006). A brief history of decision making. *Harvard Business Review*, 84(1), 32–41. https://hbr.org/2006/01/a-brief-history-of-decision-making PMID: 16447367

Buckley, R., & de Vasconcellos Pegas, F. (2012). Tourism and CSR. In *The Routledge Handbook of Tourism and the Environment* (pp. 521–530). Routledge.

Buhalis, D., & Moldavska, I. (2022). Voice Assistants in Hospitality: Using Artificial Intelligence for customer service. *Journal of Hospitality and Tourism Technology*, 13(3), 386–403. DOI: 10.1108/JHTT-03-2021-0104

Bunders, D. J., & Varró, K. (2019). Problematizing data-driven urban practices: Insights from five Dutch "smart cities". *Cities (London, England)*, 93, 145–152. DOI: 10.1016/j.cities.2019.05.004

Burrell, J. (2016). How the machine 'thinks': Understanding opacity in machine learning algorithms. *Big Data & Society*, 3(1), 1–12. DOI: 10.1177/2053951715622512

Bustos Díaz, J., & Martin-Vicario, L. (2024). Media Literacy in a Hyperconnected World: From Social Networks to Artificial Intelligencel Alfabetización Mediática En Un Mundo Hiperconectado: De Las Redes Sociales a La Inteligencia Artificial. *European Public and Social Innovation Review*, 9, 1–17. DOI: 10.31637/epsir-2024-1241

Butler, J.Jr. (1991). Toward Understanding and Measuring Conditions of Trust: Evolution of a Conditions of Trust Inventory. *Journal of Management*, 17(3), 643–663. DOI: 10.1177/014920639101700307

Butler, L. (2010). An alternative to WoS subject categories: redefining journal sets for closer alignment to a national classification scheme. *Eleventh International Conference on Science and Technology Indicators*, 62.

Cacchione, P. Z. (2016). The Evolving Methodology of Scoping Reviews. *Clinical Nursing Research*, 25(2), 115–119. DOI: 10.1177/1054773816637493 PMID: 26976609

Cai, L. (2024). Realities vs Expectations: Children's Perception and Imagination of AI. *International Journal of Technology and Design Education*, 34(5), 1687–1704. DOI: 10.1007/s10798-024-09879-5

Calo, R. (2015). Robots in American law. *U.C. Davis Law Review*, 49(1), 65–124. DOI: 10.2139/ssrn.2584400

Calo, R. (2017). Artificial Intelligence Policy: A Primer and Roadmap. *University of California, Davis Law Review*, 51(2), 399–435.

Calvano, E., Calzolari, G., Denicolò, V., & Pastorello, S. (2020). Artificial Intelligence, Algorithmic Pricing, and Collusion. *The American Economic Review*, 110(10), 3267–3297. DOI: 10.1257/aer.20190623

Calvo-Rodriguez, A. (2021). Learning with Mobile Technologies at Public Primary Schools in Costa Rica: The case of the National Program of Educational Informatics of the Ministry of Public Education and the Omar Dengo Foundation. *Journal of Universality of Global Education Issues*, 7(1).

Camilleri, M. A. (2012). Creating shared value through strategic CSR in tourism. *Camilleri, MA (2012). Creating shared value through strategic CSR in tourism. Ph. D. Dissertation University of Edinburgh, Edinburgh, UK.*https://era. ed. *ac. uk/ bitstream/handle/1842/6564/Camilleri2012. pdf.*

Cam, N. T., & Kiet, V. T. (2023). FlwrBC: Incentive Mechanism Design for Federated Learning by Using Blockchain. *IEEE Access : Practical Innovations, Open Solutions*, 11, 107855–107866. DOI: 10.1109/ACCESS.2023.3320045

Campbell, C., Plangger, K., Sands, S., Kietzmann, J., & Bates, K. (2022). How deepfakes and artificial intelligence could reshape the advertising industry: The coming reality of AI fakes and their potential impact on consumer behavior. *Journal of Advertising Research*, 62(3), 241–251. DOI: 10.2501/JAR-2022-017

Canale, D. (2021). The opacity of law: On the hidden impact of experts' opinion on legal decision-making. *Law and Philosophy*, 40(5), 509–543. DOI: 10.1007/s10982-021-09408-8

Cantele, S., & Zardini, A. (2018). Is sustainability a competitive advantage for small businesses? An empirical analysis of possible mediators in the sustainability–financial performance relationship. *Journal of Cleaner Production*, 182, 166–176. DOI: 10.1016/j.jclepro.2018.02.016

Cantrell, B., & Zhang, Z. (2018). A third intelligence. *Landscape Architecture Frontiers*, 6(2), 42. DOI: 10.15302/J-LAF-20180205

Carmody, J., Shringarpure, S., & Van de Venter, G. (2021). AI and privacy concerns: A smart meter case study. *Journal Of Information Communication And Ethics In Society*, 19(4), 492–505. DOI: 10.1108/JICES-04-2021-0042

Carroll, A. B. (1999). Corporate social responsibility: Evolution of a definitional construct. *Business & Society*, 38(3), 268–295. DOI: 10.1177/000765039903800303

Carroll, A. B. (2021). Corporate social responsibility (CSR) and the COVID-19 pandemic: Organizational and managerial implications. *Journal of Strategy and Management*, 14(3), 315–330. DOI: 10.1108/JSMA-07-2021-0145

Carstensen, T., & Ganz, K. (2023). Gendered AI: German News Media Discourse on the Future of Work. *AI & Society*. Advance online publication. DOI: 10.1007/s00146-023-01747-5

Casanova, L., & Dumas, A. (2010). Corporate social responsibility and Latin American multinationals: Is poverty a business issue? *Universia Business Review*, 25, 132–145.

Cath, C., Wachter, S., Mittelstadt, B., Taddeo, M., & Floridi, L. (2017). Artificial Intelligence and the 'Good Society': The US, EU, and UK approach. *Science and Engineering Ethics*. Advance online publication. DOI: 10.1007/s11948-017-9901-7 PMID: 28353045

Cath, C., Wachter, S., Mittelstadt, B., Taddeo, M., & Floridi, L. (2018). Artificial Intelligence and the 'Good Society': The US, EU, and UK Approach. *Science and Engineering Ethics*, 24(2), 505–528. PMID: 28353045

Cedillo-Campos, M. G. (2020). Web platform to develop collective intelligence in logistics for Latin American SMEs: The case of SmartLogistiX3. com. *Nova Scientia*, 12(25). Advance online publication. DOI: 10.21640/ns.v12i25.2452

Celma, D., Martínez-Garcia, E., & Coenders, G. (2014). Corporate social responsibility in human resource management: An analysis of common practices and their determinants in Spain. *Corporate Social Responsibility and Environmental Management*, 21(2), 82–99. DOI: 10.1002/csr.1301

CEPAL. (2021). Mipymes y el COVID-19. https://www.cepal.org/es/euromipyme/mipymes-covid-19

CEPAL. N. (2020). Universalizing access to digital technologies to address the consequences of COVID-19. *CEPAL*. https://hdl.handle.net/11362/45939

Cerdas, E. (2021). Costa Rica's educational challenges in the digital era. *La Nación*. Retrieved from https://www.nacion.com

Cezarino, L. O., Liboni, L. B., Hunter, T., Pacheco, L. M., & Martins, F. P. (2022). Corporate social responsibility in emerging markets: Opportunities and challenges for sustainability integration. *Journal of Cleaner Production*, 362, 132224. DOI: 10.1016/j.jclepro.2022.132224

Chang, J., Yen, N. Y., & Hung, J. C. (2022). Design of a NLP-empowered finance fraud awareness model: The anti-fraud chatbot for fraud detection and fraud classification as an instance. Journal Of Ambient Intelligence & Humanized Computing. *Journal of Ambient Intelligence and Humanized Computing*, 13(10), 4663–4679. DOI: 10.1007/s12652-021-03512-2

Chang, V. (2021). An ethical framework for big data and smart cities. *Technological Forecasting and Social Change*, 165(January), 120559. DOI: 10.1016/j.techfore.2020.120559

Cheah, P. C. Y., Yang, Y., & Lee, B. G. (2023). Enhancing Financial Fraud Detection through Addressing Class Imbalance Using Hybrid SMOTE-GAN Techniques. *International Journal Of Financial Studies*, 11(3), 110. DOI: 10.3390/ijfs11030110

Cheng, C., & Cai, W. (2023). Double-weight LDA extracting keywords for financial fraud detection system. *Multimedia Tools and Applications*, 83(17), 50757–50781. Advance online publication. DOI: 10.1007/s11042-023-17334-1

Cheng, Y., & Jiang, H. (2020). How Do AI-Driven Chatbots Impact User Experience? Examining Gratifications, Perceived Privacy Risk, Satisfaction, Loyalty, and Continued Use. *Journal of Broadcasting & Electronic Media*, 64(4), 592–614. DOI: 10.1080/08838151.2020.1834296

Chen, J., Shen, Y., & Ali, R. (2018). Credit Card Fraud Detection Using Sparse Autoencoder and Generative Adversarial Network. 2018 IEEE 9th Annual Information Technology, *Electronics and Mobile Communication Conference (IEMCON)*. https://doi.org/DOI: 10.1109/IEMCON.2018.8614815

Chen, L., Chen, P., & Lin, Z. (2020). Artificial intelligence in education: A review. *IEEE Access : Practical Innovations, Open Solutions*, 8, 75264–75278. DOI: 10.1109/ACCESS.2020.2988510

Chen, Y., Albert, L. J., & Jensen, S. (2021). Innovation farm: Teaching artificial intelligence through gamified social entrepreneurship in an introductory MIS course*. *Decision Sciences Journal of Innovative Education*, 20(1), 43–56. DOI: 10.1111/dsji.12253

Chen, Y., Zhai, Y., & Sun, S. (2024). The Gendered Lens of AI: Examining News Imagery across Digital Spaces. *Journal of Computer-Mediated Communication*, 29(1), zmad047. Advance online publication. DOI: 10.1093/jcmc/zmad047

Cherif, A., Badhib, A., Ammar, H., Alshehri, S., Kalkatawi, M., & Imine, A. (2023). Credit card fraud detection in the era of disruptive technologies: A systematic review. Journal Of King Saud University. Computer And Information Sciences/Ma ala am'a Al-malīk Saud : Ùlm Al- asib Wa Al-ma'lumat, 35(1), 145-174. https://doi.org/DOI: 10.1016/j.jksuci.2022.11.008

Cherre, I. (november 28, 2024). TikTok prohibirá los filtros de belleza para proteger a los menores. *La Vanguardia*. https://www.lavanguardia.com/andro4all/tiktok/tiktok-prohibira-los-filtros-de-belleza-para-proteger-a-los-menores

Chesney, B., & Citron, D. (2019). Deep fakes: A looming challenge for privacy, democracy, and national security. *California Law Review*, 107, 1753. DOI: 10.15779/Z38RV0D15J

Chesterman, S. (2024). Good models borrow, great models steal: Intellectual property rights and generative AI [Preprint]. *Policy and Society*, puae006. Advance online publication. DOI: 10.1093/polsoc/puae006

Chien, C. V. (2019). Predicting Patent Litigation. *Texas Law Review*, 97(2), 383–452.

Choi, Á. (2021). España ante la Revolución Industrial 4.0: Mercado laboral y formación. *Araucaria*, 47(47), 479–505. DOI: 10.12795/araucaria.2021.i47.21

Choi, M., & Choi, Y. (2021). Employee perceptions of hotel CSR activities during the COVID-19 pandemic. *International Journal of Contemporary Hospitality Management*, 33(10), 3355–3378. DOI: 10.1108/IJCHM-03-2021-0289

Cho, J. (2006). The mechanism of trust and distrust formation and their relational outcomes. *Journal of Retailing*, 82(1), 25–35. DOI: 10.1016/j.jretai.2005.11.002

Choongo, P. (2017). A longitudinal study of the impact of corporate social responsibility on firm performance in SMEs in Zambia. *Sustainability (Basel)*, 9(8), 1300. DOI: 10.3390/su9081300

Chui, M., Evers, M., & Zheng, A. (2020). How the bio revolution could transform the competitive landscape. *The McKinsey Quarterly*, 7, •••. https://www.mckinsey.com/~/media/McKinsey/Business%20Functions/McKinsey%20Digital/Our%20Insights/How%20the%20Bio%20Revolution%20could%20transform%20the%20competitive%20landscape/How-the-Bio-Revolution-could-transform-the-competitive-landscape.pdf

Chukwuere, J. E. (2023). Exploring Literature Review Methodologies in Information Systems Research: A Comparative Study. [ELDN]. *Education & Learning in Developing Nations*, 1(2), 38–46. DOI: 10.26480/eldn.02.2023.74.82

Citron, D. K., & Pasquale, F. (2014). The scored society: Due process for automated predictions. *Washington Law Review (Seattle, Wash.)*, 89(1), 1–33.

Claudy, M. C., Aquino, K., & Graso, M. (2022). Artificial intelligence can't be charmed: The effects of impartiality on laypeople's algorithmic preferences. *Frontiers in Psychology*, 13, 898027. DOI: 10.3389/fpsyg.2022.898027 PMID: 35846643

Cobianchi, L., Piccolo, D., Dal Mas, F., Agnoletti, V., Ansaloni, L., Balch, J., Biffl, W., Butturini, G., Catena, F., Coccolini, F., Denicolai, S., De Simone, B., Frigerio, I., Fugazzola, P., Marseglia, G., Marseglia, G. R., Martellucci, J., Modenese, M., Previtali, P., & Zese, M. (2023). Surgeons' perspectives on artificial intelligence to support clinical decision-making in trauma and emergency contexts: Results from an international survey. *World Journal of Emergency Surgery; WJES*, 18(1). Advance online publication. DOI: 10.1186/s13017-022-00467-3 PMID: 36597105

Coleman, J. S. (1990). Foundations of Social Theory. In *Foundations of Social Theory* (Vol. 69, Issue 2, p. 993). DOI: 10.2307/2579680

Coles, T., Fenclova, E., & Dinan, C. (2013). Tourism and corporate social responsibility: A critical review and research agenda. *Tourism Management Perspectives*, 6, 122–141. DOI: 10.1016/j.tmp.2013.02.001

Comisión Europea (CE). (2021). Proposal for a Regulation of the European Parliament and of the Council on Harmonised Rules in the field of Artificial Intelligence (Artificial Intelligence Act) and amending certain legislative acts of the Union. Brussels, 21.04.2021. https://eur-lex.europa.eu/legal-content/ES/TXT/?uri=CELEX:52021PC0206

Comisión Europea. (2011). Comunicación de la Comisión al Parlamento Europeo, al Consejo, al Comité Económico y Social Europeo y al Comité de las Regiones: Estrategia renovada de la UE para 2011-2014 sobre la responsabilidad social de las empresas. https://www.europarl.europa.eu/meetdocs/2009_2014/documents/com/com_com(2011)0681_/com_com(2011)0681_es.pdf

Connock, A. (2024). *Media Management and Live Experience: Sports, Culture, Entertainment and Events*. Routledge., DOI: 10.4324/9781003435167

Cortés, P. (2018). *Online Dispute Resolution for Consumers in the European Union*. Routledge., DOI: 10.4324/9780203847756

Cowell, J. M. (2012). Literature reviews as a research strategy. *The Journal of School Nursing: the Official Publication of the National Association of School Nurses*, 28(5), 326–327. DOI: 10.1177/1059840512458666 PMID: 23012244

Crane, A., Matten, D., & Spence, L. (2019). *Corporate social responsibility: Readings and cases in a global context*. Routledge. DOI: 10.4324/9780429294273

Crootof, R., Kaminski, M. E., & Price, W. N.II. (2023). Humans in the loop. *SSRN*, 76(2), 429–510. DOI: 10.2139/ssrn.4066781

Cruz, A. F., Saleiro, P., Belem, C., Soares, C., & Bizarro, P. (2021). Promoting Fairness through Hyperparameter Optimization. *2021 IEEE International Conference On Data Mining (ICDM)*. https://doi.org/DOI: 10.1109/ICDM51629.2021.00119

Cugurullo, F. (2024) 'The obscure politics of artificial intelligence: a Marxian socio-technical critique of the AI alignment problem thesis', *AI and Ethics* [Preprint]. Available at: DOI: 10.1007/s43681-024-00476-9

Cugurullo, F., Caprotti, F., Cook, M., & Karvonen, A. M Guirk, P. and Marvin, S. (2024) 'The rise of AI urbanism in post-smart cities: A critical commentary on urban artificial intelligence', *Urban Studies*. SAGE Publications Ltd, pp. 1168–1182. Available at: DOI: 10.1177/00420980231203386

Cui, X., Chang, Y., Yang, C., Cong, Z., Wang, B., & Leng, Y. (2022). Development and Trends in Artificial Intelligence in Critical Care Medicine: A Bibliometric Analysis of Related Research over the Period of 2010–2021. *Journal of Personalized Medicine*, 13(1), 50. DOI: 10.3390/jpm13010050 PMID: 36675711

Daddi, D., Boffo, V., Buragohain, D., & Iyaomolere, T. (2020). Programmes and methods for developing entrepreneurial skills in higher education. *Andragoske Studije*, 2(2), 101–123. DOI: 10.5937/AndStud2001101D

Dahlsrud, A. (2008). How corporate social responsibility is defined: An analysis of 37 definitions. *Corporate Social Responsibility and Environmental Management*, 15(1), 1–13. DOI: 10.1002/csr.132

Damioli, G., Van Roy, V., & Vertesy, D. (2021). The impact of artificial intelligence on labor productivity. *Eurasian Business Review*, 11(1), 1–25. DOI: 10.1007/s40821-020-00172-8

Dan, V. (2017). Empirical and non-empirical methods. In *International Encyclopaedia of Communication Research Methods* (pp. 1–3). Wiley. DOI: 10.1002/9781118901731.iecrm0083

Dasari, S., & Kaluri, R. (2024). An Effective Classification of DDoS Attacks in a Distributed Network by Adopting Hierarchical Machine Learning and Hyperparameters Optimization Techniques. *IEEE Access : Practical Innovations, Open Solutions*, 12, 10834–10845. DOI: 10.1109/ACCESS.2024.3352281

Das, S., & Gochhait, S. (2023). *Digital Entertainment as Next Evolution in Service Sector: Emerging Digital Solutions in Reshaping Different Industries*. Palgrave McMillan., DOI: 10.1007/978-981-19-8121-0

Dastin, J. (2018). Amazon scraps secret AI recruiting tool that showed bias against women. *Reuters*. https://www.reuters.com/article/us-amazon-com-jobs-automation-insight-idUSKCN1MK08G

Davenport, T. H., Guha, A., Grewal, D., & Breßgott, T. (2019). How artificial intelligence will change the future of marketing. *Journal of the Academy of Marketing Science*, 48(1), 24–42. DOI: 10.1007/s11747-019-00696-0

Daza, M. T., & Ilozumba, U. J. (2022). A survey of AI ethics in business literature: Maps and trends between 2000 and 2021. *Frontiers in Psychology*, 13, 1042661. DOI: 10.3389/fpsyg.2022.1042661 PMID: 36600712

De Barros, R. S. M., De Lima Cabral, D. R., Gonçalves, P. M., & De Carvalho Santos, S. G. T. (2017). RDDM: Reactive drift detection method. *Expert Systems with Applications*, 90, 344–355. DOI: 10.1016/j.eswa.2017.08.023

De Bruyn, A., Viswanathan, V., Beh, Y. S., Brock, J. K. U., & von Wangenheim, F. (2020). Artificial Intelligence and Marketing: Pitfalls and Opportunities. *Journal of Interactive Marketing*, 51(1), 91–105. DOI: 10.1016/j.intmar.2020.04.007

De Falco, S. (2019). Are smart cities global cities? A European perspective. *European Planning Studies*, 27(4), 759–783. DOI: 10.1080/09654313.2019.1568396

De Fine Licht, K., & De Fine Licht, J. (2020). Artificial intelligence, transparency, and public decision-making. *AI & Society*, 35(4), 917–926. DOI: 10.1007/s00146-020-00960-w

De Freitas, L. C., & Neves de Moura Filho, R. (2022). Aesthetic Normalization of Gender in the Instagram Application: A Portrait of the Brazilian Woman. *Computer Law & Security Report*, 47, 105753. Advance online publication. DOI: 10.1016/j.clsr.2022.105753

De Girolamo, D. (2019). Rethinking the role of the mediator: Promoting party autonomy through informed decision-making. *Journal of Law and Society*, 46(1), 64–91. DOI: 10.1111/jols.12160

De Grosbois, D. (2016). Corporate social responsibility reporting in the cruise tourism industry: A performance evaluation using a new institutional theory based model. *Journal of Sustainable Tourism*, 24(2), 245–269. DOI: 10.1080/09669582.2015.1076827

de Jong, M. D. T., Neulen, S., & Jansma, S. R. (2019). 'Citizens' intentions to participate in governmental co-creation initiatives: Comparing three co-creation configurations'. *Government Information Quarterly*, 36(3), 490–500. DOI: 10.1016/j.giq.2019.04.003

De La Cruz, J., Gómez-Luna, E., Ali, M., Vasquez, J. C., & Guerrero, J. M. (2023). *'Fault Location for Distribution Smart Grids: Literature Overview, Challenges, Solutions, and Future Trends', Energies*. MDPI., DOI: 10.3390/en16052280

Deng, W., Liang, G., Yu, C., Yao, K., Wang, C., & Zhang, X. (2023). An Early Warning Model of Telecommunication Network Fraud Based on User Portrait. Computers, Materials & Continua/Computers. *Computers, Materials & Continua*, 75(1), 1561–1576. DOI: 10.32604/cmc.2023.035016

Deo, R. C., Yaseen, Z. M., Al-Ansari, N., Nguyen-Huy, T., Langlands, T. A. M., & Galligan, L. (2020). Modern artificial intelligence model development for undergraduate student performance prediction: An investigation on engineering mathematics courses. *IEEE Access : Practical Innovations, Open Solutions*, 8, 136697–136724. DOI: 10.1109/ACCESS.2020.3010938

Derici, S. (2024). Digitalization Concept and the Historical Evolution of Digitalization. In *Developing Digital Inclusion Through Globalization and Digitalization* (pp. 90–106). IGI Global. DOI: 10.4018/979-8-3693-4111-7.ch006

Deutsch, M. (1973). The Resolution of Conflict. *The American Behavioral Scientist*, 17(2), 248–248. DOI: 10.1177/000276427301700206

di Placido, D. (2024, May 10). Apple's iPad Pro 'crush' controversy. *Forbes*. Retrieved from https://www.forbes.com/sites/danidiplacido/2024/05/09/the-backlash-against-apples-new-ipad-pro-ad-explained/

Diakopoulos, N. (2016). Accountability in Algorithmic Decision Making. *Communications of the ACM*, 59(2), 56–62. DOI: 10.1145/2844110

Diakopoulos, N. (2016). *Automating the news: How algorithms are reshaping journalism*. Columbia University Press.

Diakopoulos, N., Friedler, S. A., Pesta, B., & Wallach, H. (2020). *Fairness, accountability, and transparency in machine learning: A survey*. Springer., DOI: 10.1007/s11023-019-09506-3

Diaz Ruiz, C., & Nilsson, T. (2023). Disinformation and Echo Chambers: How Disinformation Circulates on Social Media Through Identity-Driven Controversies. *Journal of Public Policy & Marketing*, 42(1), 18–35. DOI: 10.1177/07439156221103852

Diaz, M. (2020) *Biases as Values: Evaluating Algorithms in Context*. Northwestern University. Available at: https://dataverse.harvard.edu/dataverse/algorithm-age-bias/

Díaz-Arancibia, J., Hochstetter-Diez, J., Bustamante-Mora, A., Sepúlveda-Cuevas, S., Albayay, I., & Arango-López, J. (2024). Navigating Digital Transformation and Technology Adoption: A Literature Review from Small and Medium-Sized Enterprises in Developing Countries. *Sustainability (Basel)*, 16(14), 5946. DOI: 10.3390/su16145946

Diaz-Granados, M., Diaz-Montes, J., & Parashar, M. (2015). Investigating insurance fraud using social media. *Proceedings 2015 IEEE International Conference on Big Data*, pp.1344-1349. https://doi.org/DOI: 10.1109/BigData.2015.7363893

Díez, F., Villa, A., López, A. L., & Iraurgi, I. (2020). Impact of quality management systems in the performance of educational centers: Educational policies and management processes. *Heliyon*, 6(4), e03824. Advance online publication. DOI: 10.1016/j.heliyon.2020.e03824 PMID: 32373736

Ding, J. (2018). *Deciphering China's AI Dream: The Context, Components, Capabilities, and Consequences of China's Strategy to Lead the World in AI*. Future of Humanity Institute, University of Oxford. https://www.fhi.ox.ac.uk/wp-content/uploads/Deciphering_Chinas_AI-Dream.pdf

Ding, J. (2018). Deciphering China's AI Dream: The Context, Components, Capabilities, and Consequences of China's Strategy to Lead the World in AI. Future of Humanity Institute, University of Oxford. https://www.fhi.ox.ac.uk/wp-content/uploads/Deciphering_Chinas_AI-Dream.pdf

Dingli, A., Haddod, F., & Klüver, C. (2021). *Artificial intelligence in industry 4.0* (Vol. 928). Springer International Publishing. DOI: 10.1007/978-3-030-61045-6

Dini, M., & Stumpo, G. (2018). *Mipymes en América Latina: un frágil desempeño y nuevos desafíos para las políticas de fomento*. CEPAL.

Dirks, K. T., & Ferrin, D. L. (2001). The Role of Trust in Organizational Settings. *Organization Science*, 12(4), 450–467. DOI: 10.1287/orsc.12.4.450.10640

Dittmar, E. C. (2020). Evolución, tendencias e iniciativas en materia de RSC. In Dittmar, E. C. (Ed.), *Tendencias y organización empresarial frente al nuevo entorno tecnológico: Una perspectiva multidisciplinar*. Thomson Reuters Aranzadi.

Dong, Y., Liu, N., Jalaian, B., & Li, J. (2022). EDITS: Modeling and Mitigating Data Bias for Graph Neural Networks. *Proceedings Of The ACM Web Conference 2022*. https://doi.org/DOI: 10.1145/3485447.3512173

Donohue, K. G. (2003). *Freedom from want: American liberalism and the idea of the consumer*. JHU Press.

Doshi, T. (May 11, 2022). Improving skin tone representation across Google. *Blog Google*. https://blog.google/products/search/monk-skin-tone-scale

Du Toit, A., & Kempen, E. L. (2020). Effectual Structuring of Entrepreneurship Education: Guidelines for Overcoming Inadequacies in the South African School curriculum. *Africa Education Review*, 17(4), 41–55. DOI: 10.1080/18146627.2020.1868074

Dunn, J. (1988). Ch. 5: Trust and Political Agency. In *Trust: Making and Breaking Cooperative Relations* (pp. 73–93). Basil Blackwell. DOI: 10.2307/591021

Dutta, A., Deb, T., & Pathak, S. (2020). Automated Data Harmonization (ADH) using Artificial Intelligence (AI). OPSEARCH/Opsearch, 58(2), 257-275. https://doi.org/DOI: 10.1007/s12597-020-00467-4

Dwork, C., & Minow, M. (2022). Distrust of Artificial Intelligence: Sources & Responses from Computer Science & Law. *Daedalus*, 151(2), 309–321. DOI: 10.1162/daed_a_01918

Ebner, N., Pehlivanoglu, D., & Shoenfelt, A. (2023). *Financial Fraud and Deception in Aging*. Advances In Geriatric Medicine And Research., DOI: 10.31219/osf.io/ay4jw

Edwards, L., & Veale, M. (2017). Slave to the algorithm? Why a "right to an explanation" is probably not the remedy you are looking for. *Duke Law and Technology Review*, 16(1), 18–84. DOI: 10.31228/osf.io/97upg

Ejjami, R. (2024). AI-Driven Smart Cities in France. *International Journal For Multidisciplinary Research*, 6(3), 21920. Advance online publication. DOI: 10.36948/ijfmr.2024.v06i03.21920

Elayyan, S. (2021). The future of education according to the fourth industrial revolution. *Journal of Educational Technology and Online Learning*, 4(1), 23–30. DOI: 10.31681/jetol.737193

Elkington, J. (1998). Partnerships from cannibals with forks: The triple bottom line of 21st-century business. *Environmental Quality Management*, 8(1), 37–51. DOI: 10.1002/tqem.3310080106

Elliott, K., Price, R., Shaw, P., Spiliotopoulos, T., Ng, M., Coopamootoo, K., & Van Moorsel, A. (2021). Towards an Equitable Digital Society: Artificial Intelligence (AI) and Corporate Digital Responsibility (CDR). *Society*, 58(3), 179–188. DOI: 10.1007/s12115-021-00594-8 PMID: 34149122

Enoch, M. A., & Albaugh, B. J. (2017). Review: Genetic and environmental risk factors for alcohol use disorders in American Indians and Alaskan Natives. *The American Journal on Addictions*, 26(5), 461–468. DOI: 10.1111/ajad.12420 PMID: 27599369

EQFM. (2024) *Abu Dhabi Police Becoming a Stakeholder-Centric Organisation*. Available at: https://efqm.org/case-studies/abu-dhabi-police/ (Accessed: 26 October 2024).

Espaɲol, J. B., Barayuga, S. J. R., Tariga, J. N., Eraɲa, P. L. C., Bautista, R. G., & Mayoya, M. A. (2021). Enterprising skills of hospitality management students. *American Journal of Educational Research*, 9(2), 72–76. DOI: 10.12691/education-9-2-3

Eubanks, V. (2018). *Automating inequality: How high-tech tools profile, police, and punish the poor*. St. Martin's Press.

European Commission. (2011). *A renewed EU strategy 2011-14 for Corporate Social Responsibility*. European Commission.

European Commission. (2016). *General Data Protection Regulation (GDPR)*. https://gdpr-info.eu

European Commission. (2019) Ethics guidelines for trustworthy AI. https://digital-strategy.ec.europa.eu/en/library/ethics-guidelines-trustworthy-ai

European Commission. (2021). *Proposal for a regulation laying down harmonized rules on artificial intelligence (Artificial Intelligence Act).* https://ec.europa.eu/info/business-economy-euro/banking-and-finance/financial-markets/securities-markets/financial-regulation/ai-acts_en

European Commission. (2023). The Commission welcomes the political agreement on the Artificial Intelligence Act [Press release] https://ec.europa.eu/commission/presscorner/api/files/document/print/es/ip_23_6473/IP_23_6473_ES.pdf

European Parliament & Council. (2024). *Regulation laying down harmonised rules on artificial intelligence (PE-CONS 24/24). (EC) No 300/2008, (EU) No 167/2013, (EU) No 168/2013, (EU) 2018/858, (EU) 2018/1139 and (EU) 2019/2144 and Directives 2014/90/EU, (EU) 2016/797 and (EU) 2020/1828.* Artificial Intelligence Act.

European Parliament (2016). Reglamento (UE) 2016/679 del Parlamento Europeo y del Consejo.https://www.boe.es/doue/2016/119/L00001-00088.pdf

European Parliament (2024). Reglamento (UE) 2024/1689 del Parlamento Europeo y del Consejo. https://www.boe.es/buscar/doc.php?id=DOUE-L-2024-81079

Ezrachi, A., & Stucke, M. E. (2016). *Virtual Competition: The Promise and Perils of the Algorithm-Driven Economy.* Harvard University Press. DOI: 10.4159/9780674973336

Faccia, A. (2023). National Payment Switches and the Power of Cognitive Computing against Fintech Fraud. *Big Data and Cognitive Computing*, 7(2), 76. DOI: 10.3390/bdcc7020076

Faccia, A., McDonald, J. A. K., & George, B. (2023). NLP Sentiment Analysis and Accounting Transparency: A New Era of Financial Record Keeping. *Computers*, 13(1), 5. DOI: 10.3390/computers13010005

Fang, B., Yu, J., Chen, Z., Osman, A. I., Farghali, M., Ihara, I., Hamza, E. H., Rooney, D. W., & Yap, P. S. (2023). *'Artificial intelligence for waste management in smart cities: a review', Environmental Chemistry Letters.* Springer Science and Business Media Deutschland GmbH., DOI: 10.1007/s10311-023-01604-3

Fatma, M., Rahman, Z., & Khan, I. (2016). Measuring consumer perception of CSR in tourism industry: Scale development and validation. *Journal of Hospitality and Tourism Management*, 27, 39–48. DOI: 10.1016/j.jhtm.2016.03.002

Fayoumi, M. A., Odeh, A., Keshta, I., Aboshgifa, A., AlHajahjeh, T., & Abdulraheem, R. (2022). Email phishing detection based on naïve Bayes, Random Forests, and SVM classifications: A comparative study. 2022 IEEE 12th Annual Computing And Communication Workshop And Conference (CCWC). https://doi.org/DOI: 10.1109/CCWC54503.2022.9720757

Feder, A., Keith, K. A., Manzoor, E., Pryzant, R., Sridhar, D., Wood-Doughty, Z., Eisenstein, J., Grimmer, J., Reichart, R., Roberts, M. E., Stewart, B. M., Veitch, V., & Yang, D. (2022). Causal Inference in Natural Language Processing: Estimation, Prediction, Interpretation and Beyond. *Transactions of the Association for Computational Linguistics*, 10, 1138–1158. DOI: 10.1162/tacl_a_00511

Ferraro, C., & Rojo, S. (2018). Las MIPYMES en América Latina y el Caribe: Una agenda integrada para promover la productividad y la formalización. *OIT Américas, Informes Técnicos, 7.*

Filser, M., Kraus, S., Roig-Tierno, N., Kailer, N., & Fischer, U. (2019). Entrepreneurship as catalyst for sustainable development: Opening the black box. *Sustainability (Basel)*, 11(16), 4503. DOI: 10.3390/su11164503

Finocchiaro, G. D. (2023). The regulation of artificial intelligence. *AI & Society*. Advance online publication. DOI: 10.1007/s00146-023-01650-z

Fioravante, R. (2024). Beyond the Business Case for Responsible Artificial Intelligence: Strategic CSR in Light of Digital Washing and the Moral Human Argument. *Sustainability (Basel)*, 16(3), 1232. DOI: 10.3390/su16031232

Fiore, U., De Santis, A., Perla, F., Zanetti, P., & Palmieri, F. (2019). Using generative adversarial networks for improving classification effectiveness in credit card fraud detection. *Information Sciences*, 479, 448–455. DOI: 10.1016/j.ins.2017.12.030

Firdaus, A., Anuar, N. B., Karim, A., & Razak, M. F. A. (2018). Discovering optimal features using static analysis and a genetic search based method for Android malware detection. Frontiers Of Information Technology & Electronic Engineering/Frontiers Of Informaion Technology & Electronic Engineering, 19(6), 712-736. https://doi.org/DOI: 10.1631/FITEE.1601491

Firdaus, R., Xue, Y., Gang, L., & Ali, M. S. E. (2022). Artificial Intelligence and Human Psychology in Online Transaction Fraud. *Frontiers in Psychology*, 13, 947234. Advance online publication. DOI: 10.3389/fpsyg.2022.947234 PMID: 36304851

Fisher, I., & Ziviani, J. (2004). Explanatory case studies: Implications and applications for clinical research. *Australian Occupational Therapy Journal*, 51(4), 185–191. DOI: 10.1111/j.1440-1630.2004.00446.x

Flores-Ruiz, D., & Bino-Raya, R. E., & de la O Barroso-González, M. (2016). Responsabilidad social en el sector hotelero. Análisis de caso en Córdoba (Argentina). *Journal of Globalization, Competitiveness & Governability/Revista de Globalización, Competitividad y Gobernabilidad/Revista de Globalização. Competitividade e Governabilidade*, 10(3), 116–135.

Floridi, L. (2018). Soft Ethics and the Governance of the Digital. *Philosophy & Technology*, 31(1), 1–8. DOI: 10.1007/s13347-018-0303-9 PMID: 30322997

Floridi, L., Cowls, J., Beltrametti, M., Chatila, R., Chazerand, P., Dignum, V., Luetge, C., Madelin, R., Pagallo, U., Rossi, F., Schafer, B., Valcke, P., & Vayena, E. (2018). AI4People—An ethical framework for a good AI society: Opportunities, risks, principles, and recommendations. *Minds and Machines*, 28(4), 689–707. DOI: 10.1007/s11023-018-9482-5 PMID: 30930541

Floridi, L., & Taddeo, M. (2016). What is data ethics? *Philosophical Transactions. Series A, Mathematical, Physical, and Engineering Sciences*, 374(2083), 20160360. Advance online publication. DOI: 10.1098/rsta.2016.0360 PMID: 28336805

Font, X., & Lynes, J. (2018). Corporate social responsibility in tourism and hospitality. *Journal of Sustainable Tourism*, 26(7), 1027–1042. DOI: 10.1080/09669582.2018.1488856

Forcadell, F. J., & Aracil, E. (2017). European banks' reputation for corporate social responsibility. *Corporate Social Responsibility and Environmental Management*, 24(1), 1–14. DOI: 10.1002/csr.1402

Francisco, M., & Linnér, B. (2023). AI and the governance of sustainable development. An idea analysis of the European Union, the United Nations, and the World Economic Forum. *Environmental Science & Policy*, 150, 103590. DOI: 10.1016/j.envsci.2023.103590

Frey, C. B. (2019). The technology trap: Capital, labor, and power in the age of automation. In *The technology trap*. Princeton University Press., DOI: 10.1515/9780691191959

Frey, C. B., & Osborne, M. A. (2017). The future of employment: How susceptible are jobs to computerisation? *Technological Forecasting and Social Change*, 114, 254–280. DOI: 10.1016/j.techfore.2016.08.019

Fukas, P., Rebstadt, J., Menzel, L., & Thomas, O. (2022). Towards Explainable Artificial Intelligence in Financial Fraud Detection: Using Shapley Additive Explanations to Explore Feature Importance. En Lecture notes in computer science (pp. 109-126). DOI: 10.1007/978-3-031-07472-1_7

Fullan, M., Azorín, C., Harris, A., & Jones, M. (2024). Artificial intelligence and school leadership: Challenges, opportunities and implications. *School Leadership & Management*, 44(4), 339–346. DOI: 10.1080/13632434.2023.2246856

Fu, T. (2019). China's personal information protection in a data-driven economy: A privacy policy study of Alibaba, Baidu and Tencent. *Global Media and Communication*, 15(2), 195–213. DOI: 10.1177/1742766519846644

Gai, K., Qiu, M., Sun, X., & Zhao, H. (2017). Security and Privacy Issues: A Survey on FinTech. En Lecture notes in computer science (pp. 236-247). DOI: 10.1007/978-3-319-52015-5_24

Gai, X., Sainz de Baranda Andújar, C., & Franco, Y. G. (2024). Las Fotografías Que Ilustran Las Informaciones Sobre Inteligencia Artificial En Los Medios Españoles (2017-2021). Un Análisis Desde La Perspectiva de Género[1]. *Historia y Comunicacion Social*, 29(1), 201–218. DOI: 10.5209/hics.95830

Galbusera, F., & Cina, A. (2024). Image annotation and curation in radiology: An overview for machine learning practitioners. *European Radiology Experimental*, 8(1), 11. Advance online publication. DOI: 10.1186/s41747-023-00408-y PMID: 38316659

Gallo, G. (2019). Desarrollo rural comunitario: Experiencia de la Escuela Argentina de Negocios en Zárate, Buenos Aires. *RIDAS. Revista Iberoamericana de Aprendizaje-Servicio*, (8), 162–173. DOI: 10.1344/RIDAS2019.8.11

Gálvez, C. (2024). Scientific Map of Artificial Intelligence in Communication (2004-2024) | Mapa Científico de La Inteligencia Artificial En Comunicación (2004-2024). *European Public and Social Innovation Review*, 9, 1–17. Advance online publication. DOI: 10.31637/epsir-2024-947

Gao, S., He, L., Chen, Y., Li, D., & Lai, K. (2020). Public Perception of Artificial Intelligence in Medical Care: Content Analysis of Social Media. *J Med Internet Res 2020;22(7):E16649*Https://Www.Jmir.Org/2020/7/E16649, *22*(7), e16649. DOI: 10.2196/16649

Gao, B., Wang, Y., Xie, H., Hu, Y., & Hu, Y. (2023). Artificial intelligence in advertising: Advancements, challenges, and ethical considerations in targeting, personalization, content creation, and ad optimization. *SAGE Open*, 13(4), 21582440231210759. Advance online publication. DOI: 10.1177/21582440231210759

Garbarino, E., & Lee, O. F. (2003). Dynamic Pricing in Internet Retail: Effects on Consumer Trust. *Psychology and Marketing*, 20(6), 495–513. DOI: 10.1002/mar.10084

García-Ull, F. J., & Lázaro, M. M. (2023). Gender Stereotypes in AI-Generated Images | Estereotipos de Género En Imágenes Generadas Mediante Inteligencia Artificial. *El Profesional de la Información*, 32(5), e320505. Advance online publication. DOI: 10.3145/epi.2023.sep.05

Garrett, N., Beard, N., & Fiesler, C. (2020). *More Than "If Time Allows."* AIES '20: Proceedings of the AAAI/ACM Conference on AI, Ethics, and Society. DOI: 10.1145/3375627.3375868

Garriga, M., Ruiz-Incertis, R., & Magallón-Rosa, R. (2024). Artificial Intelligence, Disinformation and Media Literacy Proposals around Deepfakes | Inteligencia Artificial, Desinformación y Propuestas de Alfabetización En Torno a Los Deepfakes. *Observatorio (OBS*)*, •••, 175–194. DOI: 10.15847/obsOBS18520242445

Gasser, U. (2023). An EU landmark for AI governance. *Science*, 380(6651), 1203. DOI: 10.1126/science.adj1627 PMID: 37319234

Gautam, A., Joshi, R. K., Narula, A., & Sharma, N. (2024). Mitigating Human Rights Violations Caused by Deepfake Technology. *Library Progress International 44*(3), 4628–4737. https://bpasjournals.com/library-science/index.php/journal/article/view/1283/800

Geca (2024). Informe 'Generación Z'. *Spain Audiovisual Hub.*https://spainaudiovisualhub.mineco.gob.es/content/dam/seteleco-hub-audiovisual/resources/pdf/GECA_Informe_generacion_Z.pdf

Gefen, D. (2000). E-commerce: The role of familiarity and trust. *Omega*, 28(6), 725–737. DOI: 10.1016/S0305-0483(00)00021-9

George, A. S. (2023). Preparing students for an AI-driven world: Rethinking curriculum and pedagogy in the age of artificial intelligence. *Partners Universal Innovative Research Publication*, 1(2), 112–136. DOI: 10.5281/zenodo.10245675

Ghezali, F., & Boudi, A. (2020). The moderating effect of information technology capabilities on the relationship between marketing mix and corporate entrepreneurship. *PSU Research Review*, 5(2), 101–119. DOI: 10.1108/PRR-12-2019-0037

Ghoddusi, H., Creamer, G. G., & Rafizadeh, N. (2019). Machine learning in energy economics and finance: A review. *Energy Economics*, 81, 709–727. DOI: 10.1016/j.eneco.2019.05.006

Giest, S. N., & Klievink, B. (2022). More than a digital system: How AI is changing the role of bureaucrats in different organizational contexts. *Public Management Review*, 26(2), 379–398. DOI: 10.1080/14719037.2022.2095001

Giffinger, R. and Gudrun, H. (2010) 'Smart cities ranking: an effective instrument for the positioning of the cities?', *ACE: architecture, city and environment*, 4(12), pp. 7–26. Available at: .DOI: 10.1007/BF02992681

Giffinger, R., Fertner, C., Kramar, H., & Meijers, E. (2007) 'City-ranking of European medium-sized cities', *Centre of Regional Science* [Preprint]. Available at: https://www.smart-cities.eu/download/smart_cities_final_report.pdf

Gomes, M. G., Da Silva, V. H. C., Pinto, L. F. R., Centoamore, P., Digiesi, S., Facchini, F., & De Oliveira Neto, G. C. (2020). Economic, Environmental and Social Gains of the Implementation of Artificial Intelligence at Dam Operations toward Industry 4.0 Principles. Sustainability, 12(9), 3604. https://doi.org/ (2025). Making AI helpful for everyone. Google IA. https://ai.googleDOI: 10.3390/su12093604Google

Gómez-García, M., Soto-Varela, R., Umaña-Mata, A. C., & Pérez-Pérez, E. (2024). Digital Transformation Training and Digital Inclusion in Costa Rica. In *From Digital Divide to Digital Inclusion: Challenges, Perspectives and Trends in the Development of Digital Competences* (pp. 149-166). Singapore: Springer Nature Singapore. https://doi.org/DOI: 10.1007/978-981-99-7645-4_7

Gongane, V. U., Munot, M. V., & Anuse, A. D. (2024). A Survey of Explainable AI Techniques for Detection of Fake News and Hate Speech on Social Media Platforms. *Journal of Computational Social Science*, 7(1), 587–623. DOI: 10.1007/s42001-024-00248-9

Gonzalez-Tamayo, L. A., Maheshwari, G., Bonomo-Odizzio, A., Herrera-Avilés, M., & Krauss-Delorme, C. (2023). Factors influencing small and medium size enterprises development and digital maturity in Latin America. *Journal of Open Innovation*, 9(2), 100069. DOI: 10.1016/j.joitmc.2023.100069

Goodfellow, I., Pouget-Abadie, J., Mirza, M., Xu, B., Warde-Farley, D., Ozair, S., Courville, A., & Bengio, Y. (2014). Generative adversarial nets. *Advances in Neural Information Processing Systems, 27.* https://proceedings.neurips.cc/paper_files/paper/2014/file/5ca3e9b122f61f8f06494c97b1afccf3-Paper.pdf

Goodwin, E. A., Burhansstipanov, L., Dignan, M., Jones, K. L., & Kaur, J. S. (2017). The Experience of Treatment Barriers and Their Influence on Quality of Life in American Indian/Alaska Native Breast Cancer Survivors. *Cancer*, 123(5), 861–868. DOI: 10.1002/cncr.30406 PMID: 27763688

Google, A. I. Blog (2019). *Reducing gender bias in Google Translate*. Retrieved from https://ai.googleblog.com/2019/12/reducing-gender-bias-in-google.html

Google. (n.d.a). *Applying AI to help solve society's biggest challenges and improve lives.*https://ai.google/advancing-ai/social-impact

Google. (n.d.b). *Our principles*https://ai.google/responsibility/principles/#our-ai-principles-in-action

Google. (n.d.c). *Communication made easier*https://sites.research.google/relate

Gorur, R., Hoon, L., & Kowal, E. (2020). *Computer Science Ethics Education in Australia – A Work in Progress. 2020 IEEE International Conference on Teaching, Assessment, and Learning for Engineering (TALE).* DOI: 10.1109/TALE48869.2020.9368375

Gössling, S. (2000). Tourism–sustainable development option? *Environmental Conservation*, 27(3), 223–224. DOI: 10.1017/S0376892900000242

Govender, K. (2023). *Age of Agency: Rise with AI.* CRC Press. DOI: 10.4324/9781032684895

Graziani, M., Dutkiewicz, L., Calvaresi, D., Amorim, J. P., Yordanova, K., Vered, M., Nair, R., Abreu, P. H., Blanke, T., Pulignano, V., Prior, J. O., Lauwaert, L., Reijers, W., Depeursinge, A., Andrearczyk, V., & Müller, H. (2023). A global taxonomy of interpretable AI: Unifying the terminology for the technical and social sciences. *Artificial Intelligence Review*, 56(4), 3473–3504. DOI: 10.1007/s10462-022-10256-8 PMID: 36092822

Gremillion, G. M., Metcalfe, J. S., Marathe, A. R., Paul, V. J., Christensen, J., Drnec, K., Haynes, B., & Atwater, C. (2016). Analysis of trust in autonomy for convoy operations. In T. George, A. K. Dutta, & M. S. Islam (Eds.), *Micro- and Nanotechnology Sensors, Systems, and Applications VIII* (Vol. 9836, Issue Conference on Micro-and Nanotechnology Sensors, Systems, and Applications VIII. DOI: 10.1117/12.2224009

Grishunin, S., Naumova, E., Burova, E., Suloeva, S., & Nekrasova, T. (2022). The Impact of Sustainability Disclosures on Value of Companies Following Digital Transformation Strategies. *International Journal of Technology*, 13(7), 1432–1441. DOI: 10.14716/ijtech.v13i7.6194

Guadagnolo, B. A., Petereit, D. G., & Coleman, C. N. (2017). Cancer Care Access and Outcomes for American Indian Populations in the United States: Challenges and Models for Progress. *Seminars in Radiation Oncology*, 27(2), 143–149. DOI: 10.1016/j.semradonc.2016.11.006 PMID: 28325240

Gunning, D., Aha, D., & McGovern, A. (2019). *Explainable artificial intelligence (XAI).* DARPA. https://www.darpa.mil/program/explainable-artificial-intelligence

Guo, Z., Cho, J., Chen, I., Sengupta, S., Hong, M., & Mitra, T. (2021). Online Social Deception and Its Countermeasures: A Survey. *IEEE Access : Practical Innovations, Open Solutions*, 9, 1770–1806. DOI: 10.1109/ACCESS.2020.3047337

Gupta, A., Pranathy, R. S., Binny, M., Chellasamy, A., Nagarathinam, A., Pachiyappan, S., & Bhagat, S. (2024). Voices of the Future: Generation Z's Views on AI's Ethical and Social Impact. *Studies in Systems. Decision and Control.*, 223, 367–386. Advance online publication. DOI: 10.1007/978-3-031-51997-0_31

Guresen, E., & Kayakutlu, G. (2011). Definition of artificial neural networks with comparison to other networks. *Procedia Computer Science*, 3, 426–433. DOI: 10.1016/j.procs.2010.12.071

Hajli, N., Saeed, U., Tajvidi, M., & Shirazi, F. (2022). Social Bots and the Spread of Disinformation in Social Media: The Challenges of Artificial Intelligence. *British Journal of Management*, 33(3), 1238–1253. DOI: 10.1111/1467-8551.12554

Haleem, A., Javaid, M., Qadri, M. A., & Suman, R. (2022). Understanding the role of digital technologies in education: A review. *Sustainable operations and computers*, 3, 275-285. https://doi.org/DOI: 10.1016/j.susoc.2022.05.004

Hallur, G. G., Prabhu, S., & Aslekar, A. (2021). Entertainment in Era of AI, Big Data & IoT. In S. Das & S. Gochhait (eds) *Digital Entertainment* (pp.87-109). Palgrave Macmillan. https://doi.org/DOI: 10.1007/978-981-15-9724-4_5

Hamburg, I., O'brien, E., & Vladut, G. (2019). Entrepreneurial learning and AI literacy to support digital entrepreneurship. *Balkan Region Conference on Engineering and Business Education, 3*(1), 132–144. DOI: 10.2478/cplbu-2020-0016

Hamilton, S. A., Ambrosy, A. P., Parikh, R. V., Tan, T. C., Fitzpatrick, J. K., Avula, H. R., Sandhu, A. T., Ku, I. A., Go, A. S., Sax, D., & Bhatt, A. S. (2024). Applying natural language processing to identify emergency department and observation encounters for worsening heart failure. *ESC Heart Failure*, 11(5), 2542–2545. Advance online publication. DOI: 10.1002/ehf2.14829 PMID: 38741373

Hamon, R., Junklewitz, H., Garrido, J. S., & Sanchez, I. (2024). Three Challenges to Secure AI Systems in the Context of AI Regulations. *IEEE Access : Practical Innovations, Open Solutions*, 12, 61022–61035. DOI: 10.1109/ACCESS.2024.3391021

Hand, D. J. (2022). Trustworthiness of statistical inference. *Journal of the Royal Statistical Society. Series A, (Statistics in Society)*, 185(1), 329–347. DOI: 10.1111/rssa.12752

Han, M. J. N., & Kim, M. J. (2021). A critical review of the smart city in relation to citizen adoption towards sustainable smart living. *Habitat International*, 108, 102312. DOI: 10.1016/j.habitatint.2021.102312

Hansen, A. V., & Fuglsang, L. (2020). Living Labs as an Innovation Tool for Public Value Creation: Possibilities and Pitfalls. *The Innovation Journal*, 25(3), 1–21.

Hansen, D. J., & Wyman, D. (2021). Beyond making a profit: Using the UN SDGs in entrepreneurship programs to help nurture sustainable entrepreneurs. *Journal of the International Council for Small Business*, 2(2), 125–133. DOI: 10.1080/26437015.2021.1881931

Hansen, E. B., & Bøgh, S. (2021). Artificial intelligence and internet of things in small and medium-sized enterprises: A survey. *Journal of Manufacturing Systems*, 58, 362–372. DOI: 10.1016/j.jmsy.2020.08.009

Harbinja, E., Edwards, L., & McVey, M. (2023). Governing ghostbots. Computer Law And Security Report. *Computer Law & Security Report*, 48, 105791. DOI: 10.1016/j.clsr.2023.105791

Hardin, R. (2004). Distrust. In Hardin, R. (Ed.), *Distrust* (pp. 3–33). Russell Sage Foundation.

Hardt, M., Price, E., & Srebro, N. (2016). Equality of opportunity in supervised learning. *Proceedings of the 30th International Conference on Neural Information Processing Systems*, 3315-3323.

Hasanujjaman, M., Chowdhury, M. Z., & Jang, Y. M. (2023). Sensor Fusion in Autonomous Vehicle with Traffic Surveillance Camera System: Detection, Localization, and AI Networking. *Sensors (Basel)*, 23(6), 3335. Advance online publication. DOI: 10.3390/s23063335 PMID: 36992043

Hasan, Z., Vaz, D., Athota, V. S., Désiré, S. S. M., & Pereira, V. (2023). Can artificial intelligence (AI) manage behavioural biases among financial planners? *Journal of Global Information Management*, 31(2), 1–18. DOI: 10.4018/JGIM.321728

Haslam, P. A. (2007). *The corporate social responsibility system in Latin America and the Caribbean. Policy Paper*. Canadian Foundation for the Americas.

Hatipoglu, B., Ertuna, B., & Salman, D. (2019). Corporate social responsibility in tourism as a tool for sustainable development: An evaluation from a community perspective. *International Journal of Contemporary Hospitality Management*, 31(6), 2358–2375. DOI: 10.1108/IJCHM-05-2018-0448

Heaton, J., & Parlikad, A. K. (2019) 'A conceptual framework for the alignment of infrastructure assets to citizen requirements within a Smart Cities framework', *Cities*, 90(April 2018), pp. 32–41. Available at: DOI: 10.1016/j.cities.2019.01.041

Heilbronner, R. L. (2011). *The worldly philosophers: The lives, times and ideas of the great economic thinkers*. Simon and Schuster.

Helfat, C. E., Kaul, A., Ketchen, D. J.Jr, Barney, J. B., Chatain, O., & Singh, H. (2023). Renewing the resource-based view: New contexts, new concepts, and new methods. *Strategic Management Journal*, 44(6), 1357–1390. DOI: 10.1002/smj.3500

Hemachandran, K. & Rodriguez, R.V. (2023). *Artificial Intelligence for Business: An Implementation Guide Containing Practical and Industry-Specific Case Studies*. https://doi.org/.DOI: 10.4324/9781003358411

Henman, P. (2020). Improving public services using artificial intelligence: Possibilities, pitfalls, governance. *Asia Pacific Journal of Public Administration*, 42(4), 209–221. DOI: 10.1080/23276665.2020.1816188

Herasimenka, A. (2022). Communication resource mobilization. *Journal of Communication*. Advance online publication. DOI: 10.1093/joc/jqac043 PMID: 37016634

Heredia Zurita, A., & Dini, M. (2021). *Análisis de las políticas de apoyo a las pymes para enfrentar la pandemia de COVID-19 en América Latina*. CEPAL.

Hernández-Mulero, N., & Berengüí, R. (2016). No Title. *Cuadernos de Psicología del Deporte*, 16(2), 37–44.

Hernández-Perlines, F., & Rung-Hoch, N. (2017). Sustainable entrepreneurial orientation in family firms. *Sustainability (Basel)*, 9(7), 1212. DOI: 10.3390/su9071212

Herrera, M. E. B. (2016). Innovation for impact: Business innovation for inclusive growth. *Journal of Business Research*, 69(5), 1725–1730. DOI: 10.1016/j.jbusres.2015.10.045

Herzog, C., & Lunn, B. K. (2018). *Issue 1* (Vol. 117). Response to the letter 'Field classification of publications in Dimensions: a first case study testing its reliability and validity.' In *Scientometrics*. Springer Netherlands., DOI: 10.1007/s11192-018-2854-z

Higgins-Desbiolles, F. (2020). The "war over tourism": Challenges to sustainable tourism in the tourism academy after COVID-19. *Journal of Sustainable Tourism*, 29(4), 551–569. DOI: 10.1080/09669582.2020.1803334

Hildebrandt, M. (2015). *Smart technologies and the end(s) of law: Novel entanglements of law and technology*. Edward Elgar Publishing. DOI: 10.4337/9781849808774

Hinojosa, H., & González-Cacho, T. (2023). The dark side of smart cities. In Cebral-Loureda, M., Rincón-Flores, E. G., & Sanchez-Ante, G. (Eds.), *What AI Can Do*. Taylor and Francis Group, LLC. DOI: 10.1201/b23345-13

Hoefsloot, F. I., Jimenez, A., Martinez, J., Miranda Sara, L., & Pfeffer, K. (2022). Eliciting design principles using a data justice framework for participatory urban water governance observatories. *Information Technology for Development*, 28(3), 617–638. DOI: 10.1080/02681102.2022.2091505

Hofstede, G. (2001). *Culture's Consequences: Comparing Values, Behaviors, Institutions, and Organizations Across Nations* (2nd ed.). SAGE Publications.

Hollebeek, L. D., & Macky, K. (2019). Digital content marketing's role in fostering consumer engagement, trust, and value: Framework, fundamental propositions, and implications. *Journal of Interactive Marketing*, 45(1), 27–41. DOI: 10.1016/j.intmar.2018.07.003

Holmes, W., & Tuomi, I. (2022). State of the art and practice in AI in education. *European Journal of Education*, 57(4), 542–570. DOI: 10.1111/ejed.12533

Hook, D. W., Porter, S. J., & Herzog, C. (2018). Dimensions: Building Context for Search and Evaluation. *Frontiers in Research Metrics and Analytics*, 3, 23. Advance online publication. DOI: 10.3389/frma.2018.00023

Horneber, D., & Laumer, S. (2023). Algorithmic accountability. *Business & Information Systems Engineering*, 65(6), 723–730. DOI: 10.1007/s12599-023-00817-8

Horng, J. S., Hsu, H., & Tsai, C. Y. (2018). An assessment model of corporate social responsibility practice in the tourism industry. *Journal of Sustainable Tourism*, 26(7), 1085–1104. DOI: 10.1080/09669582.2017.1388384

Hossain, A. T., & Masum, A. A. (2022). Does corporate social responsibility help mitigate firm-level climate change risk? *Finance Research Letters*, 47, 102791. DOI: 10.1016/j.frl.2022.102791

Houghtaling, B., Byker Shanks, C., Ahmed, S., & Rink, E. (2018). Grandmother and health care professional breastfeeding perspectives provide opportunities for health promotion in an American Indian community. *Social Science & Medicine*, 208, 80–88. DOI: 10.1016/j.socscimed.2018.05.017 PMID: 29772397

Hu, Y. & Kurylo, A.D. (2024). *Screaming out Loud in the Communication Classroom: Asian Stereotypes and the Fallibility of Image Generating Artificial Intelligence (AI). The Role of Generative AI in the Communication Classroom*. DOI: 10.4018/979-8-3693-0831-8.ch012

Huang, X., Kwiatkowska, M., Wang, S., & Wu, M. (2017). Safety Verification of Deep Neural Networks. En Lecture notes in computer science (pp. 3-29). https://doi.org/DOI: 10.1007/978-3-319-63387-9_1

Huang, M. H., & Rust, R. T. (2018). Artificial intelligence in service. *Journal of Service Research*, 21(2), 155–172. DOI: 10.1177/1094670517752459

Hua, X., Hasan, N. A. M., De Costa, F., & Qiao, W. (2024). Opportunities or Challenges? The Interplay between Artificial Intelligence and Corporate Social Responsibility Communication. *Business Systems Research*, 15(1), 131–157. DOI: 10.2478/bsrj-2024-0007

Hughes, E., & Scheyvens, R. (2016). Corporate social responsibility in tourism post-2015: A development first approach. *Tourism Geographies*, 18(5), 469–482. DOI: 10.1080/14616688.2016.1208678

Hughes, J. (2019). The Law of Intellectual Property: The Need for a Global Framework. *Intellectual Property Quarterly*, 3, 214–232.

Huh, Y. K. (2022). Legal Implications of Financial Supervision with Artificial Intelligence. *The Korean Journal of Securities Law*, 23(1), 221–250. https://www.webofscience.com/wos/alldb/full-record/KJD:ART002839443

Huq, A. Z. (2020). A right to a human decision. *Virginia Law Review*, 106(3), 611–688.

Hurley, S. L. (2003). *Justice, Luck, and Knowledge*. Harvard University Press.

Hu, X., Li, S., Huang, T., Tang, B., Huai, R., & Chen, L. (2024). How Simulation Helps Autonomous Driving: A Survey of Sim2real, Digital Twins, and Parallel Intelligence. *IEEE Transactions on Intelligent Vehicles*, 9(1), 593–612. DOI: 10.1109/TIV.2023.3312777

Hu, Y., Kuang, W., Qin, Z., Li, K., Zhang, J., Gao, Y., Li, W., & Li, K. (2021). Artificial Intelligence Security: Threats and Countermeasures. *ACM Computing Surveys*, 55(1), 1–36. DOI: 10.1145/3487890

IAB & Mazzin. (2024). *Guía para conectar con la Generación Z*.https://iabspain.es/iab-spain-y-mazinn-presentan-la-2a-edicion-de-la-guia-para-conectar-con-la-generacion-z/

Iadanza, E., Benincasa, G., Ventisette, I., & Gherardelli, M. (2022). Automatic Classification of Hospital Settings through Artificial Intelligence. *Electronics (Basel)*, 11(11), 1697. DOI: 10.3390/electronics11111697

IEEE. (2019). *IEEE 7000-2021: Standard for ethics in autonomous and intelligent systems*. IEEE. https://standards.ieee.org/standards/7000

Igwegbe, C. A., Obi, C. C., Ohale, P. E., Ahmadi, S., Onukwuli, O. D., Nwabanne, J. T., & Białowiec, A. (2023). Modelling and optimisation of electrocoagulation/flocculation recovery of effluent from land-based aquaculture by artificial intelligence (AI) approaches. *Environmental Science and Pollution Research International*, 30(27), 70897–70917. DOI: 10.1007/s11356-023-27387-2 PMID: 37160520

Innan, N., Khan, M. A., & Беннаи, M. (2023). Financial fraud detection: A comparative study of quantum machine learning models. *International Journal of Quantum Information*, 22(02), 2350044. Advance online publication. DOI: 10.1142/S0219749923500442

Instagram (n.d.). *PROGRAMS. Instagram fosters communities of support*https://about.instagram.com/community/programs

Isaacson, M. J., & Lynch, A. R. (2018). Culturally Relevant Palliative and End-of-Life Care for U.S. Indigenous Populations: An Integrative Review. *Journal of Transcultural Nursing*, 29(2), 180–191. DOI: 10.1177/1043659617720980 PMID: 28826379

Islam, M., Rashid, M., & Nuruzzaman, M. (2021). Sustainable corporate entrepreneurship of publicly traded Commercial Banks: A Developing Country perspective. *Journal of International Business and Management*. DOI: 10.37227/jibm-2021-09-1498

Ivars-Baidal, J. A., Vera-Rebollo, J. F., Perles-Ribes, J., Femenia-Serra, F., & Celdrán-Bernabeu, M. A. (2023). Sustainable tourism indicators: What's new within the smart city/destination approach? *Journal of Sustainable Tourism*, 31(7), 1556–1582. DOI: 10.1080/09669582.2021.1876075

Jain, A., Gue, I. H., & Jain, P. (2023). Research trends, themes, and insights on artificial neural networks for smart cities towards SDG-11. *Journal of Cleaner Production*, 412, 137300. Advance online publication. DOI: 10.1016/j.jclepro.2023.137300

Jaiswal, A., & Arun, C. J. (2021). Potential of Artificial Intelligence for transformation of the education system in India. *International Journal of Education and Development Using Information and Communication Technology*, 17(1), 142–158.

Jamali, D., Lund-Thomsen, P., & Jeppesen, S. (2017). SMEs and CSR in developing countries. *Business & Society*, 56(1), 11–22. DOI: 10.1177/0007650315571258

James, R. D., West, K. M., Claw, K. G., EchoHawk, A., Dodge, L., Dominguez, A., Taualii, M., Forquera, R., Thummel, K., & Burke, W. (1613–1616). EchoHawk, A., Dodge, L., Dominguez, A., Taualii, M., Forquera, R., Thummel, K., & Burke, W. (2018). Responsible research with urban American Indians and Alaska natives. *American Journal of Public Health*, 108(12), 1613–1616. Advance online publication. DOI: 10.2105/AJPH.2018.304708 PMID: 30359103

Jamshidi, S., & Hashemi, M. R. (2012). *An efficient data enrichment scheme for fraud detection using social network analysis. 2012 SIXTH INTERNATIONAL SYMPOSIUM ON TELECOMMUNICATIONS*. IST., DOI: 10.1109/ISTEL.2012.6483147

Jang, S. (2024). Recent Trends and Implications for Artificial Intelligence Regulation. Science. *Technology and Law*, 15(1), 153–174. DOI: 10.34267/cbstl.2024.15.1.153

Jannach, D., Zanker, M., Felfernig, A., & Friedrich, G. (2018). *Recommender Systems: An Introduction*. Cambridge University Press.

Jarrahi, M. H. (2018). Artificial Intelligence and the Future of Work: Human-AI Symbiosis in Organizational Decision Making. *Business Horizons*, 61(4), 577–586. DOI: 10.1016/j.bushor.2018.03.007

Järvi, H., Kähkönen, A. K., & Torvinen, H. (2018). When value co-creation fails: Reasons that lead to value co-destruction. *Scandinavian Journal of Management*, 34(1), 63–77. DOI: 10.1016/j.scaman.2018.01.002

Jasper, A. I. (2024, November 2). *AI content generation for marketing and sales*. Jasper. Retrieved from https://www.jasper.ai/

Javed, A. R., Ahmed, W., Pandya, S., Maddikunta, P. K. R., Alazab, M., & Gadekallu, T. R. (2023). *'A Survey of Explainable Artificial Intelligence for Smart Cities', Electronics*. MDPI., DOI: 10.3390/electronics12041020

Jaworska, S. (2018). Change but no climate change: Discourses of climate change in corporate social responsibility reporting in the oil industry. *International Journal of Business Communication*, 55(2), 194–219. DOI: 10.1177/2329488417753951

Jeffers, M. T. (2020). Luck and the limits of equality. *Philosophical Papers*, 49(3), 397–429. DOI: 10.1080/05568641.2020.1762114

Jenkins, H. (2004). A critique of conventional CSR theory: An SME perspective. *Journal of General Management*, 29(4), 37–57. DOI: 10.1177/030630700402900403

Jenkins, H. (2006). Small business champions for corporate social responsibility. *Journal of Business Ethics*, 67(3), 241–256. DOI: 10.1007/s10551-006-9182-6

Jesus, S., Belém, C., Balayan, V., Bento, J., Saleiro, P., Bizarro, P., & Gama, J. (2021). How can I choose an explainer? *Proceedings of the 2021 ACM Conference on Fairness, Accountability, and Transparency*, pp.805-815. https://doi.org/DOI: 10.1145/3442188.3445941

Jewani, V. K., Ajmire, P. E., Chaurasia, S., & Brijwani, G. N. (2023). Artificial Intelligence: A Smart and Empowering Approach to Women's Safety. In Ponnusamy, S., Bora, V., Daigavane, P. M., & Wazalwar, S. S. (Eds.), *Impact of AI on Advancing Women's Safety* (pp. 121–138). IGI Global., DOI: 10.4018/979-8-3693-2679-4.ch008

Jiménez, M. (2025, 21 enero). Trump barre la era Biden con una avalancha de decretos contra la inmigración, la agenda verde y la diversidad. El País. https://elpais.com/internacional/2025-01-20/trump-barre-la-era-biden-con-una-avalancha-de-decretos-contra-la-inmigracion-la-agenda-verde-y-la-diversidad.html

Jiménez, D. L., Dittmar, E. C., & Portillo, J. P. V. (2021). Cooperation and relationship in the triple helix model of innovation. *International Journal of Knowledge and Learning*, 14(1), 1–9. DOI: 10.1504/IJKL.2021.115025

Jin, Q., Lin, R., & Yang, F. (2020). E-WACGAN: Enhanced Generative Model of Signaling Data Based on WGAN-GP and ACGAN. *IEEE Systems Journal*, 14(3), 3289–3300. DOI: 10.1109/JSYST.2019.2935457

Jobin, A., Ienca, M., & Vayena, E. (2019). The global landscape of AI ethics guidelines. *Nature Machine Intelligence*, 1(9), 389–399. DOI: 10.1038/s42256-019-0088-2

Johann, M. (2022). CSR Strategy in Tourism during the COVID-19 Pandemic. *Sustainability (Basel)*, 14(7), 3773. DOI: 10.3390/su14073773

Johnson, M., Albizri, A., Harfouche, A., & Fosso-Wamba, S. (2022). Integrating human knowledge into artificial intelligence for complex and ill-structured problems: Informed artificial intelligence. *International Journal of Information Management*, 64, 102479. DOI: 10.1016/j.ijinfomgt.2022.102479

Josephng, P. S., Vasu, K. P., Phan, K. Y., Sun, J., & Wei, Z. (2024). Managing Sustainable E-Waste Resilient Infrastructure with Smart Bin. *Journal of Advanced Research in Applied Mechanics*, 118(1), 108–130. DOI: 10.37934/aram.118.1.108130

Kaal, W. A., & Vermeulen, E. P. M. (2017). How to regulate disruptive innovation – From facts to data. *SSRN*, 57(2), 169–190. DOI: 10.2139/ssrn.2808044

Kalolo, J. F. (2019). Digital revolution and its impact on education systems in developing countries. *Education and Information Technologies*, 24(1), 345–358. DOI: 10.1007/s10639-018-9778-3

Kalpokas, I., & Kalpokiene, J. (2022). *Deepfakes: A realistic assessment of potentials, risks, and policy regulation*. Springer Nature. DOI: 10.1007/978-3-030-93802-4

Kamel, D. (2024) *Dubai's new airport terminal promises easier and faster check-in enabled by AI, The National*. Available at: https://www.thenationalnews.com/business/aviation/2024/10/24/dubais-new-airport-terminal-promises-easier-and-faster-check-in-enabled-by-ai/ (Accessed: 26 October 2024).

Kaminski, M. E. (2019). The Right to Explanation, Explained. *Berkeley Technology Law Journal*, 34(1), 189–218.

Kamruzzaman, M. M. (2022). Impact of Social Media on Geopolitics and Economic Growth: Mitigating the Risks by Developing Artificial Intelligence and Cognitive Computing Tools. *Computational Intelligence and Neuroscience*, 2022, 1–12. DOI: 10.1155/2022/7988894 PMID: 35602647

Kanika, S., Singla, J., Kashif Bashir, A., Nam, Y., Ul Hasan, N., & Tariq, U. (2022). Handling Class Imbalance in Online Transaction Fraud Detection. Computers, Materials & Continua/Computers. *Computers, Materials & Continua*, 70(2), 2861–2877. DOI: 10.32604/cmc.2022.019990

Kapadiya, K., Patel, U., Gupta, R., Alshehri, M. D., Tanwar, S., Sharma, G., & Bokoro, P. N. (2022). Blockchain and AI-Empowered Healthcare Insurance Fraud Detection: An Analysis, Architecture, and Future Prospects. *IEEE Access : Practical Innovations, Open Solutions*, 10, 79606–79627. DOI: 10.1109/ACCESS.2022.3194569

Kaplan, A., & Haenlein, M. (2020). Rulers of the world, unite! The challenges and opportunities of artificial intelligence. *Business Horizons*, 63(1), 37–50. DOI: 10.1016/j.bushor.2019.09.003

Kar, A. K., Choudhary, S. K., & Singh, V. K. (2022). How can artificial intelligence impact sustainability: A systematic literature review. *Journal of Cleaner Production*, 376, 134120. DOI: 10.1016/j.jclepro.2022.134120

Kariv, D., Matlay, H., & Fayolle, A. (2019). Introduction: entrepreneurial trends meet entrepreneurial education. In *Edward Elgar Publishing eBooks*. DOI: 10.4337/9781786438232.00006

Karpinska-Krakowiak, M., & Eisend, M. (2024). Realistic Portrayals of Untrue Information: The Effects of Deepfaked Ads and Different Types of Disclosures. *Journal of Advertising*, •••, 1–11. DOI: 10.1080/00913367.2024.2306415

Karpus, J., Krueger, A., Verba, J. T., Bahrami, B., & Deroy, O. (2021). Algorithm exploitation: Humans are keen to exploit benevolent AI. *iScience*, 24(6), 102679. Advance online publication. DOI: 10.1016/j.isci.2021.102679 PMID: 34189440

Karuppiah, K., Sankaranarayanan, B., D'Adamo, I., & Ali, S. M. (2023). Evaluation of key factors for industry 4.0 technologies adoption in small and medium enterprises (SMEs): An emerging economy context. *Journal of Asia Business Studies*, 17(2), 347–370. DOI: 10.1108/JABS-05-2021-0202

Katsh, E., & Rabinovich-Einy, O. (2017). *Digital Justice: Technology and the Internet of Disputes*. Oxford University Press. DOI: 10.1093/acprof:oso/9780190464585.001.0001

Kaufmann-Kohler, G., & Schultz, T. (2004). *Online Dispute Resolution: Challenges for Contemporary Justice*. Kluwer Law International.

Kaur, D., Uslu, S., Rittichier, K. J., & Durresi, A. (2022). Trustworthy artificial intelligence: A review. *ACM Computing Surveys*, 55(2), 1–38. DOI: 10.1145/3491209

Kesa, A., & Kerikmäe, T. (2020). Artificial Intelligence and the GDPR: Inevitable Nemeses? TalTech Journal Of European Studies/TalTech. *Journal of European Studies*, 10(3), 68–90. DOI: 10.1515/bjes-2020-0022

Khan, H. U., Malik, M. Z., Nazir, S., & Khan, F. (2023). Utilizing Bio Metric System for Enhancing Cyber Security in Banking Sector: A Systematic Analysis. *IEEE Access : Practical Innovations, Open Solutions*, 11, 80181–80198. DOI: 10.1109/ACCESS.2023.3298824

Khan, S. A. R., Yu, Z., Panait, M., Janjua, L. R., & Shah, A. (Eds.). (2021). *Global corporate social responsibility initiatives for reluctant businesses*. IGI Global. DOI: 10.4018/978-1-7998-3988-0

Khokhar, M. S., Agashe, A., Deogaonkar, A., & Paralkar, T. A. (2023). Ethical Leadership and Corporate Social Responsibility in Diversified Business Groups: A Conceptual Model of Asian and Latin America. *International Journal of Professional Business Review: Int.J. Prof. Bus. Rev.*, 8(6), 19.

Khurana, D., Koli, A., Khatter, K., & Singh, S. (2023). Natural language processing: State of the art, current trends and challenges. *Multimedia Tools and Applications*, 82(3), 3713–3744. DOI: 10.1007/s11042-022-13428-4 PMID: 35855771

Kietzmann, J., Mills, A. J., & Plangger, K. (2020). Deepfakes: Perspectives on the future "reality" of advertising and branding. *International Journal of Advertising*, 40(3), 473–485. DOI: 10.1080/02650487.2020.1834211

Kim, D. J. (2019). Digital Economy and FinTech in the view of Consumer Protection. *The Journal of Comparative Private Law*, 26(3), 285–330. https://www.webofscience.com/wos/alldb/full-record/KJD:ART002501742

Kim, E., Shin, J., Kwon, Y., & Park, B. (2023). EMG-Based Dynamic Hand Gesture Recognition Using Edge AI for Human-Robot Interaction. *Electronics (Basel)*, 12(7), 1541. Advance online publication. DOI: 10.3390/electronics12071541

Kim, S., & Chung, S. (2019). Explaining organizational responsiveness to emerging regulatory pressure: The case of illegal overwork in South Korea. *Human Relations*, 72(9), 1436–1461.

King, T. C., Aggarwal, N., Taddeo, M., & Floridi, L. (2019). Artificial Intelligence Crime: An Interdisciplinary Analysis of Foreseeable Threats and Solutions. *Science and Engineering Ethics*, 26(1), 89–120. DOI: 10.1007/s11948-018-00081-0 PMID: 30767109

Kinnula, M., Durall Gazulla, E., Hirvonen, N., Malmberg, J., & Haukipuro, L. (2024). Nurturing Systems Thinking among Young People by Developing Business Ideas on Sustainable AI. *International Journal of Child-Computer Interaction*, 40, 100656. Advance online publication. DOI: 10.1016/j.ijcci.2024.100656

Kleinman, Z. (February 4, 2019). Amazon: Facial recognition bias claims are 'misleading. *BBC News*.https://www.bbc.com/news/technology-47117299

Köbis, N., Bonnefon, J. F., & Rahwan, I. (2021). Bad machines corrupt good morals. *Nature Human Behaviour*, 5(6), 679–685. DOI: 10.1038/s41562-021-01128-2 PMID: 34083752

Koh, K., Li, H., & Tong, Y. H. (2023). Corporate social responsibility (CSR) performance and stakeholder engagement: Evidence from the quantity and quality of CSR disclosures. *Corporate Social Responsibility and Environmental Management*, 30(2), 504–517. DOI: 10.1002/csr.2370

Kolk, A., & van den Buuse, D. (2012). In search of viable business models for development: Sustainable energy in developing countries. *Corporate Governance (Bradford)*, 12(4), 551–567. DOI: 10.1108/14720701211267865

Kong, D., & Liu, B. (2023). Digital Technology and Corporate Social Responsibility: Evidence from China. *Emerging Markets Finance & Trade*, 59(9), 2967–2993. DOI: 10.1080/1540496X.2023.2199122

Kong, M., Li, R., Wang, J., Li, X., Jin, S., Xie, W., Hou, M., & Cao, C. (2024). CFTNet: A robust credit card fraud detection model enhanced by counterfactual data augmentation. *Neural Computing & Applications*, 36(15), 8607–8623. DOI: 10.1007/s00521-024-09546-9

Korstanje, M. E. (2018). Dialogues with Slavoj Zizek: Placing the role of torture in context. *International Journal of Žižek Studies*, 12(2), 1–15.

Korstanje, M. E., Séraphin, H., & Gowreesunkar, V. G. (Eds.). (2020). *Post-disaster and post-conflict tourism: Toward a new management approach*. CRC Press.

Kotilainen, S., Okkonen, J., Vuorio, J., & Leisti, K. (2020). *Youth Media Education in the Age of Algorithm-Driven Social Media. The Handbook of Media Education Research.* DOI: 10.1002/9781119166900.ch10

Kotras, B. (2020). Mass personalization: Predictive marketing algorithms and the reshaping of consumer knowledge. *Big Data & Society*, 7(2), 2053951720951581. Advance online publication. DOI: 10.1177/2053951720951581

Koukal, A., Gleue, C., & Breitner, M. (2014). Enhancing Literature Review Methods-Evaluation of a Literature Search Approach based on Latent Semantic Indexing.

Kowszyk, Y., Covarrubias, A., & García, L. (2011). *El estado de la responsabilidad social empresarial en América Latina 2011*. Red Forum Empresa.

Krambia-Kapardis, M., Christodoulou, C., & Agathocleous, M. (2010). Neural networks: The panacea in fraud detection? *Managerial Auditing Journal*, 25(7), 659–678. DOI: 10.1108/02686901011061342

Kulal, A., Rahiman, H. U., Suvarna, H., Abhishek, N., & Dinesh, S. (2024). Enhancing public service delivery efficiency: Exploring the impact of AI. *Journal of Open Innovation*, 10(3), 100329. Advance online publication. DOI: 10.1016/j.joitmc.2024.100329

Kuleto, V., Ilic, M., Dumangiu, M., Rankovic, M., Martins, O. M., Paun, D., & Mihoreanu, L. (2021). Exploring opportunities and challenges of artificial intelligence and machine learning in higher education institutions. *Sustainability (Basel)*, 13(18), 10424. DOI: 10.3390/su131810424

Kulkov, I., Kulkova, J., Leone, D., Rohrbeck, R., & Menvielle, L. (2024). Standalone or run together: Artificial intelligence as an enabler for other technologies. *International Journal of Entrepreneurial Behaviour & Research*, 30(8), 2082–2105. DOI: 10.1108/IJEBR-02-2023-0169

Kumar, D., & Suthar, N. (2024). Ethical and legal challenges of AI in marketing: an exploration of solutions. *Journal of Information, Communication and Ethics in Society*, 22(1), 124-144. https://doi-org.zulib.idm.oclc.org/10.1108/JICES-05-2023-0068

Kumar, V., Gunner, S., Pregnolato, M., Tully, P., Georgalas, N., Oikonomou, G., Karatzas, S. and Tryfonas, T. (2024) 'Sense (and) the city: From Internet of Things sensors and open data platforms to urban observatories', *IET Smart Cities* [Preprint]. John Wiley and Sons Inc. Available at: .DOI: 10.1049/smc2.12081

Kumar, A., Bhattacharyya, S. S., & Krishnamoorthy, B. (2023). Automation-augmentation paradox in organizational artificial intelligence technology deployment capabilities; an empirical investigation for achieving simultaneous economic and social benefits. *Journal of Enterprise Information Management*, 36(6), 1556–1582. DOI: 10.1108/JEIM-09-2022-0307

Kumari, A., Gupta, R., & Tanwar, S. (2021). Amalgamation of blockchain and IoT for smart cities underlying 6G communication: A comprehensive review. *Computer Communications*, 172, 102–118. DOI: 10.1016/j.comcom.2021.03.005

Kumar, P. C., Cotter, K., & Cabrera, L. Y. (2024). Taking Responsibility for Meaning and Mattering: An Agential Realist Approach to Generative AI and Literacy. *Reading Research Quarterly*, 59(4), 570–578. DOI: 10.1002/rrq.570

Kumar, P., Sharma, S. K., & Dutot, V. (2023). Artificial intelligence (AI)-enabled CRM capability in healthcare: The impact on service innovation. *International Journal of Information Management*, 69, 102598. Advance online publication. DOI: 10.1016/j.ijinfomgt.2022.102598

Kumar, S., Sharma, D., Rao, S., Lim, W. M., & Mangla, S. K. (2022). Past, present, and future of sustainable finance: Insights from big data analytics through machine learning of scholarly research. Annals Of Operation Research. *Annals of Operations Research*. Advance online publication. DOI: 10.1007/s10479-021-04410-8 PMID: 35002001

Kumar, V., Rajan, B., Venkatesan, R., & Lecinski, J. (2019). Understanding the role of artificial intelligence in personalized engagement marketing. *California Management Review*, 61(4), 135–155. DOI: 10.1177/0008125619859317

Kumi, S., Snow, C., Lomotey, R. K., & Deters, R. (2024). Uncovering Concerns of Citizens Through Machine Learning and Social Network Sentiment Analysis. *IEEE Access : Practical Innovations, Open Solutions*, 12, 94885–94913. DOI: 10.1109/ACCESS.2024.3426329

Kuzniacki, B., Almada, M., Tyliński, K., & Górski, Ł. (2022). Requirements for Tax XAI Under Constitutional Principles and Human Rights. En Lecture notes in computer science (pp. 221-238). https://doi.org/DOI: 10.1007/978-3-031-15565-9_14

Laghrabli, S., Benabbou, L., & Berrado, A. (2015, October). A new methodology for literature review analysis using association rules mining. In 2015 10th International Conference on Intelligent Systems: Theories and Applications (SITA) (pp. 1-6). IEEE. DOI: 10.1109/SITA.2015.7358394

Lai, C. Y., Li, Y., & Lin, L. F. (2017). A social referral appraising mechanism for the e-marketplace. *Information & Management*, 54(3), 269–280. DOI: 10.1016/j.im.2016.07.001

Lambrecht, A., & Tucker, C. (2019). Algorithmic bias? An empirical study of apparent gender-based discrimination in the display of STEM career ads. *Management Science*, 65(7), 2966–2981. DOI: 10.1287/mnsc.2018.3093

Langenbucher, K. (2021). Zur Regulierung des Kreditscoring. *Europäische Zeitschrift Für Wirtschaftsrecht*, 22, 961–963.

Larsson, S., & Heintz, F. (2020). Transparency in artificial intelligence. *Internet Policy Review*, 9(2), 1–16. DOI: 10.14763/2020.2.1469

Latif, K. F., & Sajjad, A. (2018). Measuring corporate social responsibility: A critical review of survey instruments. *Corporate Social Responsibility and Environmental Management*, 25(6), 1174–1197. DOI: 10.1002/csr.1630

Law 15/2022, of July 12 (15917/2022), for equal treatment and non-discrimination *BOE*https://www.boe.es/buscar/pdf/2022/BOE-A-2022-11589-consolidado.pdf

Leal, A. A. (2019). Aspetos jurídicos da análise de dados na Internet (big data analytics) nos setores bancário e financeiro: proteção de dados pessoais e deveres de informação. In *FinTech—Desafios da Tecnologia Financeira* (2nd ed.). Almedina.

Leal, A. A. (2022). Decisões, algoritmos e interpretabilidade em ambiente negocial. Sobre o dever de explicação das decisões algorítmicas. *Lisbon Law Review*, 63(1–2), 65–148.

Leben, D. (2023). Explainable AI as evidence of fair decisions. *Frontiers in Psychology*, 14, 1069426. DOI: 10.3389/fpsyg.2023.1069426 PMID: 36865358

Lee, J., & Lee, K. (2021). Is the fourth industrial revolution a continuation of the third industrial revolution or something new under the sun? Analyzing technological regimes using US patent data. *Industrial and Corporate Change, 30*(1), 137-159. https://doi.org/DOI: 10.1093/icc/dtaa059

Lee, K. F., Triolo, P., & Kania, E. (2018). AI Superpowers: China, Silicon Valley, and the New World Order. Houghton Mifflin Harcourt.

Lee, K. Y., Kwon, H. Y., & Lim, J. I. (2018). Legal Consideration on the Use of Artificial Intelligence Technology and Self-regulation in Financial Sector: Focused on Robo-Advisors. En Lecture notes in computer science (pp. 323-335). https://doi.org/DOI: 10.1007/978-3-319-93563-8_27

Lee, J. D., & See, K. A. (2004). Trust in automation: Designing for appropriate reliance. *Human Factors*, 46(1), 50–80. DOI: 10.1518/hfes.46.1.50.30392 PMID: 15151155

Lee, K. (2021). A Systematic Review on Social Sustainability of Artificial Intelligence in Product Design. *Sustainability (Basel)*, 13(5), 2668. Advance online publication. DOI: 10.3390/su13052668

Lee, M., Scheepers, H., Lui, A. K. H., & Ngai, E. W. T. (2023). The implementation of artificial intelligence in organizations: A systematic literature review. *Information & Management*, 60(5), 103816. DOI: 10.1016/j.im.2023.103816

Lee, S. (2022). Corporate social responsibility and COVID-19: Research implications. *Tourism Economics*, 28(4), 863–869. DOI: 10.1177/1354816620978136

Leung, K. Y. K., & Lee, H. Y. (2023). Implementing the smart city: Who has a say? Some insights from Hong Kong. *International Journal of Urban Sciences*, 27(sup1, S1), 124–148. DOI: 10.1080/12265934.2021.1997634

Levenda, A. M. (2019). 'Mobilizing smart grid experiments: Policy mobilities and urban energy governance', *Environment and Planning C. Politics and Space*, 37(4), 634–651. DOI: 10.1177/2399654418797127

Levesque, H. (2017). *Artificial intelligence: A guide for thinking humans*. Penguin Press.

Lewicki, R. J., McAllister, D. J., & Bies, R. J. (1998). Trust and Distrust: New Relationships and Realities. *Academy of Management Review*, 23(3), 438. DOI: 10.2307/259288

Lewis, P. R., & Marsh, S. (2022). What is it like to trust a rock? A functionalist perspective on trust and trustworthiness in artificial intelligence. *Cognitive Systems Research*, 72, 33–49. DOI: 10.1016/j.cogsys.2021.11.001

Liburd, J. J., Benckendorff, P., & Carlsen, J. (2011). Tourism and quality-of-life: How does tourism measure up? *Handbook of tourism and quality-of-life research: Enhancing the lives of tourists and residents of host communities*, 105-132.

Licardo, J. T., Domjan, M., & Orehovački, T. (2024). Intelligent robotics—A systematic review of emerging technologies and trends. *Electronics (Basel)*, 13(3), 542. DOI: 10.3390/electronics13030542

Li, J. (2022). E-Commerce Fraud Detection Model by Computer Artificial Intelligence Data Mining. *Computational Intelligence and Neuroscience*, 2022, 1–9. DOI: 10.1155/2022/7498025 PMID: 35586101

Li, J., Ma, S., Qu, Y., & Wang, J. (2023). 'The impact of artificial intelligence on firms' energy and resource efficiency: Empirical evidence from China'. *Resources Policy*, 82, 103507. Advance online publication. DOI: 10.1016/j.resourpol.2023.103507

Li, L. (2020). Education supply chain in the era of Industry 4.0. *Systems Research and Behavioral Science*, 37(4), 579–592. DOI: 10.1002/sres.2702

Li, M., & Bitterly, T. B. (2024). How Perceived Lack of Benevolence Harms Trust of Artificial Intelligence Management. *The Journal of Applied Psychology*, 109(11), 1794–1816. Advance online publication. DOI: 10.1037/apl0001200 PMID: 38815093

Lima, A. M., & Casais, B. (2021). Consumer Reactions towards Femvertising: A Netnographic Study. *Corporate Communications*, 26(3), 605–621. DOI: 10.1108/CCIJ-02-2021-0018

Liñán, F., Paul, J., & Fayolle, A. (2020). SMEs and entrepreneurship in the era of globalization: Advances and theoretical approaches. *Small Business Economics*, 55(3), 695–703. DOI: 10.1007/s11187-019-00180-7

Lin, D., Zhou, Z., Weng, M., Broere, W., & Cui, J. (2024). Metro systems: Construction, operation and impacts. *Tunnelling and Underground Space Technology*, 143, 105373. Advance online publication. DOI: 10.1016/j.tust.2023.105373

Lindecrantz, E., Tjon Pian Gi, M., & Zerbi, S. (2020, April 28). Personalizing the customer experience: Driving differentiation in retail. *McKinsey and Company*. https://www.mckinsey.com/industries/retail/our-insights/personalizing-the-customer-experience-driving-differentiation-in-retail

Lin, P. (2016). Why ethics matters for autonomous cars. In Lin, L. A. P., Abney, K., & Bekey, G. A. (Eds.), *Robot ethics: The ethical and social implications of robotics* (pp. 69–85). MIT Press.

Lin, Y.-P. (2021). Media Literacy in an Age of Artificial Intelligence: An Exploratory Research from Hmc. *Taiwan Journal of East Asian Studies*, 18(1), 1–42. DOI: 10.6163/TJEAS.202106_18(1).0001

Lipton, Z. C. (2018). The mythos of model interpretability. *Communications of the ACM*, 61(12), 36–43. DOI: 10.1145/3233231

Lipuma, J., & Leon, C. (2024) 'Minorities and the AI Revolution: Examining the Literature on Equity and the Digital Divide Equity', *Academia Journals*, 16(6). Available at: https://orcid.org/0000-0002-9778-3843

Liu, X., Xie, M., Wen, X., Chen, R., Ge, Y., Duffield, N., & Wang, N. (2020). Micro-and macro-level churn analysis of large-scale mobile games. *Knowledge and Information Systems*, 62(4), 1465–1496. DOI: 10.1007/s10115-019-01394-7

Lobera, J., Fernández Rodríguez, C. J., & Torres-Albero, C. (2020). Privacy, Values and Machines: Predicting Opposition to Artificial Intelligence. *Communication Studies*, 71(3), 448–465. DOI: 10.1080/10510974.2020.1736114

Lokanan, M. (2022). The determinants of investment fraud: A machine learning and artificial intelligence approach. *Frontiers in Big Data*, 5, 961039. Advance online publication. DOI: 10.3389/fdata.2022.961039 PMID: 36299659

London, A. J. (2019). Artificial Intelligence and Black-Box Medical Decisions: Accuracy versus Explainability. *The Hastings Center Report*, 49(1), 15–21. DOI: 10.1002/hast.973 PMID: 30790315

López Jiménez, D., Dittmar, E. C., & Vargas Portillo, J. P. (2022). Nuevas estrategias publicitarias con influencers: Un examen multidisciplinar. *Revista de Ciencias Sociales*, 28(4), 63–78. DOI: 10.31876/rcs.v28i4.39117

López Jiménez, D., Dittmar, E. C., & Vargas Portillo, J. P. (2023). The Self-Regulating Jury in the Field of Interactive Advertising. *Revista de Direito. Estado e Telecomunicacoes*, 15(1), 1–30. DOI: 10.26512/lstr.v15i1.42146

López-Úbeda, P., Martín-Noguerol, T., & Luna, A. (2023). Radiology, explicability and AI: Closing the gap. *European Radiology*, 33(12), 9466–9468. DOI: 10.1007/s00330-023-09902-8 PMID: 37410108

Lorkowski, J., Kolaszyńska, O., & Pokorski, M. (2021). Artificial Intelligence and Precision Medicine: A Perspective. En Advances in experimental medicine and biology (pp. 1-11). https://doi.org/DOI: 10.1007/5584_2021_652

Lovelock, B., & Lovelock, K. (2013). *The ethics of tourism: Critical and applied perspectives*. Routledge. DOI: 10.4324/9780203854532

Low, B., Lavin, D., Du, C. R., & Fang, C. (2023). Risk-Informed and AI-Based Bias Detection on Gender, Race, and Income Using Gen-Z Survey Data. *IEEE Access : Practical Innovations, Open Solutions*, 11, 88317–88328. DOI: 10.1109/ACCESS.2023.3305636

Luhmann, N. (2018). *Trust and power*. John Wiley & Sons.

Lukic Vujadinovic, V., Damnjanovic, A., Cakic, A., Petkovic, D. R., Prelevic, M., Pantovic, V., Stojanovic, M., Vidojevic, D., Vranjes, D., & Bodolo, I. (2024). AI-Driven Approach for Enhancing Sustainability in Urban Public Transportation. *Sustainability (Basel)*, 16(17), 7763. DOI: 10.3390/su16177763

Lundberg, E., & Mozelius, P. (2024). The Potential Effects of Deepfakes on News Media and Entertainment. *AI & Society*. Advance online publication. DOI: 10.1007/s00146-024-02072-1

Lund-Durlacher, D. (2015). *Corporate social responsibility and tourism. Education for sustainability in tourism: A handbook of processes, resources, and strategies*. Springer.

Luttrell, R., Wallace, A., McCollough, C., & Lee, J. (2020). The Digital Divide: Addressing Artificial Intelligence in Communication Education. *Journalism and Mass Communication Educator*, 75(4), 470–482. DOI: 10.1177/1077695820925286

Luusua, A., Ylipulli, J., Foth, M., & Aurigi, A. (2023). *'Urban AI: understanding the emerging role of artificial intelligence in smart cities', AI and Society*. Springer Science and Business Media Deutschland GmbH., DOI: 10.1007/s00146-022-01537-5

Maashi, M., Alabduallah, B. I., & Kouki, F. (2023b). Sustainable Financial Fraud Detection Using Garra Rufa Fish Optimization Algorithm with Ensemble Deep Learning. *Sustainability (Basel)*, 15(18), 13301. DOI: 10.3390/su151813301

Macassa, G., McGrath, C., Tomaselli, G., & Buttigieg, S. C. (2021). *'Corporate social responsibility and internal stakeholders' health and well-being in Europe: A systematic descriptive review', Health Promotion International*. Oxford University Press., DOI: 10.1093/heapro/daaa071

Madanaguli, A., Srivastava, S., Ferraris, A., & Dhir, A. (2022). Corporate social responsibility and sustainability in the tourism sector: A systematic literature review and future outlook. *Sustainable Development (Bradford)*, 30(3), 447–461. DOI: 10.1002/sd.2258

Madhavi, S., Ashmita, R. S., Dakshatha, E. S., & Dhinakar, T. (2024) 'Smart Sewage System with Advanced Remote Monitoring for Efficient Urban Infrastructure Management', in *2nd International Conference on Artificial Intelligence and Machine Learning Applications: Healthcare and Internet of Things, AIMLA 2024*. Institute of Electrical and Electronics Engineers Inc. Available at: DOI: 10.1109/AIMLA59606.2024.10531479

Mahmood, A., Naveed, R. T., Ahmad, N., Scholz, M., Khalique, M., & Adnan, M. (2021). Unleashing the barriers to CSR implementation in the sme sector of a developing economy: A thematic analysis approach. *Sustainability (Basel)*, 13(22), 12710. DOI: 10.3390/su132212710

Majeed, Y., Fu, L., & He, L. (2024). Editorial: Artificial intelligence-of-things (AIoT) in precision agriculture. *Frontiers in Plant Science*, 15, 1369791. Advance online publication. DOI: 10.3389/fpls.2024.1369791 PMID: 38344185

Makhloufi, L., Laghouag, A. A., Sahli, A. A., & Belaid, F. (2021). Impact of entrepreneurial orientation on innovation capability: The mediating role of absorptive capability and organizational learning capabilities. *Sustainability (Basel)*, 13(10), 5399. DOI: 10.3390/su13105399

Makkonen, T., & Inkinen, T. (2024). Inclusive smart cities? Technology-driven urban development and disabilities. *Cities (London, England)*, 154, 105334. Advance online publication. DOI: 10.1016/j.cities.2024.105334

Mancini, S., & González, J. L. C. (2021). Role of technology transfer, innovation strategy and network: A conceptual model of innovation network to facilitate the internationalization process of SMEs. *Technology and Investment*, 12(2), 82–128. DOI: 10.4236/ti.2021.122006

Mangrulkar, S. (1990). Artificial neural systems. *ISA Transactions*, 29(1), 5–7. DOI: 10.1016/0019-0578(90)90024-F PMID: 2307576

Mannuru, N. R., Shahriar, S., Teel, Z. A., Wang, T., Lund, B. D., Tijani, S., Pohboon, C. O., Agbaji, D., Alhassan, J., Galley, J., Kousari, R., Ogbadu-Oladapo, L., Saurav, S. K., Srivastava, A., Tummuru, S. P., Uppala, S., & Vaidya, P. (2023). Artificial intelligence in developing countries: The impact of generative artificial intelligence (AI) technologies for development. *Information Development*, 02666669231200628. Advance online publication. DOI: 10.1177/02666669231200628

Mariani, M. M., Machado, I., Magrelli, V., & Dwivedi, Y. K. (2023). Artificial intelligence in innovation research: A systematic review, conceptual framework, and future research directions. *Technovation*, 122, 102623. Advance online publication. DOI: 10.1016/j.technovation.2022.102623

Marimekala, D., & Lamb, J. (2024). Impact of Generative AI Adoption in Academia and How It Influences Ethics, Cognitive Thinking and AI Singularity. *IEEE Integrated STEM Education Conference, ISEC 2024*. DOI: 10.1109/ISEC61299.2024.10664756

Marsh, S., & Dibben, M. R. (2005). Trust, untrust, distrust and mistrust - An exploration of the dark(er) side. *Lecture Notes in Computer Science*, 3477, 17–33. DOI: 10.1007/11429760_2

Martínez, R. (2016). Fraud Detection Using Deep Learning. https://cybercamp.es/cybercamp2016/sites/default/files/contenidos/material/cybercamp2016-fraud_detection_using_deep_learning-ruben_martinez.pdf

Martinez, A. R. (2010). Natural language processing. *Wiley Interdisciplinary Reviews: Computational Statistics*, 2(3), 352–357. DOI: 10.1002/wics.76

Martínez-Conesa, I., Soto-Acosta, P., & Palacios-Manzano, M. (2017). Corporate social responsibility and its effect on innovation and firm performance: An empirical research in SMEs. *Journal of Cleaner Production*, 142, 2374–2383. DOI: 10.1016/j.jclepro.2016.11.038

Martínez, P., Pérez, A., & Rodriguez del Bosque, I. (2013). Measuring corporate social responsibility in tourism: Development and validation of an efficient measurement scale in the hospitality industry. *Journal of Travel & Tourism Marketing*, 30(4), 365–385. DOI: 10.1080/10548408.2013.784154

Martinho, A., Kroesen, M., & Chorus, C. (2021). A healthy debate: Exploring the views of medical doctors on the ethics of artificial intelligence. *Artificial Intelligence in Medicine*, 121, 102190. Advance online publication. DOI: 10.1016/j.artmed.2021.102190 PMID: 34763805

Martin, K. (2018). Ethical Implications and Accountability of Algorithms. *Journal of Business Ethics*, 160(4), 835–850. DOI: 10.1007/s10551-018-3921-3

Martin, K., & Murphy, P. (2017). The Ethics of Big Data: Current and Future Challenges. *Business Horizons*, 60(2), 211–220.

Ma, S., Zhu, Z., Liu, Y., Zheng, Y., Lu, J., & Xu, J. (2024). Artificial intelligence-enabled predictive planning for sewage treatment based on improved DNN and LSTM. *Computers & Industrial Engineering*, 198, 110636. Advance online publication. DOI: 10.1016/j.cie.2024.110636

Matten, D., & Moon, J. (2004). Corporate social responsibility. *Journal of Business Ethics*, 54, 323–337.

Mayer, R. C., Davis, J. H., & Schoorman, F. D. (1995). An Integrative Model Of Organizational Trust. *Academy of Management Review*, 20(3), 709–734. DOI: 10.2307/258792

Mayiwar, L., Asutay, E., Tinghög, G., Västfjäll, D., & Barrafrem, K. (2024). Determinants of Digital Well-Being. *AI & Society*. Advance online publication. DOI: 10.1007/s00146-024-02071-2

Mazurowski, M. A. (2020). Artificial Intelligence in Radiology: Some Ethical Considerations for Radiologists and Algorithm Developers. *Academic Radiology*, 27(1), 127–129. DOI: 10.1016/j.acra.2019.04.024 PMID: 31818378

McClelland, R. S. (2022). Generative design and digital manufacturing: using AI and robots to build lightweight instrument structures. In R. B. Johnson, V. N. Mahajan, S. Thibault, & A. Padilla-Vivanco (Eds.), *CURRENT DEVELOPMENTS IN LENS DESIGN AND OPTICAL ENGINEERING XXIII* (Vol. 12217, Issue Conference on Current Developments in Lens Design and Optical Engineering XXIII Part of SPIE Optics and Photonics Conference CL-San Diego, CA, p. 37). DOI: 10.1117/12.2646476

McIntyre, J. R., Ivanaj, S., & Ivanaj, V. (Eds.). (2018). *CSR and climate change implications for Multinational Enterprises*. Edward Elgar Publishing. DOI: 10.4337/9781786437761

McKnight, D. H., Cummings, L. L., & Chervany, N. L. (1998). Initial trust formation in new organizational relationships. *Academy of Management Review*, 23(3), 473–490. DOI: 10.2307/259290

Medhat, M. (2012). Artificial intelligence methods applied for quantitative analysis of natural radioactive sources. *Annals of Nuclear Energy*, 45, 73–79. DOI: 10.1016/j.anucene.2012.02.013

Melo, I. C., Queiroz, G. A., Junior, P. N. A., de Sousa, T. B., Yushimito, W. F., & Pereira, J. (2023). Sustainable digital transformation in small and medium enterprises (SMEs): A review on performance. *Heliyon*, 9(3), e13908. Advance online publication. DOI: 10.1016/j.heliyon.2023.e13908 PMID: 36915489

Meng, N. (2024). Integration of Big Data and AI in Educational Leadership Practices: Opportunities and Challenges. *Eurasian Journal of Educational Research*, 111(111), 47–67.

Mersha, M., Lam, K., Wood, J., AlShami, A., & Kalita, J. (2024). Explainable artificial intelligence: A survey of needs, techniques, applications, and future direction. *Neurocomputing*, 128111, 128111. Advance online publication. DOI: 10.1016/j.neucom.2024.128111

Meta (n.d.a). *Responsible AI. Driven by our belief that AI should benefit everyone.* https://ai.meta.com/responsible-ai/

Meta (n.d.b). *El compromiso de Meta es proteger a las personas y darles la posibilidad de expresarse.*https://transparency.meta.com/es-es/

Meta (n.d.c). Nuestro método para explicar el sistema de clasificación. https://transparency.meta.com/features/explaining-ranking/#facebook_ai_systems

Mhlanga, D. (2020). Industry 4.0 in Finance: The Impact of Artificial Intelligence (AI) on Digital Financial Inclusion. *International Journal Of Financial Studies*, 8(3), 45. DOI: 10.3390/ijfs8030045

Miake-Lye, I. M., Hempel, S., Shanman, R., & Shekelle, P. G. (2016). What is an evidence map? A systematic review of published evidence maps and their definitions, methods, and products. *Systematic Reviews*, 5(1), 28. Advance online publication. DOI: 10.1186/s13643-016-0204-x PMID: 26864942

Michaeli, T., Romeike, R., & Seegerer, S. (2023). What Students Can Learn About Artificial intelligence – Recommendations for K-12 computing education. In *IFIP advances in information and communication technology* (pp. 196–208). DOI: 10.1007/978-3-031-43393-1_19

Mikalef, P., & Gupta, M. (2021). Artificial intelligence capability: Conceptualization, measurement calibration, and empirical study on its impact on organizational creativity and firm performance. *Information & Management*, 58(3), 103434. Advance online publication. DOI: 10.1016/j.im.2021.103434

Mill, E. R., Garn, W., Ryman-Tubb, N. F., & Turner, C. (2023). Opportunities in real time fraud detection: An explainable artificial intelligence (XAI) Research Agenda. *International Journal of Advanced Computer Science and Applications*, 14(5), 1172–1186. https://www.webofscience.com/wos/alldb/full-record/WOS:001015077500001. DOI: 10.14569/IJACSA.2023.01405121

Miller, A. P. (2018). Want less-biased decisions? use algorithms. *Harvard Business Review*. Retrieved from: https://hbr.org/2018/07/want-less-biased-decisions-use-algorithms

Miller, B., Ward, K., Burns, R., Fast, V., & Levenda, A. (2021). Worlding and provincialising smart cities: From individual case studies to a global comparative research agenda. *Urban Studies (Edinburgh, Scotland)*, 58(3), 655–673. DOI: 10.1177/0042098020976086

Minkkinen, M., Niukkanen, A., & Mäntymäki, M. (2022). What about investors? ESG analyses as tools for ethics-based AI auditing. *AI & Society*. Advance online publication. DOI: 10.1007/s00146-022-01415-0

Minsky M. (1968). *Semantic Information Processing*.

Mishra, S. (2023). Exploring the Impact of AI-Based Cyber Security Financial Sector Management. *Applied Sciences (Basel, Switzerland)*, 13(10), 5875. DOI: 10.3390/app13105875

Mishrif, A., & Khan, A. (2023). Technology adoption as survival strategy for small and medium enterprises during COVID-19. *Journal of Innovation and Entrepreneurship*, 12(1), 53. DOI: 10.1186/s13731-023-00317-9

Mistry, J. J. (2012). The role of egovernance in mitigating corruption. *Accounting and the Public Interest*, 12(1), 137–159. DOI: 10.2308/apin-10287

MIT Technology Review (2024). Vuelta al mundo por las regulaciones de la IA en 2024. Opinno. https://www.technologyreview.es/s/16069/vuelta-al-mundo-por-las-regulaciones-de-la-ia-en-2024

Mittelstadt, B. D., Allo, P., Taddeo, M., Wachter, S., & Floridi, L. (2016). The ethics of algorithms: Mapping the debate. *Big Data & Society*, 3(2), 1–21. DOI: 10.1177/2053951716679679

Mobilio, G. (2023). Your face is not new to me – Regulating the surveillance power of facial recognition technologies. *Internet Policy Review*, 12(1). Advance online publication. DOI: 10.14763/2023.1.1699

Mohapeloa, M. (2017). Developing an entrepreneurial mindset within the social sector: A review of the South African context. *African Journal of Science, Technology, Innovation and Development*, 9(5), 645–652. DOI: 10.1080/20421338.2017.1358917

Molina, M. D., & Sundar, S. S. (2022). Does distrust in humans predict greater trust in AI? Role of individual differences in user responses to content moderation. *New Media & Society*. Advance online publication. DOI: 10.1177/14614448221103534

Molina, M. D., Wang, J., Sundar, S. S., Le, T., & DiRusso, C. (2023). Reading, Commenting and Sharing of Fake News: How Online Bandwagons and Bots Dictate User Engagement. *Communication Research*, 50(6), 667–694. DOI: 10.1177/00936502211073398

Molina-Ycaza, D., & Sánchez-Riofrío, A. (2016). Obstáculos para la micro, pequeña y mediana empresa en América Latina. *Pymes. Innovación y Desarrollo*, 4(2), 21–36.

Molteni, M., & Pedrini, M. (2010). In search of socio-economic syntheses. *Journal of Management Development*, 29(7/8), 626–636. DOI: 10.1108/02621711011059059

Montero Carretero, L. (May, 28, 2023). El fin de la era del 'todo vale' para la inteligencia artificial. *ABC*https://www.abc.es/economia/fin-era-vale-inteligencia-artificial-20230528014912-nt.html

Moraes, T. (2024). Ethical AI Regulatory Sandboxes: Insights from cyberspace regulation and Internet governance. *2nd International Symposium On Trustworthy Autonomous Systems*, 10, 1-10. DOI: 10.1145/3686038.3686049

Morris, M. H., & Kuratko, D. F. (2020). The entrepreneurial journey: intention versus emergence. In *Edward Elgar Publishing eBooks* (pp. 1–16). DOI: 10.4337/9781789900224.00009

Mtapuri, O., & Giampiccoli, A. (2021). Contextualing a tourism development alternative for Argentina: A proposal for community based diffused tourism. *Journal of Spatial and Organizational Dynamics*, 9(2), 138–155.

Mulcahy, R., & Barnes, R. (2024). Sharing of misinformation by influencers. *Australasian Marketing Journal*. Advance online publication. DOI: 10.1177/14413582241273987

Muñoz-Martín, J. (2013). Ética empresarial, Responsabilidad Social Corporativa (RSC) y Creación de Valor Compartido (CVC). *Journal of Globalization, Competitiveness & Governability, 7*(3).

Murillo, D., & Lozano, J. M. (2006). SMEs and CSR: An approach to CSR in their own words. *Journal of Business Ethics*, 67(3), 227–240. DOI: 10.1007/s10551-006-9181-7

Mushtaq, A., Haq, I. U., Sarwar, M. A., Khan, A., Khalil, W., & Mughal, M. A. (2023). Multi-Agent Reinforcement Learning for Traffic Flow Management of Autonomous Vehicles. *Sensors (Basel)*, 23(5), 2373. Advance online publication. DOI: 10.3390/s23052373 PMID: 36904577

Mytnyk, B., Tkachyk, O., Shakhovska, N., Fedushko, S., & Syerov, Y. (2023). Application of Artificial Intelligence for Fraudulent Banking Operations Recognition. *Big Data and Cognitive Computing*, 7(2), 93. DOI: 10.3390/bdcc7020093

Nader, K., Toprac, P., Scott, S., & Baker, S. (2024). Public Understanding of Artificial Intelligence through Entertainment Media. *AI & Society*, 39(2), 713–726. DOI: 10.1007/s00146-022-01427-w PMID: 35400854

Nanne, A. J., Antheunis, M. L., Van Der Lee, C. G., Postma, E. O., Wubben, S., & Van Noort, G. (2020). The use of computer vision to analyze brand-related user generated image content. *Journal of Interactive Marketing*, 50(1), 156–167. https://doi-org.zulib.idm.oclc.org/10.1016/j.intmar.2019.09.003. DOI: 10.1016/j.intmar.2019.09.003

Nannini, L., Alonso-Moral, J. M., Catala, A., Lama, M., & Barro, S. (2024). Operationalizing Explainable Artificial Intelligence in the European Union Regulatory Ecosystem. *IEEE Intelligent Systems*, 39(4), 37–48. DOI: 10.1109/MIS.2024.3383155

Napal, M., Mendióroz-Lacambra, A. M., & Peñalva, A. (2020). Sustainability teaching tools in the digital age. *Sustainability (Basel)*, 12(8), 3366. DOI: 10.3390/su12083366

Narayanan, A. (2023). Understanding social media recommendation algorithms. *Knight First Amendment Institute at Columbia University*. Retrieved from: https://knightcolumbia.org/content/understanding-social-media-recommendation-algorithms

Navarro, T. (August 24, 2021). Los filtros de Instagram que ayudan a escapar de los límites del mundo físico. *El País*. https://elpais.com/ideas/2021-08-29/los-filtros-de-instagram-que-ayudan-a-escapar-de-los-limites-del-mundo-fisico.html

Nayak, S., & Chandiramani, J. (2022). A crisis that changed the banking scenario in India: Exploring the role of ethics in business. *Asian Journal Of Business Ethics*, 11(S1), 7–32. DOI: 10.1007/s13520-022-00151-4

Nesoff, E. D., Brownstein, J. N., Veazie, M., O'Leary, M., & Brody, E. A. (2017). Time-to-Treatment for Myocardial Infarction: Barriers and Facilitators Perceived by American Indians in Three Regions. *Journal of Community Health*, 42(1), 129–138. DOI: 10.1007/s10900-016-0239-x PMID: 27613739

Netflix (n.d.). *Accesibilidad en Netflix*. https://help.netflix.com/es-es/node/116022

Netflix (n.d.). *Inclusión y diversidad*.https://about.netflix.com/es_es/inclusion

Newman, E. J., & Schwarz, N. (2023). Misinformed by images: How images influence perceptions of truth and what can be done about it. *Current Opinion in Psychology*, 101778. Advance online publication. DOI: 10.1016/j.copsyc.2023.101778 PMID: 38134526

Newman, J., & Mintrom, M. (2023). Mapping the discourse on evidence-based policy, artificial intelligence, and the ethical practice of policy analysis. *Journal of European Public Policy*, 30(9), 1839–1859. DOI: 10.1080/13501763.2023.2193223

Ngah, R., Sarmidy, R., & Halil, N. H. A. (2020). Implications of generic skills on Innovative Behavior towards Opportunity Recognition in Youth. *Review of World Economics*, 11(1), 123. DOI: 10.5430/rwe.v11n1p123

Nguyen, A., Ngo, H. N., Hong, Y., Dang, B., & Nguyen, B. P. T. (2022). Ethical principles for artificial intelligence in education. *Education and Information Technologies*, 28(4), 1–21. PMID: 36254344

Nicodeme, C. (2020). Build confidence and acceptance of AI-based decision support systems - Explainable and liable AI. 13th IEEE International Conference On Human System Interaction (IEEE HSI). DOI: 10.1109/HSI49210.2020.9142668

Nieto, S. G., Yelpo, P. C., & Guzmán, K. P. (2021). Smart City Puebla: Measuring smartness. *Revista Ibero-Americana de Estratégia*, 20(1), e15793. DOI: 10.5585/riae.v20i1.15793

Nishant, R., Kennedy, M., & Corbett, J. (2020). Artificial intelligence for sustainability: Challenges, opportunities, and a research agenda. *International Journal of Information Management*, 53, 102104. DOI: 10.1016/j.ijinfomgt.2020.102104

Nour, N., & Gelfand, J. (2022). Deepfakes: A Digital Transformation Leads to Misinformation. *Grey Journal 18* (2), 85–94. https://doi.org/DOI: 10.26069/greynet-2022-000.471-gg

Novelli, C. (2022). Legal personhood for the integration of AI systems in the social context: A study hypothesis. *AI & Society*, 38(4), 1347–1359. DOI: 10.1007/s00146-021-01384-w

O'Connor, S., & Liu, H. (2024). Gender bias perpetuation and mitigation in AI technologies: Challenges and opportunities. *AI & Society*, 39(4), 2045–2057. DOI: 10.1007/s00146-023-01675-4

O'Neil, C. (2016). *Weapons of math destruction: How big data increases inequality and threatens democracy*. Crown Publishing Group.

Obermeyer, Z., Powers, B. W., Vogeli, C., & Mullainathan, S. (2019). Dissecting racial bias in an algorithm used to manage the health of populations. *Science*, 366(6464), 447–453. DOI: 10.1126/science.aax2342 PMID: 31649194

Obschonka, M., & Audretsch, D. B. (2019). Artificial intelligence and big data in entrepreneurship: A new era has begun. *Small Business Economics*, 55(3), 529–539. DOI: 10.1007/s11187-019-00202-4

OCDE. (2021). *Perspectivas económicas de América Latina 2021: Avanzando juntos hacia una mejor recuperación*. OECD Publishing.

OECD. (2019). *OECD Principles on Artificial Intelligence*. https://www.oecd.org/going-digital/ai/principles/

OECD. (2021). *Recommendation of the Council on Artificial Intelligence*. OECD. https://www.oecd.org/digital/ai/

Ogunlela, O., & Tengeh, R. (2021). The fourth industrial revolution and the future of entrepreneurial university in South Africa. *International Journal of Research in Business and Social Science (2147-4478), 10*(3), 91–100. DOI: 10.20525/ijrbs.v10i3.1103

Okai, E., Feng, X., & Sant, P. (2019) 'Smart Cities Survey', in *Proceedings - 20th International Conference on High Performance Computing and Communications, 16th International Conference on Smart City and 4th International Conference on Data Science and Systems, HPCC/SmartCity/DSS 2018*. IEEE, pp. 1726–1730. Available at: DOI: 10.1109/HPCC/SmartCity/DSS.2018.00282

Oke, A. E., Aghimien, D. O., Aigbavboa, C. O., & Akinradewo, O. I. (2020). Appraisal of the drivers of smart city development in South Africa. *Construction Economics and Building*, 20(2), 109–126. DOI: 10.5130/AJCEB.v20i2.6632

Okiye, S. E. (2024). Renewable energy construction: Role of AI for smart building infrastructures. *Journal of Inventive Engineering and Technology*, 5(3), 40–48. www.jiengtech.com

Okolo, C.T. (2021) 'AI in the Global South: Opportunities and Challenges Towards More Inclusive Governance', *International Journal of Innovative Research in Arts, Education and Technology | IJIRAET*, 2(1). Available at: https://doi.org/.DOI: 10.48028/iiprds/ijiraet.v2.i1.09

Okot, T., & Zuñiga Castro, M. (2023). Desigualdad Digital en el Sistema de Educación Pública: Estudio de Caso Fuera del Área Metropolitana de Costa Rica. *Revista De Educación Y Derecho*, (28). https://doi.org/DOI: 10.1344/REYD2023.28.41707

Okot, T., Madrigal-Mendez, P., & Solorzano-Arias, D. (2023). The internet of things (IoT) for sustainability: A framework for Costa Rica. *Journal of Technology Management & Innovation*, 18(4), 3–17. DOI: 10.4067/S0718-27242023000400003

Ongena, Y. P., Haan, M., Yakar, D., & Kwee, T. C. (2020). Patients' views on the implementation of artificial intelligence in radiology: Development and validation of a standardized questionnaire. *European Radiology*, 30(2), 1033–1040. DOI: 10.1007/s00330-019-06486-0 PMID: 31705254

Open, A. I. (2024, November 2). DALL·E 2 is an AI system that can create realistic images and art from a description in natural language. OpenAI. Retrieved from https://openai.com/index/dall-e-2/

Orbik, Z. (2022). 'CORPORATE SOCIAL RESPONSIBILITY AND THE SMART CITY CONCEPT', *Scientific Papers of Silesian University of Technology. Organization and Management Series*, 2022(165), 245–257. DOI: 10.29119/1641-3466.2022.165.18

Orduña-Malea, E., & Delgado-López-Cózar, E. (2018). Dimensions: Redescubriendo el ecosistema de la información científica. *El Profesional de la Información*, 27(2), 420–431. DOI: 10.3145/epi.2018.mar.21

Ortega Fernández, E. A., & Rodríguez Hernández, J. (2024). Sesgo en la inteligencia artificial y su impacto en el aprendizaje de estudiantes que utilizan ChatGPT. In Almazán-López, O. (Ed.), *IA, educación y medios de comunicación: modelo TRIC* (pp. 59–78). Dykinson.

Ouyang, F., Zheng, L., & Jiao, P. (2022). Artificial intelligence in online higher education: A systematic review of empirical research from 2011 to 2020. *Education and Information Technologies*, 27(6), 7893–7925. DOI: 10.1007/s10639-022-10925-9

Packin, N. G., & Lev-Aretz, Y. (2016). On social credit and the right to be unnetworked. *Columbia Business Law Review*, 2, 339–425. DOI: 10.7916/cblr.v2016i2.1739

Pagliari, M., Chambon, V., & Berberian, B. (2022). What is new with Artificial Intelligence? Human–agent interactions through the lens of social agency. *Frontiers in Psychology*, 13, 954444. Advance online publication. DOI: 10.3389/fpsyg.2022.954444 PMID: 36248519

Pai, V., & Chandra, S. (2022). Exploring Factors Influencing Organizational Adoption of Artificial Intelligence (AI) in Corporate Social Responsibility (CSR) Initiatives. *Pacific Asia Journal Of The Association For Information Systems*, 14, 82–115. DOI: 10.17705/1pais.14504

Palgan, Y. V., Mont, O., & Sulkakoski, S. (2021). Governing the sharing economy: Towards a comprehensive analytical framework of municipal governance. *Cities (London, England)*, 108, 102994. DOI: 10.1016/j.cities.2020.102994

Palmatier, R. W., Dant, R. P., Grewal, D., & Evans, K. R. (2006). Factors influencing the effectiveness of relationship marketing: A meta-analysis. *Journal of Marketing*, 70(4), 136–153. DOI: 10.1509/jmkg.70.4.136

Pandiyan, P., Saravanan, S., Usha, K., Kannadasan, R., Alsharif, M. H., & Kim, M. K. (2023). Technological advancements toward smart energy management in smart cities. *Energy Reports*, 10, 648–677. DOI: 10.1016/j.egyr.2023.07.021

Papagiannidis, E., Enholm, I. M., Mikalef, P., & Krogstie, J. (2021) 'Structuring AI resources to build an AI capability: A conceptual framework', in *ECIS*. Available at: https://www.researchgate.net/publication/351069404

Papetti, A., Gregori, F., Pandolfi, M., Peruzzini, M., & Germani, M. (2020). A method to improve workers' well-being toward human-centered connected factories. *Journal of Computational Design and Engineering*, 7(5), 630–643. DOI: 10.1093/jcde/qwaa047

Parasuraman, A., Zeithaml, V. A., & Berry, L. L. (1988). SERVQUAL: A multiple-item scale for measuring consumer perceptions of service quality. *Electronics Letters*, 64(1), 12–40. DOI: 10.1049/el:19850169

Parekh, R. (2024). Automating the design process for smart building technologies. *World Journal of Advanced Research and Reviews*, 23(2), 1213–1234. DOI: 10.30574/wjarr.2024.23.2.2461

Pašalić, I., Ćukušić, M., & Jadrić, M. (2021). Smart city research advances in Southeast Europe. *International Journal of Information Management*, 58, 102127. Advance online publication. DOI: 10.1016/j.ijinfomgt.2020.102127

Paskova, M., & Zelenka, J. (2019). How crucial is the social responsibility for tourism sustainability? *Social Responsibility Journal*, 15(4), 534–552. DOI: 10.1108/SRJ-03-2018-0057

Pasquale, F. (2015). *The Black Box Society: The Secret Algorithms That Control Money and Information*. Harvard University Press. DOI: 10.4159/harvard.9780674736061

Pasricha, S. (2023). Ethics in Computing Education: Challenges and Experience with Embedded Ethics. *arXiv (Cornell University)*. /arxiv.2303.12909DOI: 10.1145/3583781.3590240

Pastrana, N. A., & Sriramesh, K. (2014). Corporate social responsibility: Perceptions and practices among SMEs in Colombia. *Public Relations Review*, 40(1), 14–24. DOI: 10.1016/j.pubrev.2013.10.002

Pathak, K., Prakash, G., Samadhiya, A., Kumar, A., & Luthra, S. (2025). Impact of Gen-AI Chatbots on Consumer Services Experiences and Behaviors: Focusing on the Sensation of Awe and Usage Intentions through a Cybernetic Lens. *Journal of Retailing and Consumer Services*, 82, 104120. Advance online publication. DOI: 10.1016/j.jretconser.2024.104120

Pathak, R., & Spezzano, F. (2024). Algorithmic contribution to misinformation. *ACM Transactions on the Web*. Advance online publication. DOI: 10.1145/3616088

Pavlou, P. A., & Gefen, D. (2005). Psychological contract violation in online marketplaces: Antecedents, consequences, and moderating role. *Information Systems Research*, 16(4), 372–399. DOI: 10.1287/isre.1050.0065

Peinado-Vara, E. (2011). RSE en América Latina. In Vives, A., & Peinado-Vara, E. (Eds.), *La responsabilidad social de la empresa en América Latina* (pp. 65–82). Banco Interamericano de Desarrollo.

Peña Miranda, D. D., & Serra Cantallops, A. (2012). Responsabilidad social empresarial en el sector turístico: Estudio de caso en empresa de alojamiento de la ciudad de Santa Marta, Colombia. *Estudios y perspectivas en turismo, 21*(6), 0-0.

Pérez-delHoyo, R., Mora, H., Nolasco-Vidal, J. M., Abad-Ortiz, R., & Mollá-Sirvent, R. A. (2021). Addressing new challenges in smart urban planning using Information and Communication Technologies. *Systems Research and Behavioral Science*, 38(3), 342–354. DOI: 10.1002/sres.2787

Perrini, F., Russo, A., & Tencati, A. (2007). CSR strategies of SMEs and large firms. Evidence from Italy. *Journal of Business Ethics*, 74(3), 285–300. DOI: 10.1007/s10551-006-9235-x

Peter, O., Pradhan, A., & Mbohwa, C. (2023). Industrial internet of things (IIoT): Opportunities, challenges, and requirements in manufacturing businesses in emerging economies. *Procedia Computer Science*, 217, 856–865. DOI: 10.1016/j.procs.2022.12.282

Peterson, M. (2017). *An introduction to decision theory* (2nd ed.). Cambridge University Press., DOI: 10.1017/9781316585061

Pham, T. D., Dwyer, L., Su, J. J., & Ngo, T. (2021). COVID-19 impacts of inbound tourism on Australian economy. *Annals of Tourism Research*, 88, 103179. DOI: 10.1016/j.annals.2021.103179 PMID: 36540369

Piccininni, M. (2022). Counterfactual fairness: The case study of a food delivery platform's reputational-ranking algorithm. *Frontiers in Psychology*, 13, 1015100. DOI: 10.3389/fpsyg.2022.1015100 PMID: 36389466

Pigola, A., da Costa, P. R., Carvalho, L. C., Silva, L. F. D., Kniess, C. T., & Maccari, E. A. (2021). Artificial intelligence-driven digital technologies to the implementation of the sustainable development goals: A perspective from Brazil and Portugal. *Sustainability (Basel)*, 13(24), 13669. DOI: 10.3390/su132413669

Pinheiro, A. F., Santos, W. B., & De Lima Neto, F. B. (2023). Intelligent Framework to Support Technology and Business Specialists in the Public Sector. *IEEE Access : Practical Innovations, Open Solutions*, 11, 15655–15679. DOI: 10.1109/ACCESS.2023.3243195

Png, M. T. (2022) 'At the Tensions of South and North: Critical Roles of Global South Stakeholders in AI Governance', in *ACM International Conference Proceeding Series*. Association for Computing Machinery, pp. 1434–1445. Available at: DOI: 10.1145/3531146.3533200

Politi, V. (2024). Who ought to look towards the horizon? A qualitative study on the collective social responsibility of scientific research. *European Journal for Philosophy of Science*, 14(2), 19. Advance online publication. DOI: 10.1007/s13194-024-00580-x

Popenici, S. A. D., & Kerr, S. (2017). Exploring the impact of artificial intelligence on teaching and learning in higher education. *Research and Practice in Technology Enhanced Learning*, 12(1), 22. DOI: 10.1186/s41039-017-0062-8 PMID: 30595727

Popescu, C. (2019). Adaptive Sustainable academic management practices. In *IntechOpen eBooks*. DOI: 10.5772/intechopen.87018

Popescu, S.M., Mansoor, S., Wani, O.A., Kumar, S.S., Sharma, V., Sharma, A., Arya, V.M., Kirkham, M.B., Hou, D., Bolan, N. and Chung, Y.S. (2024) 'Artificial intelligence and IoT driven technologies for environmental pollution monitoring and management', *Frontiers in Environmental Science*. Frontiers Media SA. Available at: .DOI: 10.3389/fenvs.2024.1336088

Porto, J. B., & Oliveira, M. (2020). The smart cities methodology based on public value: The first evaluation cycle. *BAR - Brazilian Administration Review*, 17(1), e190048. Advance online publication. DOI: 10.1590/1807-7692bar2020190048

Prasad, T. V. S. R. K., Srinivas, K., & Srinivas, C. (2017). Decentralized production-distribution planning in multi-echelon supply chain network using intelligent agents. *OPSEARCH*, 54(2), 217–232. DOI: 10.1007/s12597-016-0277-2

Prates, M. O. R., Avelar, P. H., & Lamb, L. C. (2020). Assessing Gender Bias in Machine Translation: A Case Study with Google Translate. *Neural Computing & Applications*, 32(10), 6363–6381. DOI: 10.1007/s00521-019-04144-6

Qiu, S., & Luo, Y. (2024). How to detect and forecast corporate fraud by media reports? An approach using machine learning and qualitative comparative analysis. *Journal of Forecasting*, 43(1), 58–80. DOI: 10.1002/for.3022

Qureshi, M. I., Khan, N., Raza, H., Imran, A., & Ismail, F. (2021). *Digital technologies in education 4.0. Does it enhance the effectiveness of learning?*http://hdl.handle.net/123456789/25661

Rabah, K. (2018). Convergence of AI, IoT, big data and blockchain: a review. *The lake institute Journal, 1*(1), 1-18.

Radwan, E. K. A., & Russo, A. (2024). Web-Based Corporate Social Responsibility Disclosure Practices: A Systematic Literature Review and Research Directions. *Corporate Social Responsibility and Environmental Management*, 31(5), 5049–5106. DOI: 10.1002/csr.2841

Rafieian, O. and Yoganarasimhan, H. (2023). AI and personalization. *Artificial Intelligence in Marketing*, 77-102. DOI: 10.1108/S1548-643520230000020004

Rahwan, I., Cebrian, M., & Robles, D.. (2019). Machine behaviour. *Nature*, 568(7753), 477–486. DOI: 10.1038/s41586-019-1138-y PMID: 31019318

Ramdhani, M. A., & Ramdhani, A. (2014). Verification of research logical framework based on literature review. *International Journal of Basic and Applied Science*, 3(2), 1–9.

Ramírez-Solis, E. R., Llonch-Andreu, J., & Malpica-Romero, A. D. (2022). How beneficial are relational capital and technology orientation for innovation? Evidence from Mexican SMEs. *International Journal of Innovation Studies*, 6(1), 1–10. DOI: 10.1016/j.ijis.2022.02.001

Ranard, B. L., Park, S., Jia, Y., Zhang, Y., Alwan, F., Celi, L. A., & Lusczek, E. R. (2024). Minimizing bias when using artificial intelligence in critical care medicine. *Journal of Critical Care*, 82, 154796. DOI: 10.1016/j.jcrc.2024.154796 PMID: 38552451

Ranchordás, S. (2020). Nudging citizens through technology in smart cities. *International Review of Law Computers & Technology*, 34(3), 254–276. DOI: 10.1080/13600869.2019.1590928

Ranchordás, S., & Goanta, C. (2020). The New City Regulators: Platform and Public Values in Smart and Sharing Cities. *Computer Law & Security Report*, 36, 105375. Advance online publication. DOI: 10.1016/j.clsr.2019.105375

Rapp, A., Di Lodovico, C., Torrielli, F., & Di Caro, L. (2025). How Do People Experience the Images Created by Generative Artificial Intelligence? An Exploration of People's Perceptions, Appraisals, and Emotions Related to a Gen-AI Text-to-Image Model and Its Creations. *International Journal of Human-Computer Studies*, 193, 103375. Advance online publication. DOI: 10.1016/j.ijhcs.2024.103375

Razaque, A., Alotaibi, B., Alotaibi, M., Hussain, S., Alotaibi, A., & Jotsov, V. (2022). Clickbait detection using deep recurrent neural network. *Applied Sciences (Basel, Switzerland)*, 12(1), 504. DOI: 10.3390/app12010504

Reed, C. (2020). *Law, Technology and the Internet*. Cambridge University Press., DOI: 10.1017/CBO9780511808791

Reinert Lyra, F., & Barbosa de Souza, M. J. (2015). Responsabilidad social corporativa en el sector turístico: Un estudio de caso en el Parque Temático Beto Carrero World (Santa Catarina-Brasil). *Estudios y Perspectivas en Turismo*, 24(2), 264–278.

Rempel, J. K., Holmes, J. G., & Zanna, M. P. (1985). Trust in Close Relationships. *Journal of Personality and Social Psychology*, 49(1), 95–112. DOI: 10.1037/0022-3514.49.1.95 PMID: 11474726

Revell, A., Stokes, D., & Chen, H. (2010). Small businesses and the environment: Turning over a new leaf? *Business Strategy and the Environment*, 19(5), 273–288. DOI: 10.1002/bse.628

Ribeiro, M. T., Singh, S., & Guestrin, C. (2016). "Why should I trust you?": Explaining the predictions of any classifier. *Proceedings of the 22nd ACM SIGKDD International Conference on Knowledge Discovery and Data Mining*, 1135-1144.

Ridzuan, N. N., Masri, M., Anshari, M., Fitriyani, N. L., & Syafrudin, M. (2024). AI in the Financial Sector: The Line between Innovation, Regulation and Ethical Responsibility. *Information (Basel)*, 15(8), 432. DOI: 10.3390/info15080432

Riedl, R., Hogeterp, S. A., & Reuter, M. (2024). Do patients prefer a human doctor, artificial intelligence, or a blend, and is this preference dependent on medical discipline? Empirical evidence and implications for medical practice. *Frontiers in Psychology*, 15, 1422177. Advance online publication. DOI: 10.3389/fpsyg.2024.1422177 PMID: 39188871

Rival Technologies. (May 11, 2023). *YouTube, Netflix and Amazon are Gen Z's Top Brands in 2023, New Research From Rival Group Finds.*https://www.rivaltech.com/gen-z-brand-power-index

Rojas-Berrio, S., Rincon-Novoa, J., Sánchez-Monrroy, M., Ascúa, R., & Montoya-Restrepo, L. A. (2022). Factors influencing 4.0 technology adoption in manufacturing SMEs in an emerging country. *Journal of Small Business Strategy*, 32(3), 67–83. DOI: 10.53703/001c.34608

Rossi, U. (2022). The existential threat of urban social extractivism: Urban revival and the extinction crisis in the European South. *Antipode*, 54(3), 892–913. DOI: 10.1111/anti.12802

Rotter, J. B. (1967). A new scale for the measurement of interpersonal trust. *Journal of Personality*, 35(4), 651–665. DOI: 10.1111/j.1467-6494.1967.tb01454.x PMID: 4865583

Rouhani, B. D., Samragh, M., Javaheripi, M., Javidi, T., & Koushanfar, F. (2018). DeepFense. 2018 IEEE/ACM INTERNATIONAL CONFERENCE ON COMPUTER-AIDED DESIGN (ICCAD). *Digest ofTechnical Papers*, 1–8. Advance online publication. DOI: 10.1145/3240765.3240791

Rousseau, D. M., Sitkin, S. B., Burt, R. S., & Camerer, C. (1998). Not so different after all: A cross-discipline view of trust. *Academy of Management Review*, 23(3), 393–404. DOI: 10.5465/amr.1998.926617

Rousseau, R., & Leuven, K. U. (2018). The Australian and New Zealand Fields of Research (FoR) Codes. *ISSI Newsletter*, 14(3), 59–61.

Rule, C. (2017). *The New Handshake: Online Dispute Resolution and the Future of Consumer Protection*. American Bar Association.

Rumrill, P. D., Fitzgerald, S. M., & Merchant, W. R. (2010). Using scoping literature reviews as a means of understanding and interpreting existing literature. *Work (Reading, Mass.)*, 35(3), 399–404. DOI: 10.3233/WOR-2010-0998 PMID: 20364059

Runway, M. L. (2024, November 2). Introducing Act-One – Generate expressive character performances inside [Alpha. Retrieved from https://app.runwayml.com/video-tools/teams/]. *GEN*, 3, •••.

Russell, S. J., & Norvig, P. (1995). Artificial intelligence: A modern approach. *Choice (Chicago, Ill.)*, 33(03), 33–1577. DOI: 10.5860/CHOICE.33-1577

Russell, S., & Norvig, P. (2020). *Artificial Intelligence: A Modern Approach* (4th ed.). Pearson.

Ruster, A. (2020). Willenserklärungen Mittels Autonomer Systeme? Zum Vertragsschluss bei Einsatz künstlicher Intelligenz (Teil 2). *Juristische Rundschau*, 12(12), 639–649. DOI: 10.1515/juru-2020-0059

Ryman-Tubb, N. F., Krause, P., & Garn, W. (2018). How Artificial Intelligence and machine learning research impacts payment card fraud detection: A survey and industry benchmark. *Engineering Applications of Artificial Intelligence*, 76, 130–157. DOI: 10.1016/j.engappai.2018.07.008

Sabharwal, R., Miah, S. J., Wamba, S. F., & Cook, P. (2024). Extending application of explainable artificial intelligence for managers in financial organizations. Annals Of Operation Research. *Annals of Operations Research*. Advance online publication. DOI: 10.1007/s10479-024-05825-9

Sadabadi, A. A., Rahimirad, Z., & Nikijoo, I. (2024). Enhancing cross-sector partnerships in energy saving through social entrepreneurship: A social network analysis approach. *Energy Research & Social Science*, 109, 103412. Advance online publication. DOI: 10.1016/j.erss.2024.103412

Sakyoud, Z., Aaroud, A., & Akodadi, K. (2023). Optimization of purchasing business process in Moroccan public universities based on COBIT and artificial intelligence techniques. *Kybernetes*, 53(5), 1607–1635. DOI: 10.1108/K-02-2022-0167

Sallam, M., Salim, N. A., Al-Tammemi, A. B., Barakat, M., Fayyad, D., Hallit, S., Harapan, H., Hallit, R., & Mahafzah, A. (2023). ChatGPT Output Regarding Compulsory Vaccination and COVID-19 Vaccine Conspiracy: A Descriptive Study at the Outset of a Paradigm Shift in Online Search for Information. *Cureus*, 15(2). Advance online publication. DOI: 10.7759/cureus.35029 PMID: 36819954

Sánchez Vergara, J. I., Papaoikonomou, E., & Ginieis, M. (2021). Exploring the strategic communication of the sharing city project through frame analysis: The case of Barcelona sharing city. *Cities (London, England)*, 110, 103082. DOI: 10.1016/j.cities.2020.103082

Sanchez-Acedo, A., Carbonell-Alcocer, A., Gertrudix, M. & Rubio-Tamayo, J.L. (2024). The Challenges of Media and Information Literacy in the Artificial Intelligence Ecology: Deepfakes and Misinformation. *Communication and Society 37* (4 Special), 223–39. .DOI: 10.15581/003.37.4.223-239

Sánchez-Cruzado, C., Santiago Campión, R., & Sánchez-Compaña, M. T. (2021). Teacher digital literacy: The indisputable challenge after COVID-19. *Sustainability (Basel)*, 13(4), 1858. DOI: 10.3390/su13041858

Sandoval, J. D. P., Arciniega-Nevárez, J. A., Delgado-Galván, X., Ramos, H. M., Pérez-Sánchez, M., López-Jiménez, P. A., & Mora Rodríguez, J. (2023). Street Lighting and Charging Stations with PATs Location Applying Artificial Intelligence. *Water (Basel)*, 15(4), 616. Advance online publication. DOI: 10.3390/w15040616

Saunkeah, B., Beans, J. A., Peercy, M. T., Hiratsuka, V. Y., & Spicer, P. (2021). Extending Research Protections to Tribal Communities. *The American Journal of Bioethics*, 21(10), 5–12. DOI: 10.1080/15265161.2020.1865477 PMID: 33449863

Savage, N. (2019). How AI and neuroscience drive each other forwards. *Nature*, 571(7766), S15–S17. DOI: 10.1038/d41586-019-02212-4 PMID: 31341311

Scepanovič, S. (2019, June). The fourth industrial revolution and education. *In 2019 8th Mediterranean Conference on Embedded Computing (MECO)* (pp. 1-4). IEEE. DOI: 10.1109/MECO.2019.8760114

Schepman, A., & Rodway, P. (2023). The General Attitudes towards Artificial Intelligence Scale (GAAIS): Confirmatory Validation and Associations with Personality, Corporate Distrust, and General Trust. *International Journal of Human-Computer Interaction*, 39(13), 2724–2741. DOI: 10.1080/10447318.2022.2085400

Schnarch, A. (2013). *Marketing para Pymes: un enfoque para Latinoamérica*. Alfaomega.

Schneider, D., & Weber, K. (2024). AI for decision support: What are possible futures, social impacts, regulatory options, ethical conundrums and agency constellations? TATuP - Zeitschrift Für Technikfolgenabschätzung In Theorie Und Praxis, 33(1), 8-54. DOI: 10.14512/tatup.33.1.08

Scholz, L. H. (2021). Algorithms and contract law. In *The Cambridge Handbook of the Law of Algorithms* (pp. 141–152). Cambridge University Press.

Schwab, K. (2024). The Fourth Industrial Revolution: what it means, how to respond1. In *Handbook of Research on Strategic Leadership in the Fourth Industrial Revolution* (pp. 29-34). Edward Elgar Publishing. https://doi.org/DOI: 10.4337/9781802208818.00008

Schwab, K., & Zahidi, S. (2018). The future of jobs report. In *World Economic Forum* (pp. 1-133).

Schwab, K. (2017). *The fourth industrial revolution*. Crown Currency.

Schwaeke, J., Peters, A., Kanbach, D. K., Kraus, S., & Jones, P. (2024). The new normal: The status quo of AI adoption in SMEs. *Journal of Small Business Management*, •••, 1–35. DOI: 10.1080/00472778.2024.2379999

Schwartz, P. M. (2019). Data Protection Law and the Ethical Use of Analytics. *Berkeley Technology Law Journal*, 34(2), 1121–1178.

Searle, J. (1980). Minds, brains, and programs. *Behavioral and Brain Sciences*, 3(3), 417–424. DOI: 10.1017/S0140525X00005756

Sedkaoui, S., & Benaichoub, R. (2024). Generative AI as a Transformative Force for Innovation: A Review of Opportunities, Applications and Challenges. *European Journal of Innovation Management*. Advance online publication. DOI: 10.1108/EJIM-02-2024-0129

Sedky, M. H., Moniri, M., & Chibelushi, C. C. (2005). Smart video surveillance for workplace applications: Implications, technologies and requirements. In J. J. Villanueva (Ed.), *Proceedings of the 5th IASTED International Conference on Visualization, Imaging, and Image Processing, VIIP 2005* (Issues 5th IASTED International Conference on Visualization, Imaging, and Image Processing, pp. 737–742).

Selbst, A., & Powles, J. (2018, January). "Meaningful information" and the right to explanation. In *conference on fairness, accountability and transparency* (pp. 48-48). PMLR. https://proceedings.mlr.press/v81/selbst18a.html

Selvaraj, R., Kuthadi, V. M., & Baskar, S. (2023). Smart building energy management and monitoring system based on artificial intelligence in smart city. *Sustainable Energy Technologies and Assessments*, 56, 103090. Advance online publication. DOI: 10.1016/j.seta.2023.103090

Sengupta, S., Basak, S., Saikia, P., Paul, S., Tsalavoutis, V., Atiah, F., Ravi, V., & Peters, A. (2020). A review of deep learning with special emphasis on architectures, applications and recent trends. *Knowledge-Based Systems*, 194, 105596. DOI: 10.1016/j.knosys.2020.105596

Seo, K., Tang, J., Roll, I., Fels, S., & Yoon, D. (2021). The impact of artificial intelligence on learner-instructor interaction in online learning. *International Journal of Educational Technology in Higher Education*, 18(1), 1–23. DOI: 10.1186/s41239-021-00292-9 PMID: 34778540

Shao, C., Hui, P. M., Cui, P., Jiang, X., & Peng, Y. (2018). Tracking and Characterizing the Competition of Fact Checking and Misinformation: Case Studies. *IEEE Access : Practical Innovations, Open Solutions*, 6, 75327–75341. DOI: 10.1109/ACCESS.2018.2881037

Sharifani, K., & Amini, M. (2023) 'Machine Learning and Deep Learning: A Review of Methods and Applications', *World Information Technology and Engineering Journal*, 10(7), pp. 3897–3904. Available at: https://www.researchgate.net/publication/371011515

Sharma, A., Garg, A., & Sujeet, K. (2021). Artificial Intelligence and Intellectual Property: Evolving Strategies for IP Management. *Journal of Intellectual Property Rights*, 26(1), 22–31.

Sharma, P. (2019). Digital revolution of education 4.0. *International Journal of Engineering and Advanced Technology*, 9(2), 3558–3564. DOI: 10.35940/ijeat.A1293.129219

Sharma, S., Singh, G., Islam, N., & Dhir, A. (2022). Why do SMEs adopt artificial intelligence-based chatbots? *IEEE Transactions on Engineering Management*, 71, 1773–1786. DOI: 10.1109/TEM.2022.3203469

Sharpley, R. (2020). Tourism, sustainable development and the theoretical divide: 20 years on. *Journal of Sustainable Tourism*, 28(11), 1932–1946. DOI: 10.1080/09669582.2020.1779732

Sherman, E. (2018, September 27). Burger King skewers AI mania in hilarious ad, but hits one tone-deaf note. *Inc.* Retrieved from https://adage.com/article/digital-marketing-ad-tech-news/burger-king-generative-ai-contest-builds-fans-weird-whoppers/2540371

Shneiderman, B. (2020). Bridging the Gap Between Ethics and Practice. *ACM Transactions on Interactive Intelligent Systems*, 10(4), 1–31. DOI: 10.1145/3419764

Shoaib, M. R., Wang, Z., Ahvanooey, M. T., & Zhao, J. (2023). Deepfakes, misinformation, and disinformation in the era of frontier AI, generative AI, and large AI models. In *2023 International Conference on Computer and Applications (ICCA)* (pp. 1-7). IEEE DOI: 10.1109/ICCA59364.2023.10401723

Siddiqui, S., & Sposato, M. (2021). Influential factors in physician burnout in the United Arab Emirates. *International Journal of Work Organisation and Emotion*, 12(3), 249–267. DOI: 10.1504/IJWOE.2021.118994

Sigfrids, A., Leikas, J., Salo-Pöntinen, H., & Koskimies, E. (2023). Human-centricity in AI governance: A systemic approach. *Frontiers in Artificial Intelligence*, 6, 976887. DOI: 10.3389/frai.2023.976887 PMID: 36872934

Simos, T. E., Katsikis, V. N., & Mourtas, S. D. (2022). A multi-input with multi-function activated weights and structure determination neuronet for classification problems and applications in firm fraud and loan approval. *Applied Soft Computing*, 127, 109351. DOI: 10.1016/j.asoc.2022.109351

Sina, A. (2023). Open AI and its Impact on Fraud Detection in Financial Industry. Journal of Knowledge Learning and Science Technology ISSN: 2959-6386 (online), 2(3), 263-281. DOI: 10.60087/jklst.vol2.n3.p281

Sindi, S., & Woodman, R. (2021). Implementing commercial autonomous road haulage in freight operations: An industry perspective. *Transportation Research Part A, Policy and Practice*, 152, 235–253. DOI: 10.1016/j.tra.2021.08.003

Singh, K., Kolar, P., Nanduri, S., Seetha Ram, V., & Kumar, D. (2024). CSR and smart city progress: A proposed model for urban development. *Letters in Spatial and Resource Sciences*, 17(1), 3. Advance online publication. DOI: 10.1007/s12076-023-00367-3

Sirdeshmukh, D., Singh, J., & Sabol, B. (2002). Consumer trust, value, and loyalty in relational exchanges. *Journal of Marketing*, 66(1), 15–37. DOI: 10.1509/jmkg.66.1.15.18449

Sirmon, D. G., Hitt, M. A., & Ireland, R. D. (2007). Managing Firm Resources in Dynamic Environments to Create Value: Looking inside the Black Box. *Academy of Management Review*, 32(1), 273–292. DOI: 10.5465/amr.2007.23466005

Sison, A., Ferrero, I., Ruiz, P. G., & Kim, T. W. (2023). Editorial: Artificial intelligence (AI) ethics in business. *Frontiers in Psychology*, 14, 1258721. Advance online publication. DOI: 10.3389/fpsyg.2023.1258721 PMID: 37771802

Šiuškaitė, D., Pilinkienė, V., & Zvirdauskas, D. (2019). The conceptualization of the sharing economy as a business model. *The Engineering Economist*, 30(3), 373–381. DOI: 10.5755/j01.ee.30.3.21253

Sivathanu, B., Pillai, R., & Metri, B. (2023). Customers' online shopping intention by watching AI-based deepfake advertisements. *International Journal of Retail & Distribution Management*, 51(1), 124–145. DOI: 10.1108/IJRDM-12-2021-0583

Six, F. E., & Latusek, D. (2023). Distrust: A critical review exploring a universal distrust sequence. *Journal of Trust Research*, 13(1), 1–23. DOI: 10.1080/21515581.2023.2184376

Skewes, M. C., Gonzalez, V. M., Gameon, J. A., FireMoon, P., Salois, E., Rasmus, S. M., Lewis, J. P., Gardner, S. A., Ricker, A., & Reum, M. (2020). Health Disparities Research with American Indian Communities: The Importance of Trust and Transparency. *American Journal of Community Psychology*, 66(3–4), 302–313. DOI: 10.1002/ajcp.12445 PMID: 32652706

Smith, P. (2024, May 10). Apple ad fail shows why we fear AI. *Financial Review*. https://www.afr.com/technology/apple-ad-fail-shows-why-we-fear-ai-20240510-p5jcgo

Smuha, N. A. (2021) *FROM A 'RACE TO AI' TO A 'RACE TO AI REGULATION': REGULATORY COMPETITION FOR ARTIFICIAL INTELLIGENCE, Innovation & Technology*. Available at: www.cifar.ca/ai/pan-canadian-

Snee, B. J., & Smulowitz, S. M. (2021). It's Alive!: Reanimating the Author in the Age of Artificially Intelligent Advertising. *Popular Culture Studies Journal, 9*(1), 249-264. https://www.mpcaaca.org/_files/ugd/5a6d69_8e82e21052d34aa8b5b744fc56f30913.pdf

Söderberg, S. (2017) *ISO 26000 and OECD Guidelines.*

Söllner, M., Benbasat, I., Gefen, D., Leimeister, J. M., & Pavlou, P. A. (2016). *Trust.* MIS Quarterly Research Curations., DOI: 10.25300/MISQ/2019/curations/10312016

Solove, D. J. (2006). *The Digital Person: Technology and Privacy in the Information Age.* NYU Press.

Soni, N., Sharma, E. K., Singh, N., & Kapoor, A. (2019). *Impact of Artificial Intelligence on Businesses: from Research, Innovation, Market Deployment to Future Shifts in Business Models.* http://arxiv.org/abs/1905.02092

Sood, P., Sharma, C., Nijjer, S., & Sakhuja, S. (2023). Review the role of artificial intelligence in detecting and preventing financial fraud using natural language processing. *International Journal of System Assurance Engineering and Management*, 14(6), 2120–2135. DOI: 10.1007/s13198-023-02043-7

Sorosrungruang, T., Ameen, N., & Hackley, C. (2024). How real is real enough? Unveiling the diverse power of generative AI-enabled virtual influencers and the dynamics of human responses. *Psychology and Marketing*, 41(12), 3124–3143. Advance online publication. DOI: 10.1002/mar.22105

Soundararajan, V., Jamali, D., & Spence, L. J. (2018). Small business social responsibility: A critical multilevel review, synthesis and research agenda. *International Journal of Management Reviews*, 20(4), 934–956. DOI: 10.1111/ijmr.12171

Souza, M. A., Gouveia, H. T. V., Ferreira, A. A., De Lima Neta, R. M., Neto, O. N., Da Silva Lira, M. M., Torres, G. L., & De Aquino, R. R. B. (2024). Detection of Non-Technical Losses on a Smart Distribution Grid Based on Artificial Intelligence Models. *Energies*, 17(7), 1729. DOI: 10.3390/en17071729

Spence, L. J. (2016). Small business social responsibility: Expanding core CSR theory. *Business & Society*, 55(1), 23–55. DOI: 10.1177/0007650314523256

Sposato, M. (2015). Methodological approaches to research in China. *International Journal of Chinese Culture and Management*, 3(4), 403–412. DOI: 10.1504/IJCCM.2015.070355

Sposato, M. (2024). Are leaders born or made? Asking the right question. *Development and Learning in Organizations*, 38(3), 1–3. DOI: 10.1108/DLO-05-2023-0123

Sposato, M. (2024). Leadership training and development in the age of artificial intelligence. *Development and Learning in Organizations*, 38(4), 4–7. DOI: 10.1108/DLO-12-2023-0256

Sposato, M. (2025). Developing Digital Leadership Skills for AI-Driven Research Environments. In *Impacts of Generative AI on the Future of Research and Education* (pp. 235–254). IGI Global., DOI: 10.4018/979-8-3693-0884-4.ch010

Springer, J. (2024, June 5). 5 ways Coke is using AI to enhance its marketing. *AdAge*.https://adage.com/article/digital-marketing-ad-tech-news/how-coke-using-ai-enhance-marketing/2563521

Stahlschmidt, S., & Stephen, D. (2020). Comparison of web of science, scopus and dimensions databases. KB forschungspoolprojekt, 1-37. https://www.bibliometrie.info/downloads/DZHW-Comparison-DIM-SCP-WOS.PDF

Stanford Institute for Human-Centered Artificial Intelligence (HAI). (2022). *Capstone projects on ethical AI solutions for nonprofits.* Stanford University. https://hai.stanford.edu

Stanford University. (2024). Stanford HAI and Stanford Robotics Center Launch New Partnership (2024, 29 octubre). Stanford HAI. https://hai.stanford.edu/news/stanford-hai-and-stanford-robotics-center-launch-new-partnership

Staniškienė, E., & Stankevičiūtė, Ž. (2018). Social sustainability measurement framework: The case of employee perspective in a CSR-committed organisation. *Journal of Cleaner Production*, 188, 708–719. DOI: 10.1016/j.jclepro.2018.03.269

Starke, G., & Ienca, M. (2022). Misplaced Trust and Distrust: How Not to Engage with Medical Artificial Intelligence. *Cambridge Quarterly of Healthcare Ethics*, •••, 1–10. DOI: 10.1017/S0963180122000445 PMID: 36263755

Stavrakakis, I., Gordon, D., Tierney, B., Becevel, A., Murphy, E., Dodig-Crnkovic, G., Dobrin, R., Schiaffonati, V., Pereira, C., Tikhonenko, S., Gibson, J. P., Maag, S., Agresta, F., Curley, A., Collins, M., & O'Sullivan, D. (2021). The teaching of computer ethics on computer science and related degree programmes. a European survey. *International Journal of Ethics Education*, 7(1), 101–129. DOI: 10.1007/s40889-021-00135-1

Stearns, P. N. (2020). *The industrial revolution in world history*. Routledge., DOI: 10.4324/9781003050186

Sterbenk, Y., Champlin, S., Windels, K., & Shelton, S. (2022). Is Femvertising the New Greenwashing? Examining Corporate Commitment to Gender Equality. *Journal of Business Ethics*, 177(3), 491–505. DOI: 10.1007/s10551-021-04755-x

Stix, C. (2017). *Asilomar AI Principles*. Future of Life Institute. https://futureoflife.org/ai-principles/

Stoian, C., & Gilman, M. (2017). Corporate social responsibility that "pays": A strategic approach to CSR for SMEs. *Journal of Small Business Management*, 55(1), 5–31. DOI: 10.1111/jsbm.12224

Strelcenia, E., & Prakoonwit, S. (2023). A Survey on GAN Techniques for Data Augmentation to Address the Imbalanced Data Issues in Credit Card Fraud Detection. *Machine Learning And Knowledge Extraction*, 5(1), 304–329. DOI: 10.3390/make5010019

Subiela-Hernández, B. H., Gómez-Company, A., & Vizcaíno-Laorga, R. (2023). Retos y oportunidades en la lucha contra la desinformación y los derechos de autor en Periodismo: MediaVerse (IA, blockchain y smart contracts). *Estudios sobre el Mensaje Periodístico*, 29(4), 869–880. DOI: 10.5209/esmp.88081

Sulaiman, A., Nagu, B., Kaur, G., Karuppaiah, P., Alshahrani, H., Al Reshan, M. S., AlYami, S., & Shaikh, A. (2023). Artificial Intelligence-Based Secured Power Grid Protocol for Smart City. *Sensors (Basel)*, 23(19), 8016. Advance online publication. DOI: 10.3390/s23198016 PMID: 37836846

Sung, C. S., & Park, J. Y. (2021). Design of an intelligent video surveillance system for crime prevention: Applying deep learning technology. *Multimedia Tools and Applications*, 80(26–27), 34297–34309. DOI: 10.1007/s11042-021-10809-z

Sun, M., & Zhang, J. (2020). Research on the application of block chain big data platform in the construction of new smart city for low carbon emission and green environment. *Computer Communications*, 149, 332–342. DOI: 10.1016/j.comcom.2019.10.031

Surroca, J., Tribó, J. A., & Waddock, S. (2010). Corporate responsibility and financial performance: The role of intangible resources. *Strategic Management Journal*, 31(5), 463–490. DOI: 10.1002/smj.820

Szpilko, D., Naharro, F. J., Lăzăroiu, G., Nica, E., & de la Torre Gallegos, A. (2023). Artificial intelligence in the smart city - a literature review. *Engineering Management in Production and Services*, 15(4), 53–75. DOI: 10.2478/emj-2023-0028

Taher, S. S., Ameen, S. Y., & Ahmed, J. A. (2024). Advanced Fraud Detection in Blockchain Transactions: An Ensemble Learning and Explainable AI Approach. Engineering, Technology And Applied Science Research/Engineering, Technology And. *Applied Scientific Research*, 14(1), 12822–12830. DOI: 10.48084/etasr.6641

Talaei, J., Yang, A., Takishova, T., & Masialeti, M. (2024). How Does Cost Leadership Strategy Suppress the Performance Benefits of Explainability of AI Applications in Organizations? *Journal of Global Information Management*, 32(1), 1–23. DOI: 10.4018/JGIM.354062

Tamajón, L. G., & Font, X. (2013). Corporate social responsibility in tourism small and medium enterprises evidence from Europe and Latin America. *Tourism Management Perspectives*, 7, 38–46. DOI: 10.1016/j.tmp.2013.03.002

Tam, K. Y., & Ho, S. Y. (2005). Web personalization as a persuasion strategy: An elaboration likelihood model perspective. *Information Systems Research*, 16(3), 271–291. DOI: 10.1287/isre.1050.0058

Tan, S. Y., & Taeihagh, A. (2020). Smart city governance in developing countries: A systematic literature review. *Sustainability (Basel)*, 12(3), 1–29. DOI: 10.3390/su12030899

Tan, Z., Liu, B., & Wu, A. (2022). Artificial Intelligence and Feature Identification Based Global Perception of Power Consumer: Definition, Structure, and Applications. *Frontiers in Energy Research*, 10, 907027. Advance online publication. DOI: 10.3389/fenrg.2022.907027

Taveekitworachai, P., Gursesli, M. C., Abdullah, F., Chen, S., Cala, F., Guazzini, A., Lanata, A., & Thawonmas, R. (2023). Journey of ChatGPT from Prompts to Stories in Games: The Positive, the Negative, and the Neutral. *IEEE International Conference on Consumer Electronics* - Berlin, ICCE-Berlin, 202–3. https://doi.org/ DOI: 10.1109/ICCE-Berlin58801.2023.10375663

Taylor, L. (2021). The taming of chaos: Optimal cities and the state of the art in urban systems research. *Urban Studies (Edinburgh, Scotland)*, 58(15), 3196–3202. DOI: 10.1177/00420980211012838

Tene, O., & Polonetsky, J. (2013). Big data for all: Privacy and user control in the age of analytics. *Northwestern Journal of Technology and Intellectual Property*, 11(5), 239–273.

Thelwall, M. (2018). Dimensions: A competitor to Scopus and the Web of Science? *Journal of Informetrics*, 12(2), 430–435. DOI: 10.1016/j.joi.2018.03.006

Thomas, D. R. (2006). A general inductive approach for analyzing qualitative evaluation data. *The American Journal of Evaluation*, 27(2), 237–246. DOI: 10.1177/1098214005283748

Tiwari, T., Albino, J., & Batliner, T. S. (2015). Challenges faced in engaging American Indian mothers in an early childhood caries preventive trial. *International Journal of Dentistry*, 2015, 1–5. Advance online publication. DOI: 10.1155/2015/179189 PMID: 26089905

Tiwary, N., Noah, S. A. M., Fauzi, F., & Yee, T. S. (2024). Max Explainability Score–A quantitative metric for explainability evaluation in knowledge graph-based recommendations. *Computers & Electrical Engineering*, 116, 109190. DOI: 10.1016/j.compeleceng.2024.109190

Trappey, A. J., Wu, C. Y., Taghaboni-Dutta, F., & Trappey, C. V. (2017). Using patent data for technology forecasting: China RFID patent analysis. *Advanced Engineering Informatics*, 31, 105–120.

Tricco, A. C., Antony, J., Zarin, W., Strifler, L., Ghassemi, M., Ivory, J., Perrier, L., Hutton, B., Moher, D., & Straus, S. E. (2015). A scoping review of rapid review methods. *BMC Medicine*, 13(1), 224. Advance online publication. DOI: 10.1186/s12916-015-0465-6 PMID: 26377409

Truby, J. (2020). Governing Artificial Intelligence to benefit the UN Sustainable Development Goals. *Sustainable Development (Bradford)*, 28(4), 946–959. DOI: 10.1002/sd.2048

Tseng, C. Y., & Ting, P. H. (2013). Patent analysis for technology development of artificial intelligence: A country-level comparative study. *Innovation (North Sydney, N.S.W.)*, 15(4), 463–475. DOI: 10.5172/impp.2013.15.4.463

Tseng, S., & Fogg, B. J. (1999). Credibility and computing technology. *Communications of the ACM*, 42(5), 39–44. DOI: 10.1145/301353.301402

Tufekci, Z. (2018). *Twitter and tear gas: The power and fragility of networked protest*. Yale University Press.

Turyakira, P., Venter, E., & Smith, E. (2014). The impact of corporate social responsibility factors on the competitiveness of small and medium-sized enterprises. *Suid-Afrikaanse Tydskrif vir Ekonomiese en Bestuurswetenskappe*, 17(2), 157–172. DOI: 10.4102/sajems.v17i2.443

Ubeda, M. A. S., Cerna, Y. A. H., Hurtado, M. J., del Socorro Villanueva, J., & Castro, C. M. (2024). Turismo sostenible desde la responsabilidad social de las empresas turísticas. *Revista Torreón Universitario, 13*(36).

UNESCO. (2021). Artificial Intelligence in education: Challenges and opportunities. Retrieved from https://www.unesco.org

United Arab Emirates Government. (2023). *UAE Vision 2030 and National Agenda.* Retrieved from https://www.government.ae/en/about-the-uae/strategies-initiatives-and-awards/federal-governments-strategies-and-plans/uae-vision-2030

United Nations (2015) *TRANSFORMING OUR WORLD: THE 2030 AGENDA FOR SUSTAINABLE DEVELOPMENT.*

United Nations Global Compact & Accenture. (2024). *Inteligencia artificial generativa para los objetivos mundiales. Guía del sector privado para acelerar el desarrollo sostenible con la tecnología.*https://www.pactomundial.org/biblioteca/inteligencia-artificial-generativa-para-los-objetivos-mundiales/

United Nations. (2015). *Sustainable Development Goals.* United Nations. https://sdgs.un.org/goals

United Nations. (2016) *United Nations Sustainability Goals.* Available at: https://sdgs.un.org/goals (Accessed: 11 October 2024).

United Nations. (2021). *People-Smart Sustainable Cities.* People-Smart Sustainable Cities., DOI: 10.18356/9789210052658

United Nations. (2024). *Progress towards the Sustainable Development Goals: Report of the Secretary-General* (A/79/79-E/2024/54). United Nations. https://unstats.un.org/sdgs

Van Audenhove, L., Vermeire, L., Van den Broeck, W., & Demeulenaere, A. (2024). Data literacy in the new EU DigComp 2.2 framework how DigComp defines competences on artificial intelligence, internet of things and data. Information and Learning Sciences, 125(5/6), 406-436.

Van Bekkum, M., & Borgesius, F. Z. (2021). Digital welfare fraud detection and the Dutch SyRI judgment. *European Journal of Social Security*, 23(4), 323–340. DOI: 10.1177/13882627211031257

Van Den Berg, M., Gerlings, J., & Kim, J. (2024). Empirical Research on Ensuring Ethical AI in Fraud Detection of Insurance Claims: A Field Study of Dutch Insurers. En Communications in computer and information science (pp. 106-114). https://doi.org/DOI: 10.1007/978-3-031-50485-3_9

Van der Sloot, B., & Wagensveld, Y. (2022). Deepfakes: Regulatory challenges for the synthetic society. *Computer Law & Security Report*, 46, 105716. DOI: 10.1016/j.clsr.2022.105716

Van Laar, E., van Deursen, A. J., van Dijk, J. A., & De Haan, J. (2019). Determinants of 21st-century digital skills: A large-scale survey among working professionals. *Computers in Human Behavior*, 100, 93–104. DOI: 10.1016/j.chb.2019.06.017

Van Leeuwen, C., Smets, A., Jacobs, A., & Ballon, P. (2021). Blind Spots in AI: The Role of Serendipity and Equity in Algorithm-Based Decision-Making. *SIGKDD Explorations*, 23(1), 42–49. DOI: 10.1145/3468507.3468514

Van, B., & Gómez, H. (2015). *Pyme de avanzada: Motor del desarrollo en América Latina*. Universidad de los. *Andes (Salta)*.

Vance, A., Elie-dit-cosaque, C., & Straub, D. W. (2008). Examining trust in information technology artifacts: The effects of system quality and culture. *Journal of Management Information Systems*, 24(4), 73–100. DOI: 10.2753/MIS0742-1222240403

Veale, M., & Edwards, L. (2018). Clarity, surprises, and further questions in the GDPR's provisions on automated decision-making and profiling. *Computer Law & Security Review*, 34(2), 398–404. DOI: 10.1016/j.clsr.2017.12.002

Vegesna, V. V. (2023). Privacy-Preserving Techniques in AI-Powered Cyber Security: Challenges and Opportunities. *International Journal of Machine Learning for Sustainable Development*, 5, 1–8.

Verma, S., Sharma, R., Deb, S., & Maitra, D. (2021). Artificial intelligence in marketing: Systematic review and future research direction. *International Journal of Information Management Data Insights*, 1(1), 100002. DOI: 10.1016/j.jjimei.2020.100002

Vermesan, O., & Friess, P. (2014). *Internet of things applications-from research and innovation to market deployment*. Taylor & Francis.

Vinuesa, R., Azizpour, H., Leite, I., Aken, M. V., & Schiebinger, L. (2020). The role of artificial intelligence in achieving the Sustainable Development Goals. *Nature Communications*, 11(1), 233. DOI: 10.1038/s41467-019-14108-y PMID: 31932590

Vives, A. (2014). Guías para la responsabilidad social en las PyMEs: Efectividad de herramientas de autoevaluación. *Journal of Globalization. Competitiveness and Governability*, 8(2), 29–54. DOI: 10.3232/GCG.2014.V8.N2.02

Voigt, P., & Von dem Bussche, A. (2017). *The EU General Data Protection Regulation (GDPR): A practical guide*. Springer. DOI: 10.1007/978-3-319-57959-7

Voldsund, K. H., Hasleberg, H., & Bragelien, J. J. (2020). *Entrepreneurship Education Through Sustainable Value Creation. 2020 IEEE Global Engineering Education Conference (EDUCON)*. DOI: 10.1109/EDUCON45650.2020.9125171

Volgger, M., & Huang, S. S. (2019). Scoping irresponsible behaviour in hospitality and tourism: Widening the perspective of CSR. *International Journal of Contemporary Hospitality Management*, 31(6), 2526–2543. DOI: 10.1108/IJCHM-05-2018-0367

Wachter, S., Mittelstadt, B., & Floridi, L. (2017). Why a right to explanation of automated decision-making does not exist in the General Data Protection Regulation. *International Data Privacy Law*, 7(2), 76–99. DOI: 10.1093/idpl/ipx005

Walters, R., Trakman, L., & Zeller, B. (2019). Jurisdictional [Comparative] Differences. En DATA PROTECTION LAW: A COMPARATIVE ANALYSIS OF ASIA-PACIFIC AND EUROPEAN APPROACHES (pp. 265-290). https://doi.org/ DOI: 10.1007/978-981-13-8110-2_11

Wang, G., Frederick, R., Duan, J., Wong, W., Rupar, V., Li, W., & Bai, Q. (2024). Detecting misinformation through Framing Theory: the Frame Element-based Model. arXiv preprint arXiv:2402.15525.

Wang, C., & Teo, T. S. H. (2020). Online service quality and perceived value in mobile government success: An empirical study of mobile police in China. *International Journal of Information Management*, 52, 102076. DOI: 10.1016/j.ijinfomgt.2020.102076

Wang, H., Fu, T., Du, Y., Gao, W., Huang, K., Liu, Z., Chandak, P., Liu, S., Van Katwyk, P., Deac, A., Anandkumar, A., Bergen, K., Gomes, C. P., Ho, S., Kohli, P., Lasenby, J., Leskovec, J., Liu, T. Y., Manrai, A., & Zitnik, M. (2023). *'Scientific discovery in the age of artificial intelligence', Nature*. Nature Research., DOI: 10.1038/s41586-023-06221-2

Wang, J., You, S., Zong, Y., & Træholt, C. (2017) 'EnergyLab Nordhavn: An integrated community energy system towards green heating and e-mobility', in *IEEE Transportation Electrification Conference and Expo, Asia Pacific (ITEC Asia Pacific)*. IEEE. DOI: 10.1109/ITEC-AP.2017.8080846

Wang, S., Wang, H., Jiang, Y., Li, P., & Yang, W. (2021). Understanding students' participation of intelligent teaching: An empirical study considering artificial intelligence usefulness, interactive reward, satisfaction, university support and enjoyment. *Interactive Learning Environments*, 31(9), 1–17.

Wang, T., Lund, B. D., Marengo, A., Pagano, A., Mannuru, N. R., Teel, Z. A., & Pange, J. (2023). Exploring the potential impact of artificial intelligence (AI) on international students in higher education: Generative AI, chatbots, analytics, and international student success. *Applied Sciences (Basel, Switzerland)*, 13(11), 6716. DOI: 10.3390/app13116716

Wang, Y. (2021). Artificial intelligence in educational leadership: A symbiotic role of human-artificial intelligence decision-making. *Journal of Educational Administration*, 59(3), 256–270. DOI: 10.1108/JEA-10-2020-0216

Wan-Jan, W. S. (2006). Defining corporate social responsibility. *Journal of Public Affairs*, 6(3–4), 176–184. DOI: 10.1002/pa.227

Weber, M. T., Schaaf, J., Storf, H., Wagner, T. O., Berger, A., & Noll, R. (2024). Editing Physicians' Responses Using GPT-4 for Academic Research. *Studies in Health Technology and Informatics*. Advance online publication. DOI: 10.3233/SHTI240019 PMID: 38682512

Wedel, M., & Kamakura, W. A. (2000). *Market segmentation: Conceptual and methodological foundations*. Springer Science and Business Media. DOI: 10.1007/978-1-4615-4651-1

West, S. M., Whittaker, M., & Crawford, K. (2019). Discriminating systems: Gender, race, and power in AI. *AI Now Institute Report 2019*. https://ainowinstitute.org/aienow19.pdf

Wille, S. M., Kemp, K. A., Greenfield, B. L., & Walls, M. L. (2017). Barriers to healthcare for American indians experiencing homelessness. *Journal of Social Distress and the Homeless*, 26(1), 1–8. DOI: 10.1080/10530789.2016.1265211 PMID: 29375241

Wilson, C., & van der Velden, M. (2022). Sustainable AI: An integrated model to guide public sector decision-making. *Technology in Society*, 68, 101926. DOI: 10.1016/j.techsoc.2022.101926

Wilson, H. J., Daugherty, P. R., & Bianzino, N. (2017). The Jobs That Artificial Intelligence Will Create. *MIT Sloan Management Review*, 58(4), 14–16.

Win, K. T., & Beydoun, G. (2020). Preface: Towards the Next Generation of Information Systems: Enhancing Traceability and Transparency. AJIS. Australasian Journal Of Information Systems/AJIS. Australian Journal Of Information Systems. *AJIS. Australasian Journal of Information Systems*, 24. Advance online publication. DOI: 10.3127/ajis.v24i0.2823

Wirtz, B. W., Göttel, V., & Daiser, P. (2019). Artificial intelligence and the digital transformation of business models. *Electronic Markets*, 29, 535–551. DOI: 10.1007/s12525-019-00354-3

Wirtz, J., Patterson, P. G., Kunz, W. H., Gruber, T., Lu, V. N., Paluch, S., & Martins, A. (2018). Brave new world: Service robots in the frontline. *Journal of Service Management*, 29(5), 907–931. DOI: 10.1108/JOSM-04-2018-0119

Woolgar, S. (1985). Why not a sociology of machines? the case of sociology and artificial intelligence. *Sociology*, 19(4), 557–572. DOI: 10.1177/0038038585019004005

World Bank. (2018). World Development Report 2018: Learning to Realize Education's Promise. *Washington, DC: World Bank*. https://hdl.handle.net/10986/28340

World Economic Forum. (2020, August), *Schools of the Future Defining New Models of Education for the Fourth Industrial Revolution*. Geneva: World Economic Forum. https://www.weforum.org/publications/schools-of-the-future-defining-new-models-of-education-for-the-fourth-industrial-revolution/

Wright, S. (2019). Artificial intelligence ethics and governance: Challenges and opportunities. *AI & Society*, 34(3), 553–561. DOI: 10.1007/s00146-019-00879-6

Wu, L. (2022). Definition, manipulation, and detection. *SIGKDD Explorations*. Advance online publication. DOI: 10.1145/3373464.3373475

Xia, Q., Chiu, T. K., Zhou, X., Chai, C. S., & Cheng, M. (2022). Systematic literature review on opportunities, challenges, and future research recommendations of artificial intelligence in education. *Computers and Education: Artificial Intelligence*, 4, 100118.

Xie, J., Dmour, A. A., & Lakys, Y. (2022). Application of Nonlinear Fractional Differential Equations in Computer Artificial Intelligence Algorithms. *Applied Mathematics And Nonlinear Sciences*, 8(1), 1145–1154. DOI: 10.2478/amns.2022.2.0101

Xing, B., Marwala, L., & Marwala, T. (2018). *Adopt fast, adapt quick: Adaptive approaches in the South African context*. Springer Singapore., DOI: 10.1007/978-981-13-0194-0

Xiong, T., Ma, Z., Li, Z., & Dai, J. (2021). The analysis of influence mechanism for internet financial fraud identification and user behavior based on machine learning approaches. *International Journal of System Assurance Engineering and Management*, 13(S3), 996–1007. DOI: 10.1007/s13198-021-01181-0

Xu, M., David, J. M., & Kim, S. H. (2018). The fourth industrial revolution: Opportunities and challenges. *International journal of financial research, 9*(2), 90-95. https://doi.org/DOI: 10.5430/ijfr.v9n2p90

Xu, D., Fan, S., & Kankanhalli, M. (2023). Combating misinformation in the era of generative AI models. In *Proceedings of the 31st ACM International Conference on Multimedia* (pp. 9291-9298) DOI: 10.1145/3581783.3612704

Yang, J., Tang, Z., Guan, Z., Hua, W., Wei, M., Wang, C., & Gu, C. (2021). Automatic Feature Engineering-Based Optimization Method for Car Loan Fraud Detection. *Discrete Dynamics in Nature and Society*, 2021, 1–10. DOI: 10.1155/2021/6077540

Yang, X., Li, H., Ni, L., & Li, T. (2021). Application of Artificial Intelligence in Precision Marketing. *Journal of Organizational and End User Computing*, 33(4), 209–219. DOI: 10.4018/JOEUC.20210701.oa10

Yang, X., Zhang, C., Sun, Y., Pang, K., Li, J., Wa, S., & Lv, C. (2023). FinChain-BERT: A High-Accuracy Automatic Fraud Detection Model Based on NLP Methods for Financial Scenarios. *Information (Basel)*, 14(9), 499. DOI: 10.3390/info14090499

Yaraziz, M. S., Jalili, A., Gheisari, M., & Liu, Y. (2022). Recent trends towards privacy-preservation in Internet of Things, its challenges and future directions. *IET Circuits, Devices & Systems*, 17(2), 53–61. DOI: 10.1049/cds2.12138

Yerima, S. Y., & Bashar, A. (2022). *Semi-supervised novelty detection with one class SVM for SMS spam detection. 2022 29TH INTERNATIONAL CONFERENCE ON SYSTEMS, SIGNALS AND IMAGE PROCESSING.* IWSSIP., DOI: 10.1109/IWSSIP55020.2022.9854496

Yeung, K. (2018). Algorithmic Regulation: A Critical Interrogation. *Regulation & Governance*, 12(4), 505–523. DOI: 10.1111/rego.12158

Yigitcanlar, T., Corchado, J. M., Mehmood, R., Li, R. Y. M., Mossberger, K., & Desouza, K. (2021). Responsible urban innovation with local government artificial intelligence (Ai): A conceptual framework and research agenda. *Journal of Open Innovation*, 7(1), 1–16. DOI: 10.3390/joitmc7010071

Yılmazdogan, O. C., Secilmis, C., & Cicek, D. (2015). The effect of corporate social responsibility (CSR) perception on tourism students' intention to work in sector. *Procedia Economics and Finance*, 23, 1340–1346. DOI: 10.1016/S2212-5671(15)00321-4

Yin, R. K. (2009). *Case study research: Design and methods* (Vol. 5). sage.

YouTube. (n.d.). *¿Cómo evita YouTube los sesgos?*https://www.youtube.com/intl/ALL_es/howyoutubeworks/our-commitments/preventing-bias/

YouTube. (n.d.). *Nuestro enfoque sobre la IA*.https://www.youtube.com/intl/ALL_es/howyoutubeworks/our-commitments/responsible-ai/

Zaimi, R., Hafidi, M., & Lamia, M. (2023). A deep learning approach to detect phishing websites using CNN for privacy protection. *Intelligent Decision Technologies*, 17(3), 713–728. DOI: 10.3233/IDT-220307

Zajko, M. (2023). Automated government benefits and welfare surveillance. *Surveillance & Society*, 21(3), 246–258. https://www.webofscience.com/wos/alldb/full-record/WOS:001078822300002. DOI: 10.24908/ss.v21i3.16107

Zandbergen, D., & Uitermark, J. (2020). In search of the Smart Citizen: Republican and cybernetic citizenship in the smart city. *Urban Studies (Edinburgh, Scotland)*, 57(8), 1733–1748. DOI: 10.1177/0042098019847410

Zand, D. (1972). Trust and managerial problem solving. *Administrative Science Quarterly*, 17(2), 229–239. DOI: 10.2307/2393957

Zanfardini, M., Aguirre, P., & Tamagni, L. (2016). The evolution of CSR's research in tourism context: A review from 1992 to 2012. *Anatolia*, 27(1), 38–46. DOI: 10.1080/13032917.2015.1083207

Zarsky, T. Z. (2016). Incompatible: The GDPR in the Age of Big Data. *Seton Hall Law Review*, 47(4), 995–1020.

Zarsky, T. Z. (2016). The trouble with algorithmic decisions: An analytic road map to examine efficiency and fairness in automated and opaque decision-making. *Science, Technology & Human Values*, 41(1), 118–132. DOI: 10.1177/0162243915605575

Zawacki-Richter, O., Marín, V. I., Bond, M., & Gouverneur, F. (2019). Systematic review of research on artificial intelligence applications in higher education—Where are the educators? *International Journal of Educational Technology in Higher Education*, 16(1), 1–27. DOI: 10.1186/s41239-019-0171-0

Zeng, Y., Chen, P., & Luo, W. (2021). The Role of Data Ethics in AI Development. *International Journal of Information Management*, 56, 102208.

Zhai, X., Chu, X., Chai, C. S., Jong, M. S. Y., Istenic, A., Spector, M., Liu, J.-B., Yuan, J., & Li, Y. (2021). A Review of Artificial Intelligence (AI) in Education from 2010 to 2020. *Complexity*, 2021(1), 8812542. DOI: 10.1155/2021/8812542

Zhang, D., Mishra, S., Brynjolfsson, E., Etchemendy, J., Ganguli, D., Grosz, B., Lyons, T., Manyika, J., Niebles, J. C., Sellitto, M., Shoham, Y., Clark, J., & Perrault, R. (2021). *The AI Index 2021 Annual Report.* AI Index Steering Committee, Human-Centered AI Institute, Stanford University.

Zhang, D., Mishra, S., Brynjolfsson, E., Etchemendy, J., Ganguli, D., Grosz, B., Lyons, T., Manyika, J., Niebles, J. C., Sellitto, M., Shoham, Y., Clark, J., & Perrault, R. (2022). *The AI Index 2022 Annual Report.* AI Index Steering Committee, Stanford Institute for Human-Centered AI, Stanford University.

Zhang, T., Qin, Y., & Li, Q. (2021). Trusted Artificial Intelligence: Technique Requirements and Best Practices. 2021 INTERNATIONAL CONFERENCE ON CYBERWORLDS (CW 2021), pp.303-306. https://doi.org/DOI: 10.1109/CW52790.2021.00058

Zhang, B. H., Lemoine, B., & Dastin, J. (2018). Mitigating bias in algorithmic decision-making systems: A survey of fairness techniques. *Proceedings of the 2018 IEEE International Conference on Data Science and Advanced Analytics (DSAA)*, 279-288.

Zhang, D., Mishra, S., Brynjolfsson, E., Etchemendy, J., Ganguli, D., Grosz, B., Lyons, T., Manyika, J., Niebles, J. C., Sellitto, M., Shoham, Y., Clark, J., & Perrault, R. (2022). *The AI Index 2022 Annual Report. AI Index Steering Committee, Stanford Institute for Human-Centered AI.* Stanford University.

Zhang, L., Chen, Y., & Yin, Y. (2021). AI-enabled patent intelligence for competitive technical analysis. *Technological Forecasting and Social Change*, 163, 120442.

Zhang, L., Fu, K., & Liu, X. (2022). Artificial intelligence in education: ethical issues and its regulations. *Proceedings of the 5th International Conference on Big Data and Education*, 1-6. DOI: 10.1145/3524383.3524406

Zhang, W., Zhang, S., Chen, J., & Huang, H. (2023). *CCFD-GAN: Credit Card Fraud Detection Based on Generative Adversarial Networks Enhanced by Penalty Mechanism. 2023 INTERNATIONAL JOINT CONFERENCE ON NEURAL NETWORKS.* IJCNN., DOI: 10.1109/IJCNN54540.2023.10191810

Zhang, Z. (2021). The impact of digital technologies on entrepreneurship education. *Advances in Social Science, Education and Humanities Research. Advances in Social Science, Education and Humanities Research.* Advance online publication. DOI: 10.2991/assehr.k.210407.088

Zhao, J., & Fariñas, B. G. (2022). Artificial Intelligence and Sustainable Decisions. *European Business Organization Law Review*, 24(1), 1–39. DOI: 10.1007/s40804-022-00262-2

Zhao, L., Yang, M. M., Wang, Z., & Michelson, G. (2023). Trends in the Dynamic Evolution of Corporate Social Responsibility and Leadership: A Literature Review and Bibliometric Analysis. *Journal of Business Ethics*, 182(1), 135–157. DOI: 10.1007/s10551-022-05035-y

Zheng, X., Gildea, E., Chai, S., Zhang, T., & Wang, S. (2023). Data Science in Finance: Challenges and Opportunities. *AI*, 5(1), 55–71. DOI: 10.3390/ai5010004

Zheng, X., Li, J., Lu, M., & Wang, F. (2024). New Paradigm for Economic and Financial Research With Generative AI: Impact and Perspective. *IEEE Transactions on Computational Social Systems*, 11(3), 1–11. DOI: 10.1109/TCSS.2023.3334306

Zhou, Y., Li, H., Xiao, Z., & Qiu, J. (2023). A user-centered explainable artificial intelligence approach for financial fraud detection. *Finance Research Letters*, 58, 104309. DOI: 10.1016/j.frl.2023.104309

Zhu, T., Ye, D., Wang, W., Zhou, W., & Yu, P. (2021). More Than Privacy: Applying Differential Privacy in Key Areas of Artificial Intelligence. *IEEE Transactions on Knowledge and Data Engineering*, 1. Advance online publication. DOI: 10.1109/TKDE.2020.3014246

Zhu, T., & Yu, P. S. (2019). Applying Differential Privacy Mechanism in Artificial Intelligence. *39th IEEE International Conference On Distributed Computing Systems (ICDCS)*. DOI: 10.1109/ICDCS.2019.00159

Zhu, X., Ao, X., Qin, Z., Chang, Y., Liu, Y., He, Q., & Li, J. (2021). Intelligent financial fraud detection practices in post-pandemic era. *Innovation (Cambridge (Mass.))*, 2(4), 100176. DOI: 10.1016/j.xinn.2021.100176 PMID: 34806059

Ziosi, M., Hewitt, B., Juneja, P., Taddeo, M., & Floridi, L. (2024). Smart cities: Reviewing the debate about their ethical implications. *AI & Society*, 39(3), 1185–1200. DOI: 10.1007/s00146-022-01558-0 PMID: 36212227

Zizek, S. (2003). *The puppet and the dwarf: the perverse core of Christianity*. Verso. DOI: 10.7551/mitpress/5706.001.0001

Zizek, S. (2015). *The Universal Excemption*. Bloomsbury.

Zorrilla-Muñoz, V., Moyano, D. L., Marcos Carvajal, C., & Agulló-Tomás, M. S. (2024). Towards Equitable Representations of Ageing: Evaluation of Gender, Territories, Aids and Artificial Intelligence. *Land (Basel)*, 13(8), 1304. Advance online publication. DOI: 10.3390/land13081304

Zuboff, S. (2019). *The Age of Surveillance Capitalism: The Fight for a Human Future at the New Frontier of Power*. PublicAffairs.

Züger, T., & Asghari, H. (2022). AI for the public. How public interest theory shifts the discourse on AI. *AI & Society*, 38(2), 815–828. DOI: 10.1007/s00146-022-01480-5

Zuiderveen Borgesius, F. (2018). Discrimination, artificial intelligence, and algorithmic decision-making. *Council of Europe, Directorate General of Democracy*, 42. https://hdl.handle.net/11245.1/7bdabff5-c1d9-484f-81f2-e469e03e2360

# About the Contributors

**Martin Sposato** is an Associate Professor at the College of Business, Zayed University, Dubai, UAE. He holds a PhD in Leadership. His research interests include leadership, artificial intelligence in organizations, postcolonialism as a theoretical lens, Indigenous (Chinese) theories and conceptualizations of Human Resource Management (HRM), gender in organizations, and reflexivity in research.

**Eduardo Carlos Dittmar** is an economist holding a PhD in Economic and Business Sciences. He brings extensive teaching expertise at both undergraduate and graduate levels. His scholarly work encompasses fundamental and applied research, resulting in a contribution of over 50 peer-reviewed publications and book chapters. Throughout his career, he has maintained active involvement in various research groups and served on editorial boards of multiple academic journals. His research interests focus on new technologies, corporate social responsibility, strategic marketing, and business ethics.

***

**Park Beede**, an associate professor at Zayed University, specializing in advertising and marketing. Having started his career in the United States, Park has taught throughout New Zealand, Australia and the United Arab Emirates. In addition to teaching, he also worked in leading advertising agencies and client companies for many years. His research interests include advertising, branding, and consumer behavior.

**Matthew Brown** PhD, MA, BA (Hons), HND, Dip PolGov (Open), PGCHE, MCIM, MIDM, MCIPR, FCMI, FHEA is a Senior Lecturer in Marketing at Middlesex University Dubai, UAE. A member of the Chartered Institute of Marketing and a Fellow of the Chartered Management Institute, Matthew holds a

MA in Management from London Southbank University. His research interesting include Marketing innovation, digital technology and smart cities.

**Víctor Manuel Castillo Girón** has been responsible for various research and academic management projects. Author and co-author of more than 150 published research papers. Lecturer and organizer of nearly two hundred national and international academic events. He has coordinated around 25 evaluation and accreditation processes for undergraduate and graduate educational programs, as well as coordinated around twenty technical groups for the creation of new study programs. Over more than three decades he has directed nearly sixty undergraduate theses and taught undergraduate and graduate courses related to regional development and sustainability; food policy and economics; leadership and management skills; research methodology; organization theory, management of educational institutions, among others. He has received various recognitions for his research, teaching, institutional management and outreach activities. He has been director and member of more than a dozen editorial boards of various national and international scientific journals.

**Areej ElSayary** is an expert in Science, Technology, Engineering, Art, and Mathematics (STEAM), curriculum design and development, teaching and learning, assessment, and school accreditation. She is also a certified associate for the Blackboard Academy, a Fellow for the Higher Education Academy (FHEA), an Editor, and a researcher. She is an Approved Accreditation Lead inspector from the New England Association of Schools and Colleges NEASC & Council of International School CIS. She is also an approved visitor by CAEP accreditation. She was the graduate program coordinator at the College of Education at Zayed University and is currently an Associate Professor and Assistant Chair for the General Education Department at the College of Interdisciplinary Studies. Her research interests include educational technology, cognitive development, positive psychology and well-being, Human-computer interaction, entrepreneurship, innovation, design-thinking, Interdisciplinary STE(A)M, and assessment. She has published her work internationally and has presented papers at conferences. Dr. Areej has also conducted several teacher training programs across the United Arab Emirates. Furthermore, she is a Mental Health Ambassador at Zayed University, specializing in positive and cyber psychology. Additionally, she was awarded to be a Certified AI Lead Assessor by IEEE.

**Cristina Gallego-Gomez** has a Master's Degree in Business Organization and another one in Business Communication at the Rey Juan Carlos University. She is a doctoral candidate in the Business Administration PHD Program at the Rey Juan

Carlos. She is an IT organizational Consultant in the digital areas of firms from 2008. She works at Capgemini, Spain, where she is specialized in channels in the Financial Services for big size firms leading their industries. She has done research in the management of CRM and ERP systems where she has published articles in indexed journals and presented communications in International venues.

**Maximiliano E. Korstanje** is editor in chief of International Journal of Safety and Security in Tourism (UP Argentina) and Editor in Chief Emeritus of International Journal of Cyber Warfare and Terrorism (IGI-Global US). Korstanje is Senior Researchers in the Department of Economics at University of Palermo, Argentina. In 2015 he was awarded as Visiting Research Fellow at School of Sociology and Social Policy, University of Leeds, UK and the University of La Habana Cuba. In 2017 is elected as Foreign Faculty Member of AMIT, Mexican Academy in the study of Tourism, which is the most prominent institutions dedicated to tourism research in Mexico. He had a vast experience in editorial projects working as advisory member of Elsevier, Routledge, Springer, IGI global and Cambridge Scholar publishing. Korstanje had visited and given seminars in many important universities worldwide. He has also recently been selected to take part of the 2018 Albert Nelson Marquis Lifetime Achievement Award. a great distinction given by Marquis Who´s Who in the world.

**María-Elena Lindez-Macarro**, professor in the Department of Financial Economics and Accounting at the Universidad Rey Juan Carlos (URJC). She obtained her degree in Economics at the University of Granada, and continued her postgraduate studies with the Master in Tax and Financial Consultancy in a National and International Framework at the URJC, where she has been teaching since March 2022. Her doctoral thesis focuses on the causes and consequences of digital financial fraud that especially affects the elderly. She has published articles on this topic in journals such as the International Journal of Bank Marketing.

**Carmen Llovet** holds a European PhD in Communication and she is a lecturer and researcher at the School of Communication and Arts at Nebrija University. She has been a visiting researcher at Southern Illinois University, Radboud University and Glasgow Caledonian University. Furthermore, she has been a visiting professor at the American Business School of Paris and at the Universidad Panamericana in Mexico. Within the group PROVULDIG -Responsible Communication and vulnerable audiences- at Complutense University of Madrid she has conducted the european project Integra_Lab, empowering emotional self-care in elderly adults by the acquisition of digital skills and creativity. She is also a member of the research group INNOMEDIA at Nebrija University. Her professional career started as a journalist in the information agencies Europa Press and Aceprensa and as a PR in the communication agency Beconfluence.

**David López Jiménez** obtained his Law degree from the Complutense University of Madrid. He obtained one PhD (with European mention) from the Seville University and another PhD from the Rey Juan Carlos University. He has an Extraordinary Doctoral Award. He has leaded research stays in different European countries. He is the author of several monographs, some of them published by the prestigious publisher Thomson Reuters and Marcial Pons, as well as more than 200 publications in various scientific journals, book chapters, book reviews, and comments about national and international law.

**Tom Okot** is a Professor and Senior Researcher at Universidad Latinoamericana de Ciencia y Tecnología (Costa Rica), where he serves as Chair of the Business School. With extensive experience, he specializes in business innovation, sustainable development, technology integration, and tourism economics. His research, published in international journals, has contributed to collaborations with academia, NGOs, and UN agencies. He has led programs in Africa, Latin America, and the Caribbean, focusing on monitoring, evaluation, capacity-building, and public-private partnerships. He has managed multidisciplinary projects aimed at socioeconomic resilience and sustainable business practices. Before his current role, he held research and advisory positions with international NGOs, shaping policy frameworks. He is also an Advisory Board member of the Rhombus Journal, where he supports scholarly discussions on emerging business paradigms.

**Jenny Patricia Vargas Portillo** is a PhD with the highest qualification, three master's degrees, an Advanced Studies Diploma and numerous specialization courses. The research carried out involves both basic and applied exploration. The lines she has been working involves, among others, Consumer Behavior, Marketing and New Technologies (Interactive Advertising and Electronic Commerce). She has been teaching and doing research in different countries of the world. She has been a professor at undergraduate and graduate levels. Likewise, she has directed a significant number of Bachelor and Master theses.

**Félix Velicia-Martín** has been director of the Expert Course in Marketing and Commercial Management at the University of Seville. He is a member of the Institute of Economics and Business of the University of Seville (IUSEN) and of the NECE Research Unit in Business Sciences of the Beira Interior University (UBI). He has published in national and international high impact journals in the field of marketing, education, and ICT, as well as numerous contributions to national and international conferences. He has participated as a researcher in national R&D projects (Ministry of Science and Technology) as well as in projects of excellence (Junta de Andalucía). He is currently Principal Researcher of the Andalusian Research Plan Research Group SEJ-642: "Society, Business, Sustainable Development and Digital Transformation". He has taught in different courses and masters related to the field of Business Management and Marketing. He has advised companies and public institutions in the field of quality and in the development and implementation of marketing plans.

**Felix Villalba-Romero** obtained his PhD from Universidad Autonoma de Madrid (Spain) in 2017. Under predoc and postdoc research contracts he worked for University of Central Lancashire (UK), during the period 2015-2020, associated with several European Research projects. In 2020 he was hired as lecturer and later as assistant professor by Universidad Rey Juan Carlos and currently teaches at Universidad de Malaga, both located in Spain. He has published papers and book chapters in high-impact journals and publishers. In the professional field, he has extensive work experience in several countries as an executive and director of large corporations, in areas of management and finance.

# Index

## A



## B



## C



## D

## E



## F



## G



## I



## L



## M



## N

www.ingramcontent.com/pod-product-compliance
Lightning Source LLC
LaVergne TN
LVHW080354011026
849161LV00009B/2299